THE HERO™
BOOK ONE

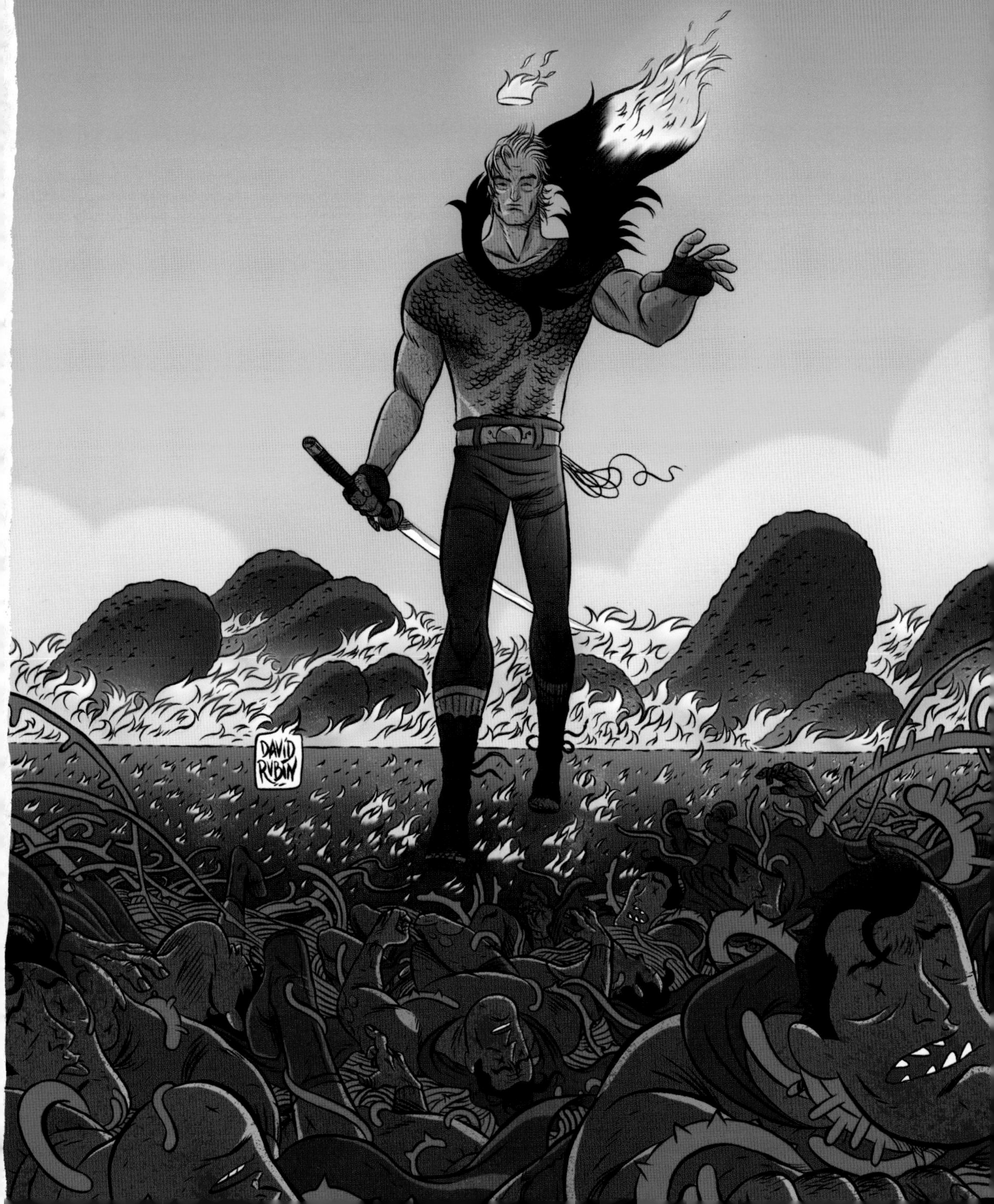
DAVID RUBIN

DARK HORSE BOOKS
MILWAUKIE, OREGON

FIRST PUBLISHED BY **ASTIBERRI EDICIONES**

PRESIDENT & PUBLISHER **MIKE RICHARDSON**

EDITOR, ENGLISH-LANGUAGE EDITION **SIERRA HAHN**

ASSISTANT EDITOR, ENGLISH-LANGUAGE EDITION **SPENCER CUSHING**

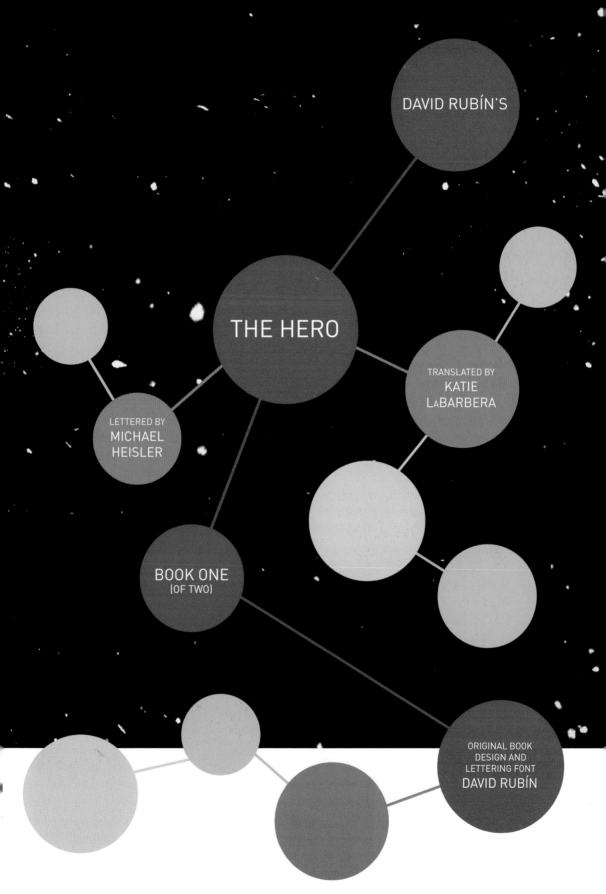

DAVID RUBÍN'S

THE HERO

TRANSLATED BY
KATIE
LaBARBERA

LETTERED BY
MICHAEL
HEISLER

BOOK ONE
(OF TWO)

ORIGINAL BOOK
DESIGN AND
LETTERING FONT
DAVID RUBÍN

SPECIAL THANKS TO LAUREANO DOMÍNGUEZ OF ASTIBERRI EDICIONES.

PRODUCTION, ENGLISH-LANGUAGE EDITION
CHRISTINA McKENZIE

BOOK DESIGN, ENGLISH-LANGUAGE EDITION
JIMMY PRESLER

NEIL HANKERSON EXECUTIVE VICE PRESIDENT / TOM WEDDLE CHIEF FINANCIAL OFFICER /
RANDY STRADLEY VICE PRESIDENT OF PUBLISHING / MICHAEL MARTENS VICE PRESIDENT
OF BOOK TRADE SALES / SCOTT ALLIE EDITOR IN CHIEF / MATT PARKINSON VICE PRESIDENT
OF MARKETING / DAVID SCROGGY VICE PRESIDENT OF PRODUCT DEVELOPMENT / DALE
LaFOUNTAIN VICE PRESIDENT OF INFORMATION TECHNOLOGY / DARLENE VOGEL SENIOR
DIRECTOR OF PRINT, DESIGN, AND PRODUCTION / KEN LIZZI GENERAL COUNSEL / DAVEY
ESTRADA EDITORIAL DIRECTOR / CHRIS WARNER SENIOR BOOKS EDITOR / DIANA SCHUTZ
EXECUTIVE EDITOR / CARY GRAZZINI DIRECTOR OF PRINT AND DEVELOPMENT / LIA RIBACCHI
ART DIRECTOR / CARA NIECE DIRECTOR OF SCHEDULING / MARK BERNARDI DIRECTOR OF
DIGITAL PUBLISHING

PUBLISHED BY DARK HORSE BOOKS / A DIVISION OF DARK HORSE COMICS, INC.
10956 SE MAIN STREET / MILWAUKIE, OR 97222

FIRST EDITION: JUNE 2015
ISBN 978-1-61655-670-9

10 9 8 7 6 5 4 3 2 1

PRINTED IN CHINA

INTERNATIONAL LICENSING: (503) 905-2377 / COMIC SHOP LOCATOR SERVICE: (888) 266-4226

THIS VOLUME REPRINTS EL HÉROE LIBRO UNO, ORIGINALLY PUBLISHED IN SPANISH BY
ASTIBERRI EDICIONES.

TABLE OF CONTENTS

[redacted]

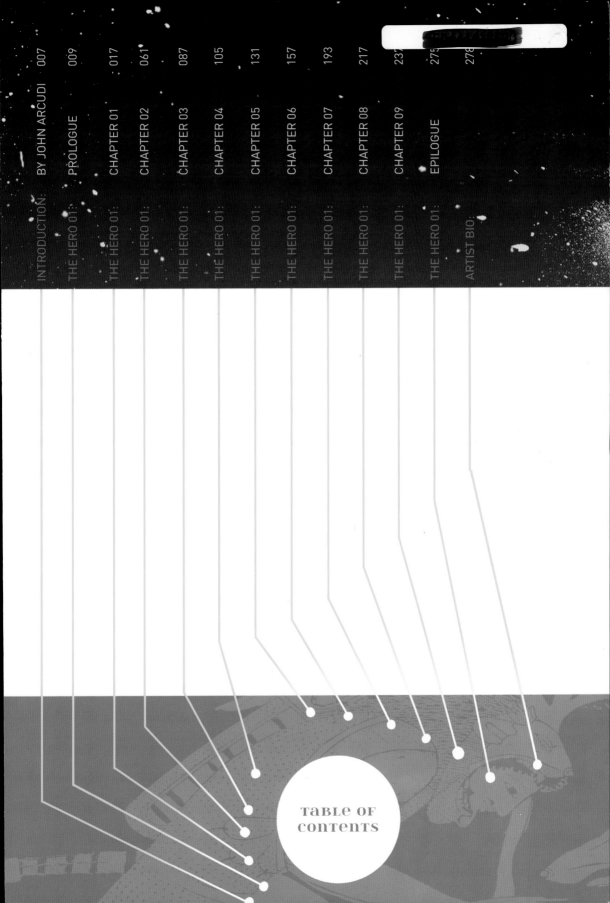

Pablo Picasso once said, "Talent borrows; genius steals."

Or was that Oscar Wilde? Well, Picasso had to steal it from somewhere, right?

But what about reinvention? Where on that scale, from talent to genius, will you find the creator who makes a wholly original work out of something that's been around for literally thousands of years? That's exactly what David Rubín has done with The Hero, and you will love him for it.

The myth of Heracles (more commonly known by his Latin name, Hercules) is about as familiar a story as you can find in Western culture. His name has entered the English language as an adjective, and his twelve labors—in toto and separately—serve as similes and metaphors alike. No surprise then that it's a staple of the entertainment industry, this dependable narrative that even children can pick up on—but why, exactly? Very possibly because this myth is a virtual archetype of the monomyth, or hero's journey, as described by Joseph Campbell in his book The Hero with a Thousand Faces. Hercules's journey parallels the growth of civilization and spirituality, rife with symbology and cultural significance. More than that, it's a potent analogy for the coming of age every one of us understands on something like a primal level. Sadly, all of this is more or less ignored in the literally dozens of versions of the Heracles character trotted out in the last hundred years or so in film, comics, etc. Ignored largely because taking Campbell's rather dense analysis and making it entertaining is something of a Herculean task—but not for David.

You'll find in The Hero no tired and predictable retread of what you already know; nor is it a dry and sententious parsing of phrases and theories. Rubín instead gives us a lively, funny, exciting, and bitingly satirical work that is as refreshingly new and original as it is deeply resonant and important.

His recontextualizing of the entire Heracles myth is accomplished mostly by setting the story in a modern world, but one that is more fabulous than actually representative of anything you'll experience in the twenty-first century. Yet it's recognizable enough to be immediately accessible to anybody who's ever heard of American Idol or been to a mall at Christmas. All the fantastic elements one would expect are still here (monsters, nymphs, and jealous gods), but the everyday is found in this book as well (motorcycles, personalized jerseys, iPods, and cell phones). Then again, what could be more fantastic than toting a computer around in your pocket? And there it is right there. The lines between what is real to the reader, what seems plausible, and the utterly fantastic are blurred. The larger narrative becomes more expansive, the themes more relevant. But in a paradoxical turn, the story is surprisingly personal and even intimate as a result of this.

There's so much more going on here, but to talk further about the writing, the story itself, risks spoiling the experience for you. Then again, what can be said about the art that you can't see for yourself by skipping ahead a few pages? It's all there, and what you'll see is more than dynamic lines and pictures. There's a vitality to David's drawing and color art that challenges the widely accepted limits of the comic page. As playful as it is potent, his artwork is explosive, hilarious, sad, and dramatic. It is whatever it needs to be to relate this evolving and complex adventure.

Rubín, a true cartoonist (meaning the whole nine yards is his responsibility—plot, script, and art), isn't just a guy who can draw well. Really, there are quite a few people who can do that. But the largely undiscussed—or at least, the poorly understood—art of storytelling is something else entirely. The aim for any comics artist should be to get across the setting, the action, and all the details of the tale clearly. If the reader doesn't get what's going on, then the story doesn't matter. So clarity is the goal, and anything beyond that is gravy. In The Hero, David Rubín gives you lots and lots of gravy!

His artfully designed two-page spreads are the best illustrations of this. While eye-catchingly beautiful, they do not distract or confuse the reader. How this is accomplished may not be plain, but the effect is. The invisible art of communicating has no better exemplar than this remarkable marriage of words and pictures. You have here the unified voice and vision of a true artist: a creator who takes his craft seriously, who sees the abundant promise of a medium that others may miss, and who has the talent, maybe even the genius, to deliver on that potential.

So, would Joseph Campbell approve of all this monkeying with the monomyth? Who knows—but it makes for great comics!

John Arcudi
February 21, 2015

John Arcudi is cocreator of the cult favorite Major Bummer and writer of the critically acclaimed The Creep, A God Somewhere, and Rumble. He's also pretty well known for collaborating with Mike Mignola on B.P.R.D.

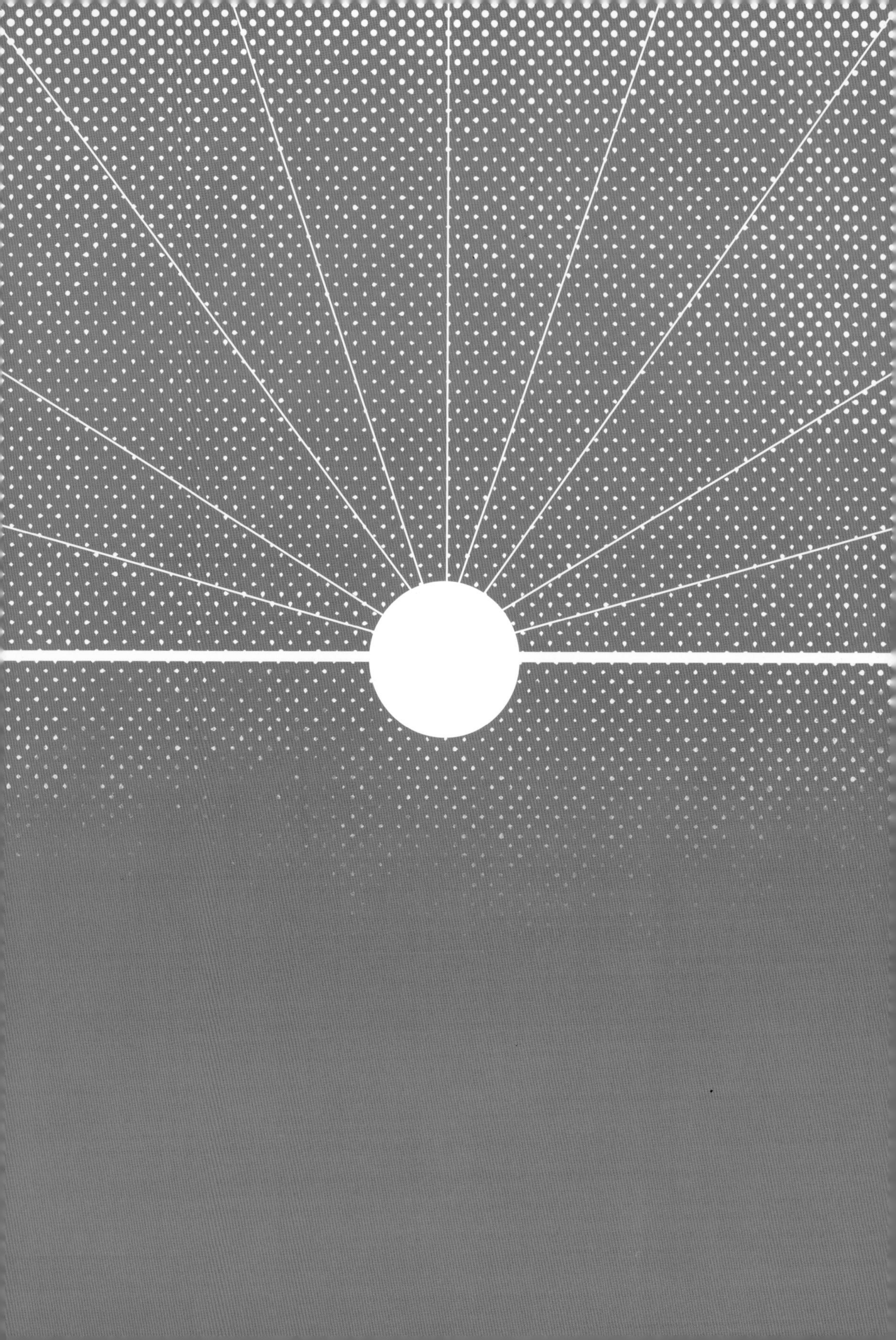

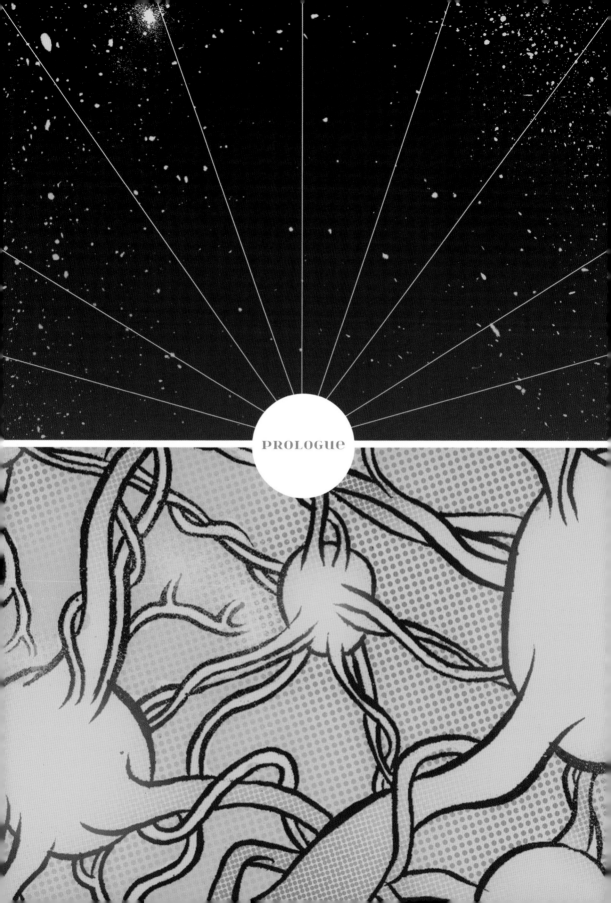

PROLOGUE

THIS IS HOW IT ALL BEGINS.
THE CURTAIN OF REALITY DROPS
TO SHOW US A WHOLE CONSTELLATION
OF EVENTS, PEOPLE, AND ACTIONS.

FICTION PREVAILS!
GIVING SHAPE TO A WORLD
THAT FINDS ITSELF HALFWAY
BETWEEN THE MYTHICAL AND THE HUMAN,
WHERE THE IMPOSSIBLE
BECOMES SYNONYMOUS
WITH EVERYDAY LIFE AND, AT THE SAME TIME,
WITH THE INCREDIBLE DOGMA OF FAITH.

DOZENS OF REIMAGINED AND REINVENTED
LIVES HOP ONSTAGE
WITH THE SOLE PURPOSE
OF COMPELLING, OF ENTERTAINING--
NEW GAZES FROM WHICH WE CAN
JUDGE EVENTS THAT HAVE HAPPENED
A THOUSAND AND ONE TIMES BEFORE.

HOLD THIS BOOK WITH ALL YOUR STRENGTH,
AS IT IS GIVING BIRTH TO THE STORY OF THE BOY
WHO GREW WITHOUT LOVE,
THE STORY OF THE MAN
WHO LOVED EVERYONE ELSE
MUCH MORE THAN HE LOVED HIMSELF,
THE STORY OF THE CHAMPION THAT,
WITH ALL HIS TRIUMPHS AND BLUNDERS,
BEFORE, NOW, AND FOREVER,
WILL BE KNOWN AS...

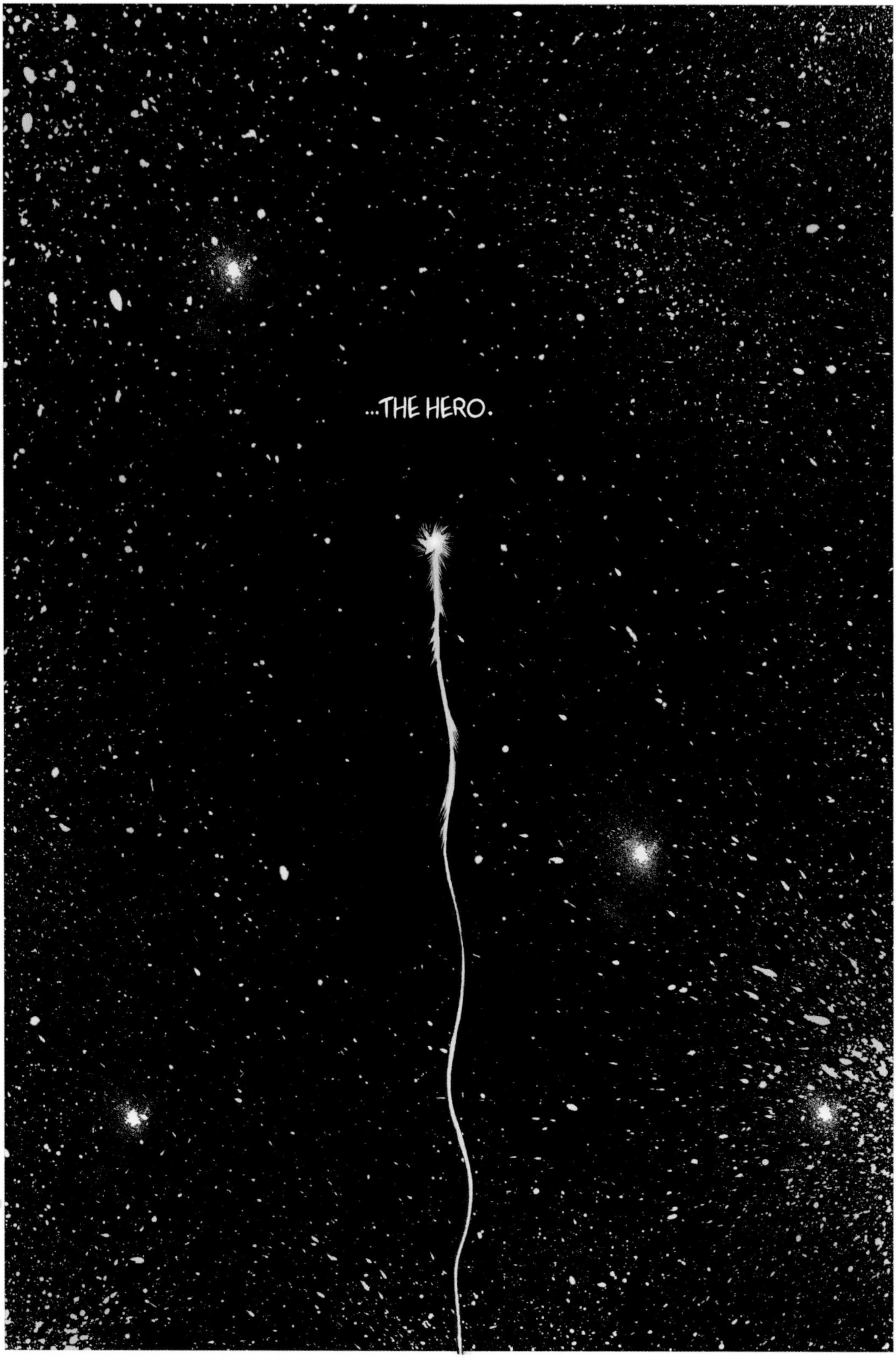
...THE HERO.

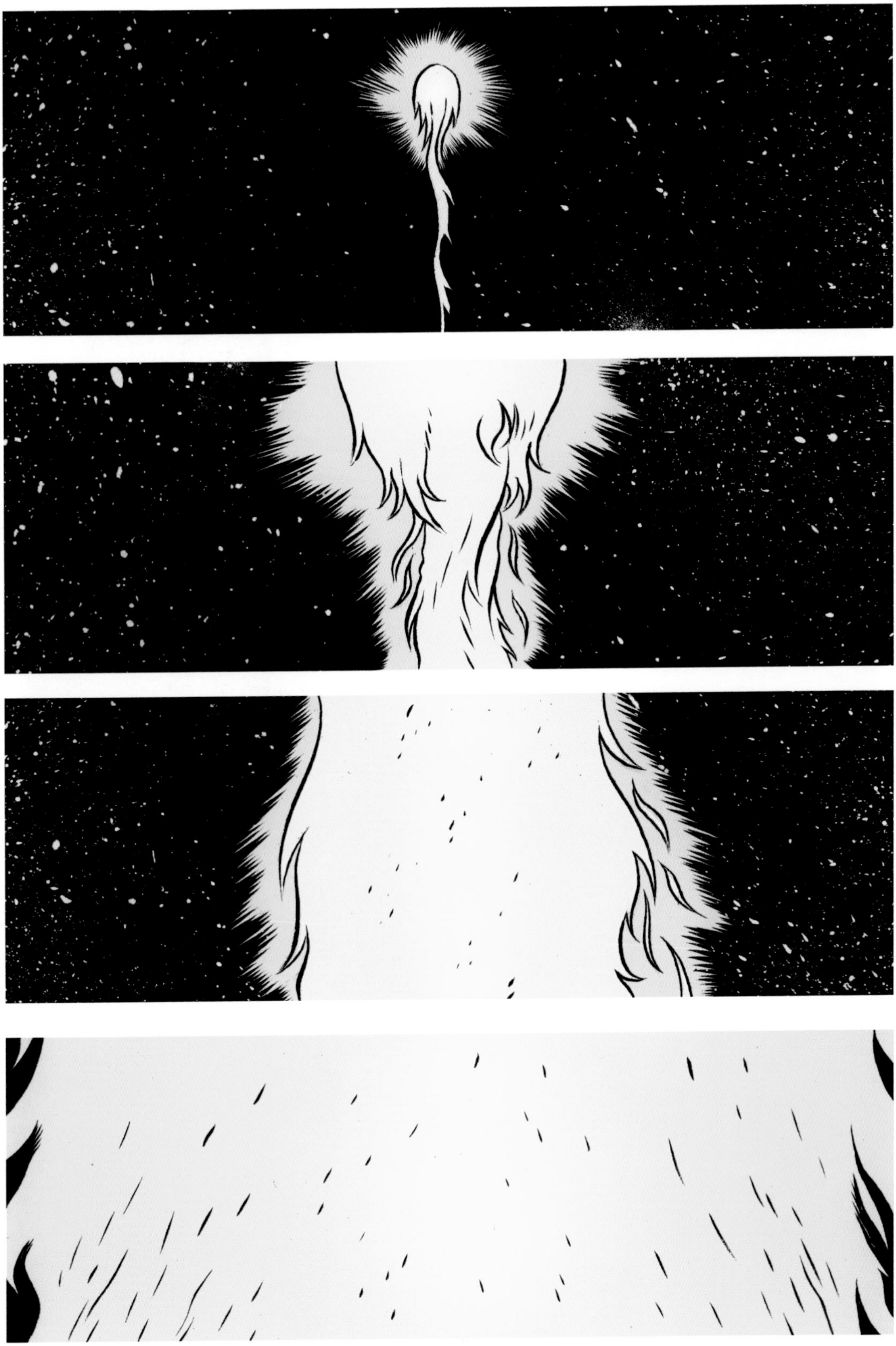

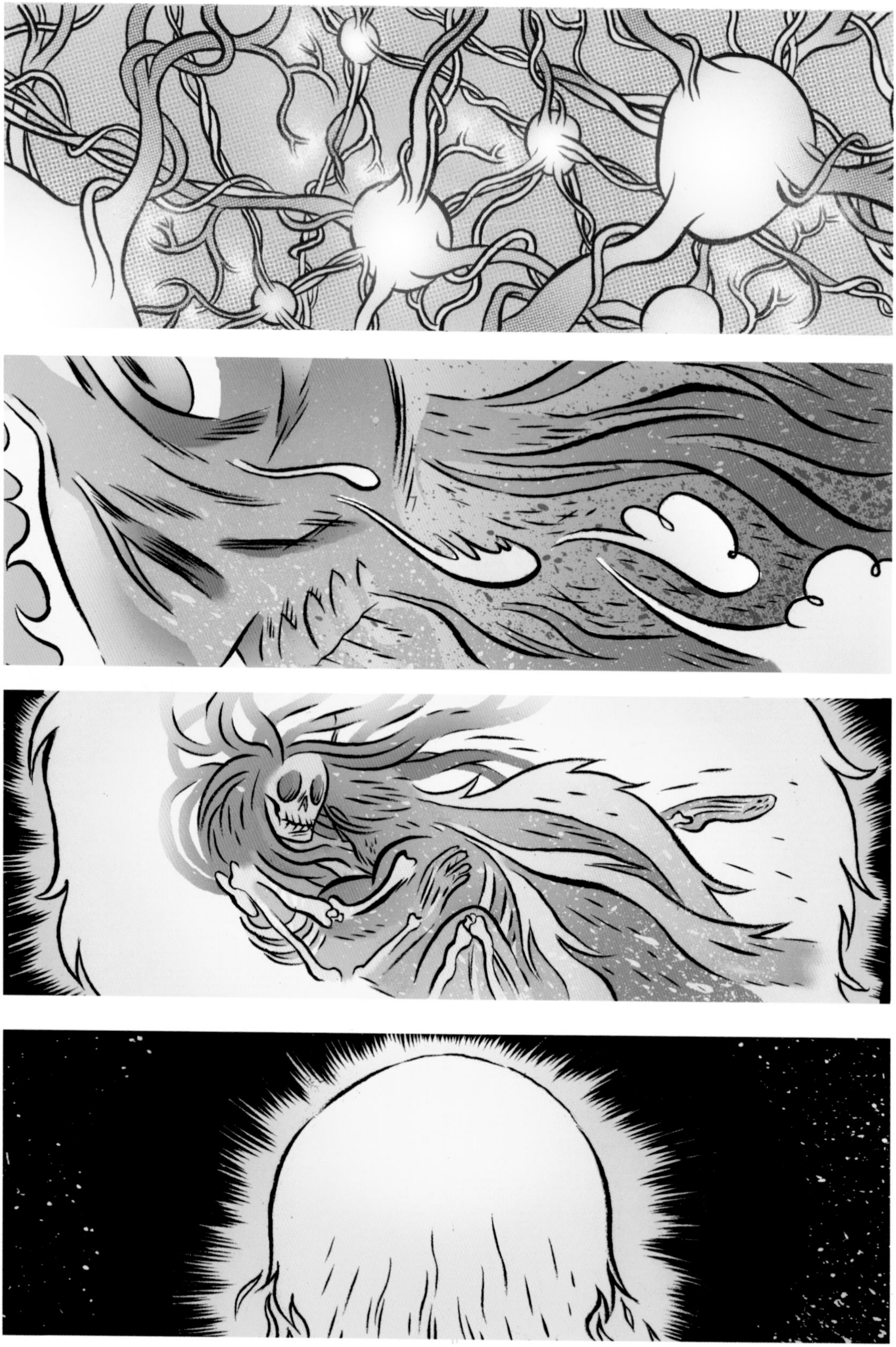

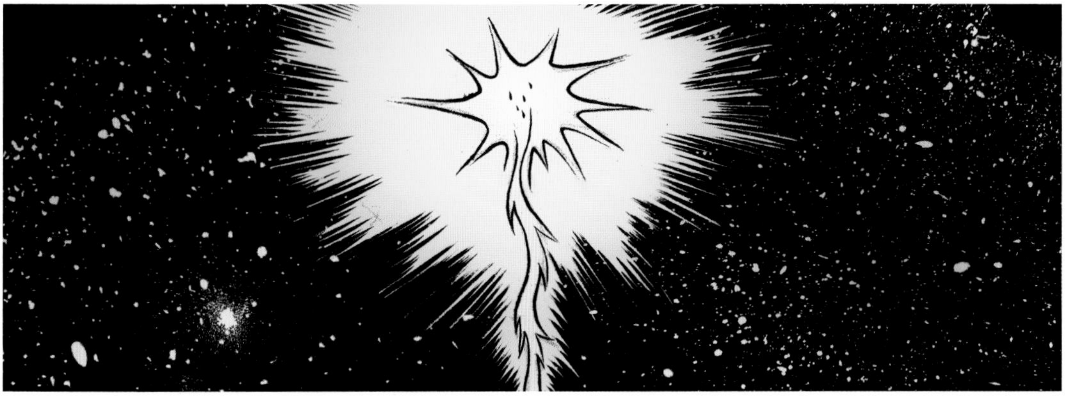

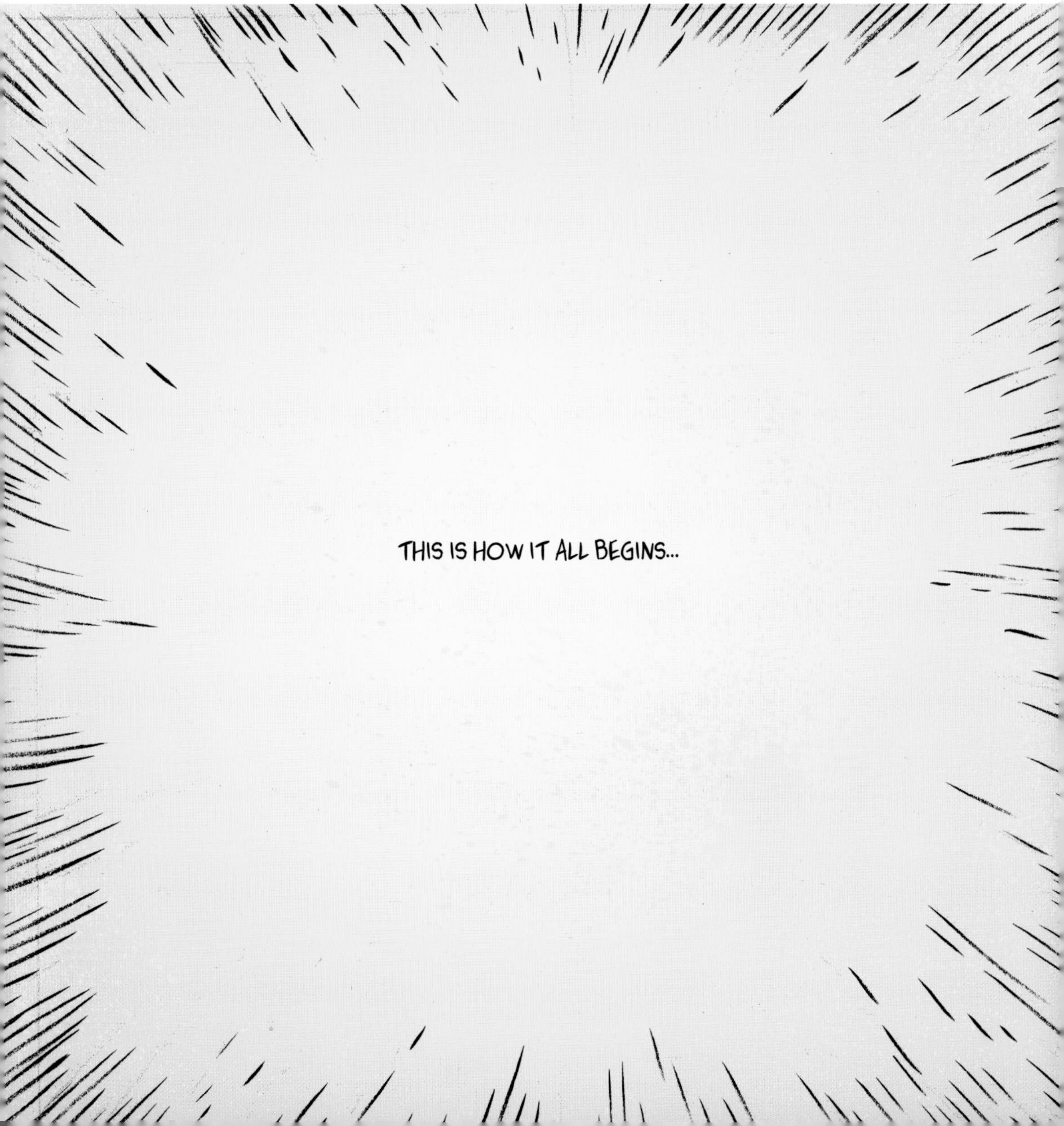
THIS IS HOW IT ALL BEGINS...

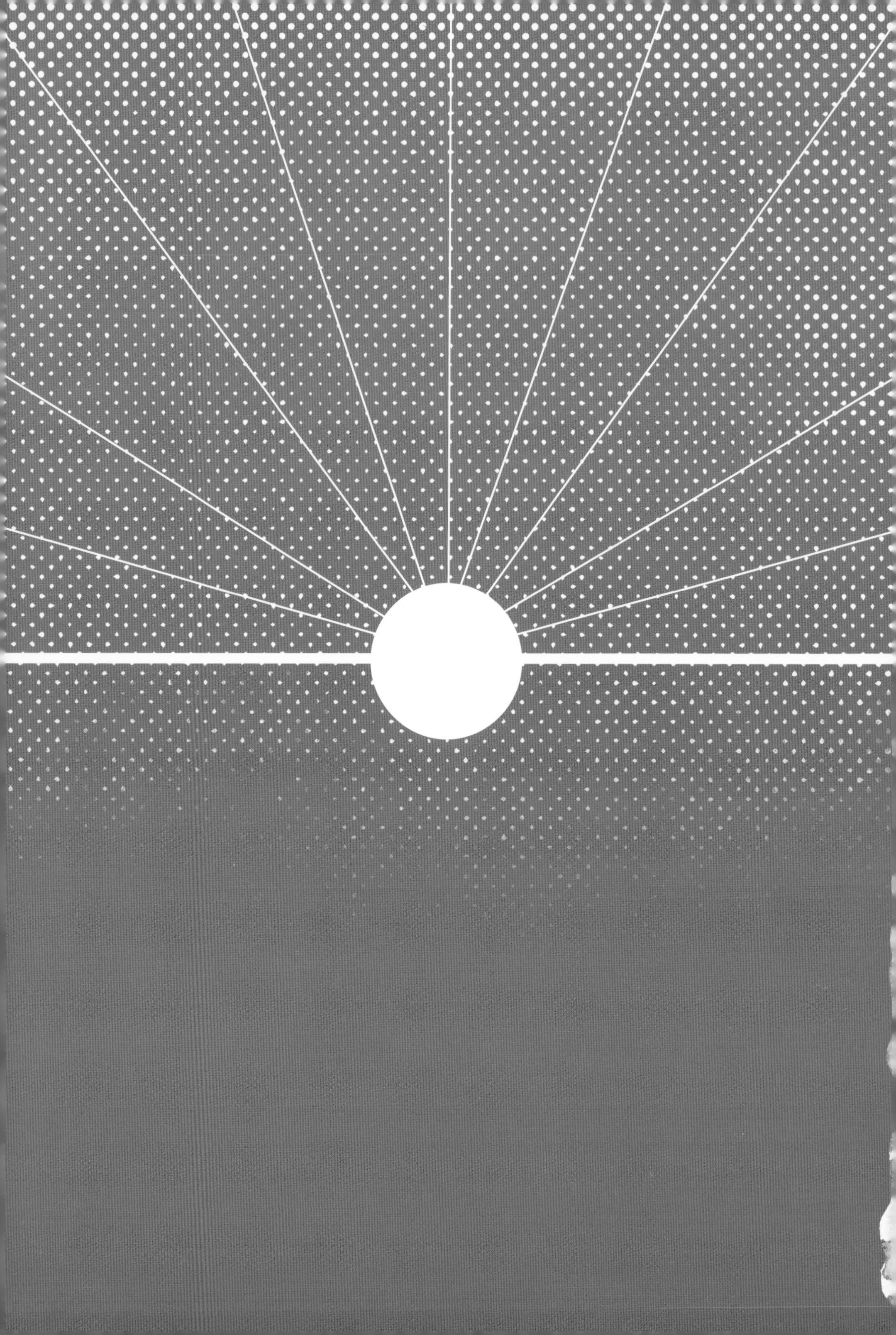

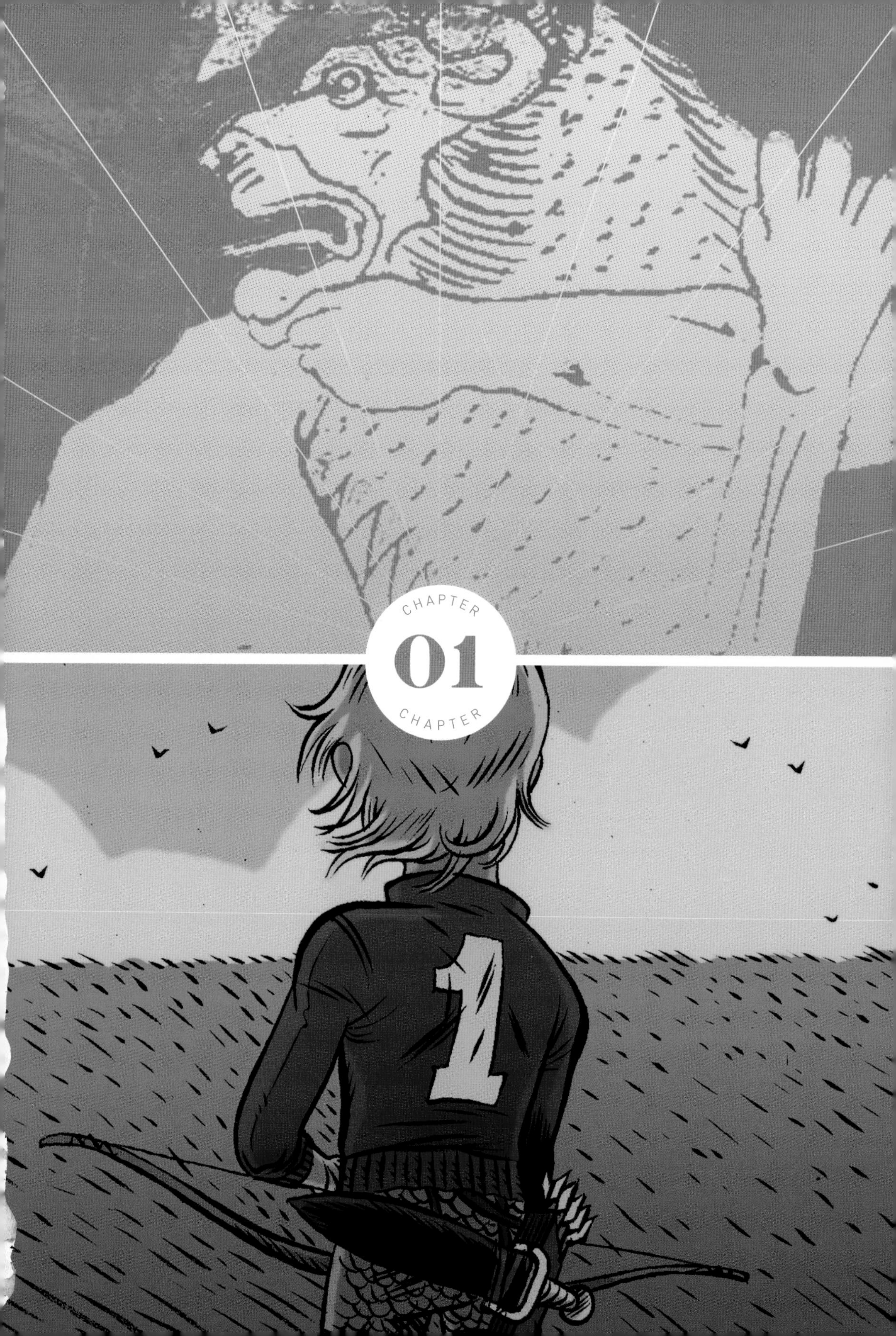
CHAPTER
01
CHAPTER
1

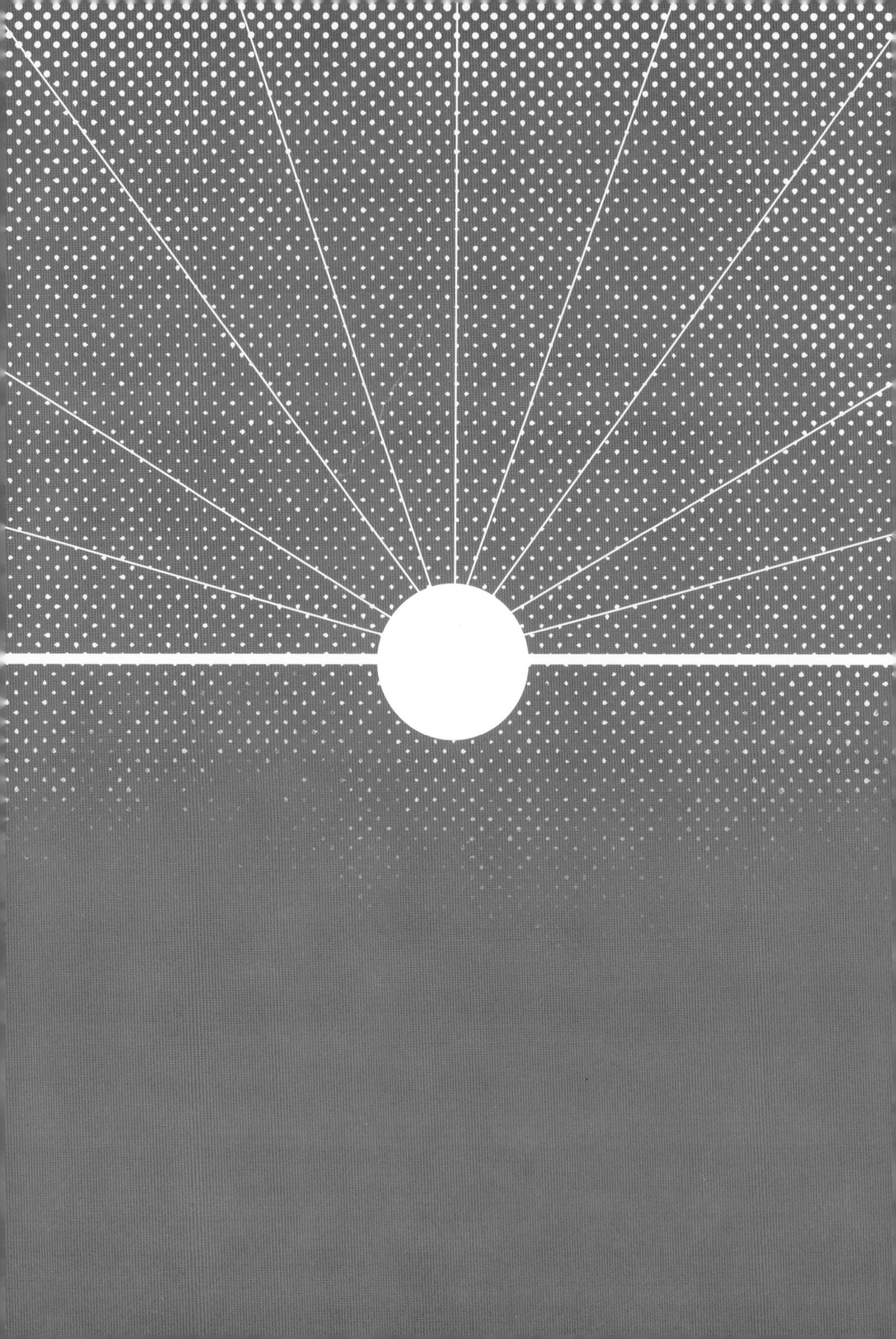

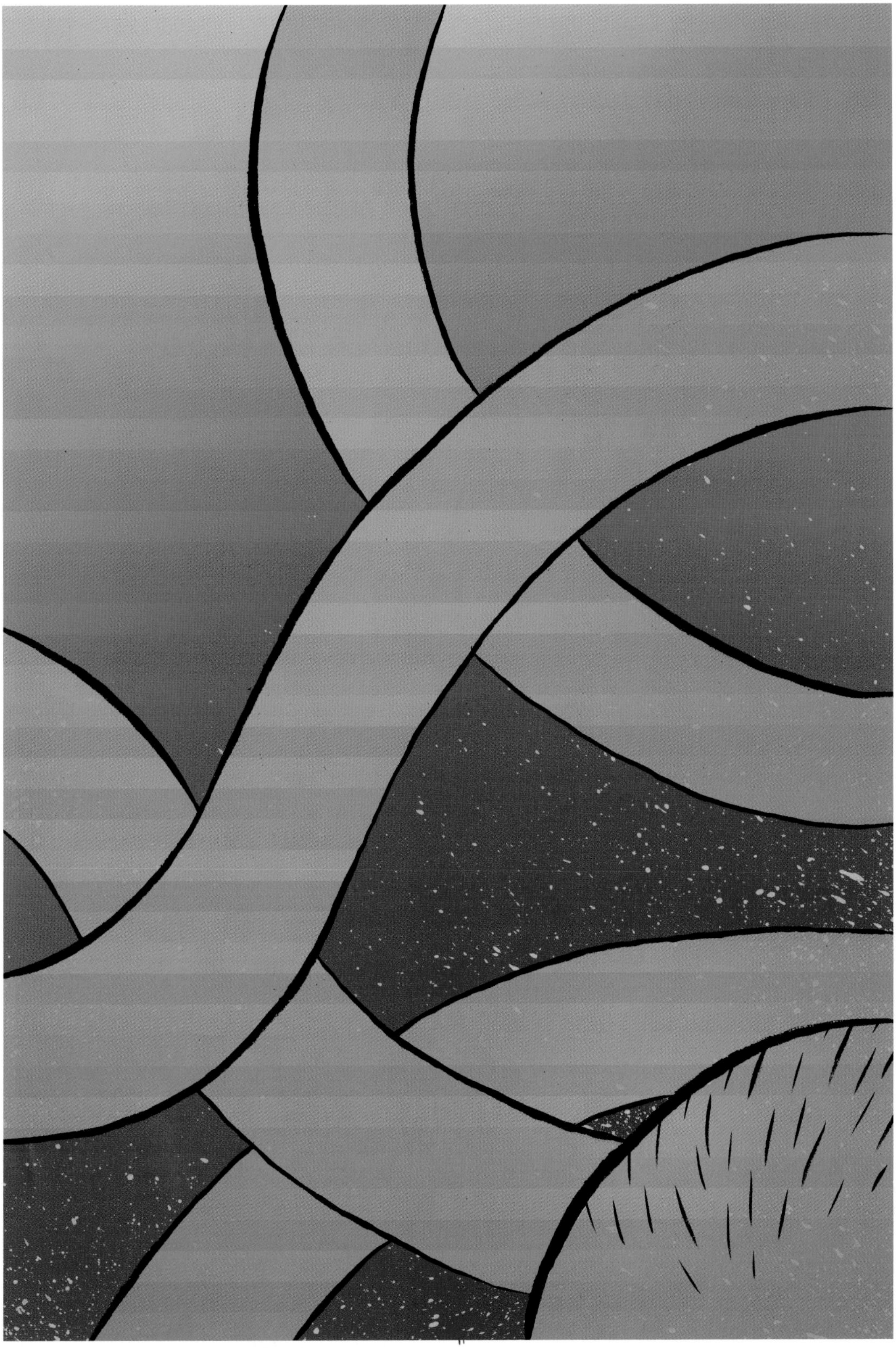

name__EURYSTHEUS
TIME UNTIL BIRTH__
      03m_02w_06d

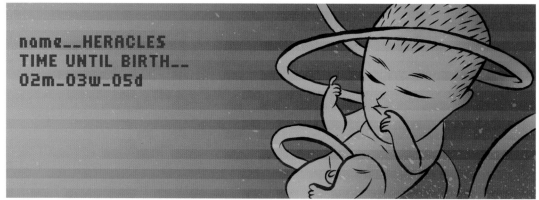

name__HERACLES
TIME UNTIL BIRTH__
02m_03w_05d

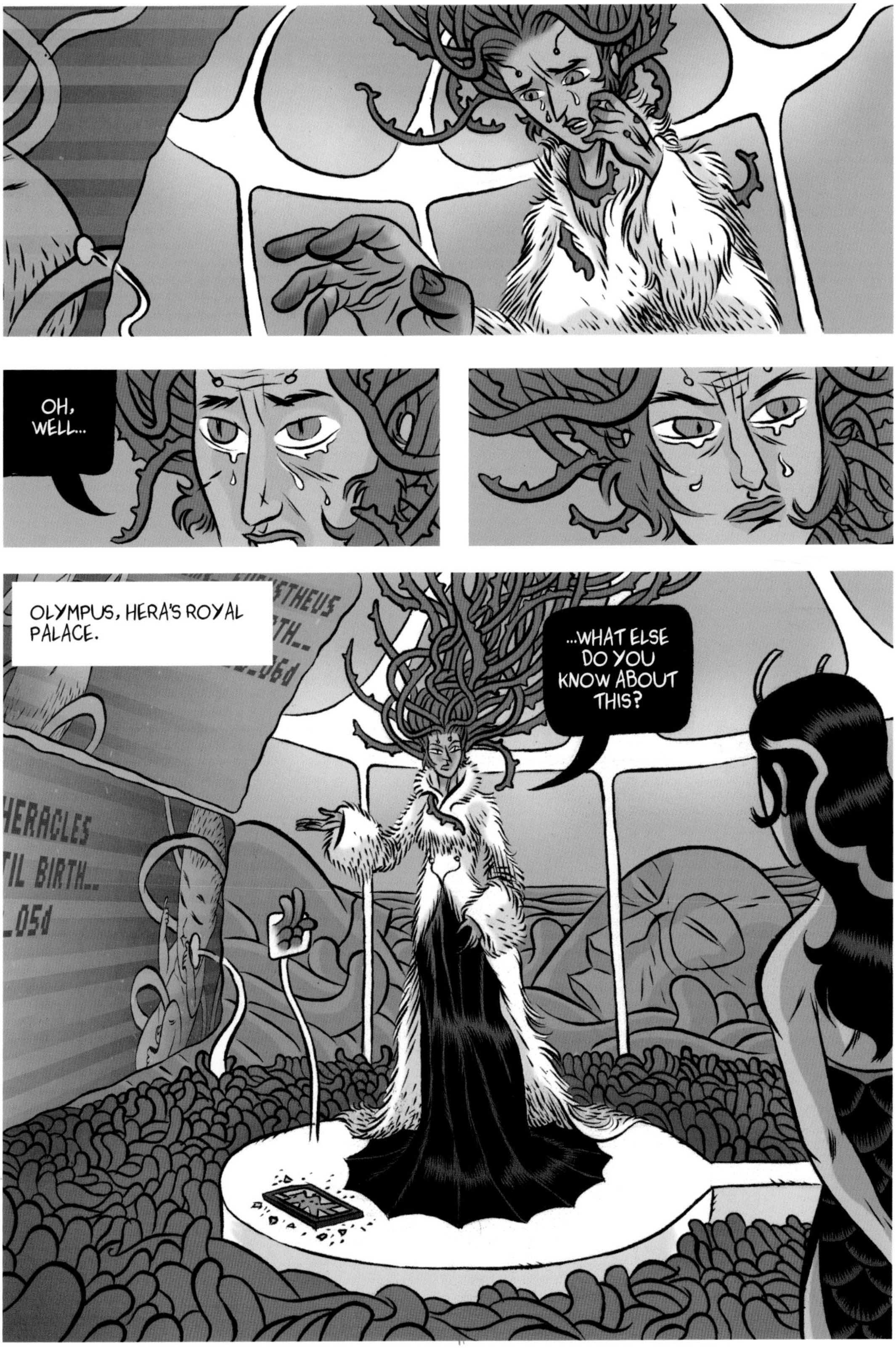
OH, WELL...
OLYMPUS, HERA'S ROYAL PALACE.
...WHAT ELSE DO YOU KNOW ABOUT THIS?
HERACLES

FATE HAS DETERMINED THAT THE BABY WHO IS BORN FIRST WILL RULE OVER THE OTHER.

EURYSTHEUS WILL BECOME A TYRANT, EAGER TO CONQUER AND ALWAYS HUNGRY FOR POWER...

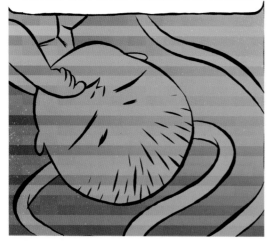

...AND HERACLES WILL BE A GREAT HERO.

HMMM ...

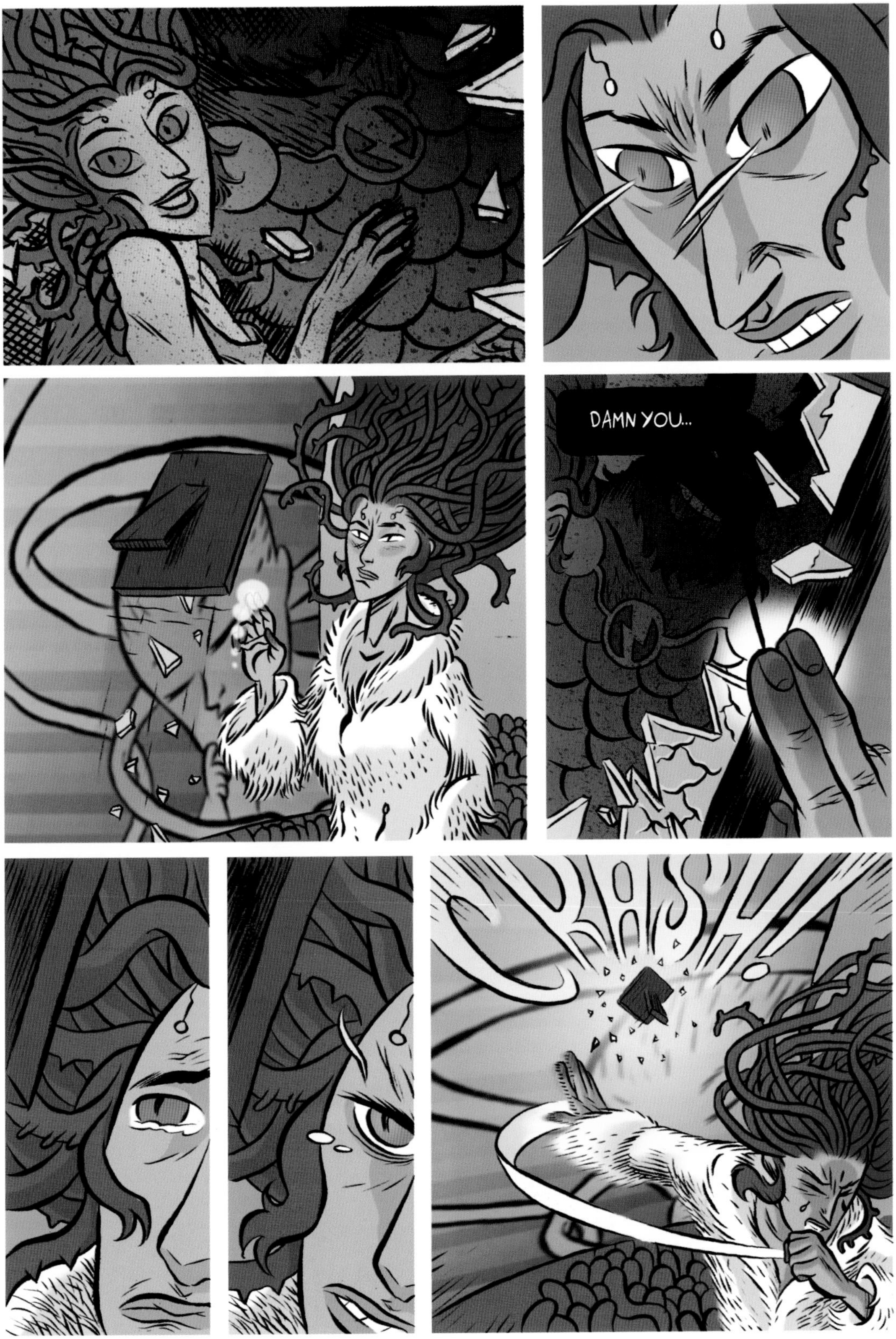
DAMN YOU...
CRASH!

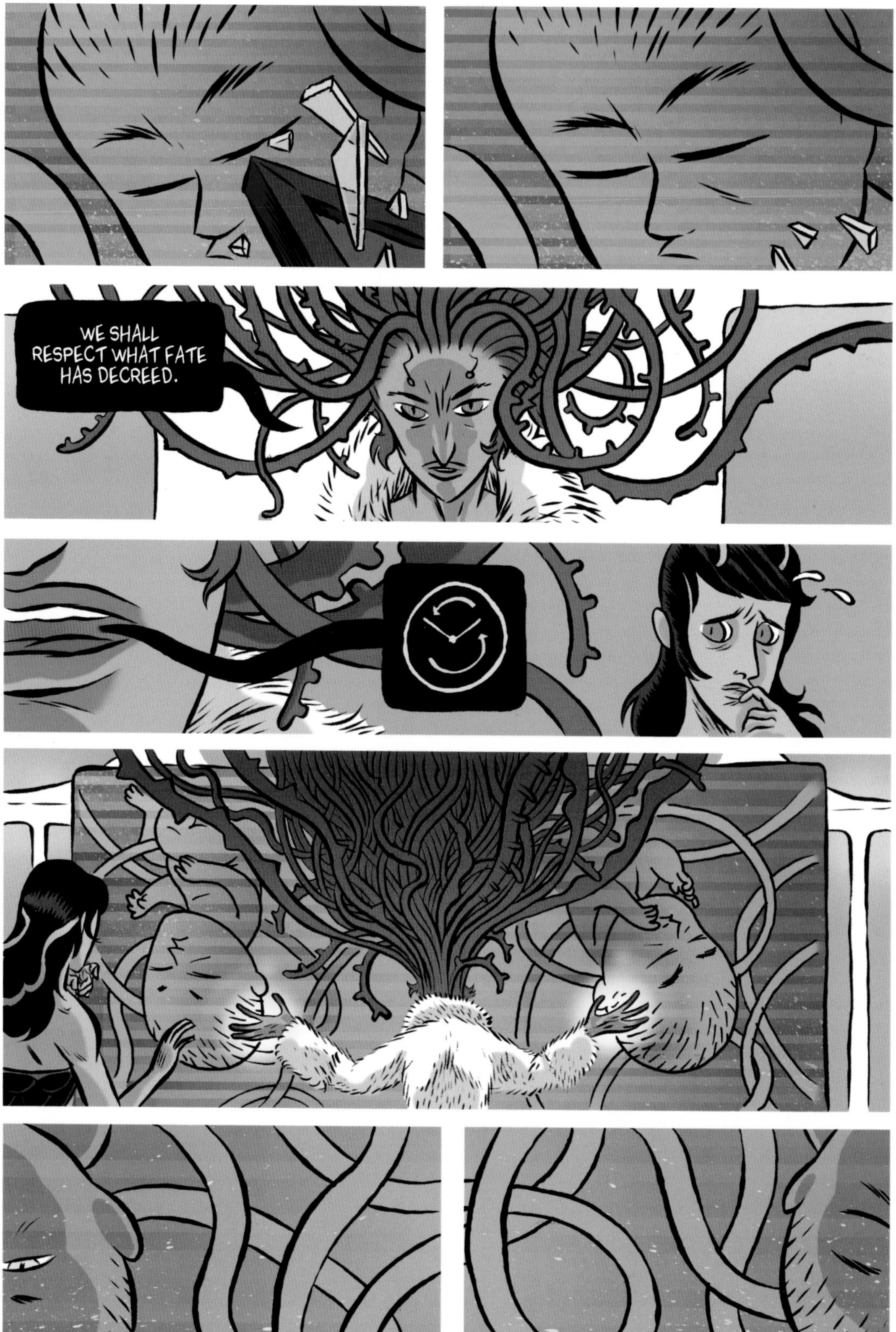
WE SHALL RESPECT WHAT FATE HAS DECREED.

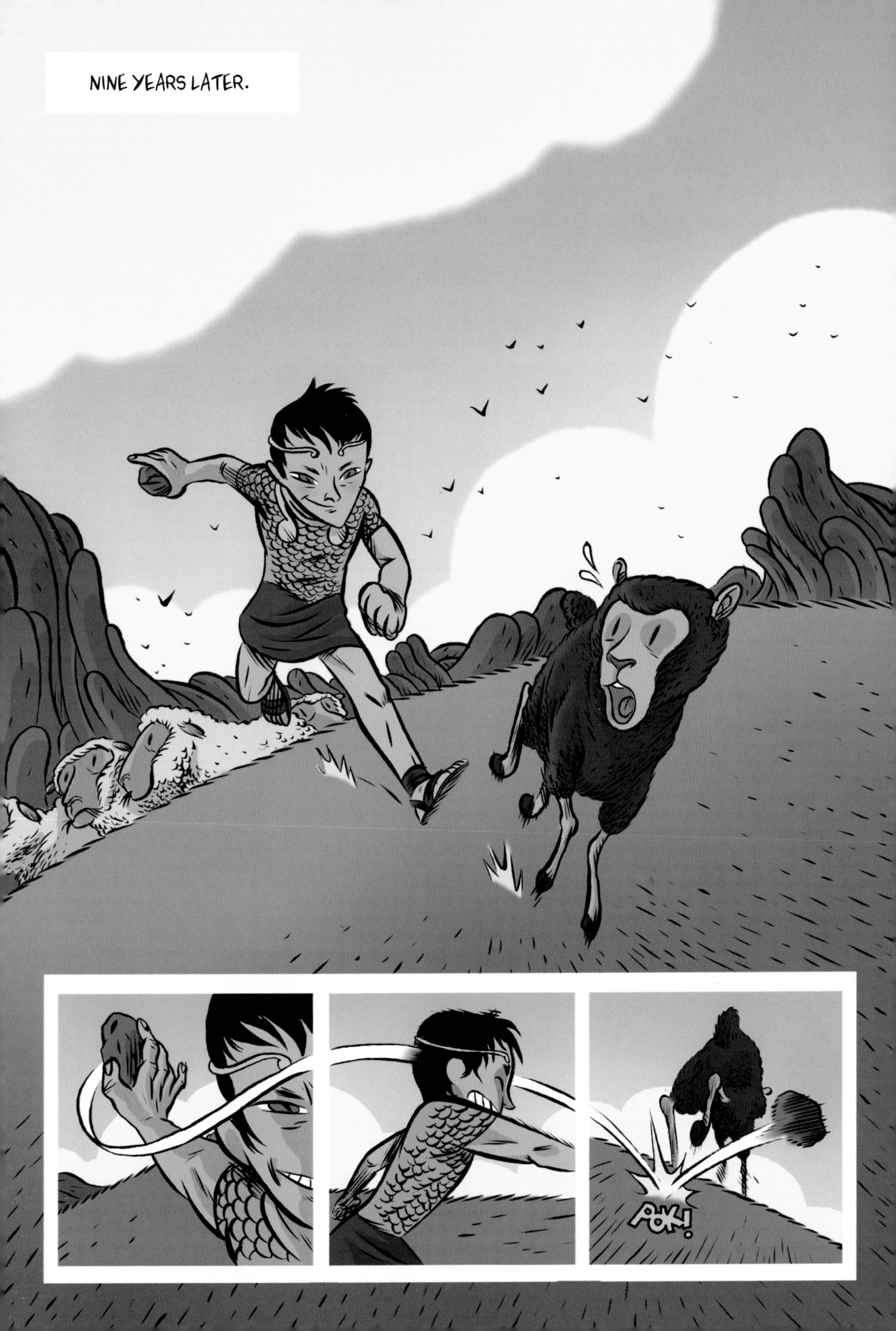
NINE YEARS LATER.
POK!

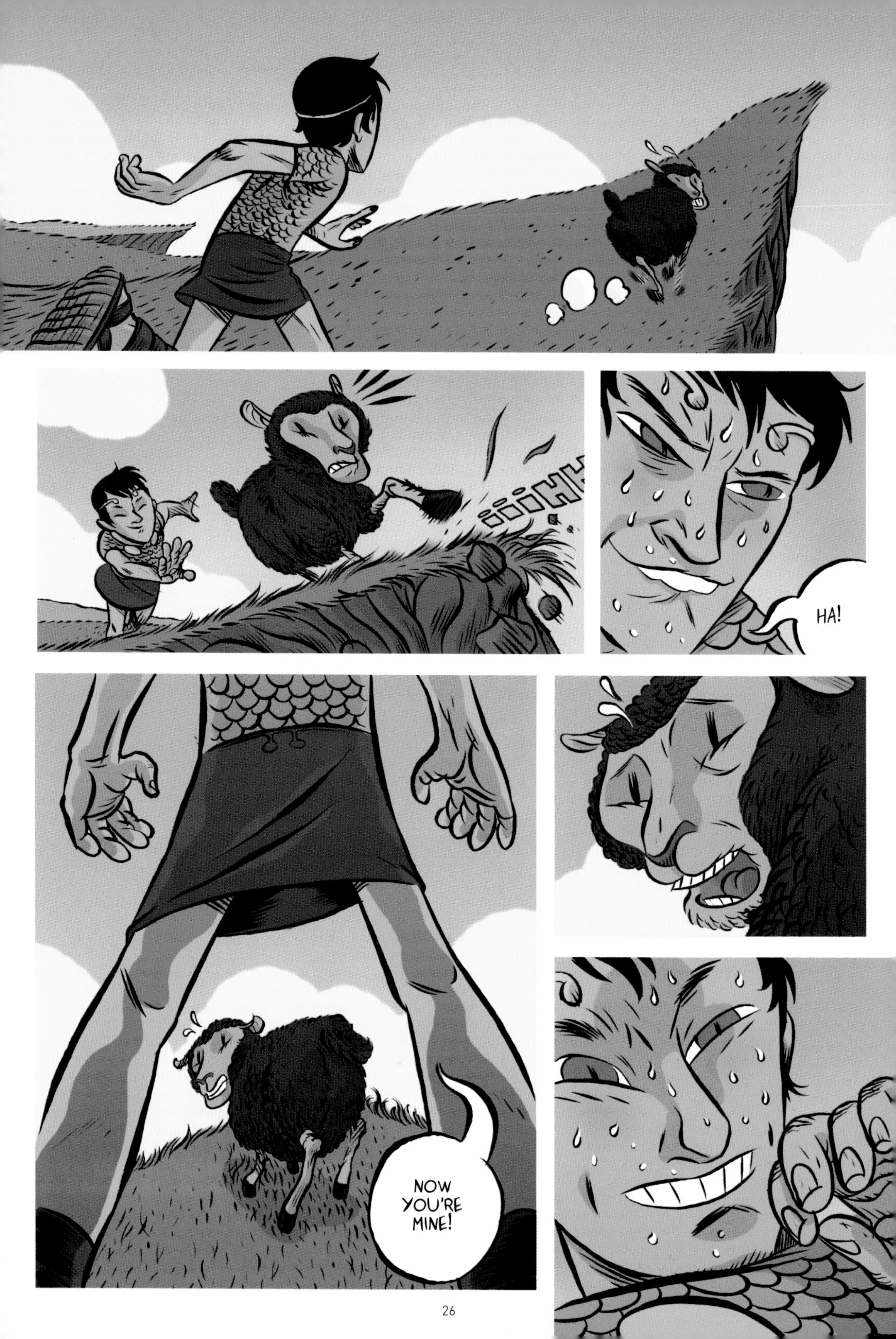
HA!
NOW YOU'RE MINE!

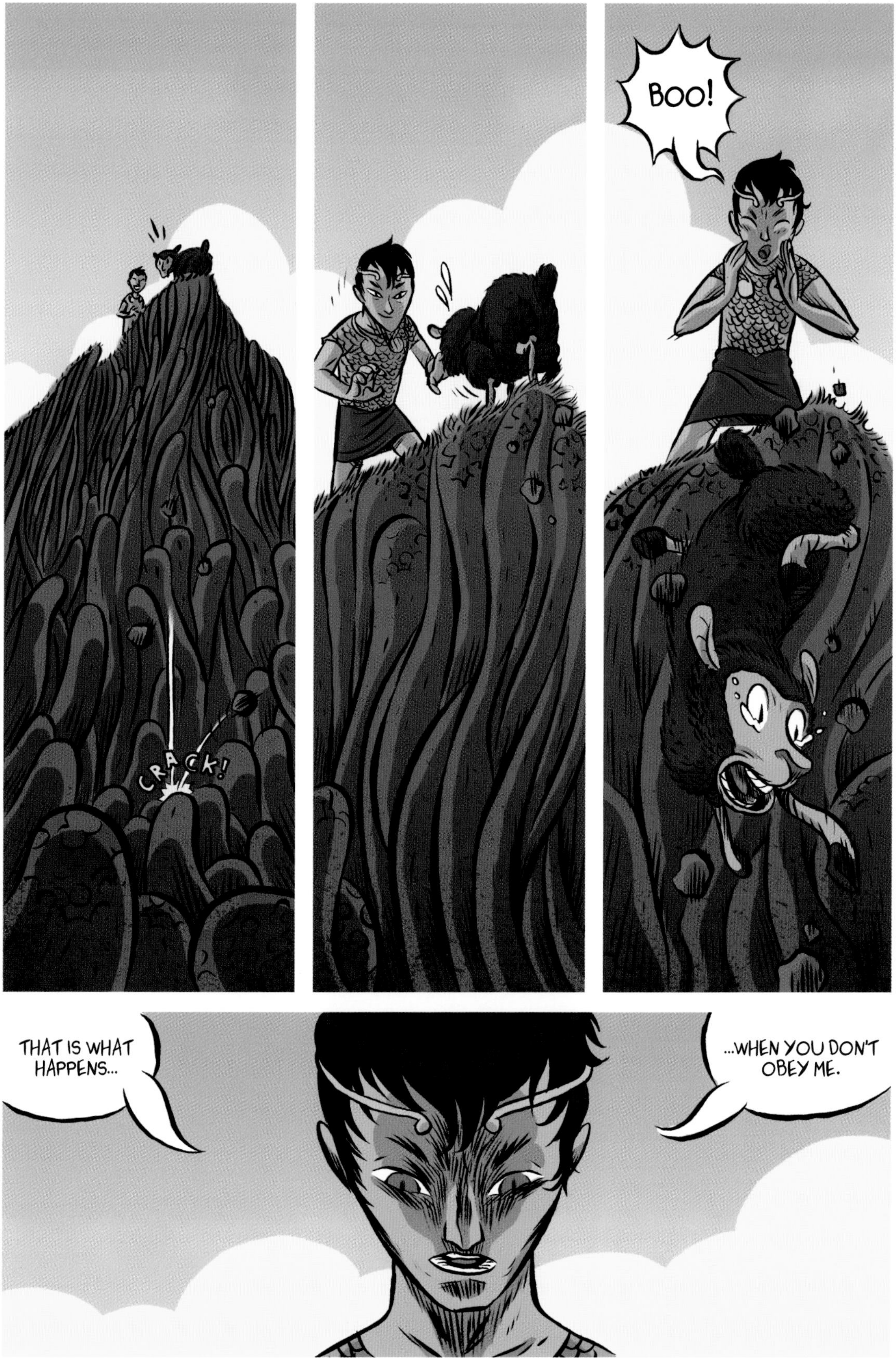
CRACK!
BOO!
THAT IS WHAT HAPPENS...
...WHEN YOU DON'T OBEY ME.

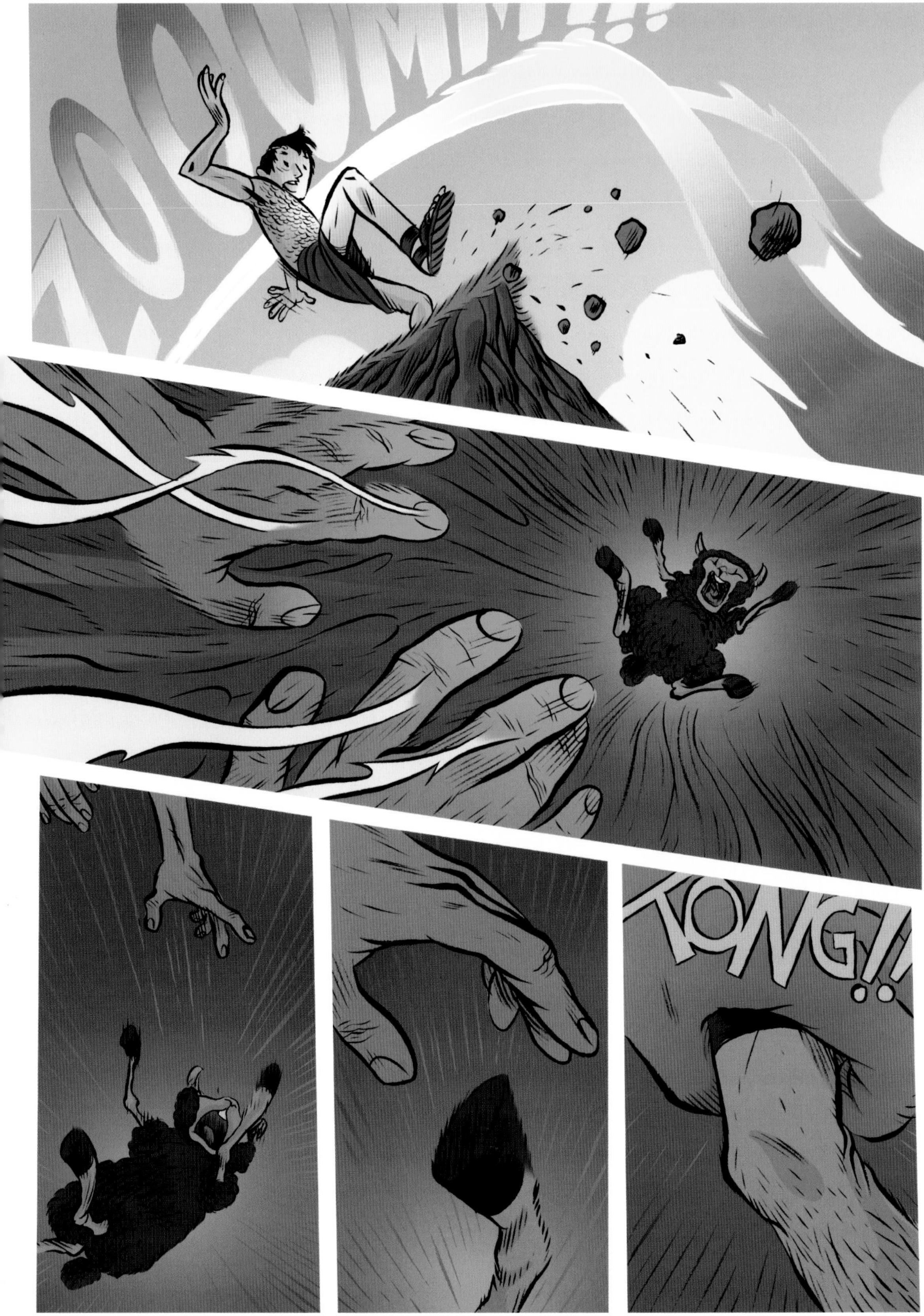
TONG!!

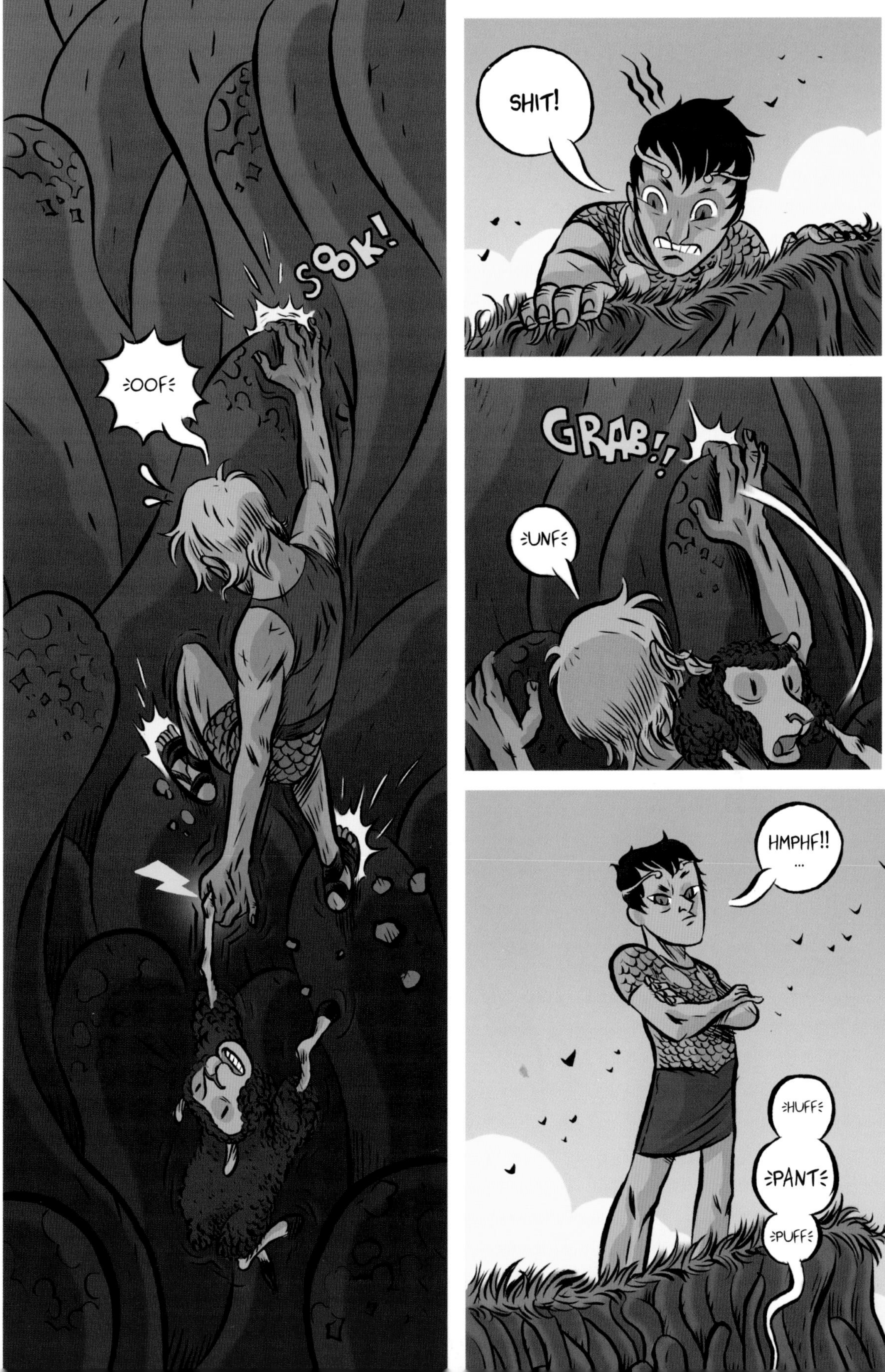
SOOK!
OOF
SHIT!
GRAB!!
UNF
HMPHF!!
...
HUFF
PANT
PUFF

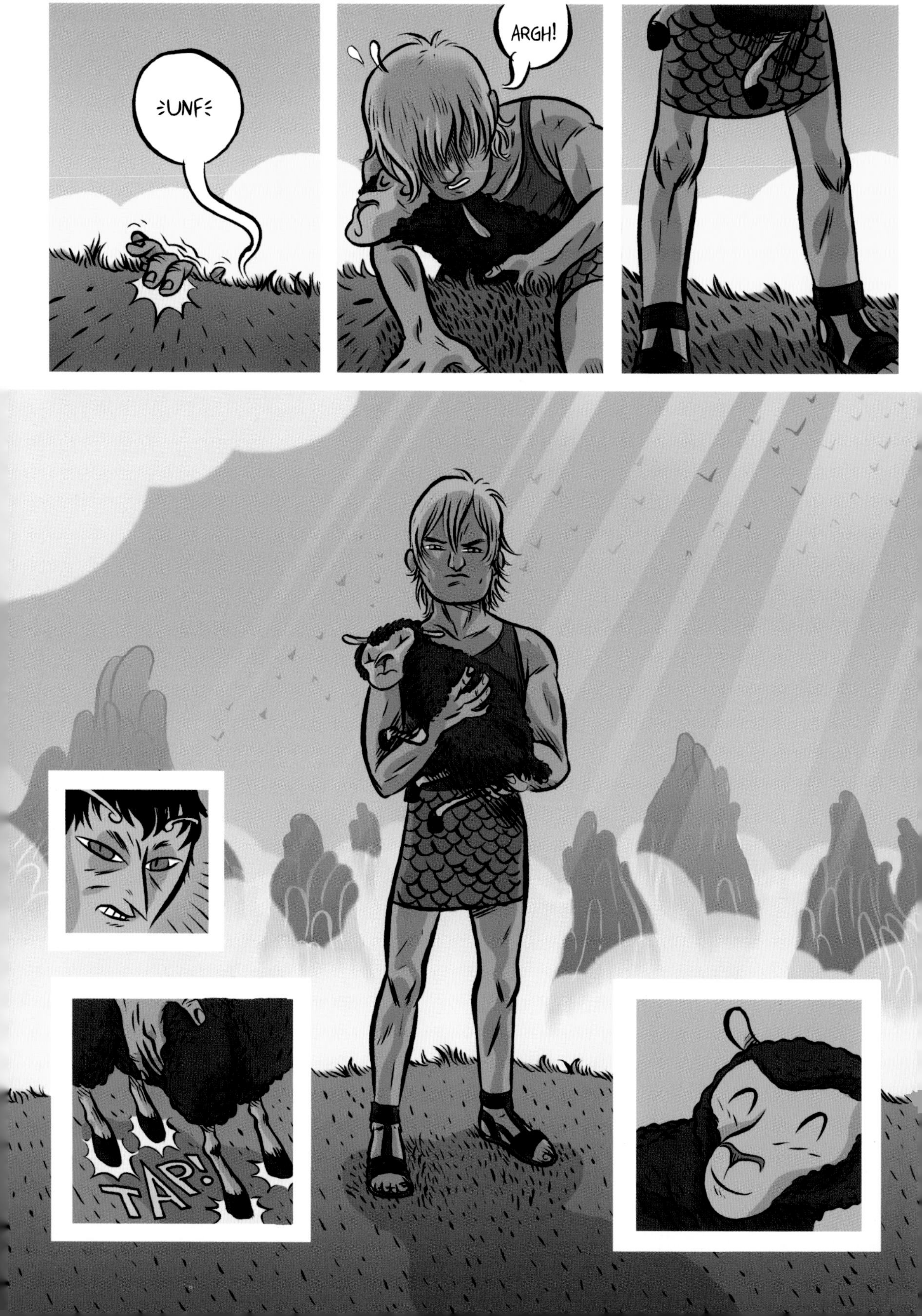
UNF
ARGH!
TAP!

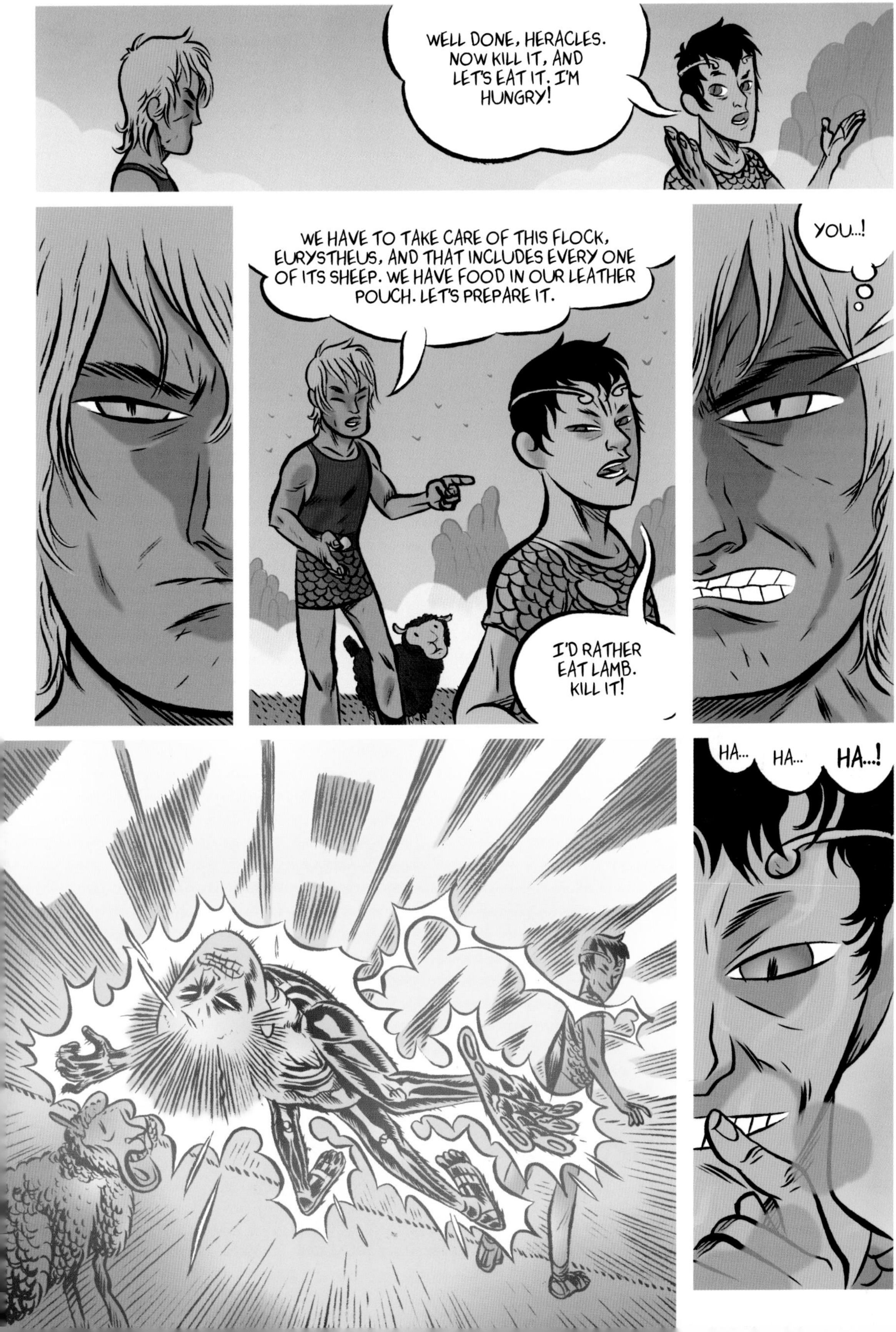
WELL DONE, HERACLES. NOW KILL IT, AND LET'S EAT IT. I'M HUNGRY!
WE HAVE TO TAKE CARE OF THIS FLOCK, EURYSTHEUS, AND THAT INCLUDES EVERY ONE OF ITS SHEEP. WE HAVE FOOD IN OUR LEATHER POUCH. LET'S PREPARE IT.
I'D RATHER EAT LAMB. KILL IT!
YOU...!
HA... HA... HA...!

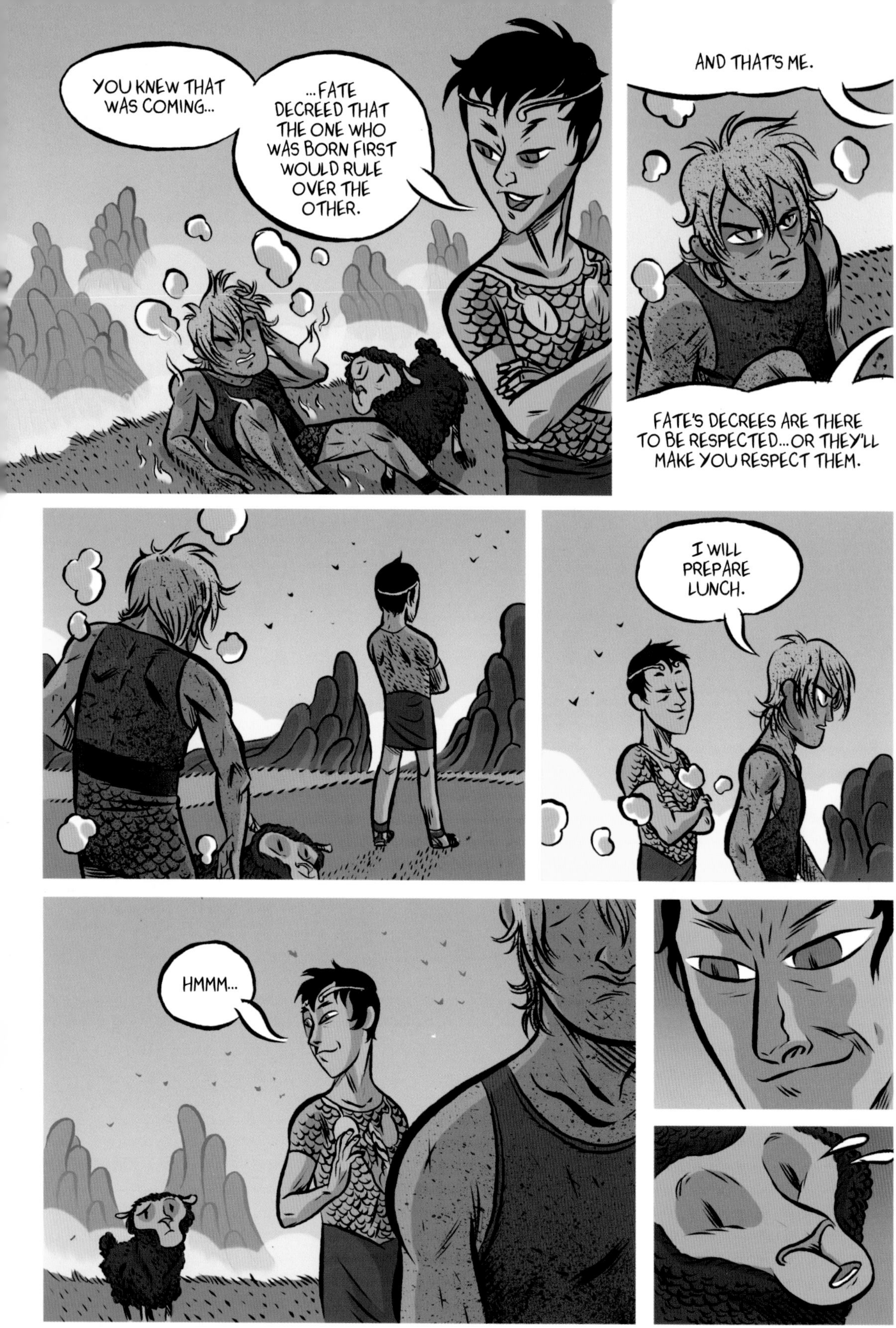
YOU KNEW THAT WAS COMING...
...FATE DECREED THAT THE ONE WHO WAS BORN FIRST WOULD RULE OVER THE OTHER.
AND THAT'S ME.
FATE'S DECREES ARE THERE TO BE RESPECTED...OR THEY'LL MAKE YOU RESPECT THEM.
I WILL PREPARE LUNCH.
HMMM...

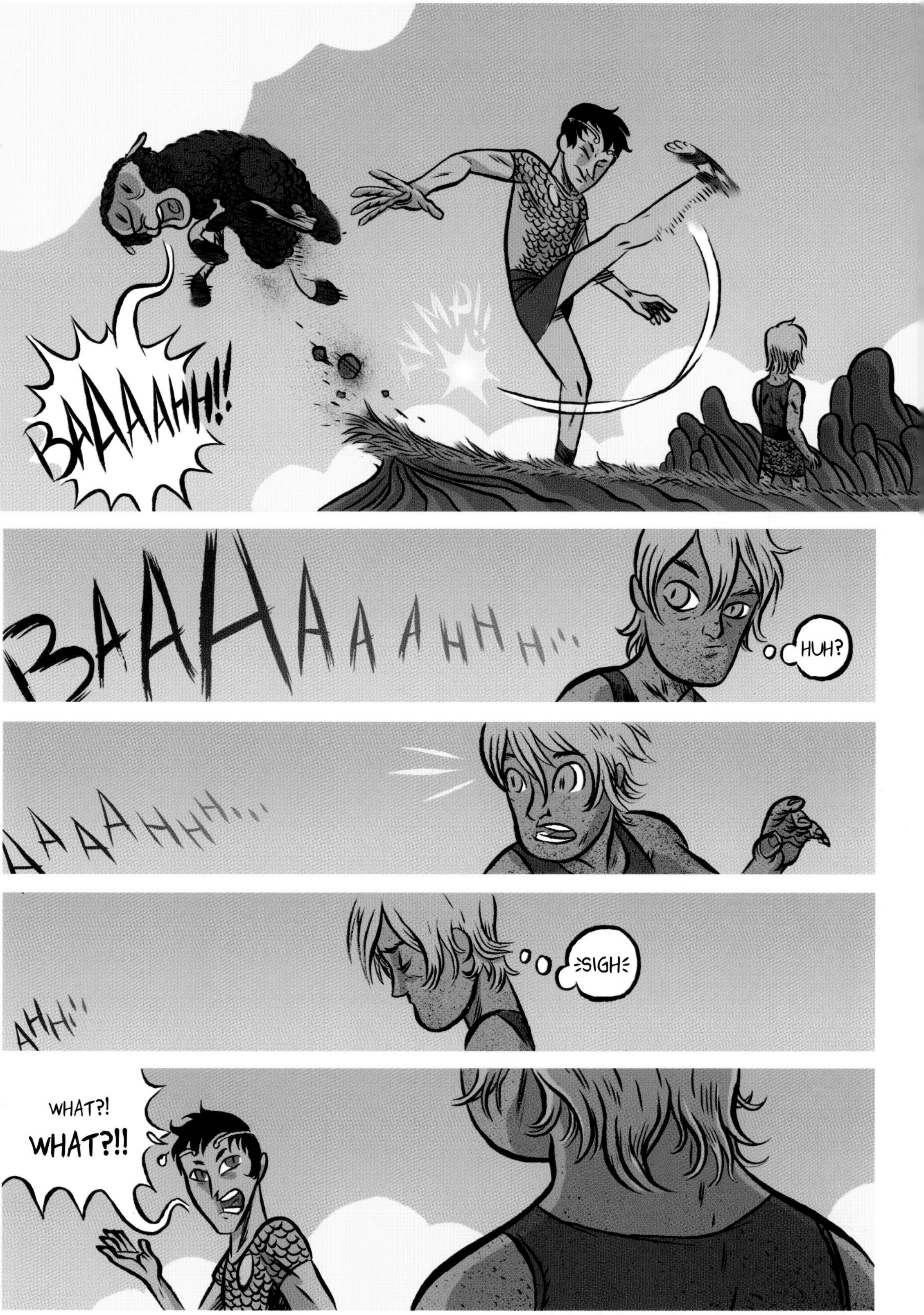
BAAAAHH!!
TVMP!!
BAAHAAAAHHH...
HUH?
AAAAAHHH...
AHH
SIGH
WHAT?!
WHAT?!!

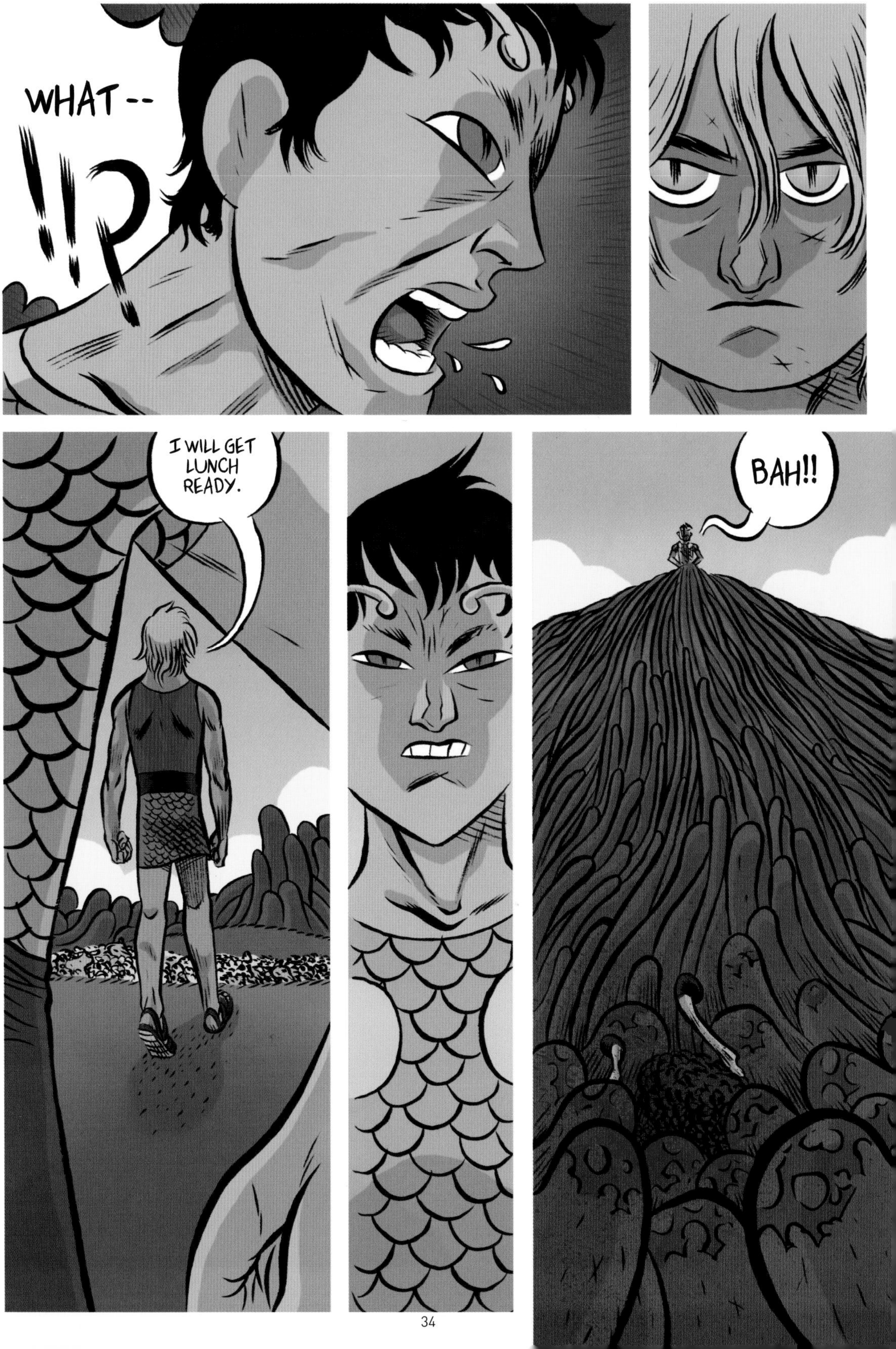
WHAT --
!!?
I WILL GET LUNCH READY.
BAH!!

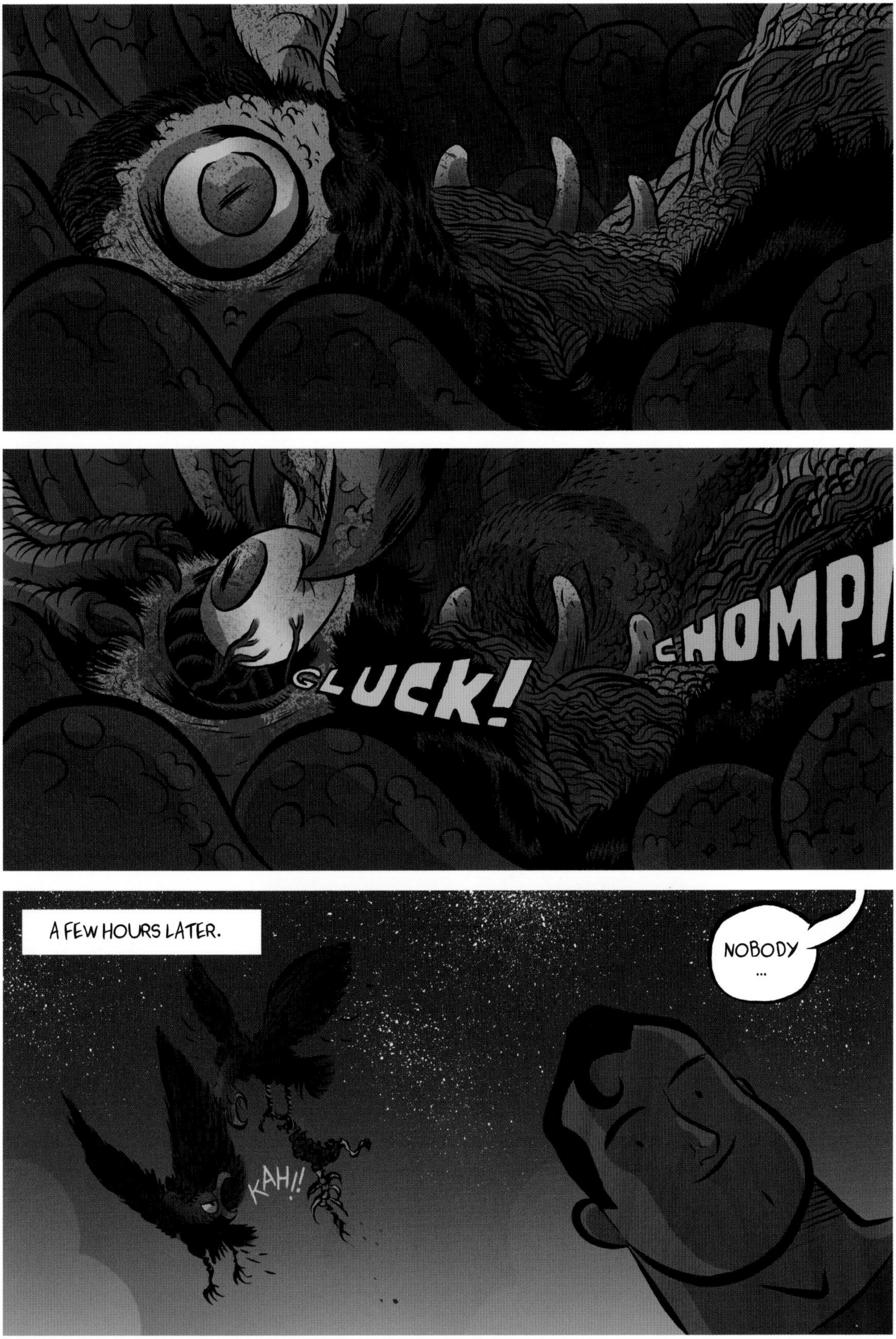
GLUCK!
CHOMP!
A FEW HOURS LATER.
NOBODY
...
KAH!!

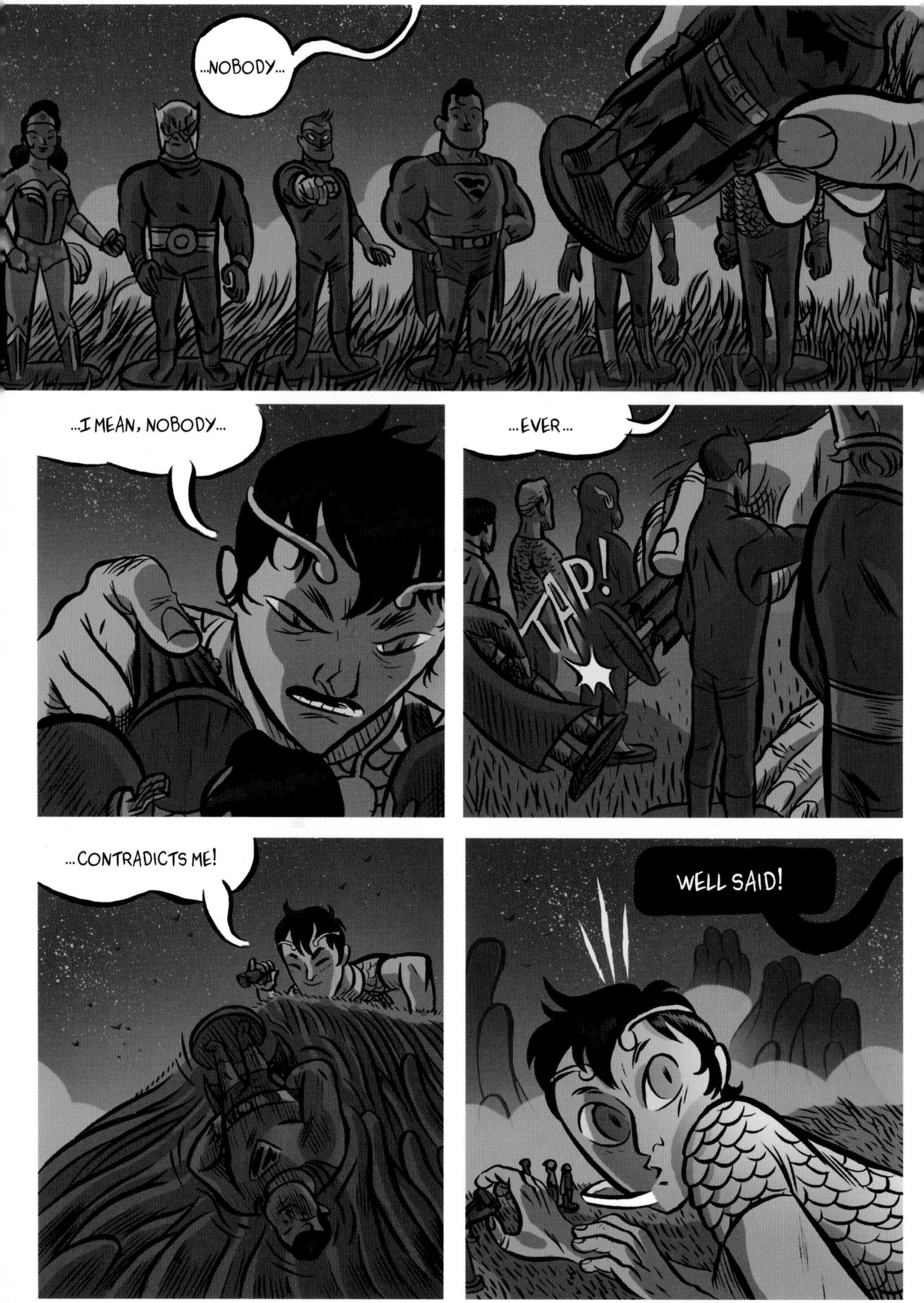
...NOBODY...
...I MEAN, NOBODY...
...EVER...
TAP!
...CONTRADICTS ME!
WELL SAID!

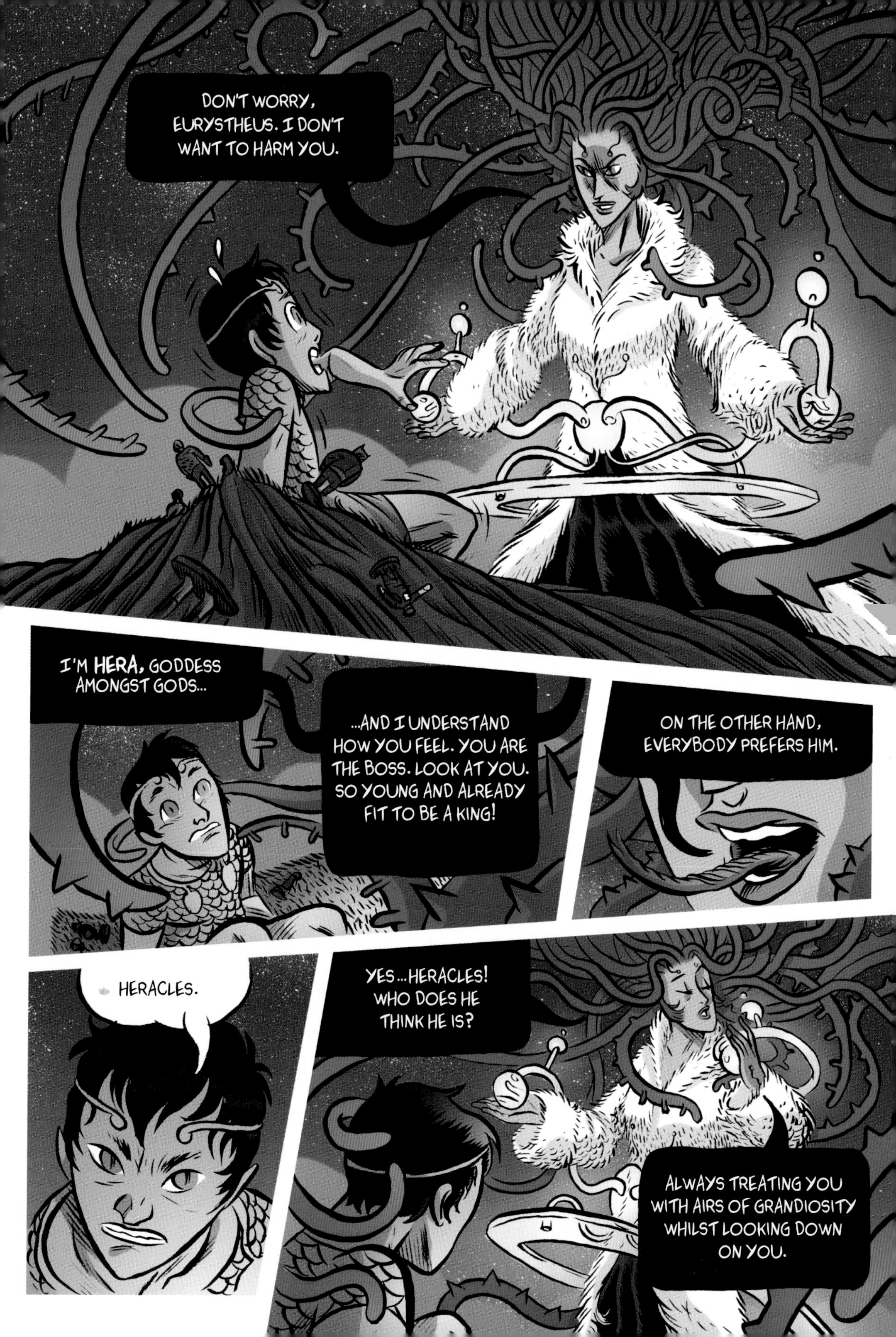

DON'T WORRY, EURYSTHEUS. I DON'T WANT TO HARM YOU.
I'M HERA, GODDESS AMONGST GODS...
...AND I UNDERSTAND HOW YOU FEEL. YOU ARE THE BOSS. LOOK AT YOU. SO YOUNG AND ALREADY FIT TO BE A KING!
ON THE OTHER HAND, EVERYBODY PREFERS HIM.
HERACLES.
YES...HERACLES! WHO DOES HE THINK HE IS?
ALWAYS TREATING YOU WITH AIRS OF GRANDIOSITY WHILST LOOKING DOWN ON YOU.

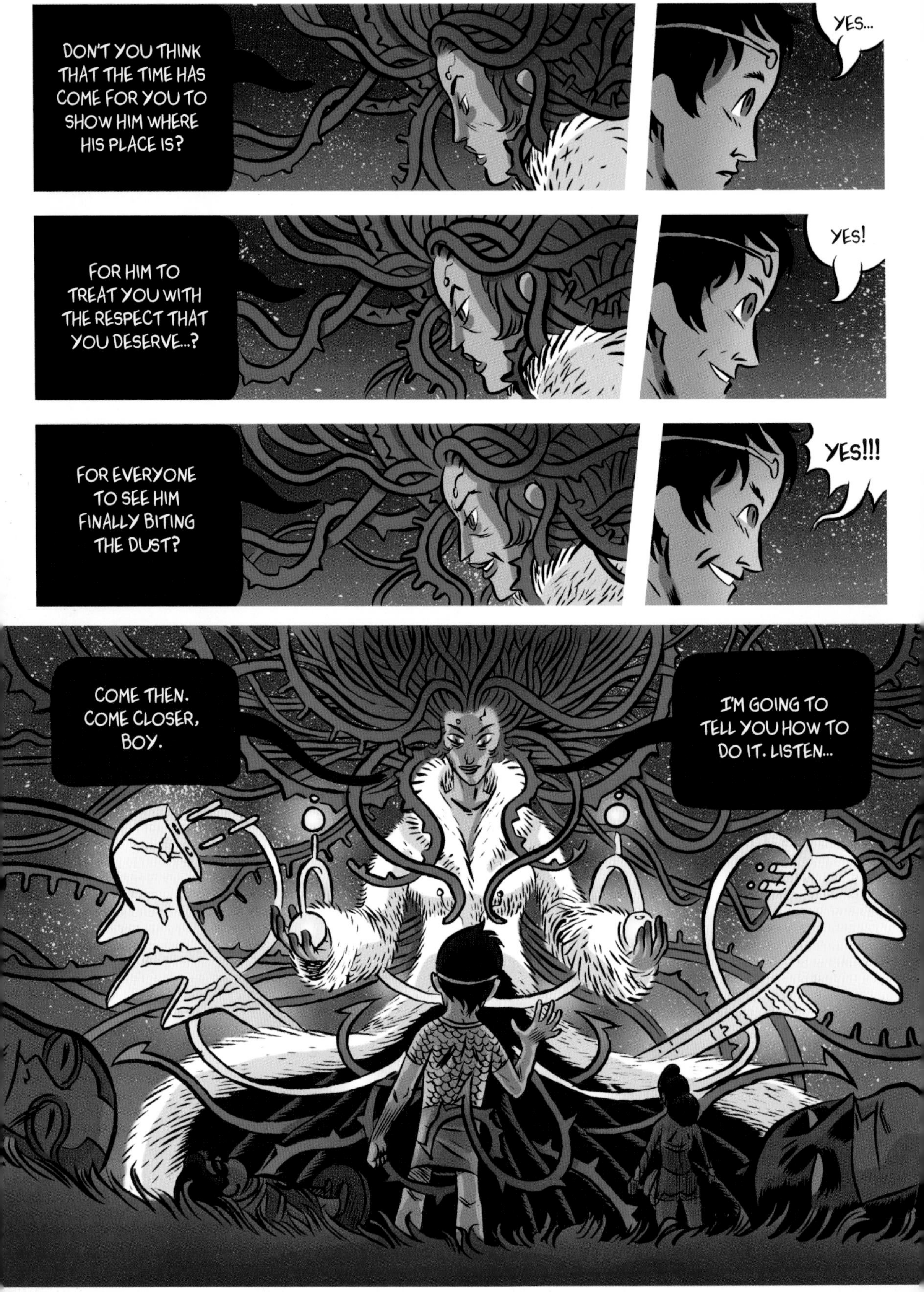
DON'T YOU THINK THAT THE TIME HAS COME FOR YOU TO SHOW HIM WHERE HIS PLACE IS?
YES...
FOR HIM TO TREAT YOU WITH THE RESPECT THAT YOU DESERVE...?
YES!
FOR EVERYONE TO SEE HIM FINALLY BITING THE DUST?
YES!!!
COME THEN. COME CLOSER, BOY.
I'M GOING TO TELL YOU HOW TO DO IT. LISTEN...

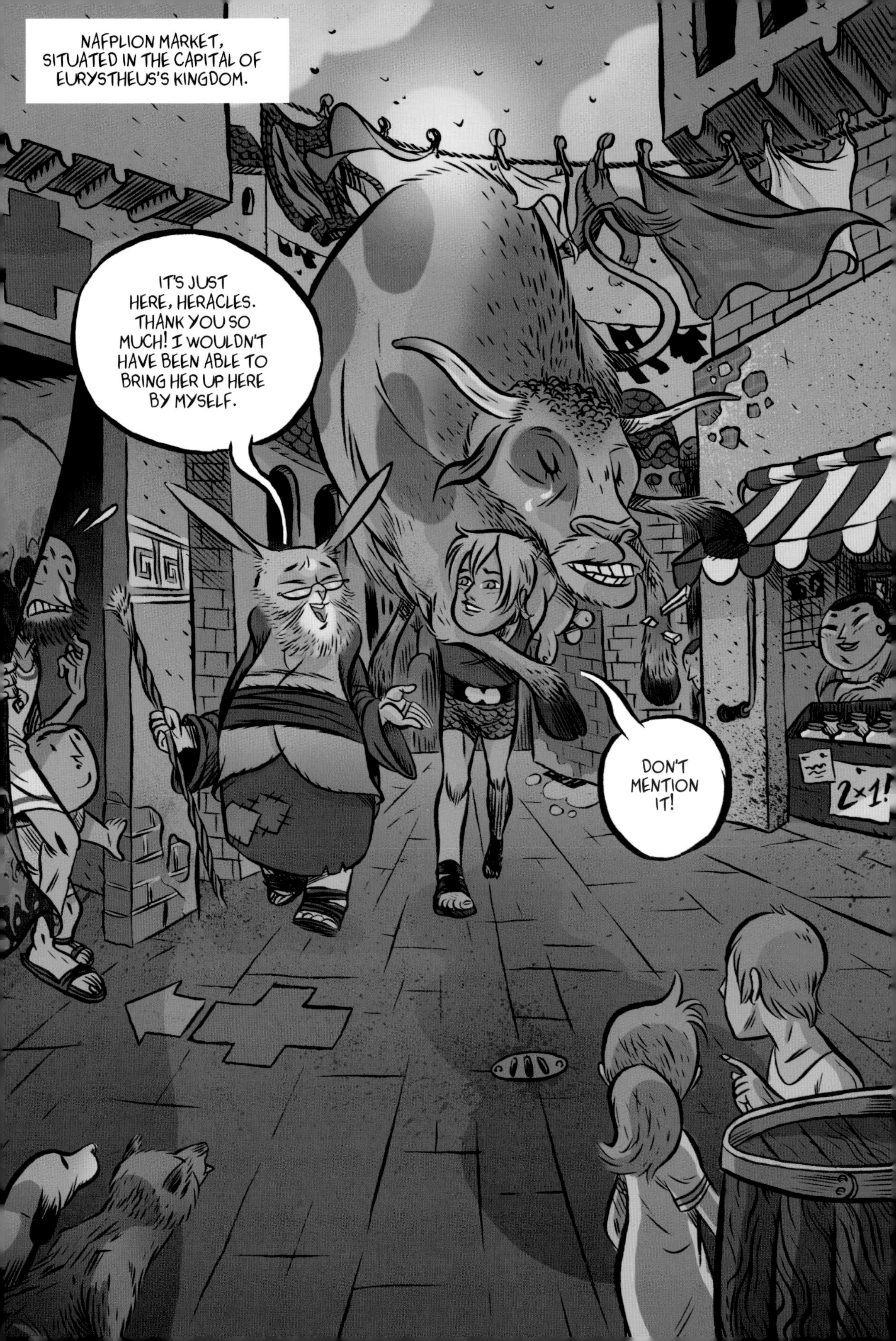
NAFPLION MARKET, SITUATED IN THE CAPITAL OF EURYSTHEUS'S KINGDOM.
IT'S JUST HERE, HERACLES. THANK YOU SO MUCH! I WOULDN'T HAVE BEEN ABLE TO BRING HER UP HERE BY MYSELF.
DON'T MENTION IT!
2×1!

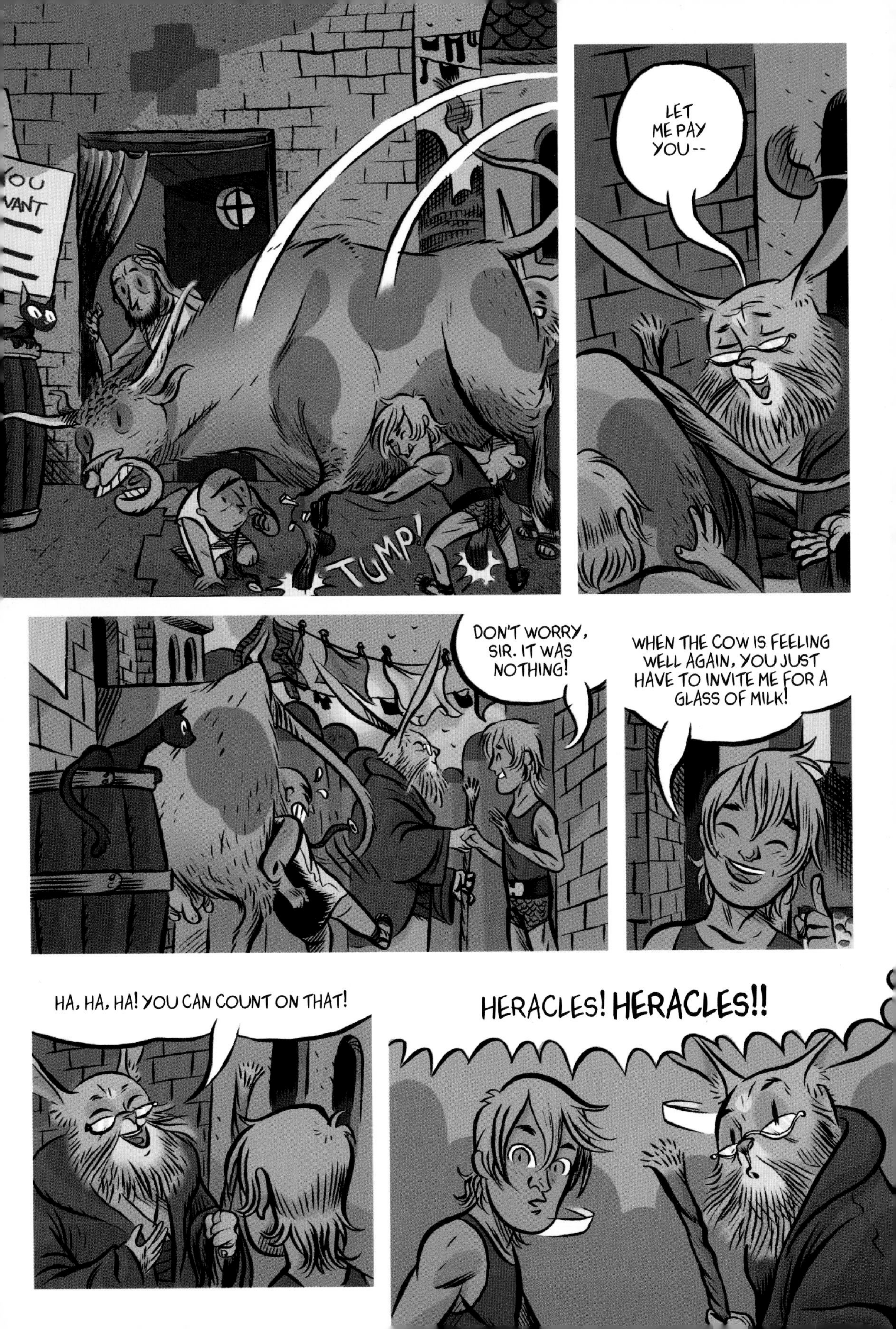
YOU
WANT
TUMP!
LET ME PAY YOU--
DON'T WORRY, SIR. IT WAS NOTHING!
WHEN THE COW IS FEELING WELL AGAIN, YOU JUST HAVE TO INVITE ME FOR A GLASS OF MILK!
HA, HA, HA! YOU CAN COUNT ON THAT!
HERACLES! HERACLES!!

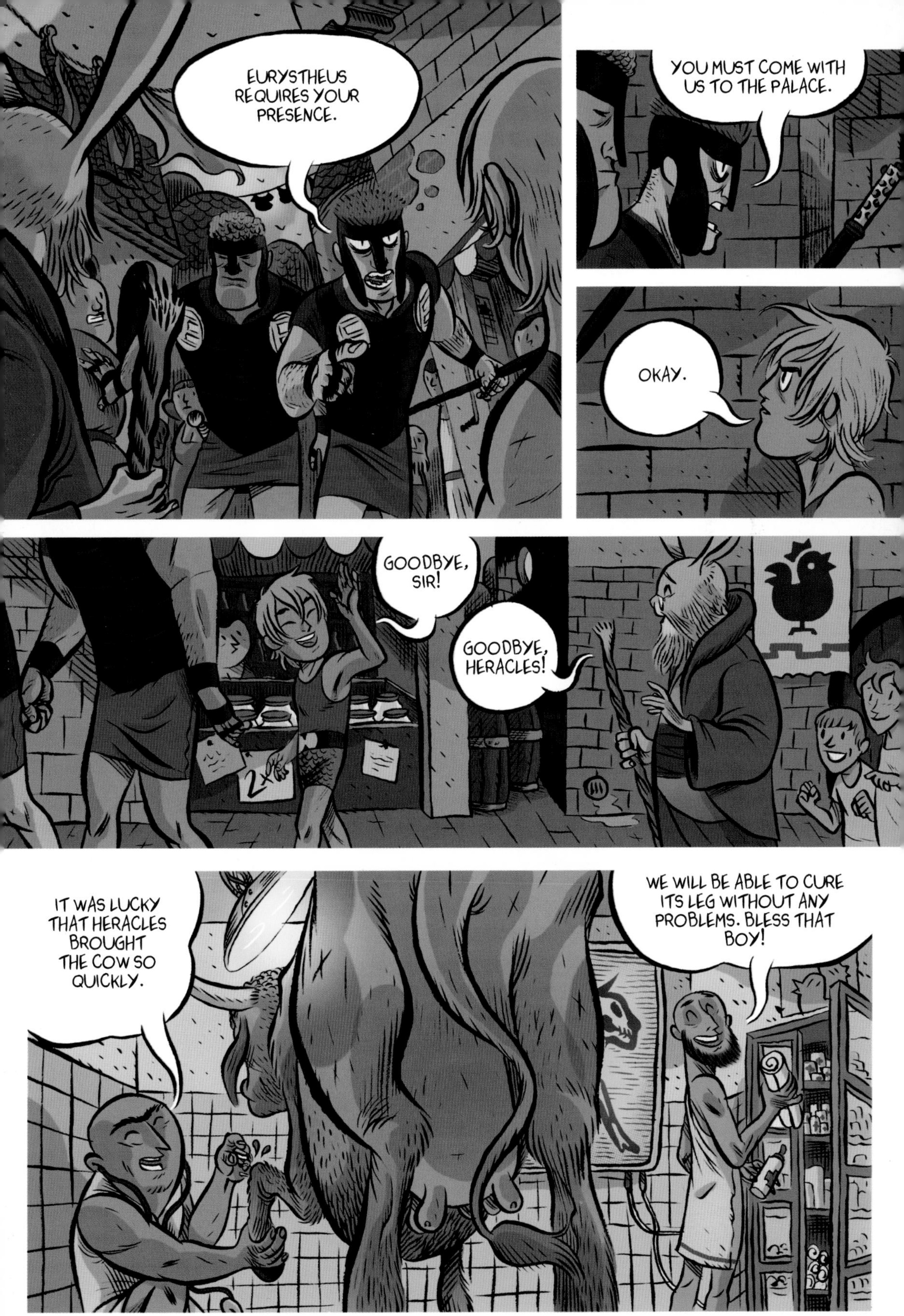
EURYSTHEUS REQUIRES YOUR PRESENCE.
YOU MUST COME WITH US TO THE PALACE.
OKAY.
GOODBYE, SIR!
GOODBYE, HERACLES!
IT WAS LUCKY THAT HERACLES BROUGHT THE COW SO QUICKLY.
WE WILL BE ABLE TO CURE ITS LEG WITHOUT ANY PROBLEMS. BLESS THAT BOY!

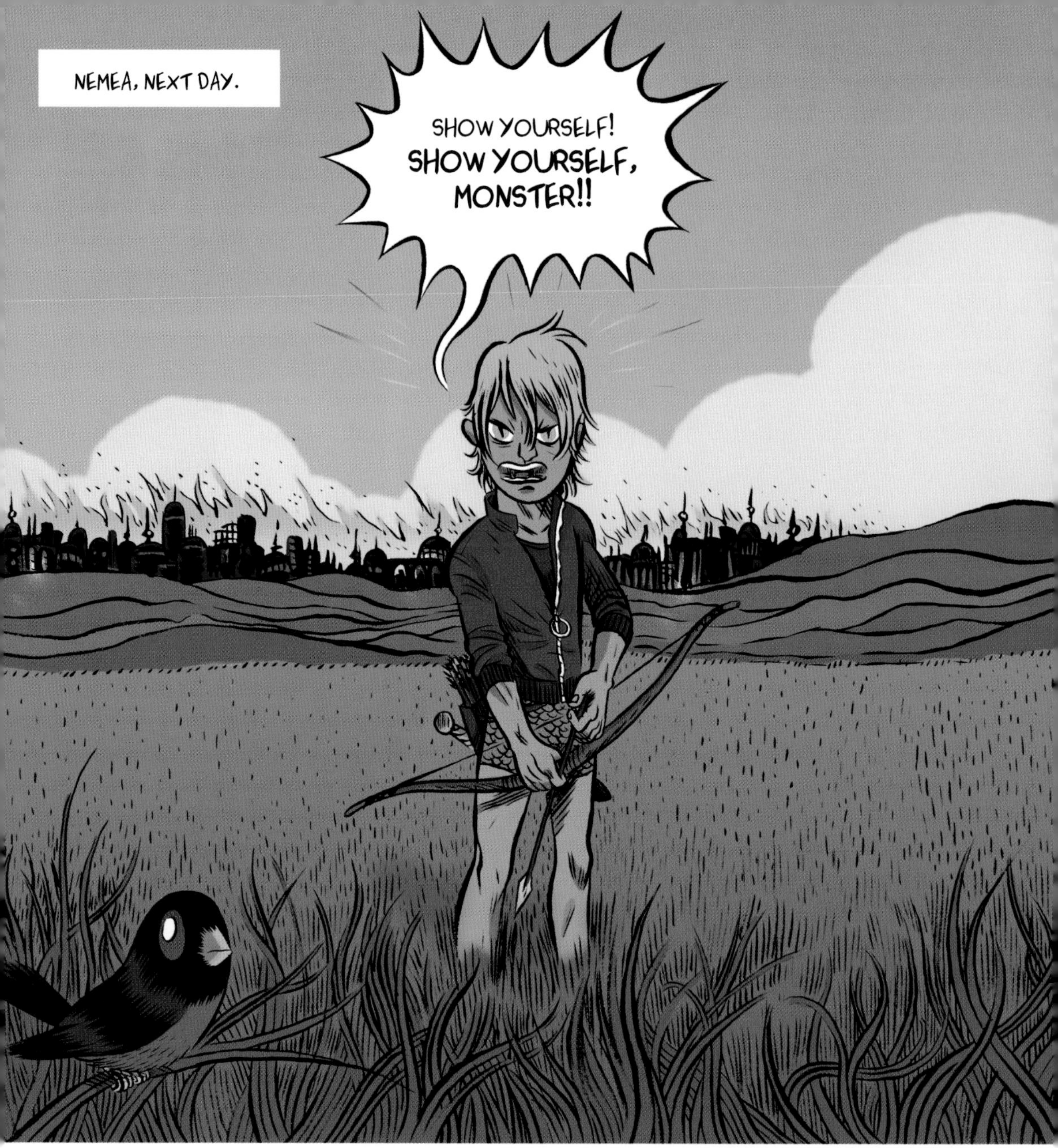
NEMEA, NEXT DAY.
SHOW YOURSELF! SHOW YOURSELF, MONSTER!!

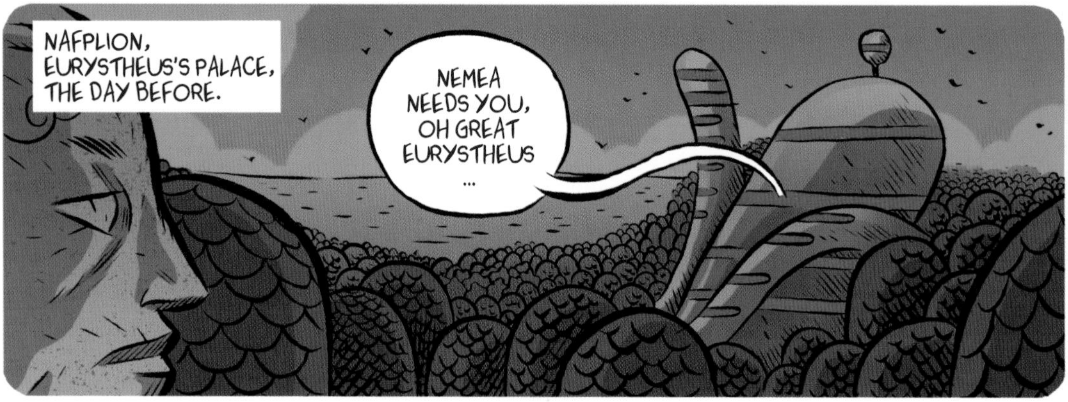
NAFPLION, EURYSTHEUS'S PALACE, THE DAY BEFORE.
NEMEA NEEDS YOU, OH GREAT EURYSTHEUS ...

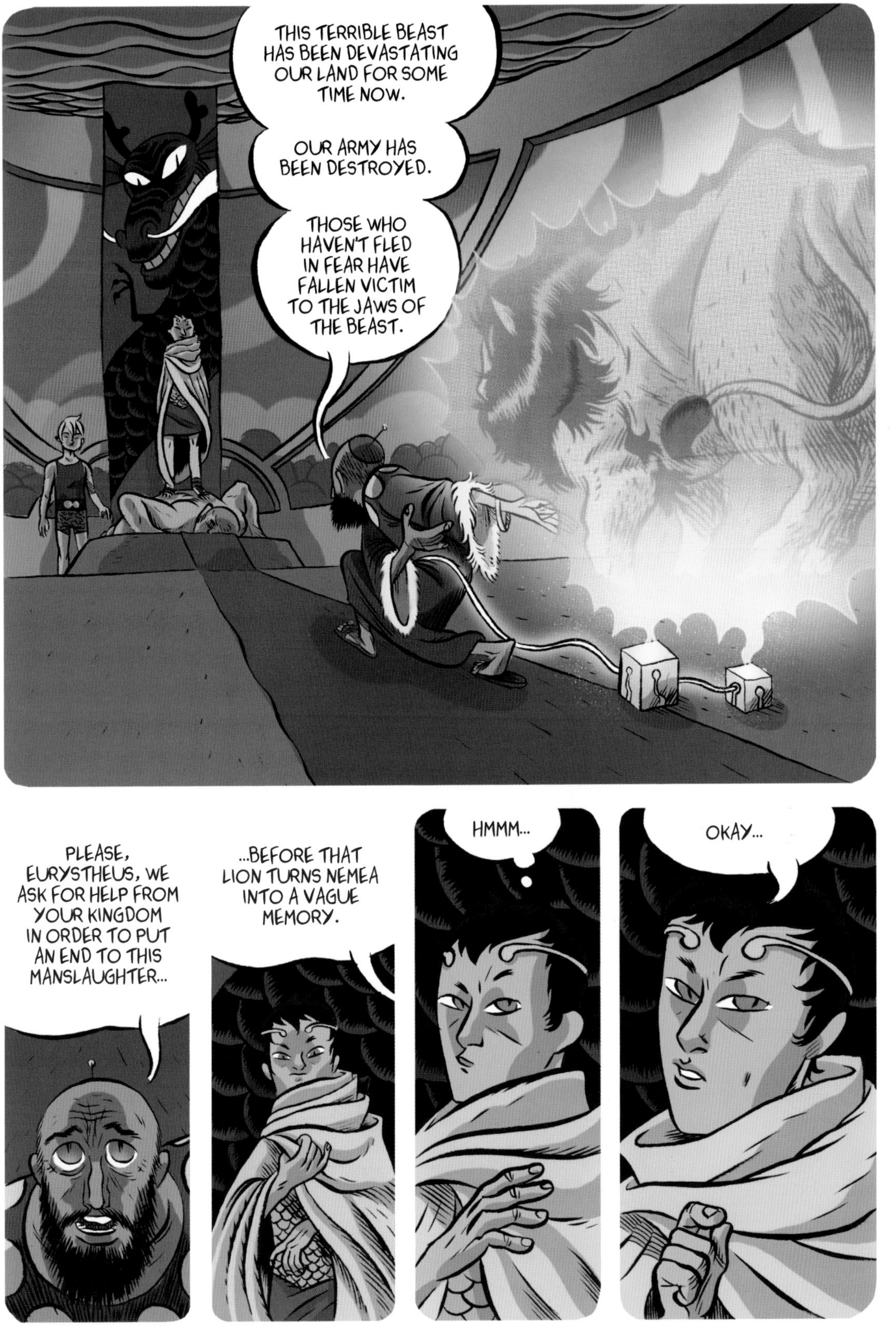
THIS TERRIBLE BEAST HAS BEEN DEVASTATING OUR LAND FOR SOME TIME NOW.
OUR ARMY HAS BEEN DESTROYED.
THOSE WHO HAVEN'T FLED IN FEAR HAVE FALLEN VICTIM TO THE JAWS OF THE BEAST.
PLEASE, EURYSTHEUS, WE ASK FOR HELP FROM YOUR KINGDOM IN ORDER TO PUT AN END TO THIS MANSLAUGHTER...
...BEFORE THAT LION TURNS NEMEA INTO A VAGUE MEMORY.
HMMM...
OKAY...

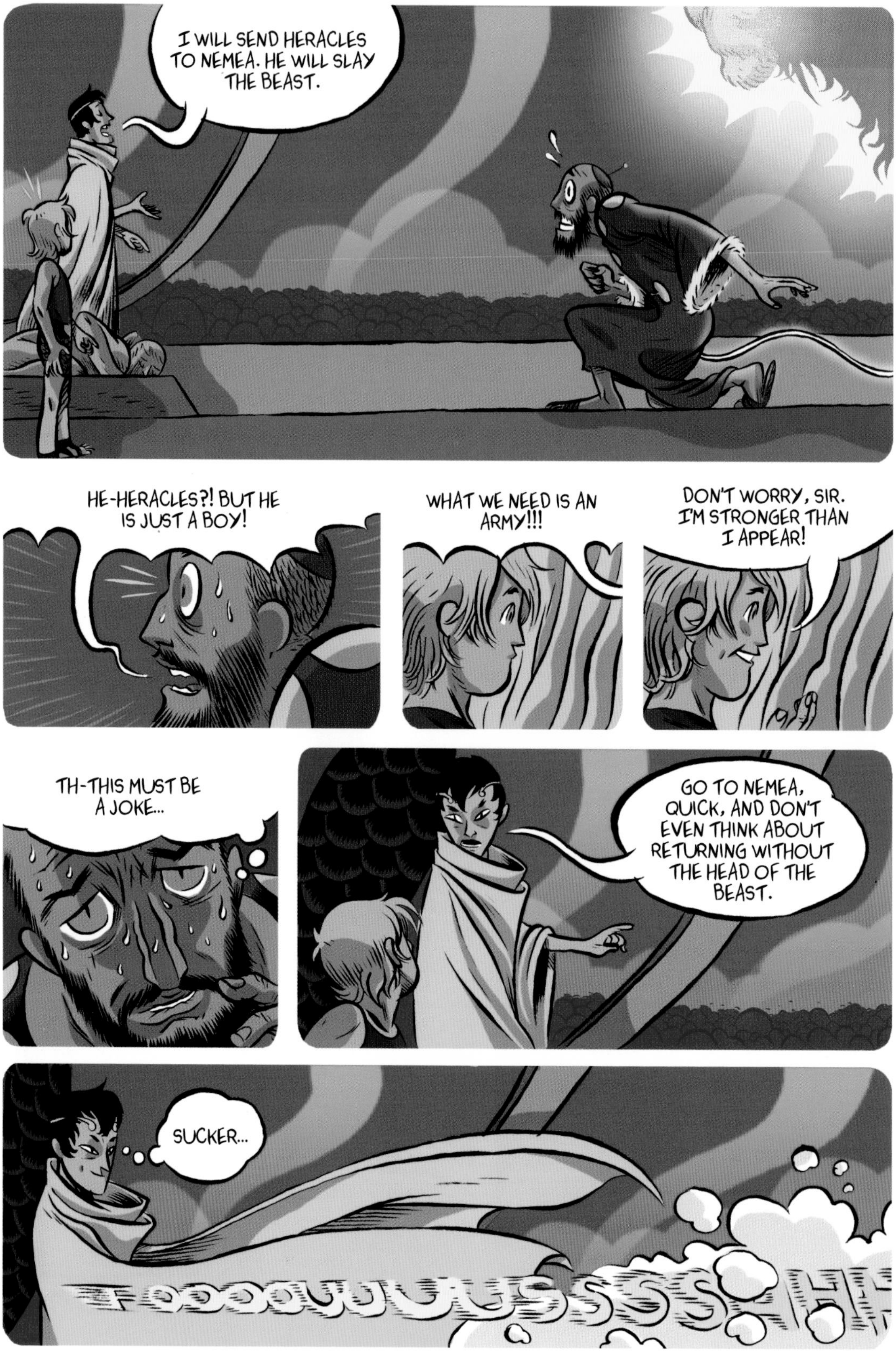
I WILL SEND HERACLES TO NEMEA. HE WILL SLAY THE BEAST.
HE-HERACLES?! BUT HE IS JUST A BOY!
WHAT WE NEED IS AN ARMY!!!
DON'T WORRY, SIR. I'M STRONGER THAN I APPEAR!
TH-THIS MUST BE A JOKE...
GO TO NEMEA, QUICK, AND DON'T EVEN THINK ABOUT RETURNING WITHOUT THE HEAD OF THE BEAST.
SUCKER...
FOOOOOWWUUUSSSSSHH

WELL...

...LET'S TALK ABOUT THE PAYMENT I SHALL RECEIVE FOR THIS SERVICE...

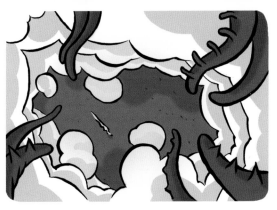

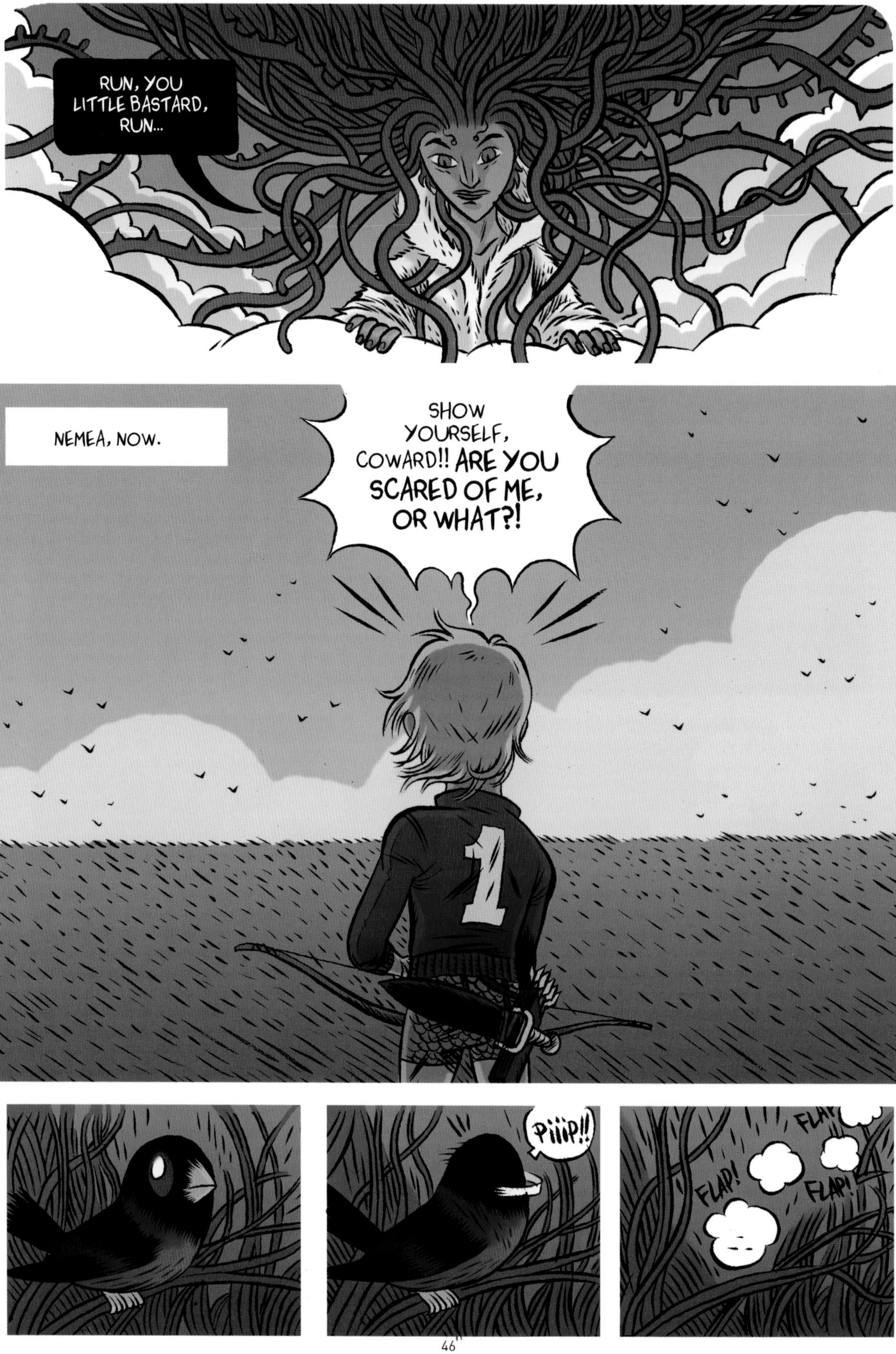
RUN, YOU LITTLE BASTARD, RUN...
NEMEA, NOW.
SHOW YOURSELF, COWARD!! ARE YOU SCARED OF ME, OR WHAT?!
Piiip!!
FLAP!
FLAP!
FLAP!

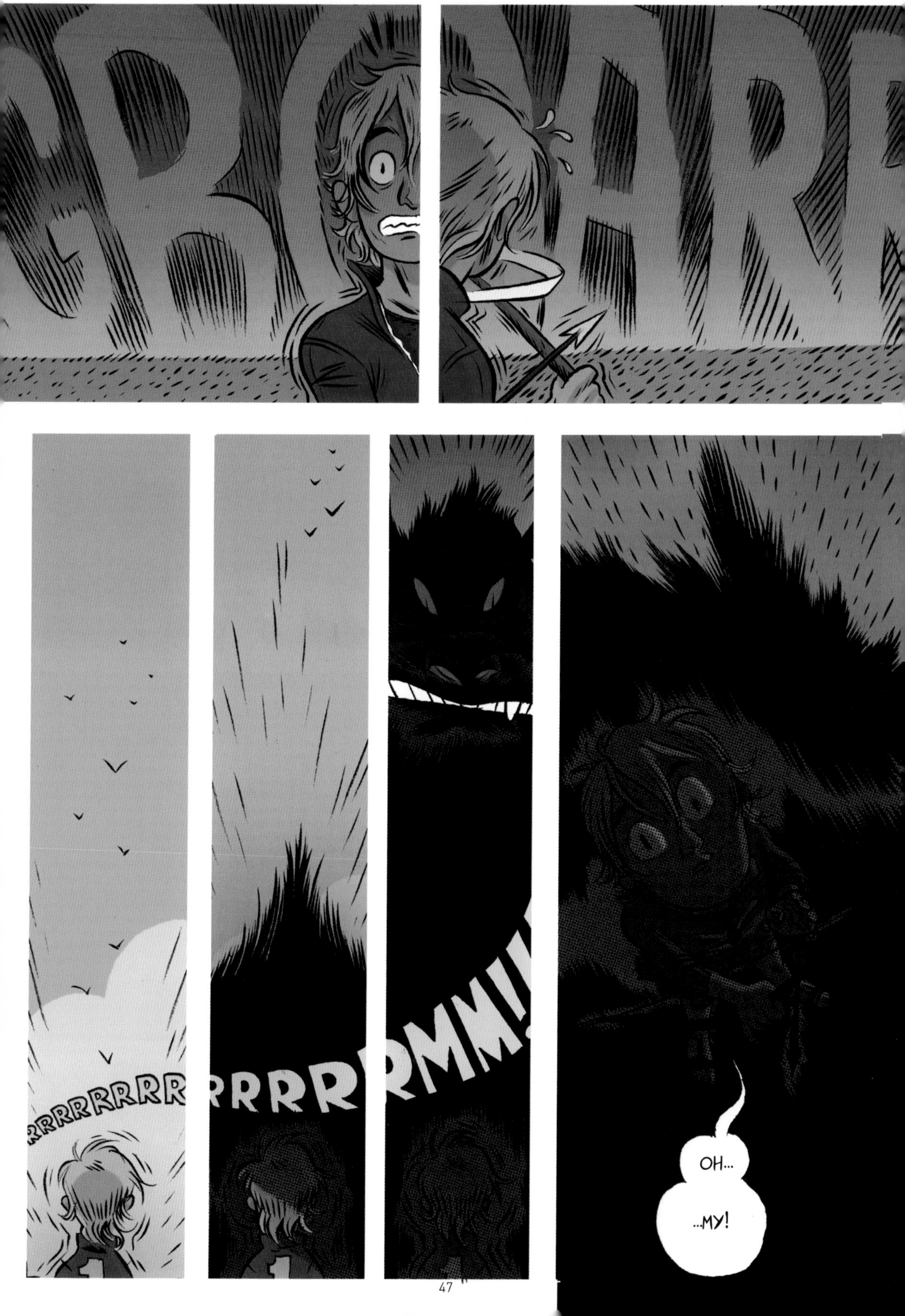
RRRRRRRRRRRRRRMM!!
OH...
...MY!

PRRMMGGGG!!!!

SSSSSHHHHH

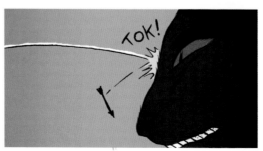

TOK!

OOPS!

48

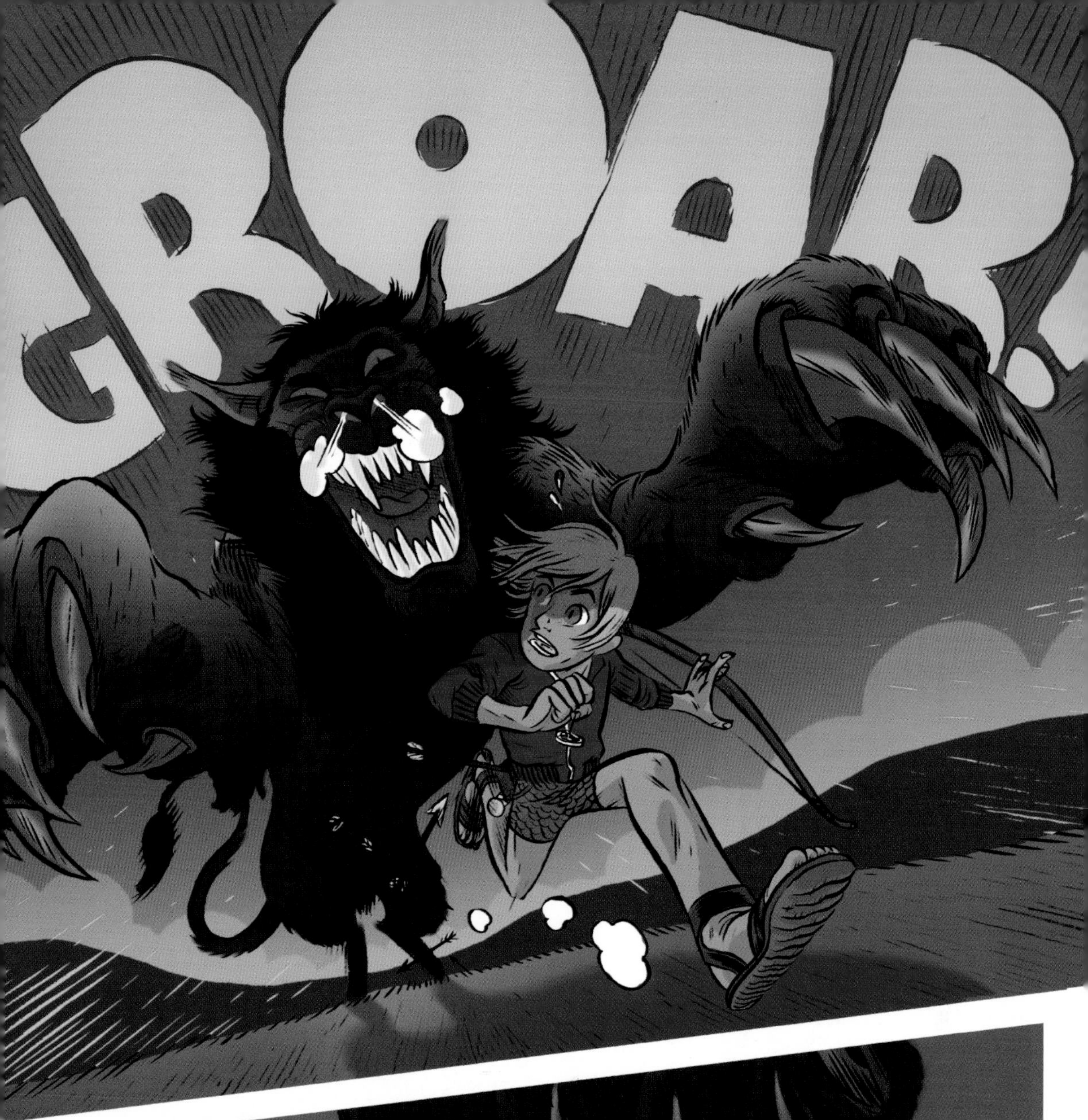
ROAR!

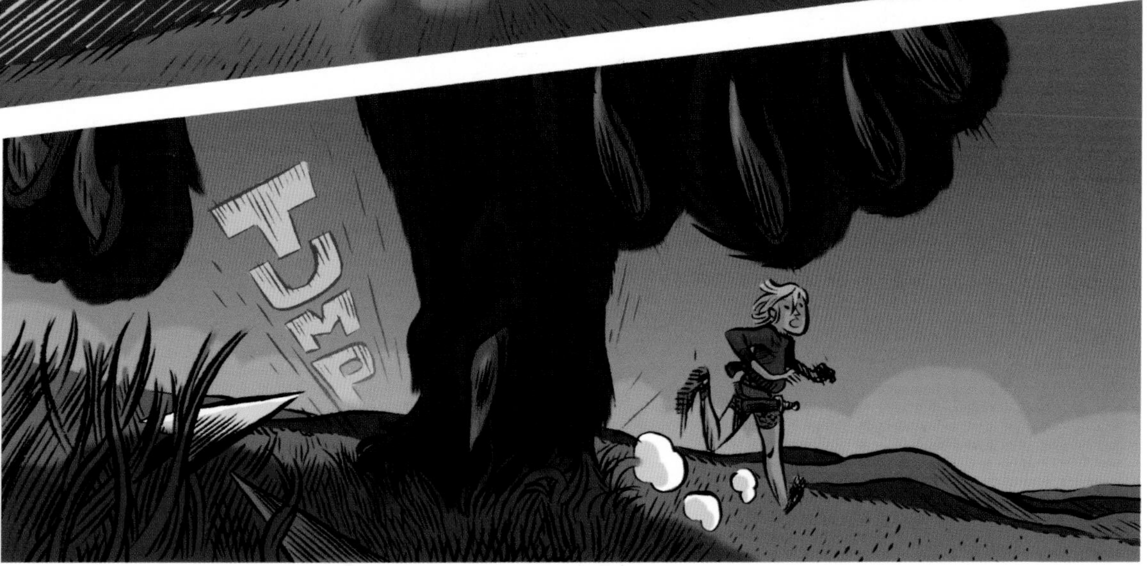
JUMP

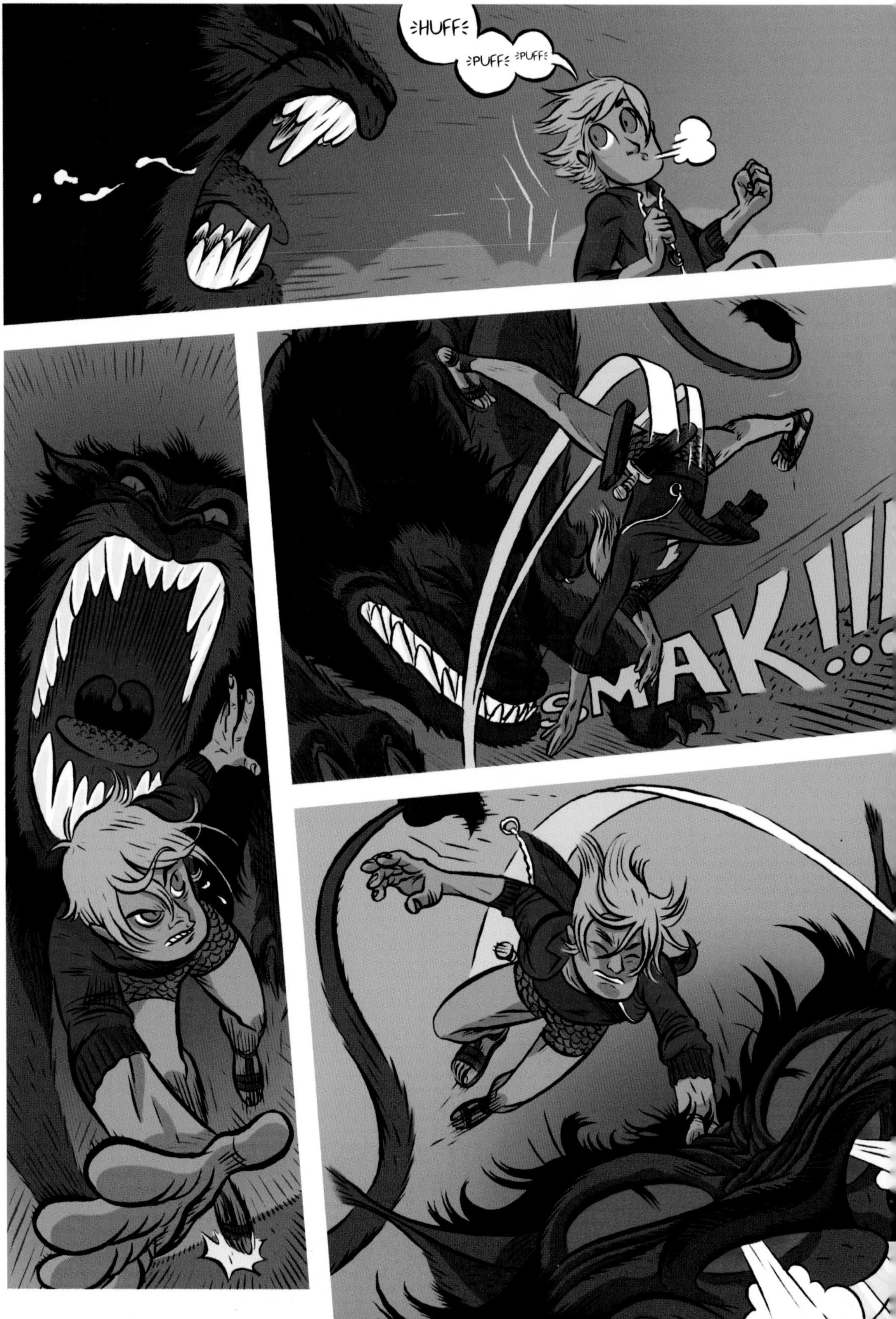
HUFF
PUFF PUFF
SMAK!!!

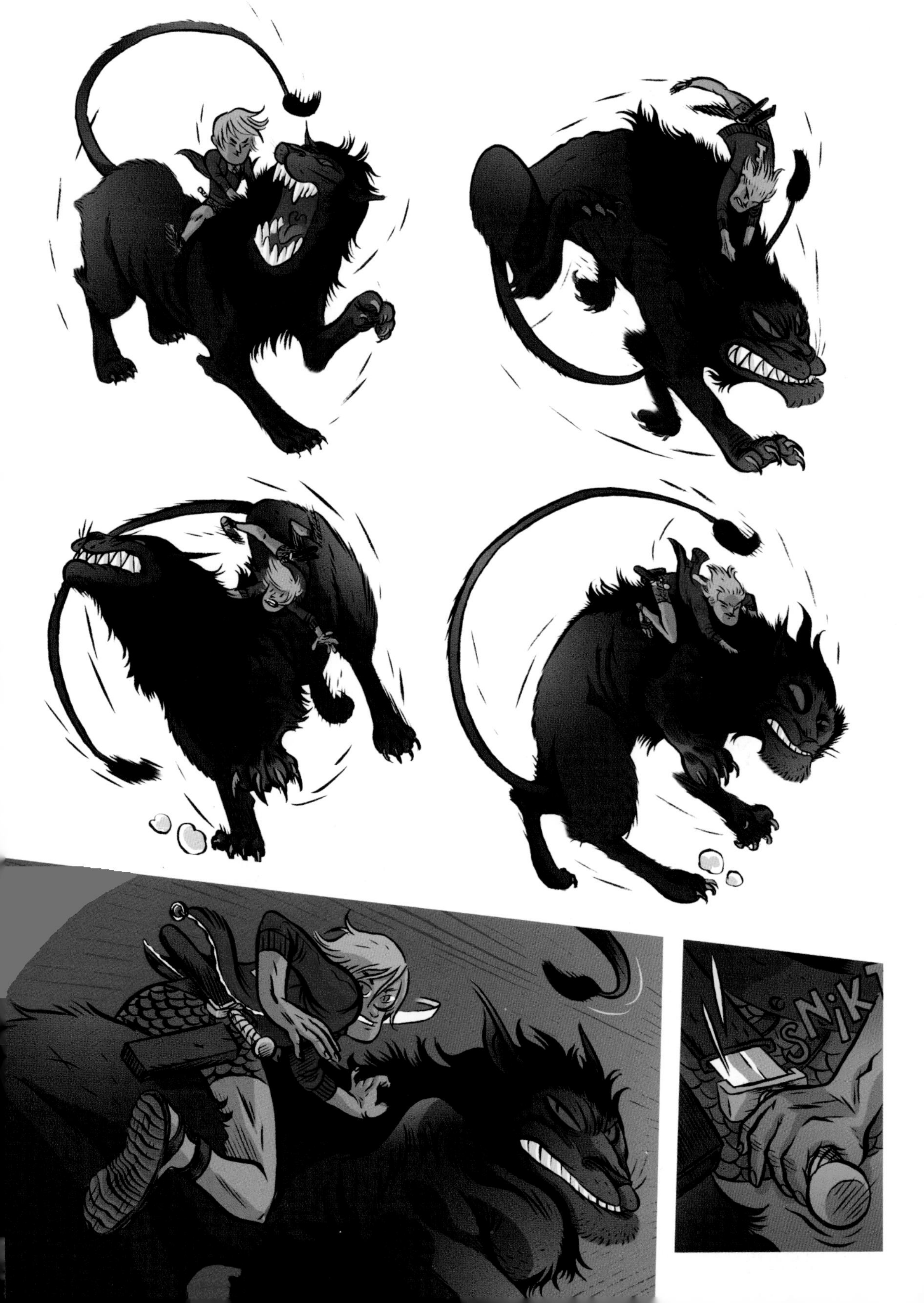
SNIKT

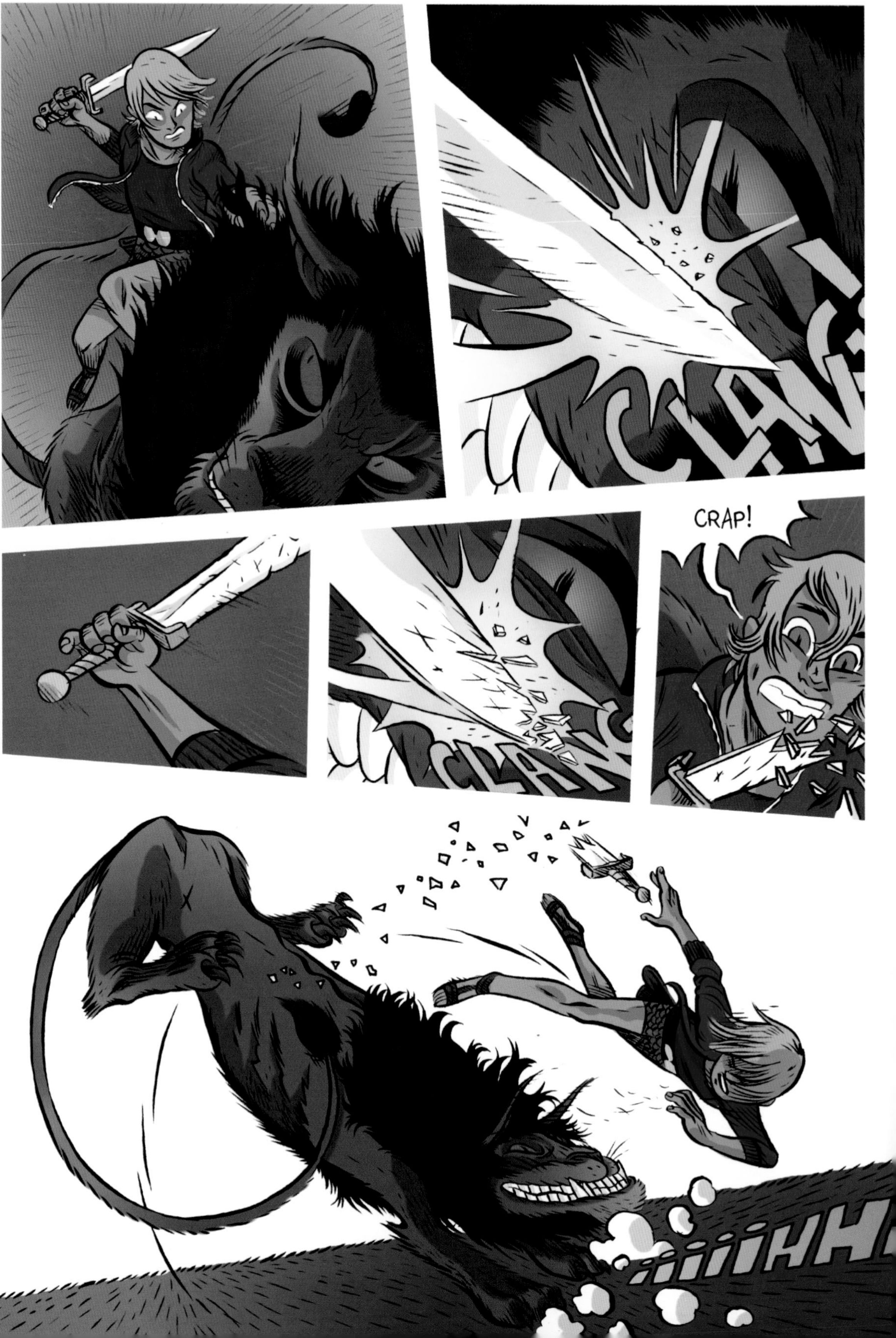
CRAP!

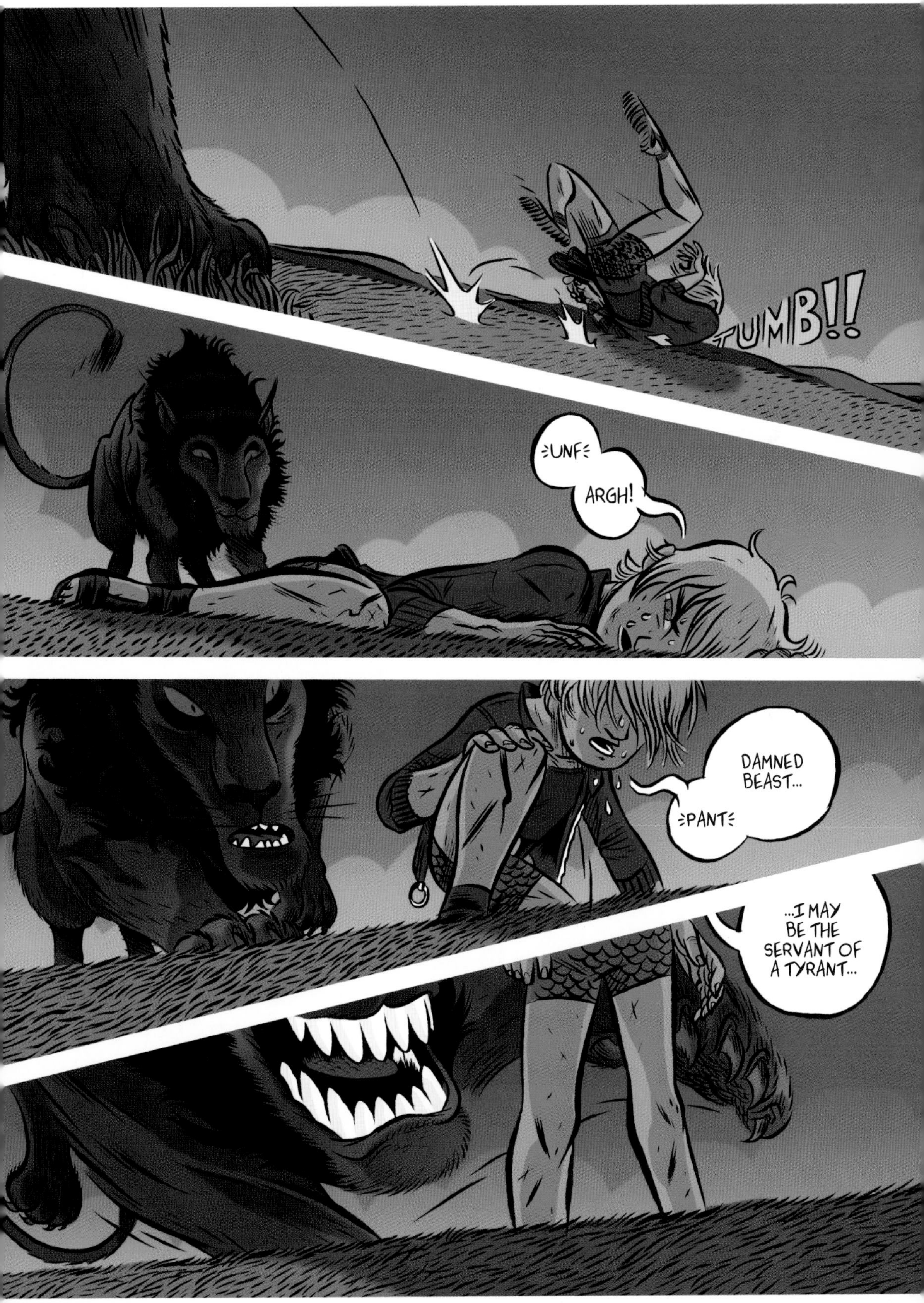
TUMB!!
UNF
ARGH!
DAMNED BEAST...
PANT
...I MAY BE THE SERVANT OF A TYRANT...

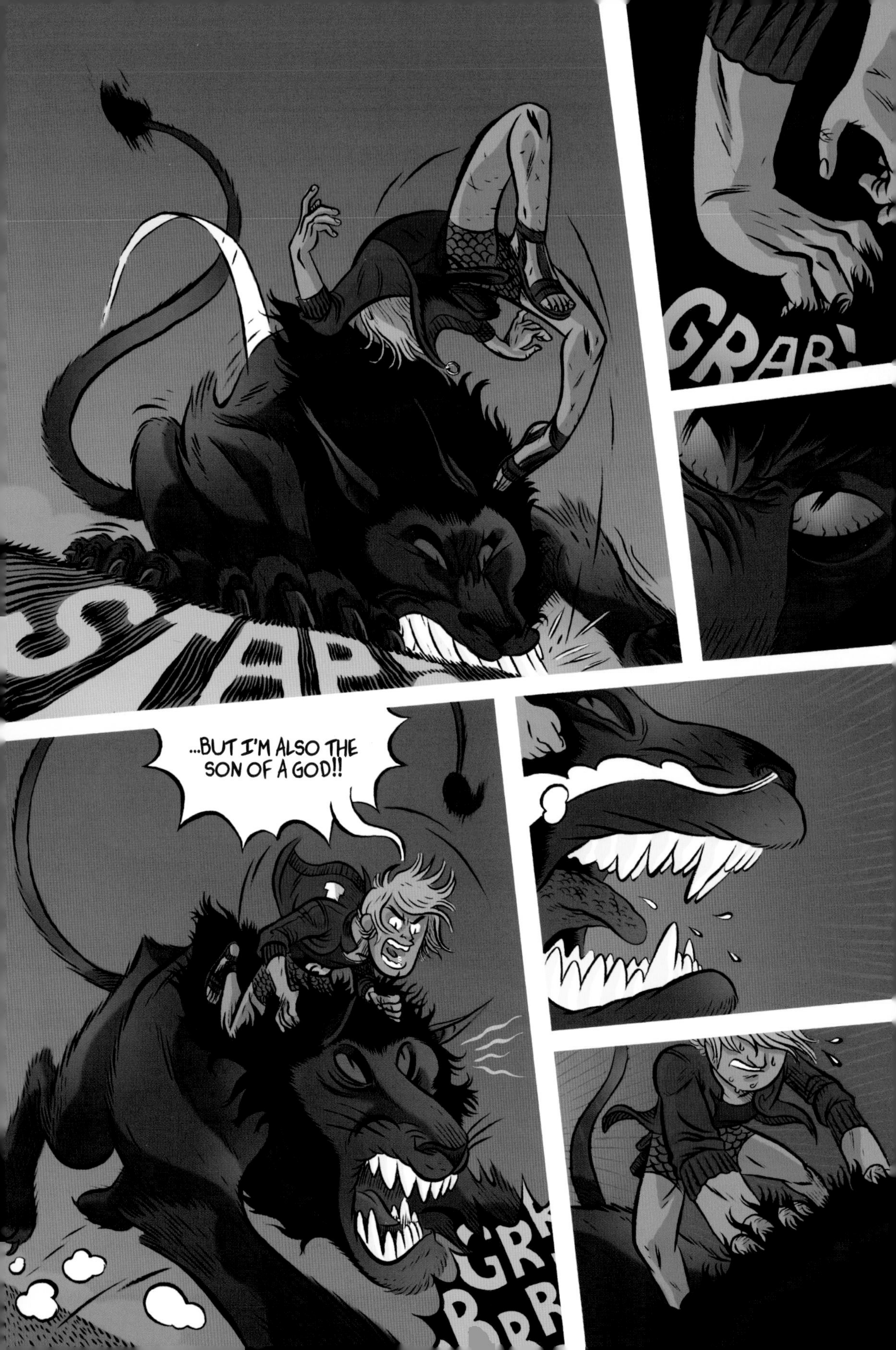
GRAB!
SLAP
...BUT I'M ALSO THE SON OF A GOD!!
GRR
RRR

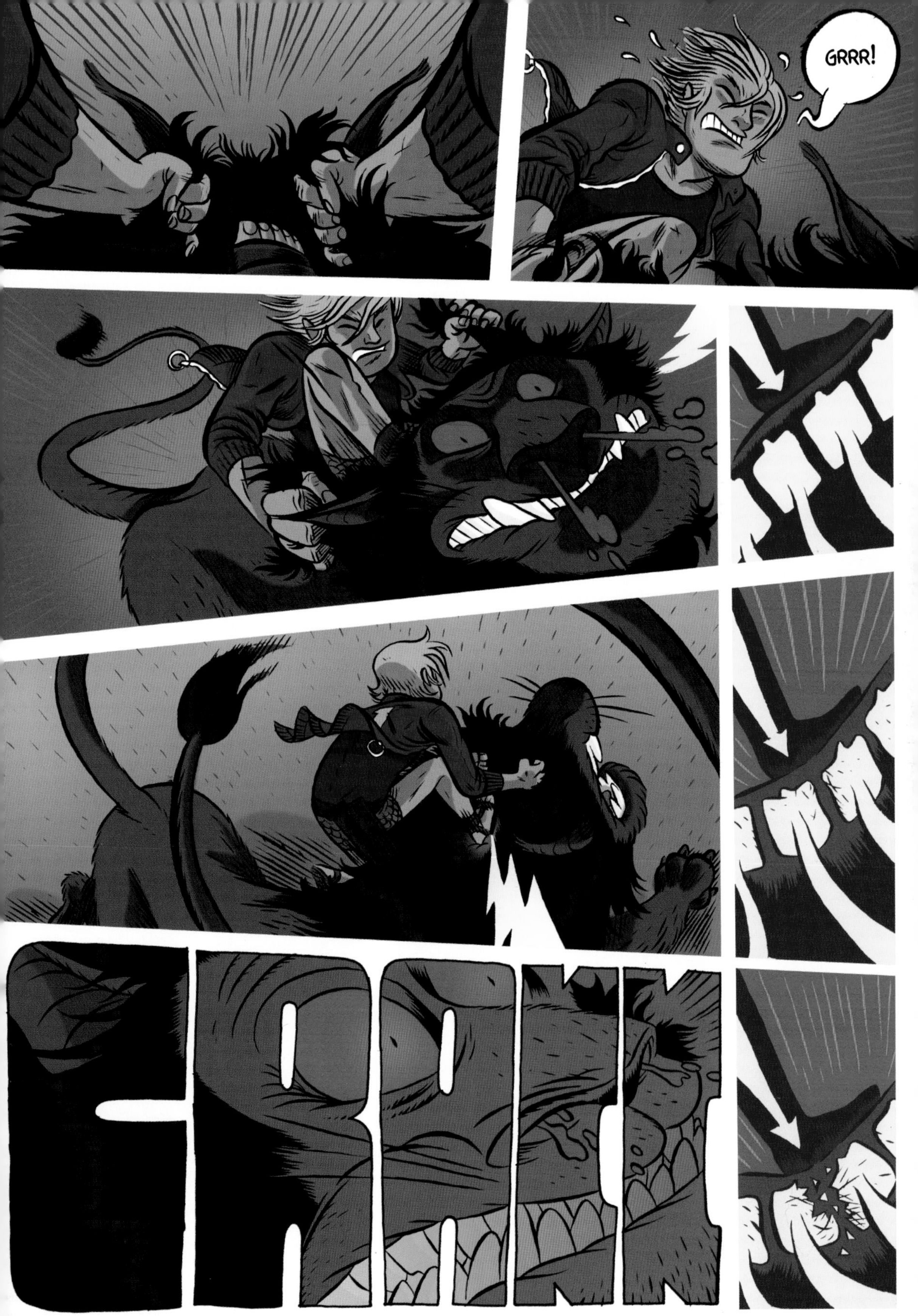
GRRR!
CRACK

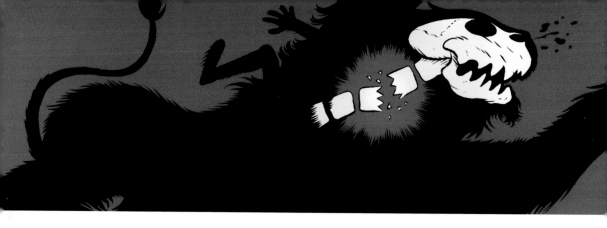

TOOOMMB

TELL...

...TELL EURYSTHEUS...

...TELL HIM...

...MISSION ACCOMPLISHED.

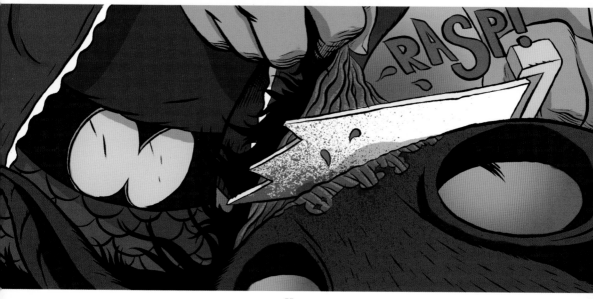
RASP!

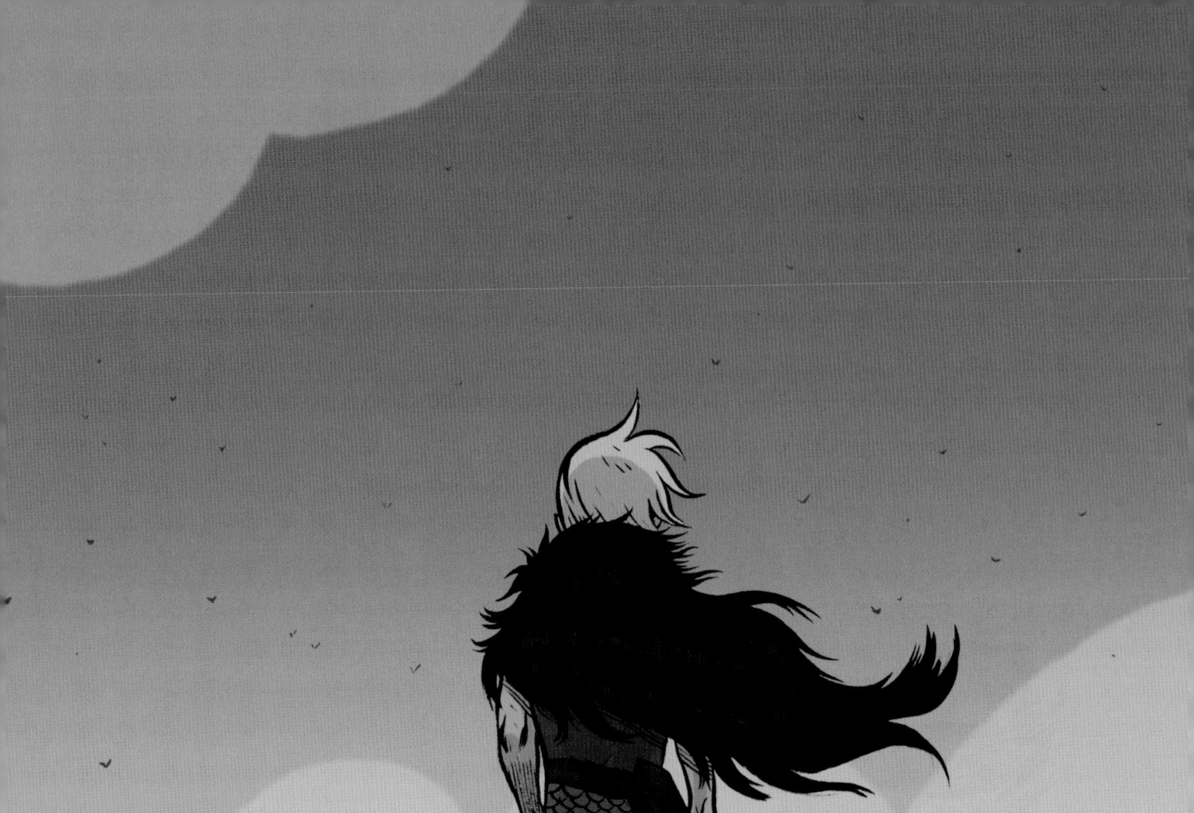

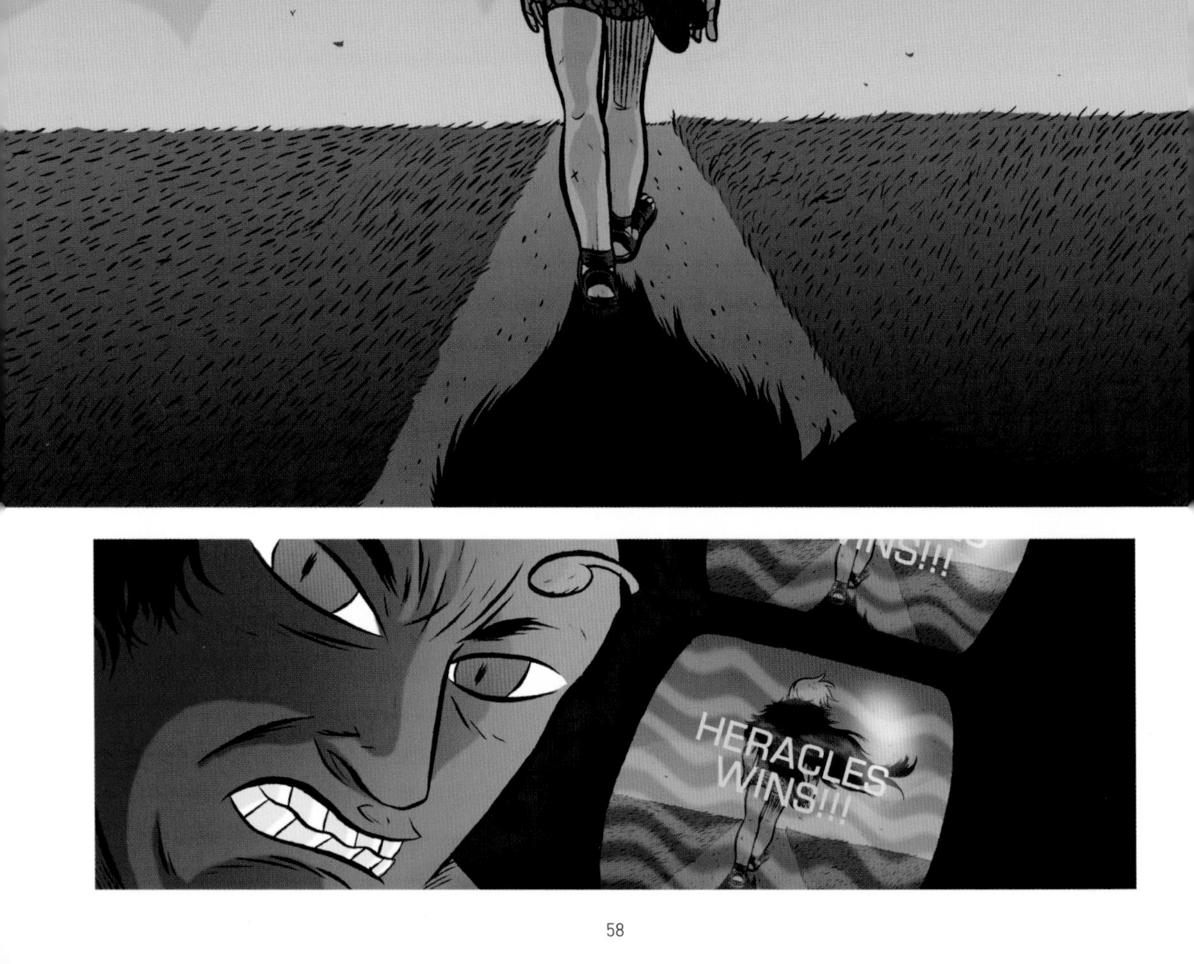
HERACLES WINS!!!

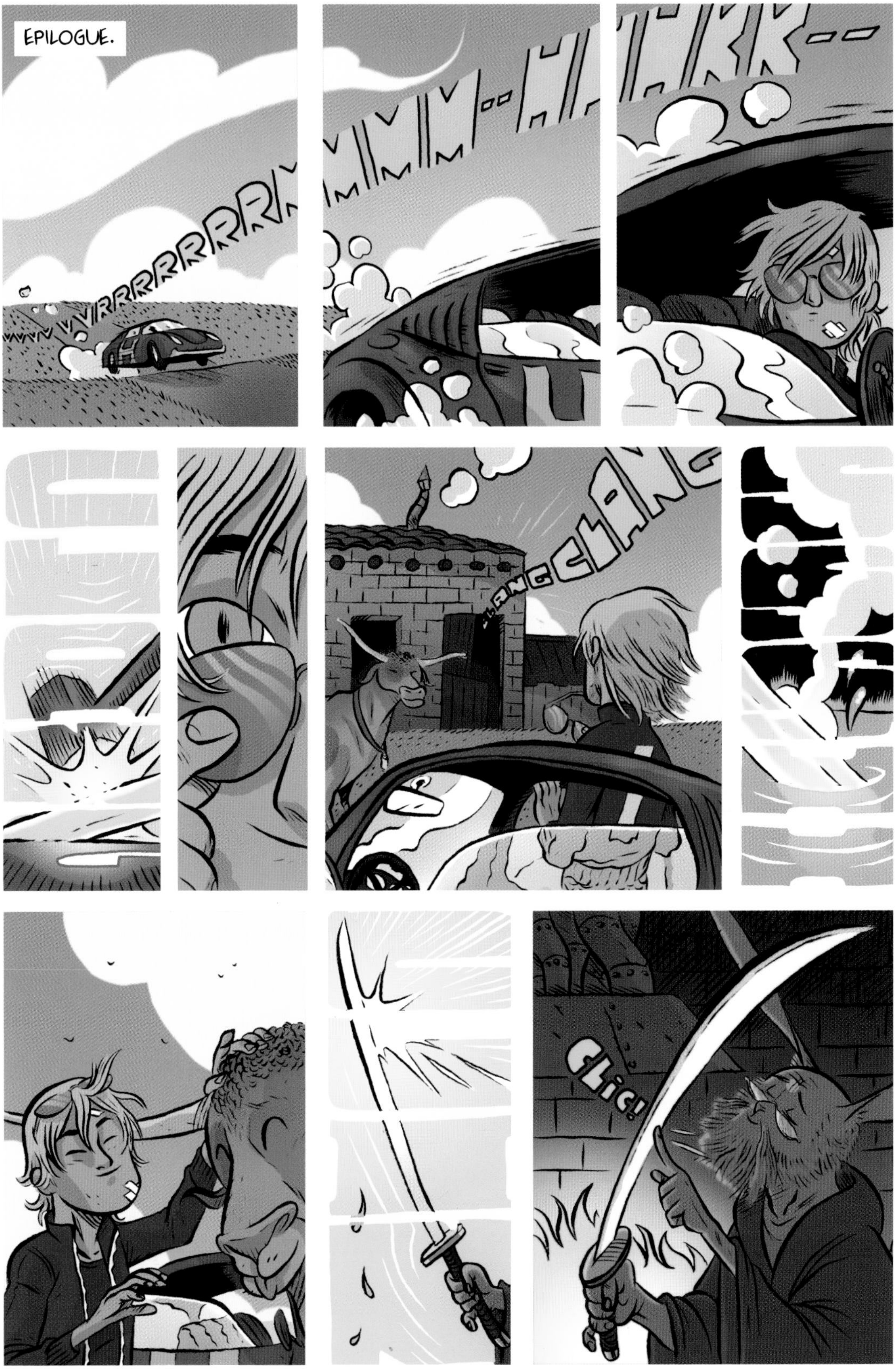
EPILOGUE.
VVVVVVRRRRRRRRR
MMMM--
HHHRRK--
CLANG CLANG
CLIC!

SLICE!!

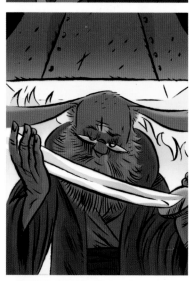

END OF CHAPTER ONE.

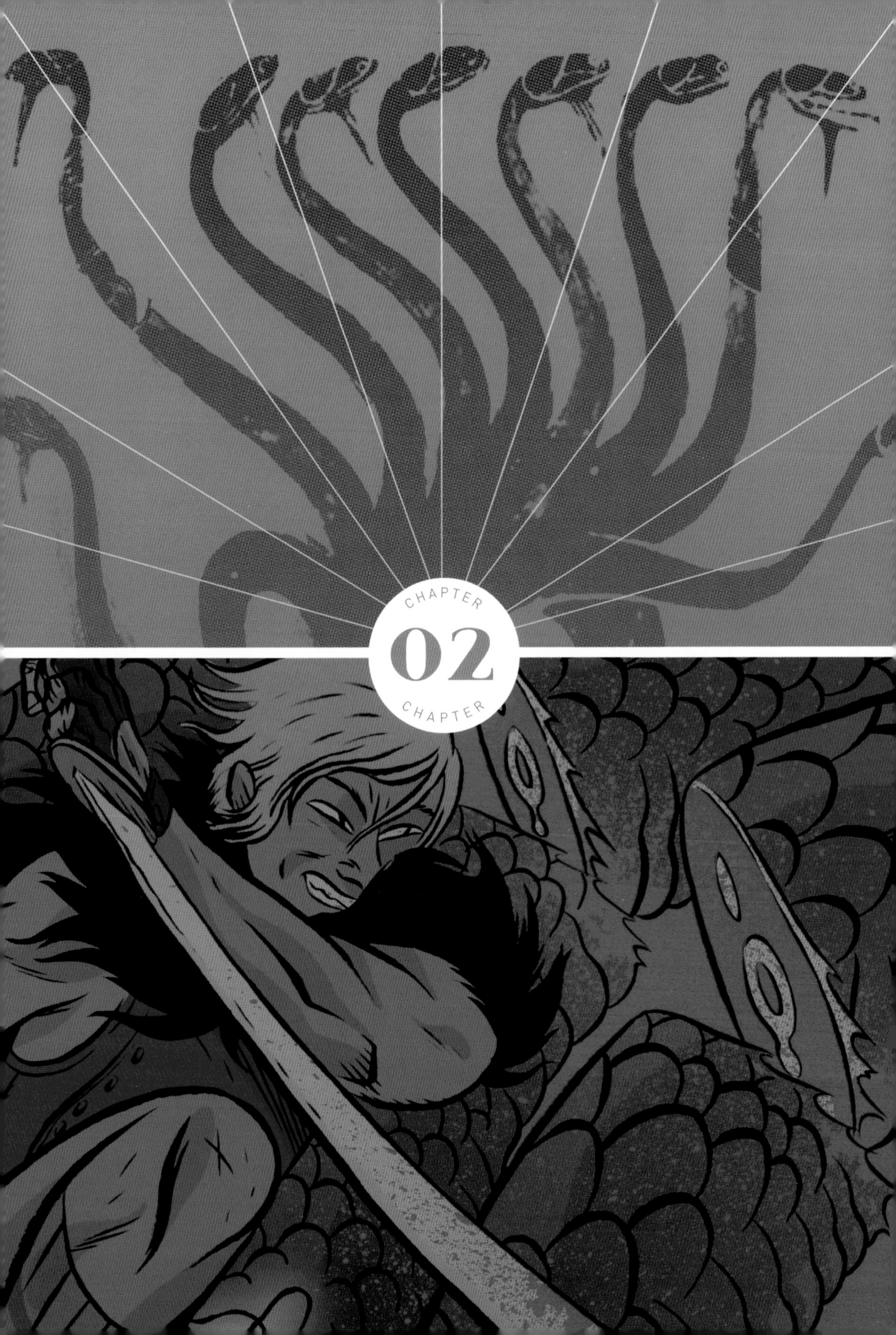
CHAPTER
02
CHAPTER

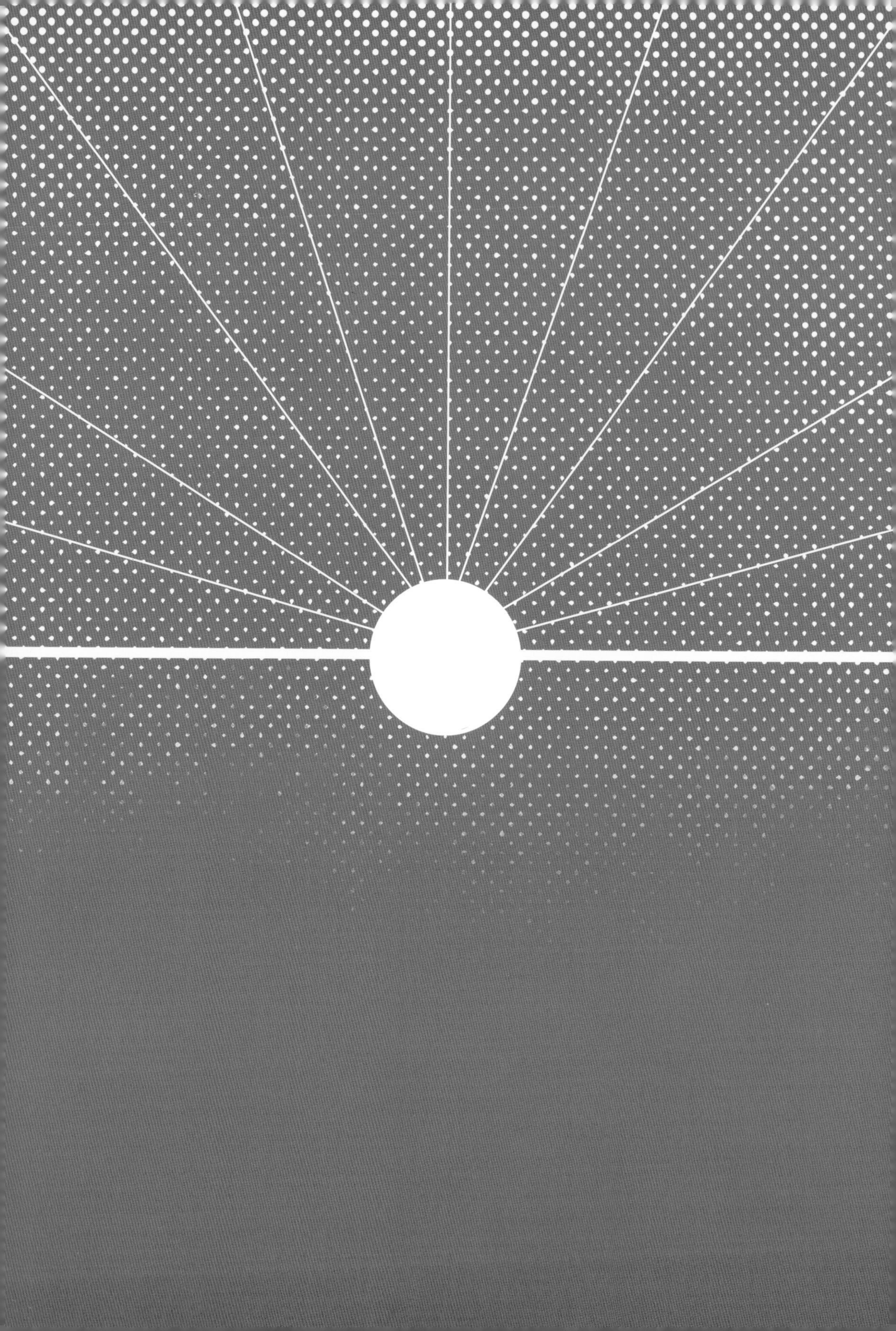

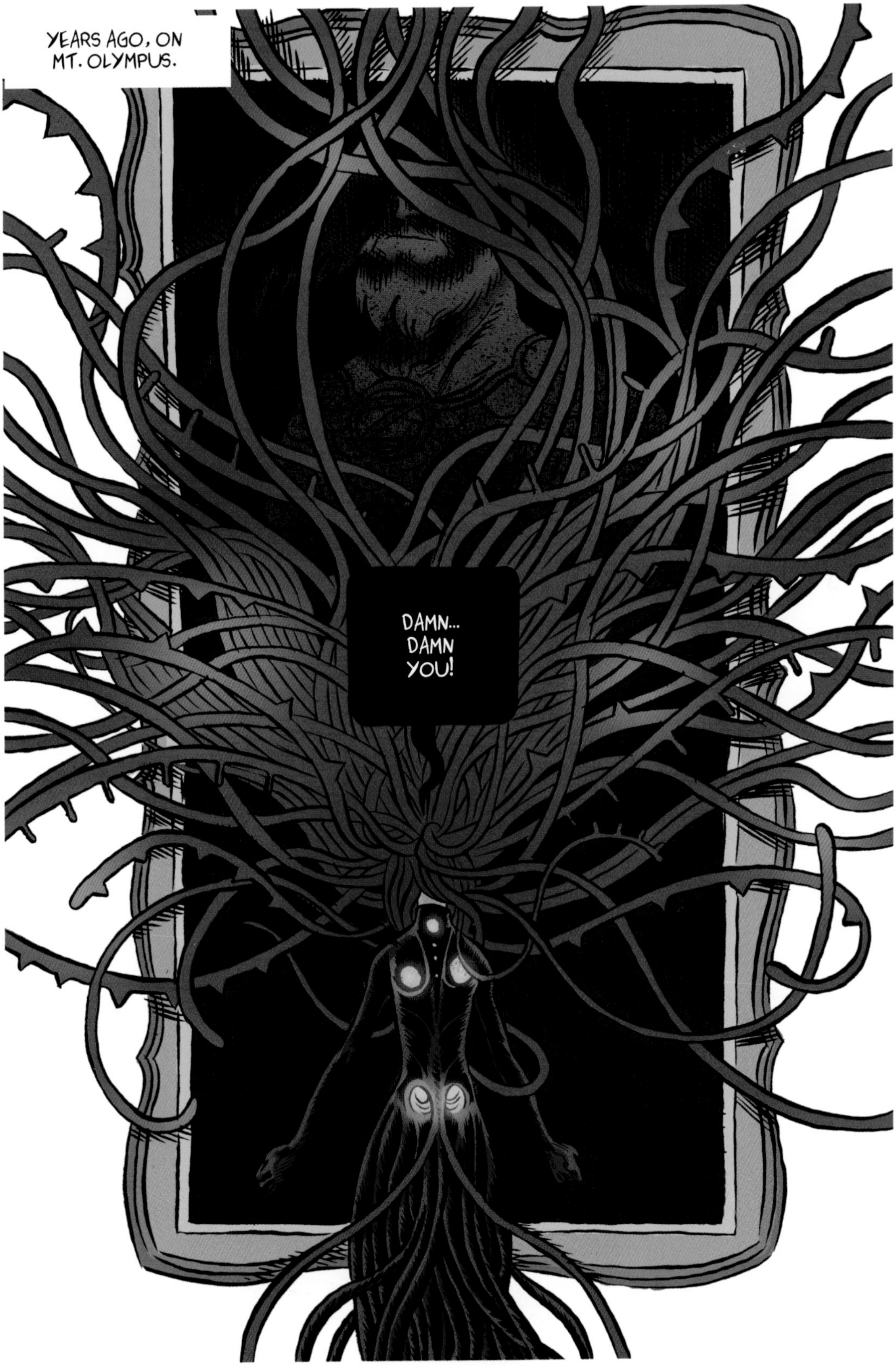
YEARS AGO, ON MT. OLYMPUS.
DAMN... DAMN YOU!

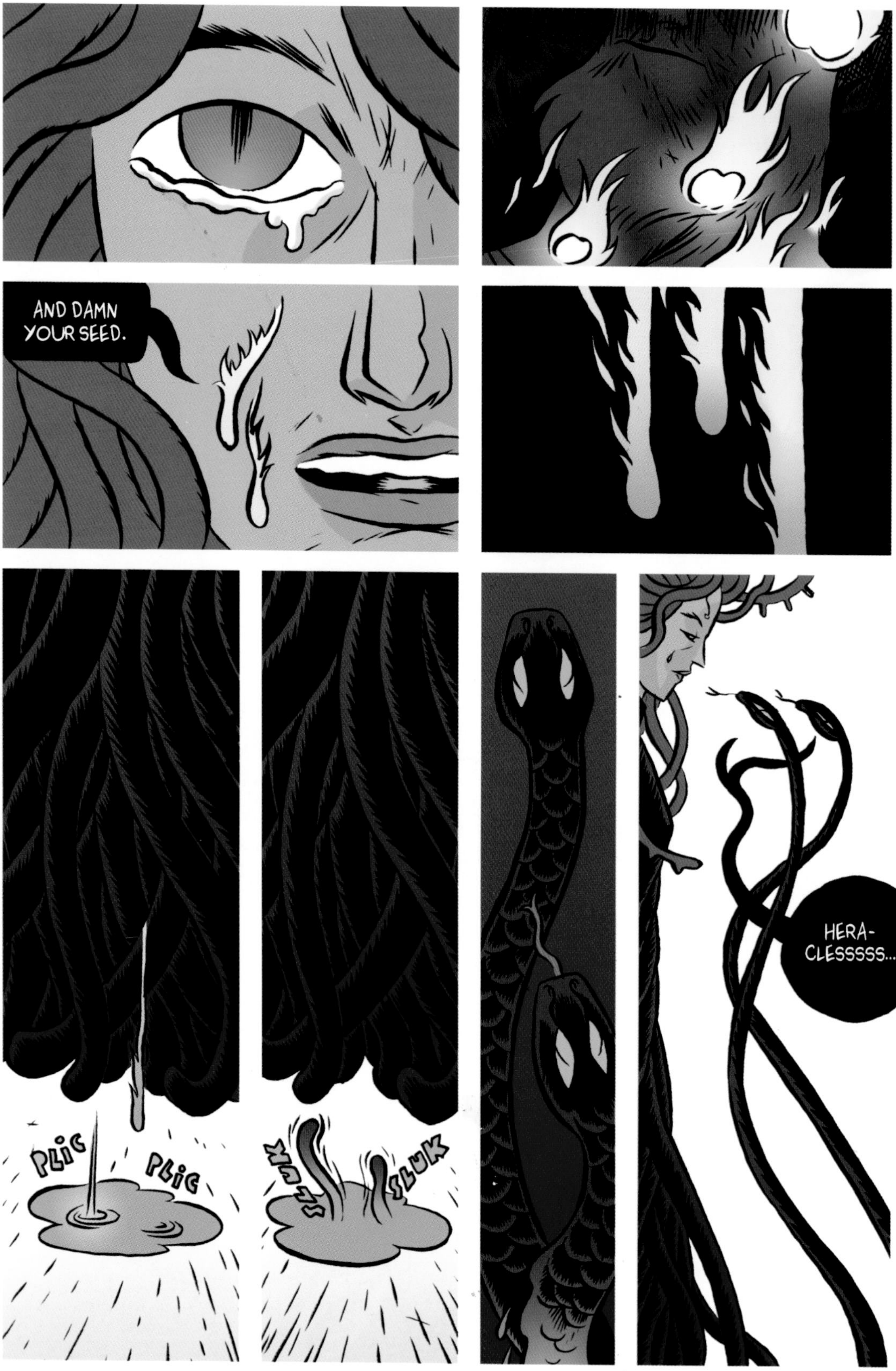
AND DAMN YOUR SEED.
PLIC
PLIC
SLUK
SLUK
HERA-CLESSSSS...

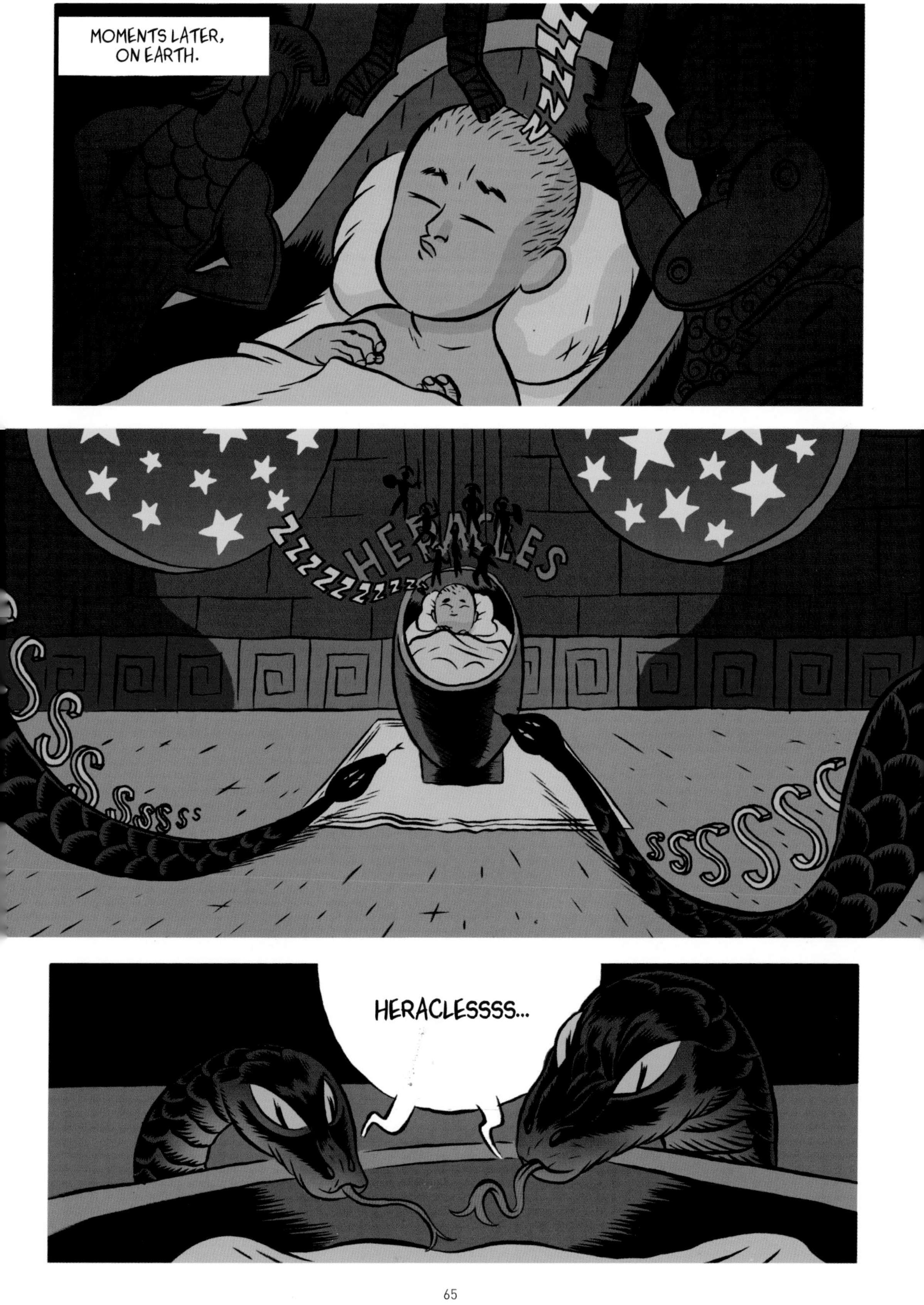
MOMENTS LATER, ON EARTH.
HERACLESSSS...

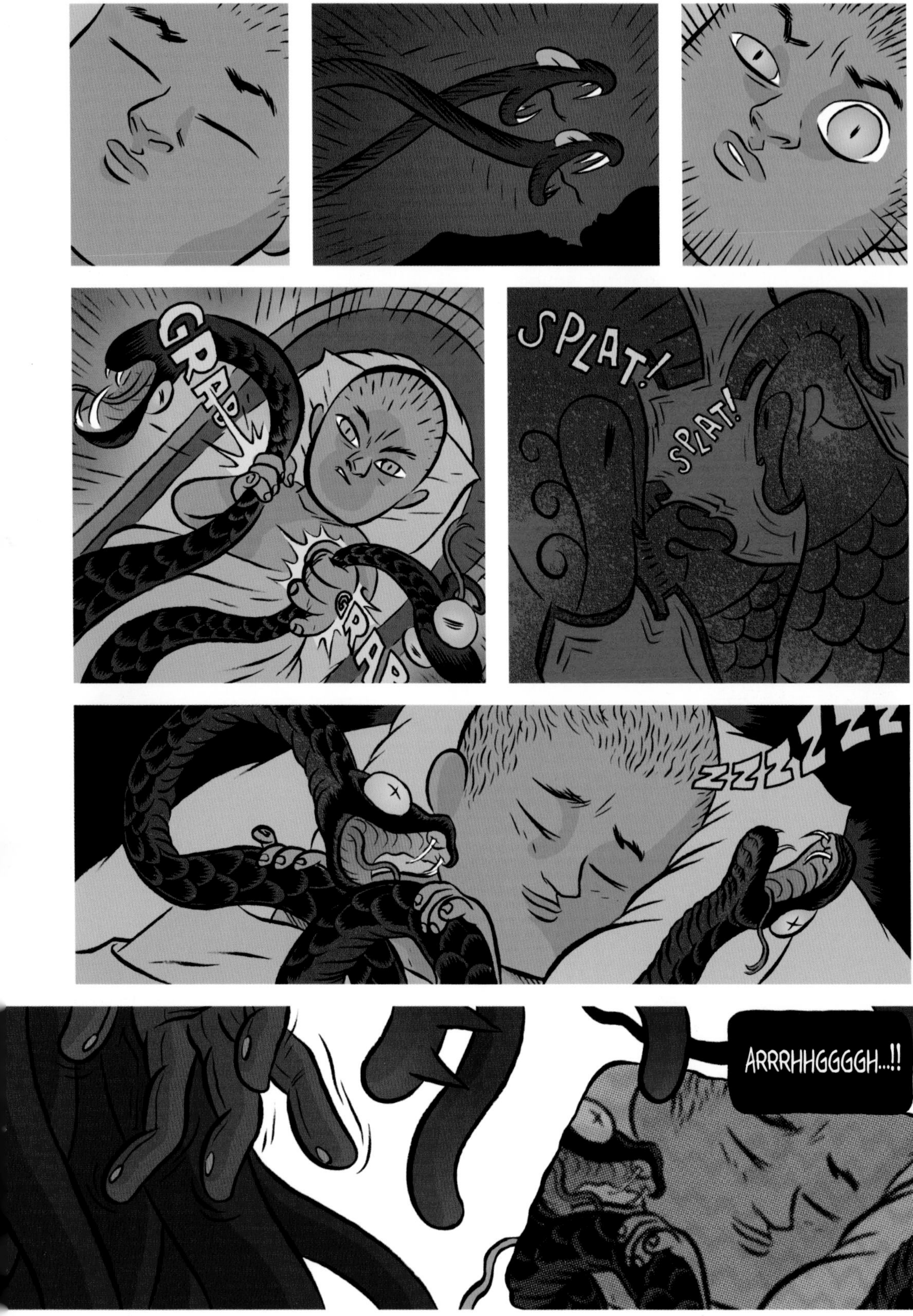
GRAB
GRAB
SPLAT!
SPLAT!
ZZZZZZ
ARRRHHGGGGH...!!

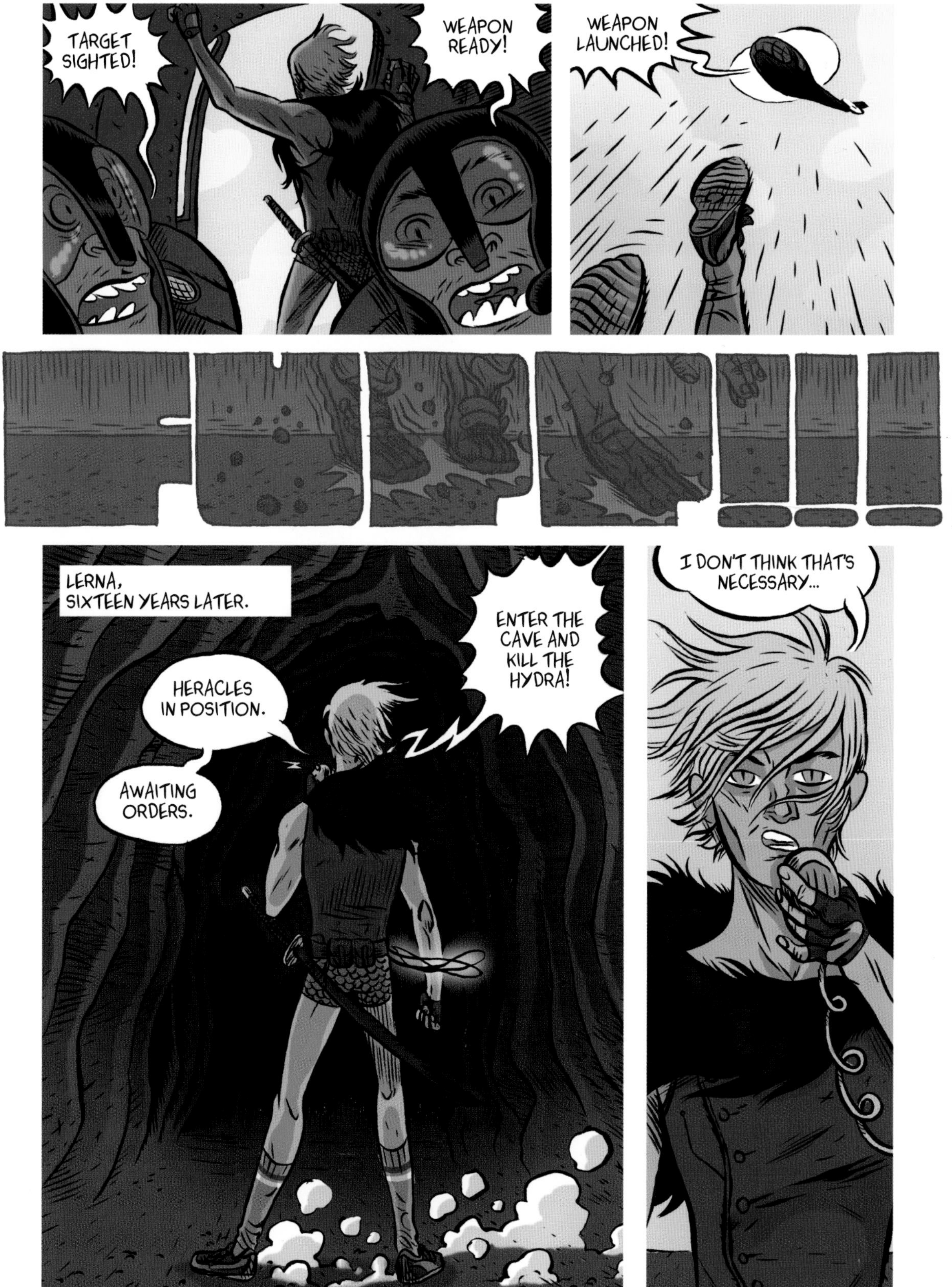
TARGET SIGHTED!
WEAPON READY!
WEAPON LAUNCHED!
LERNA, SIXTEEN YEARS LATER.
HERACLES IN POSITION.
AWAITING ORDERS.
ENTER THE CAVE AND KILL THE HYDRA!
I DON'T THINK THAT'S NECESSARY...

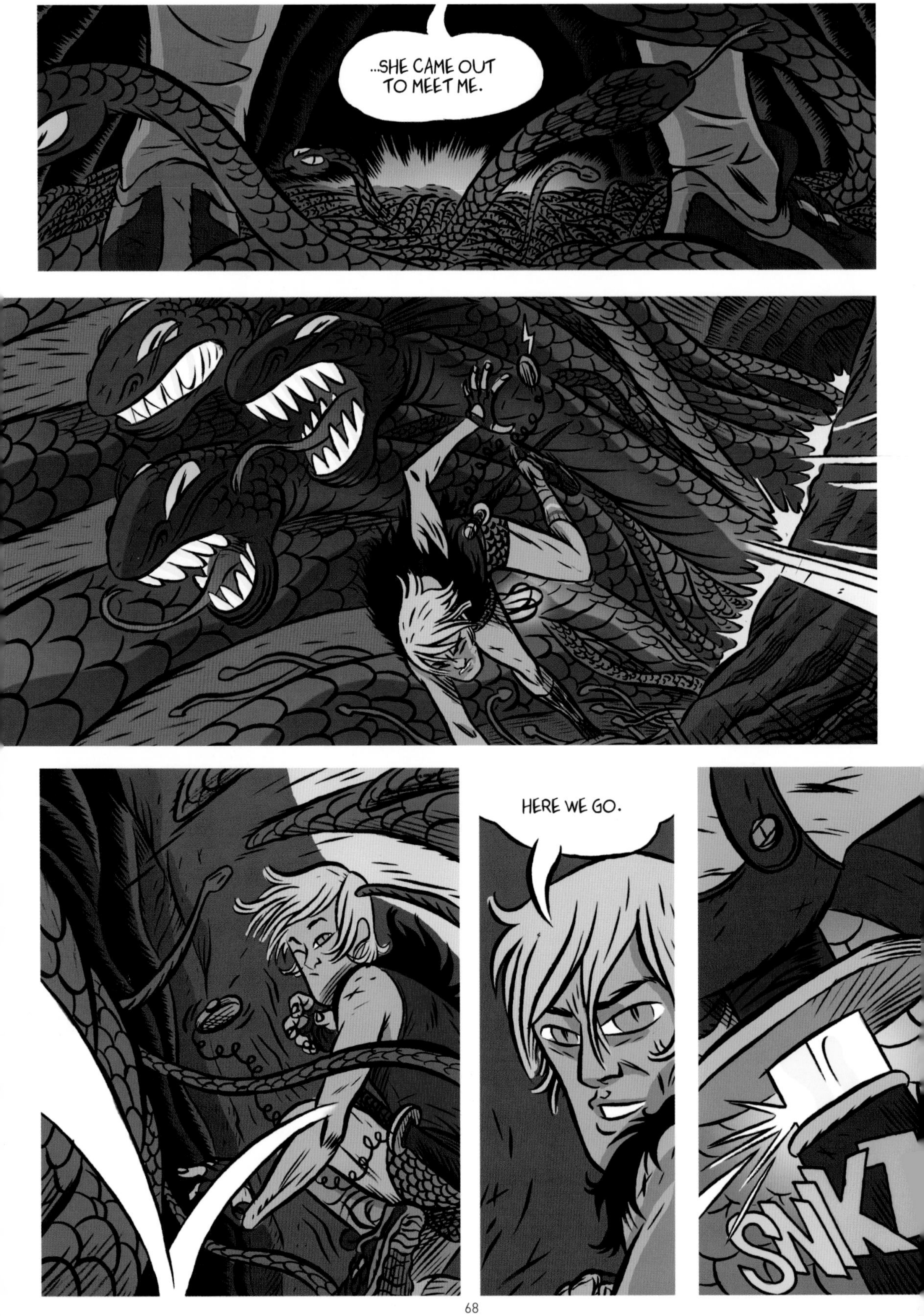
...SHE CAME OUT TO MEET ME.
HERE WE GO.
SNK

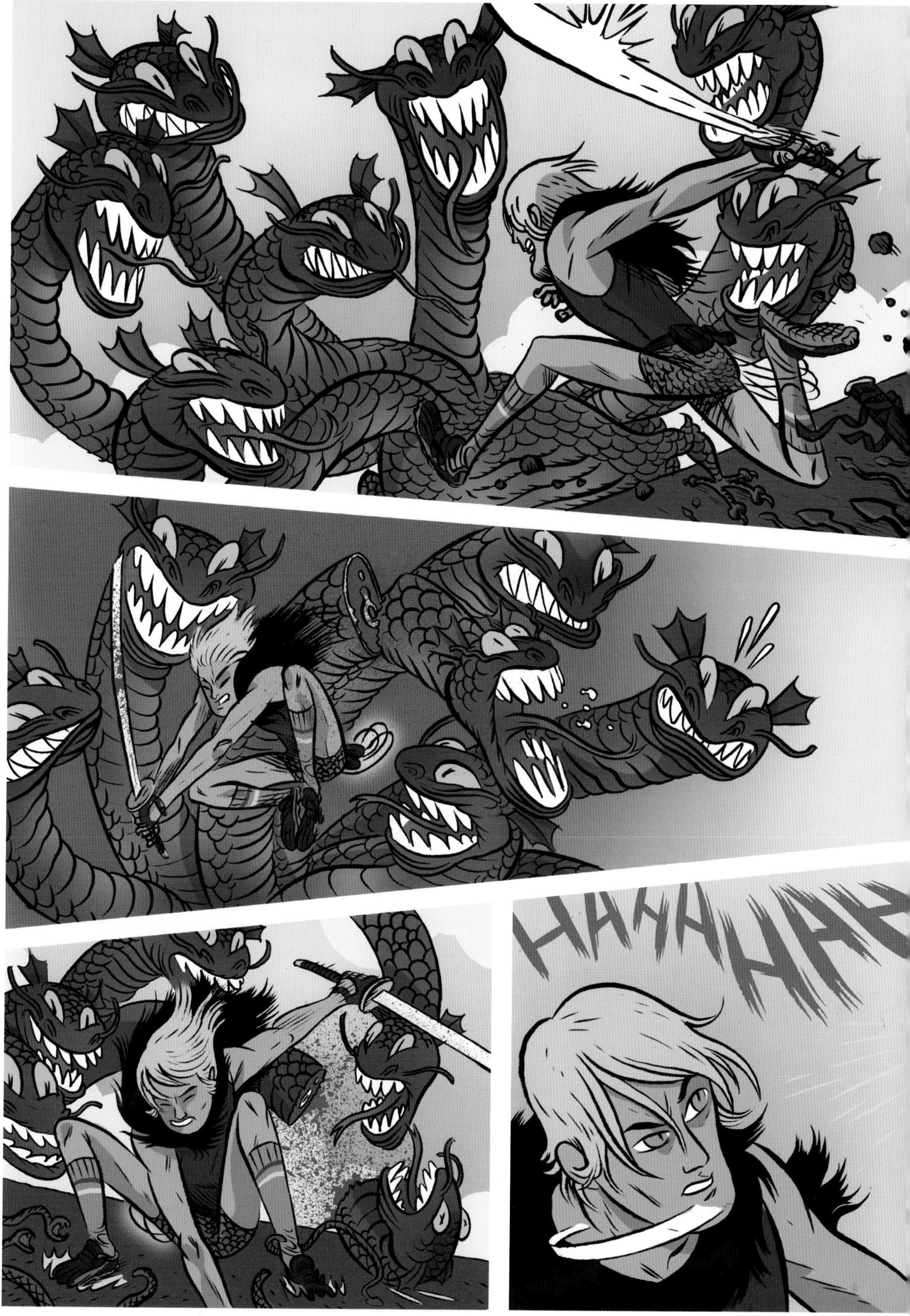
HAHAHA

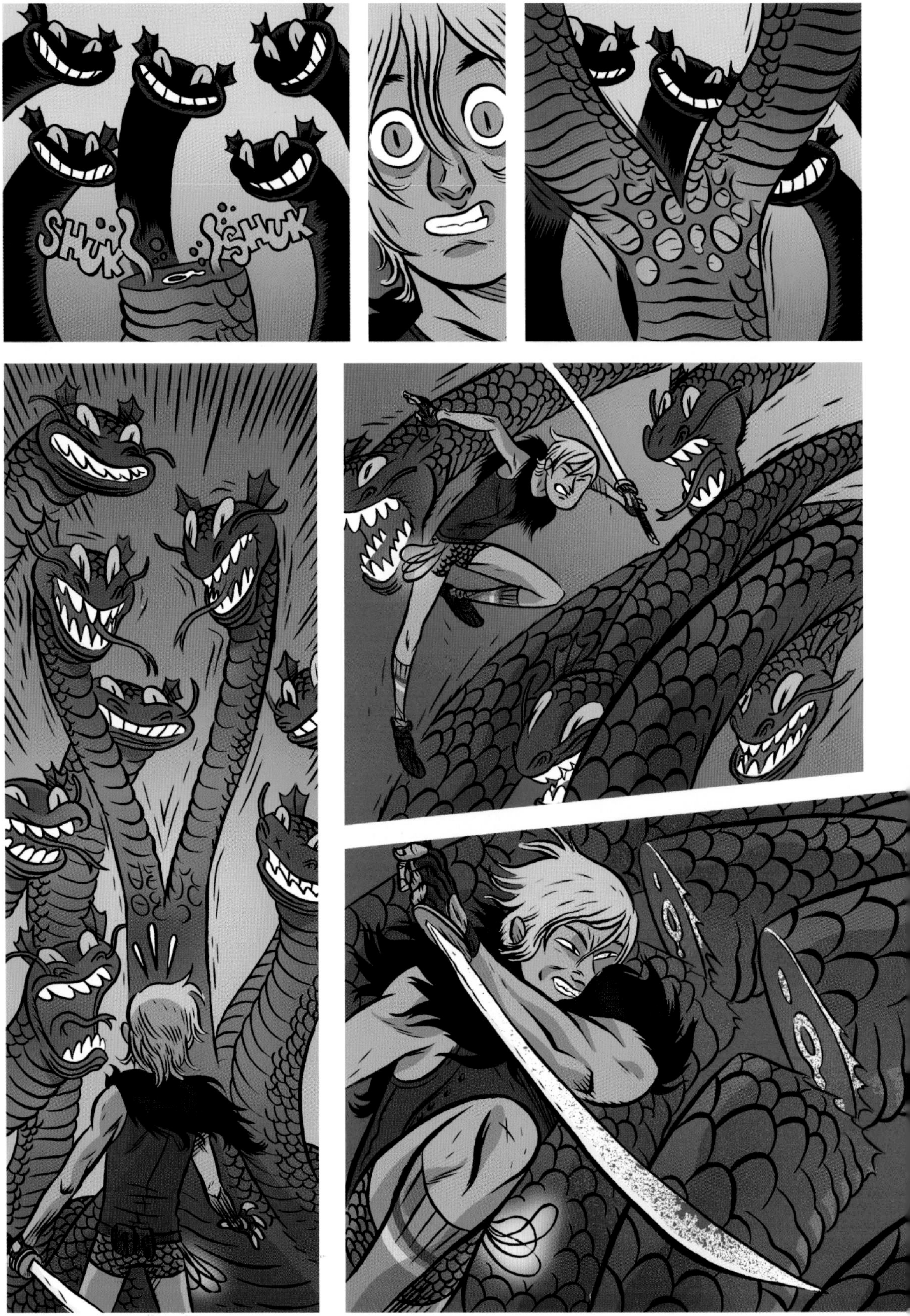
SHUK
SHUK

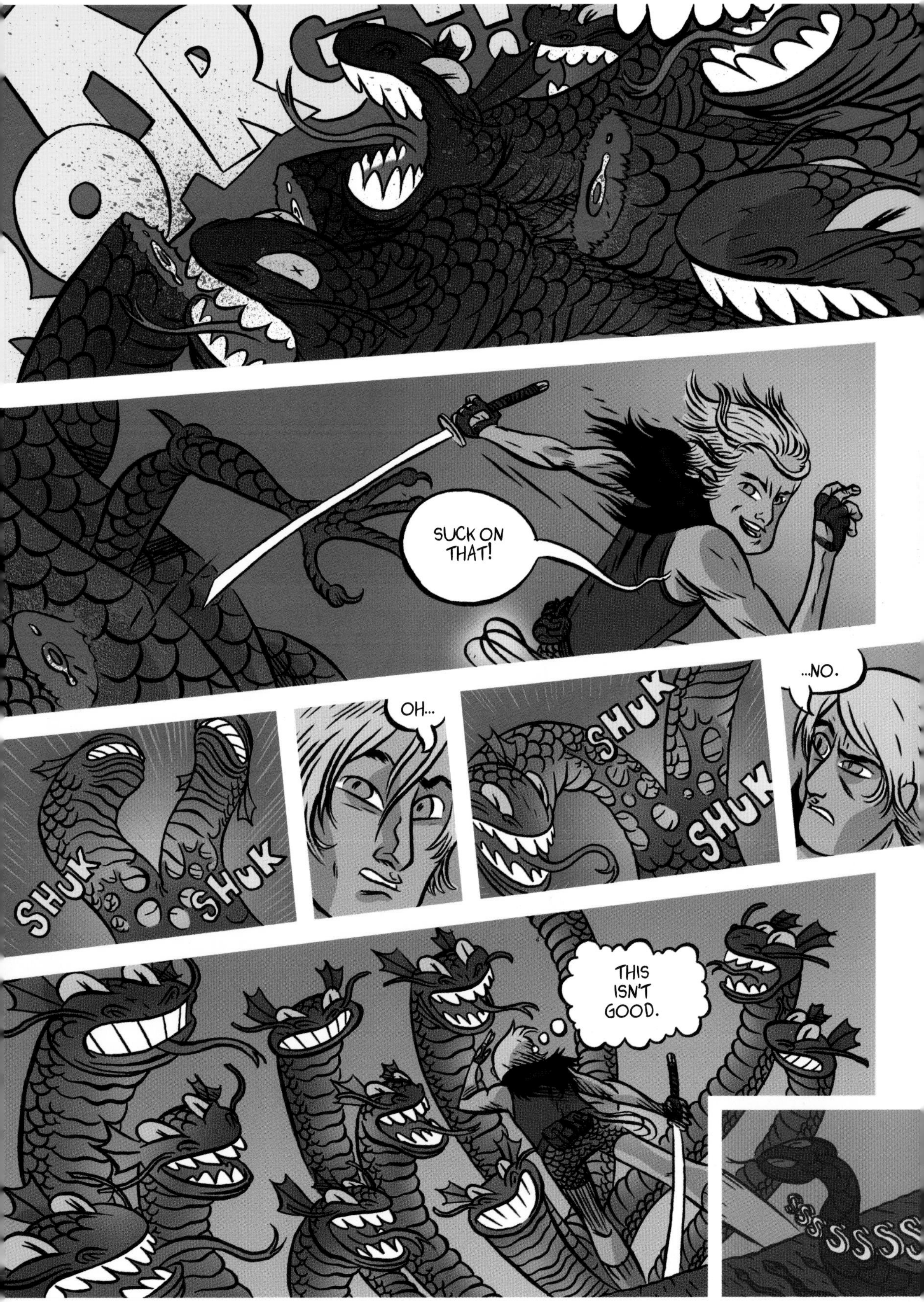
SUCK ON THAT!
OH...
...NO.
SHUK SHUK
SHUK SHUK
THIS ISN'T GOOD.
SSSSSS

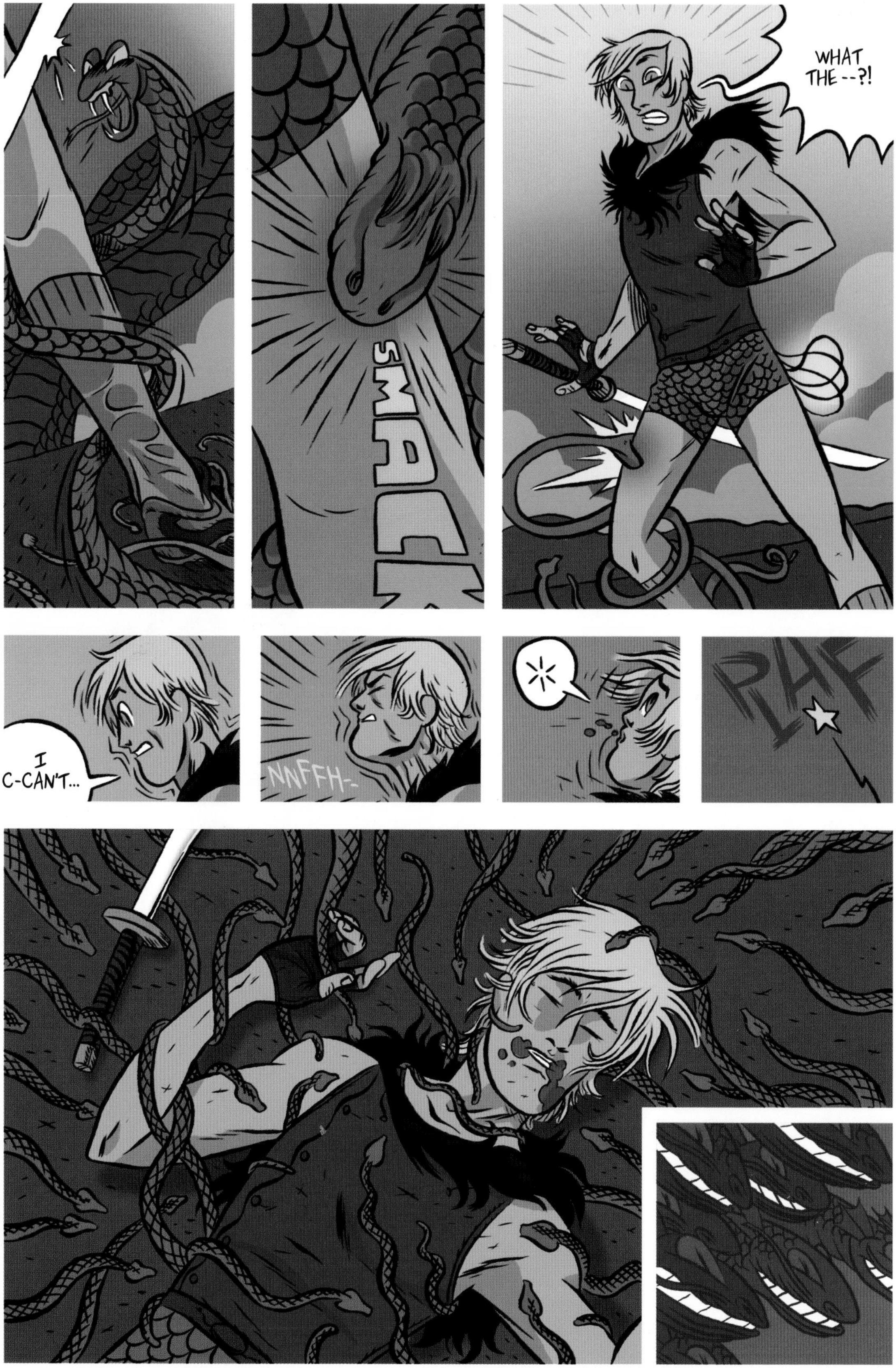
SMACK
WHAT THE --?!
I C-CAN'T...
NNFFH-
PLAF

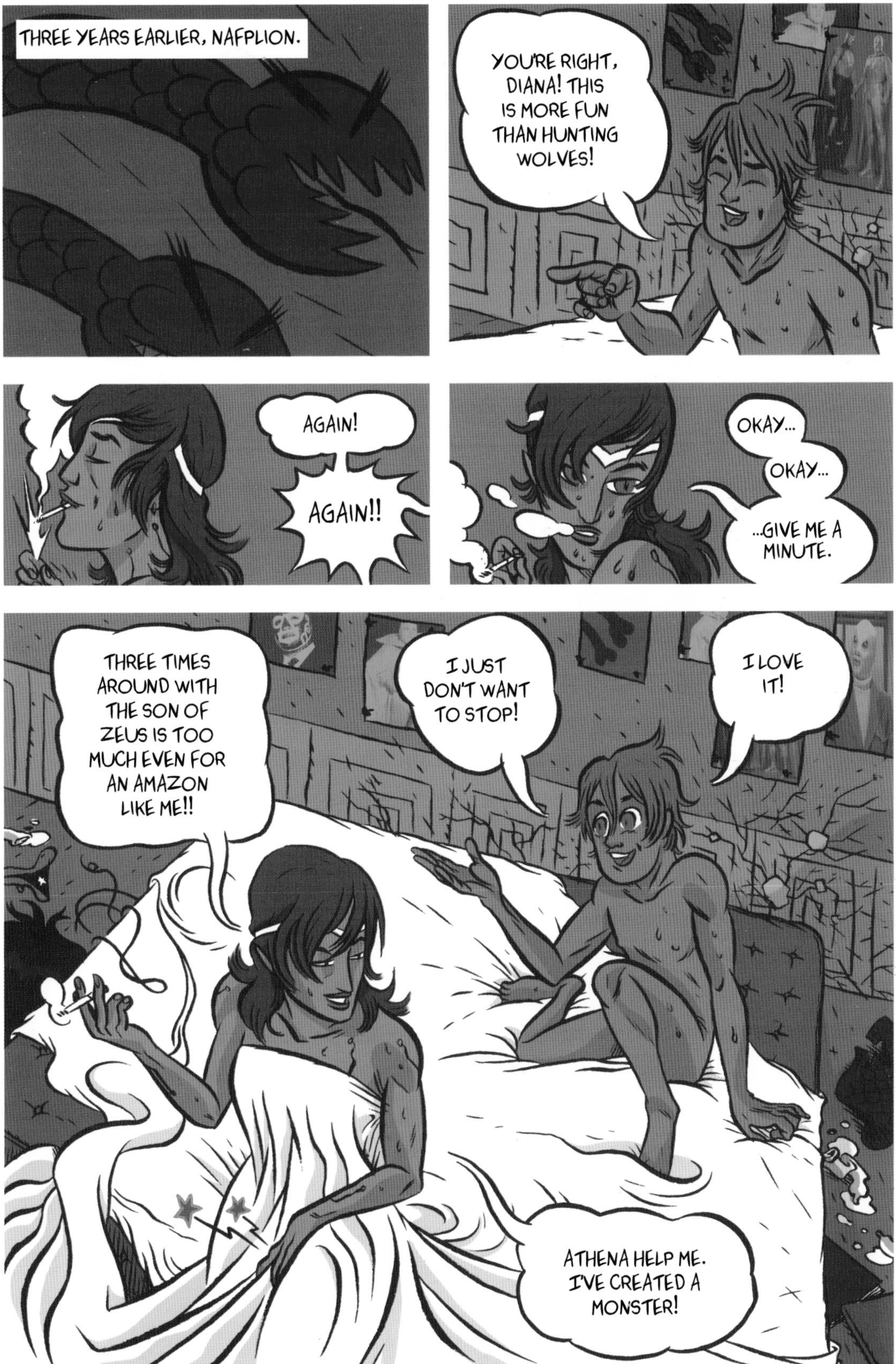
THREE YEARS EARLIER, NAFPLION.
YOU'RE RIGHT, DIANA! THIS IS MORE FUN THAN HUNTING WOLVES!
AGAIN!
AGAIN!!
OKAY...
OKAY...
...GIVE ME A MINUTE.
THREE TIMES AROUND WITH THE SON OF ZEUS IS TOO MUCH EVEN FOR AN AMAZON LIKE ME!!
I JUST DON'T WANT TO STOP!
I LOVE IT!
ATHENA HELP ME. I'VE CREATED A MONSTER!

SSSHH... WAIT.

FUP

COF
COF
COF

WHAT IS IT? WASN'T I ANY GOOD?

YOU WERE TOO GOOD.

I CAN HARDLY BELIEVE IT WAS YOUR FIRST TIME.

LOOK, I WANT TO GIVE YOU A GIFT, IN RETURN FOR THE WONDERFUL TIME I'VE HAD.

HUH?

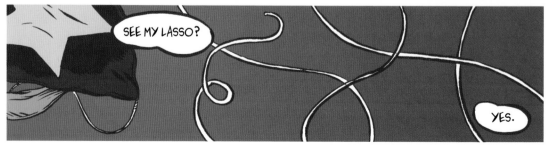

SEE MY LASSO?

YES.

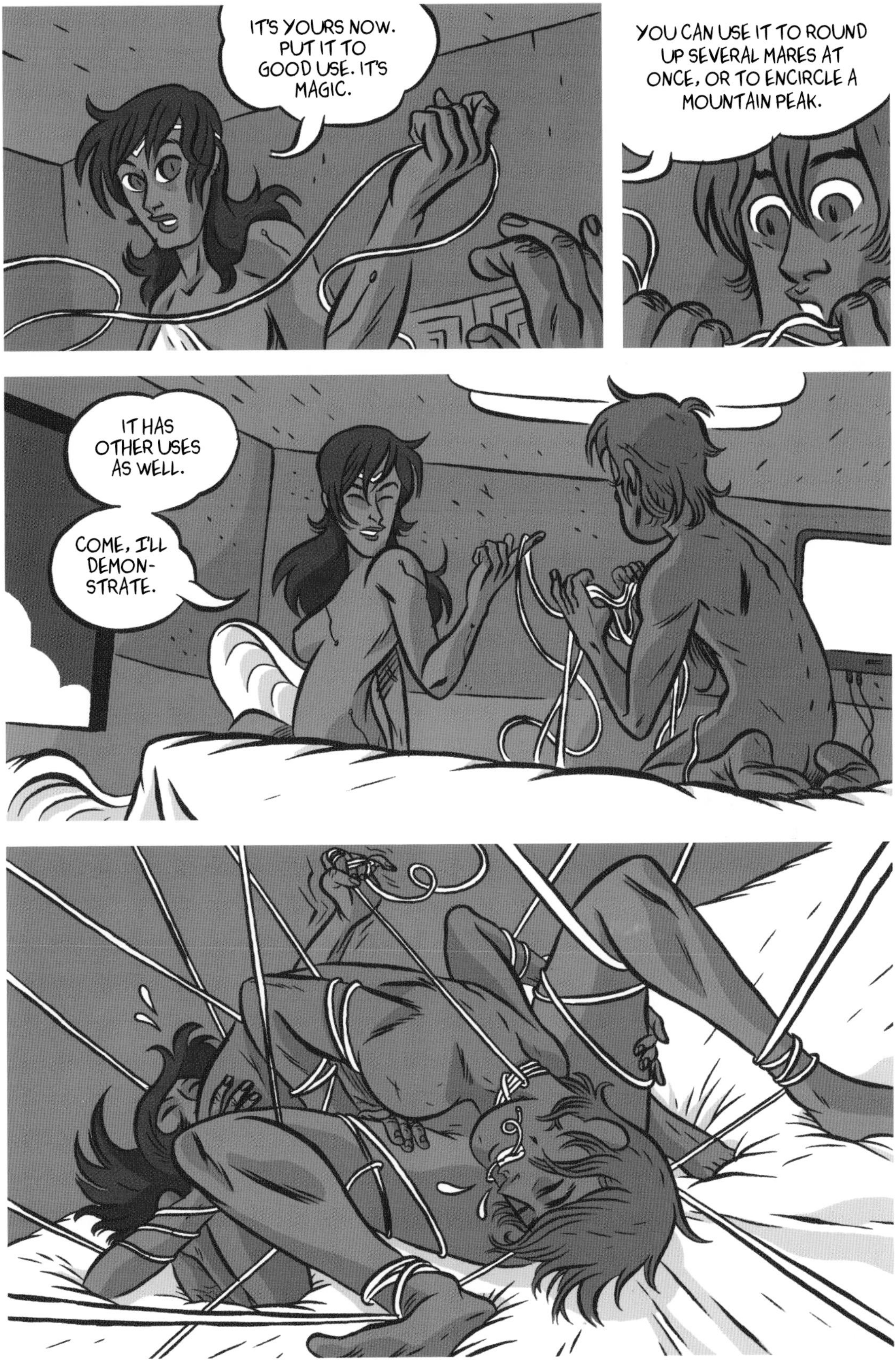
IT'S YOURS NOW. PUT IT TO GOOD USE. IT'S MAGIC.
YOU CAN USE IT TO ROUND UP SEVERAL MARES AT ONCE, OR TO ENCIRCLE A MOUNTAIN PEAK.
IT HAS OTHER USES AS WELL.
COME, I'LL DEMON-STRATE.

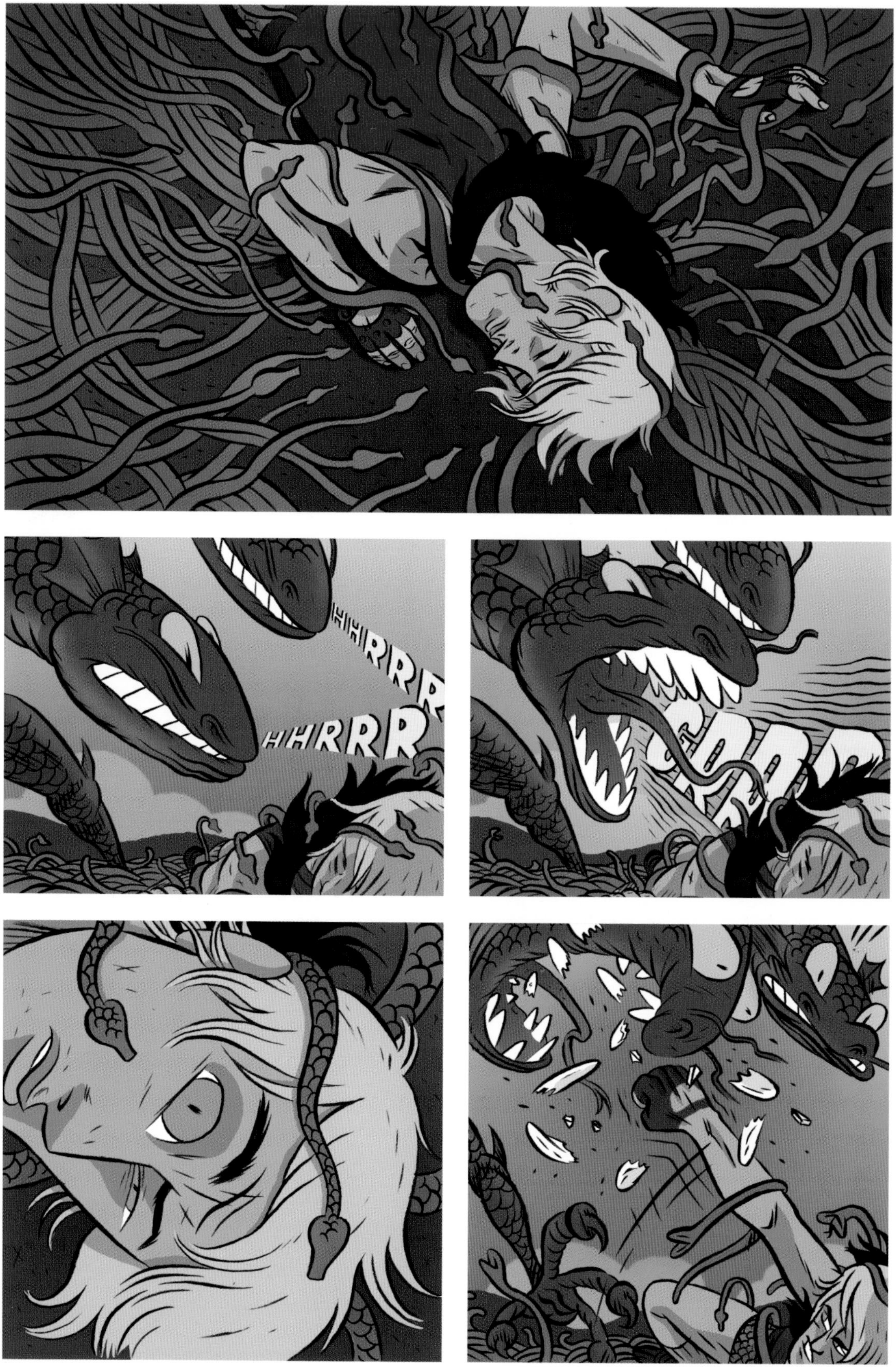
HHRRRR
HHRRRR

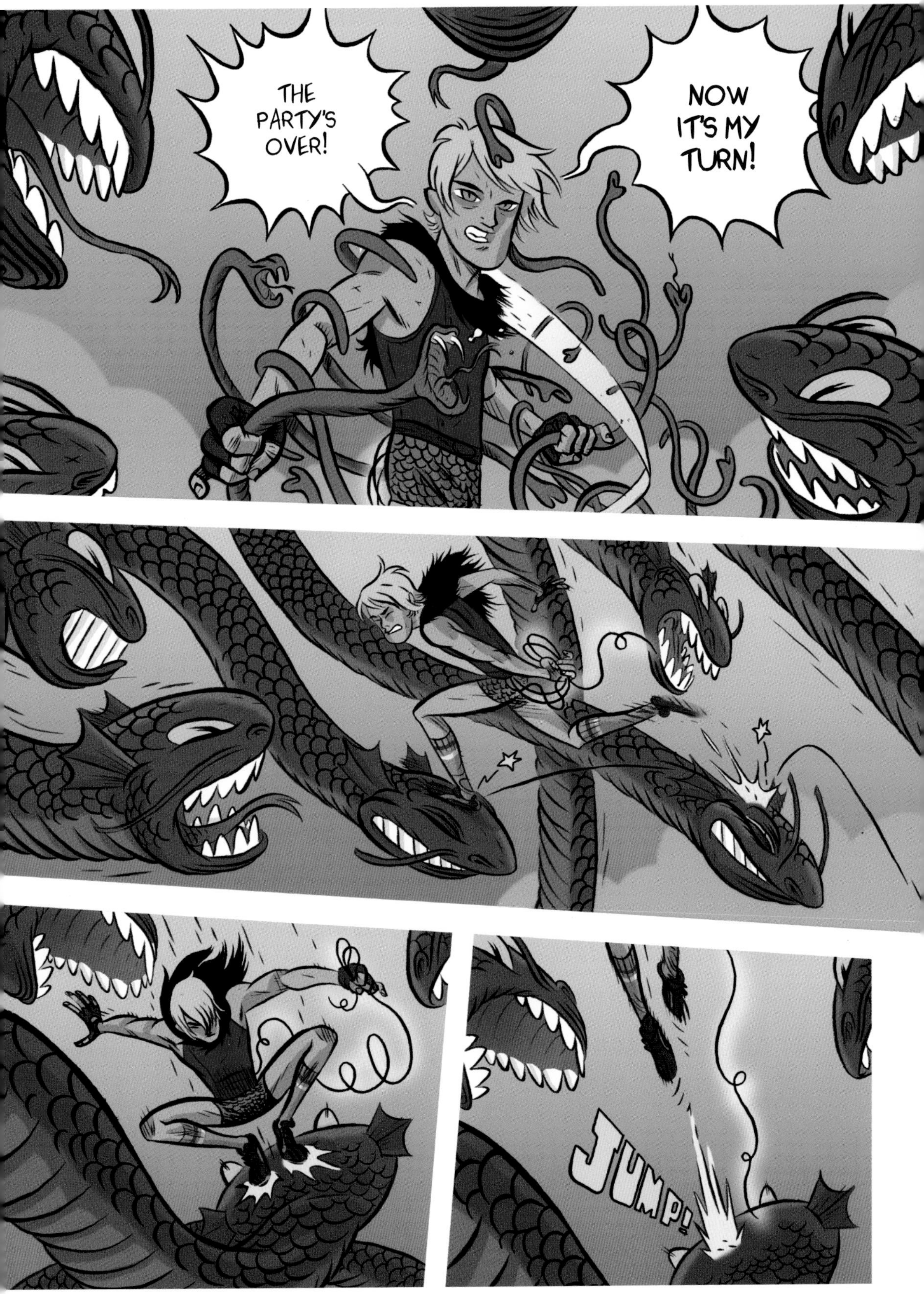
THE PARTY'S OVER!
NOW IT'S MY TURN!
JUMP!

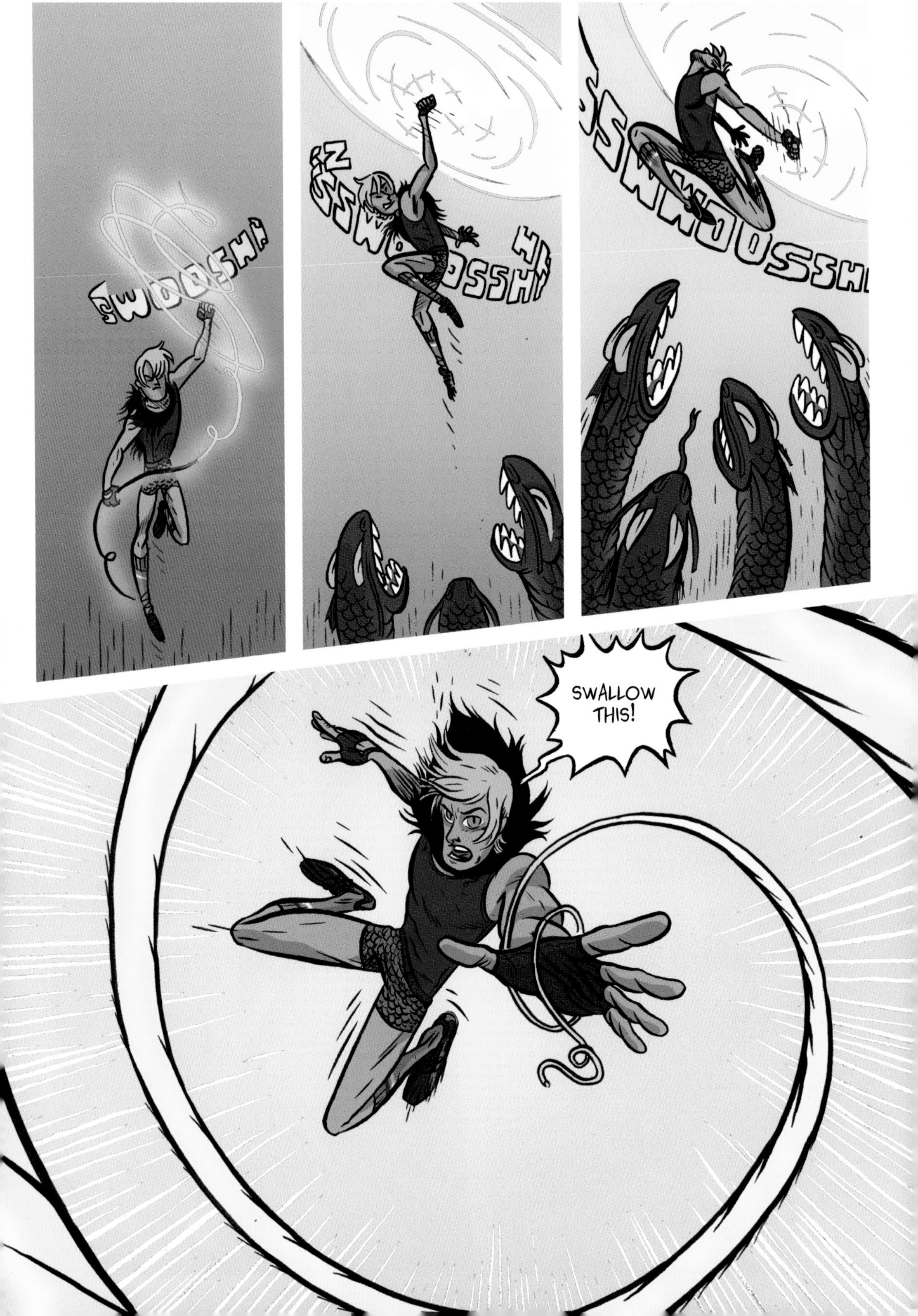
SWALLOW THIS!

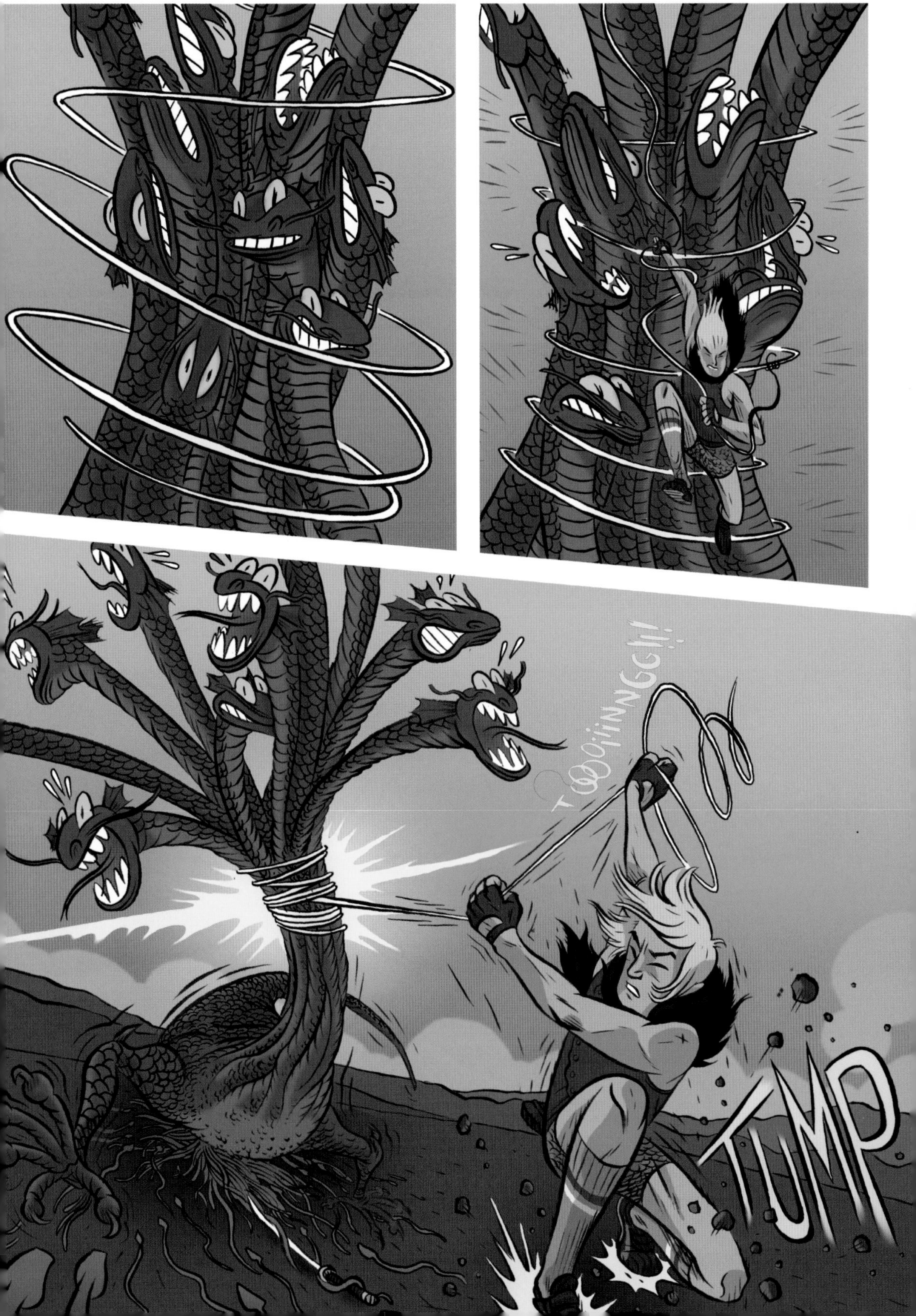
TOOOOiiiNNGG!!!
TUMP

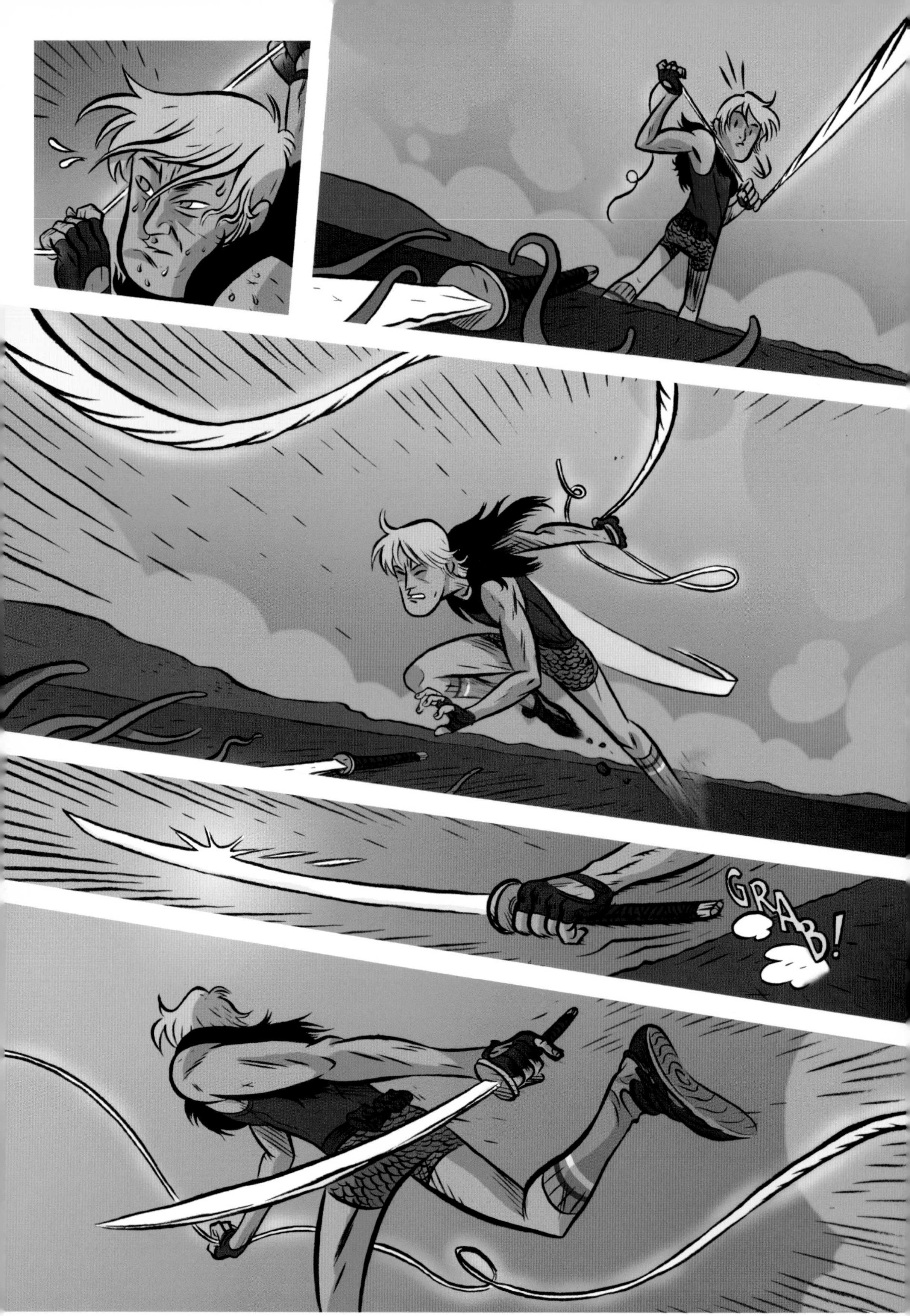
GRAB!

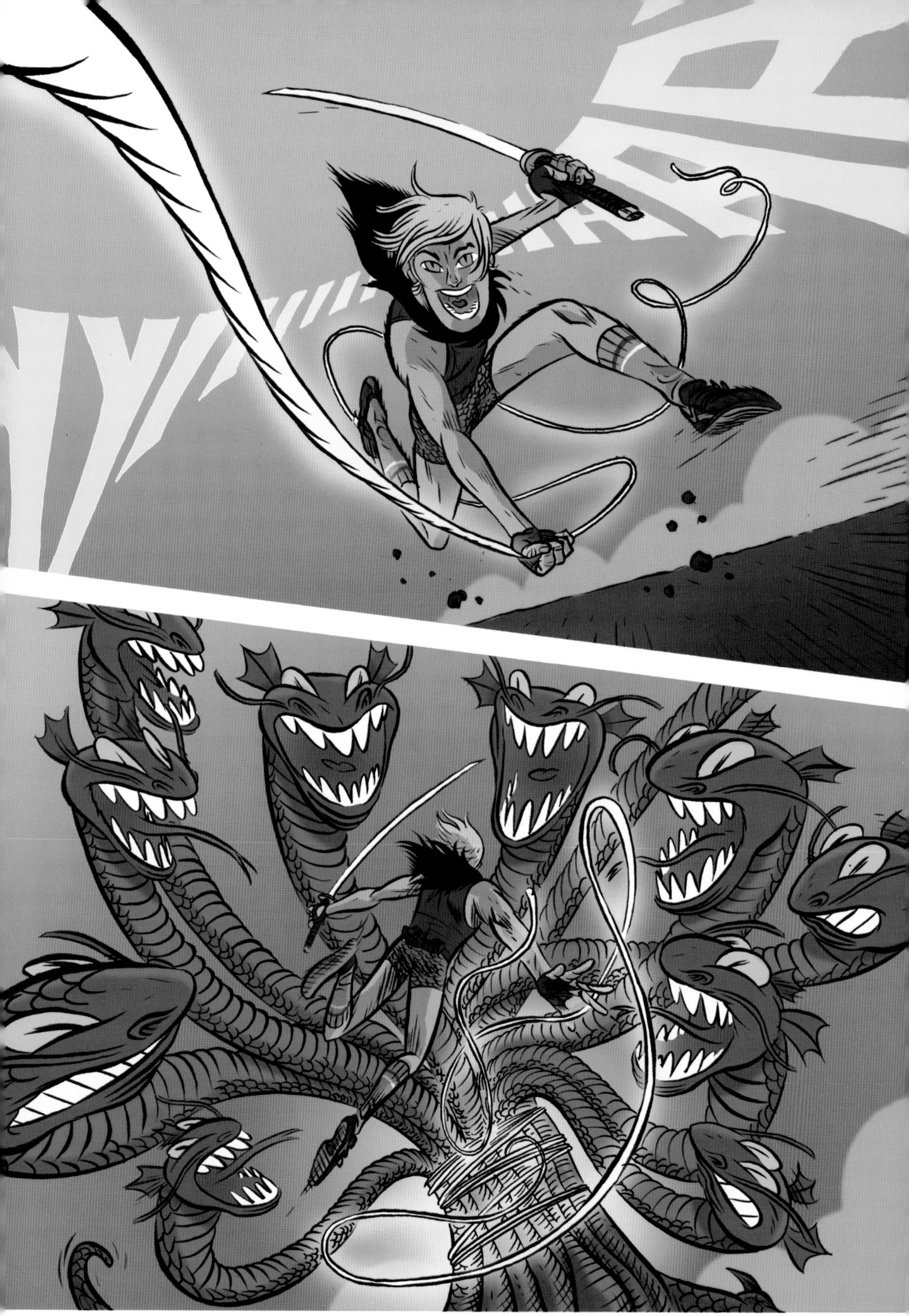

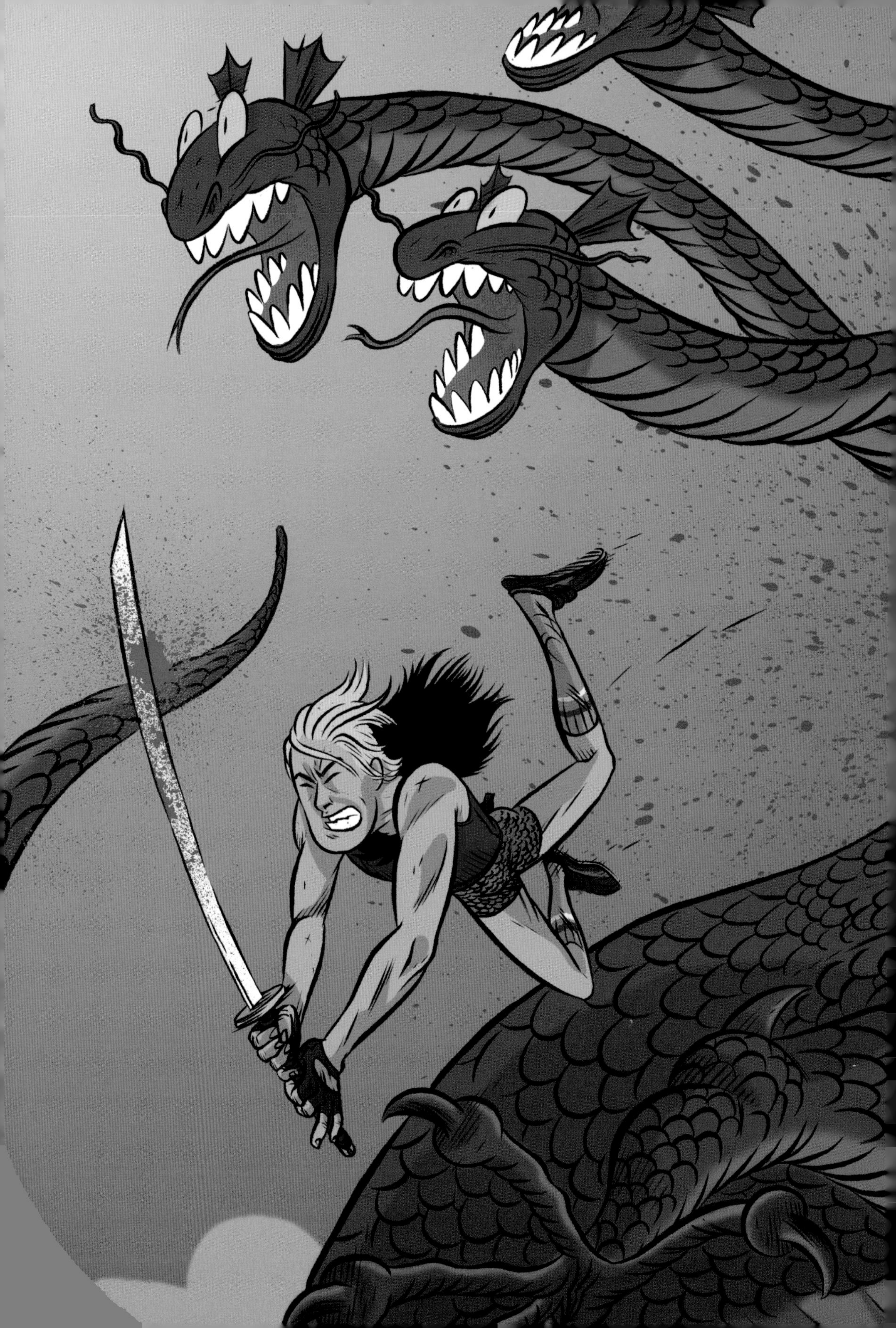

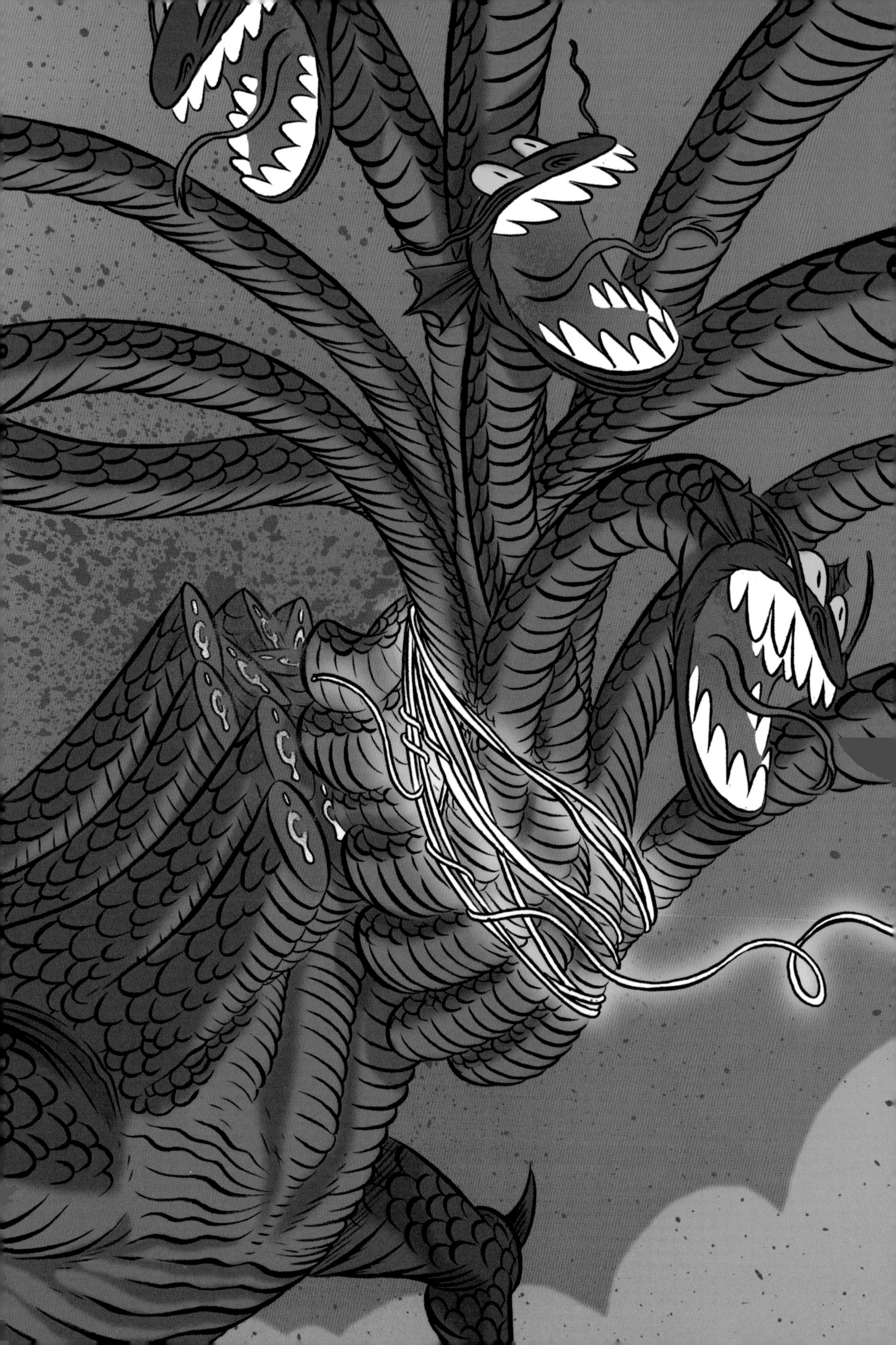

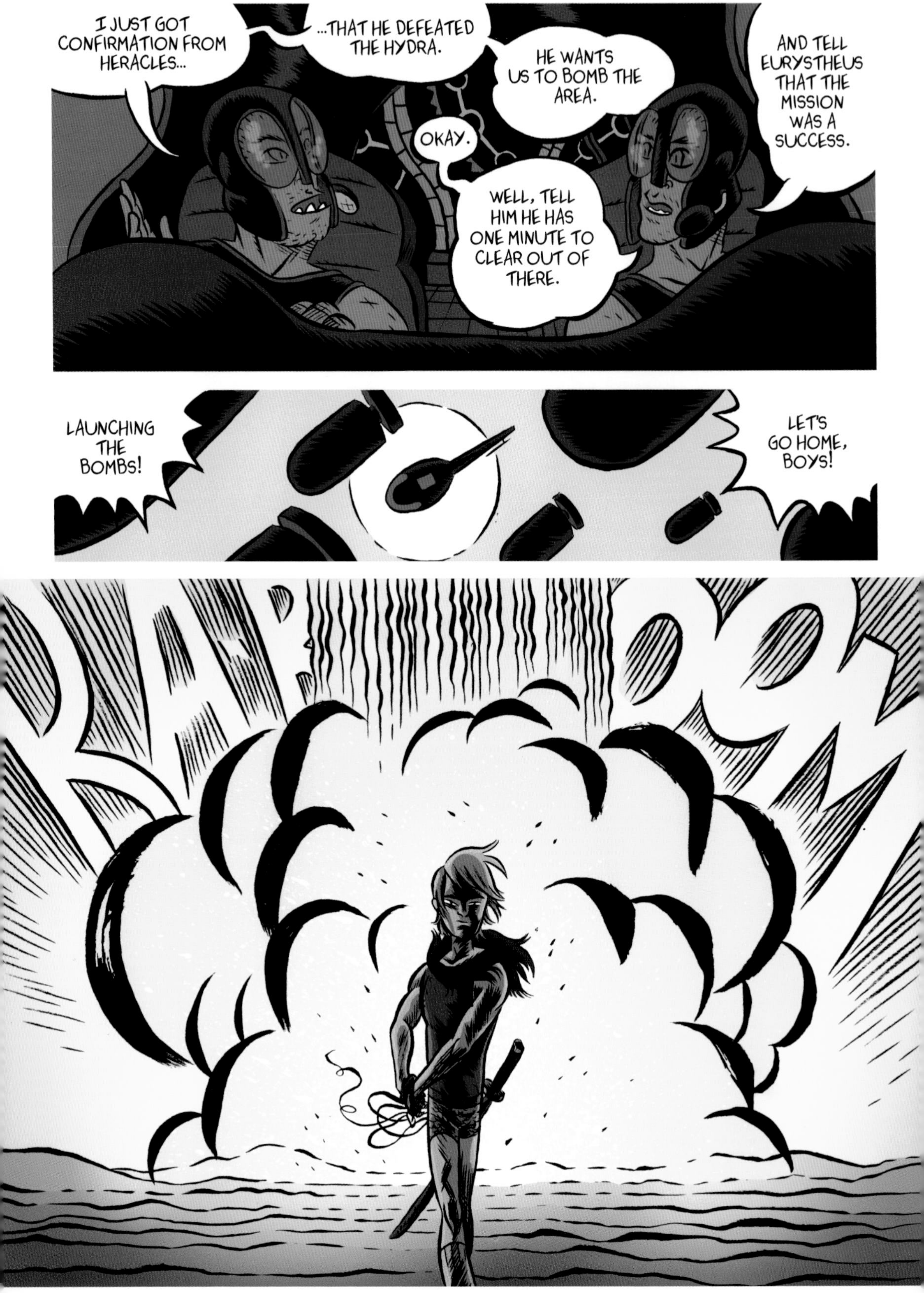
I JUST GOT CONFIRMATION FROM HERACLES...
...THAT HE DEFEATED THE HYDRA.
HE WANTS US TO BOMB THE AREA.
AND TELL EURYSTHEUS THAT THE MISSION WAS A SUCCESS.
OKAY.
WELL, TELL HIM HE HAS ONE MINUTE TO CLEAR OUT OF THERE.
LAUNCHING THE BOMBS!
LET'S GO HOME, BOYS!

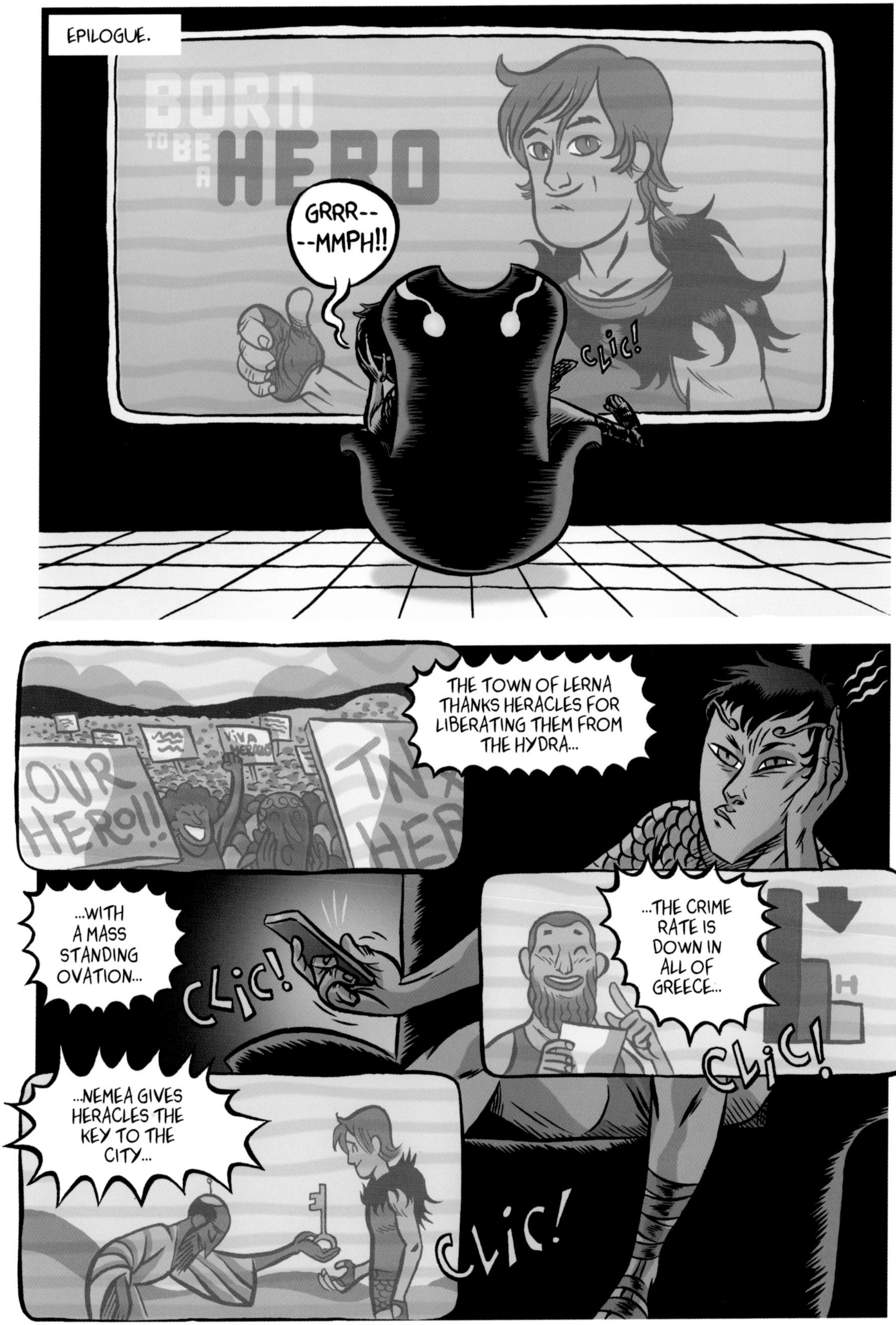
EPILOGUE.
BORN TO BE A HERO
GRRR-- --MMPH!!
CLIC!
OUR HERO!!
VIVA HERACLES
THE TOWN OF LERNA THANKS HERACLES FOR LIBERATING THEM FROM THE HYDRA...
...WITH A MASS STANDING OVATION...
CLIC!
...THE CRIME RATE IS DOWN IN ALL OF GREECE...
CLIC!
...NEMEA GIVES HERACLES THE KEY TO THE CITY...
CLIC!

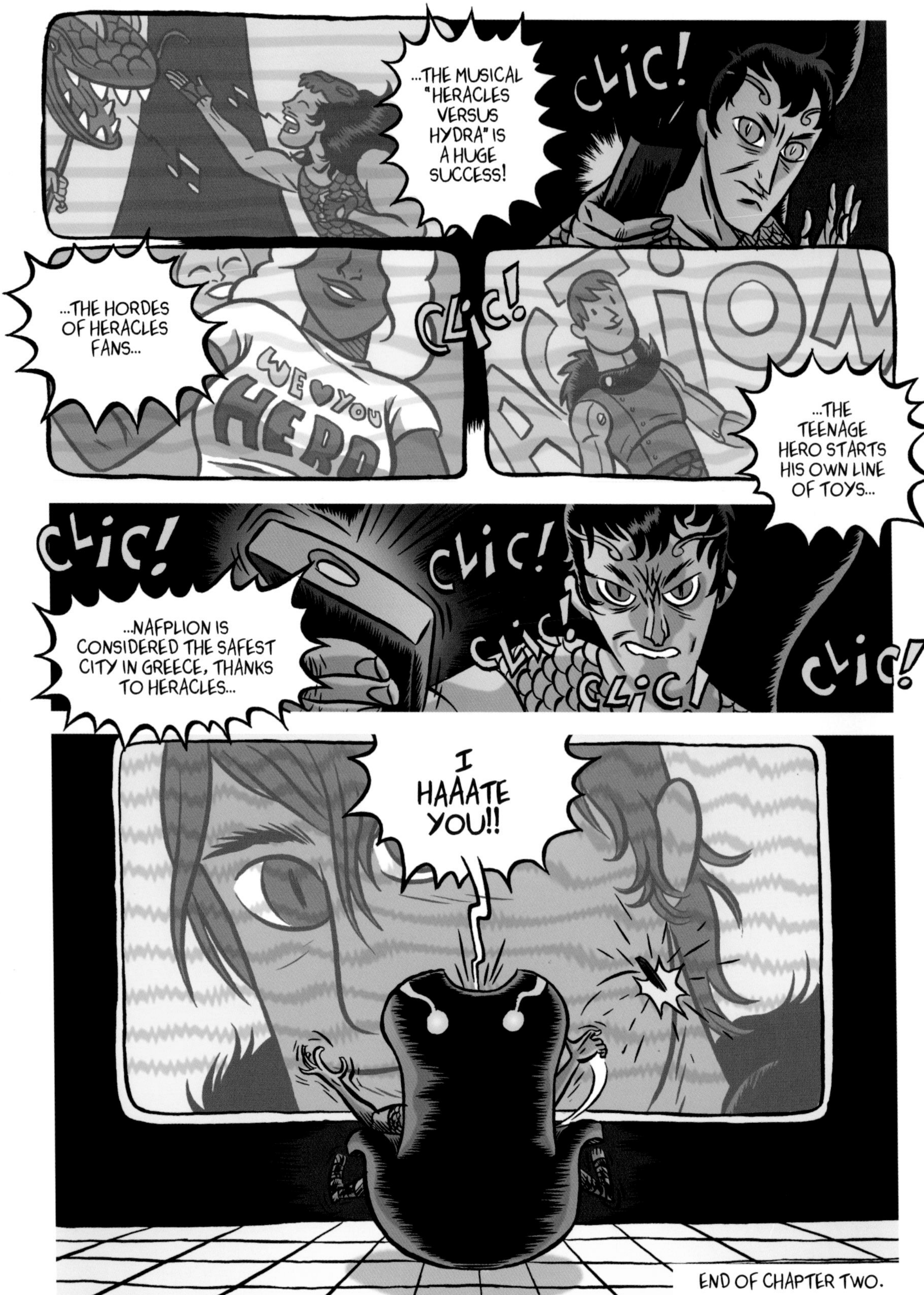
...THE MUSICAL "HERACLES VERSUS HYDRA" IS A HUGE SUCCESS!
CLIC!
...THE HORDES OF HERACLES FANS...
WE ♥ YOU HERO
CLIC!
...THE TEENAGE HERO STARTS HIS OWN LINE OF TOYS...
CLIC!
CLIC!
CLIC!
CLIC!
CLIC!
...NAFPLION IS CONSIDERED THE SAFEST CITY IN GREECE, THANKS TO HERACLES...
I HAAATE YOU!!
END OF CHAPTER TWO.

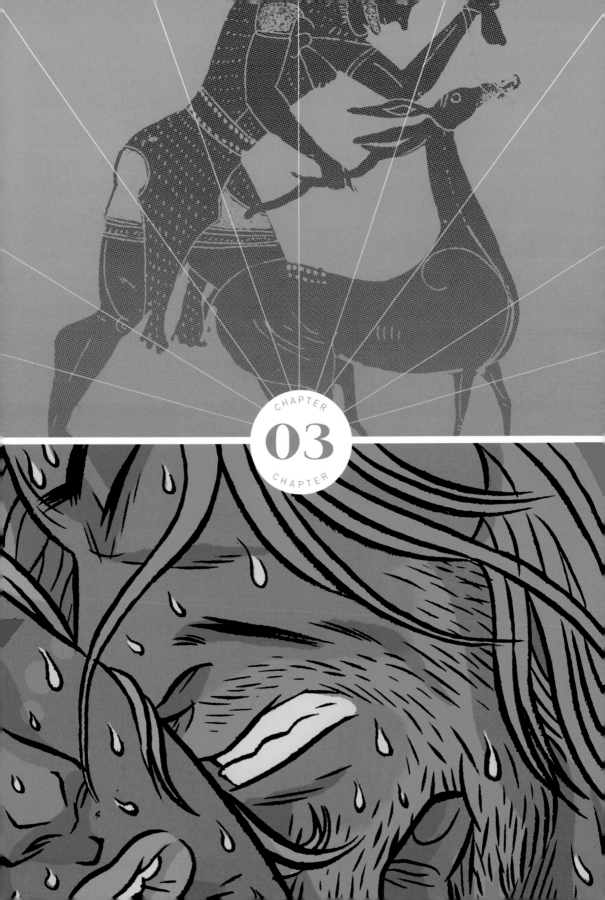

CHAPTER
03
CHAPTER

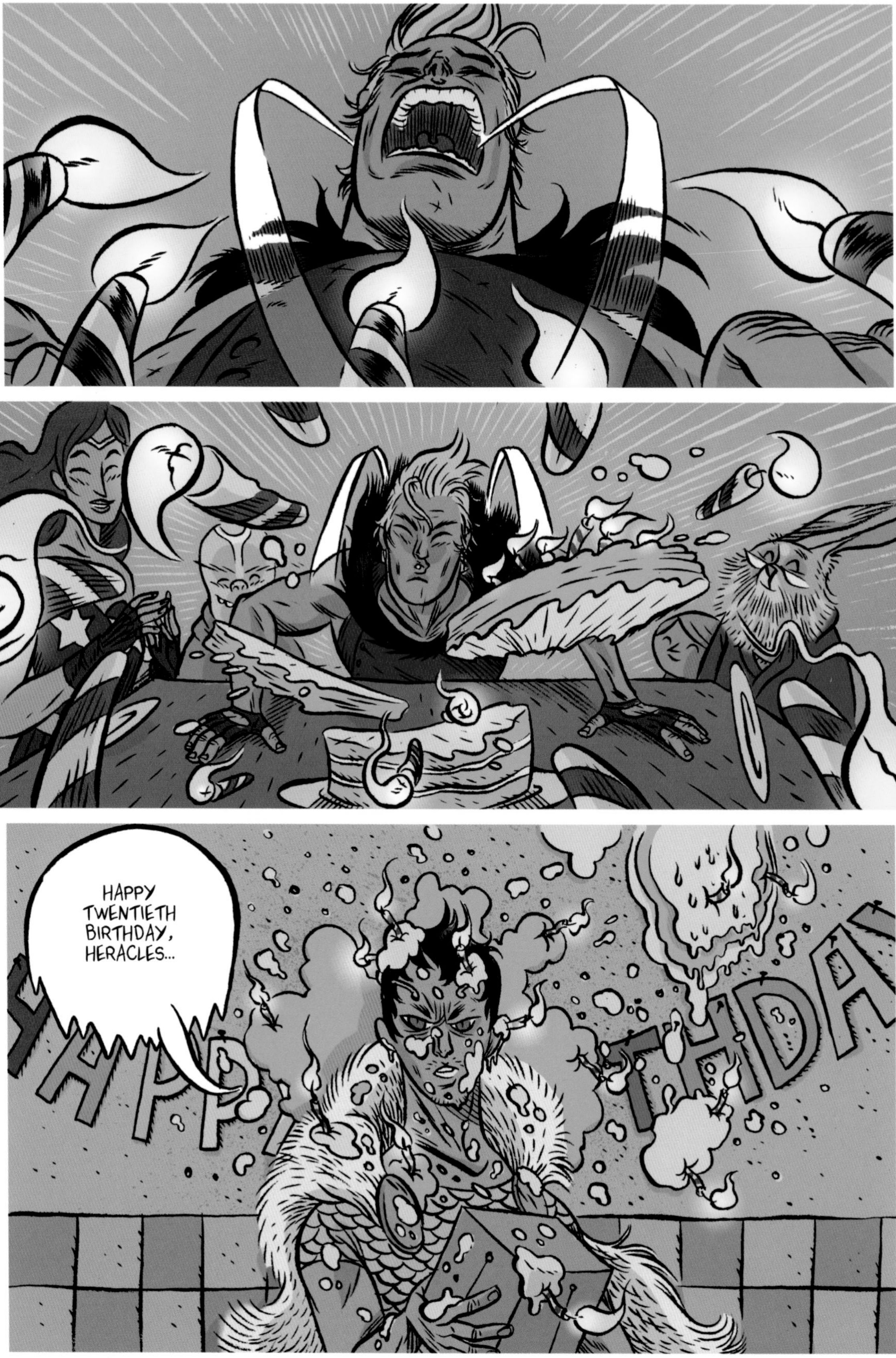
HAPPY TWENTIETH BIRTHDAY, HERACLES...

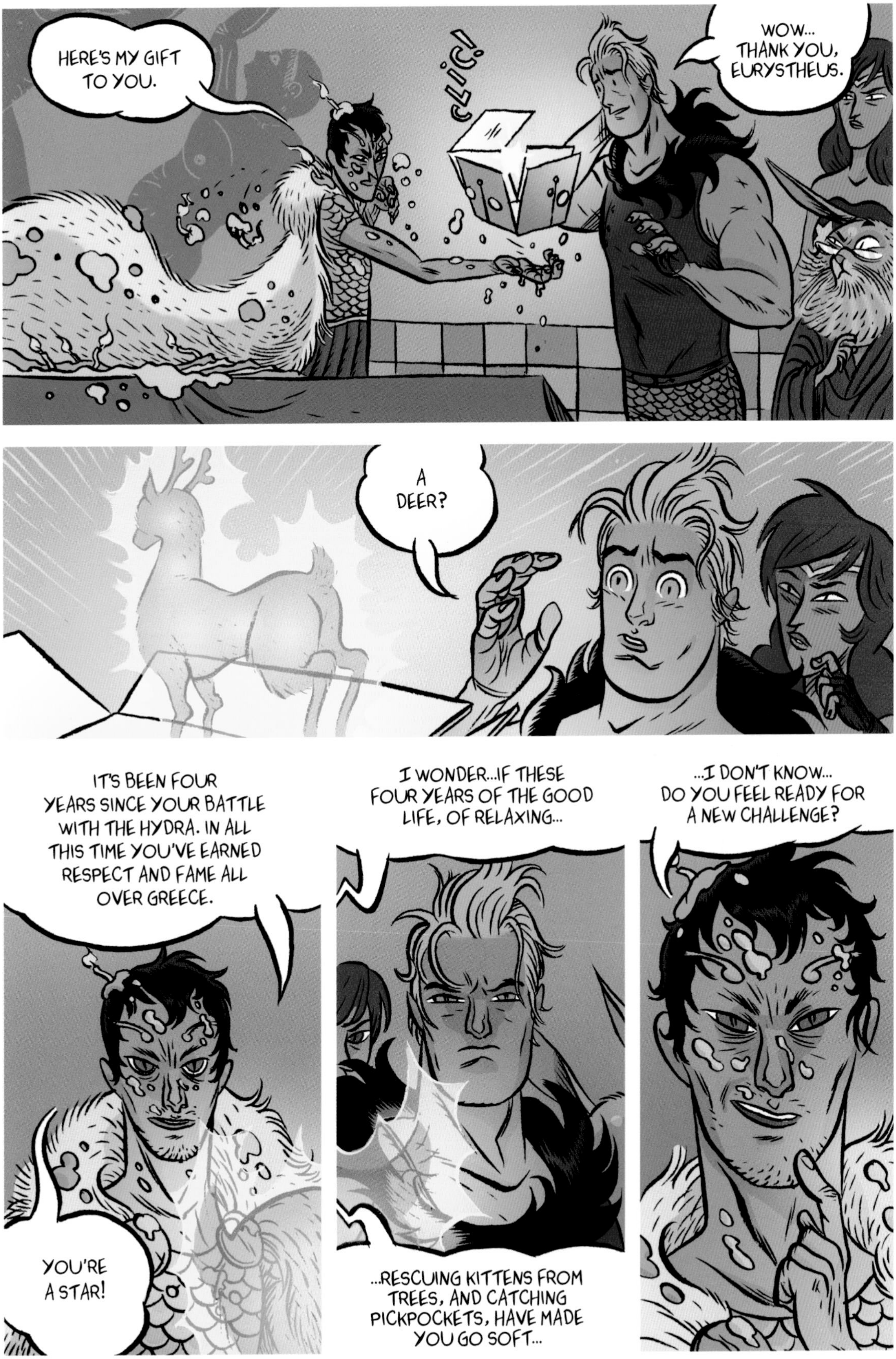
HERE'S MY GIFT TO YOU.
CLIC!
WOW... THANK YOU, EURYSTHEUS.
A DEER?
IT'S BEEN FOUR YEARS SINCE YOUR BATTLE WITH THE HYDRA. IN ALL THIS TIME YOU'VE EARNED RESPECT AND FAME ALL OVER GREECE.
YOU'RE A STAR!
I WONDER...IF THESE FOUR YEARS OF THE GOOD LIFE, OF RELAXING...
...RESCUING KITTENS FROM TREES, AND CATCHING PICKPOCKETS, HAVE MADE YOU GO SOFT...
...I DON'T KNOW... DO YOU FEEL READY FOR A NEW CHALLENGE?

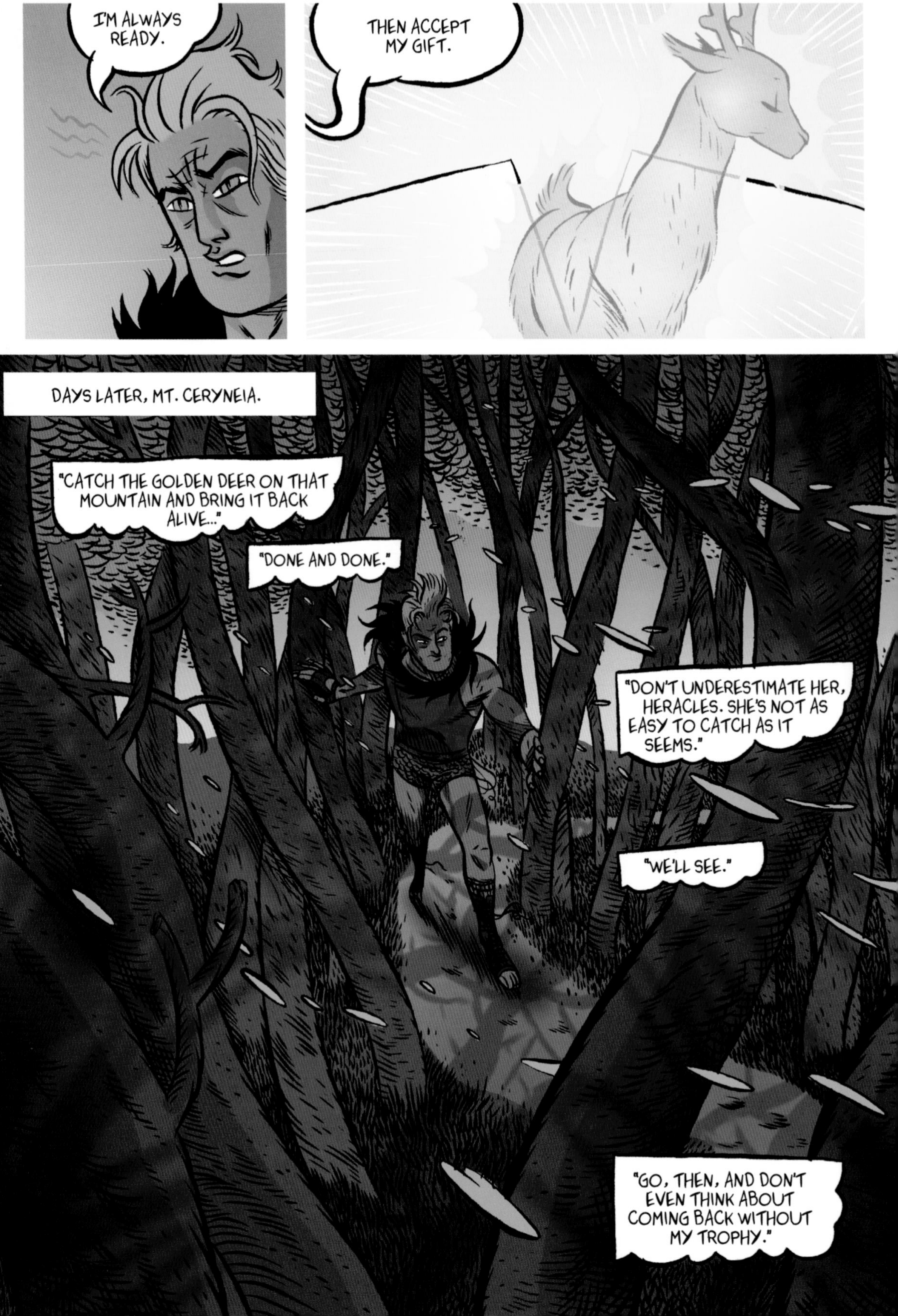
I'M ALWAYS READY.
THEN ACCEPT MY GIFT.
DAYS LATER, MT. CERYNEIA.
"CATCH THE GOLDEN DEER ON THAT MOUNTAIN AND BRING IT BACK ALIVE..."
"DONE AND DONE."
"DON'T UNDERESTIMATE HER, HERACLES. SHE'S NOT AS EASY TO CATCH AS IT SEEMS."
"WE'LL SEE."
"GO, THEN, AND DON'T EVEN THINK ABOUT COMING BACK WITHOUT MY TROPHY."

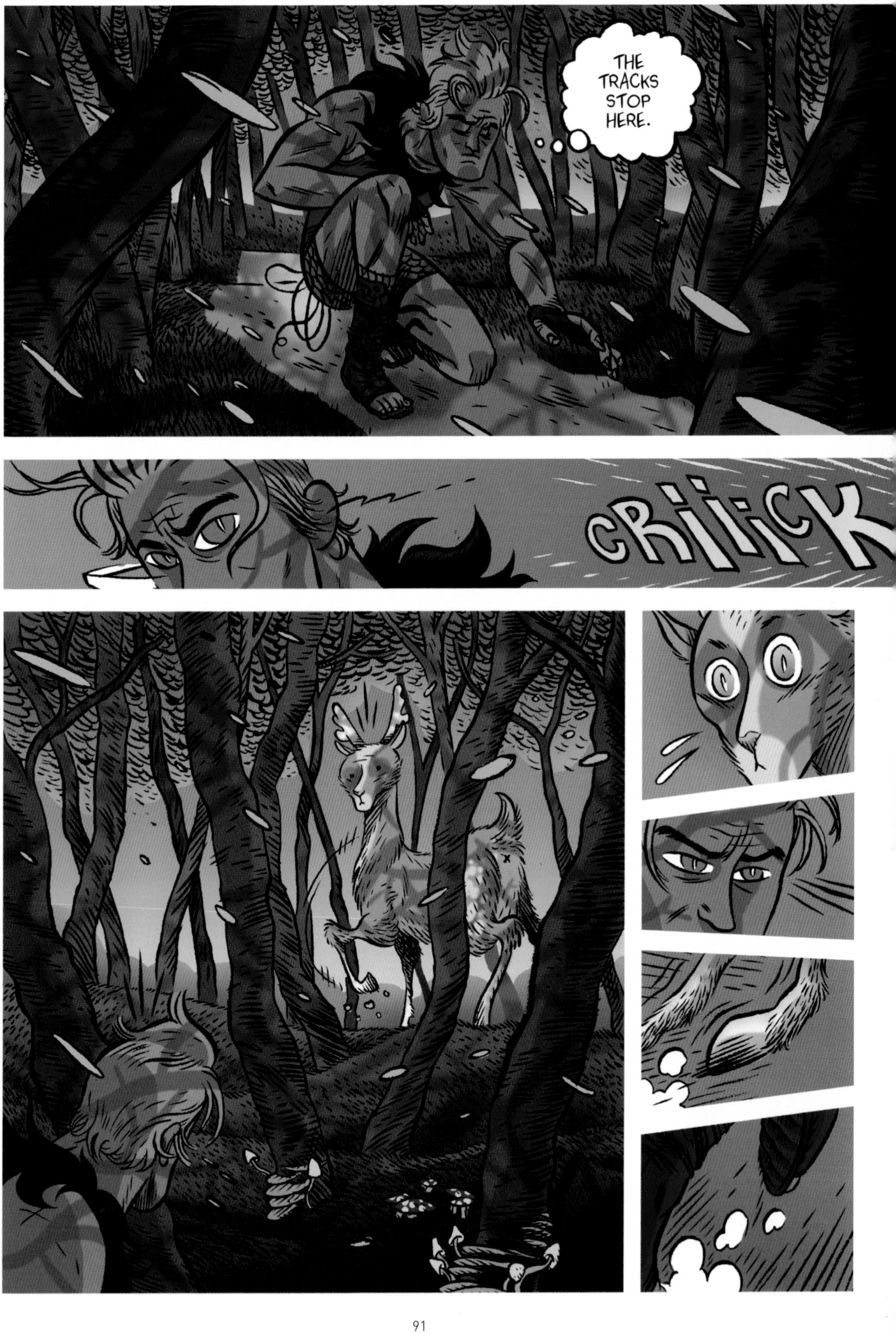
THE TRACKS STOP HERE.
CRIIICK

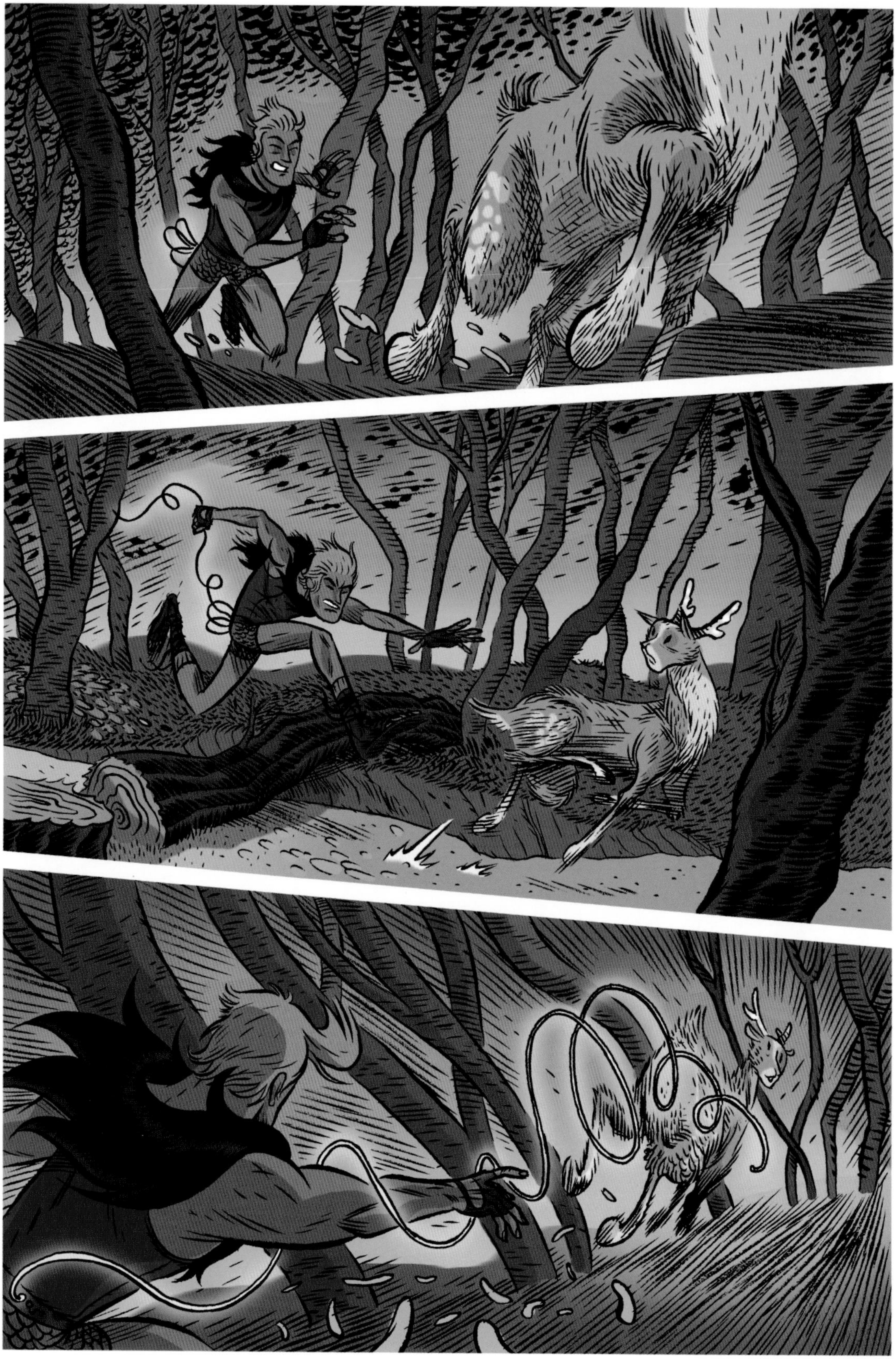

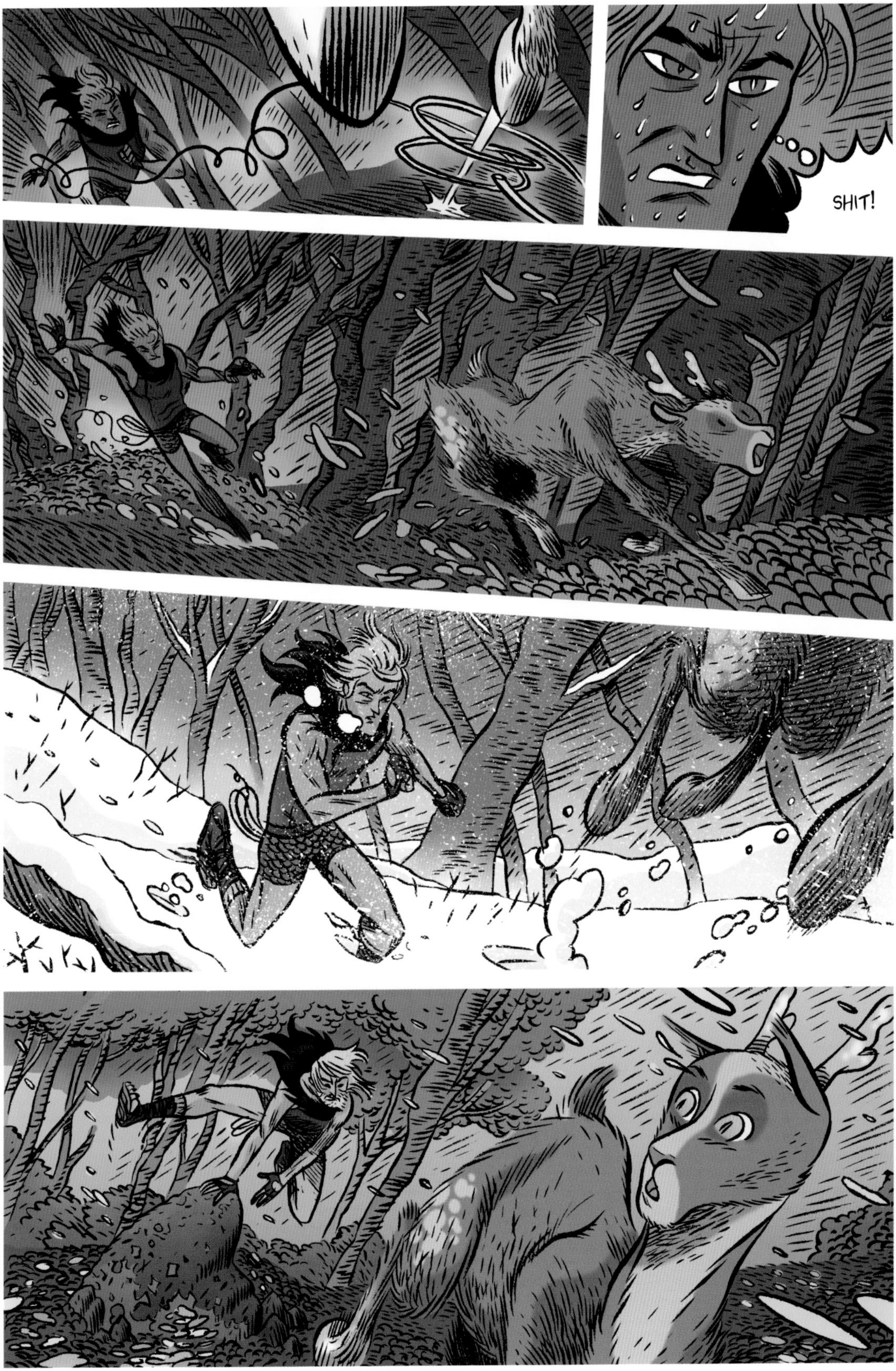
SHIT!

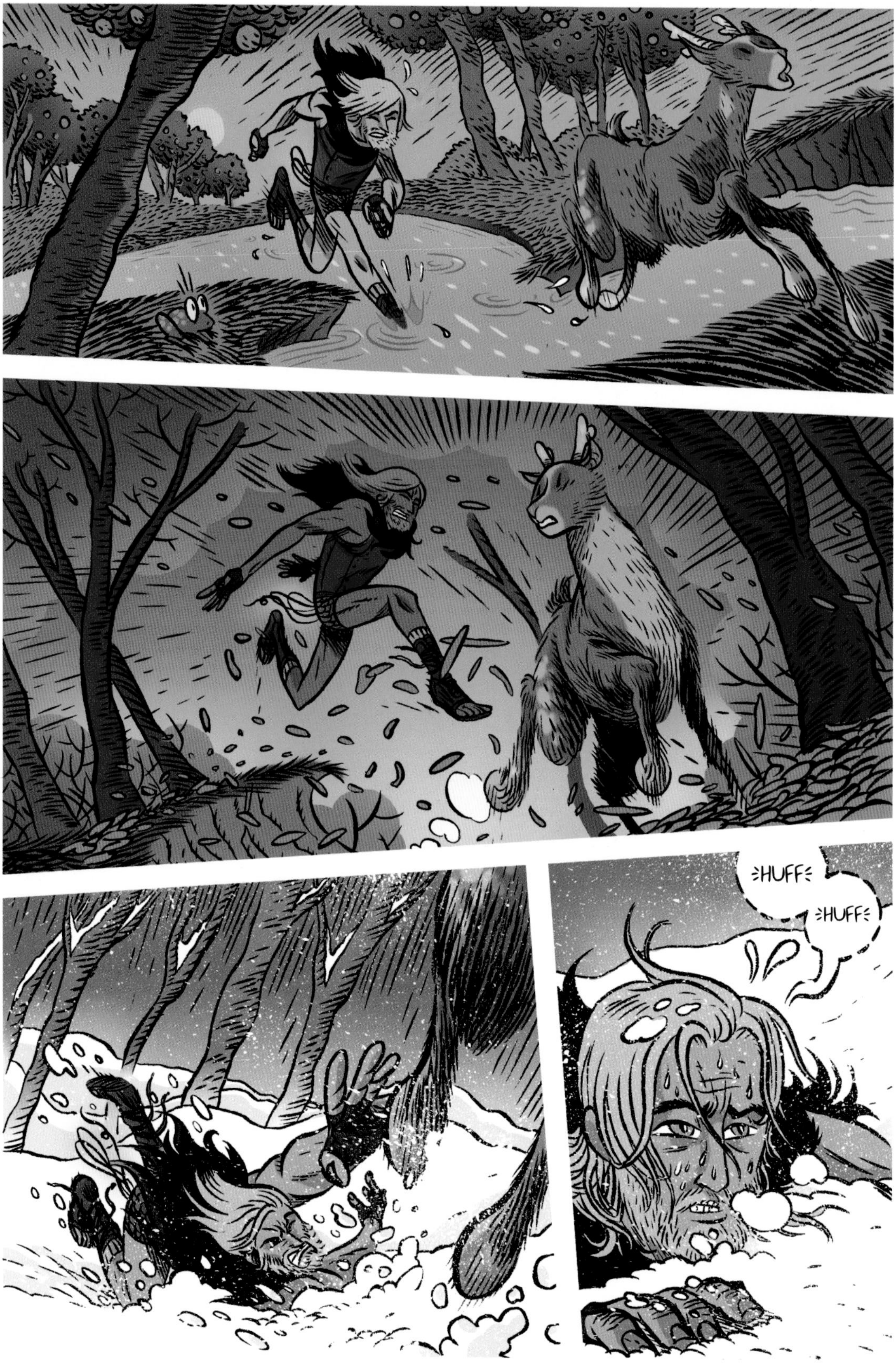
HUFF
HUFF

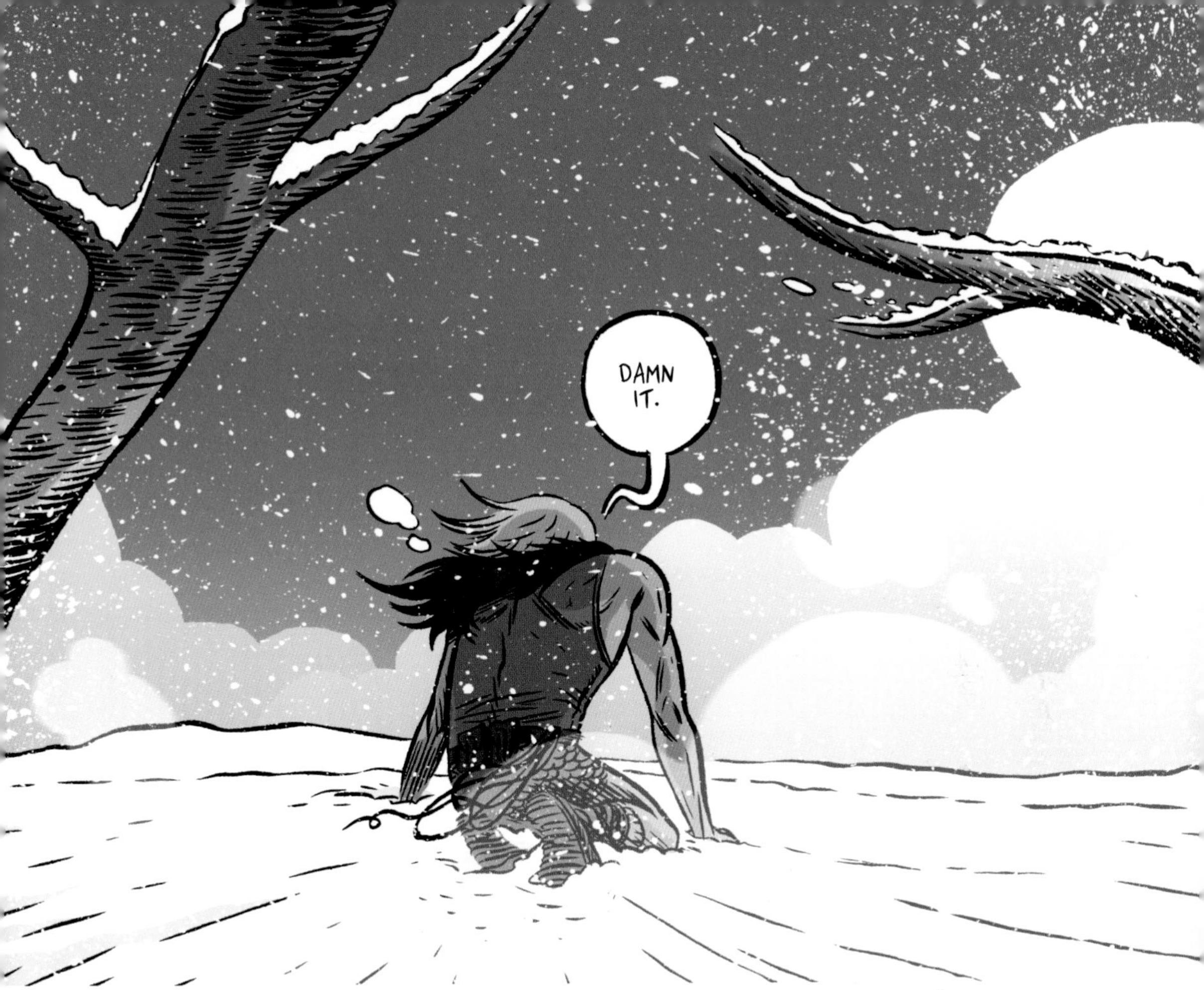
DAMN IT.

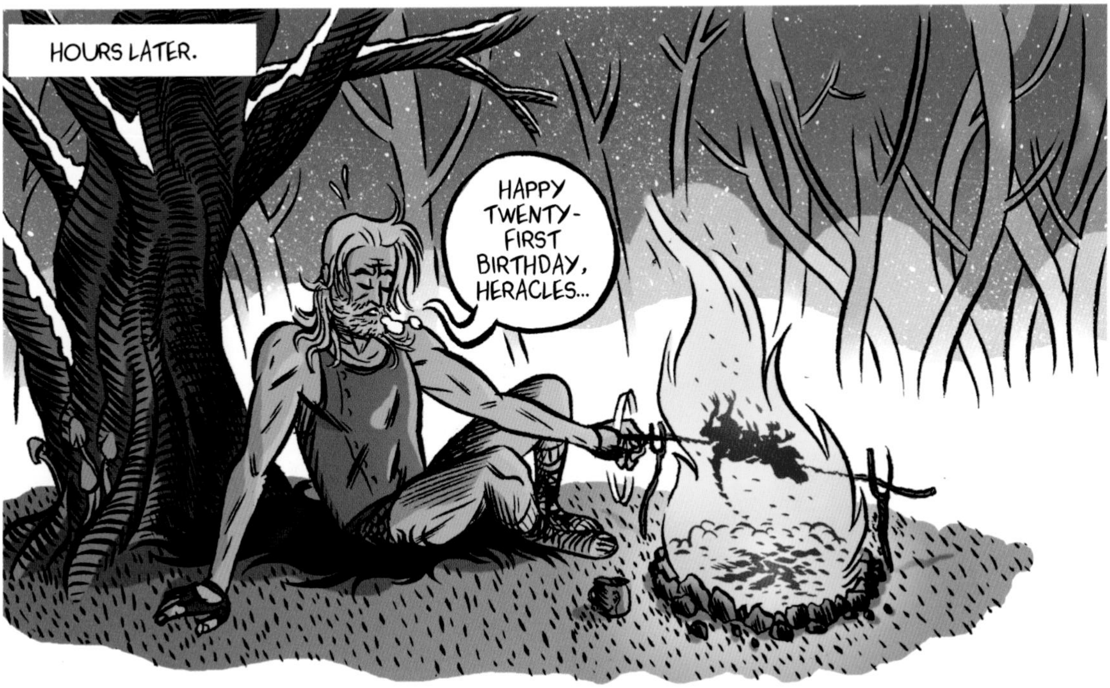
HOURS LATER.
HAPPY TWENTY-FIRST BIRTHDAY, HERACLES...

Z Z Z Z Z Z

CRAV

96

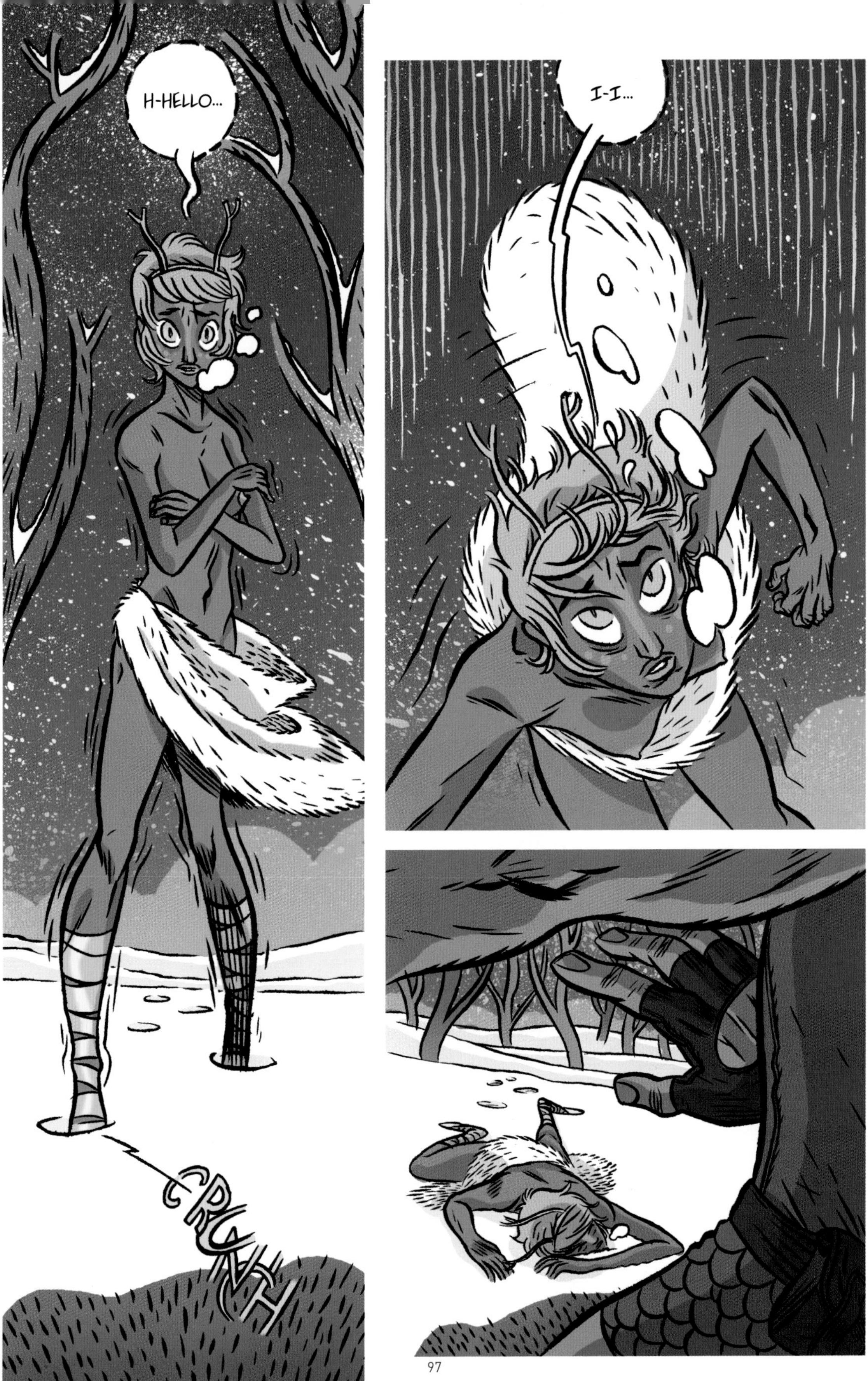
H-HELLO...
CRUNCH
I-I...

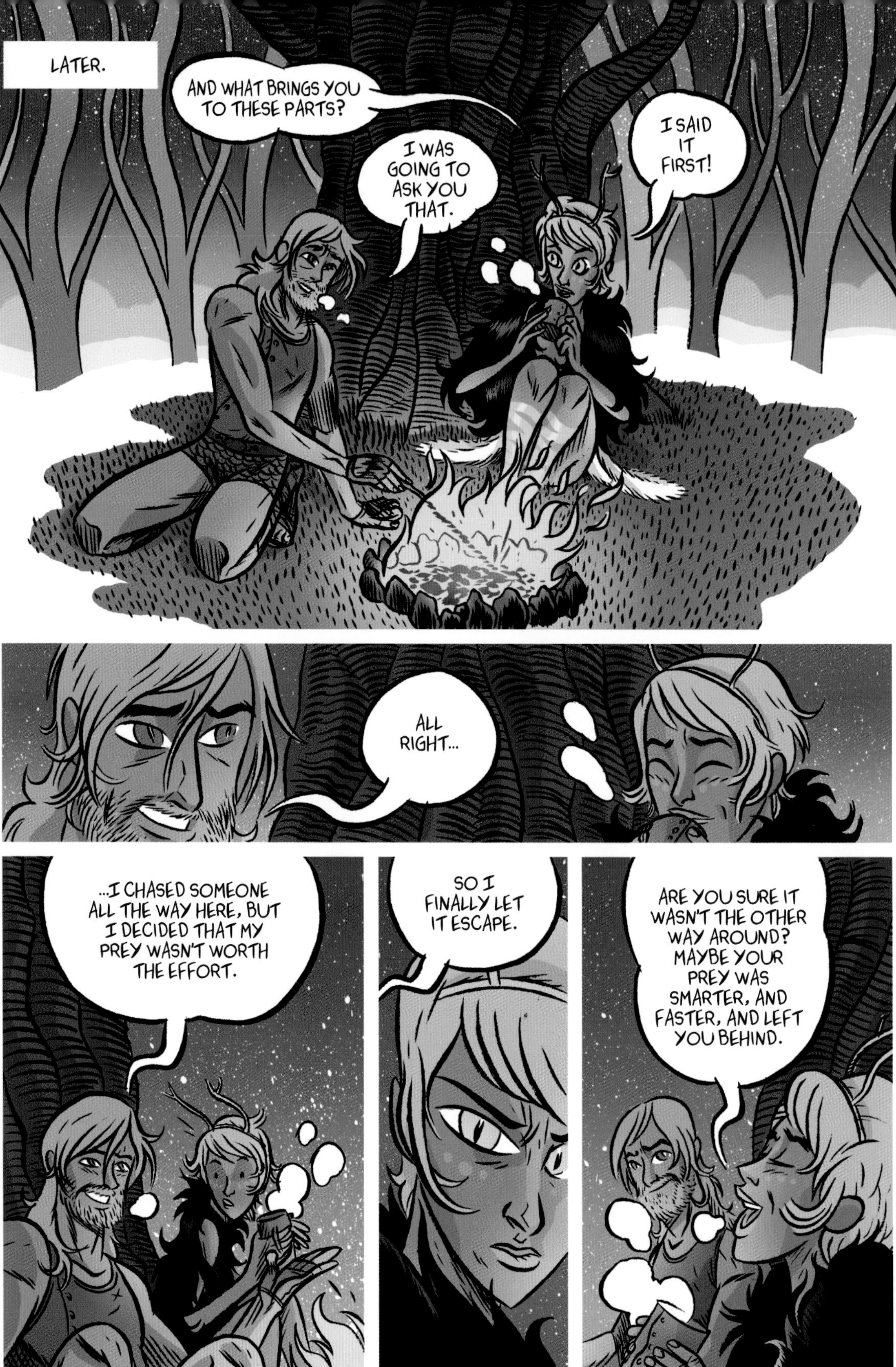
LATER.
AND WHAT BRINGS YOU TO THESE PARTS?
I WAS GOING TO ASK YOU THAT.
I SAID IT FIRST!
ALL RIGHT...
...I CHASED SOMEONE ALL THE WAY HERE, BUT I DECIDED THAT MY PREY WASN'T WORTH THE EFFORT.
SO I FINALLY LET IT ESCAPE.
ARE YOU SURE IT WASN'T THE OTHER WAY AROUND? MAYBE YOUR PREY WAS SMARTER, AND FASTER, AND LEFT YOU BEHIND.

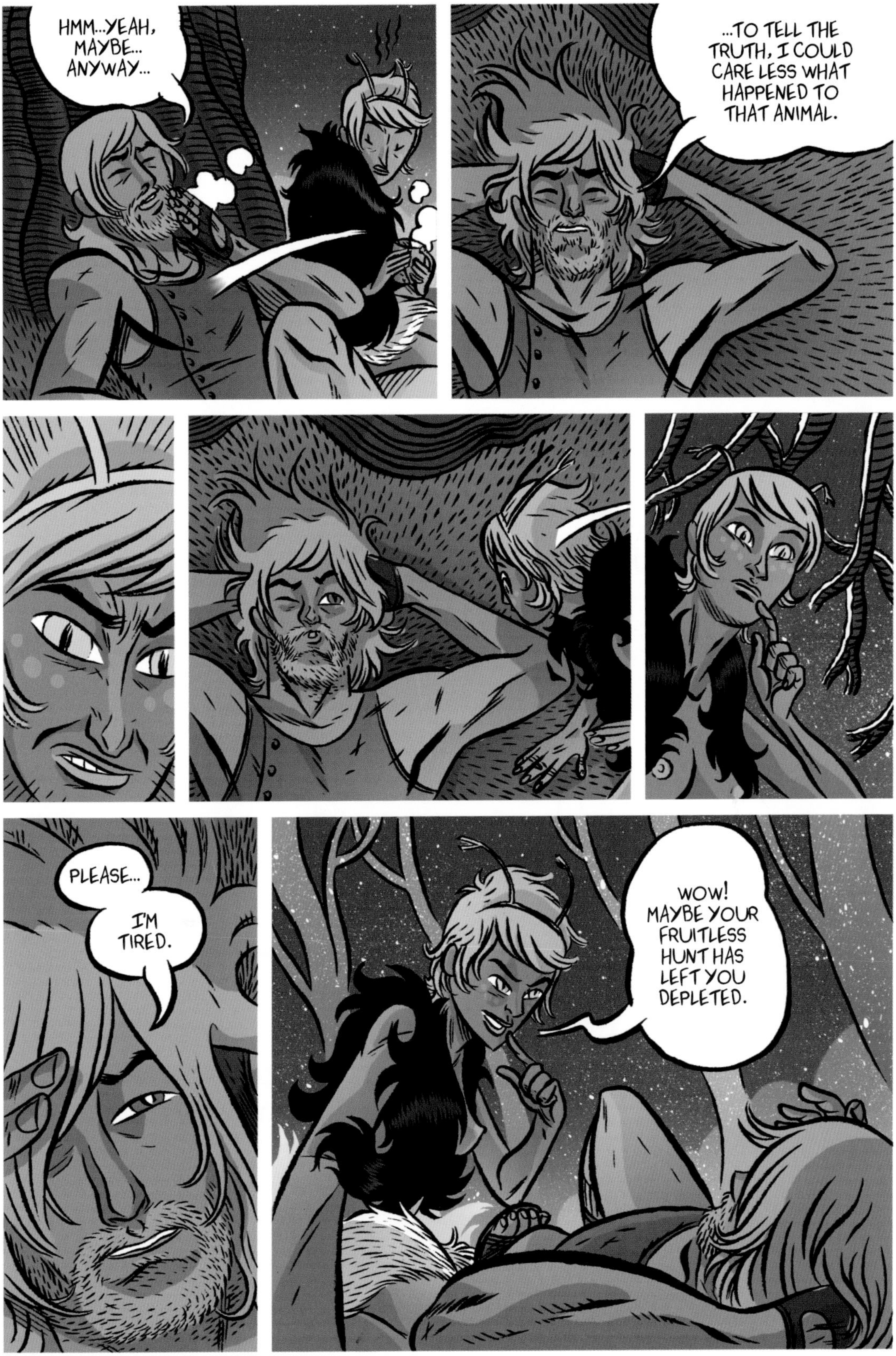
HMM...YEAH, MAYBE... ANYWAY...
...TO TELL THE TRUTH, I COULD CARE LESS WHAT HAPPENED TO THAT ANIMAL.
PLEASE...
I'M TIRED.
WOW! MAYBE YOUR FRUITLESS HUNT HAS LEFT YOU DEPLETED.

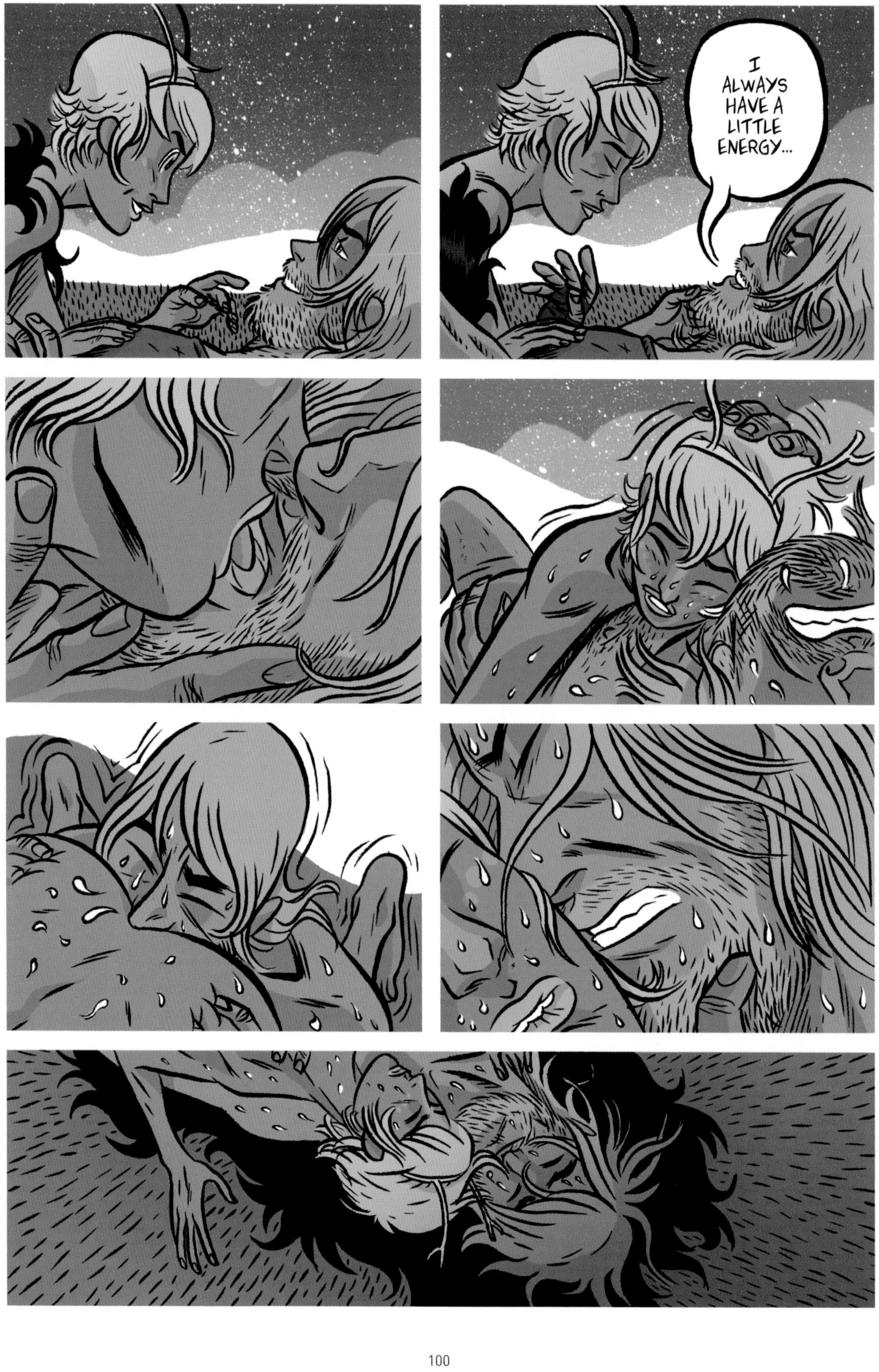
I ALWAYS HAVE A LITTLE ENERGY...

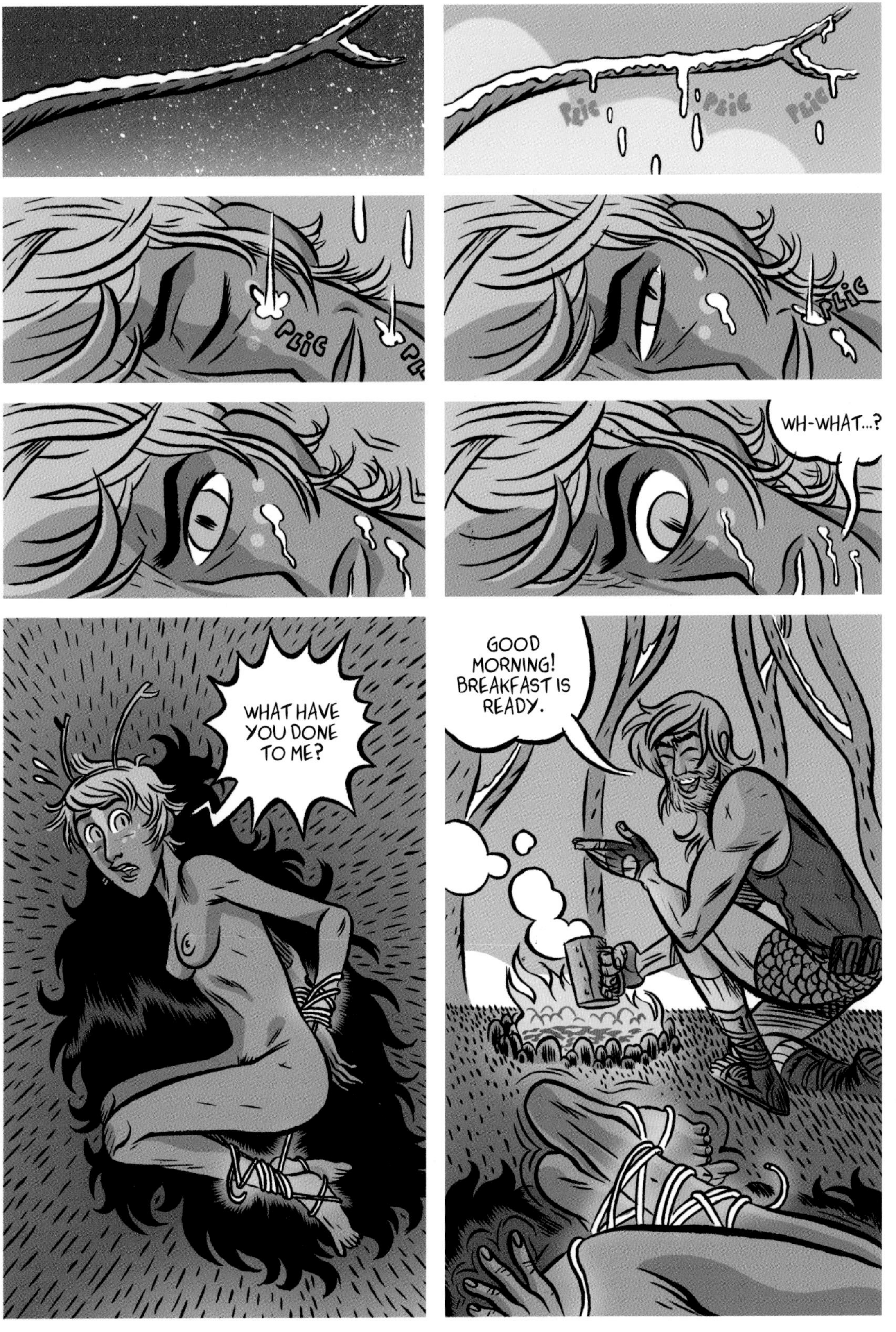
PLIC
PLIC
PLIC
PLIC
PLIC
WH-WHAT...?
WHAT HAVE YOU DONE TO ME?
GOOD MORNING! BREAKFAST IS READY.

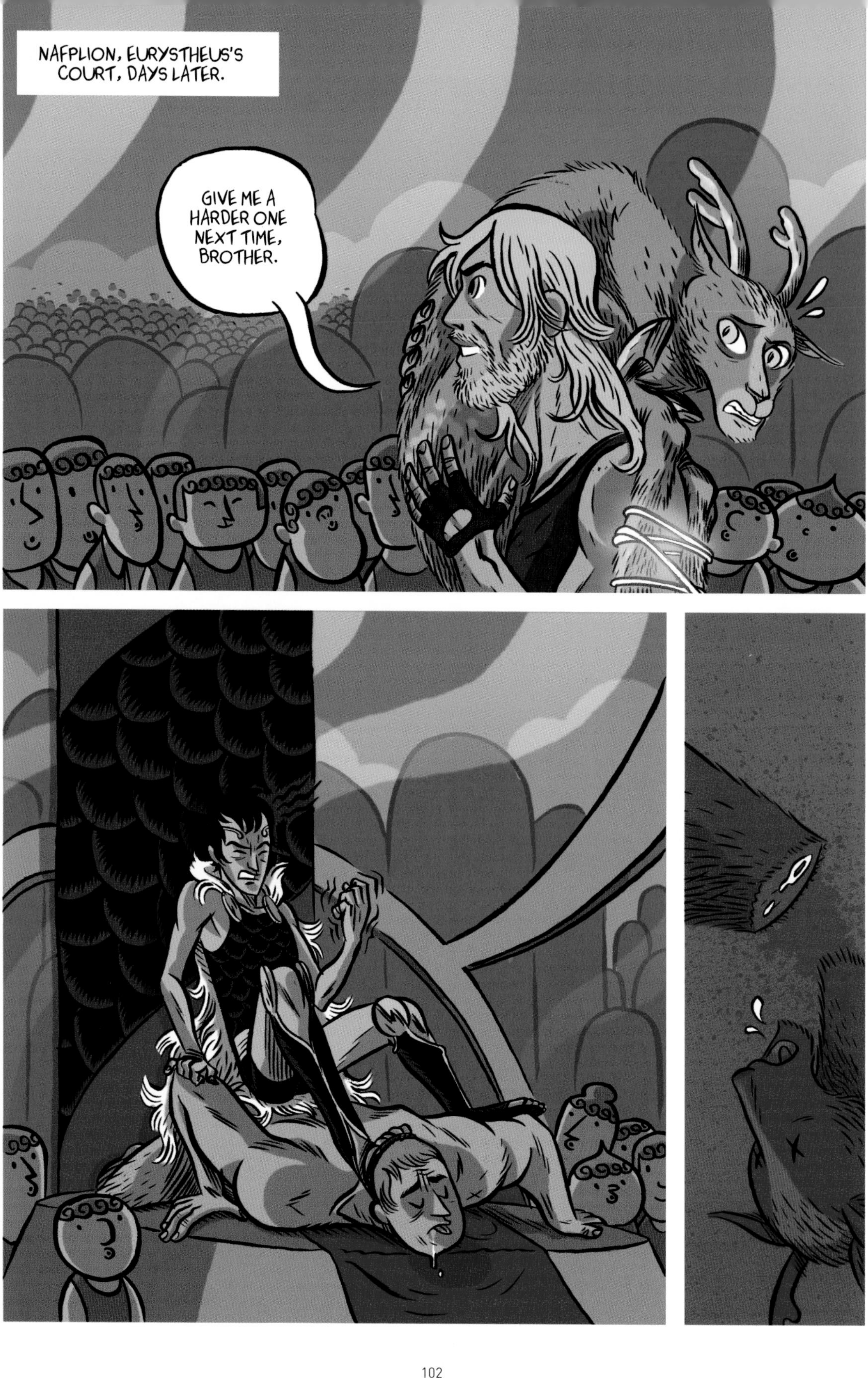
NAFPLION, EURYSTHEUS'S COURT, DAYS LATER.
GIVE ME A HARDER ONE NEXT TIME, BROTHER.

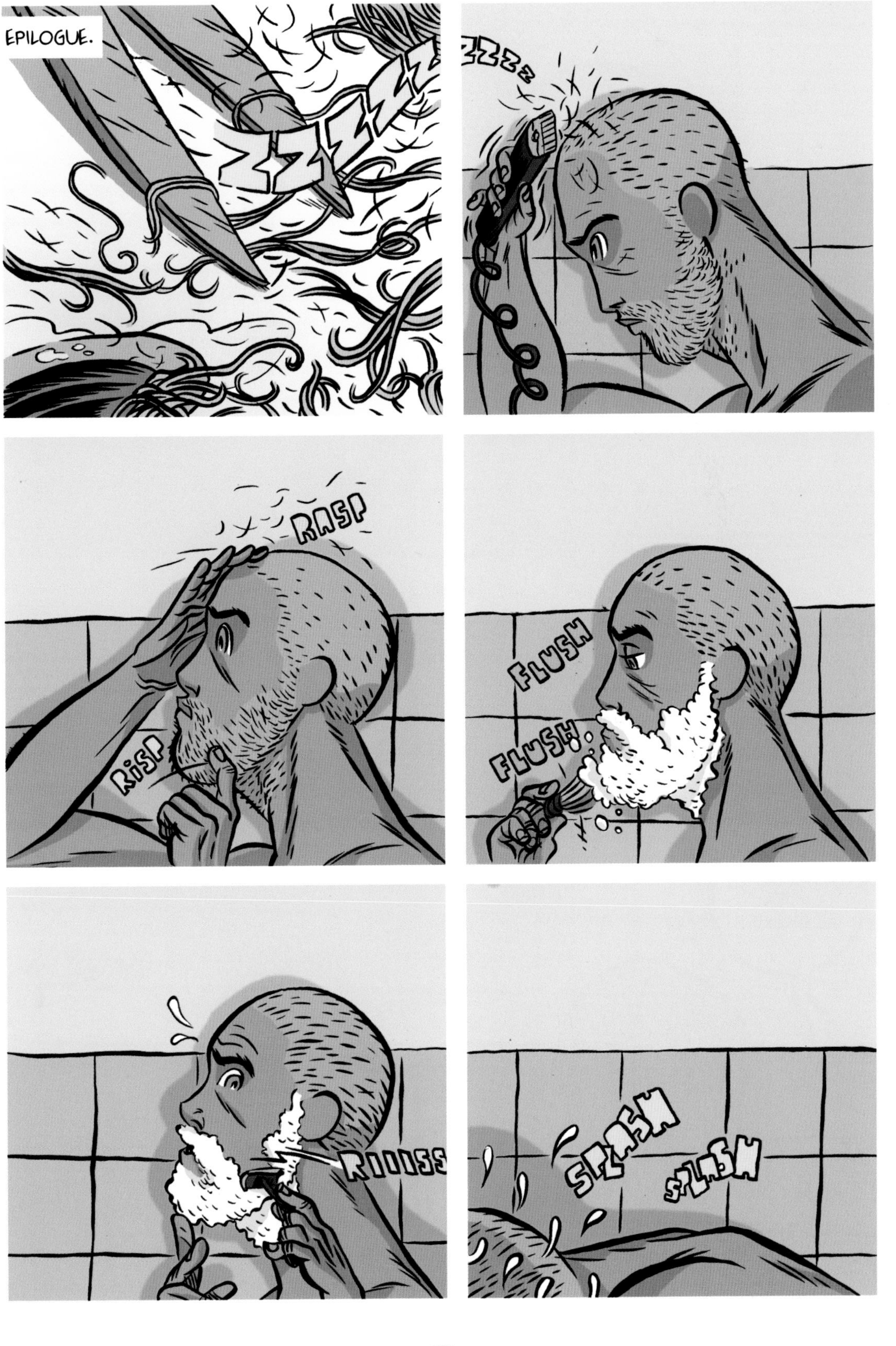
EPILOGUE.
ZZZZZZZZZZz
RASP
RiSP
FLUSH
FLUSH
RIIISS
SPLASH
SPLASH

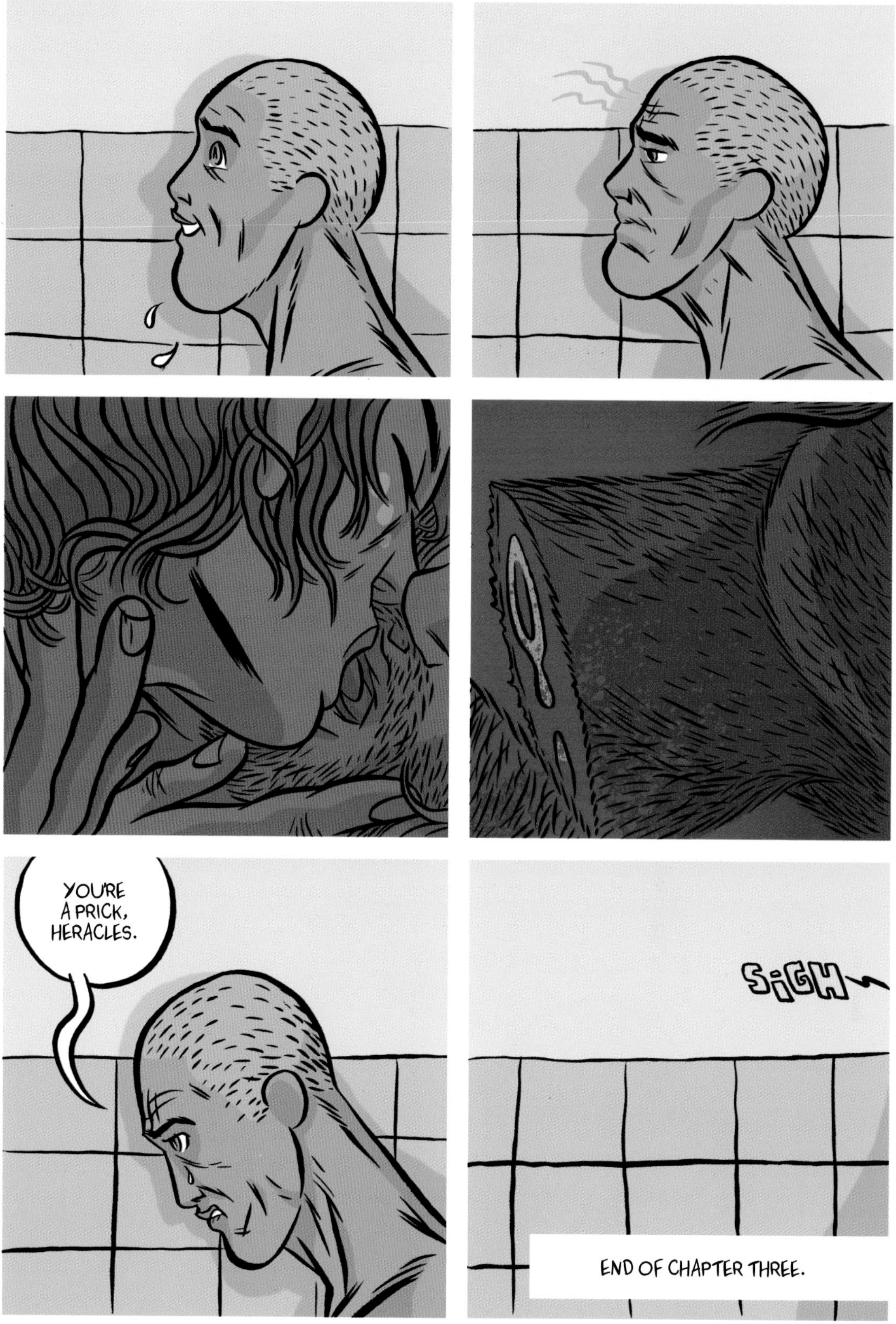
YOU'RE A PRICK, HERACLES.
SIGH
END OF CHAPTER THREE.

CHAPTER 04

CHAPTER

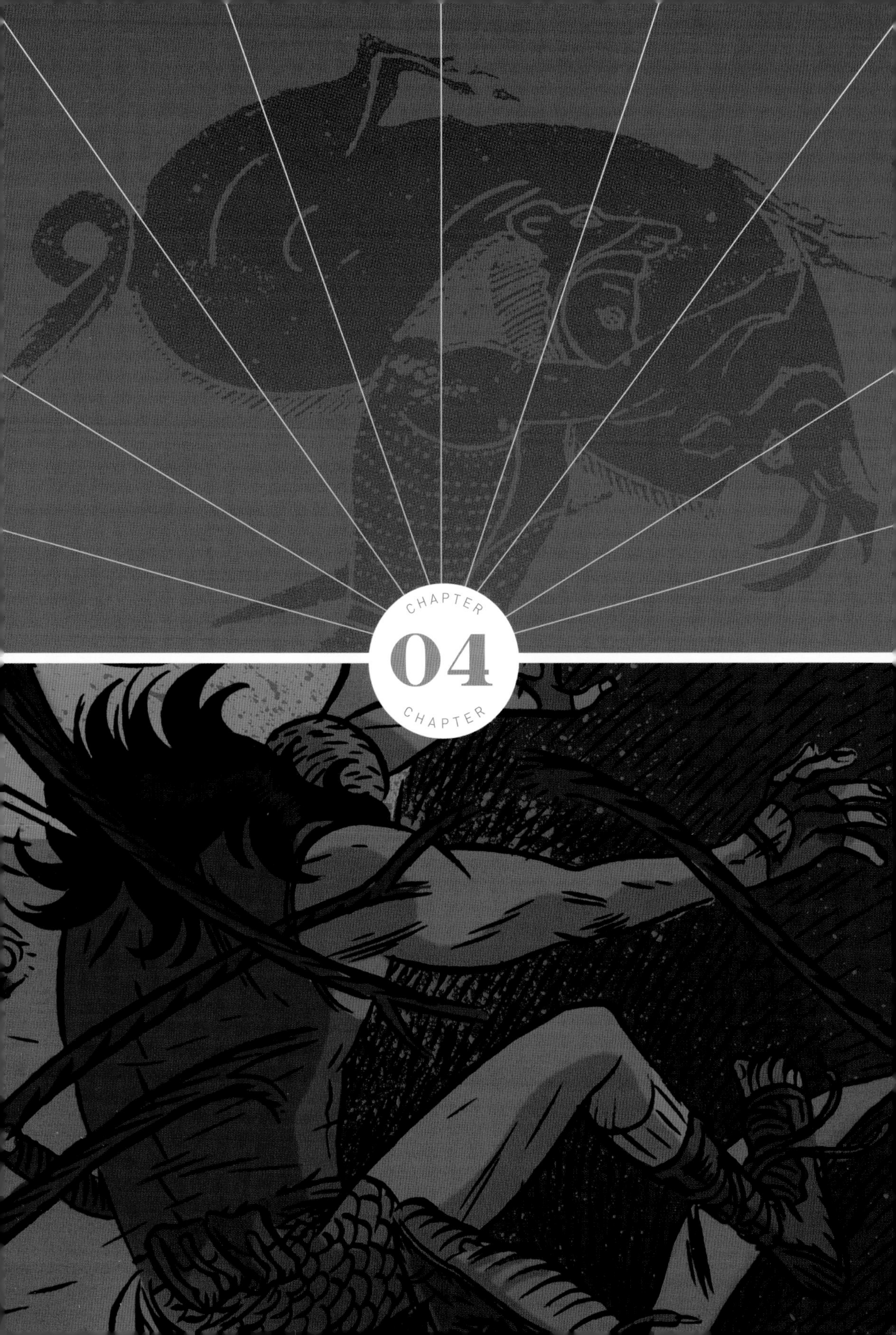

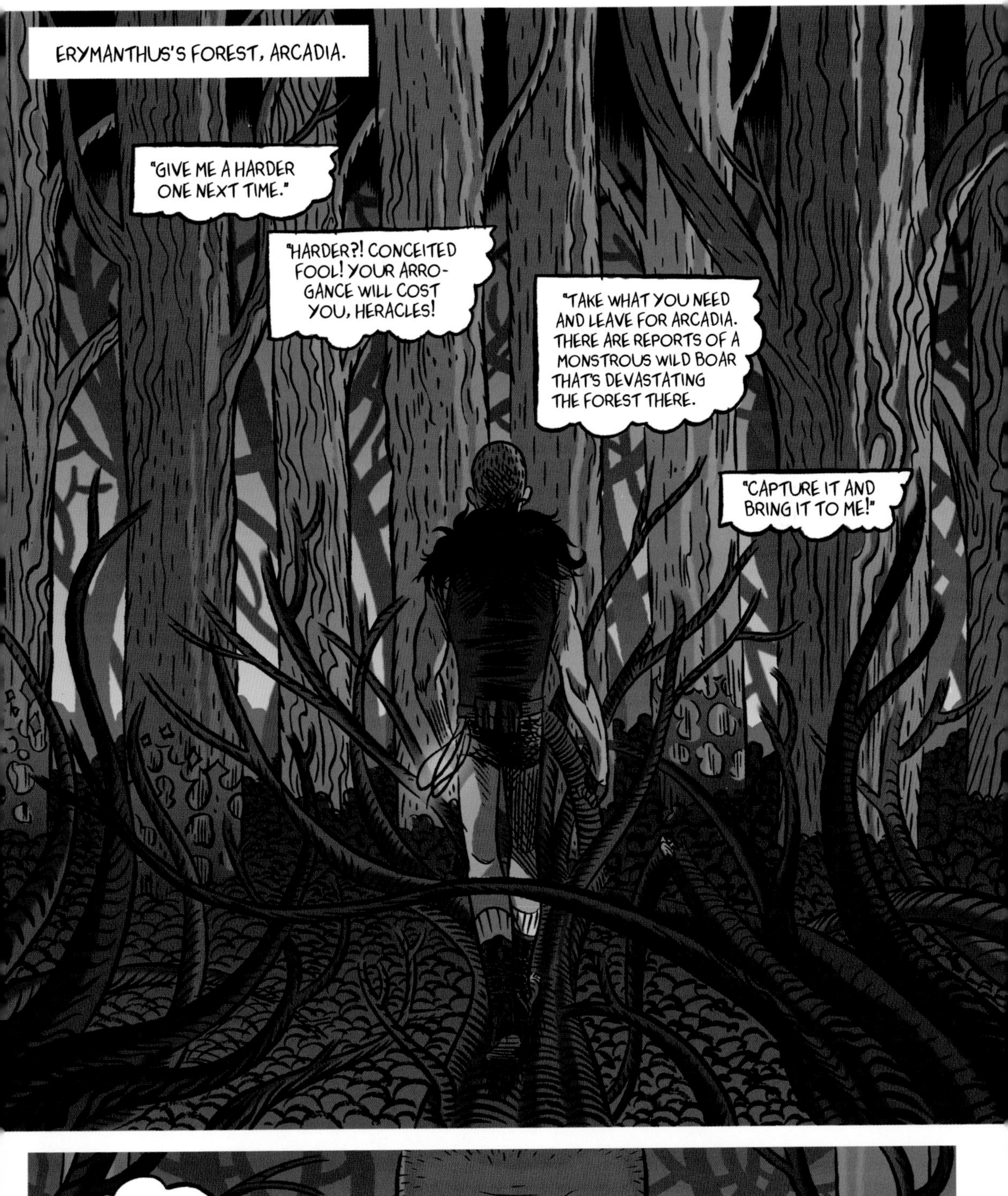
ERYMANTHUS'S FOREST, ARCADIA.
"GIVE ME A HARDER ONE NEXT TIME."
"HARDER?! CONCEITED FOOL! YOUR ARRO-GANCE WILL COST YOU, HERACLES!
"TAKE WHAT YOU NEED AND LEAVE FOR ARCADIA. THERE ARE REPORTS OF A MONSTROUS WILD BOAR THAT'S DEVASTATING THE FOREST THERE.
"CAPTURE IT AND BRING IT TO ME!"

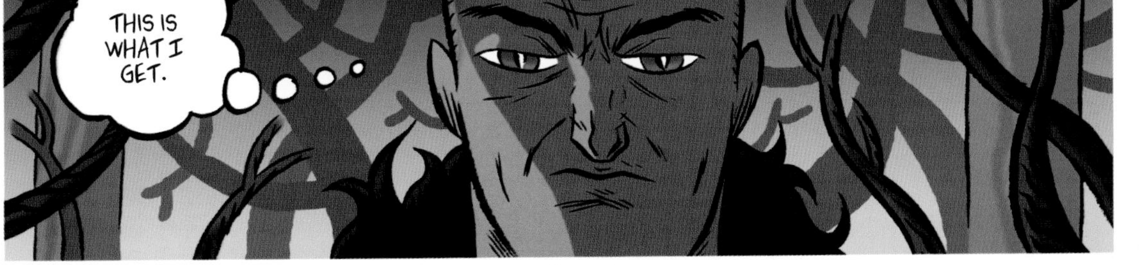
THIS IS WHAT I GET.

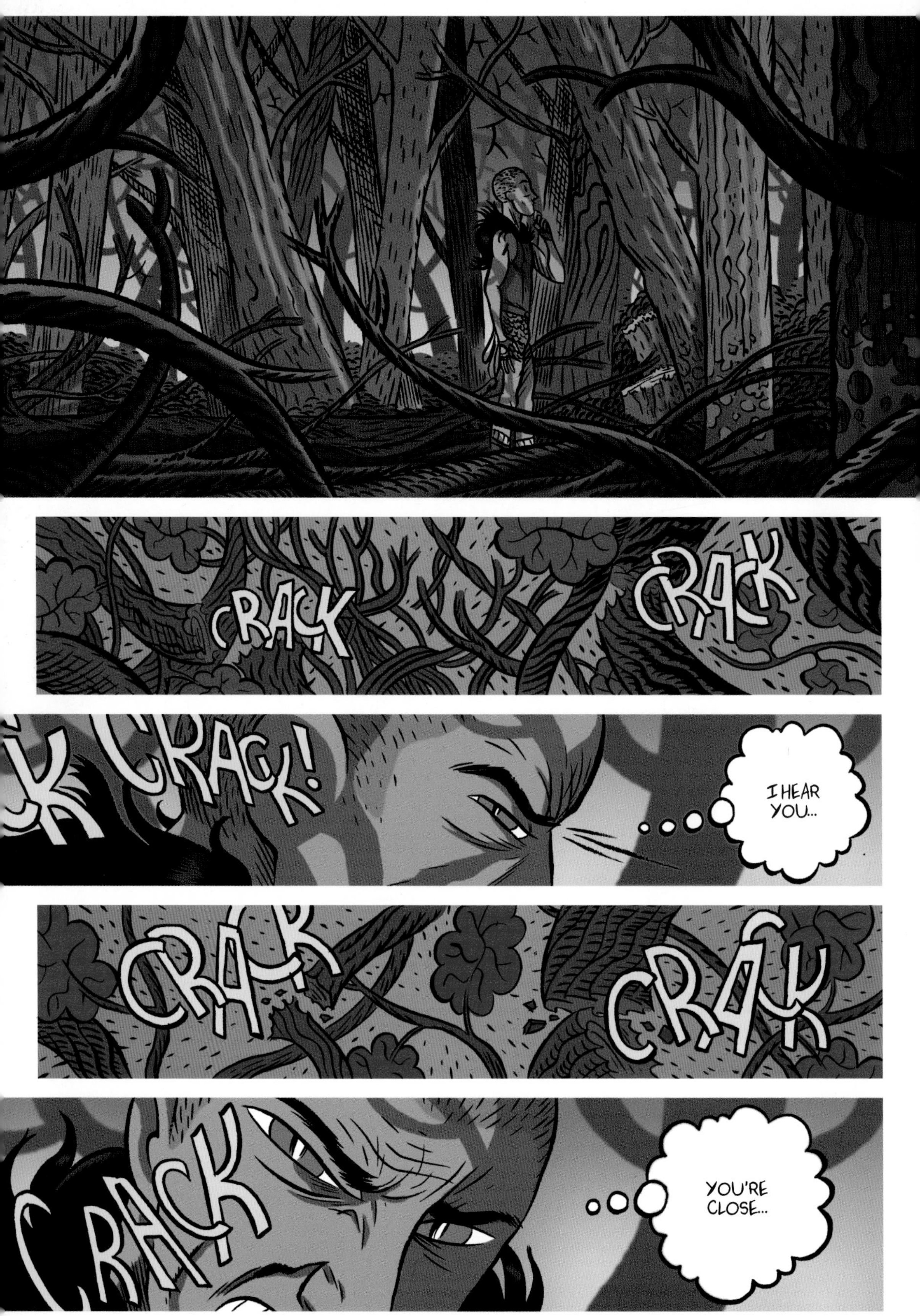
CRACK
CRACK
CRACK!
I HEAR YOU...
CRACK
CRACK
CRACK
YOU'RE CLOSE...

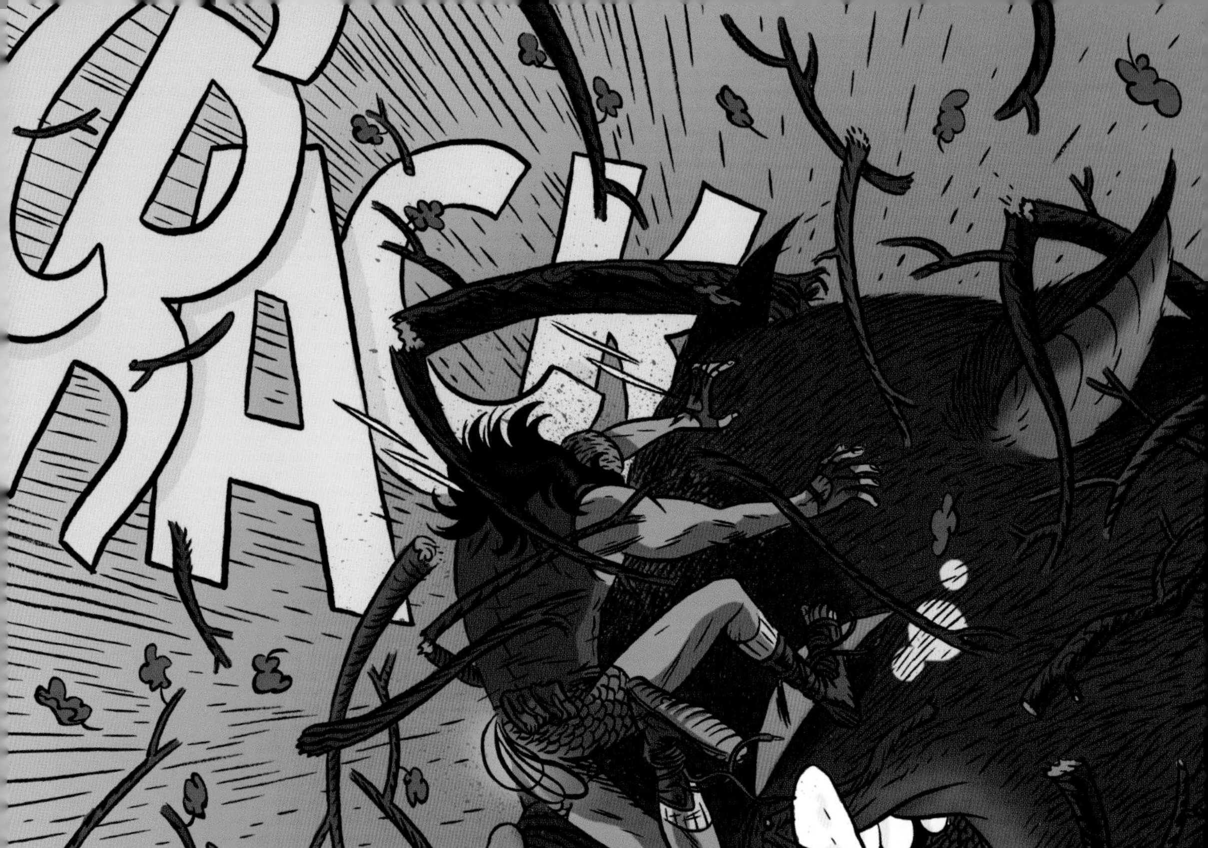

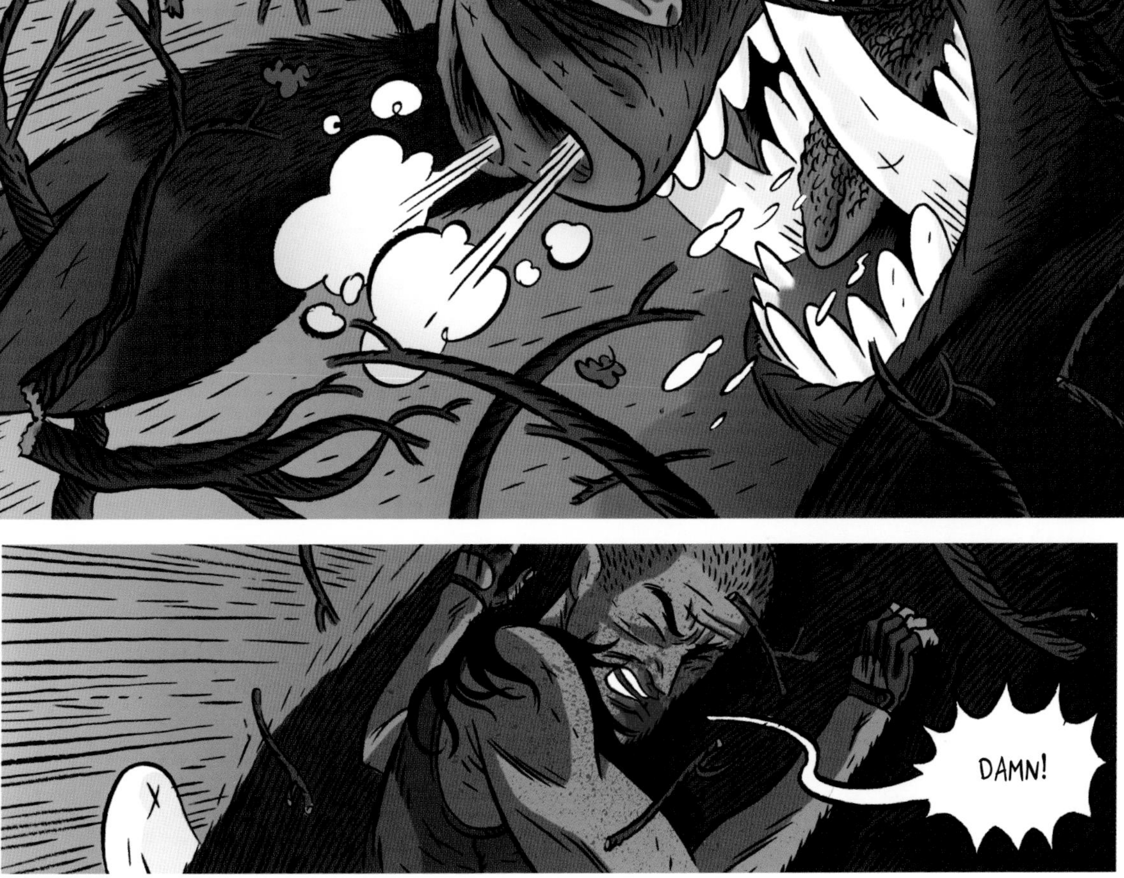
DAMN!

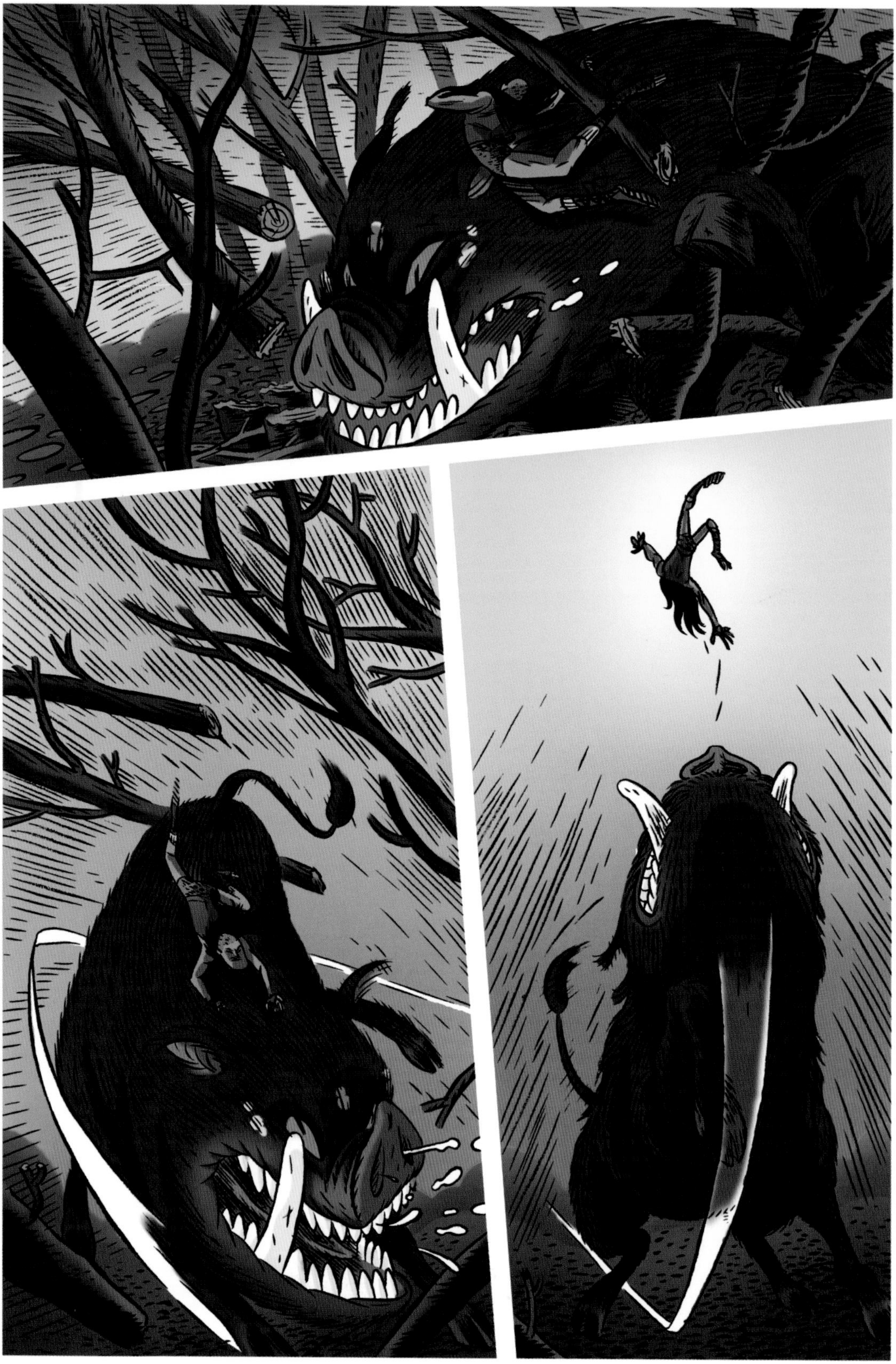

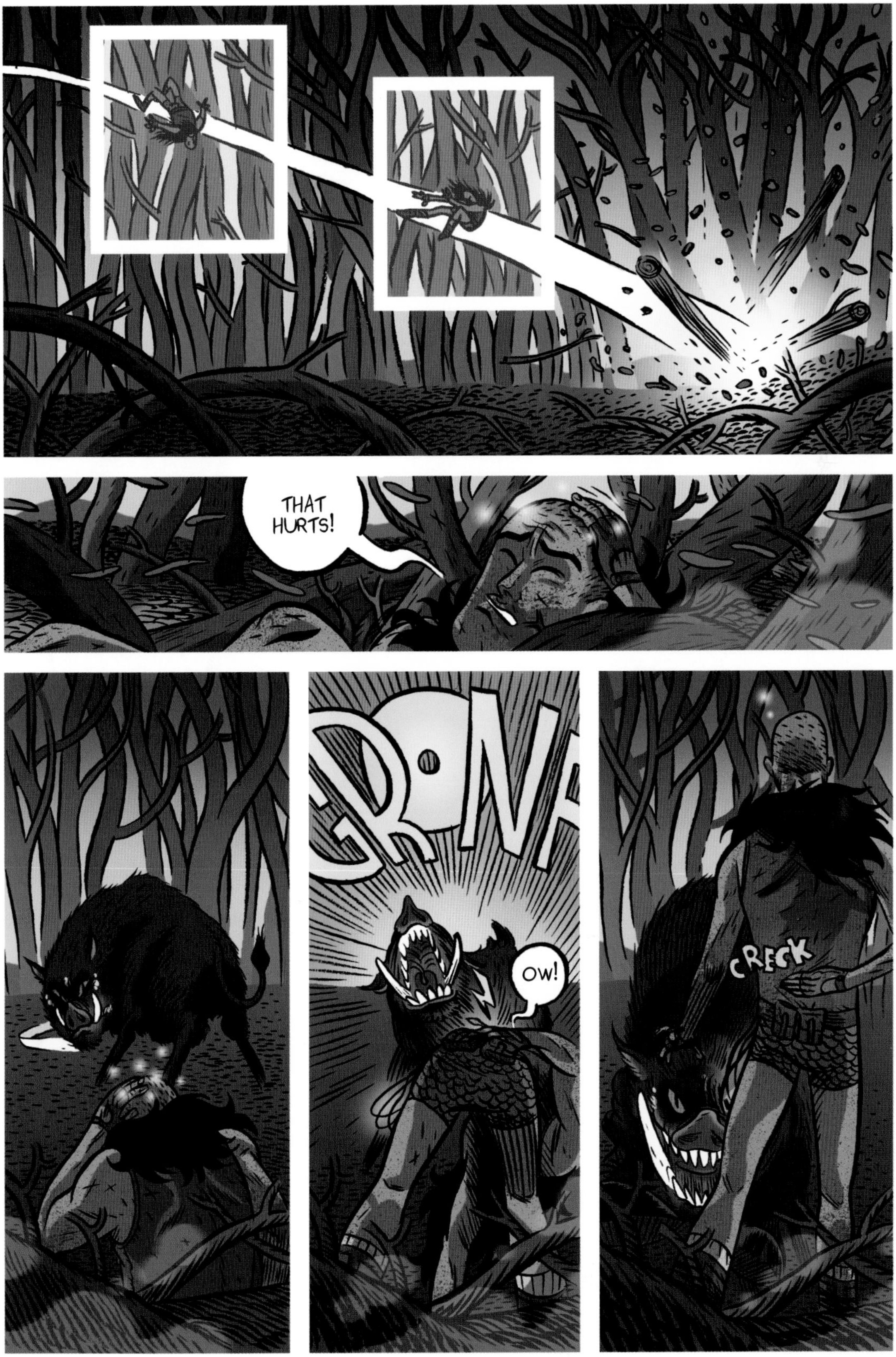
THAT HURTS!
CRONA
OW!
CRECK

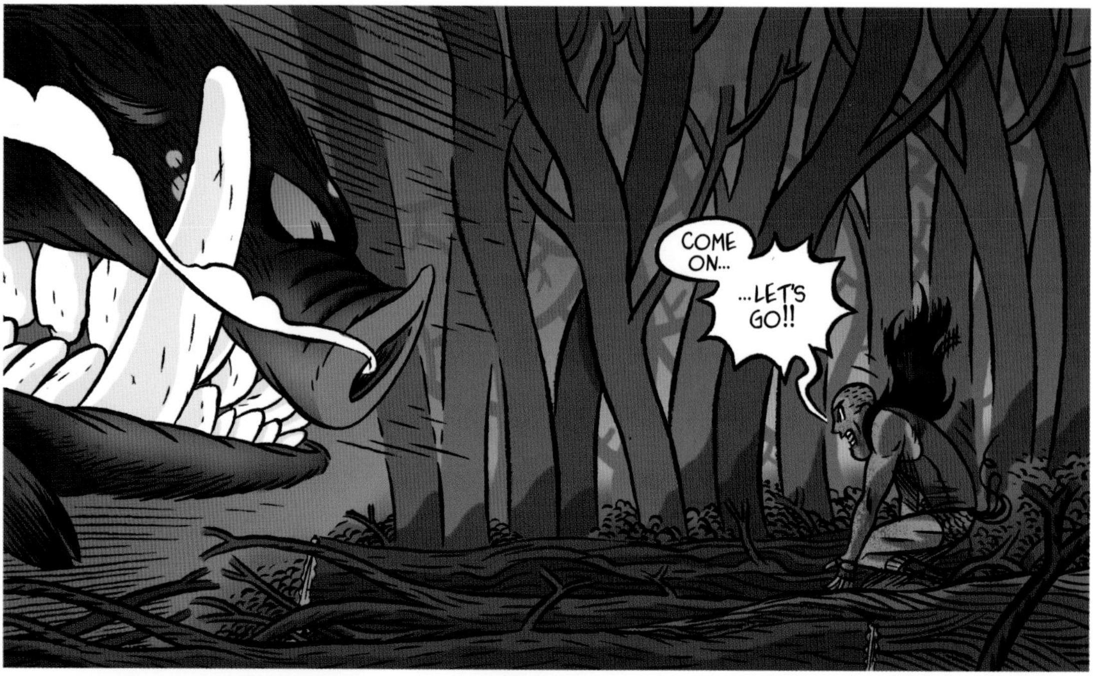
COME ON...
...LET'S GO!!

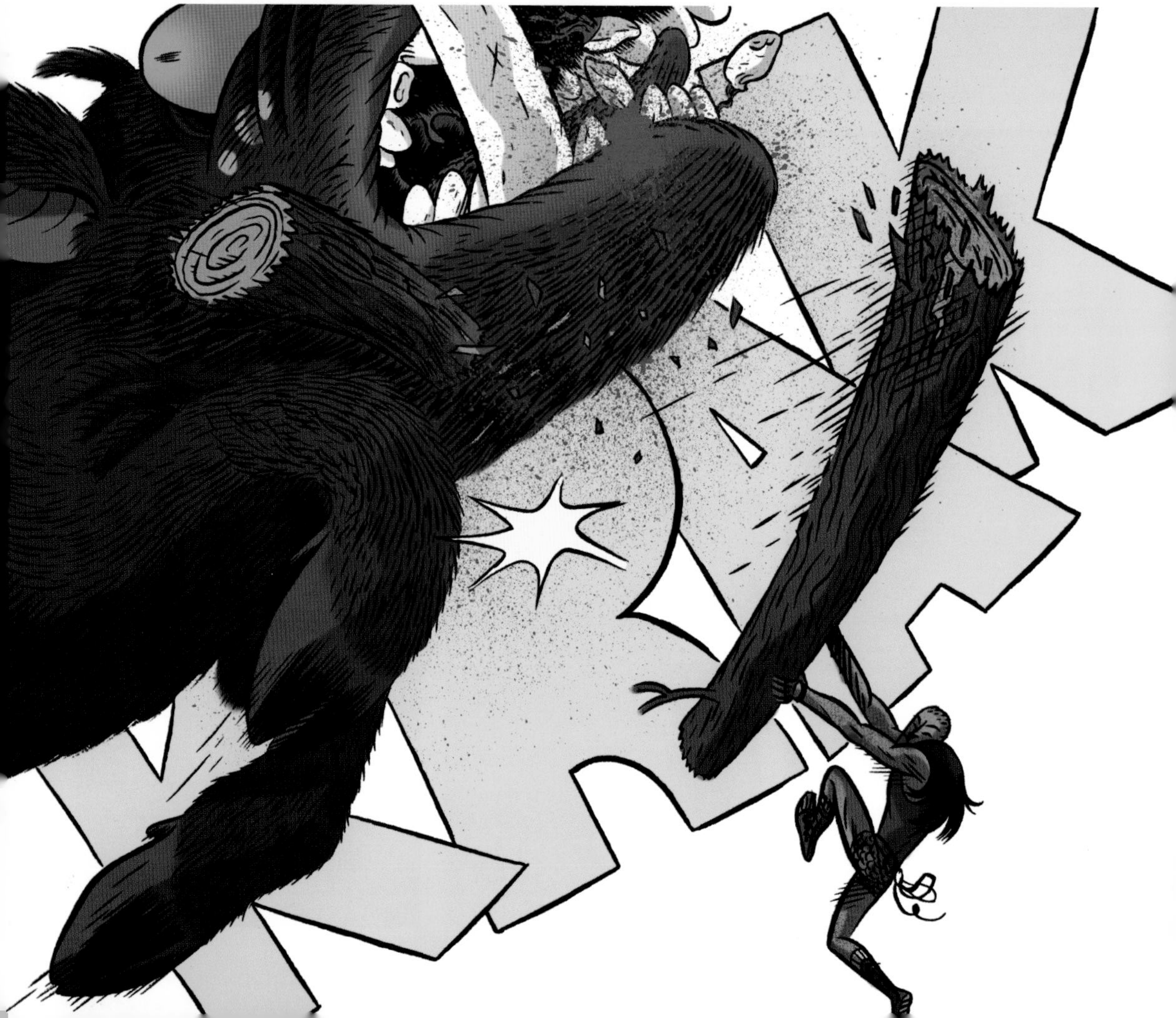

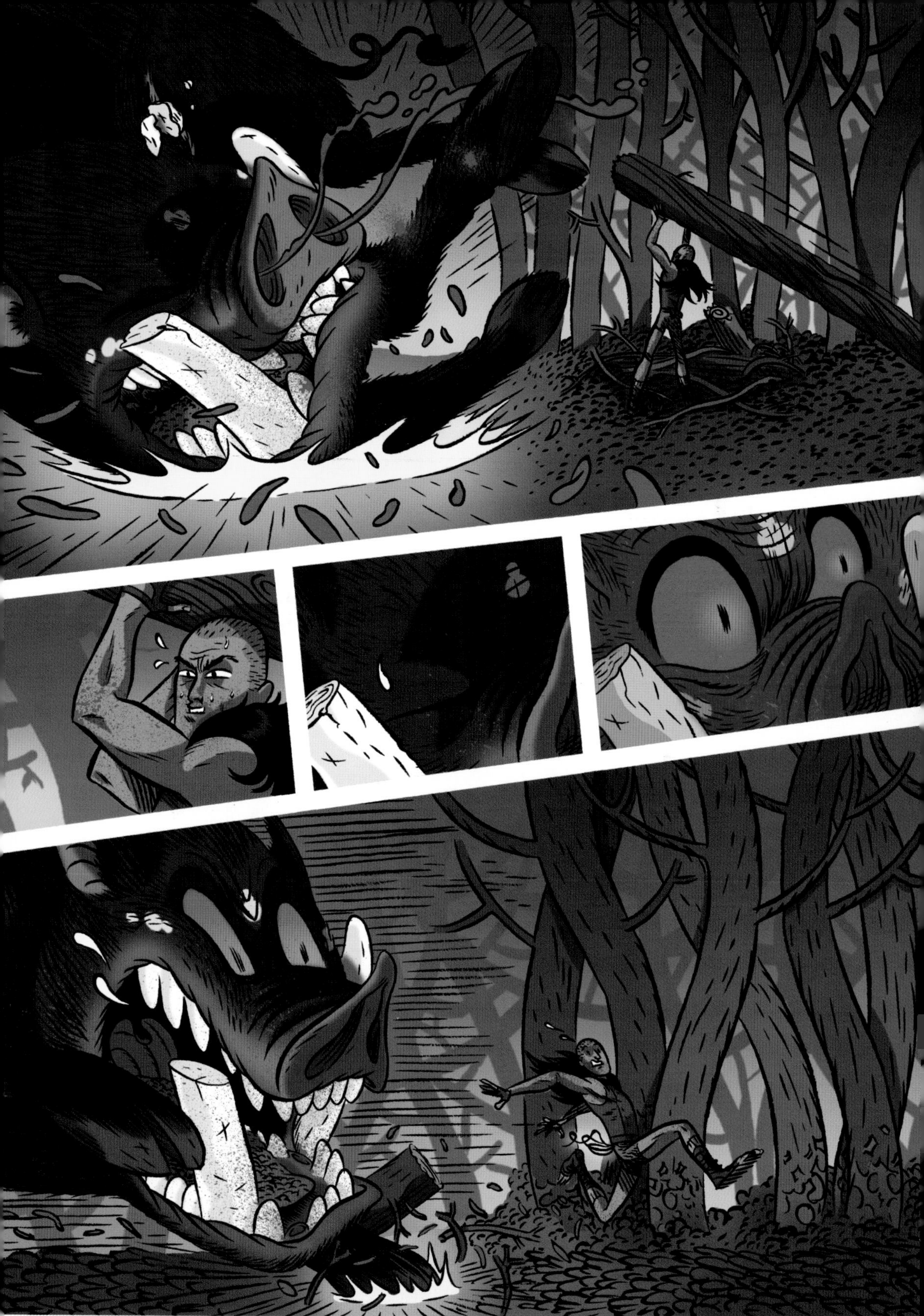

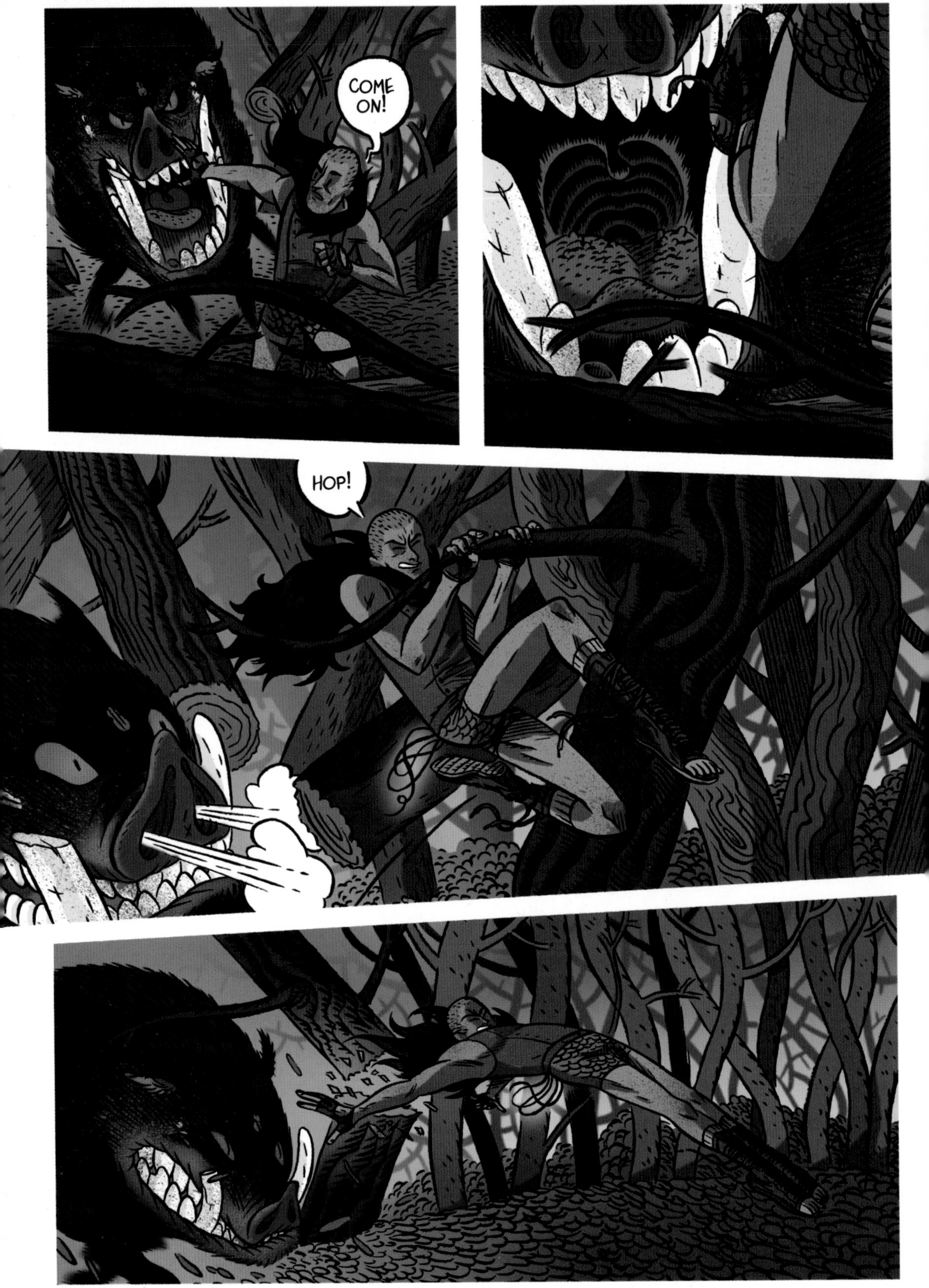
COME ON!
HOP!

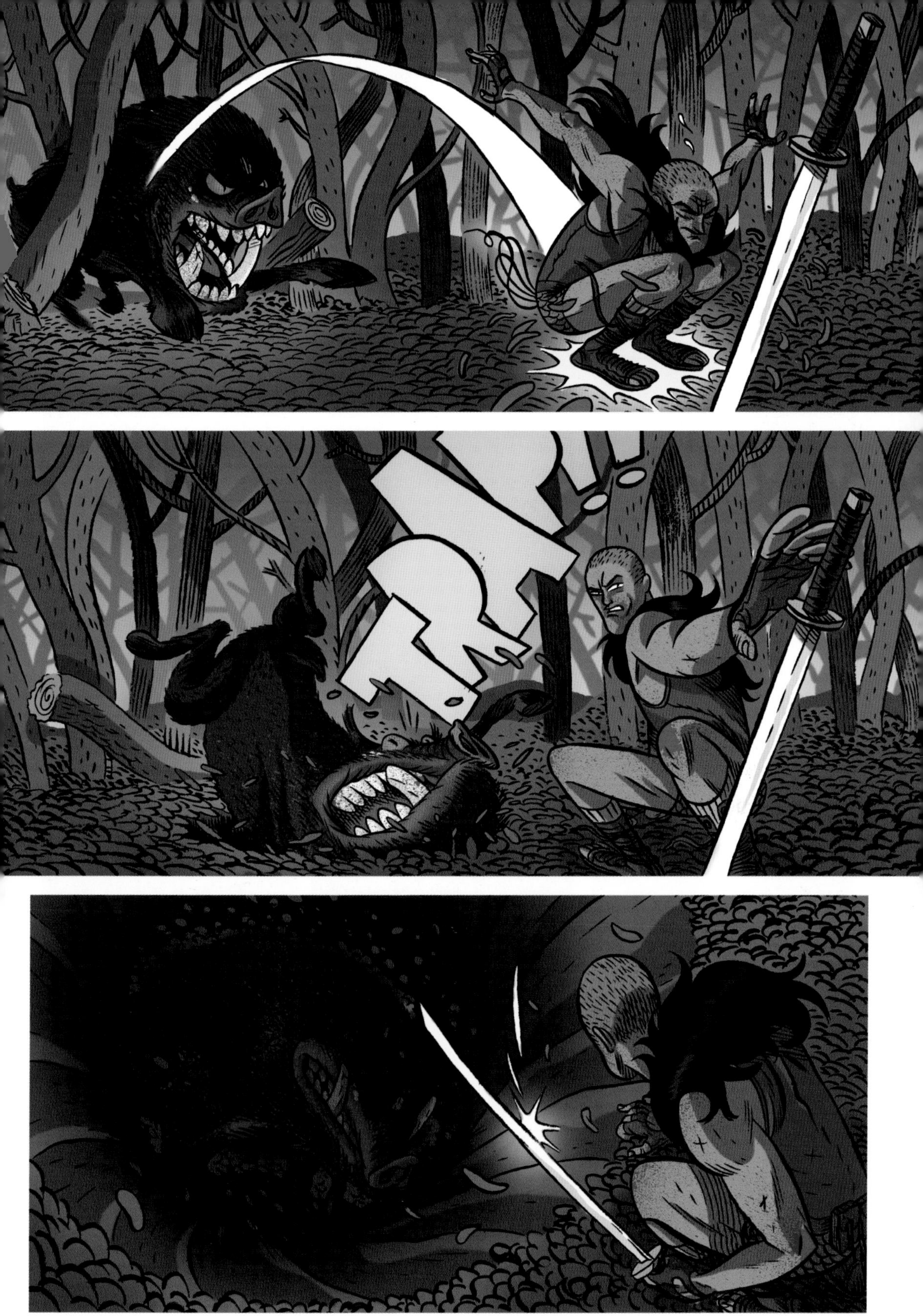

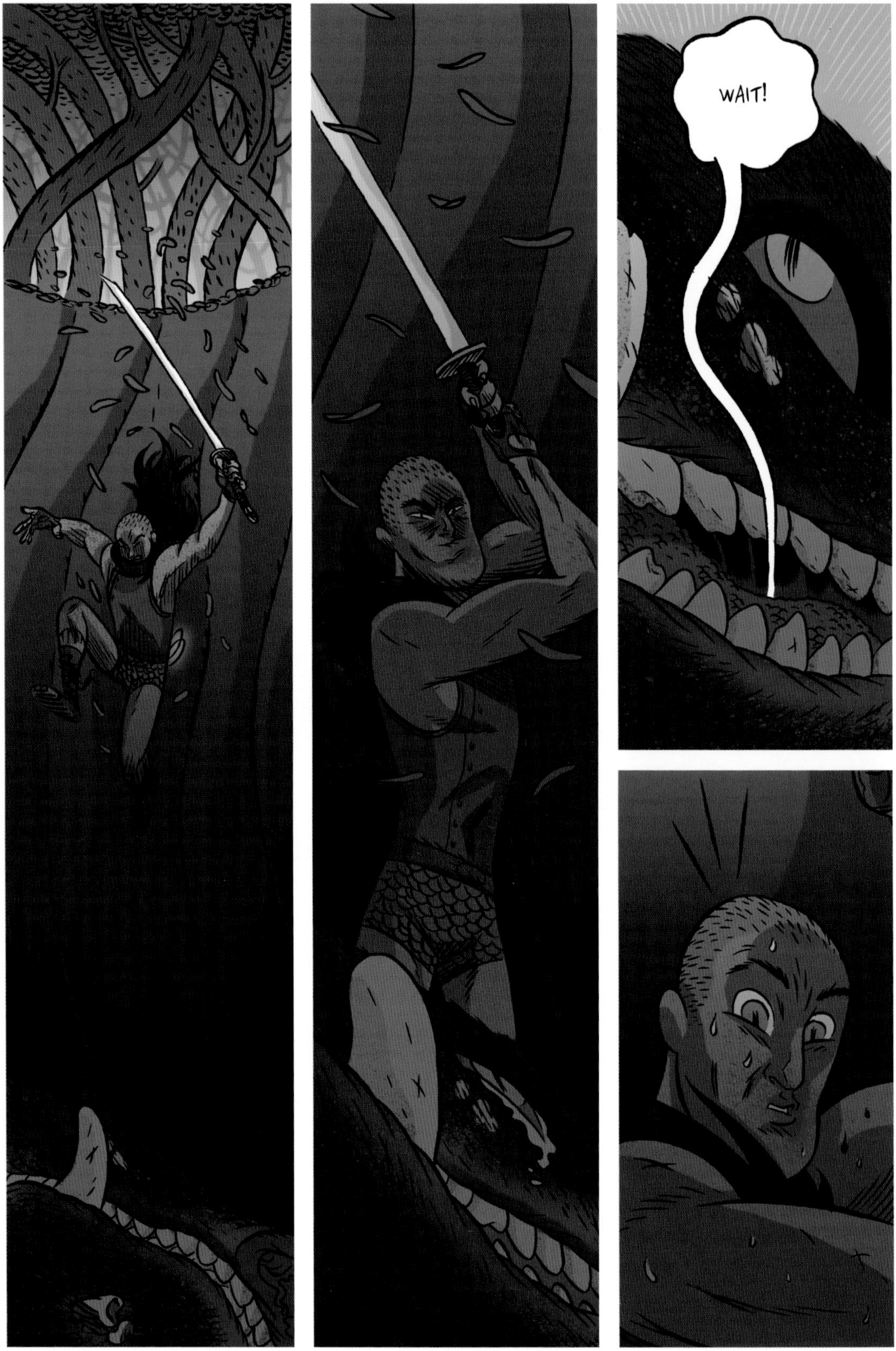
WAIT!

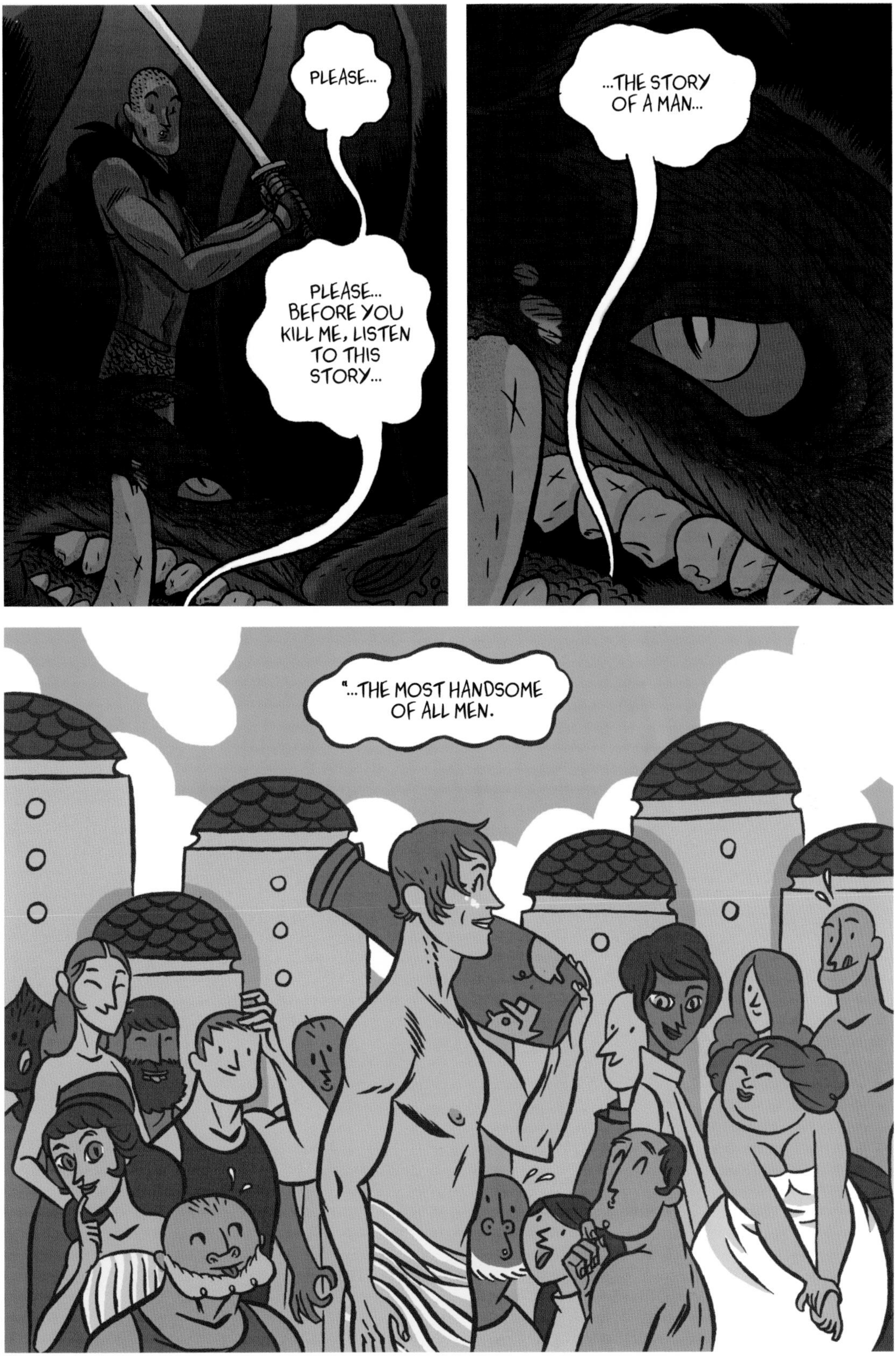
PLEASE...
PLEASE... BEFORE YOU KILL ME, LISTEN TO THIS STORY...
...THE STORY OF A MAN...
"...THE MOST HANDSOME OF ALL MEN.

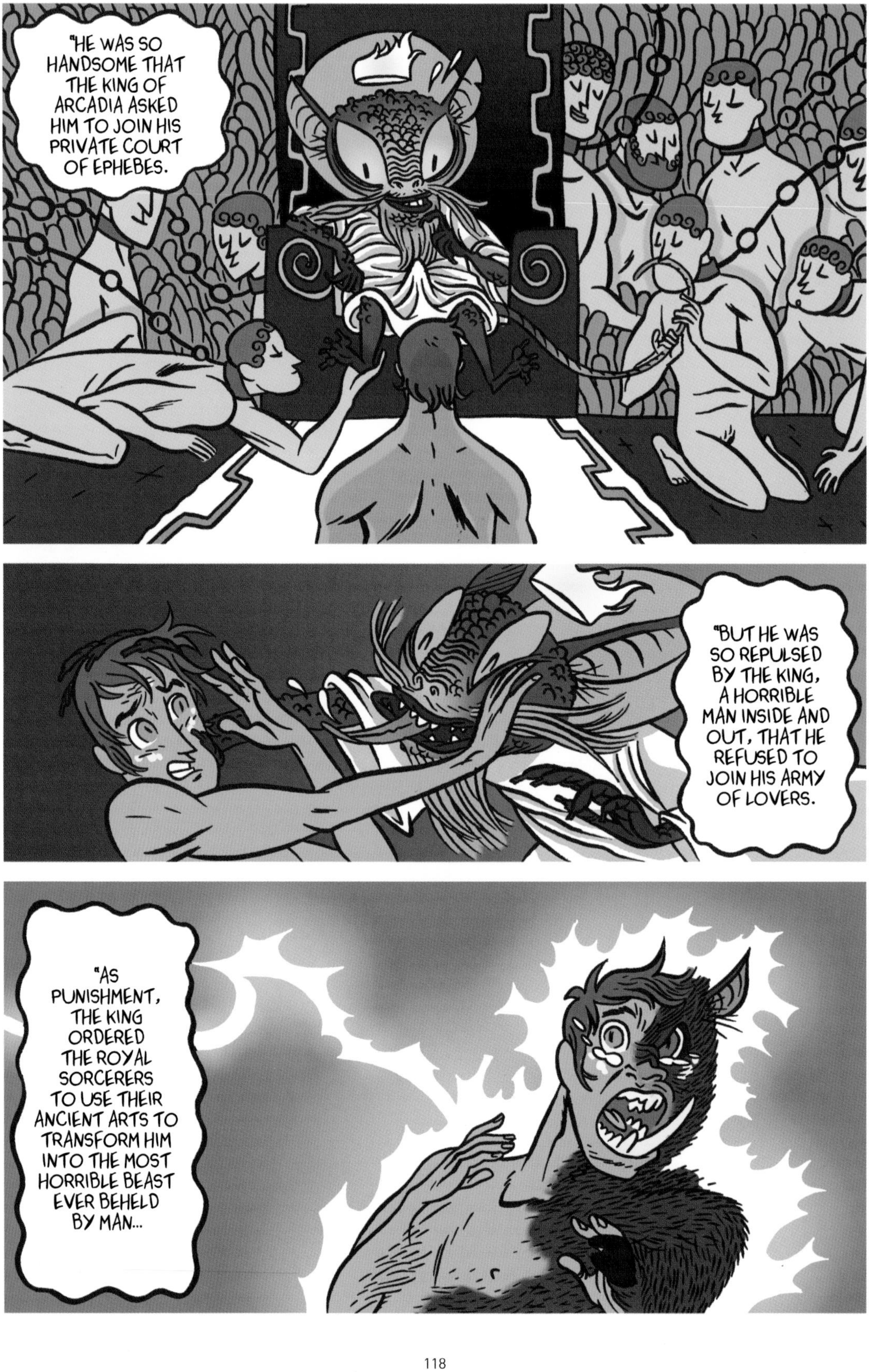
"HE WAS SO HANDSOME THAT THE KING OF ARCADIA ASKED HIM TO JOIN HIS PRIVATE COURT OF EPHEBES.
"BUT HE WAS SO REPULSED BY THE KING, A HORRIBLE MAN INSIDE AND OUT, THAT HE REFUSED TO JOIN HIS ARMY OF LOVERS.
"AS PUNISHMENT, THE KING ORDERED THE ROYAL SORCERERS TO USE THEIR ANCIENT ARTS TO TRANSFORM HIM INTO THE MOST HORRIBLE BEAST EVER BEHELD BY MAN...

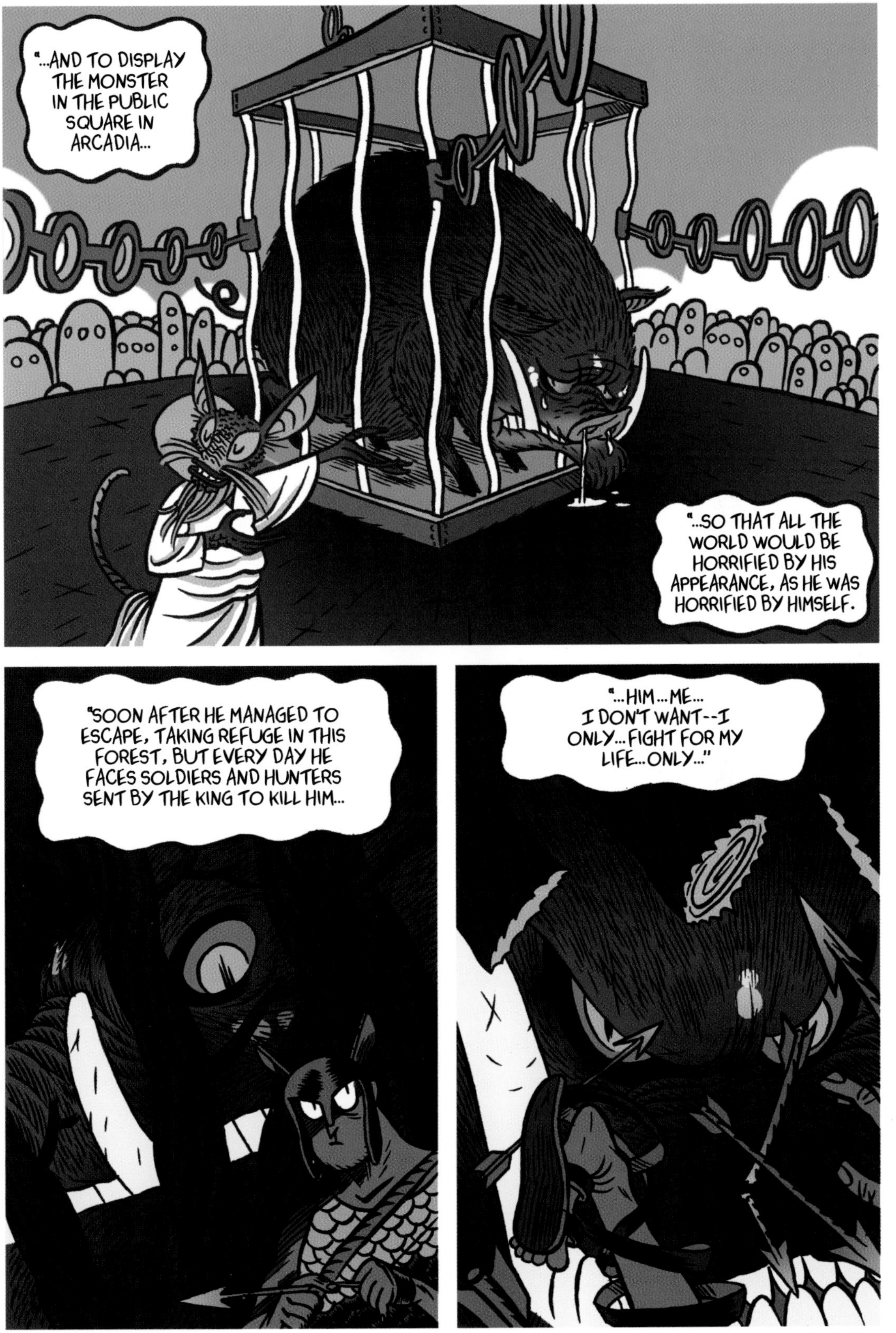
"...AND TO DISPLAY THE MONSTER IN THE PUBLIC SQUARE IN ARCADIA...
"...SO THAT ALL THE WORLD WOULD BE HORRIFIED BY HIS APPEARANCE, AS HE WAS HORRIFIED BY HIMSELF.
"SOON AFTER HE MANAGED TO ESCAPE, TAKING REFUGE IN THIS FOREST, BUT EVERY DAY HE FACES SOLDIERS AND HUNTERS SENT BY THE KING TO KILL HIM...
"...HIM...ME... I DON'T WANT--I ONLY...FIGHT FOR MY LIFE...ONLY..."

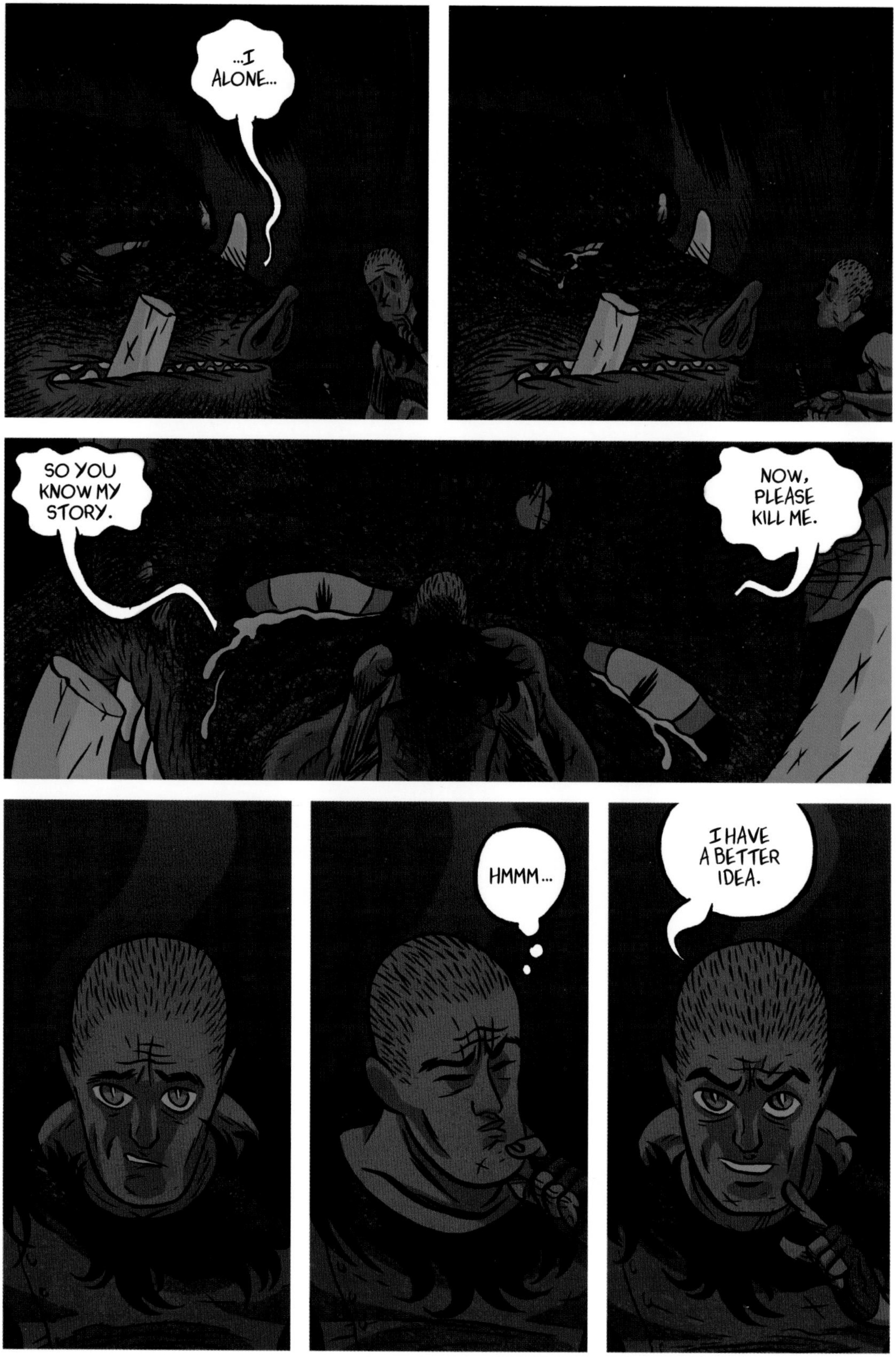
...I ALONE...
SO YOU KNOW MY STORY.
NOW, PLEASE KILL ME.
HMMM...
I HAVE A BETTER IDEA.

ARCADIA, SLAVE MARKET.

YES.

NO.

YES.

THIS ONE, TOO.

THIS ONE...

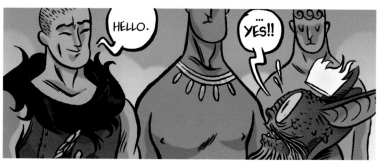

HELLO.

...YES!!

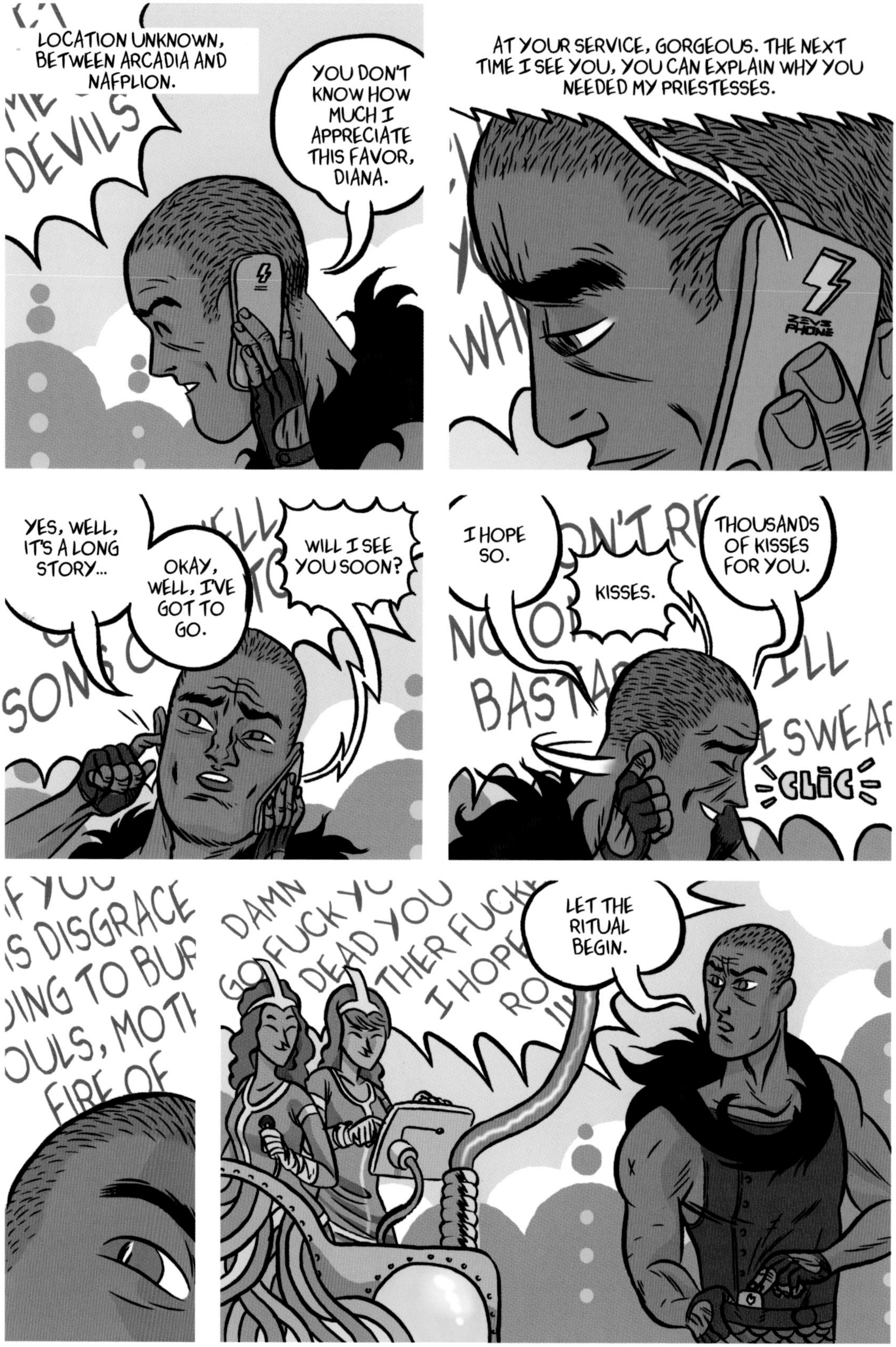
LOCATION UNKNOWN, BETWEEN ARCADIA AND NAFPLION.
YOU DON'T KNOW HOW MUCH I APPRECIATE THIS FAVOR, DIANA.
AT YOUR SERVICE, GORGEOUS. THE NEXT TIME I SEE YOU, YOU CAN EXPLAIN WHY YOU NEEDED MY PRIESTESSES.
ZEUS PHONE
YES, WELL, IT'S A LONG STORY...
OKAY, WELL, I'VE GOT TO GO.
WILL I SEE YOU SOON?
I HOPE SO.
KISSES.
THOUSANDS OF KISSES FOR YOU.
CLIC
LET THE RITUAL BEGIN.

GOD DAMN
MOTHER
FUCKERS
SONS OF
BITCHES
LET ME
GO YOU

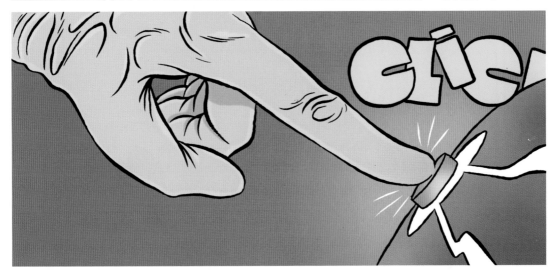

123

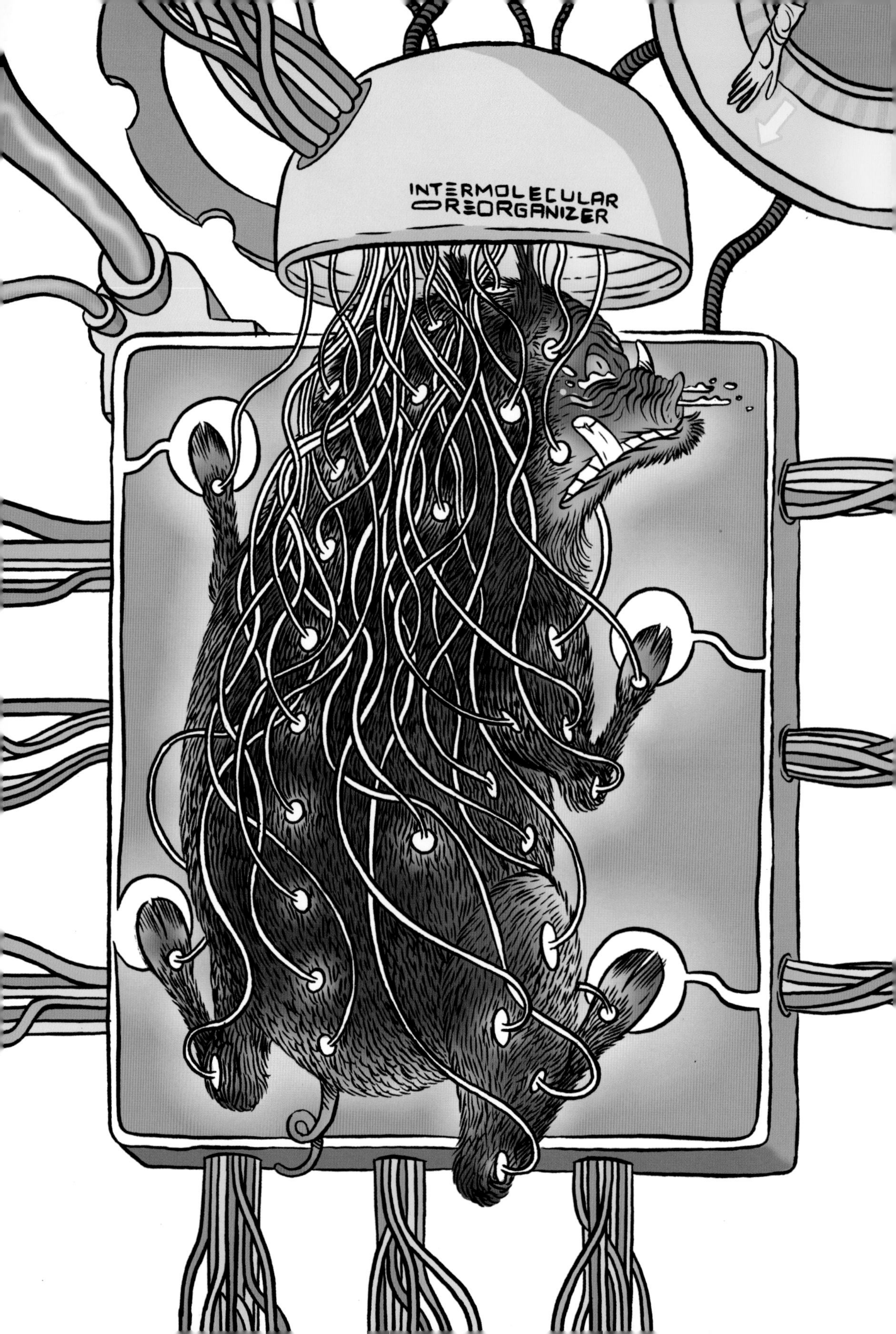
INTERMOLECULAR
REORGANIZER

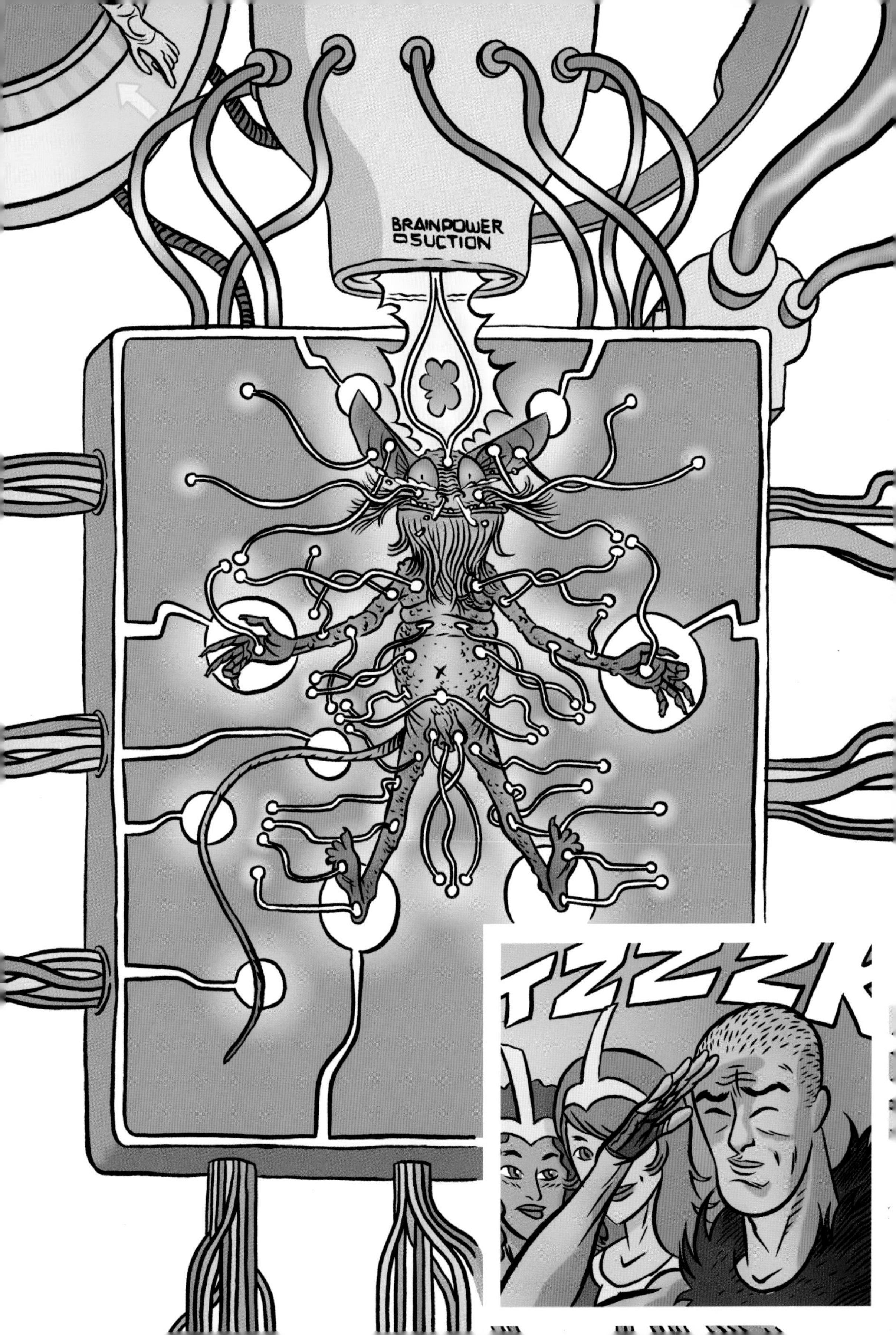
BRAINPOWER
SUCTION
TZZZR

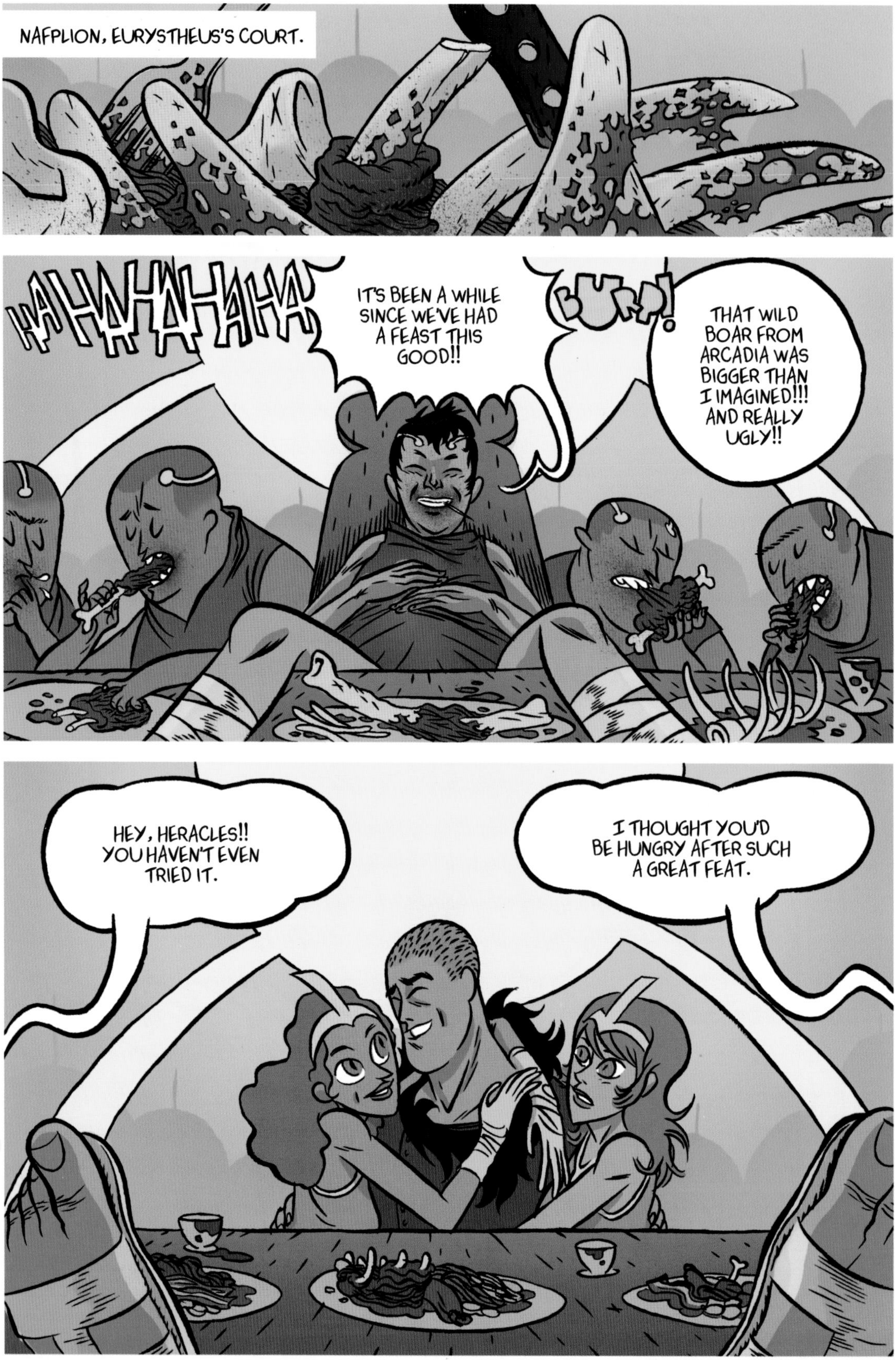
NAFPLION, EURYSTHEUS'S COURT.
HAHAHAHAHAHA
IT'S BEEN A WHILE SINCE WE'VE HAD A FEAST THIS GOOD!!
BURP!
THAT WILD BOAR FROM ARCADIA WAS BIGGER THAN I IMAGINED!!! AND REALLY UGLY!!
HEY, HERACLES!! YOU HAVEN'T EVEN TRIED IT.
I THOUGHT YOU'D BE HUNGRY AFTER SUCH A GREAT FEAT.

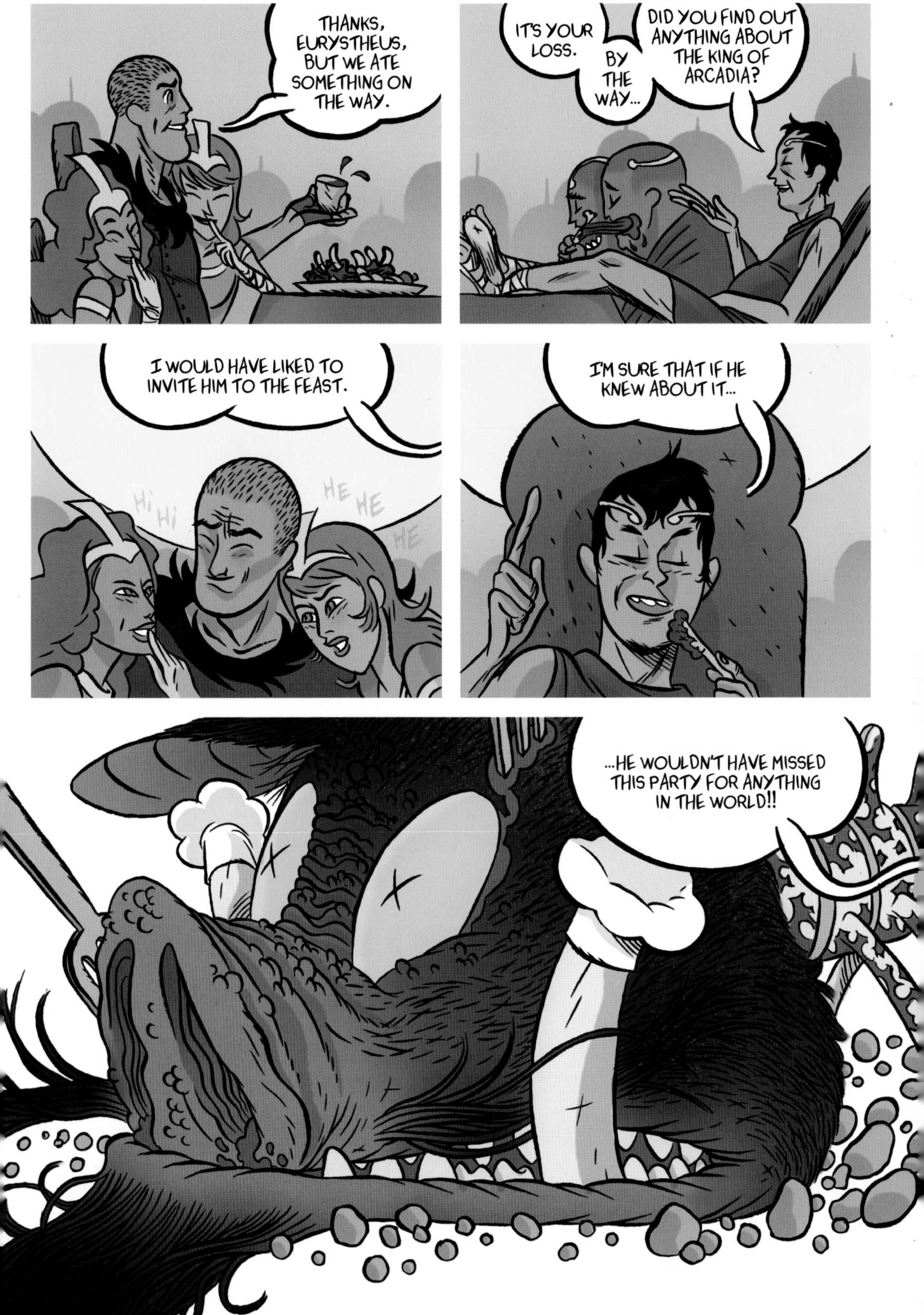
THANKS, EURYSTHEUS, BUT WE ATE SOMETHING ON THE WAY.
IT'S YOUR LOSS.
BY THE WAY...
DID YOU FIND OUT ANYTHING ABOUT THE KING OF ARCADIA?
I WOULD HAVE LIKED TO INVITE HIM TO THE FEAST.
HI HI
HE HE HE
I'M SURE THAT IF HE KNEW ABOUT IT...
...HE WOULDN'T HAVE MISSED THIS PARTY FOR ANYTHING IN THE WORLD!!

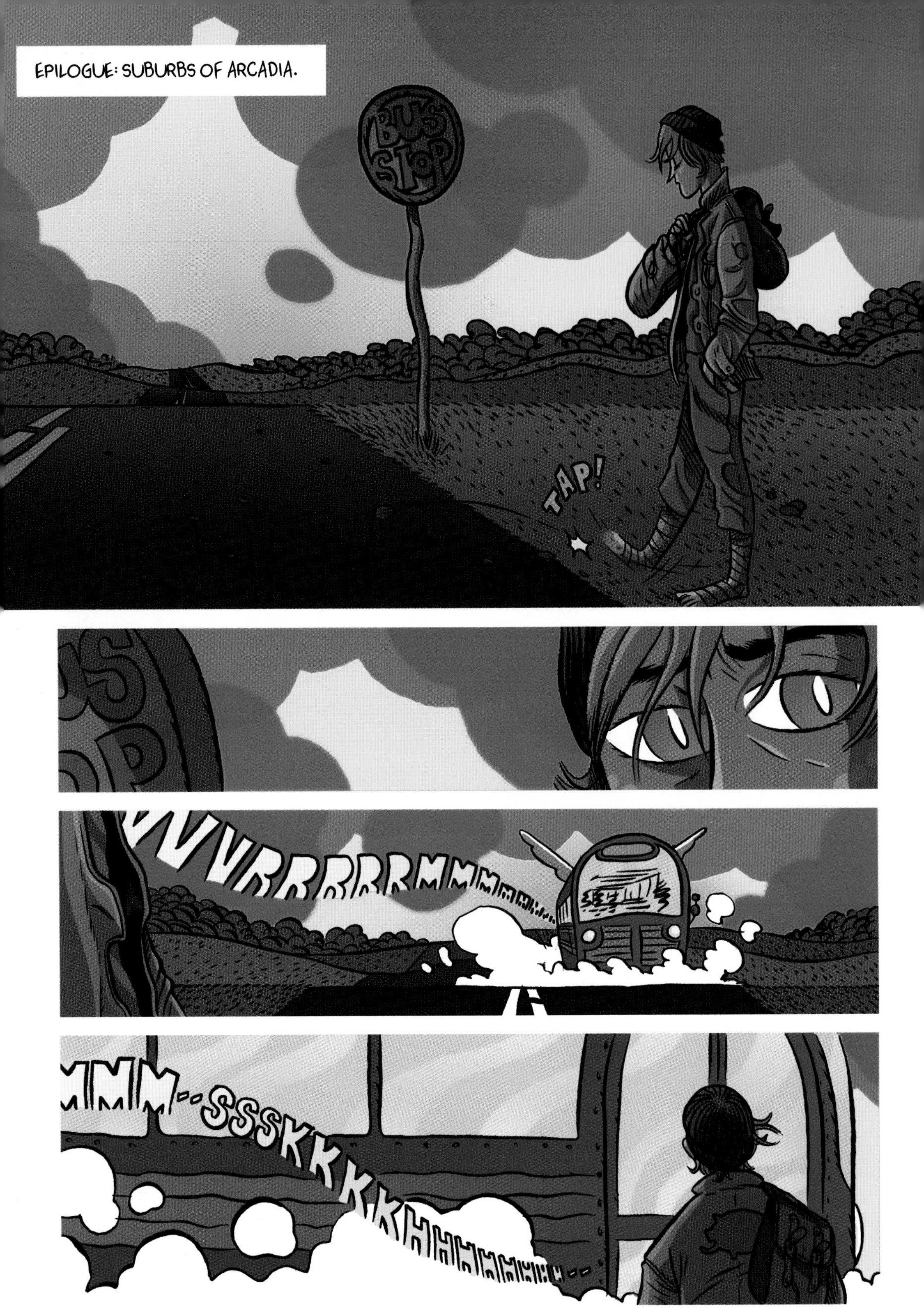
EPILOGUE: SUBURBS OF ARCADIA.
BUS STOP
TAP!
VVVRRRRRRMMMM...
MMMM--SSSKKKKHHHHHHHHH--

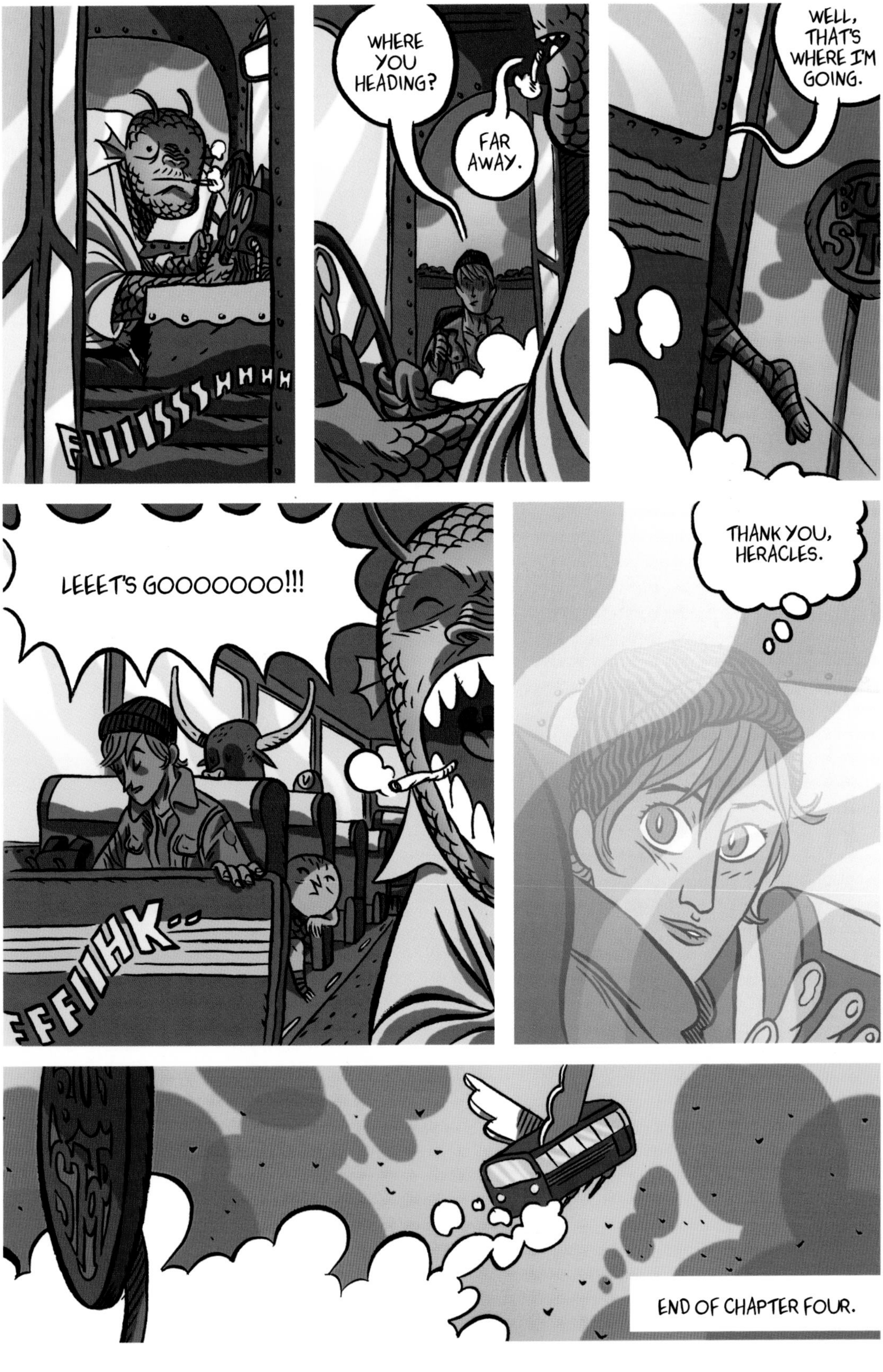
FIIIISSSSHHHH
WHERE YOU HEADING?
FAR AWAY.
WELL, THAT'S WHERE I'M GOING.
LEEET'S GOOOOOOO!!!
FFFIIHK..
THANK YOU, HERACLES.
END OF CHAPTER FOUR.

CHAPTER

05

CHAPTER

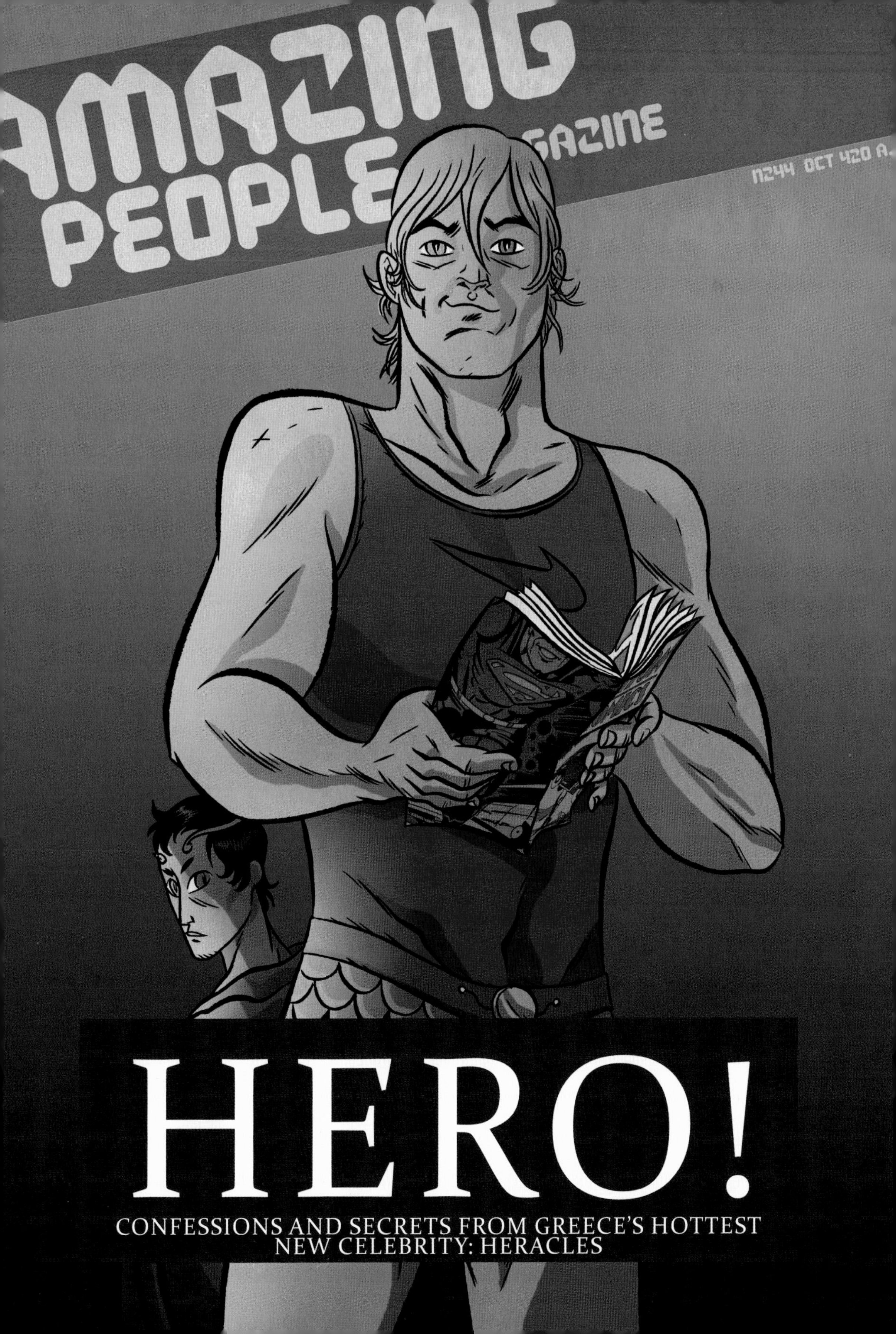
AMAZING
PEOPLE
GAZINE
N244 OCT 420 A.
HERO!
CONFESSIONS AND SECRETS FROM GREECE'S HOTTEST NEW CELEBRITY: HERACLES

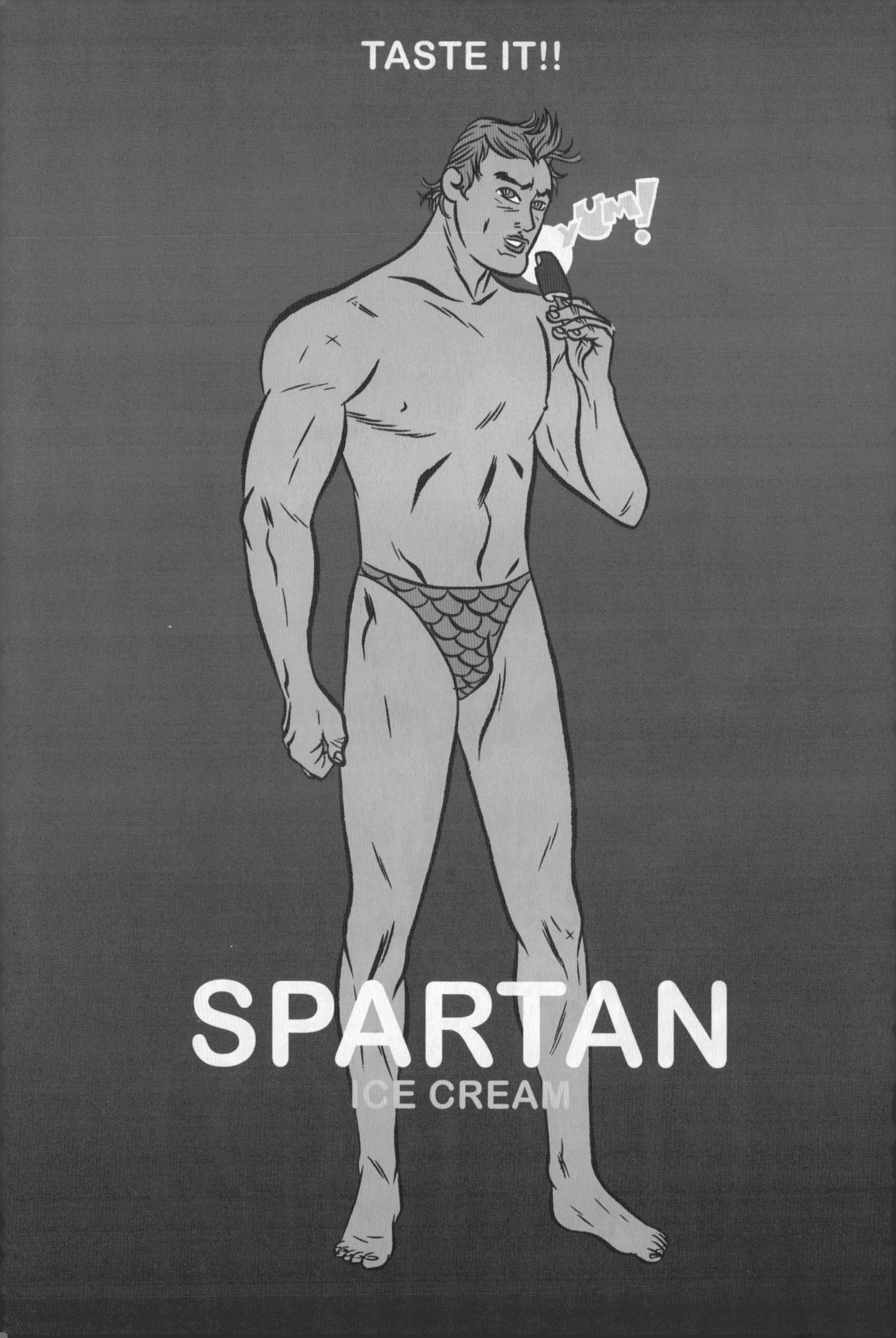
TASTE IT!!
YUM!
SPARTAN
ICE CREAM

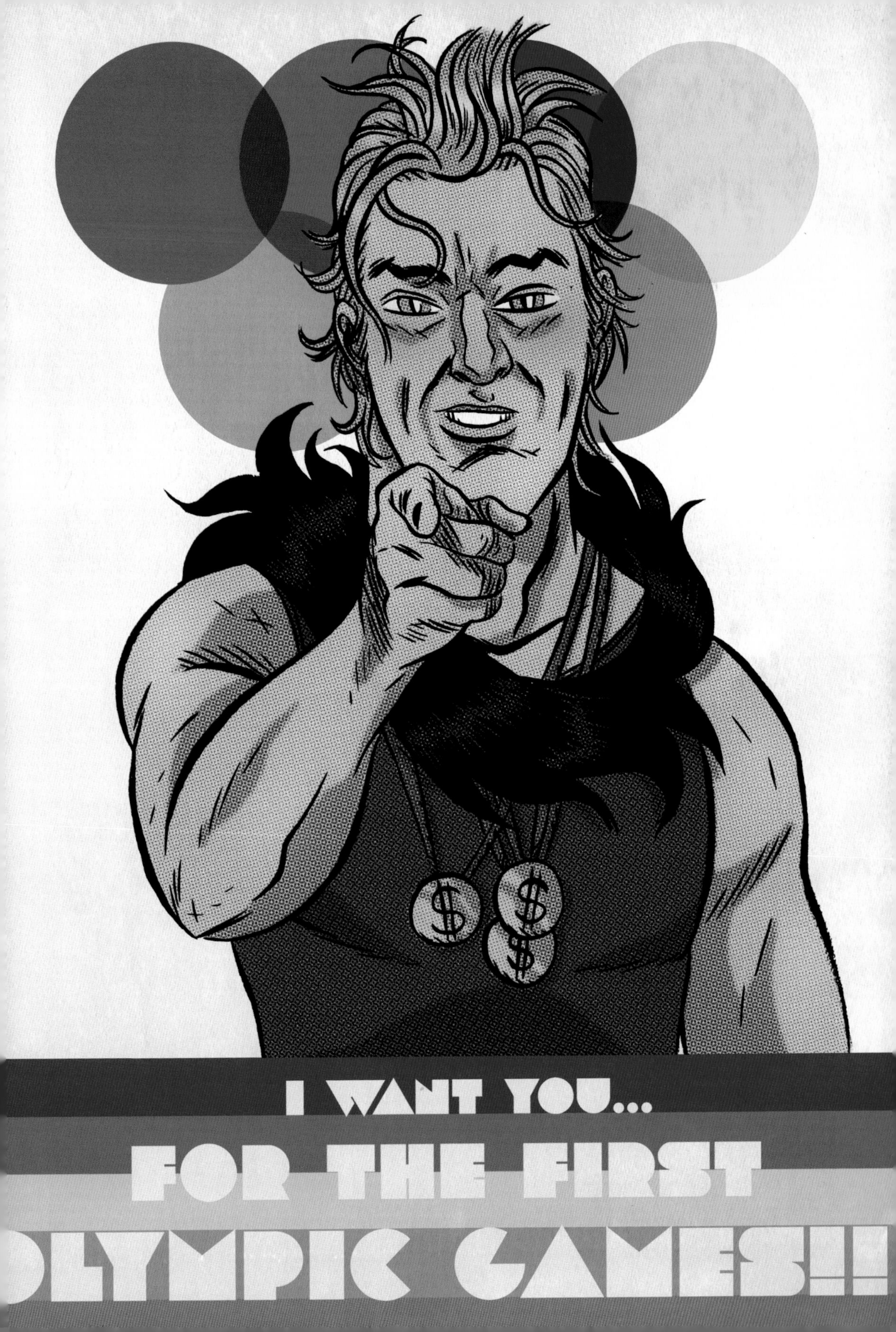
I WANT YOU...
FOR THE FIRST
OLYMPIC GAMES!!!

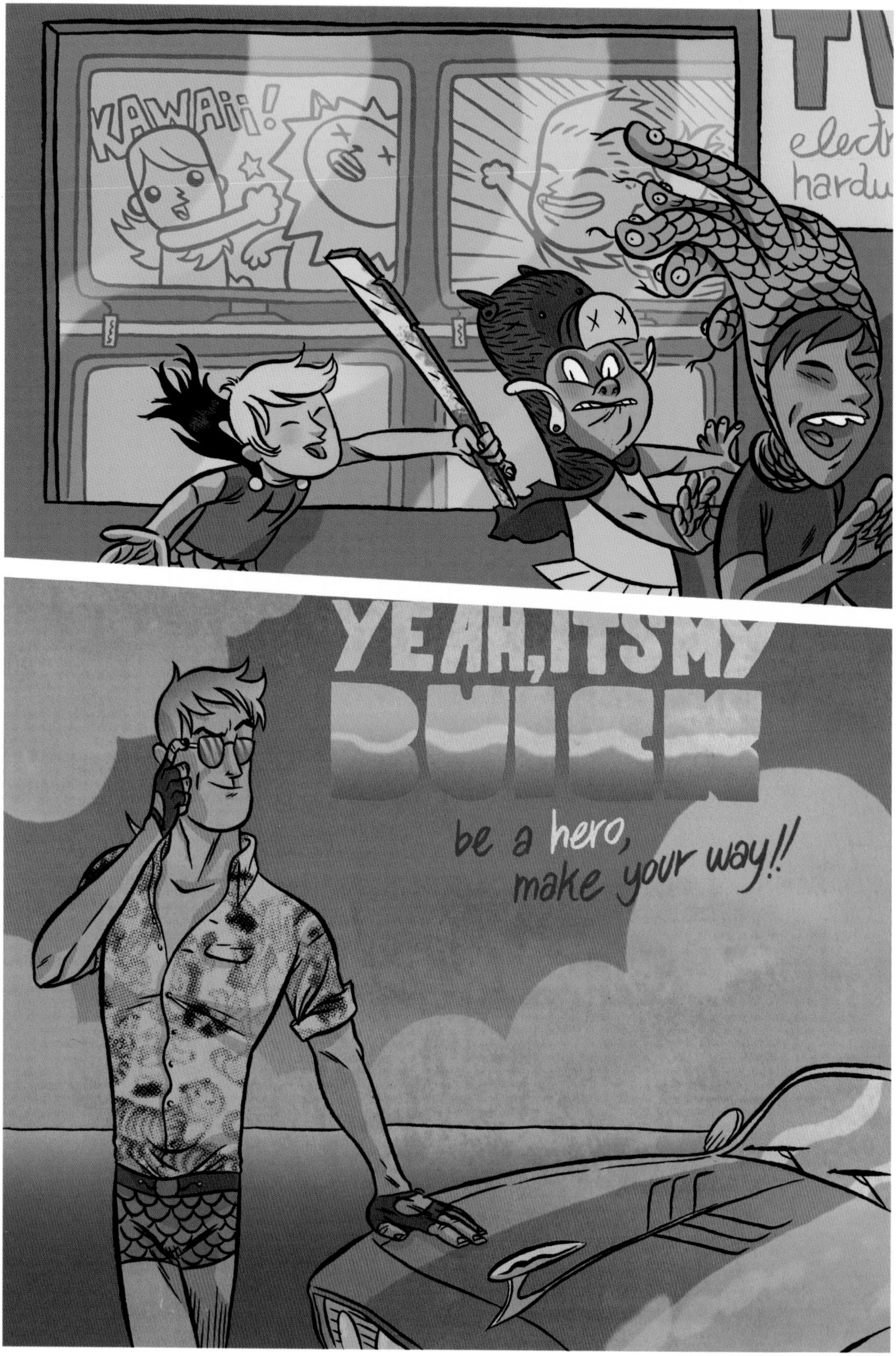
KAWAii!
YEAH, ITS MY
BUICK
be a hero,
make your way!!

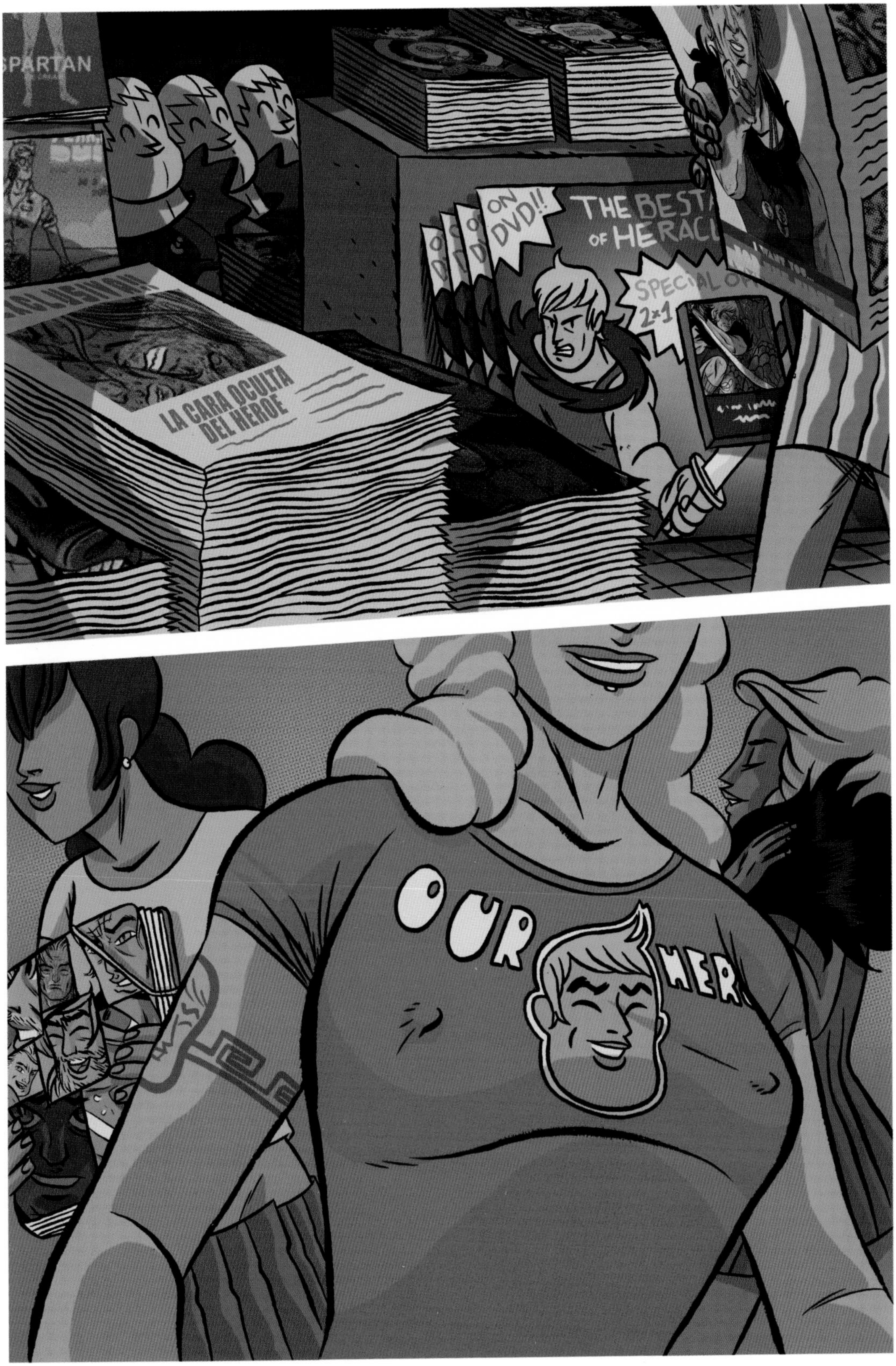
SPARTAN
ON DVD!!
THE BESTA
OF HERACL
SPECIAL OF
2x1
LA CARA OCULTA DEL HEROE
OUR HER

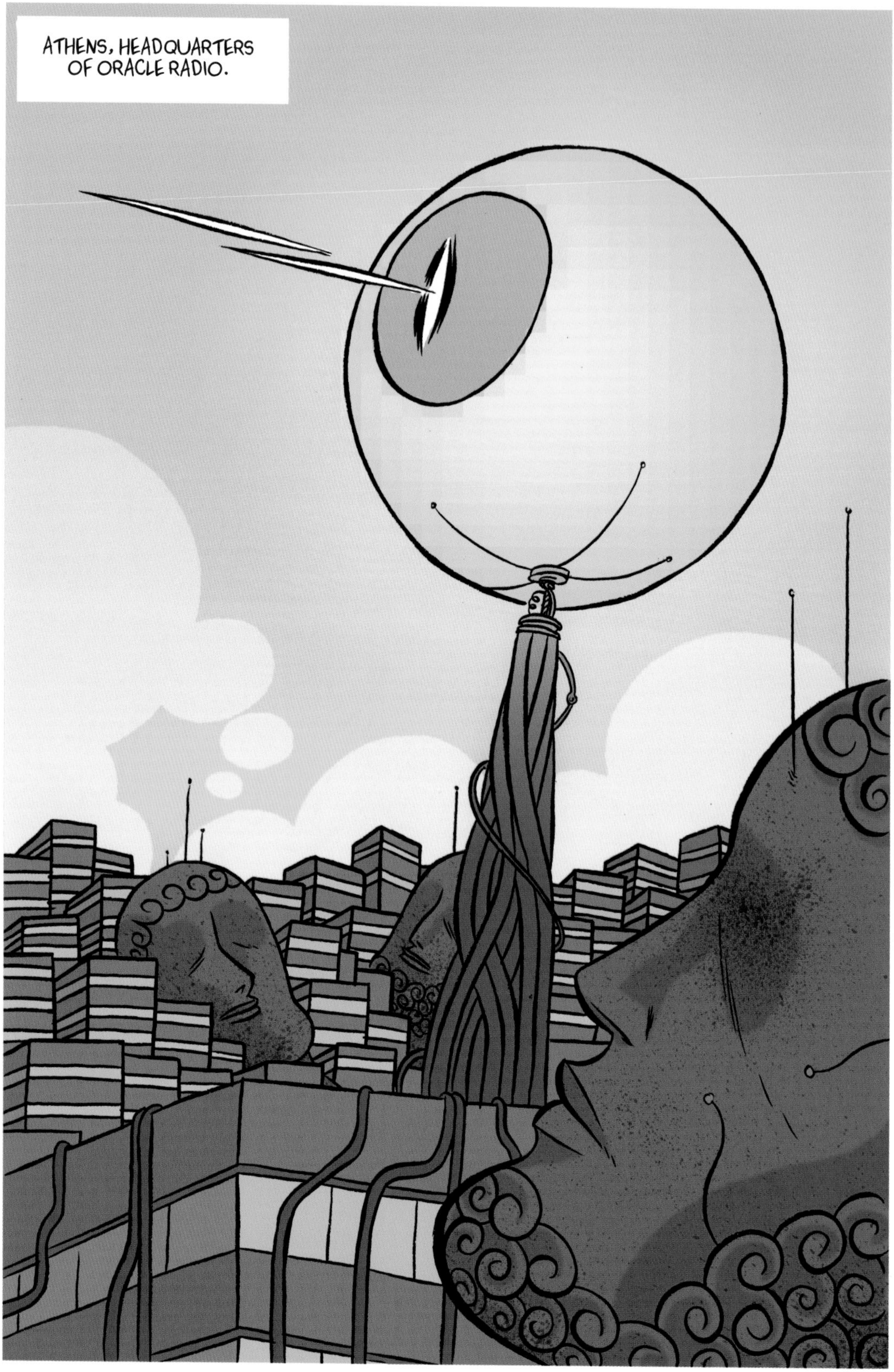
ATHENS, HEADQUARTERS OF ORACLE RADIO.

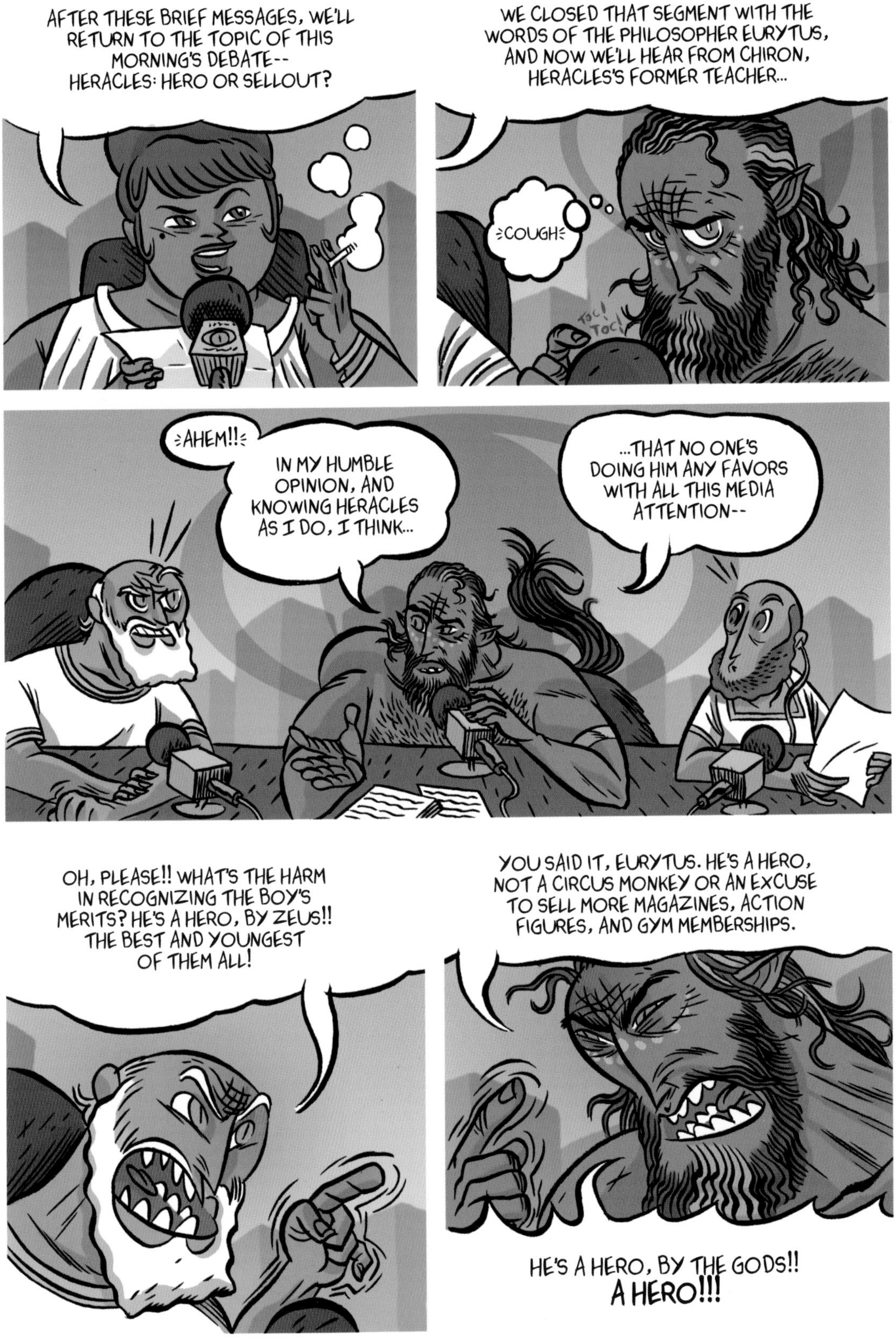
AFTER THESE BRIEF MESSAGES, WE'LL RETURN TO THE TOPIC OF THIS MORNING'S DEBATE-- HERACLES: HERO OR SELLOUT?
WE CLOSED THAT SEGMENT WITH THE WORDS OF THE PHILOSOPHER EURYTUS, AND NOW WE'LL HEAR FROM CHIRON, HERACLES'S FORMER TEACHER...
COUGH
TOC! TOC!
AHEM!!
IN MY HUMBLE OPINION, AND KNOWING HERACLES AS I DO, I THINK...
...THAT NO ONE'S DOING HIM ANY FAVORS WITH ALL THIS MEDIA ATTENTION--
OH, PLEASE!! WHAT'S THE HARM IN RECOGNIZING THE BOY'S MERITS? HE'S A HERO, BY ZEUS!! THE BEST AND YOUNGEST OF THEM ALL!
YOU SAID IT, EURYTUS. HE'S A HERO, NOT A CIRCUS MONKEY OR AN EXCUSE TO SELL MORE MAGAZINES, ACTION FIGURES, AND GYM MEMBERSHIPS.
HE'S A HERO, BY THE GODS!! A HERO!!!

YES, OF COURSE! AND ACCORDING TO YOU, A HERO DOESN'T DESERVE THE CITY'S THANKS FOR HIS DEEDS, CORRECT?

HE DESERVES RECOGNITION AND THANKS, YES, BUT NOT SO THAT IT MAKES HIM A CELEBRITY WIMP!

AH, HA, HA! WHAT'S HAPPENING, CHIRON, IS THAT YOU'RE GETTING EATEN UP WITH JEALOUSY SEEING WHAT YOUR PUPIL HAS ACHIEVED...

...BY AGE TWENTY-ONE! FEATS MUCH MORE MEMORABLE THAN YOURS!

BUT...!

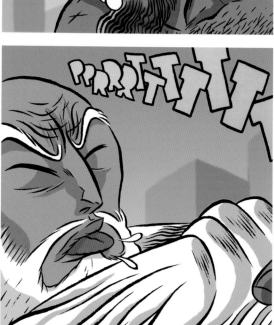

HOW DARE YOU!!! THERE'S NO GREATER PRIDE FOR ME THAN SEEING MY MOST BELOVED STUDENT BECOME ONE OF THE GREATEST HEROES THE WORLD HAS EVER KNOWN!!!

PRRRRTTTTT

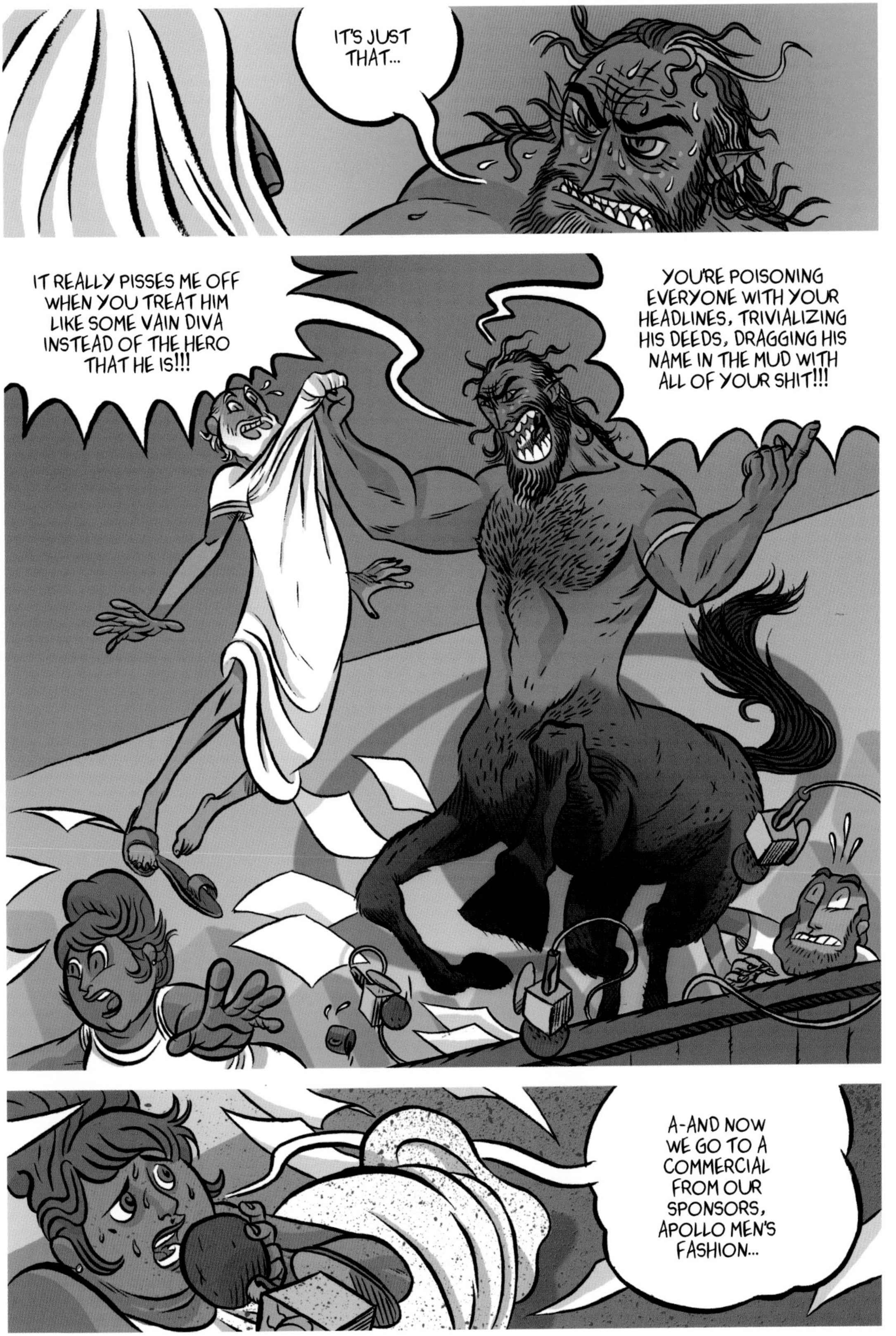
IT'S JUST THAT...
IT REALLY PISSES ME OFF WHEN YOU TREAT HIM LIKE SOME VAIN DIVA INSTEAD OF THE HERO THAT HE IS!!!
YOU'RE POISONING EVERYONE WITH YOUR HEADLINES, TRIVIALIZING HIS DEEDS, DRAGGING HIS NAME IN THE MUD WITH ALL OF YOUR SHIT!!!
A-AND NOW WE GO TO A COMMERCIAL FROM OUR SPONSORS, APOLLO MEN'S FASHION...

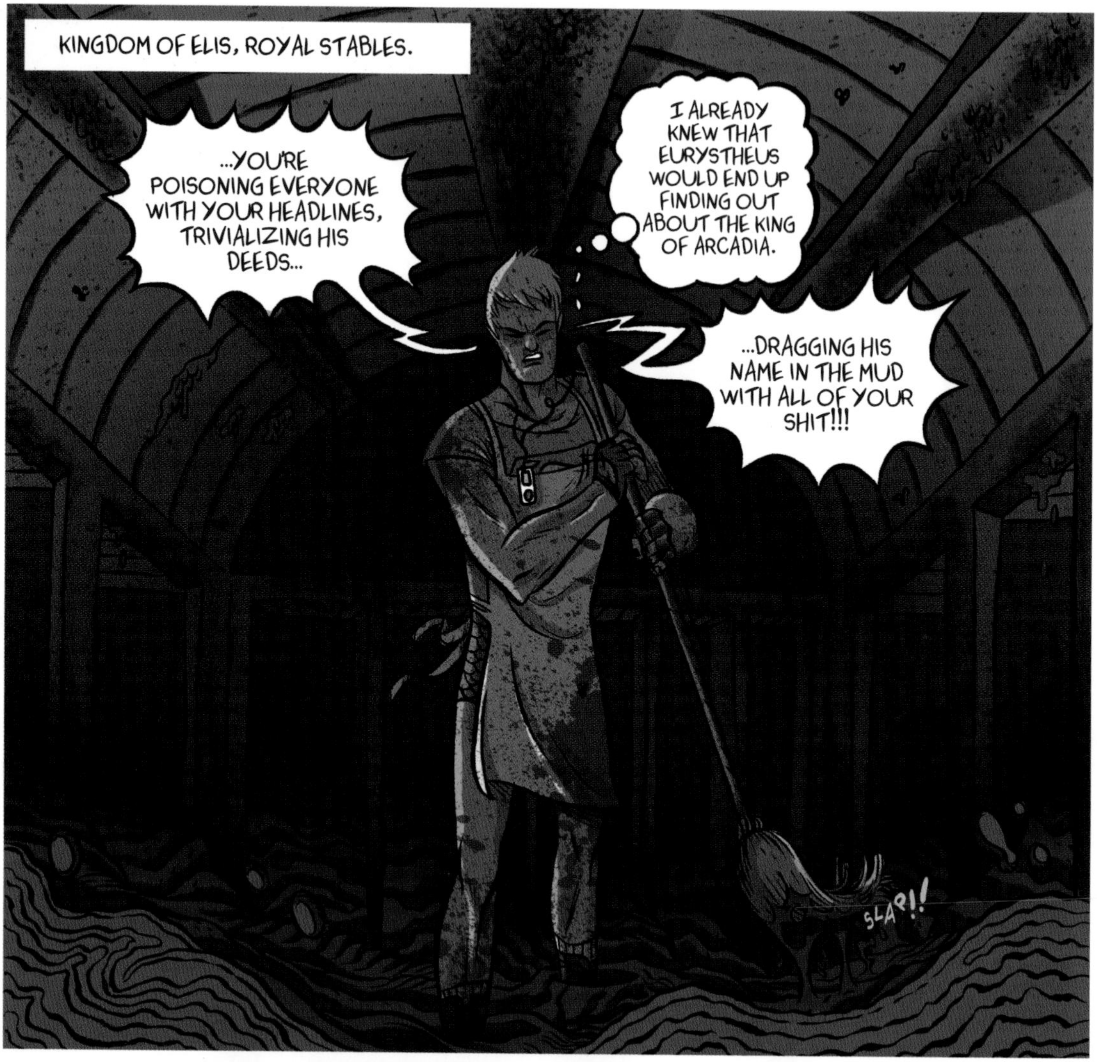
KINGDOM OF ELIS, ROYAL STABLES.
...YOU'RE POISONING EVERYONE WITH YOUR HEADLINES, TRIVIALIZING HIS DEEDS...
I ALREADY KNEW THAT EURYSTHEUS WOULD END UP FINDING OUT ABOUT THE KING OF ARCADIA.
...DRAGGING HIS NAME IN THE MUD WITH ALL OF YOUR SHIT!!!
SLAP!!

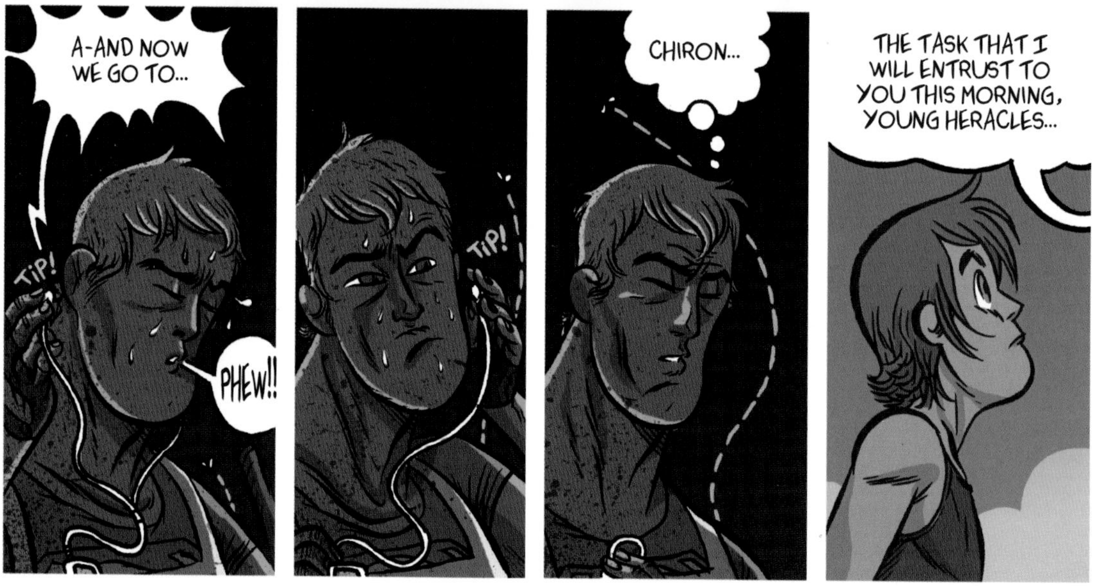
A-AND NOW WE GO TO...
TIP!
PHEW!!
TIP!
CHIRON...
THE TASK THAT I WILL ENTRUST TO YOU THIS MORNING, YOUNG HERACLES...

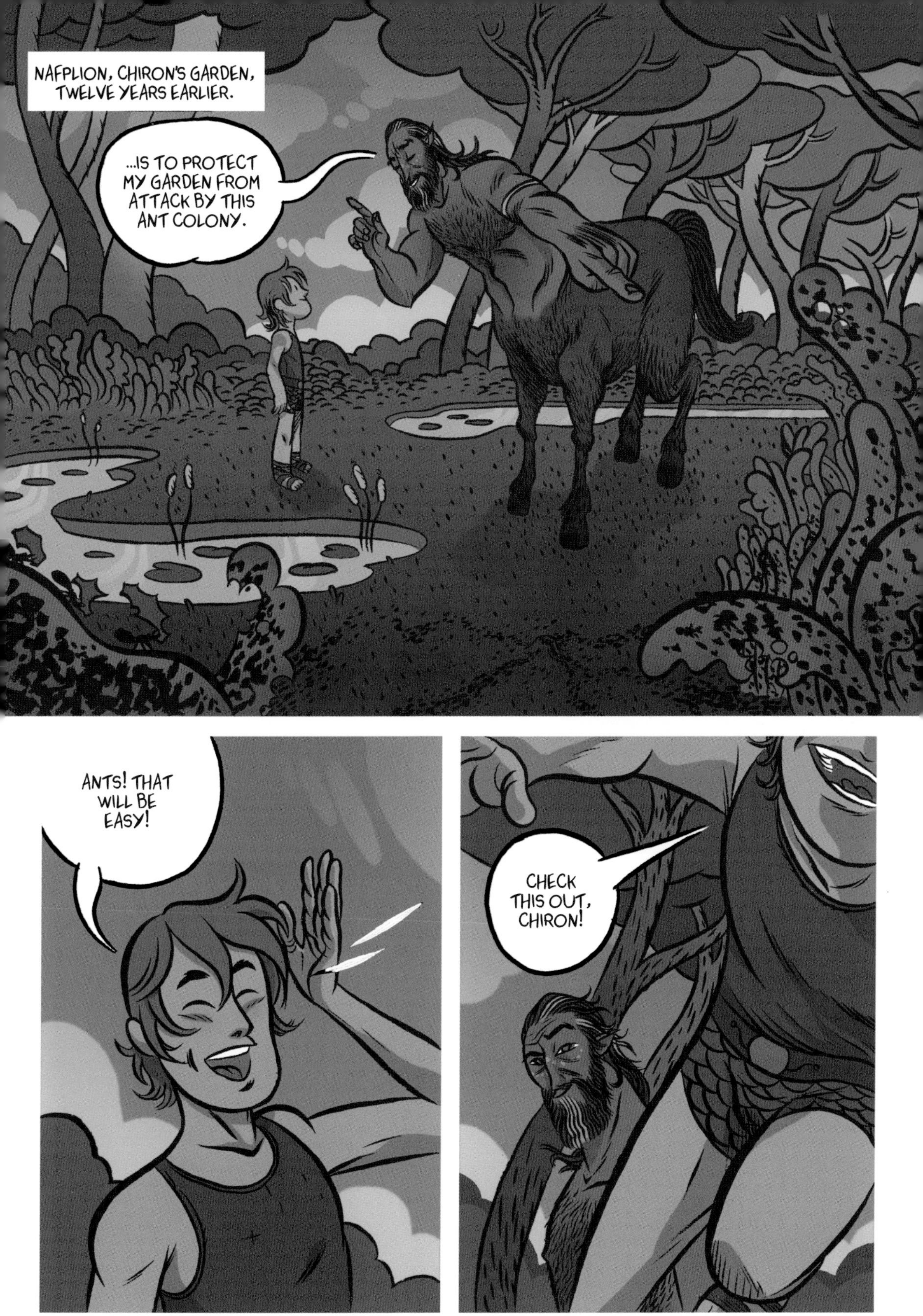
NAFPLION, CHIRON'S GARDEN, TWELVE YEARS EARLIER.
...IS TO PROTECT MY GARDEN FROM ATTACK BY THIS ANT COLONY.
ANTS! THAT WILL BE EASY!
CHECK THIS OUT, CHIRON!

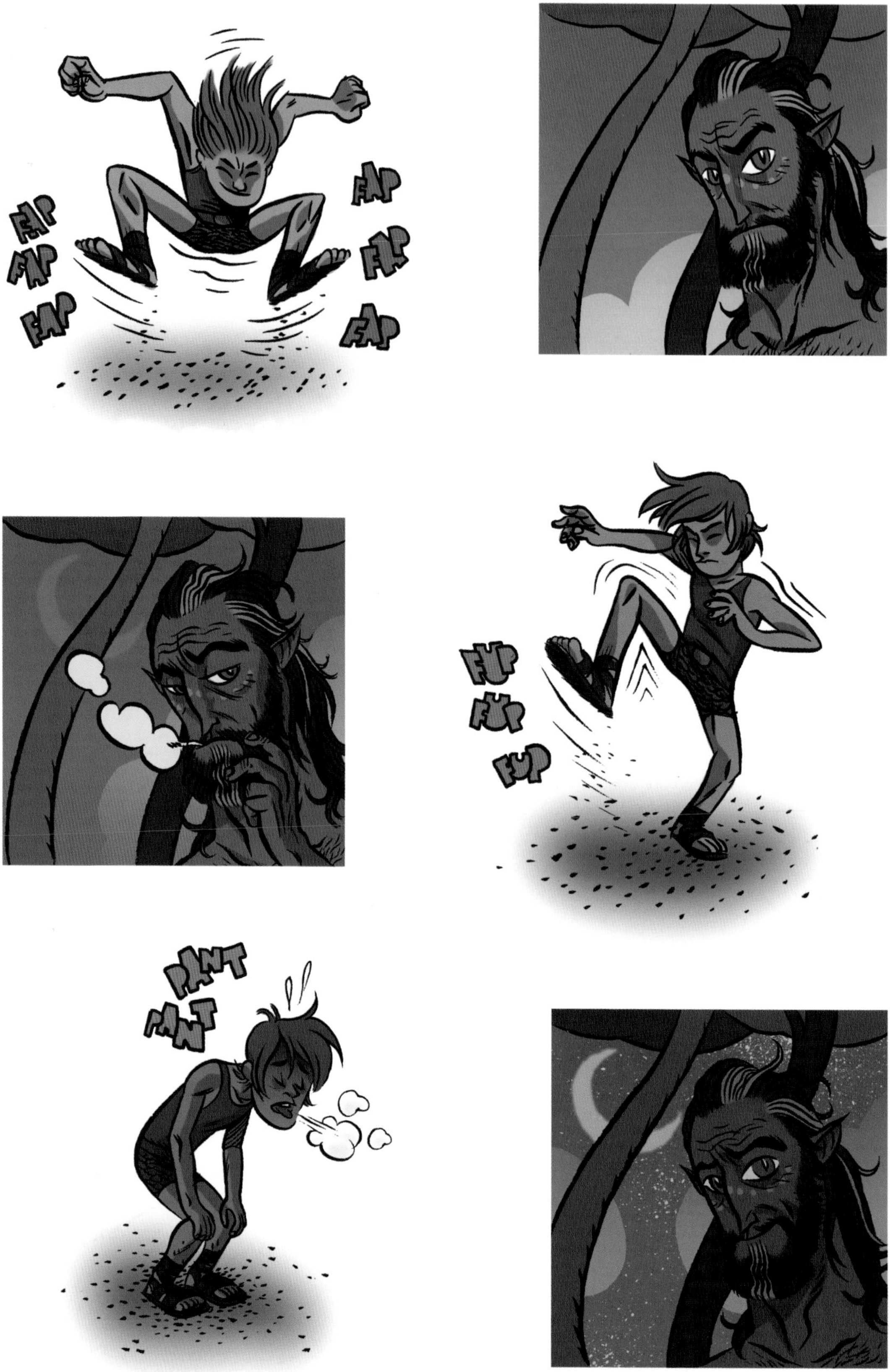
FAP
FAP
FAP
FAP
FAP
FAP
FUP
FUP
FUP
PANT
PANT

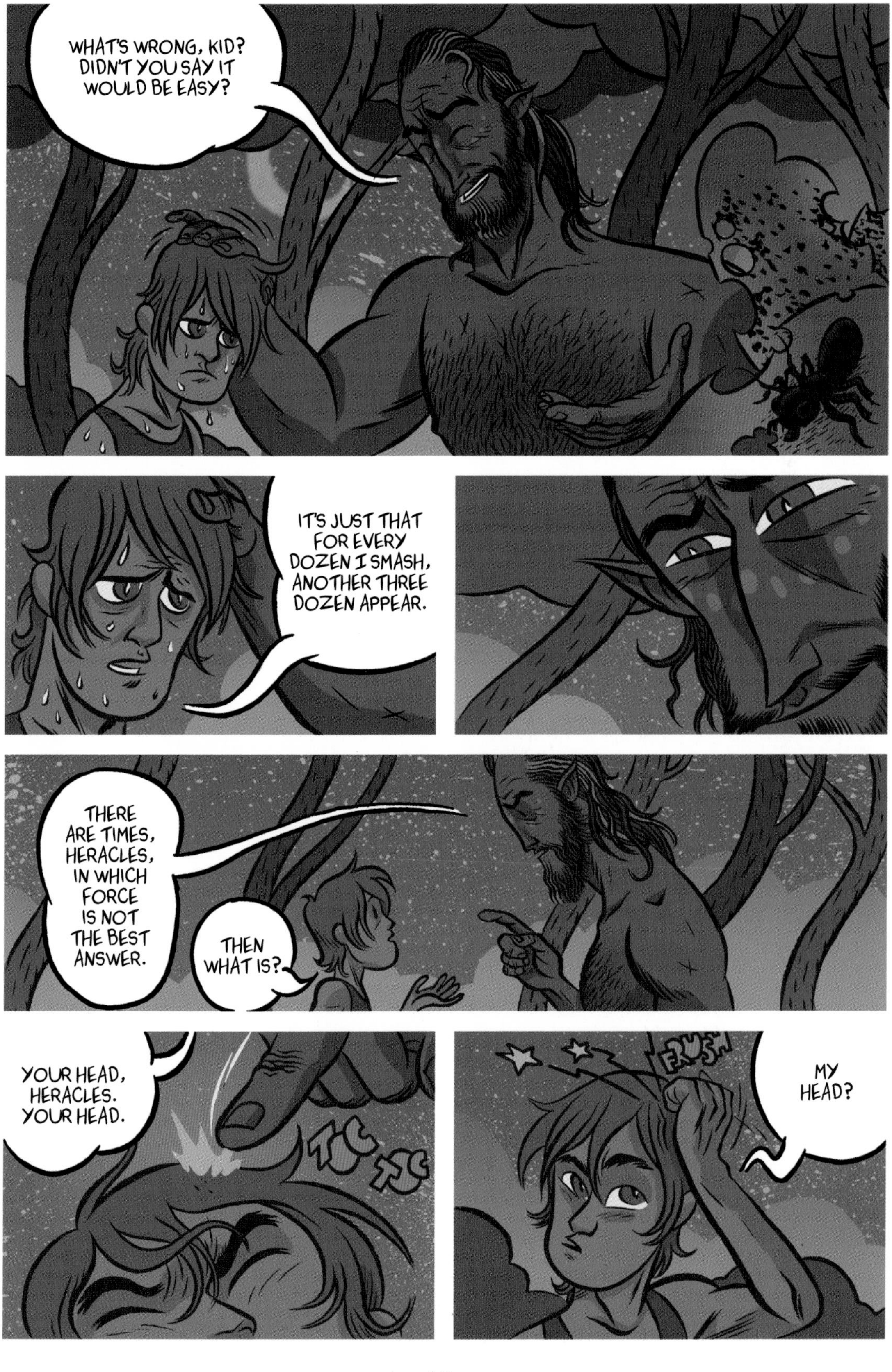
WHAT'S WRONG, KID? DIDN'T YOU SAY IT WOULD BE EASY?
IT'S JUST THAT FOR EVERY DOZEN I SMASH, ANOTHER THREE DOZEN APPEAR.
THERE ARE TIMES, HERACLES, IN WHICH FORCE IS NOT THE BEST ANSWER.
THEN WHAT IS?
YOUR HEAD, HERACLES. YOUR HEAD.
TOC TOC
MY HEAD?

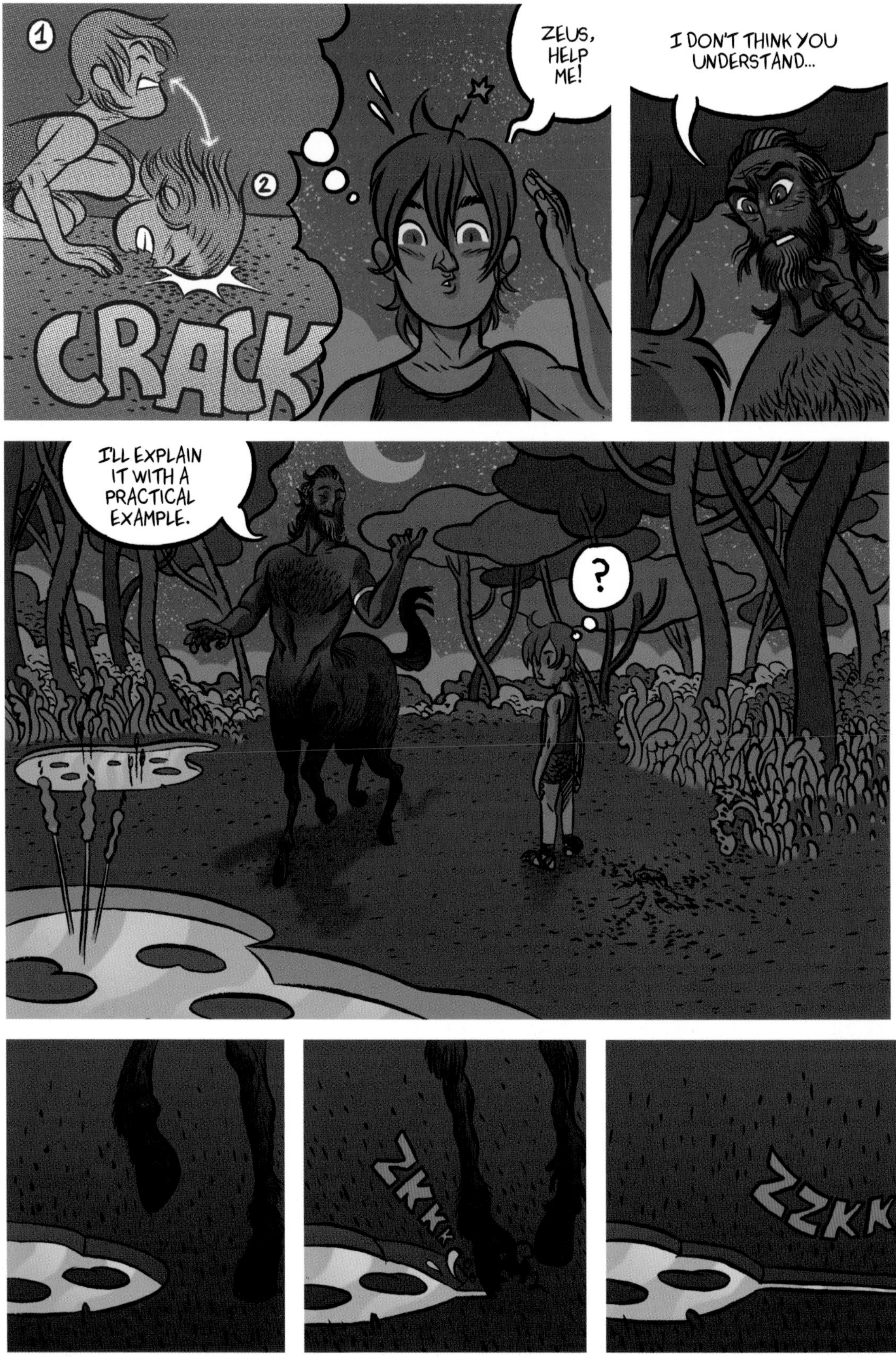
1
2
CRACK
ZEUS, HELP ME!
I DON'T THINK YOU UNDERSTAND...
I'LL EXPLAIN IT WITH A PRACTICAL EXAMPLE.
?
ZKKK
ZZKKK

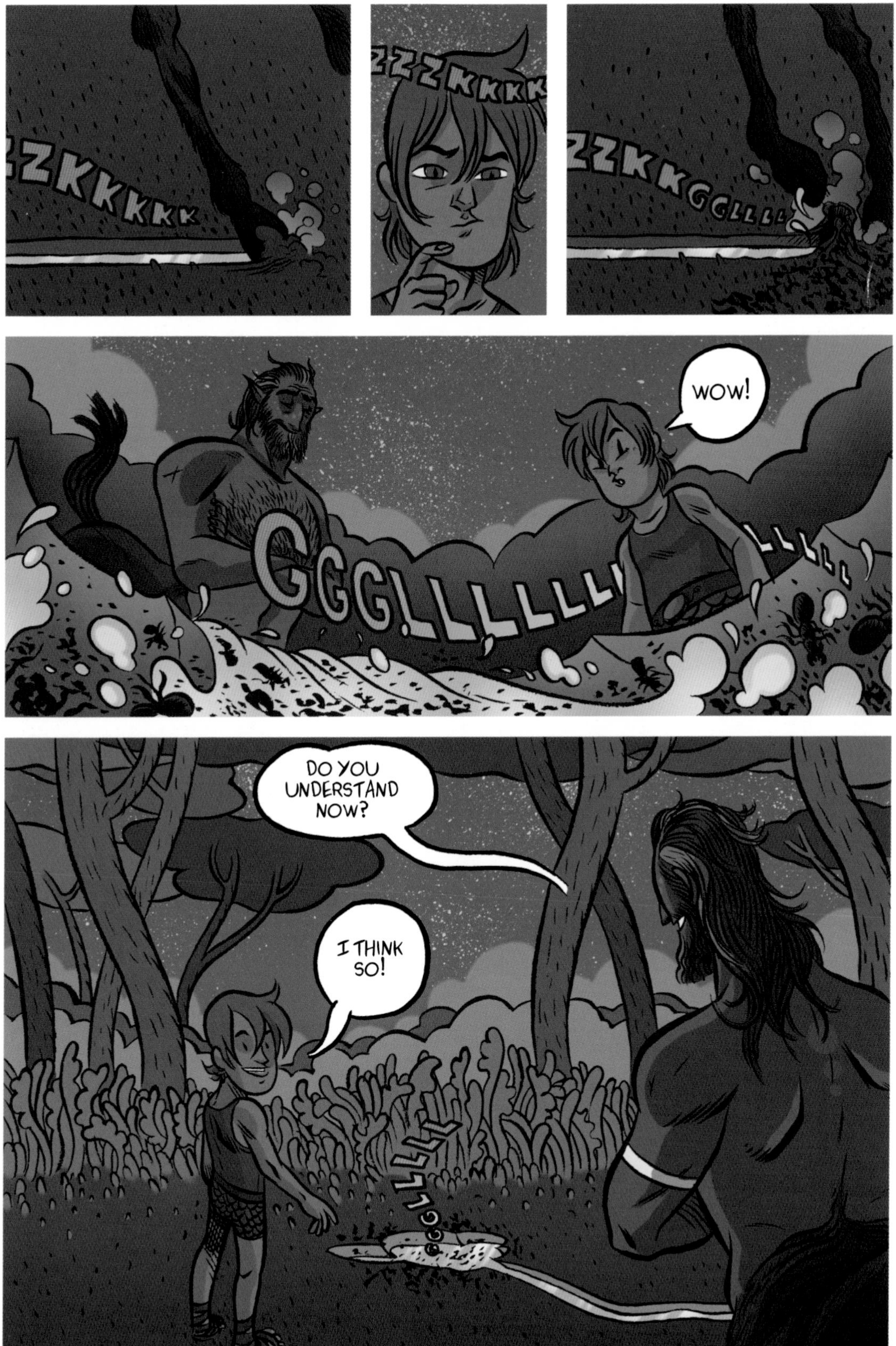
ZZKKKKKK
ZZZKKKK
ZZKKGGLLLL
GGGLLLLLLLLLLLLL
WOW!
DO YOU UNDERSTAND NOW?
I THINK SO!
GGLLLLL

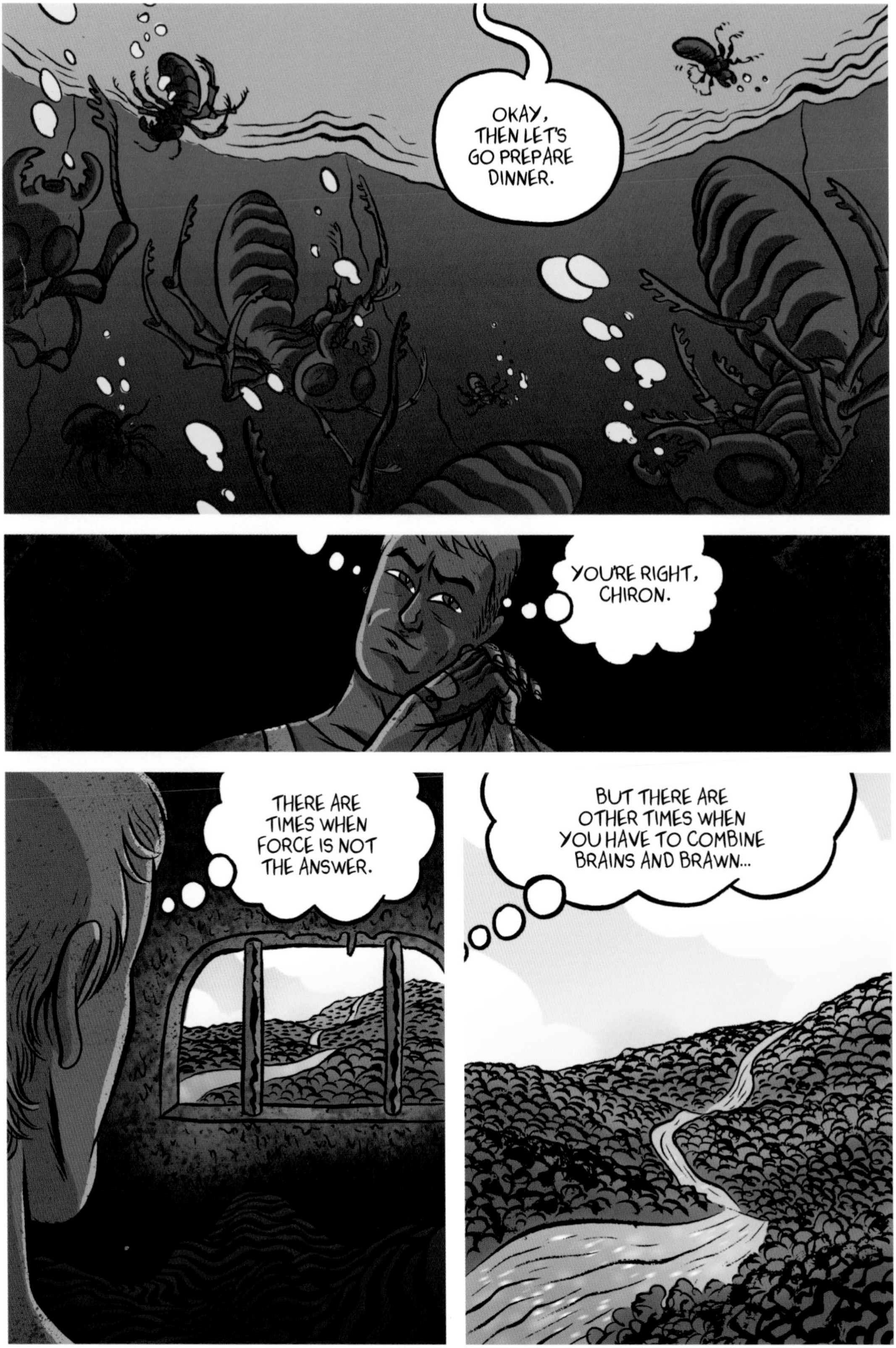
OKAY, THEN LET'S GO PREPARE DINNER.
YOU'RE RIGHT, CHIRON.
THERE ARE TIMES WHEN FORCE IS NOT THE ANSWER.
BUT THERE ARE OTHER TIMES WHEN YOU HAVE TO COMBINE BRAINS AND BRAWN...

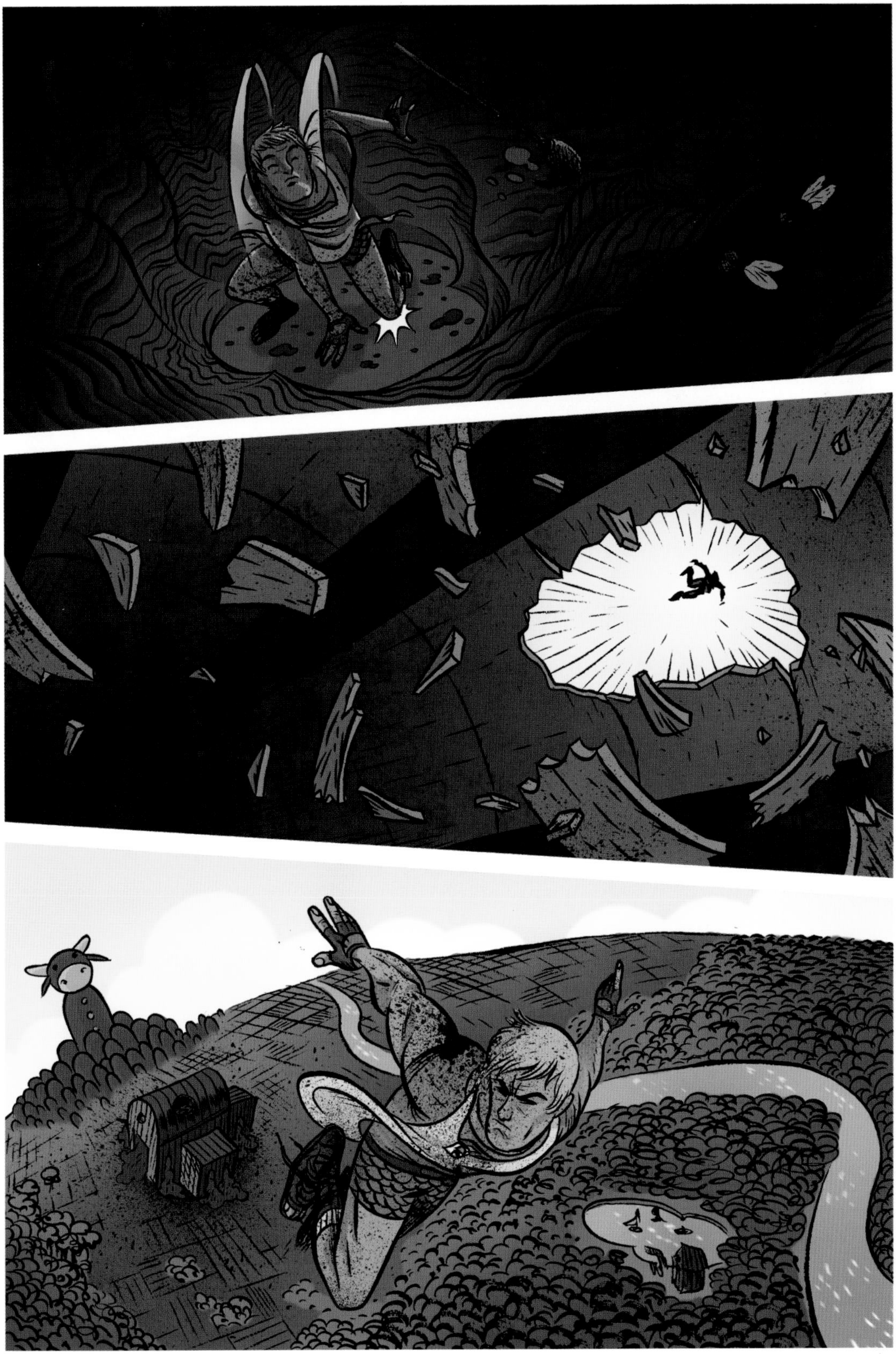

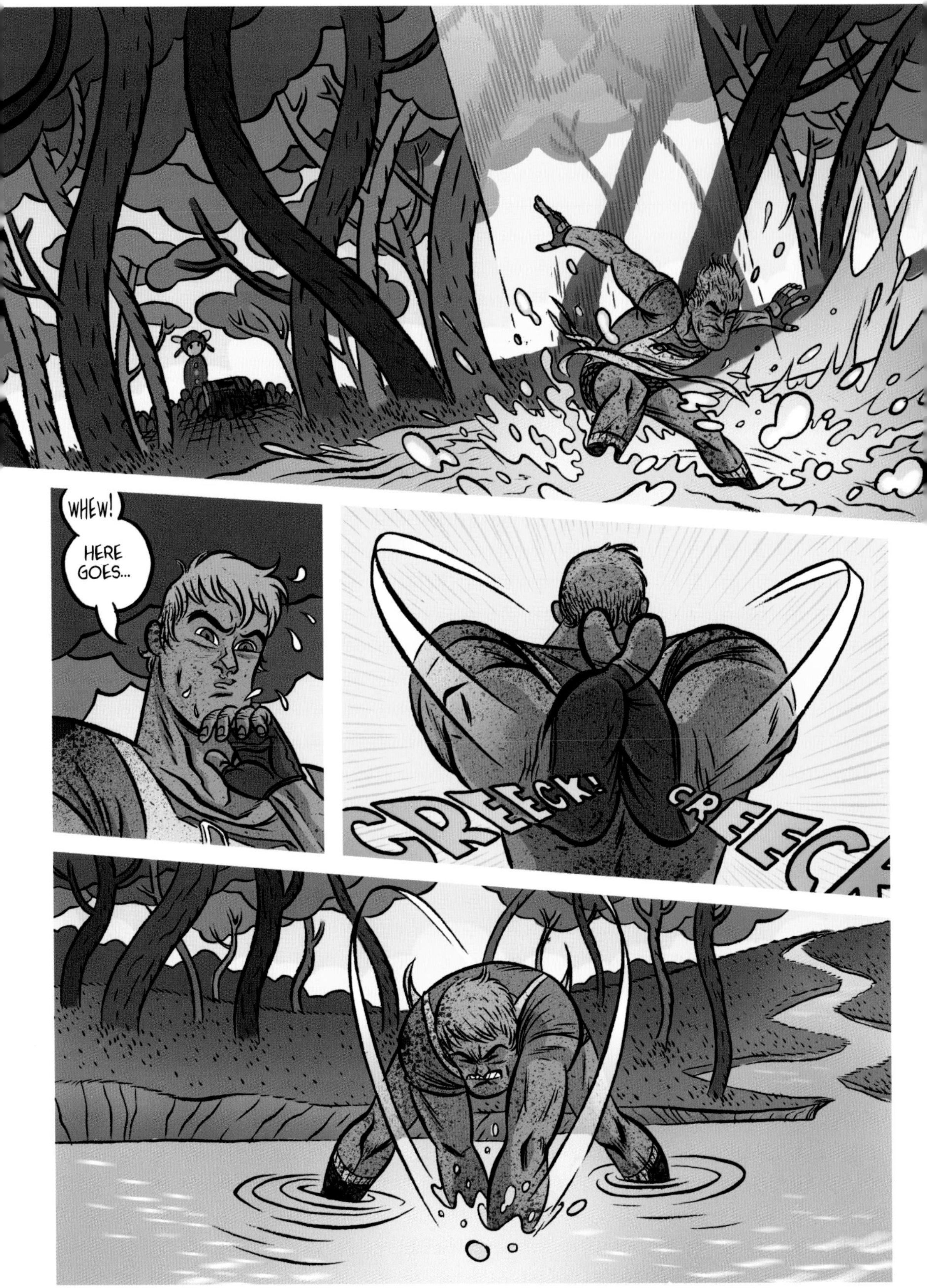
WHEW!
HERE GOES...
CREECK!
CREEC

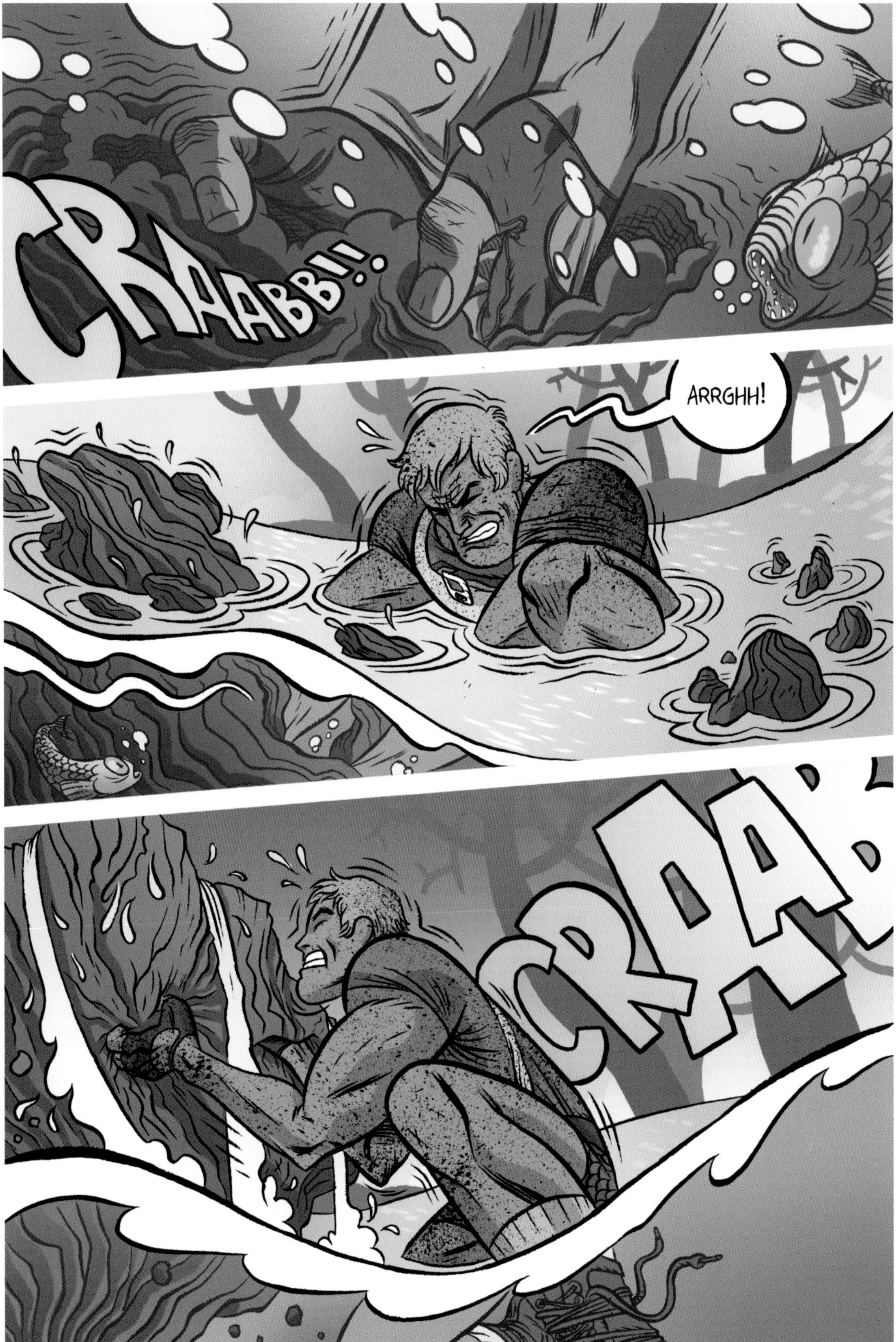
CRAABB!!
ARRGHH!
CRAA

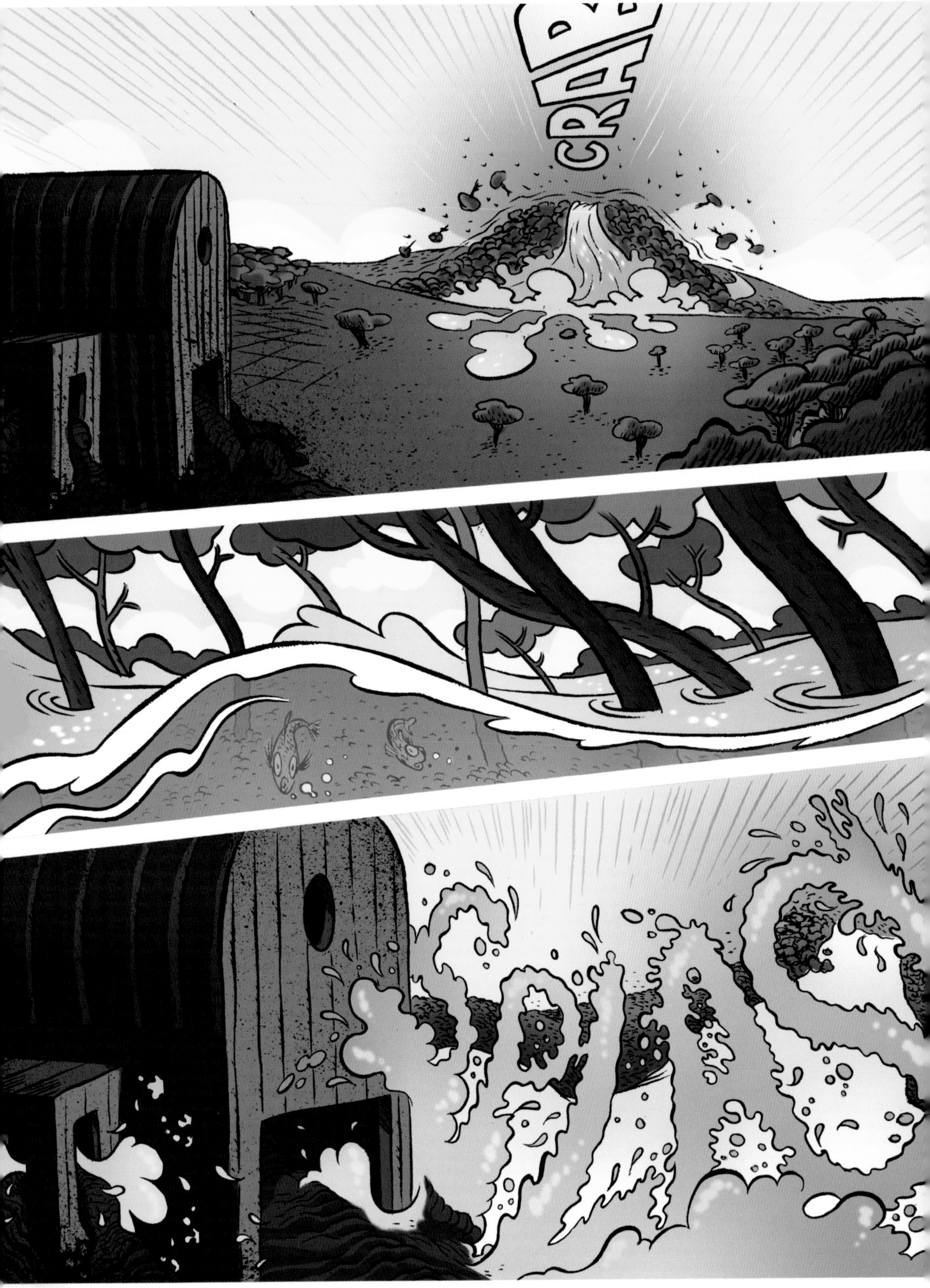
CRA

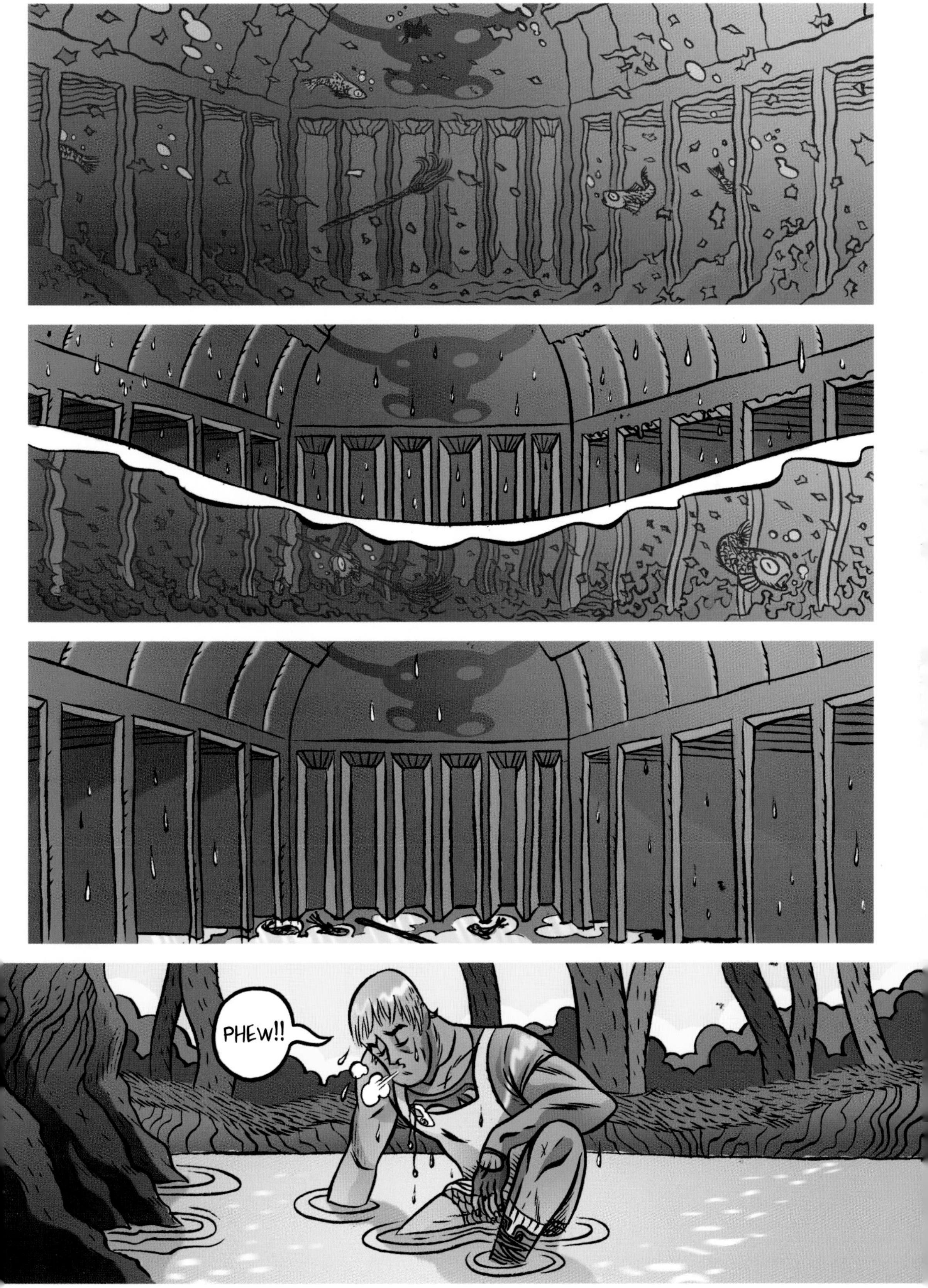
PHEW!!

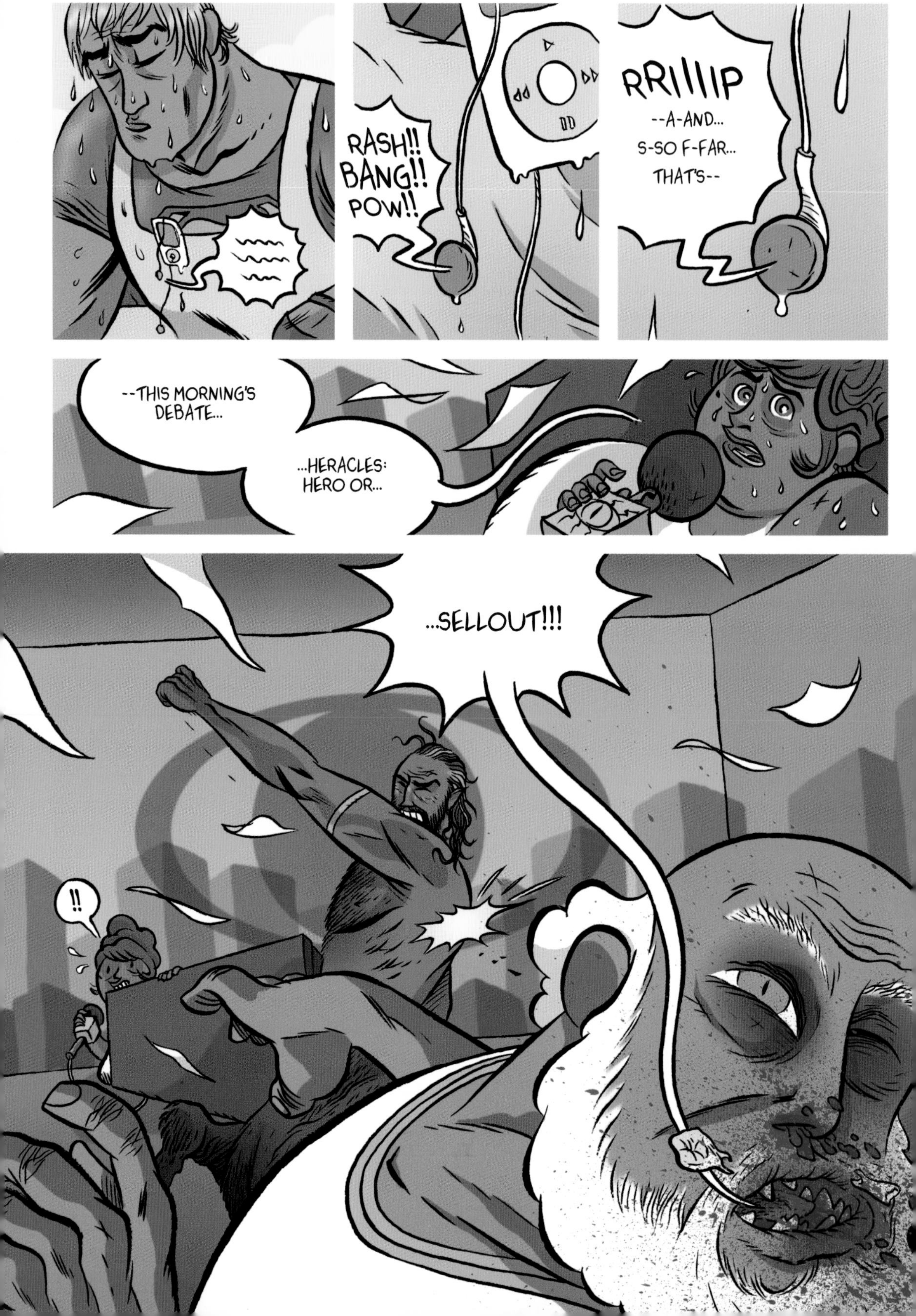
RASH!! BANG!! POW!!
RRIIIIIP
--A-AND... S-SO F-FAR... THAT'S--
--THIS MORNING'S DEBATE...
...HERACLES: HERO OR...
...SELLOUT!!!
!!

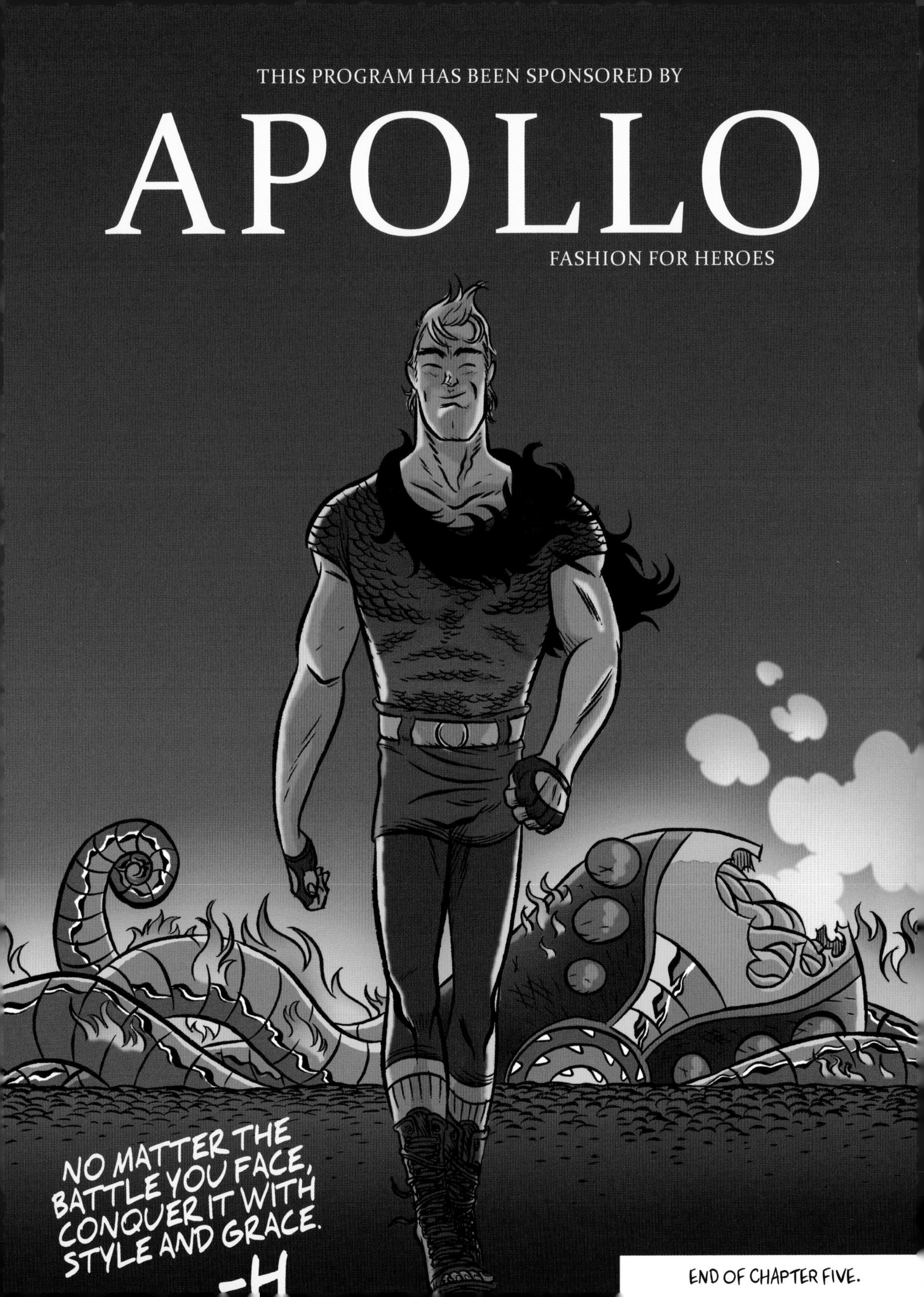

THIS PROGRAM HAS BEEN SPONSORED BY
APOLLO
FASHION FOR HEROES
NO MATTER THE BATTLE YOU FACE, CONQUER IT WITH STYLE AND GRACE.
-H
END OF CHAPTER FIVE.

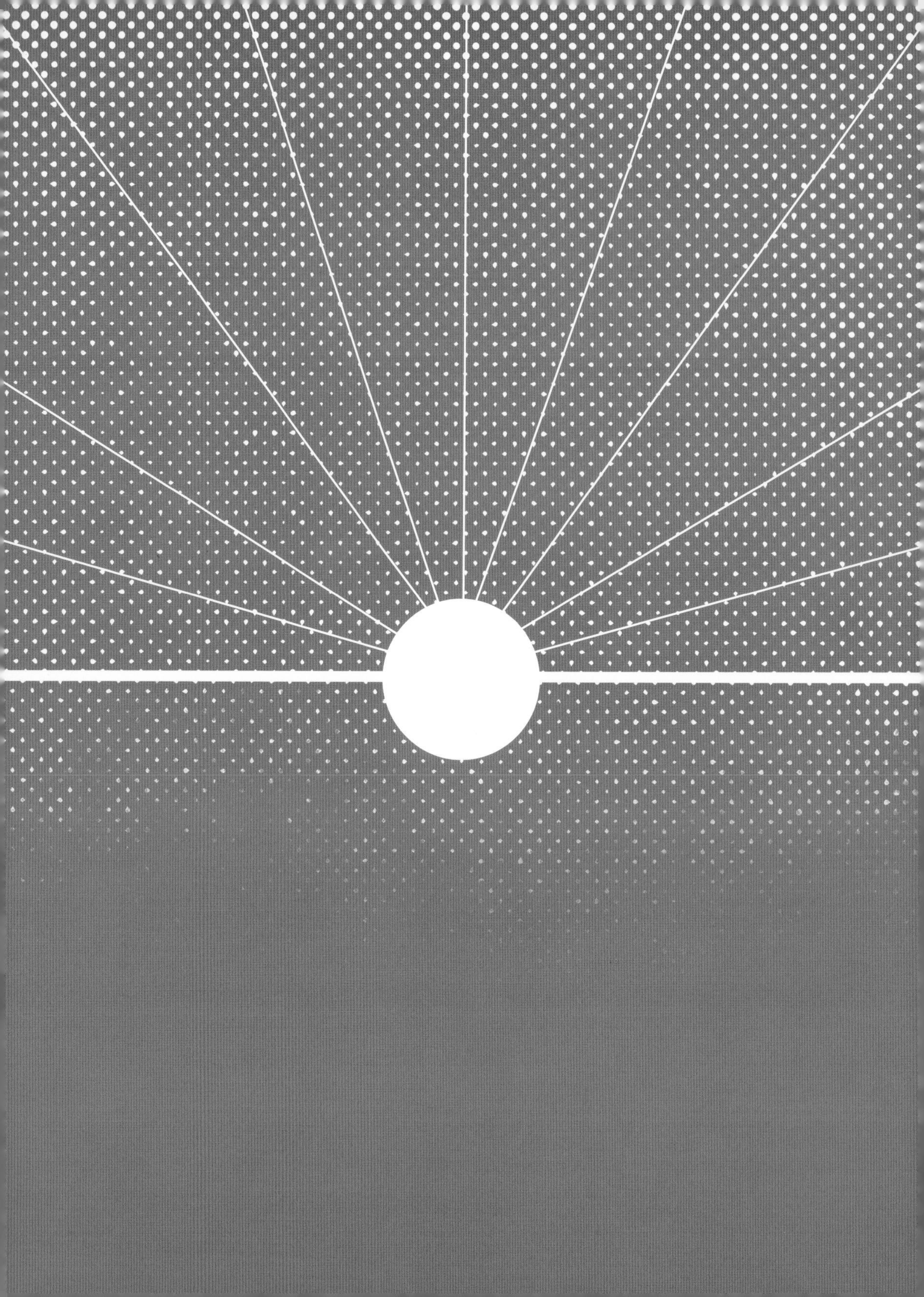

CHAPTER
06
CHAPTER

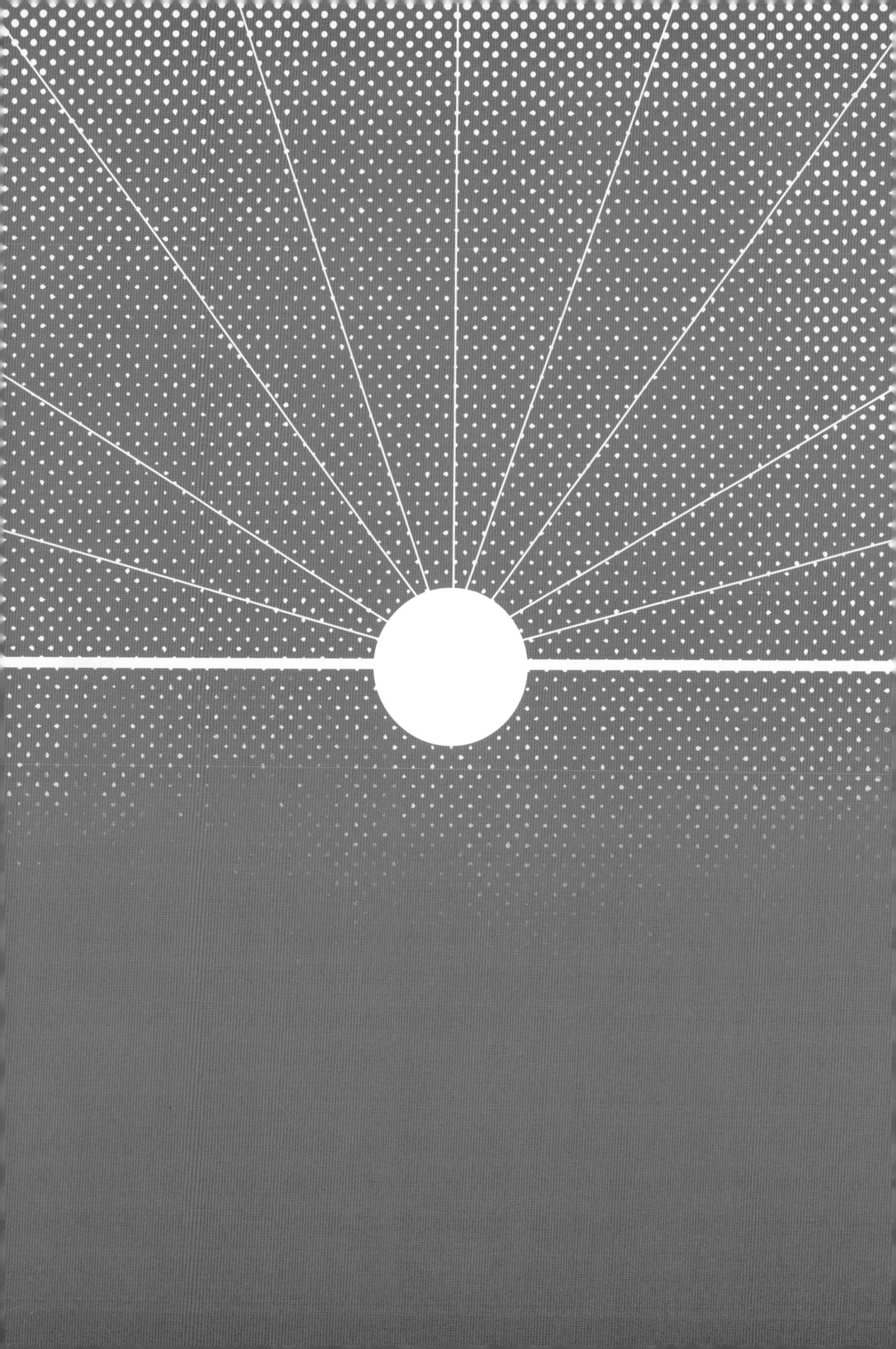

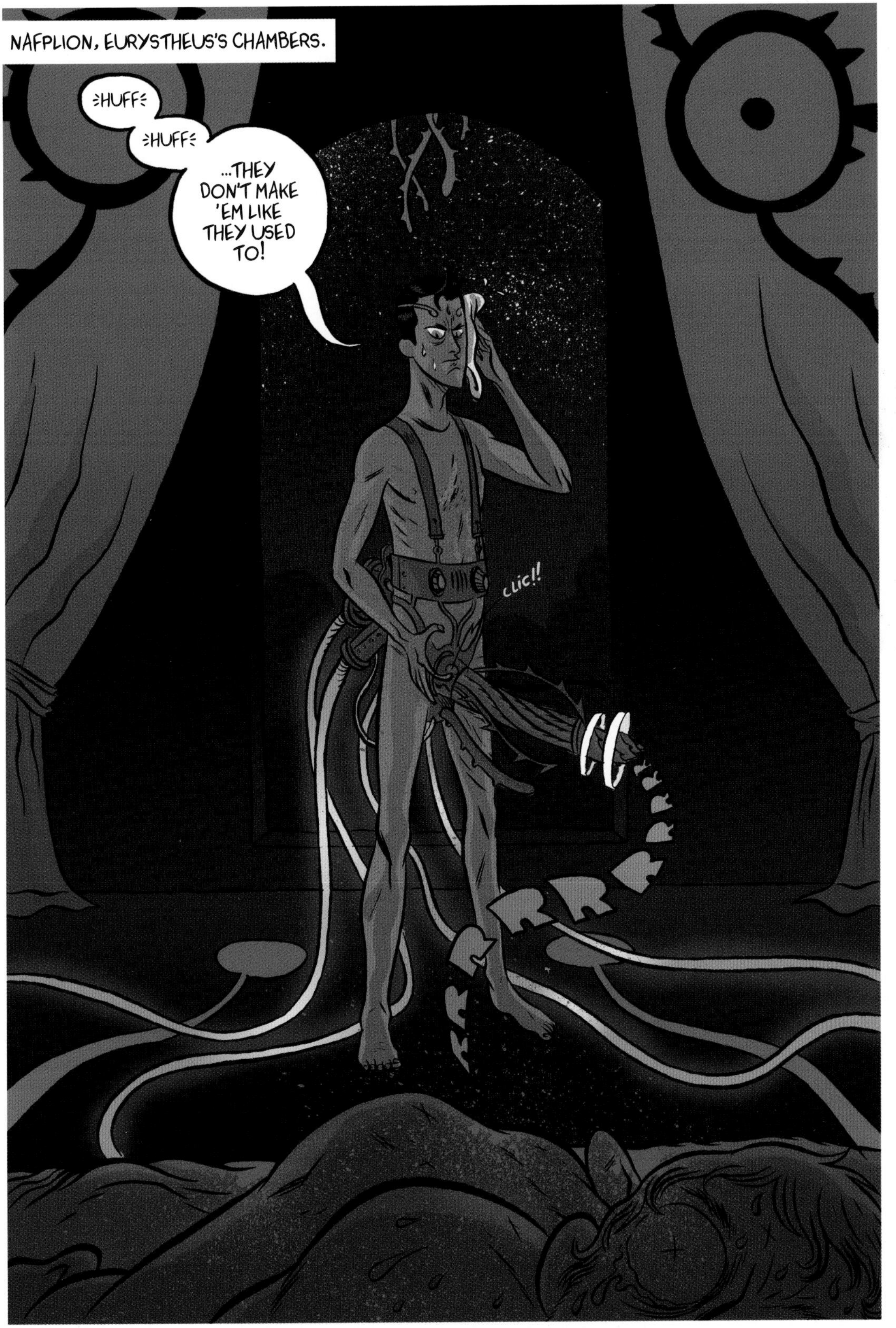
NAFPLION, EURYSTHEUS'S CHAMBERS.
HUFF
HUFF
...THEY DON'T MAKE 'EM LIKE THEY USED TO!
CLIC!!

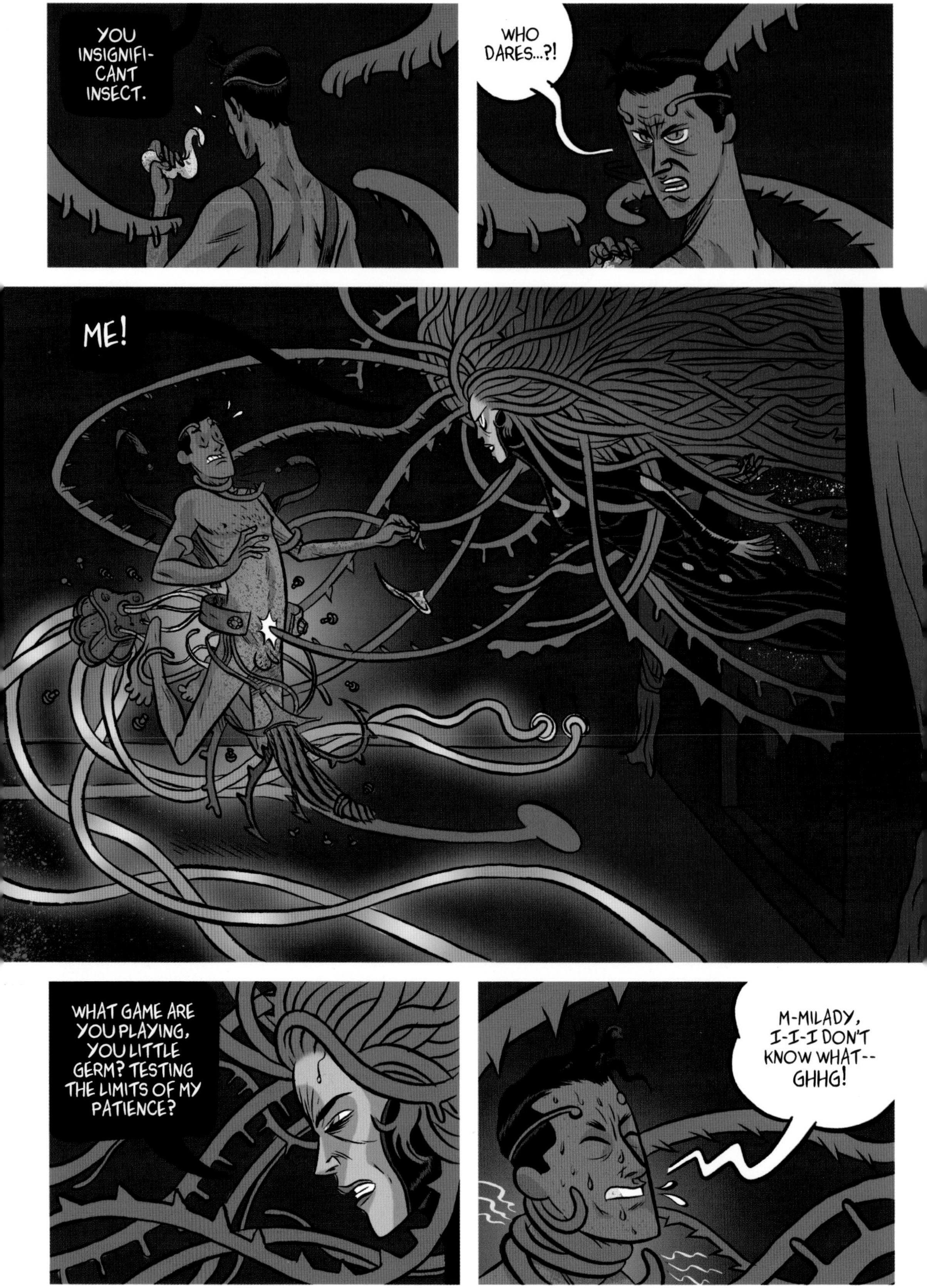
YOU INSIGNIFI-CANT INSECT.
WHO DARES...?!
ME!
WHAT GAME ARE YOU PLAYING, YOU LITTLE GERM? TESTING THE LIMITS OF MY PATIENCE?
M-MILADY, I-I-I DON'T KNOW WHAT-- GHHG!

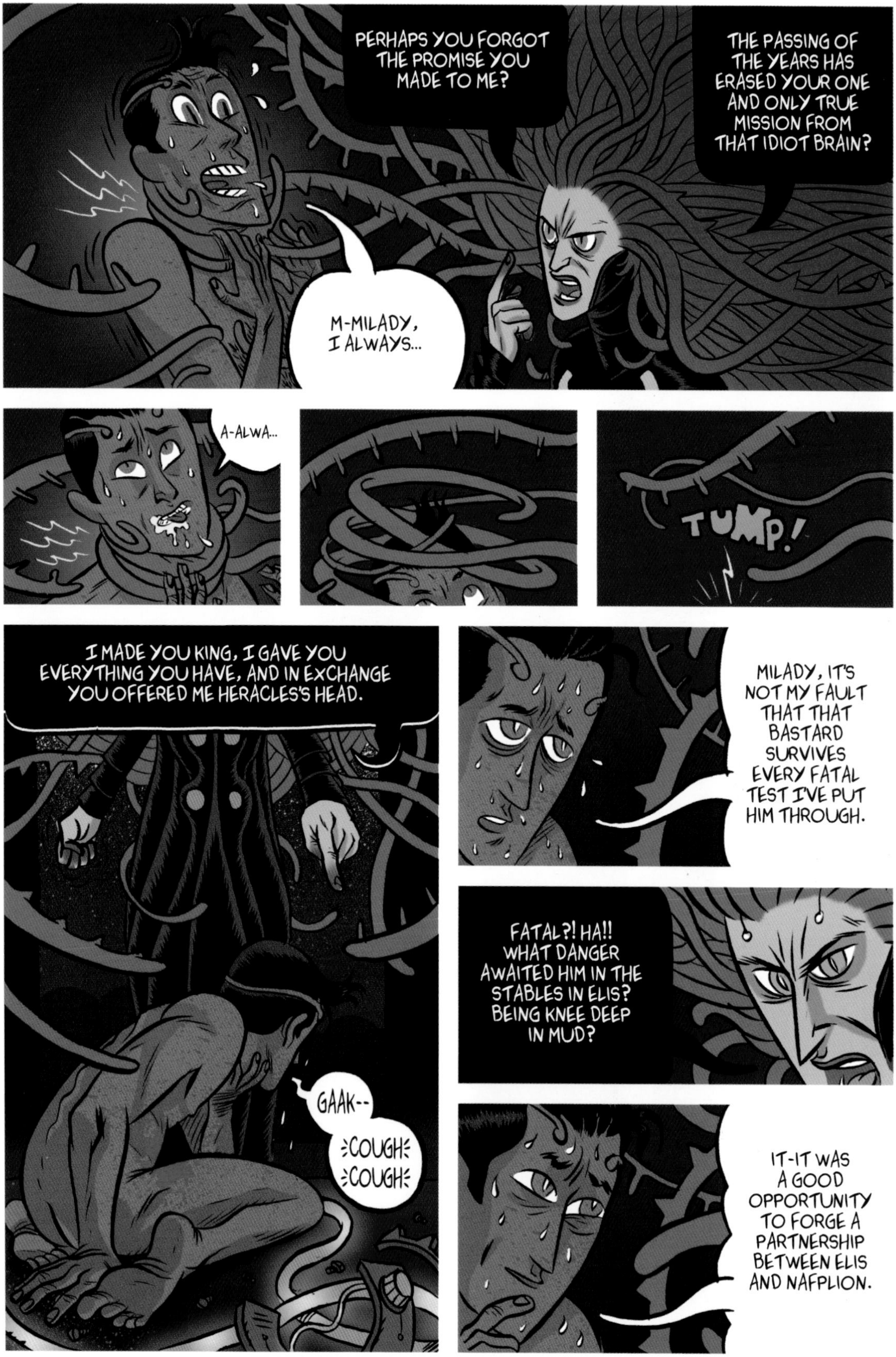
PERHAPS YOU FORGOT THE PROMISE YOU MADE TO ME?
THE PASSING OF THE YEARS HAS ERASED YOUR ONE AND ONLY TRUE MISSION FROM THAT IDIOT BRAIN?
M-MILADY, I ALWAYS...
A-ALWA...
TUMP!
I MADE YOU KING, I GAVE YOU EVERYTHING YOU HAVE, AND IN EXCHANGE YOU OFFERED ME HERACLES'S HEAD.
GAAK--
COUGH
COUGH
MILADY, IT'S NOT MY FAULT THAT THAT BASTARD SURVIVES EVERY FATAL TEST I'VE PUT HIM THROUGH.
FATAL?! HA!! WHAT DANGER AWAITED HIM IN THE STABLES IN ELIS? BEING KNEE DEEP IN MUD?
IT-IT WAS A GOOD OPPORTUNITY TO FORGE A PARTNERSHIP BETWEEN ELIS AND NAFPLION.

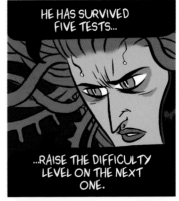
HE HAS SURVIVED FIVE TESTS...

...RAISE THE DIFFICULTY LEVEL ON THE NEXT ONE.

O-OF COURSE, MILADY. I'LL SEND HIM TO HIS DEATH, I ASSURE YOU.

YOU BETTER, EURYSTHEUS...

...YOU BETTER.

PLOP!

WHORE.

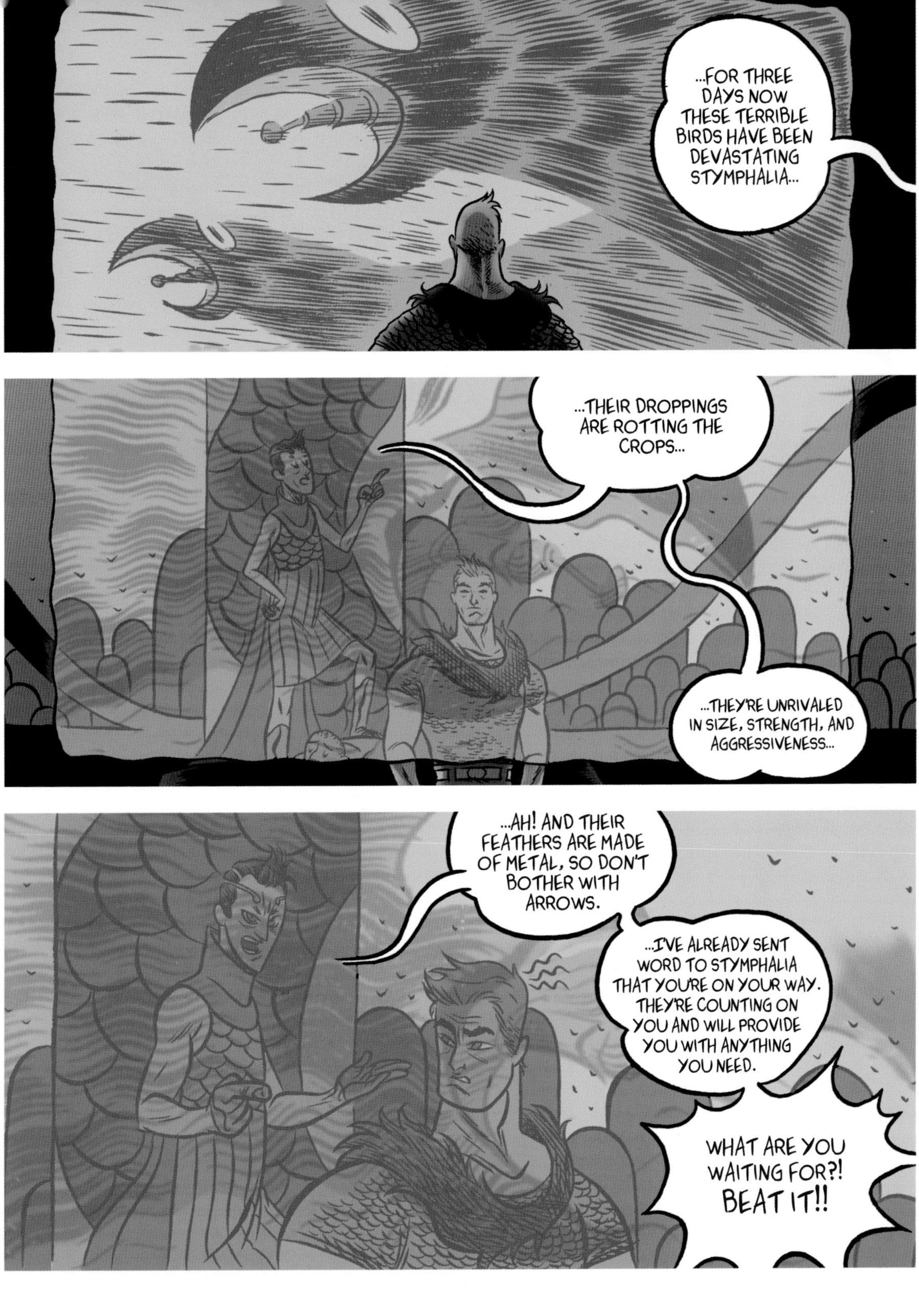
...FOR THREE DAYS NOW THESE TERRIBLE BIRDS HAVE BEEN DEVASTATING STYMPHALIA...
...THEIR DROPPINGS ARE ROTTING THE CROPS...
...THEY'RE UNRIVALED IN SIZE, STRENGTH, AND AGGRESSIVENESS...
...AH! AND THEIR FEATHERS ARE MADE OF METAL, SO DON'T BOTHER WITH ARROWS.
...I'VE ALREADY SENT WORD TO STYMPHALIA THAT YOU'RE ON YOUR WAY. THEY'RE COUNTING ON YOU AND WILL PROVIDE YOU WITH ANYTHING YOU NEED.
WHAT ARE YOU WAITING FOR?! BEAT IT!!

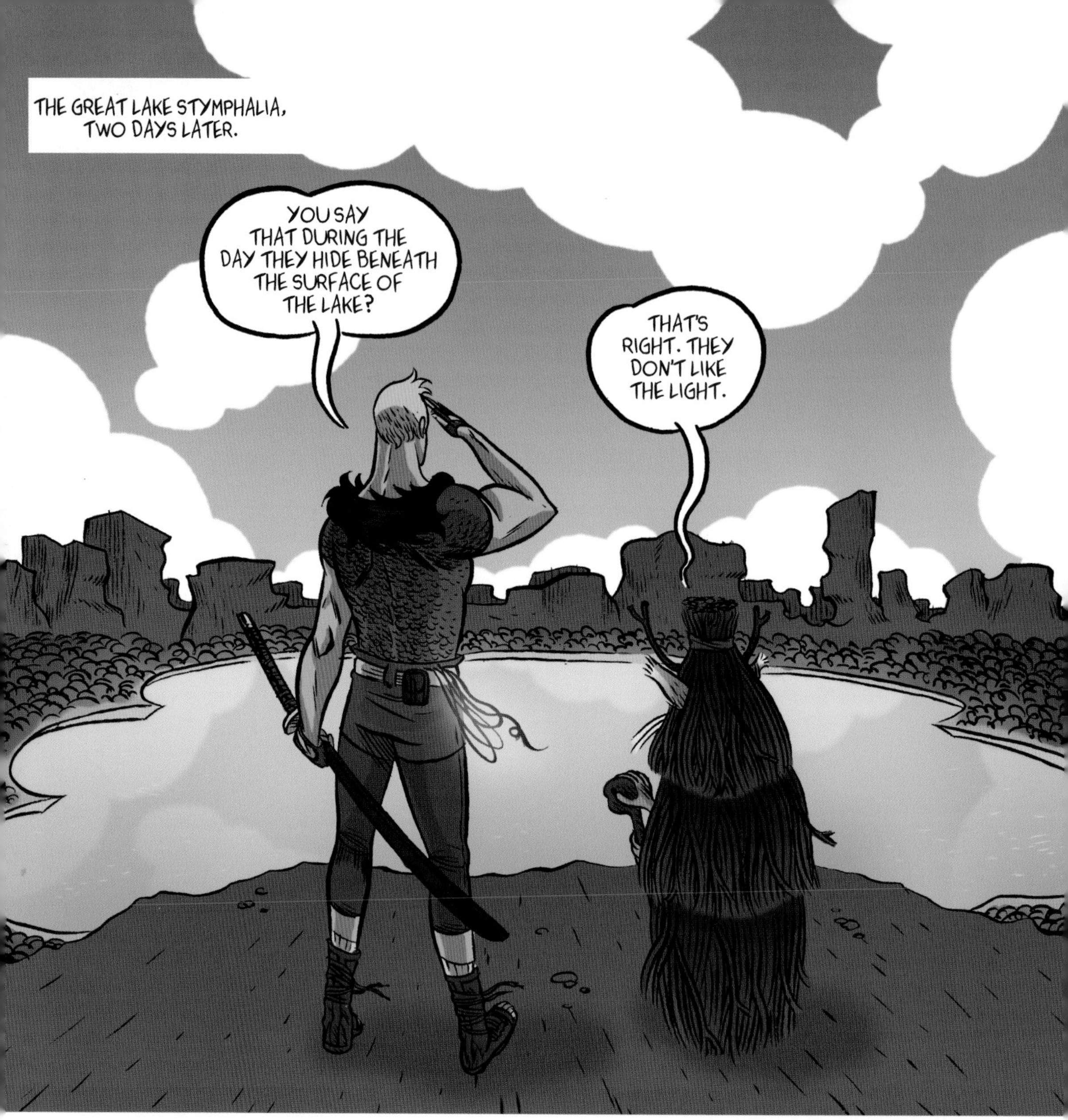
THE GREAT LAKE STYMPHALIA,
TWO DAYS LATER.
YOU SAY THAT DURING THE DAY THEY HIDE BENEATH THE SURFACE OF THE LAKE?
THAT'S RIGHT. THEY DON'T LIKE THE LIGHT.

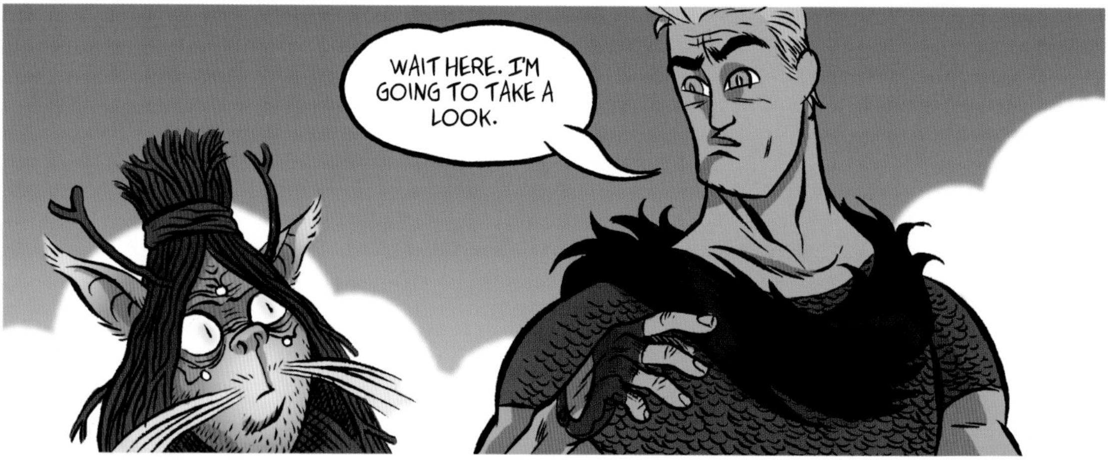
WAIT HERE. I'M GOING TO TAKE A LOOK.

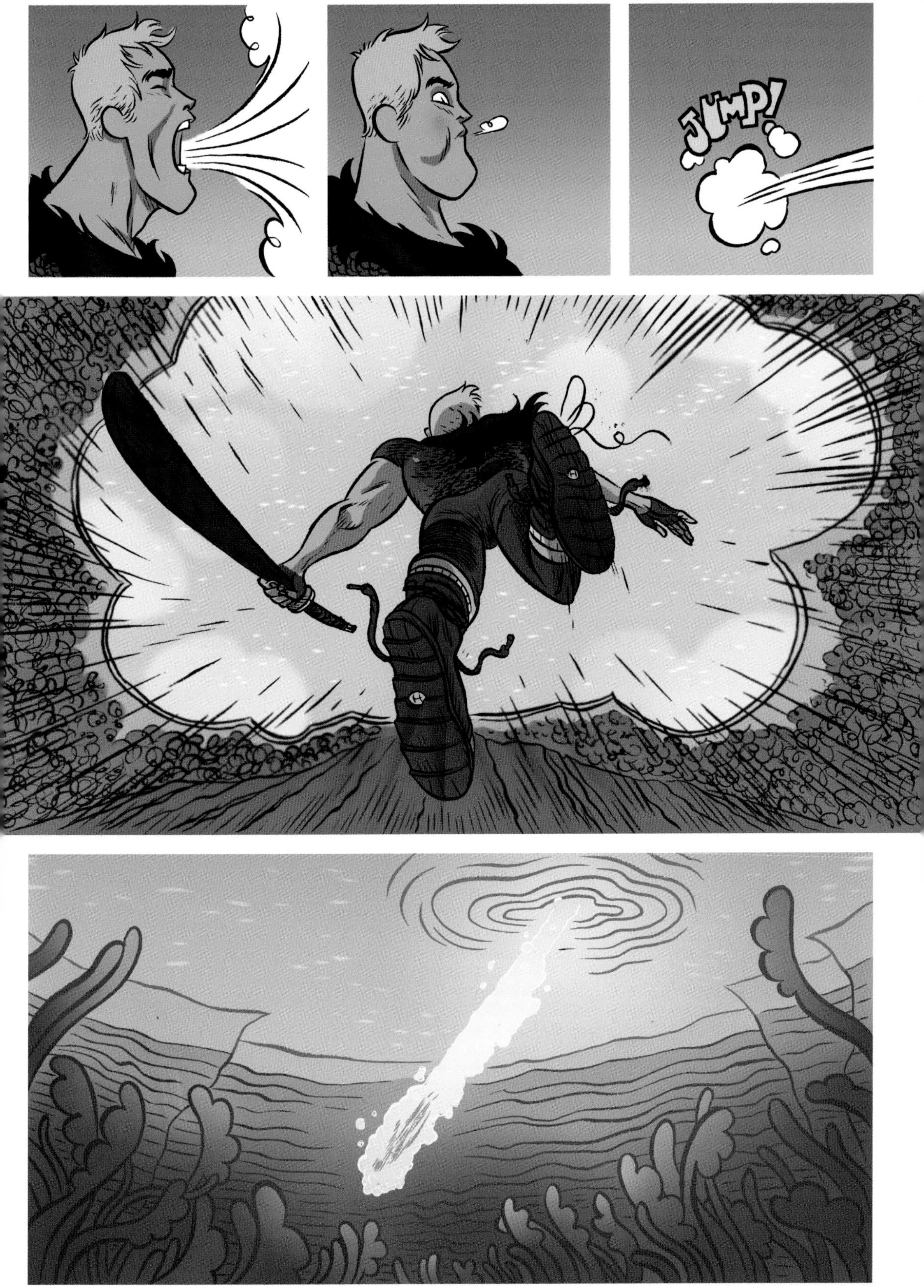
JUMP!

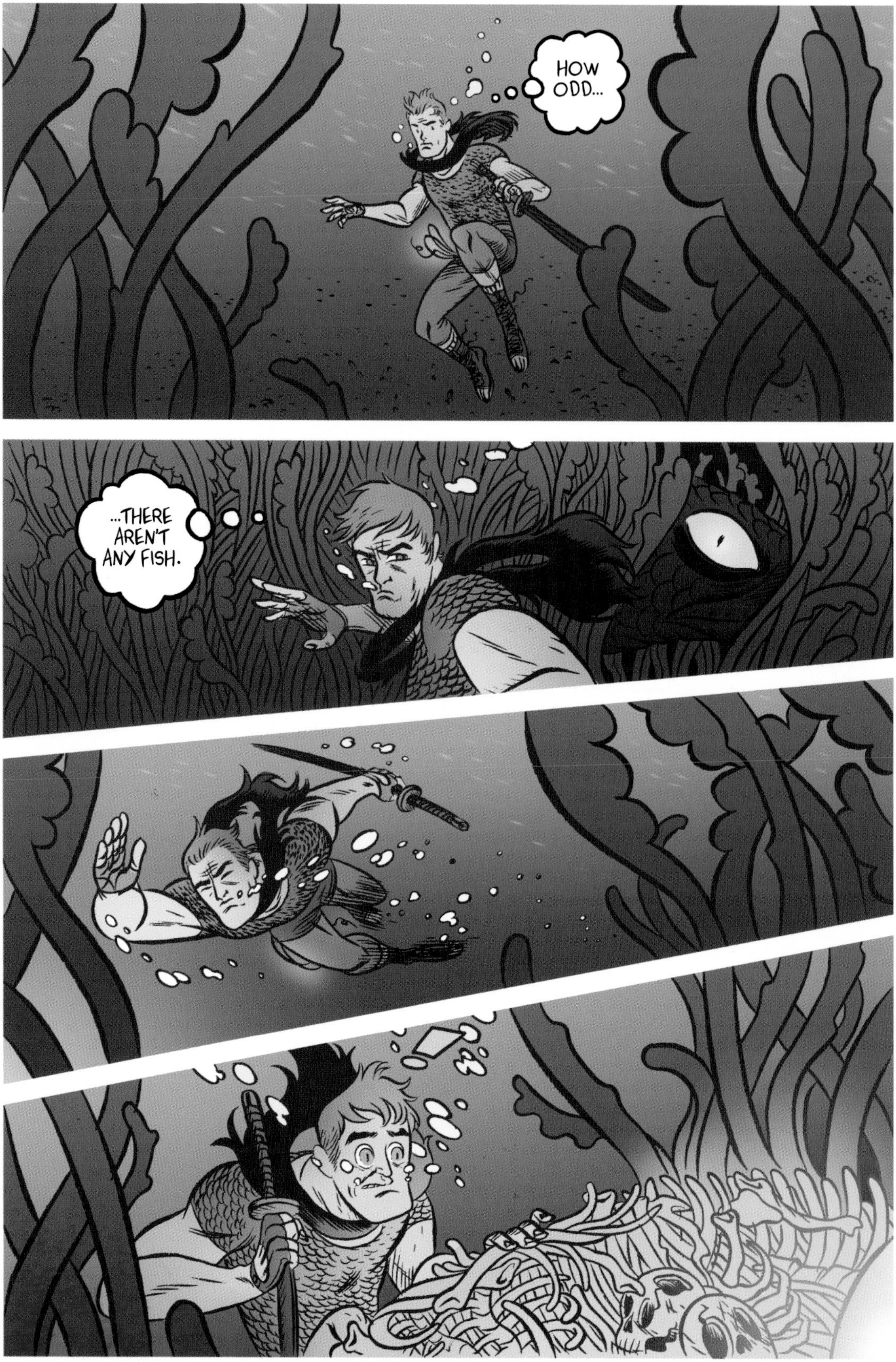
HOW ODD...
...THERE AREN'T ANY FISH.

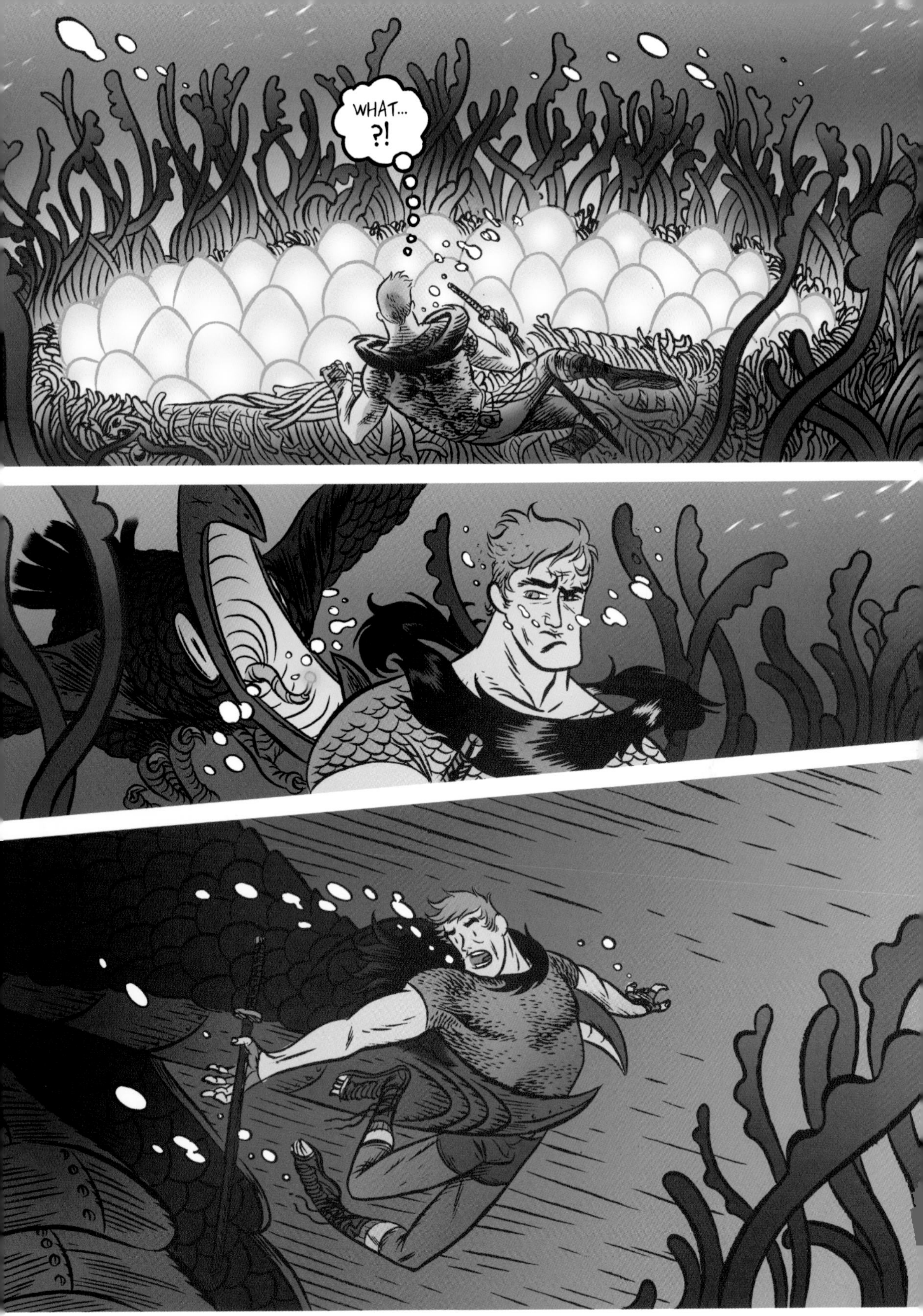
WHAT...
?!

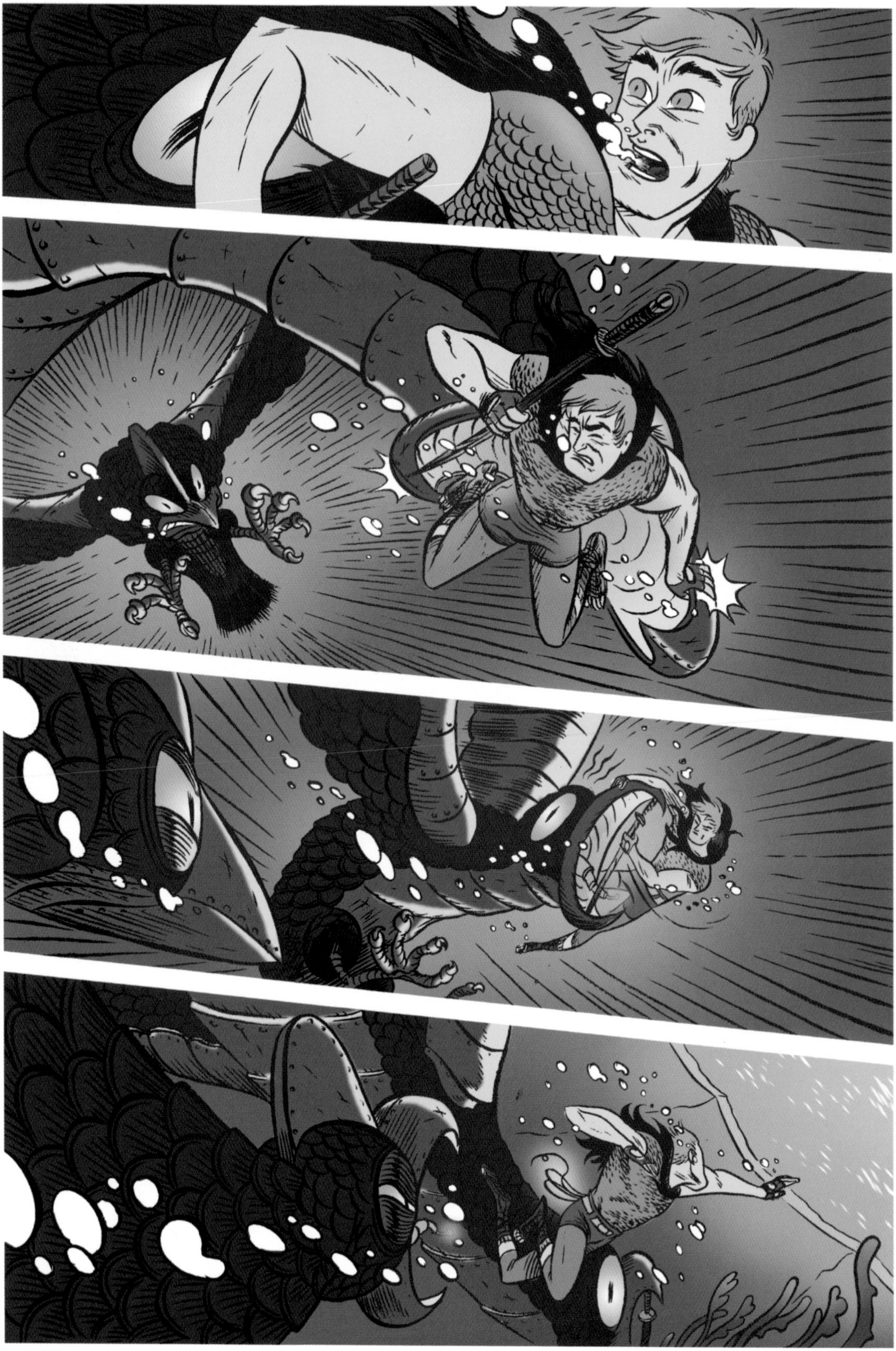

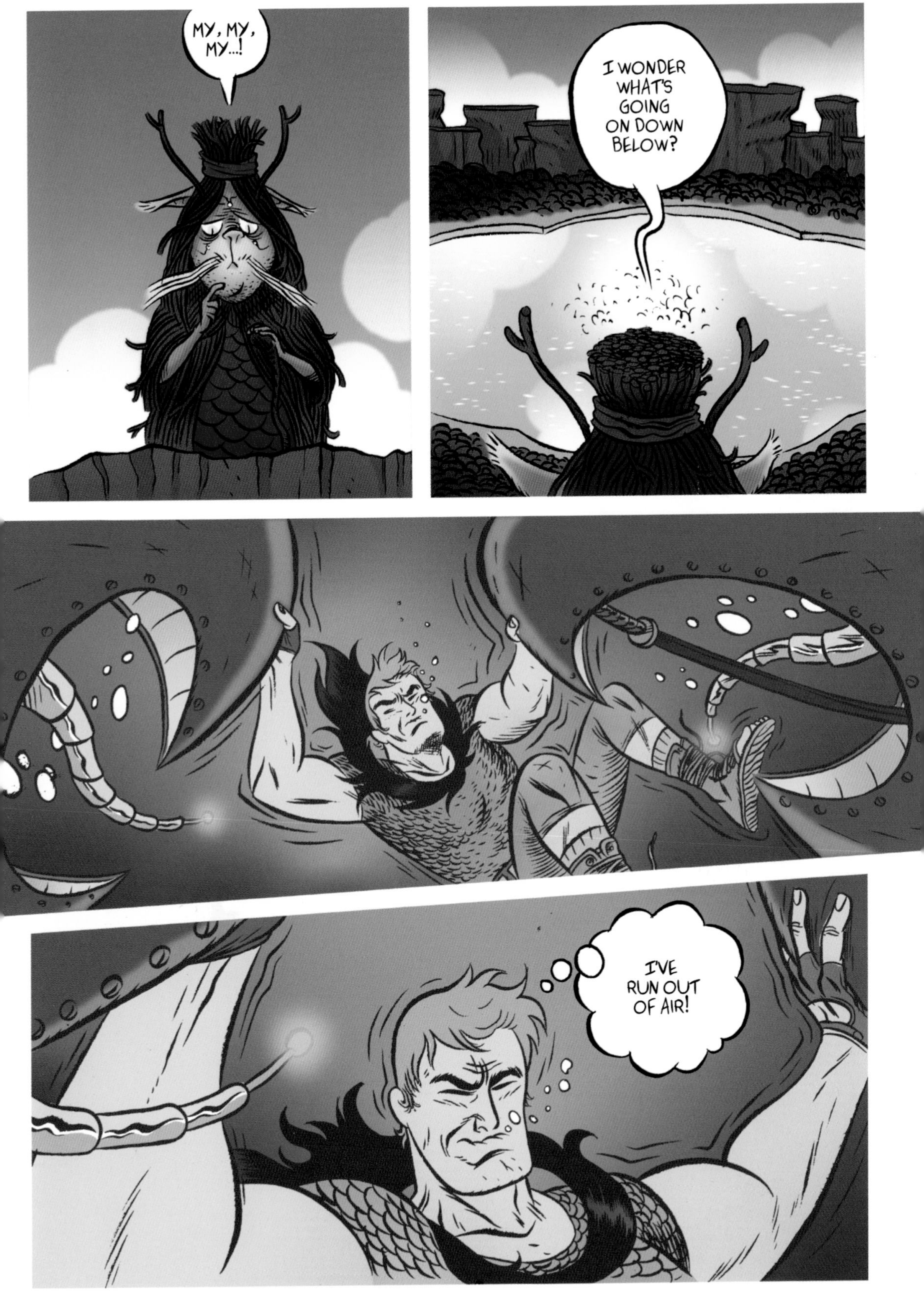
MY, MY, MY...!
I WONDER WHAT'S GOING ON DOWN BELOW?
I'VE RUN OUT OF AIR!

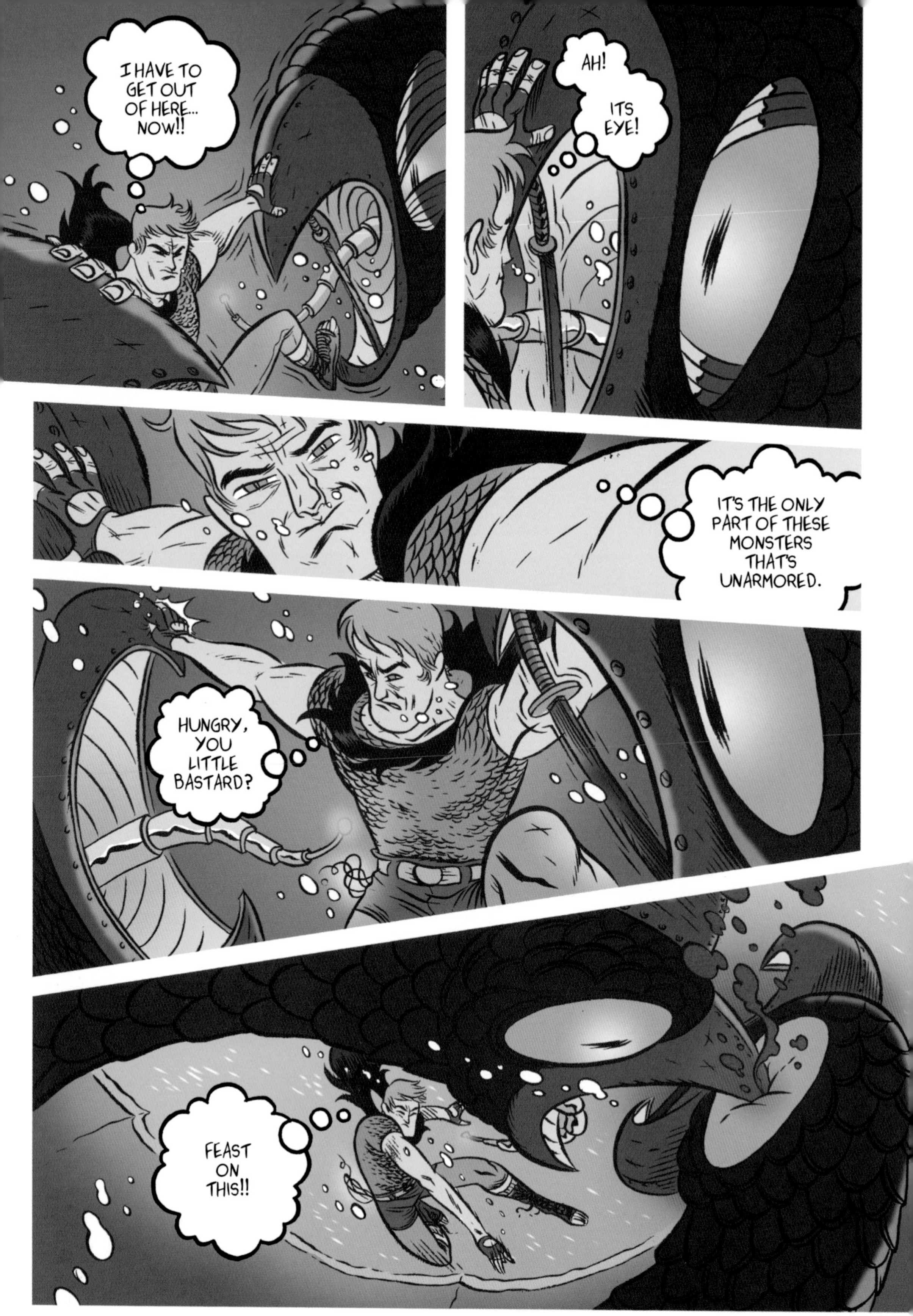
I HAVE TO GET OUT OF HERE... NOW!!
AH!
ITS EYE!
IT'S THE ONLY PART OF THESE MONSTERS THAT'S UNARMORED.
HUNGRY, YOU LITTLE BASTARD?
FEAST ON THIS!!

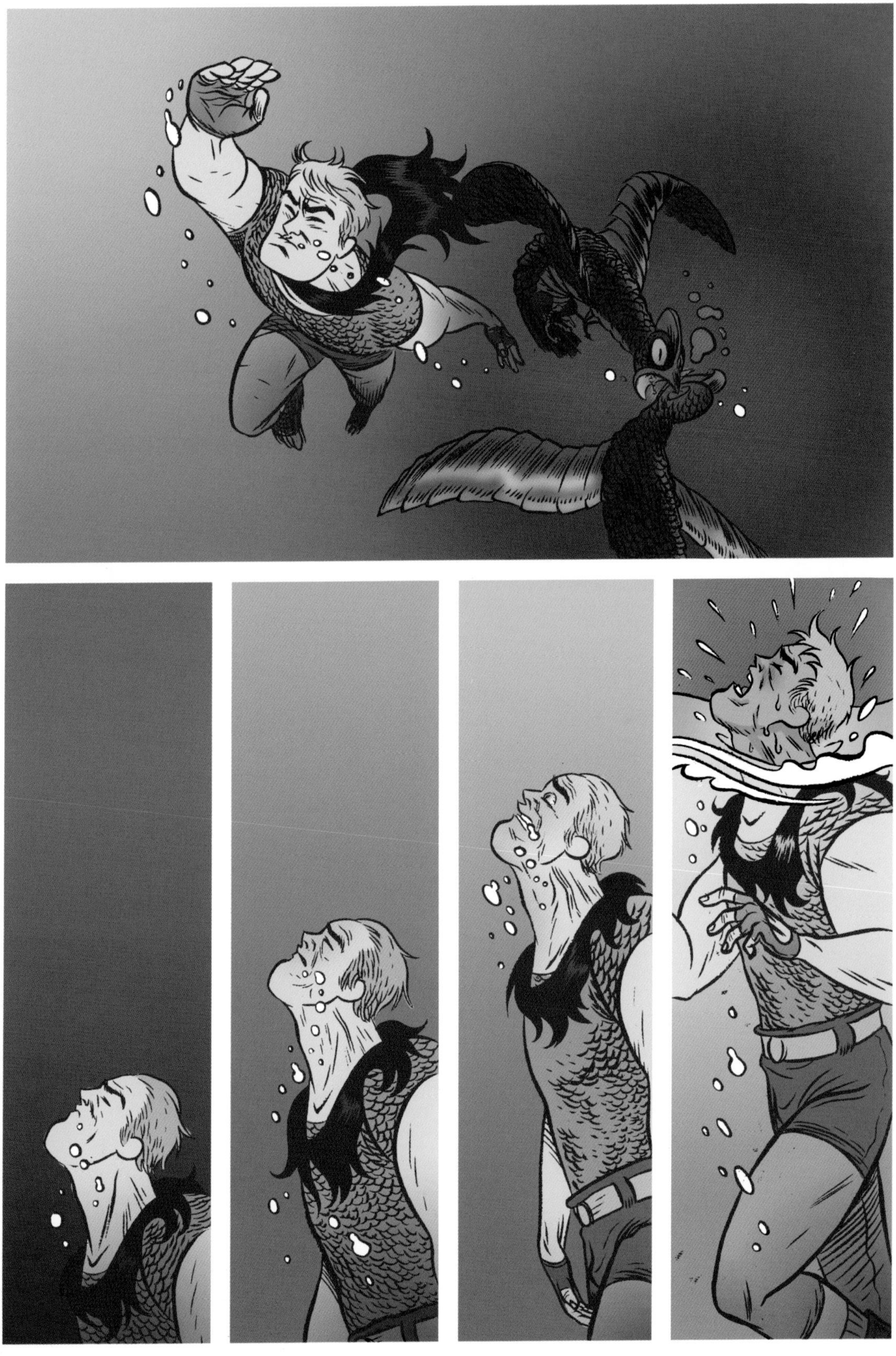

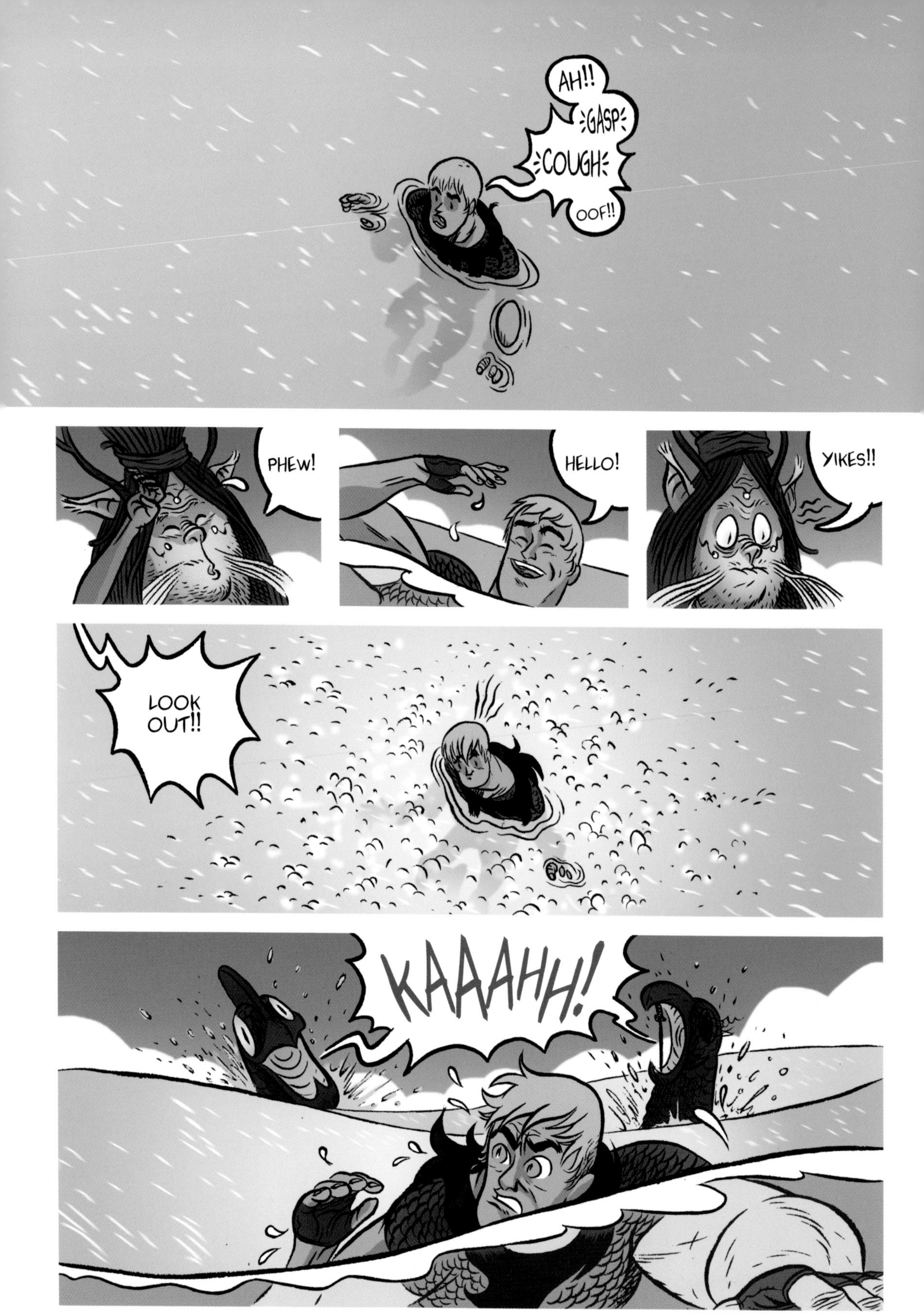
AH!!
GASP
COUGH
OOF!!
PHEW!
HELLO!
YIKES!!
LOOK OUT!!
KAAAHH!

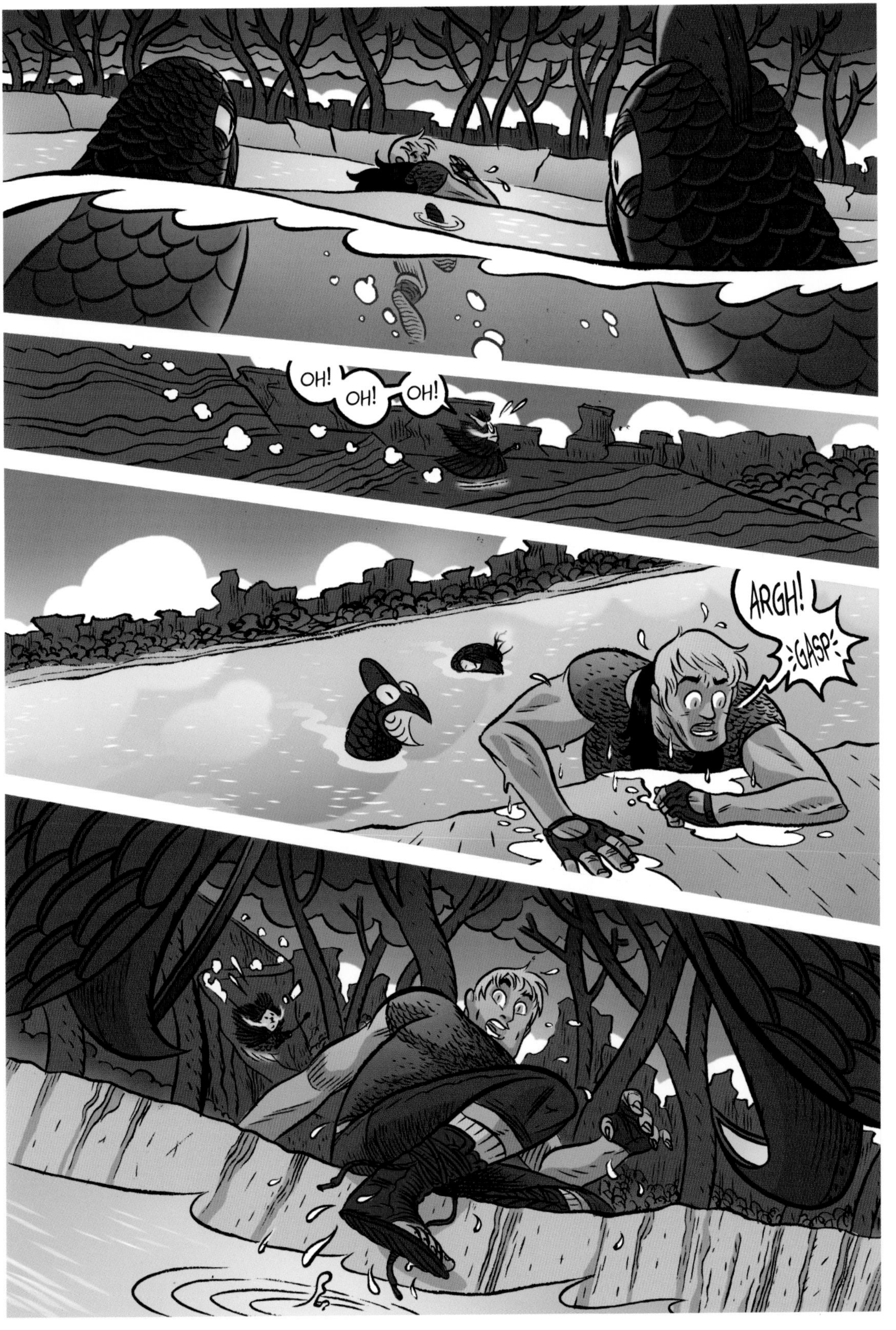
OH!
OH!
OH!
ARGH!
GASP

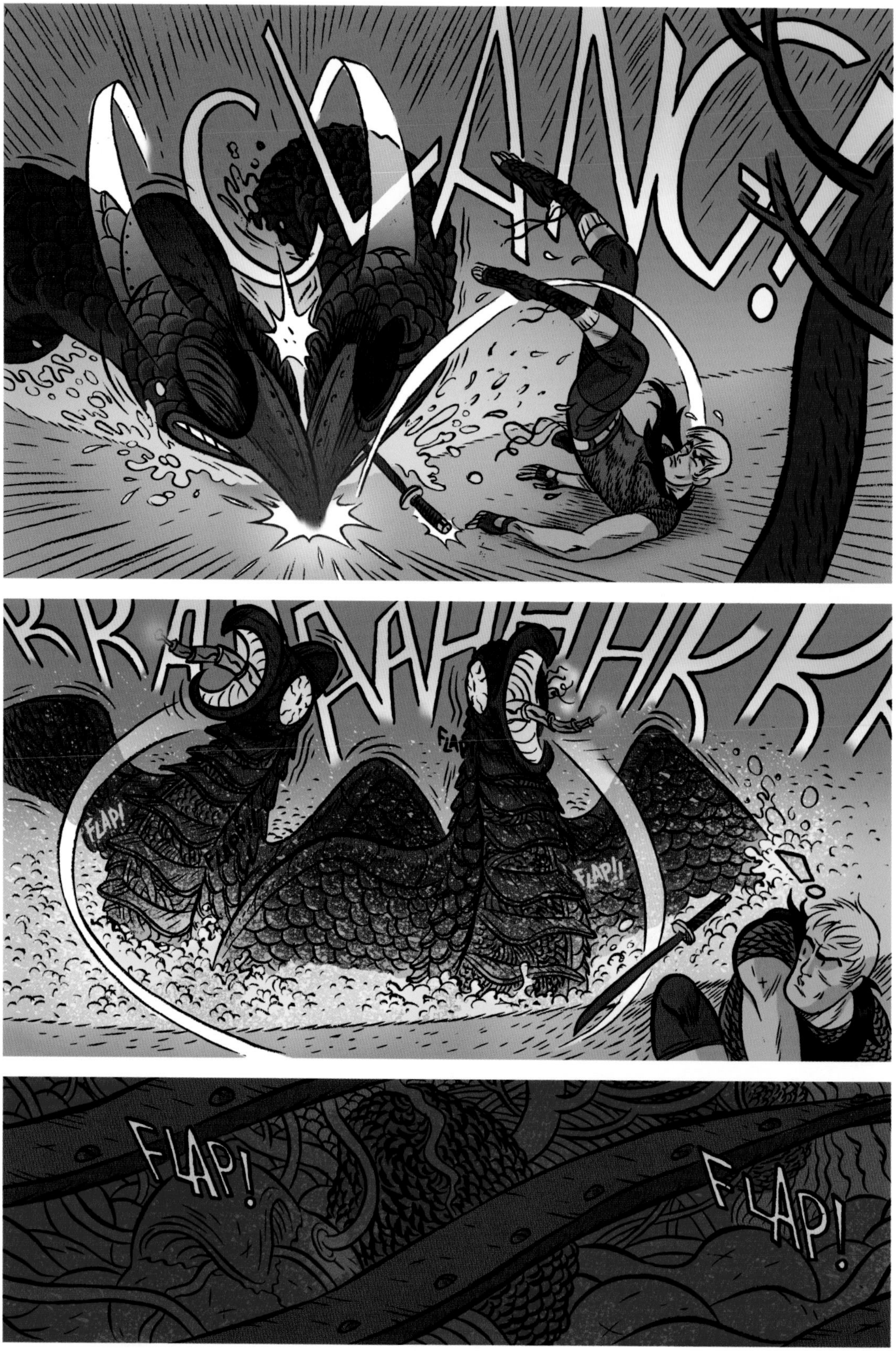
CLANG!
FLAP!
FLAP!!
FLAP!
FLAP!

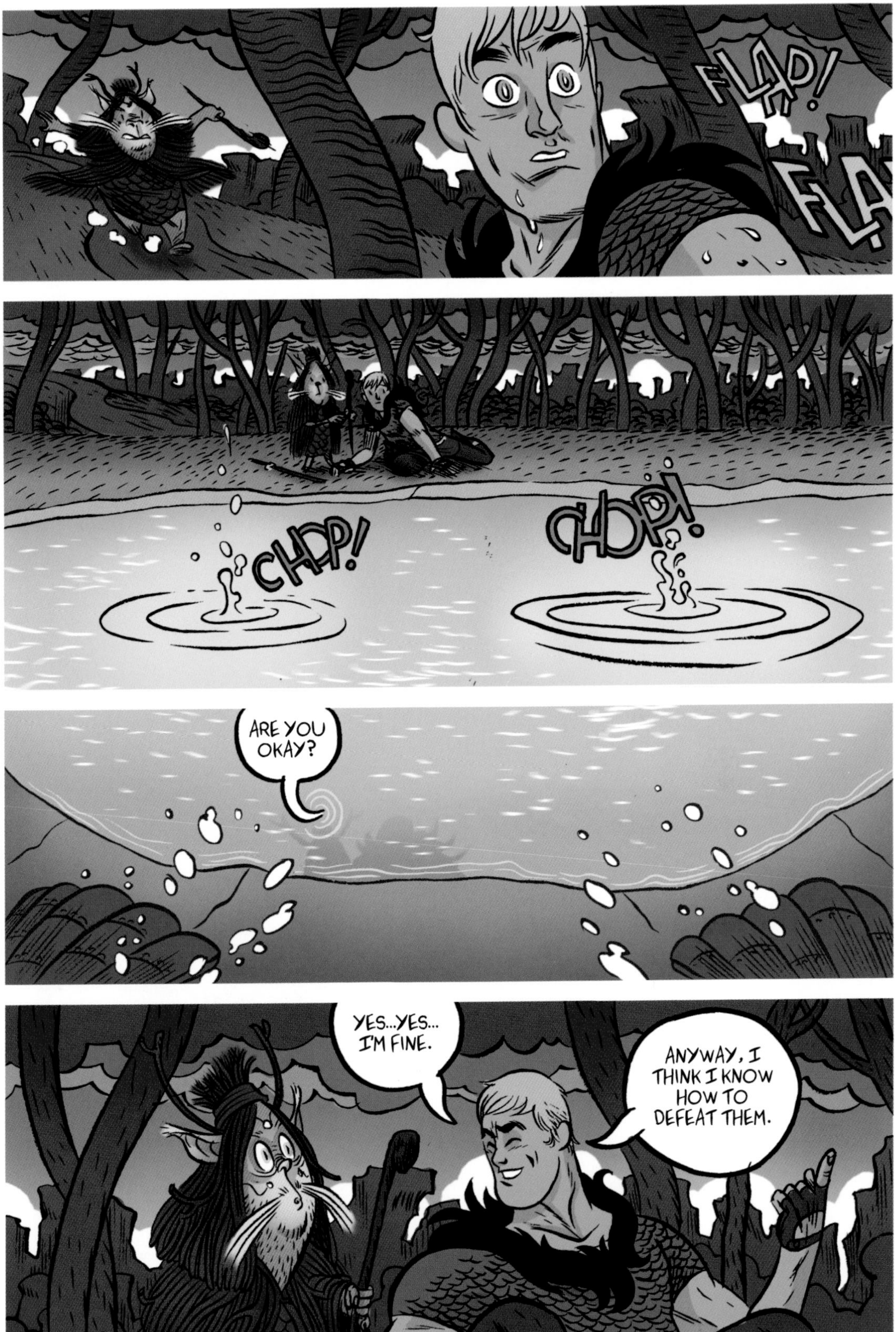
FLAP!
FLA
CHOP!
CHOP!
ARE YOU OKAY?
YES...YES... I'M FINE.
ANYWAY, I THINK I KNOW HOW TO DEFEAT THEM.

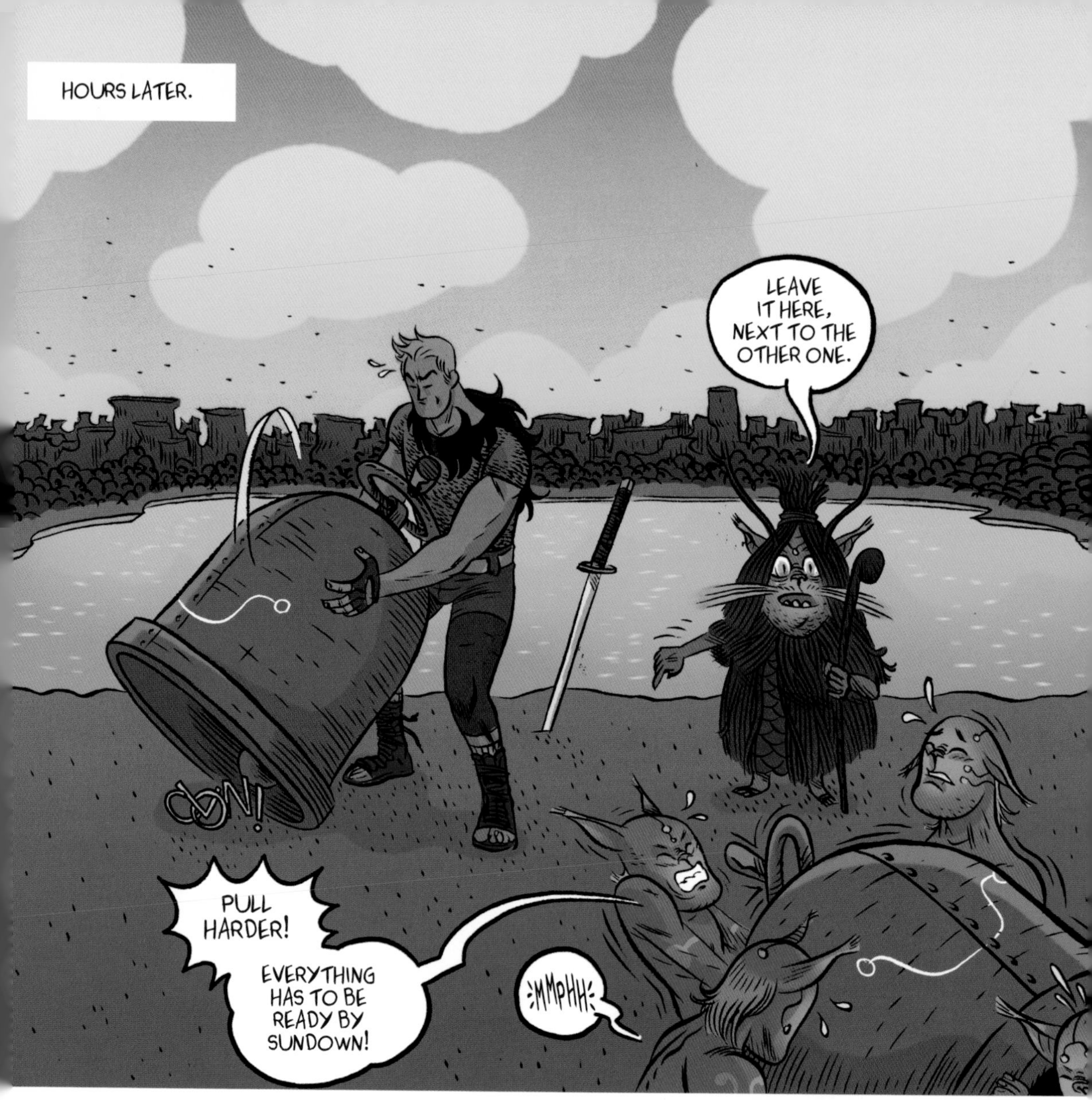
HOURS LATER.
LEAVE IT HERE, NEXT TO THE OTHER ONE.
DON!
PULL HARDER!
EVERYTHING HAS TO BE READY BY SUNDOWN!
MMPHH

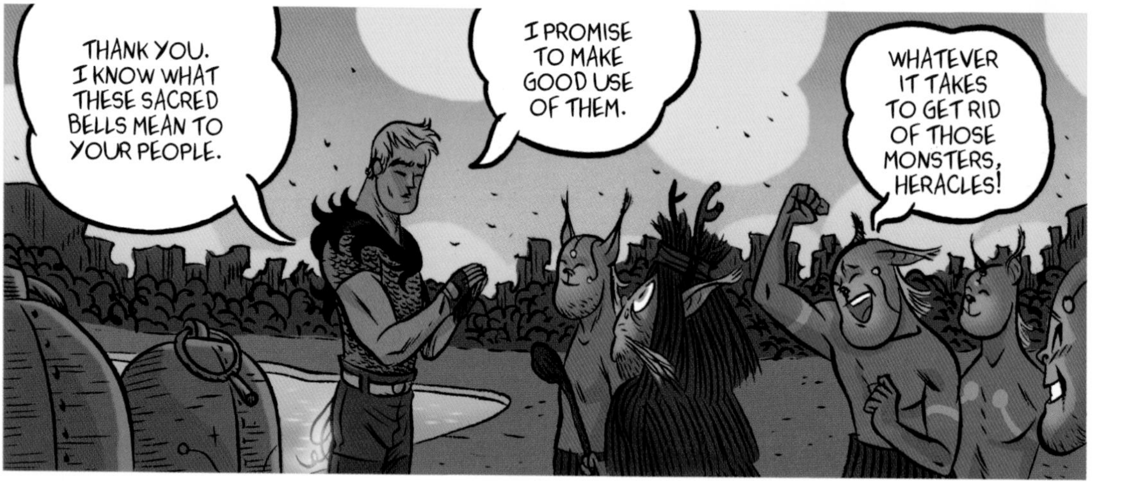
THANK YOU. I KNOW WHAT THESE SACRED BELLS MEAN TO YOUR PEOPLE.
I PROMISE TO MAKE GOOD USE OF THEM.
WHATEVER IT TAKES TO GET RID OF THOSE MONSTERS, HERACLES!

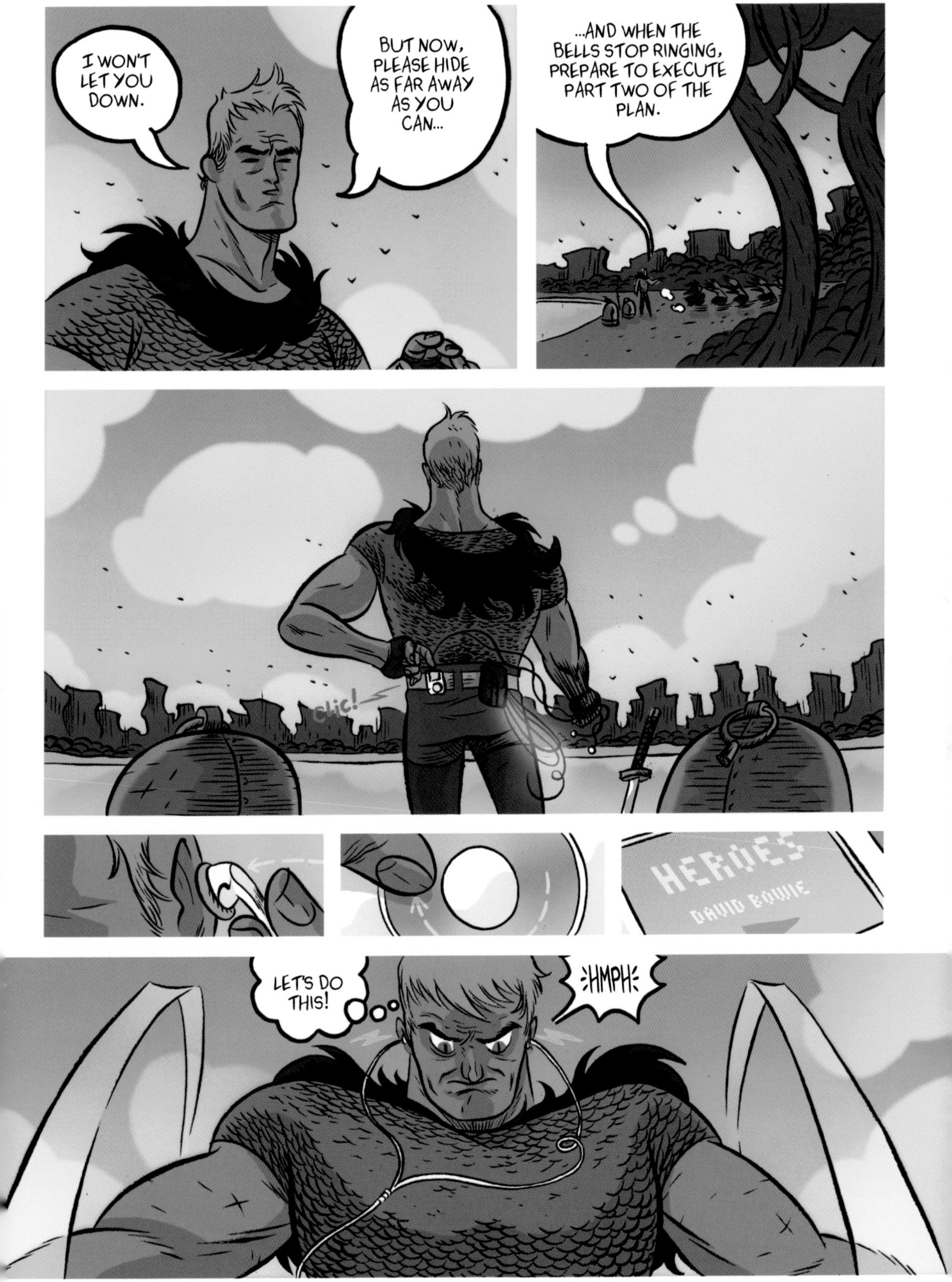
I WON'T LET YOU DOWN.
BUT NOW, PLEASE HIDE AS FAR AWAY AS YOU CAN...
...AND WHEN THE BELLS STOP RINGING, PREPARE TO EXECUTE PART TWO OF THE PLAN.
CLIC!
HEROES
DAVID BOWIE
LET'S DO THIS!
HMPH

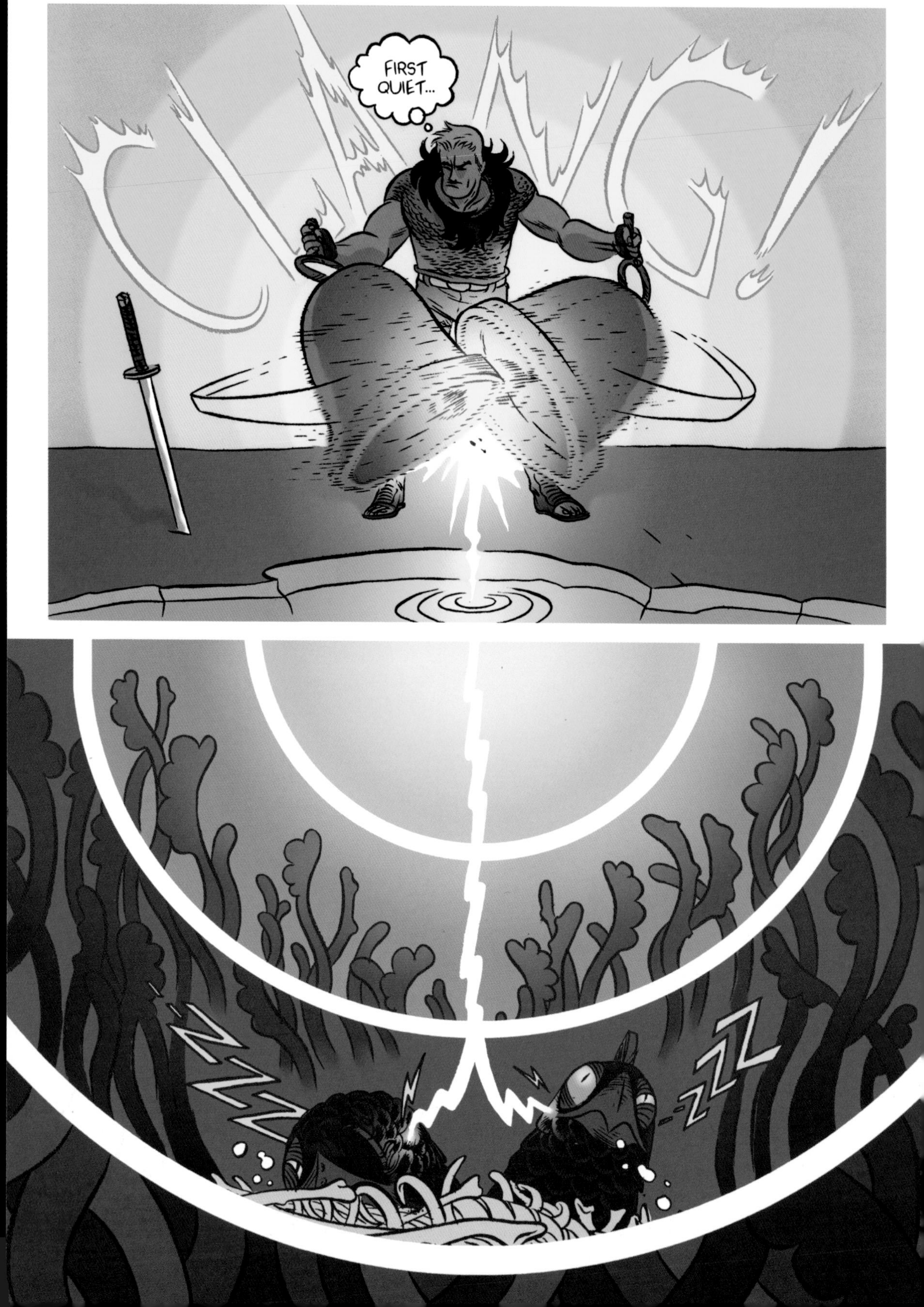
FIRST QUIET...
CLANG!

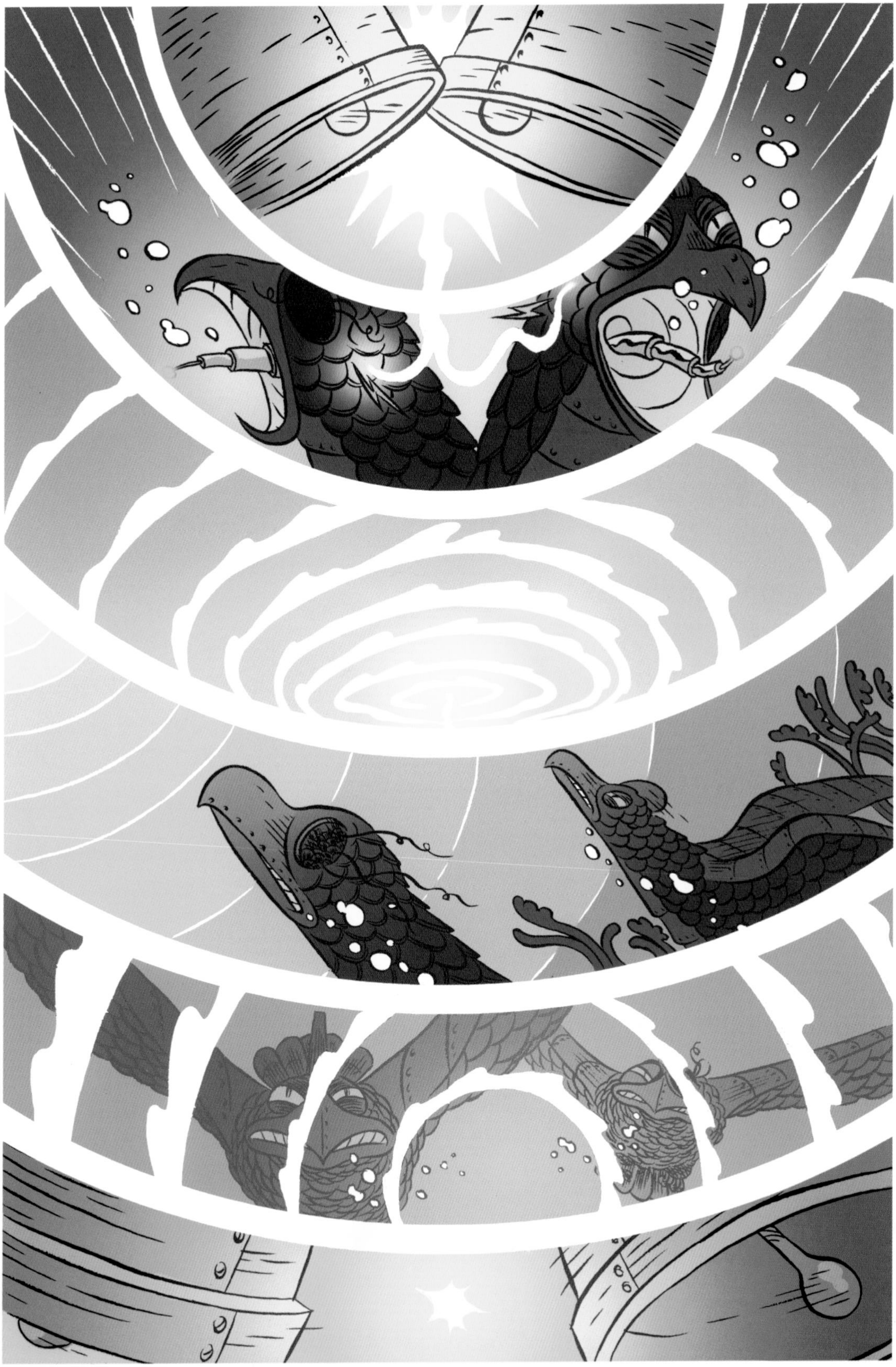

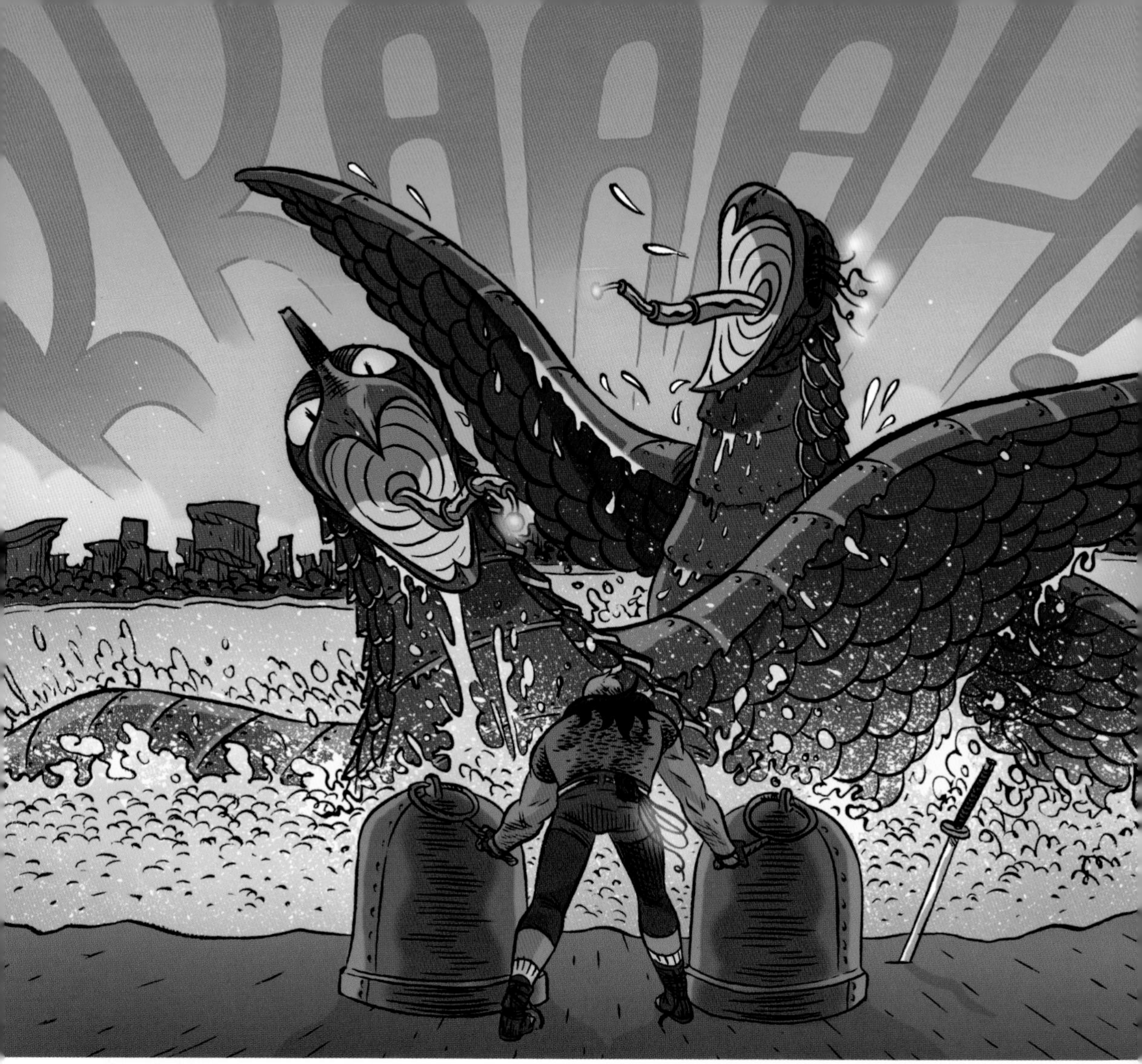

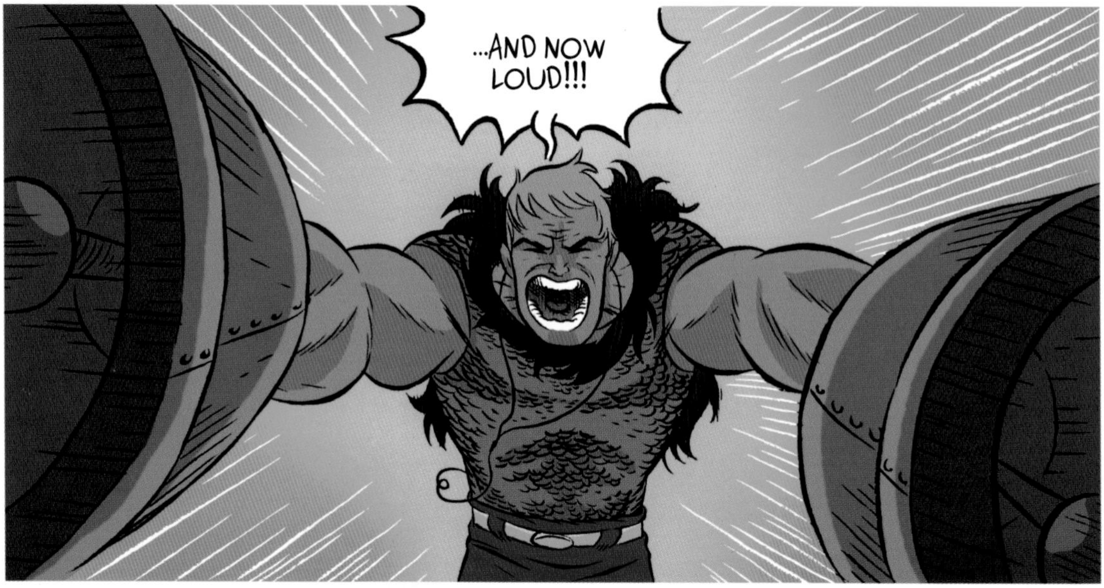
...AND NOW LOUD!!!

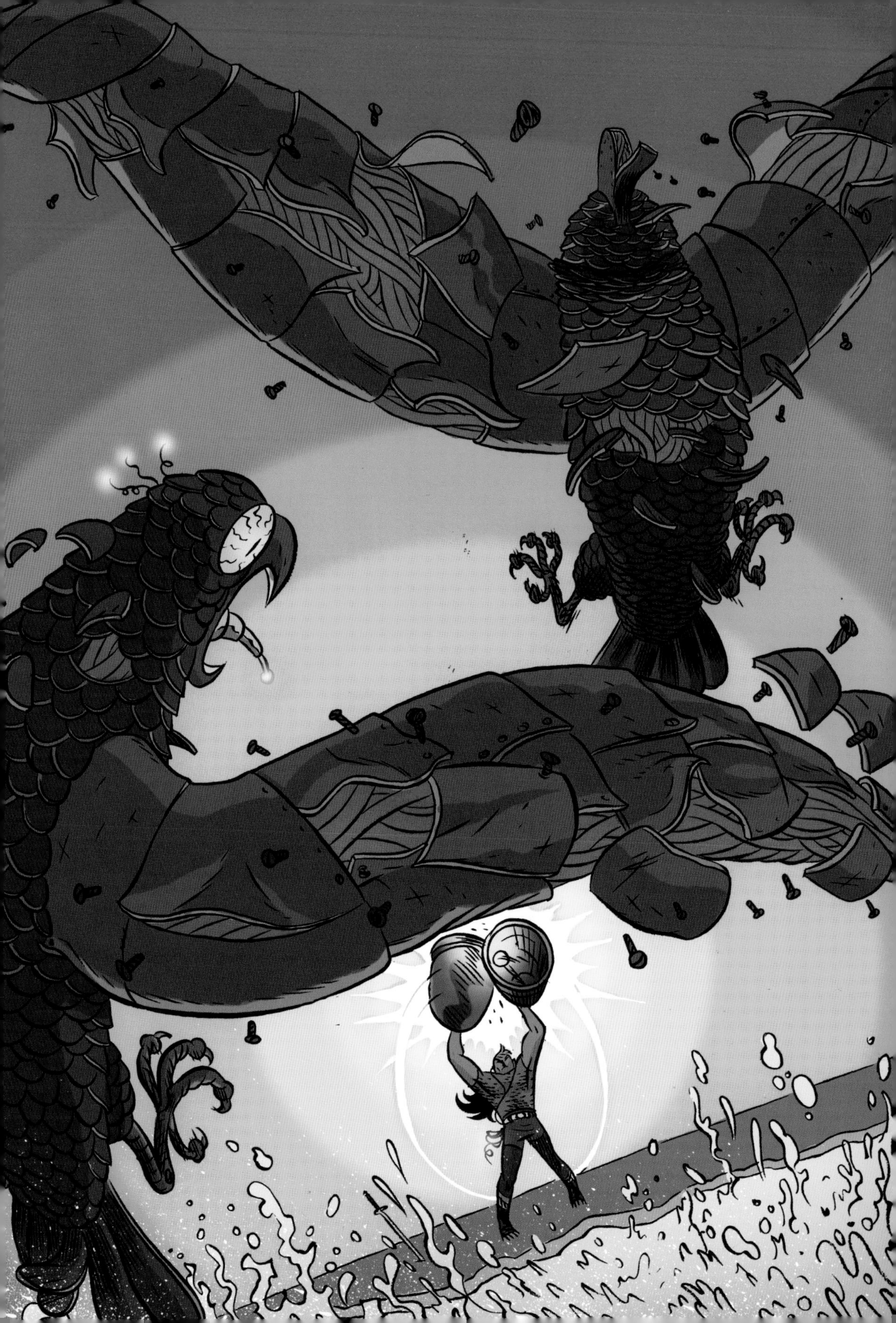

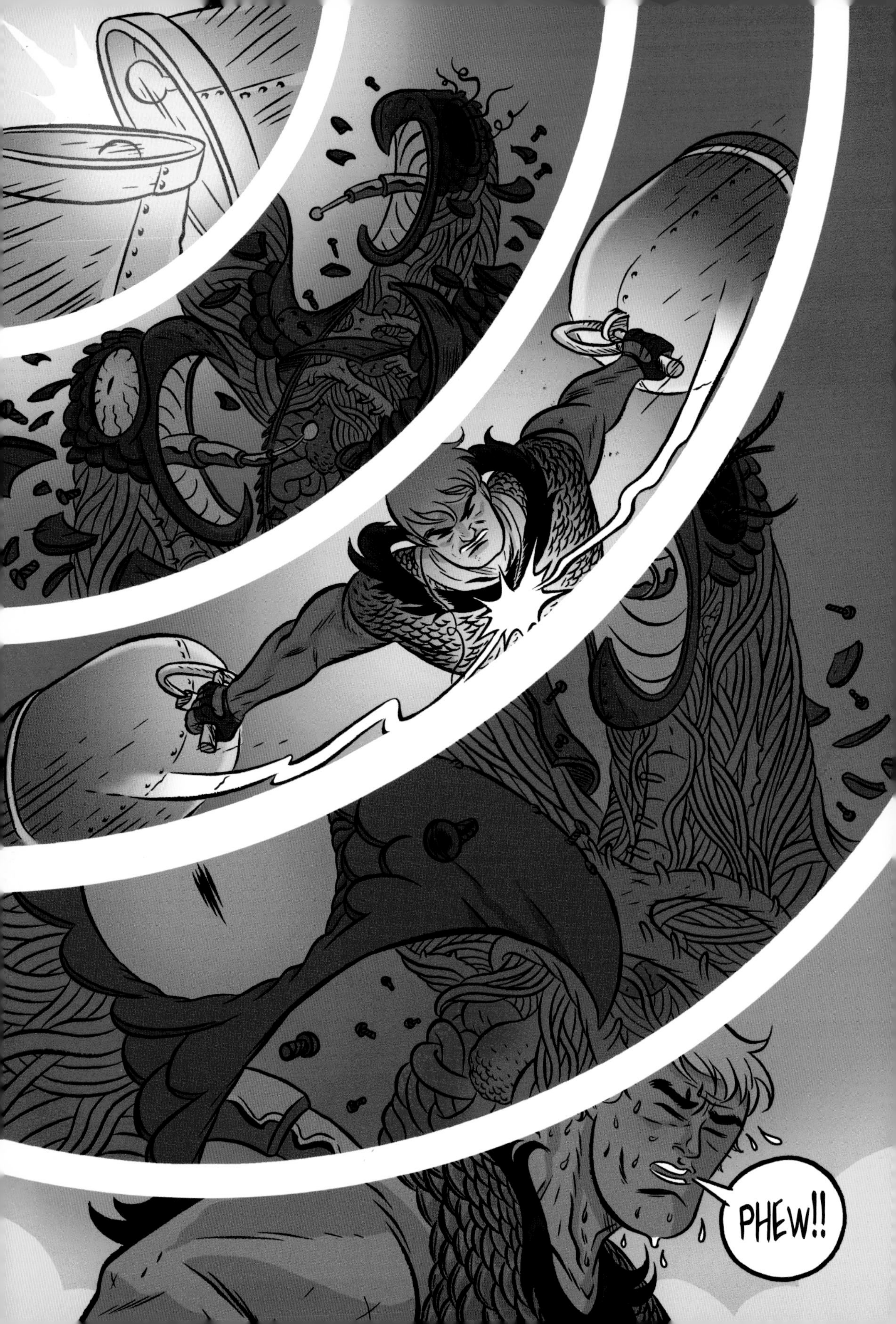
PHEW!!

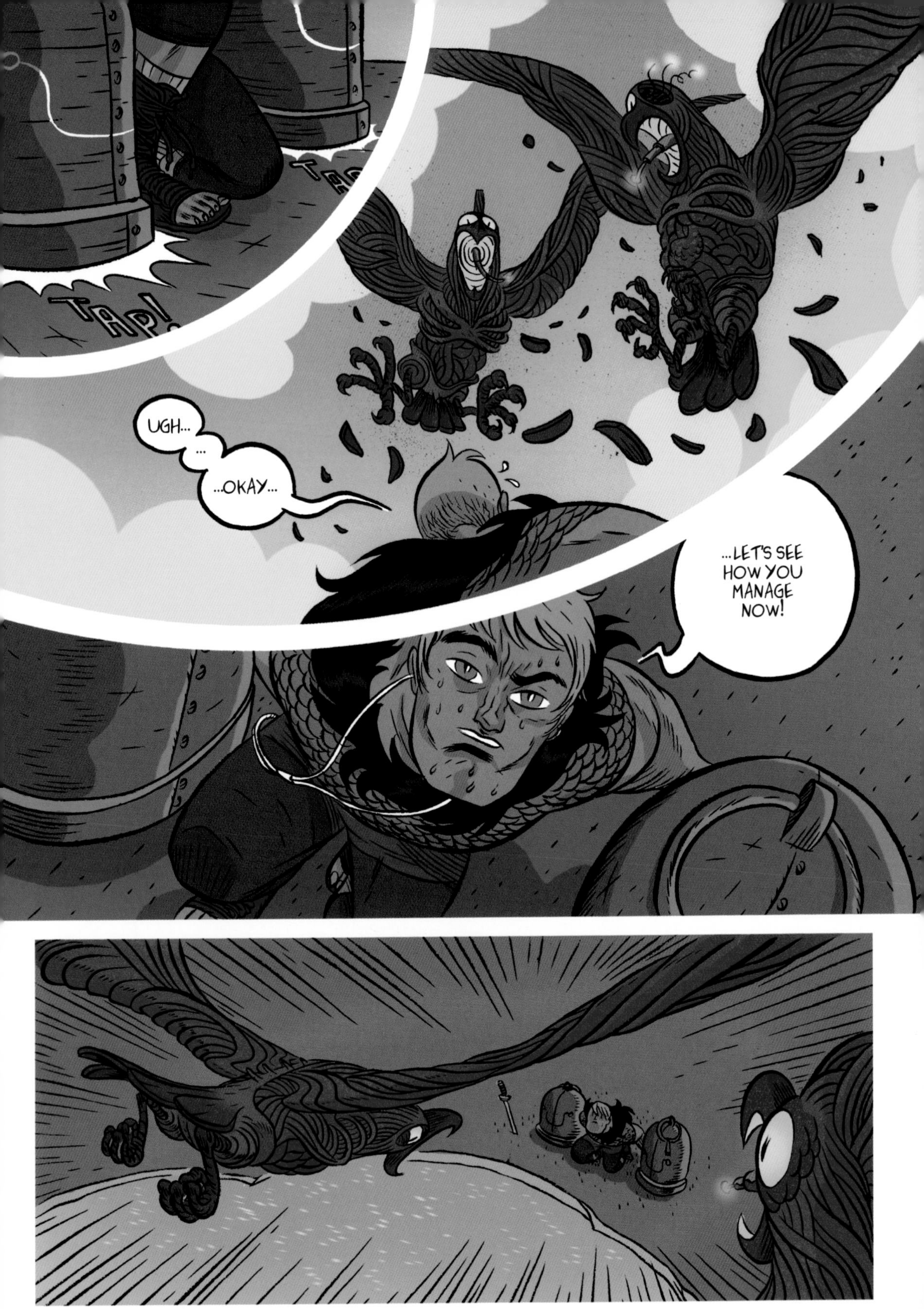

TAP!
TAP!
UGH... ... ...OKAY...
...LET'S SEE HOW YOU MANAGE NOW!

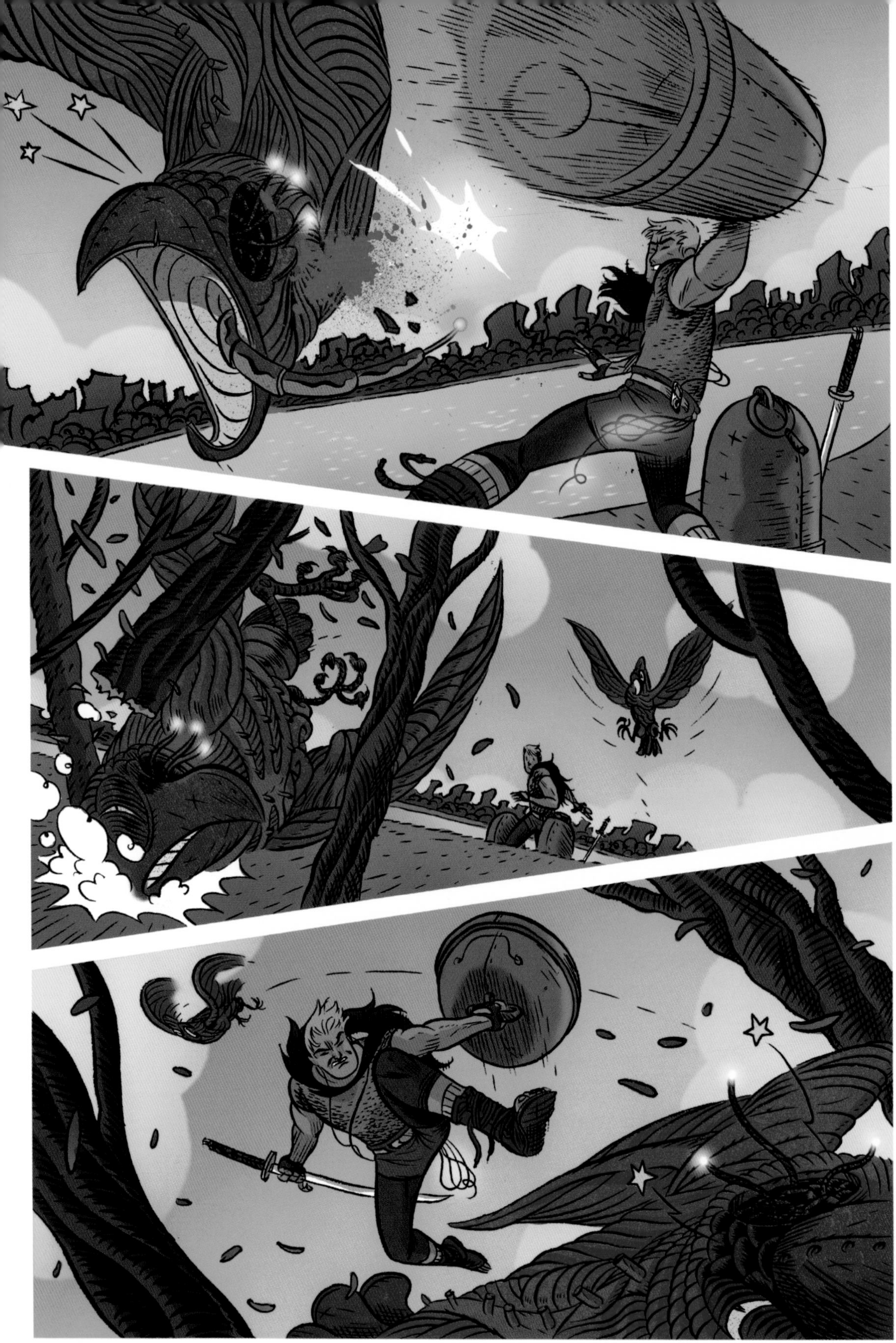

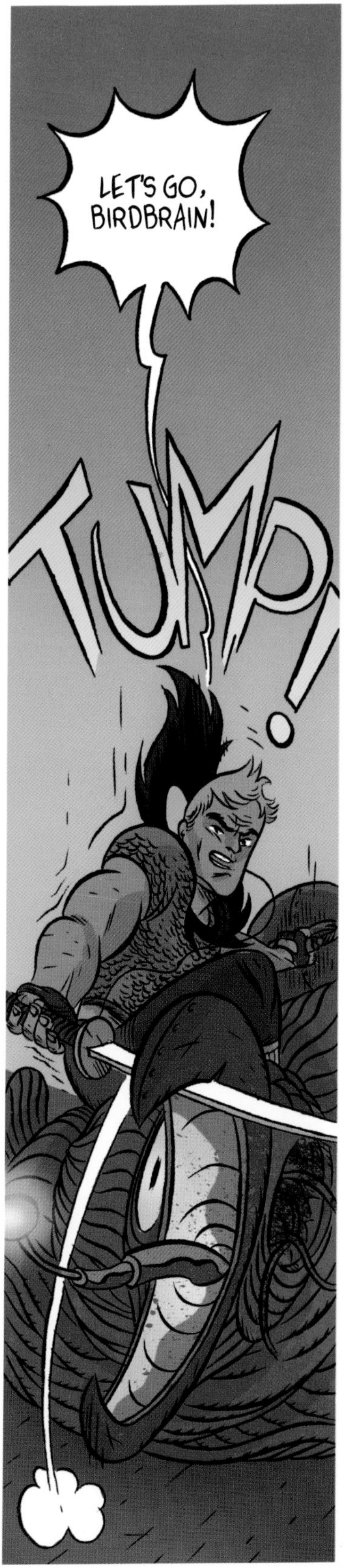
LET'S GO, BIRDBRAIN!
TUMP!

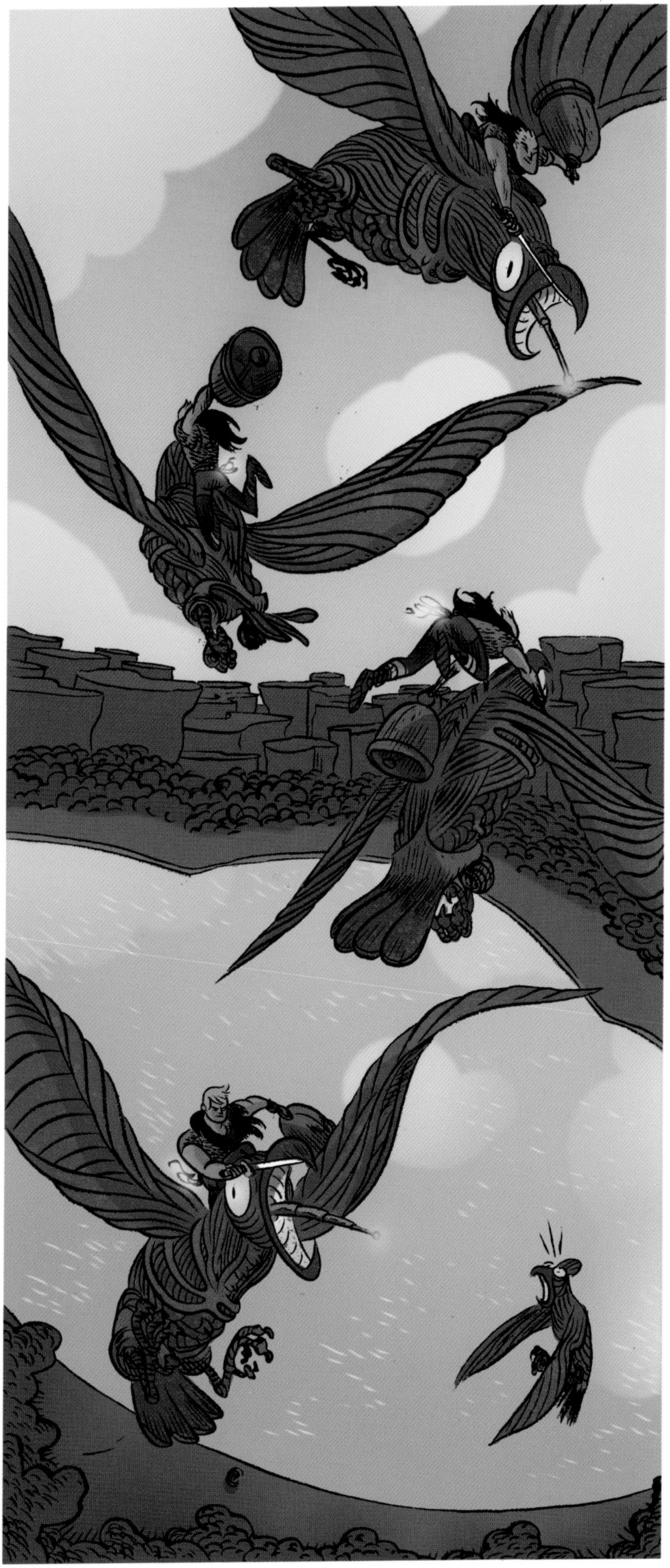

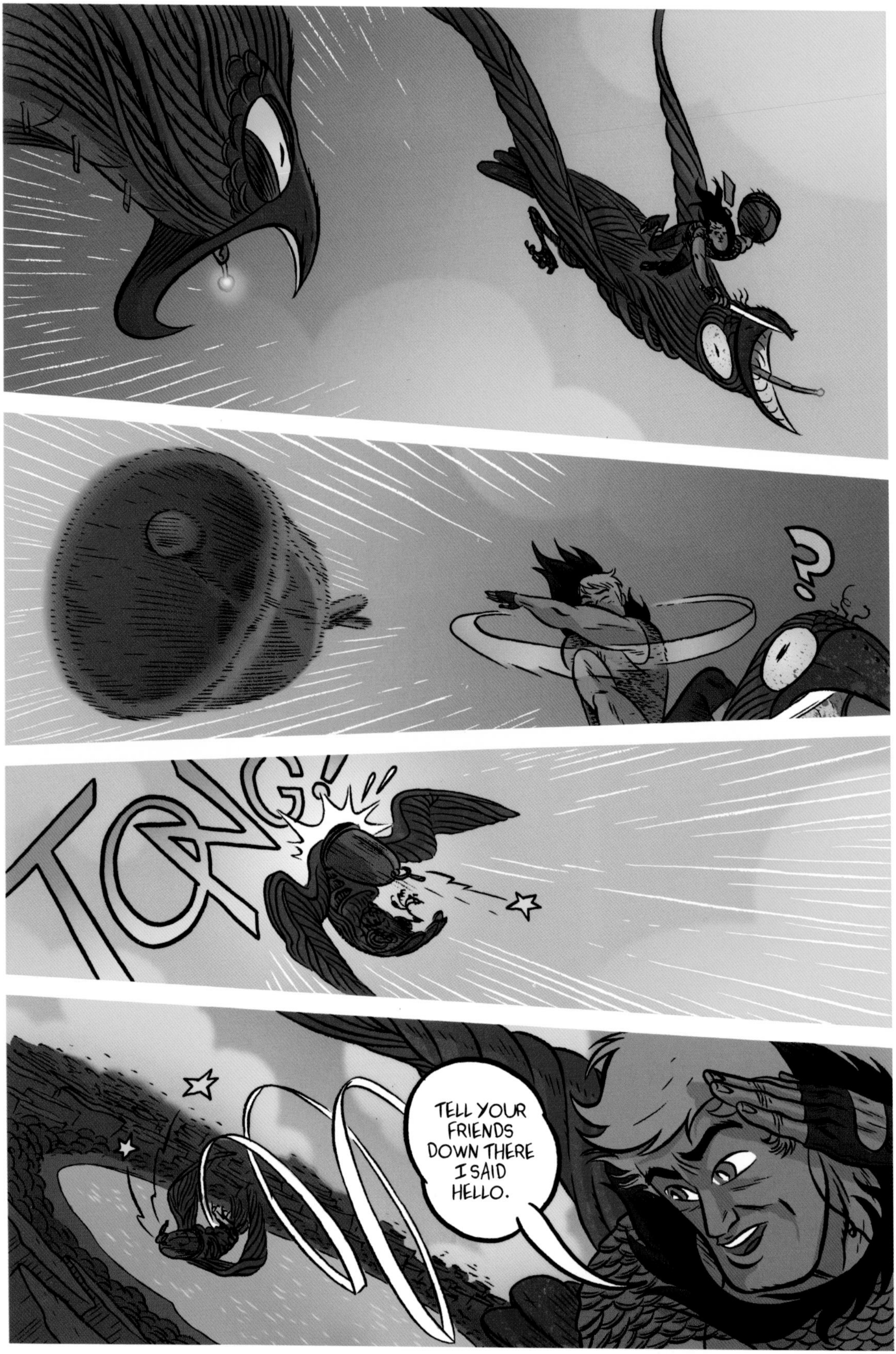
TONG!
TELL YOUR FRIENDS DOWN THERE I SAID HELLO.

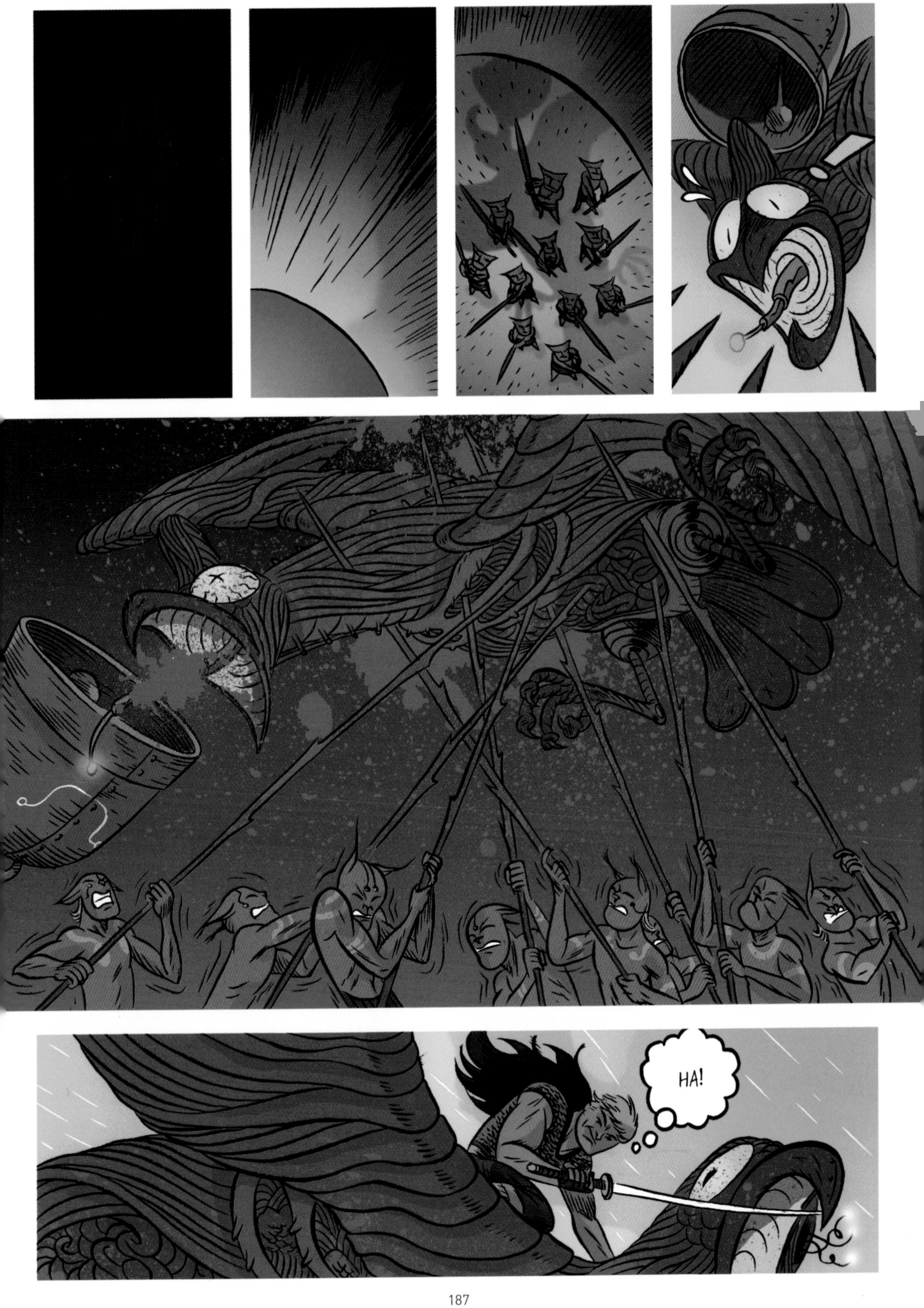
HA!

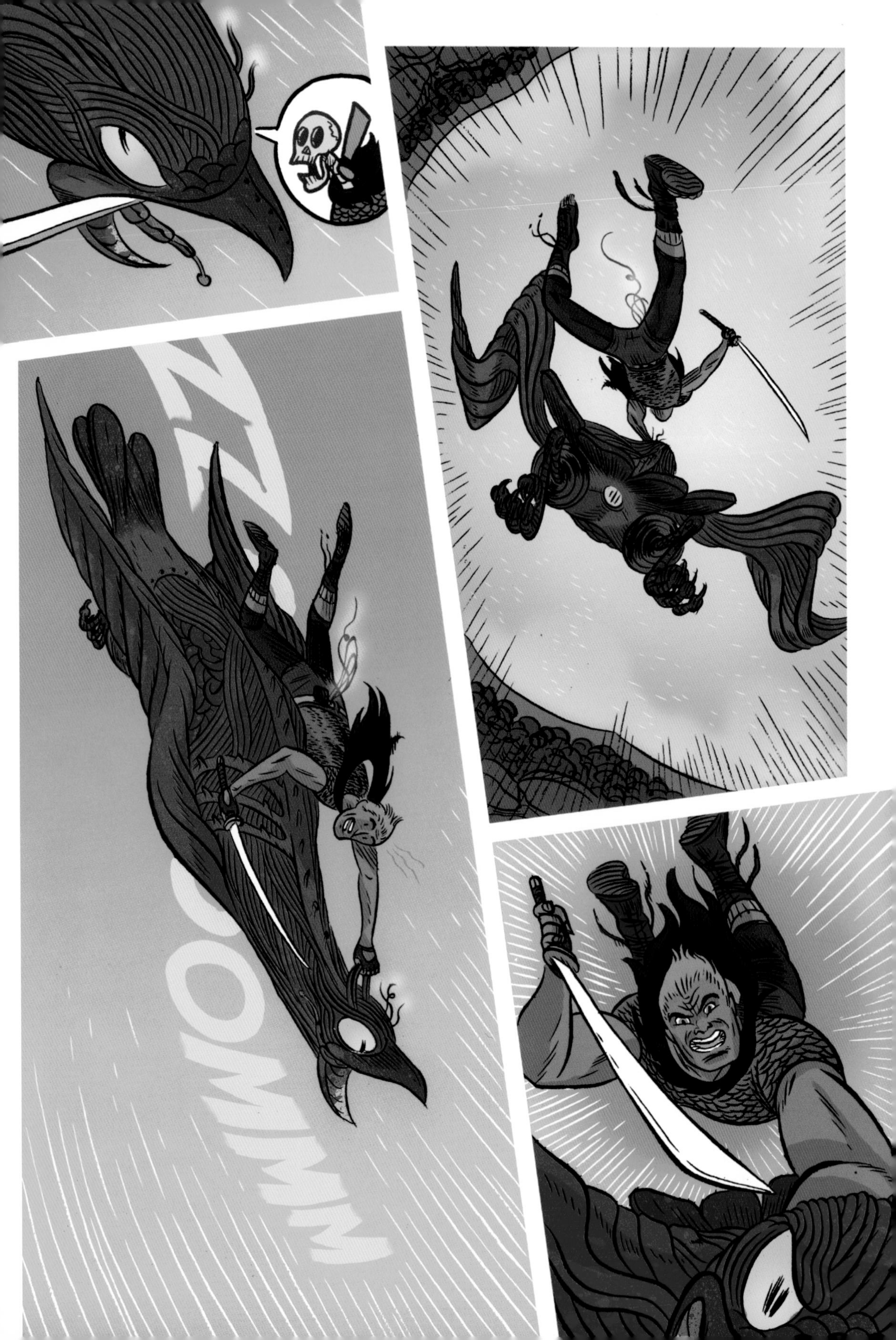

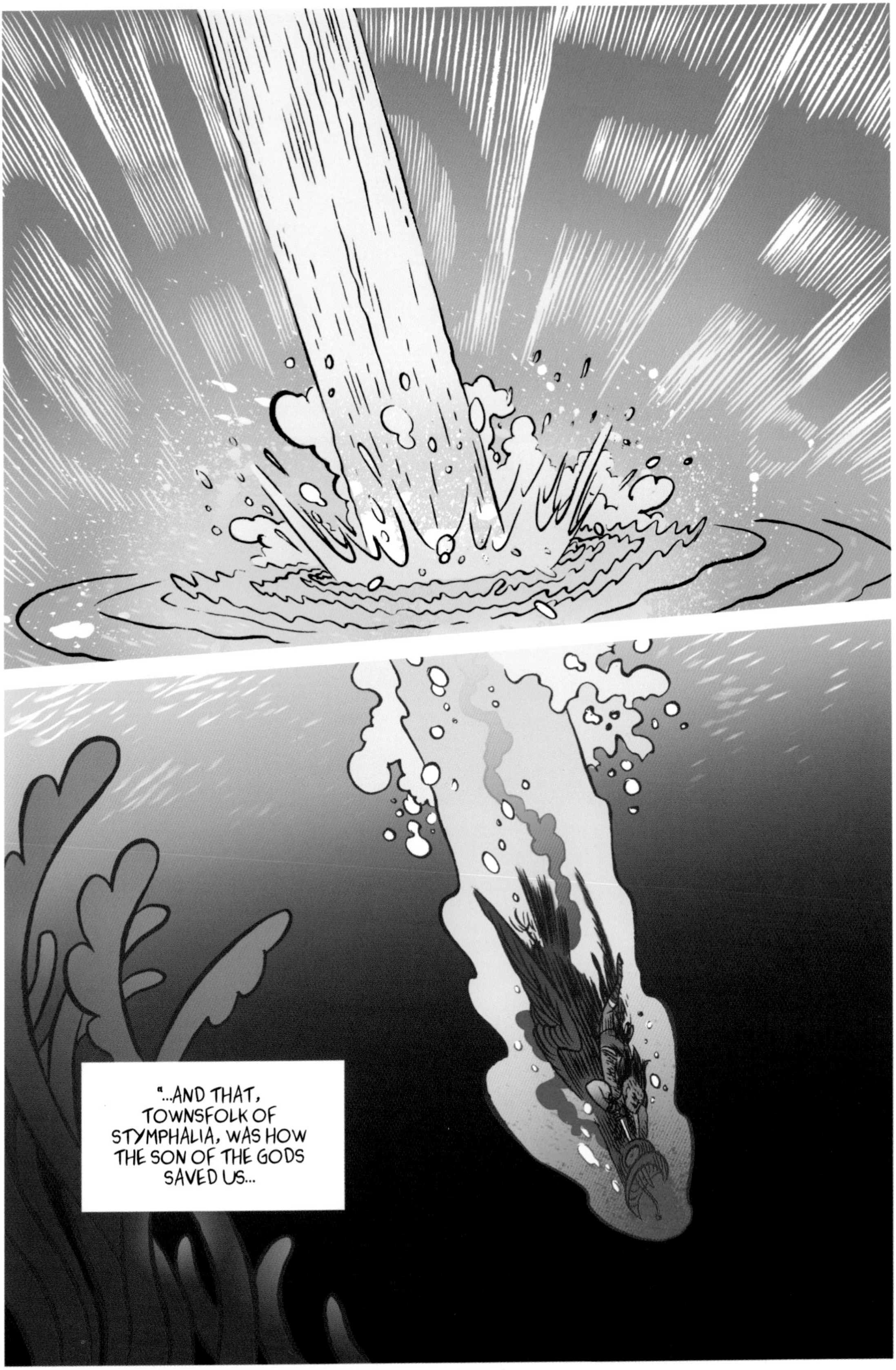
"...AND THAT, TOWNSFOLK OF STYMPHALIA, WAS HOW THE SON OF THE GODS SAVED US...

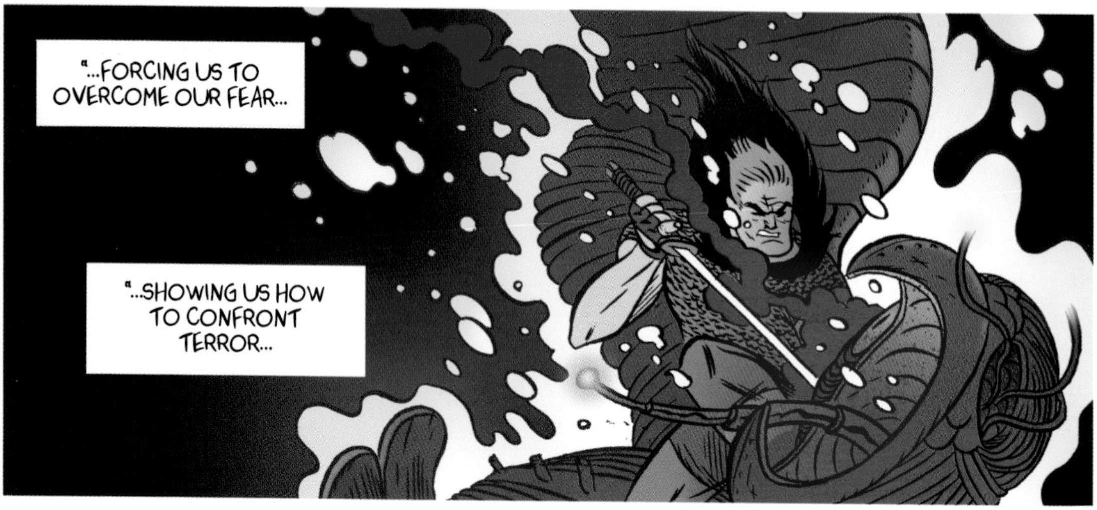
"...FORCING US TO OVERCOME OUR FEAR...
"...SHOWING US HOW TO CONFRONT TERROR...

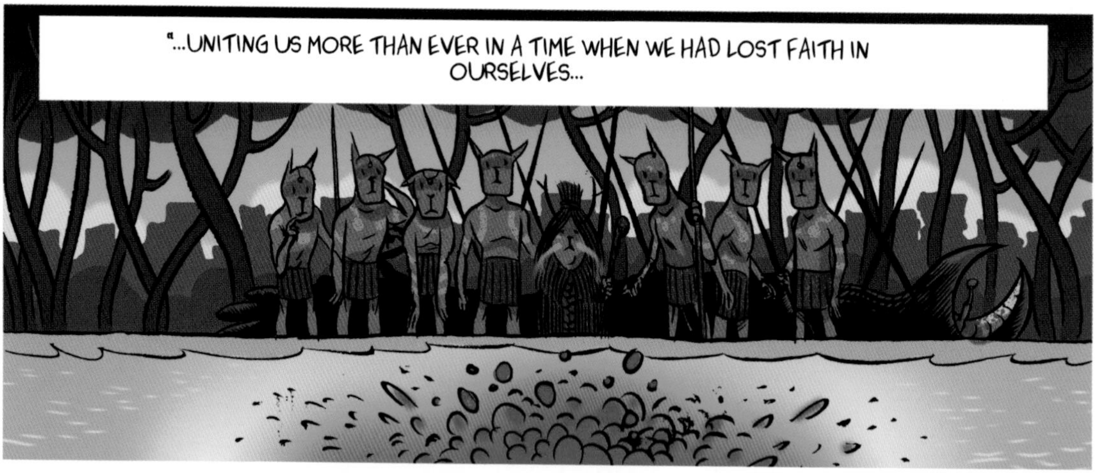
"...UNITING US MORE THAN EVER IN A TIME WHEN WE HAD LOST FAITH IN OURSELVES...

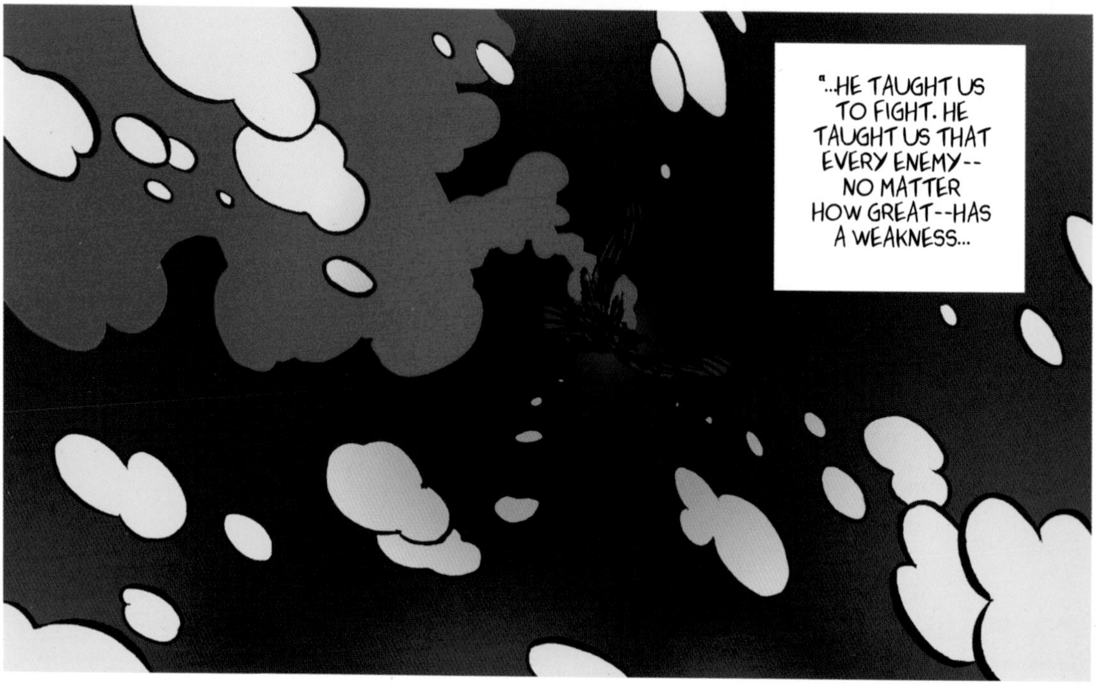
"...HE TAUGHT US TO FIGHT. HE TAUGHT US THAT EVERY ENEMY--NO MATTER HOW GREAT--HAS A WEAKNESS...

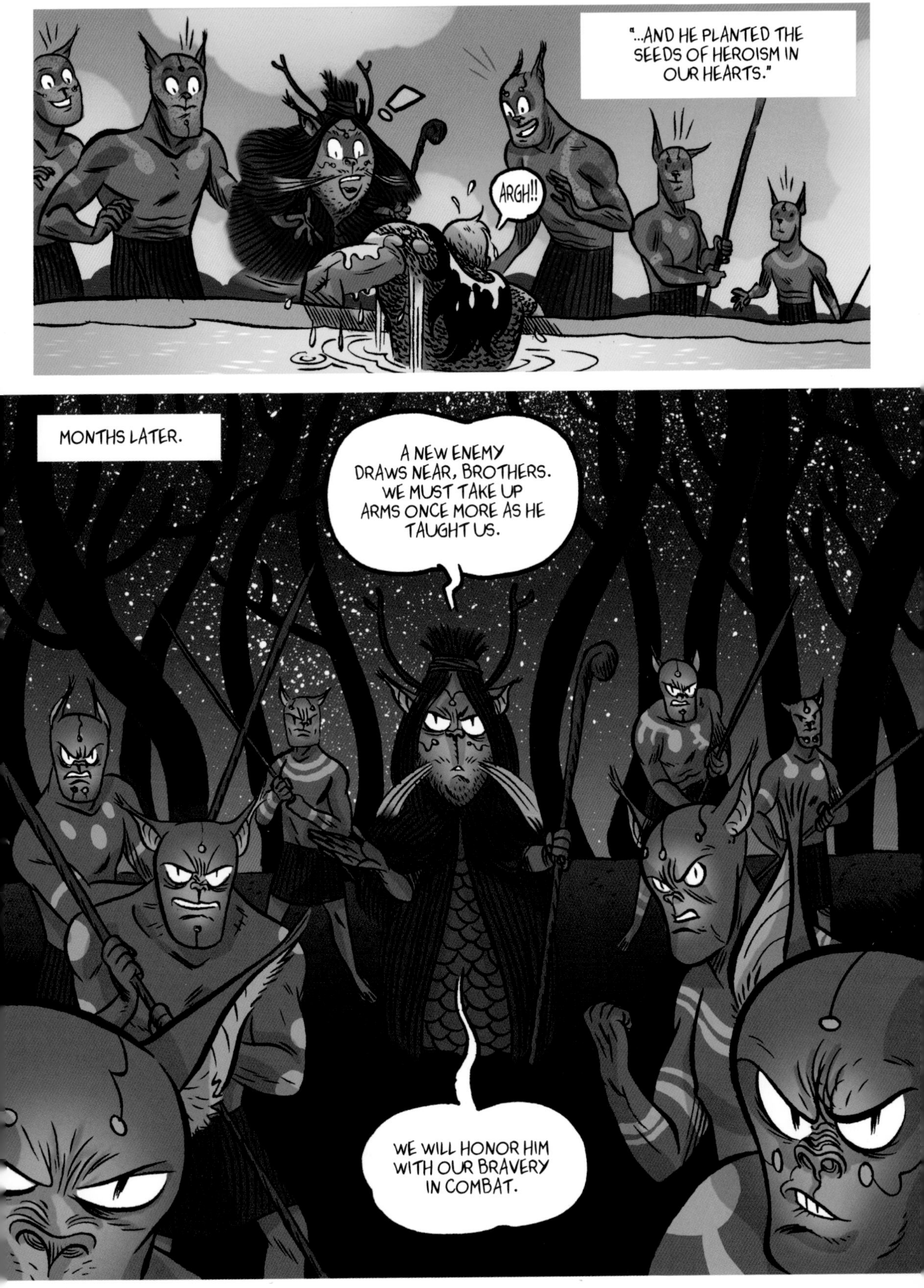
"...AND HE PLANTED THE SEEDS OF HEROISM IN OUR HEARTS."
ARGH!!
MONTHS LATER.
A NEW ENEMY DRAWS NEAR, BROTHERS. WE MUST TAKE UP ARMS ONCE MORE AS HE TAUGHT US.
WE WILL HONOR HIM WITH OUR BRAVERY IN COMBAT.

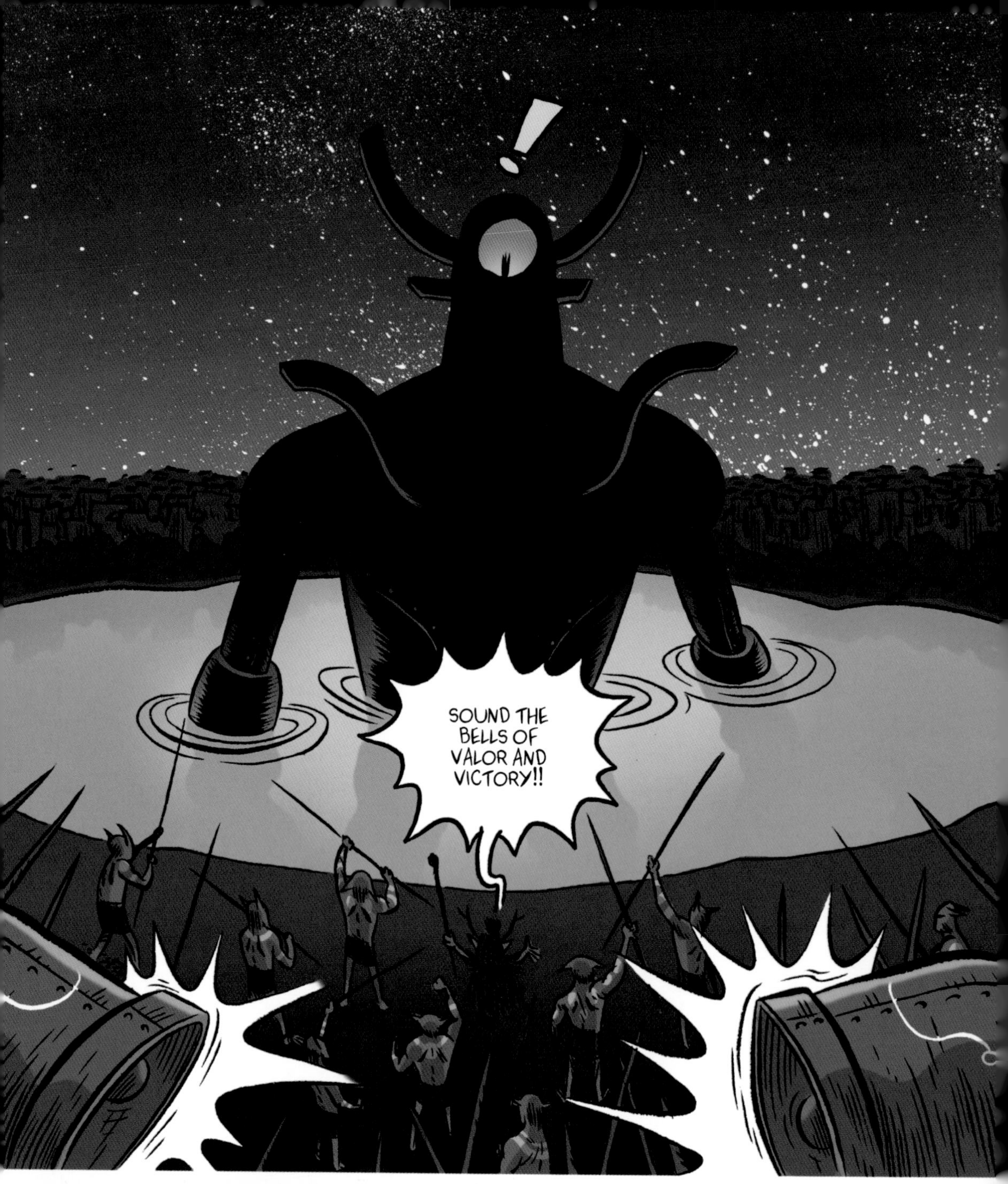
!
SOUND THE BELLS OF VALOR AND VICTORY!!

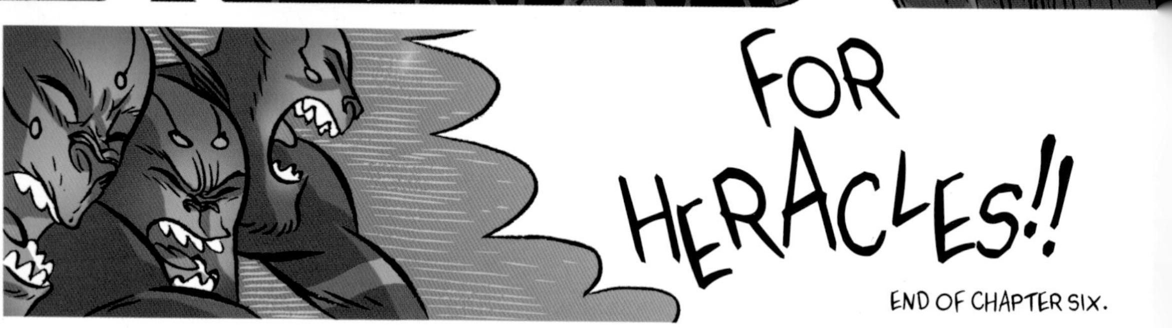
FOR HERACLES!!
END OF CHAPTER SIX.

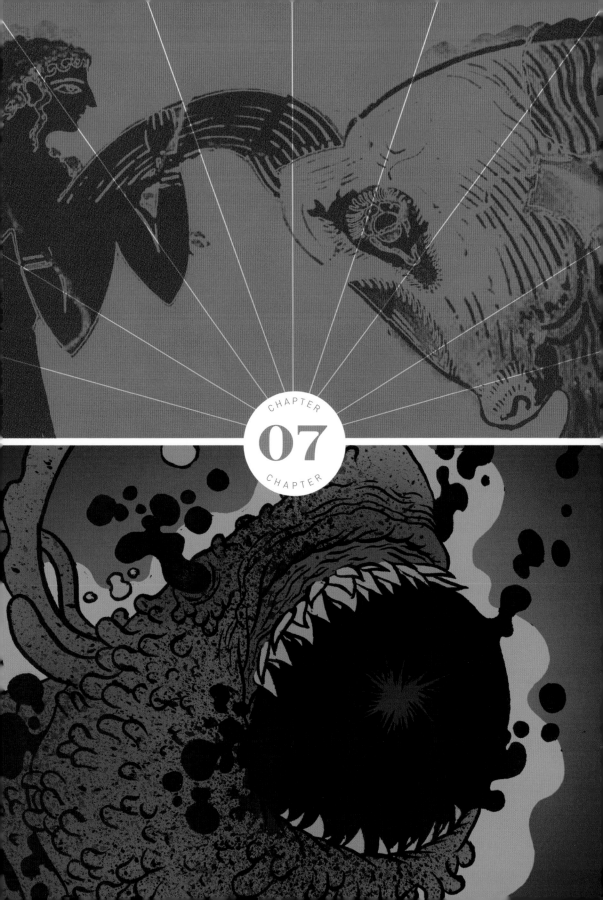

CHAPTER

07

CHAPTER

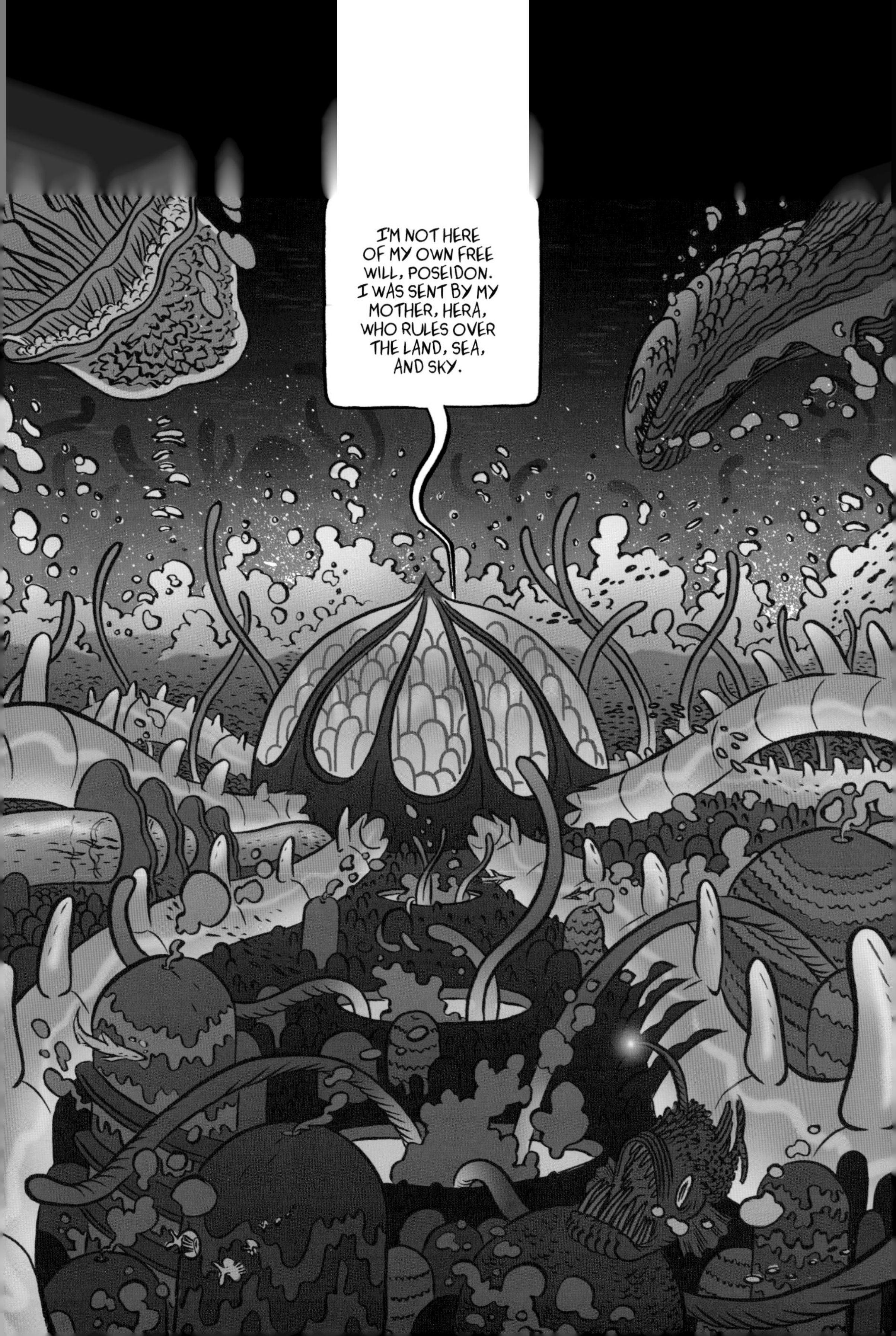
I'M NOT HERE OF MY OWN FREE WILL, POSEIDON. I WAS SENT BY MY MOTHER, HERA, WHO RULES OVER THE LAND, SEA, AND SKY.

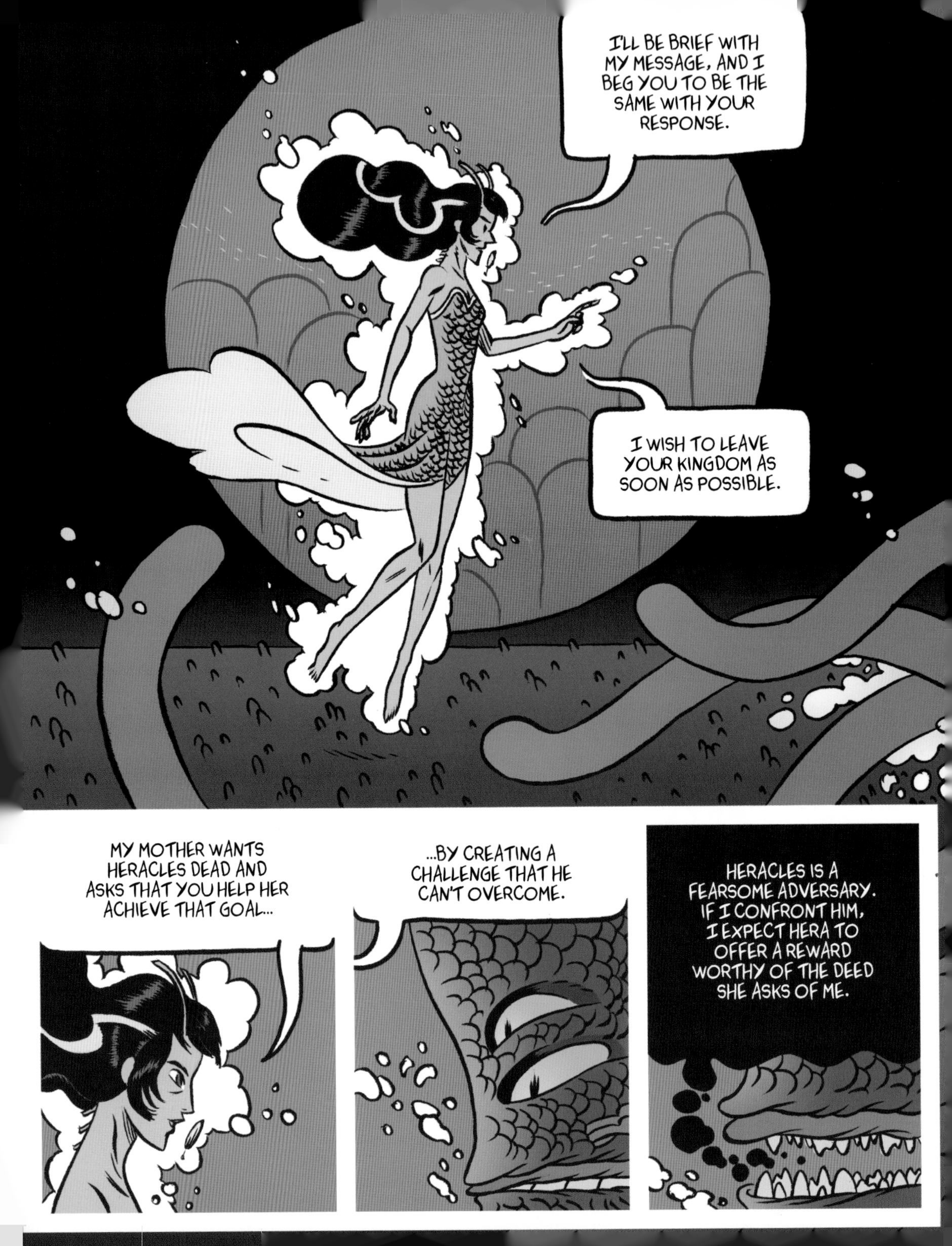

I'LL BE BRIEF WITH MY MESSAGE, AND I BEG YOU TO BE THE SAME WITH YOUR RESPONSE.
I WISH TO LEAVE YOUR KINGDOM AS SOON AS POSSIBLE.
MY MOTHER WANTS HERACLES DEAD AND ASKS THAT YOU HELP HER ACHIEVE THAT GOAL...
...BY CREATING A CHALLENGE THAT HE CAN'T OVERCOME.
HERACLES IS A FEARSOME ADVERSARY. IF I CONFRONT HIM, I EXPECT HERA TO OFFER A REWARD WORTHY OF THE DEED SHE ASKS OF ME.

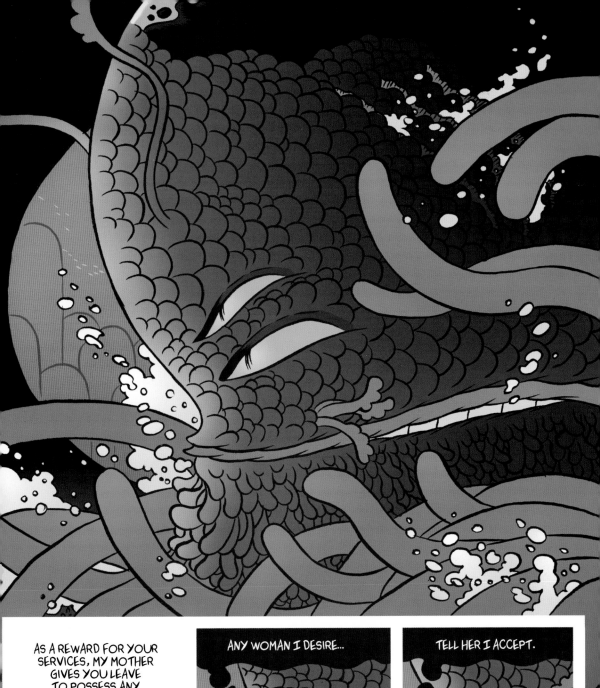

AS A REWARD FOR YOUR SERVICES, MY MOTHER GIVES YOU LEAVE TO POSSESS ANY WOMAN ON LAND THAT YOU DESIRE.

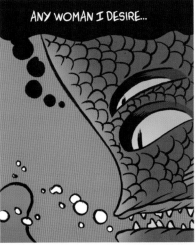

ANY WOMAN I DESIRE...

TELL HER I ACCEPT.

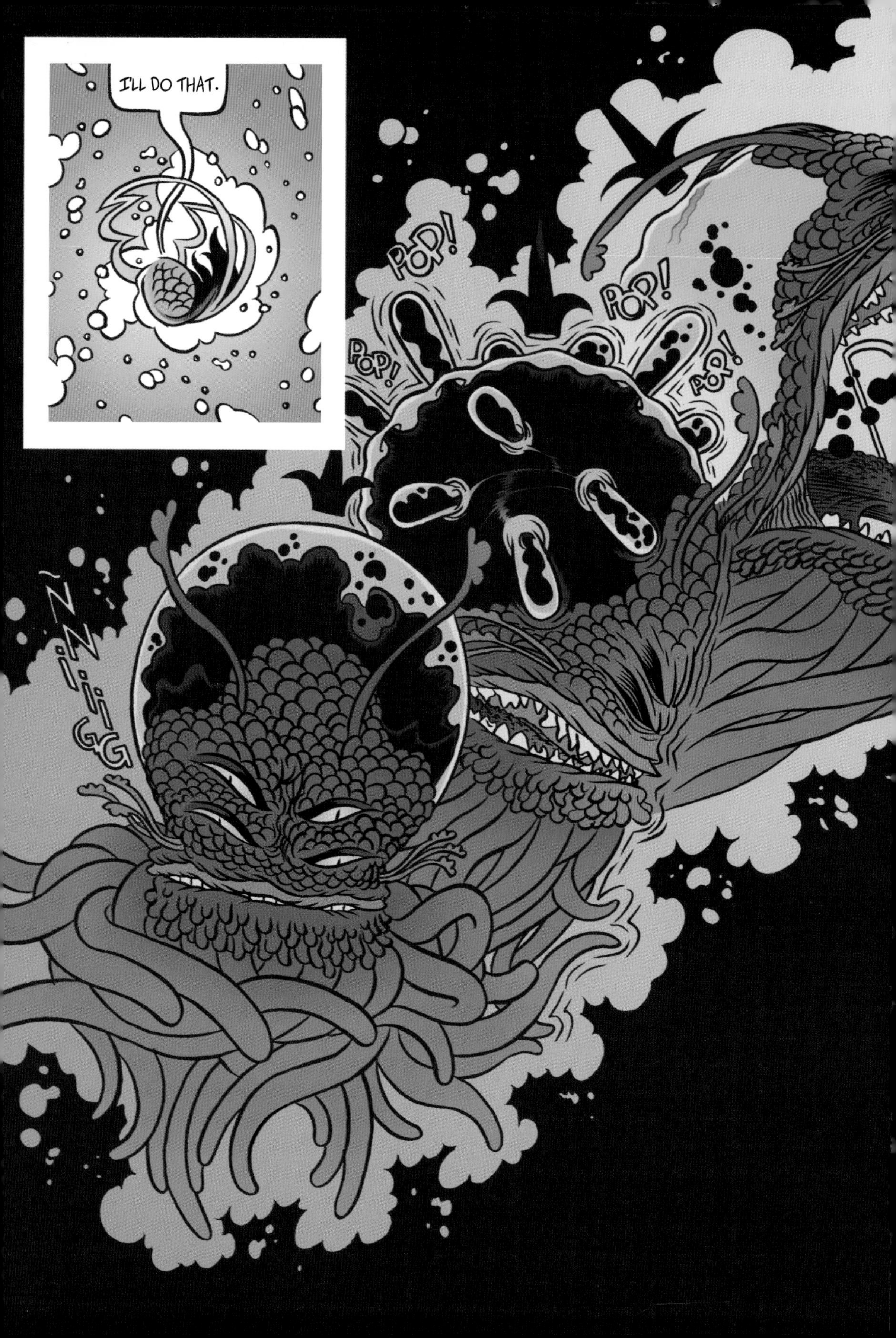
I'LL DO THAT.
POP!
POP!
POP!
POP!
~ZZiiiGG

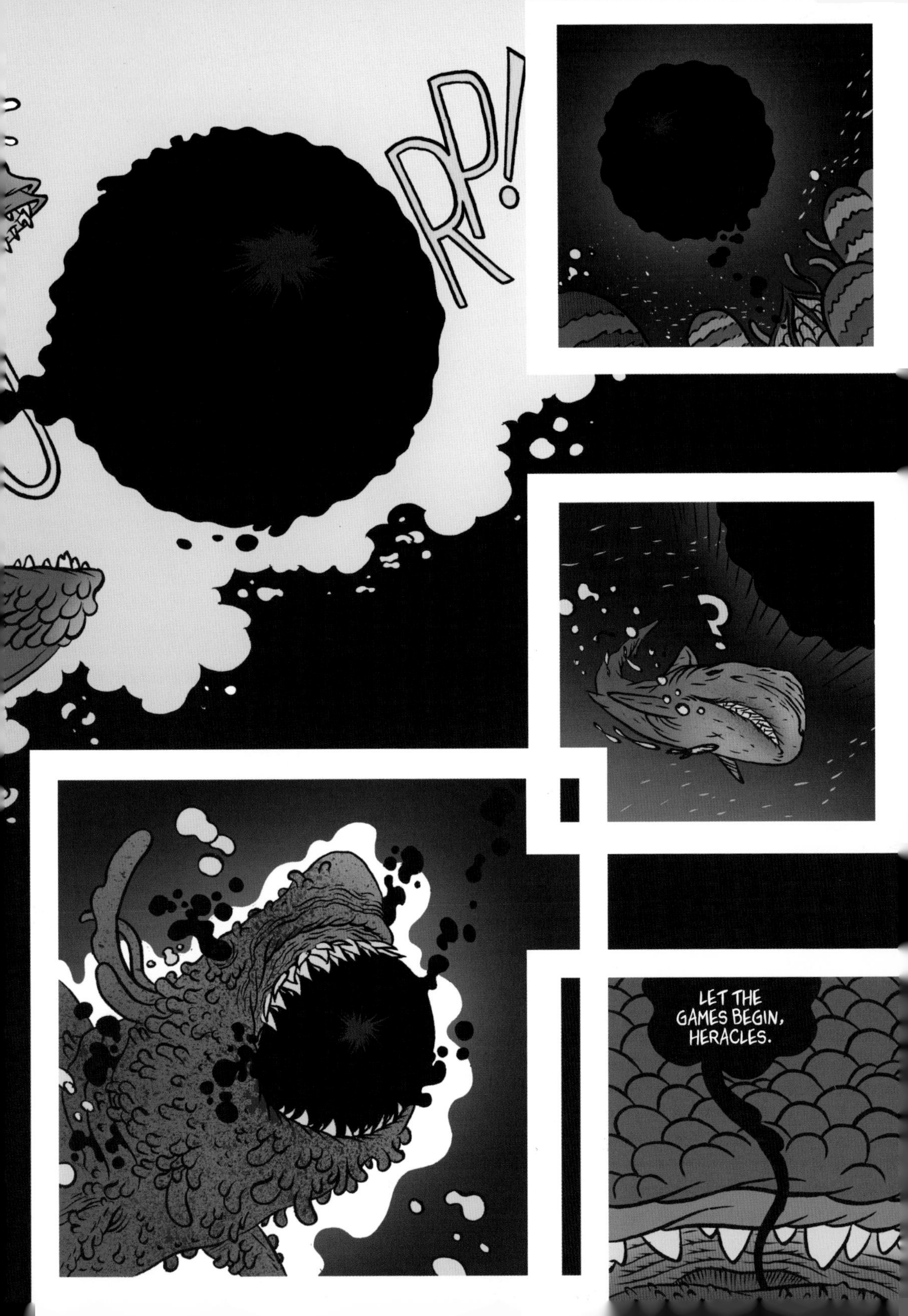
RP!
?
LET THE GAMES BEGIN, HERACLES.

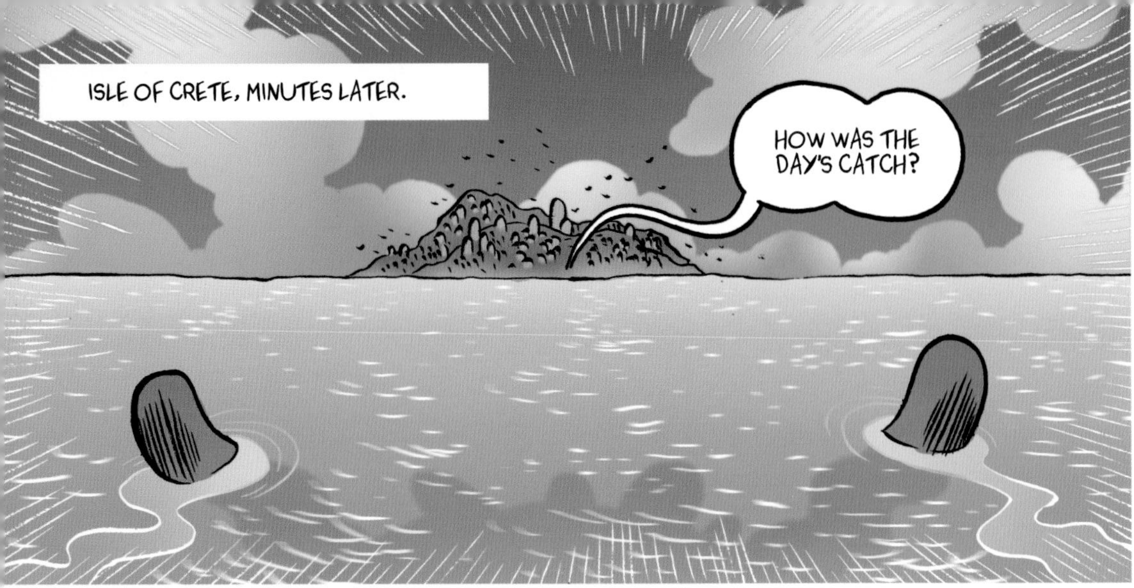
ISLE OF CRETE, MINUTES LATER.
HOW WAS THE DAY'S CATCH?

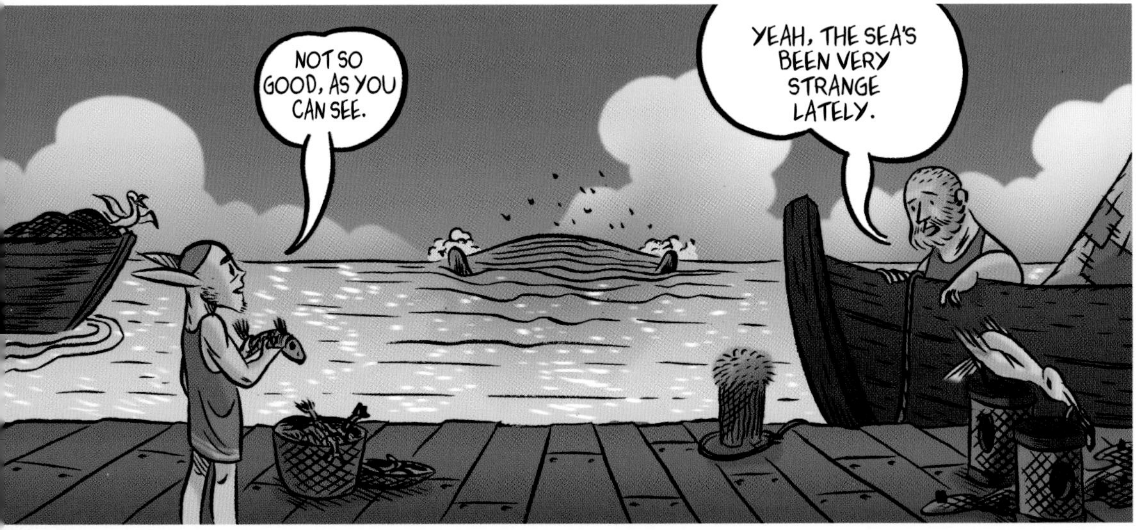
NOT SO GOOD, AS YOU CAN SEE.
YEAH, THE SEA'S BEEN VERY STRANGE LATELY.

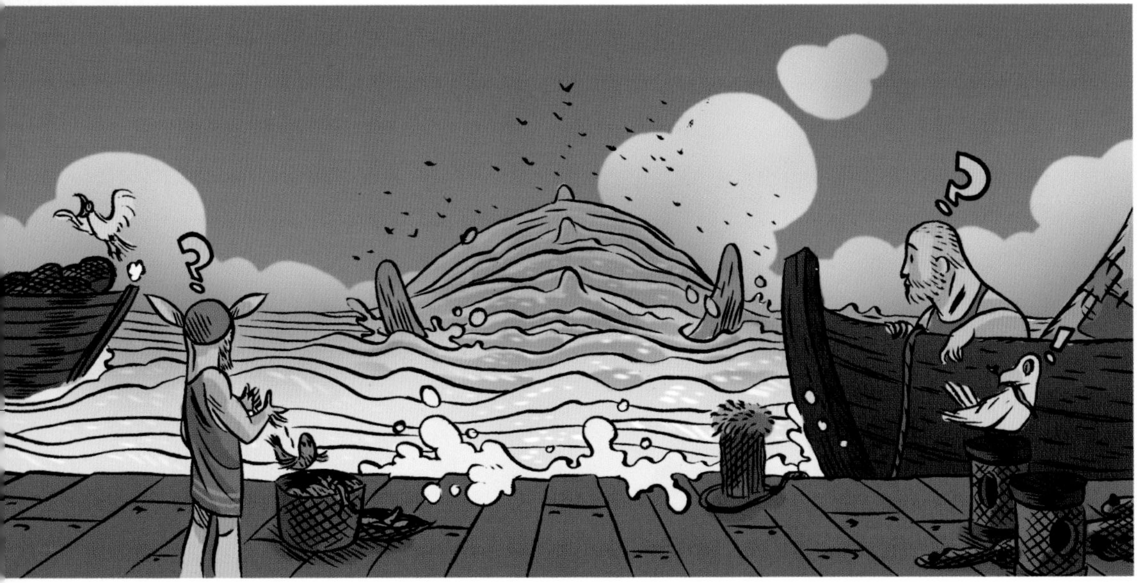
?
?

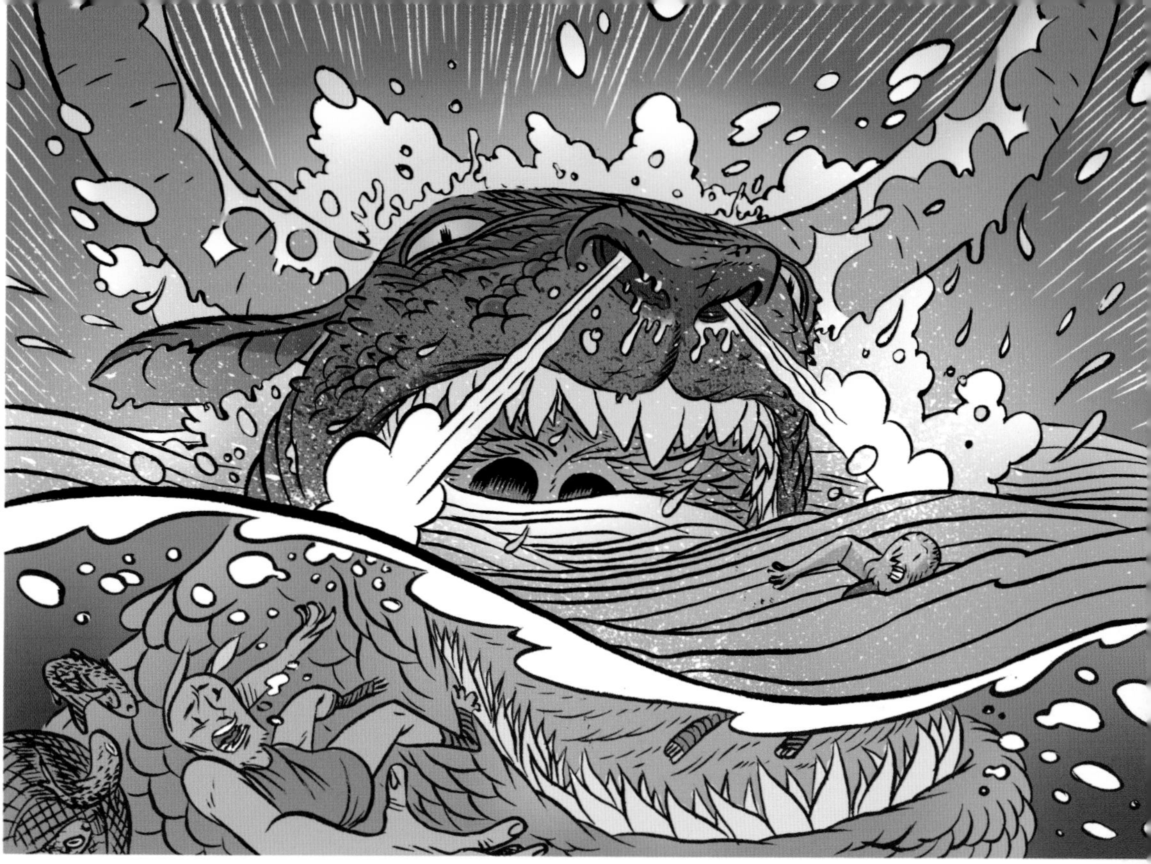

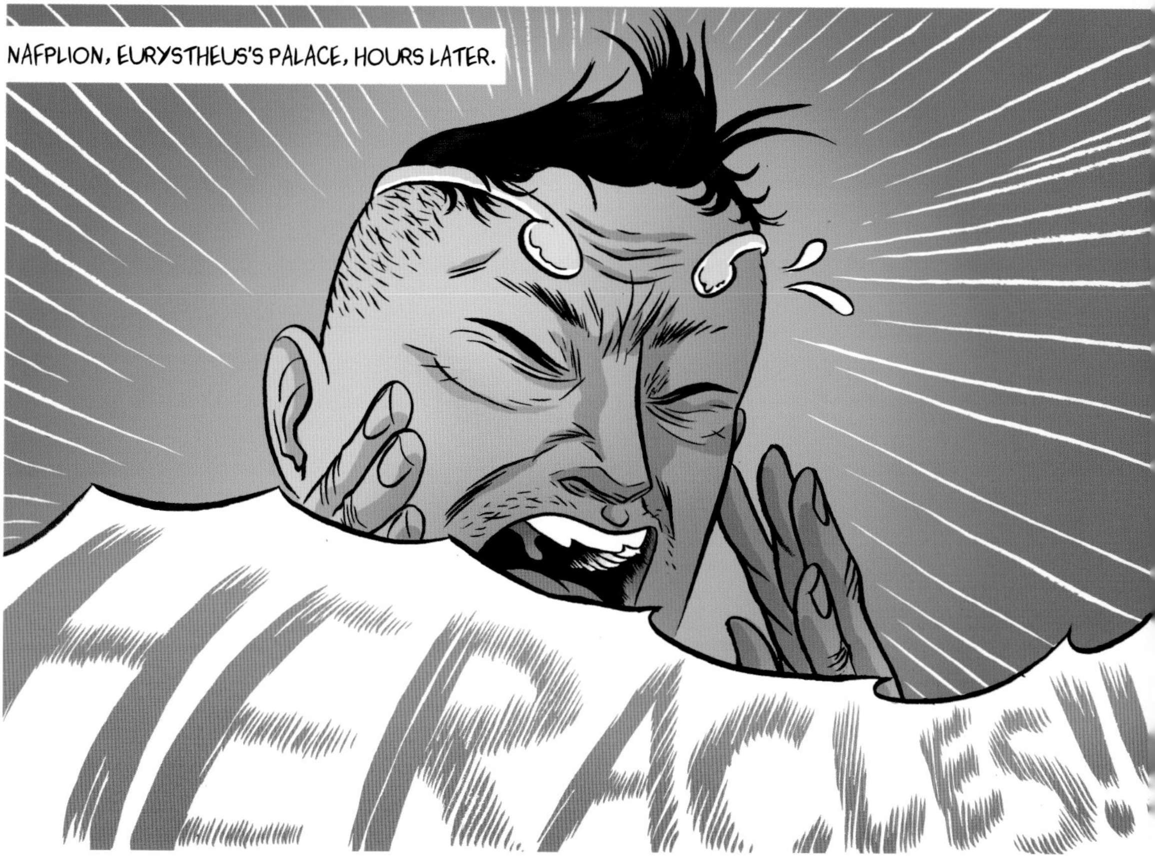
NAFPLION, EURYSTHEUS'S PALACE, HOURS LATER.
HERACLES!!

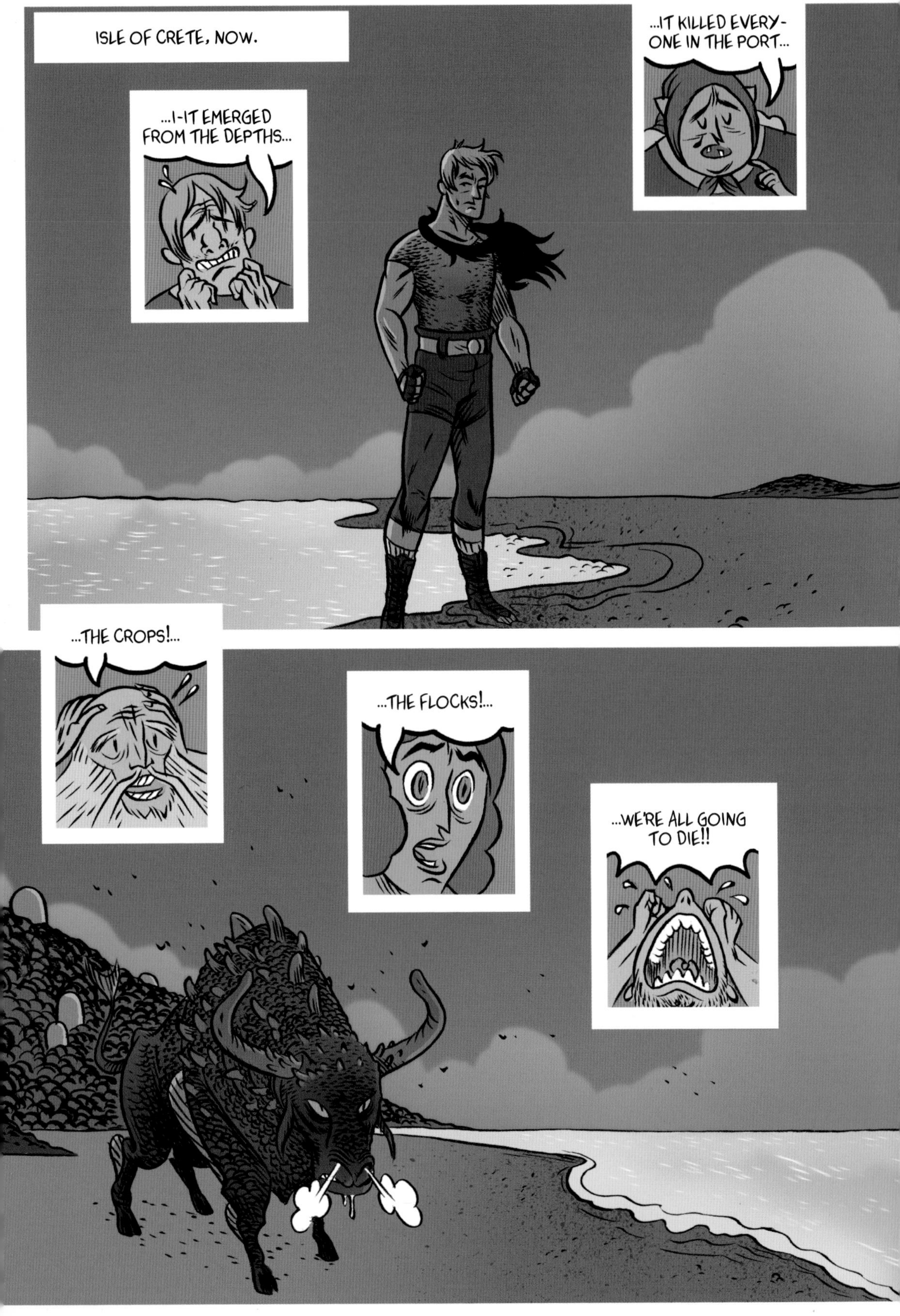
ISLE OF CRETE, NOW.
...I-IT EMERGED FROM THE DEPTHS...
...IT KILLED EVERY-ONE IN THE PORT...
...THE CROPS!...
...THE FLOCKS!...
...WE'RE ALL GOING TO DIE!!

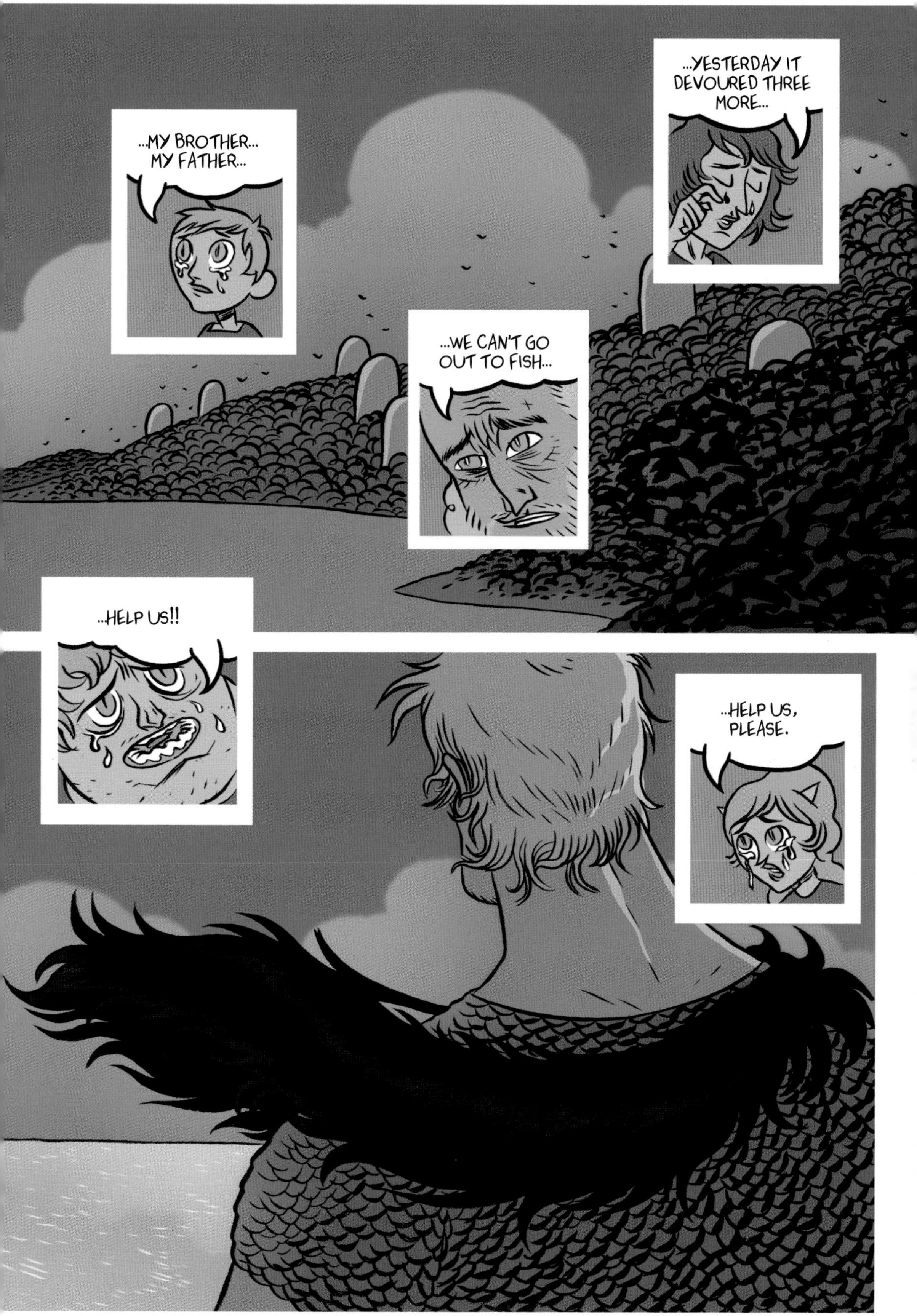
...MY BROTHER... MY FATHER...
...WE CAN'T GO OUT TO FISH...
...YESTERDAY IT DEVOURED THREE MORE...
...HELP US!!
...HELP US, PLEASE.

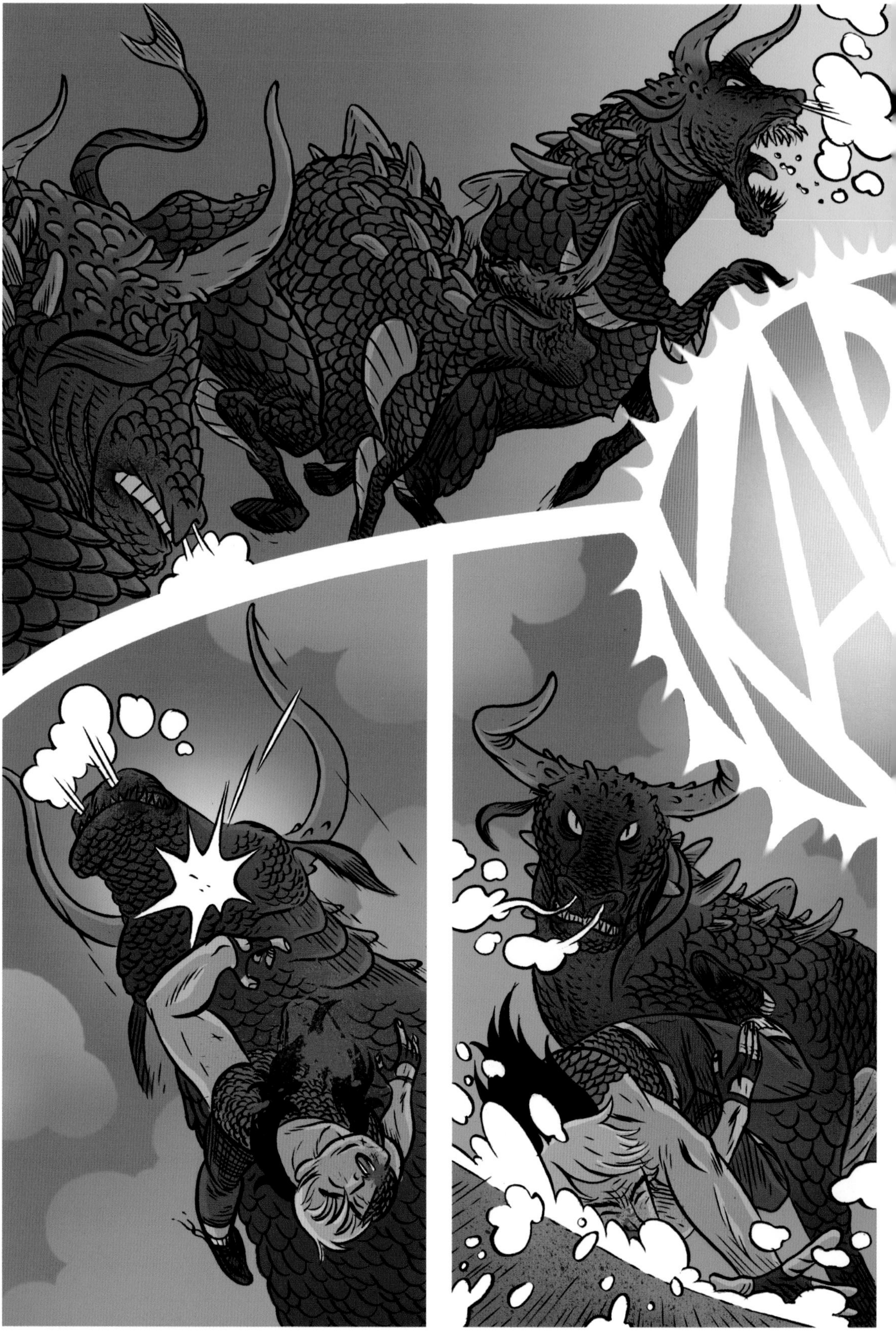

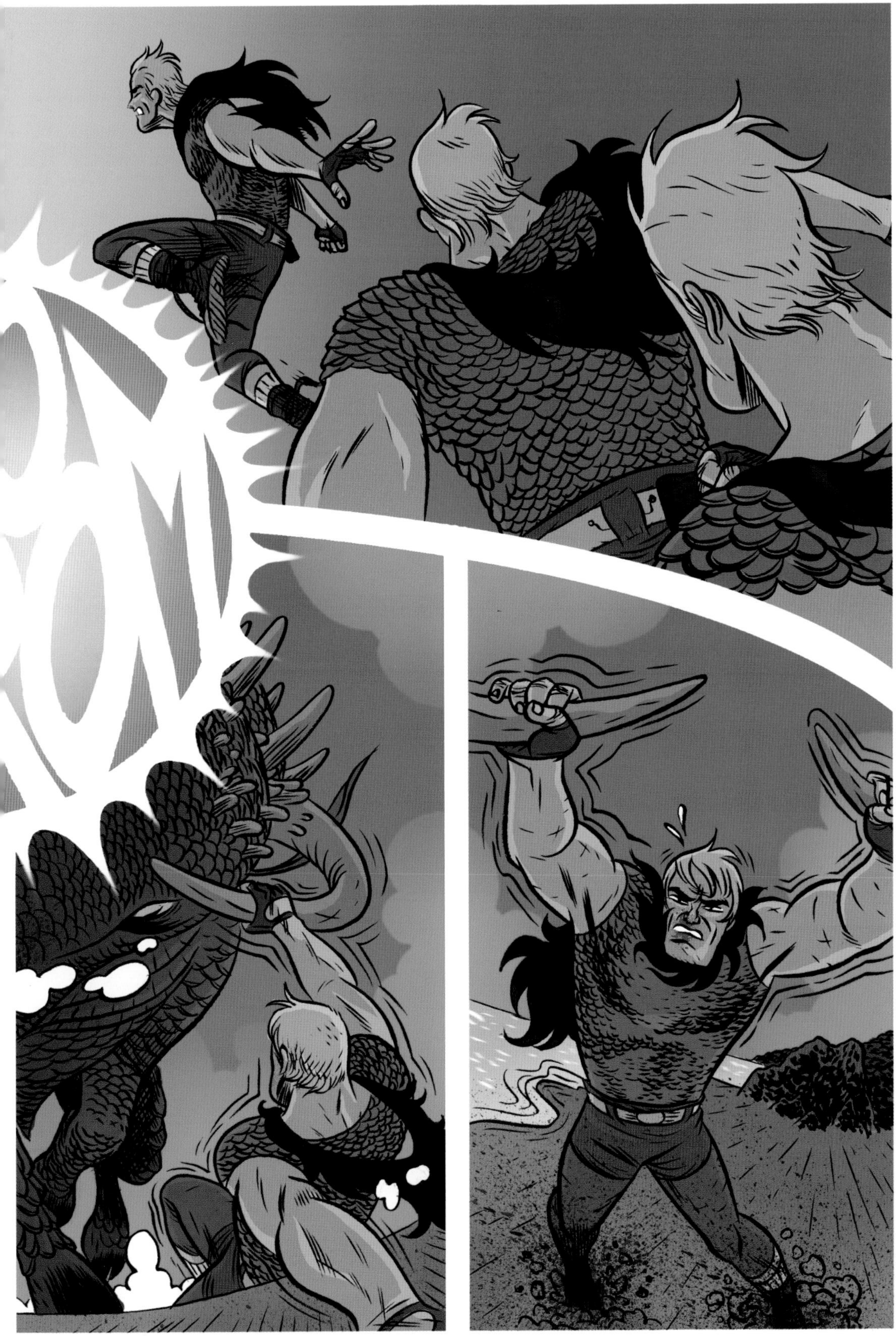

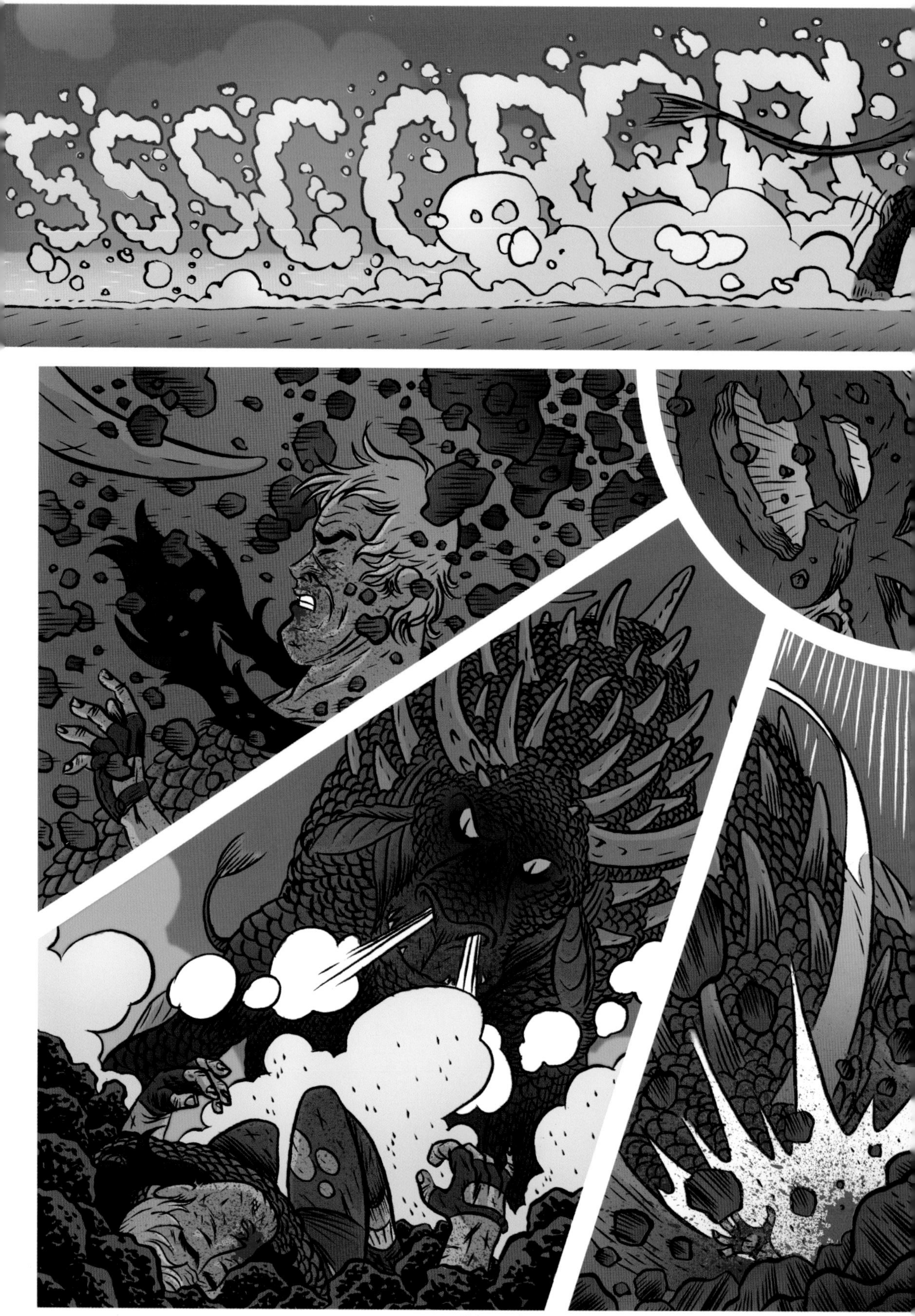
SSSGCRRR

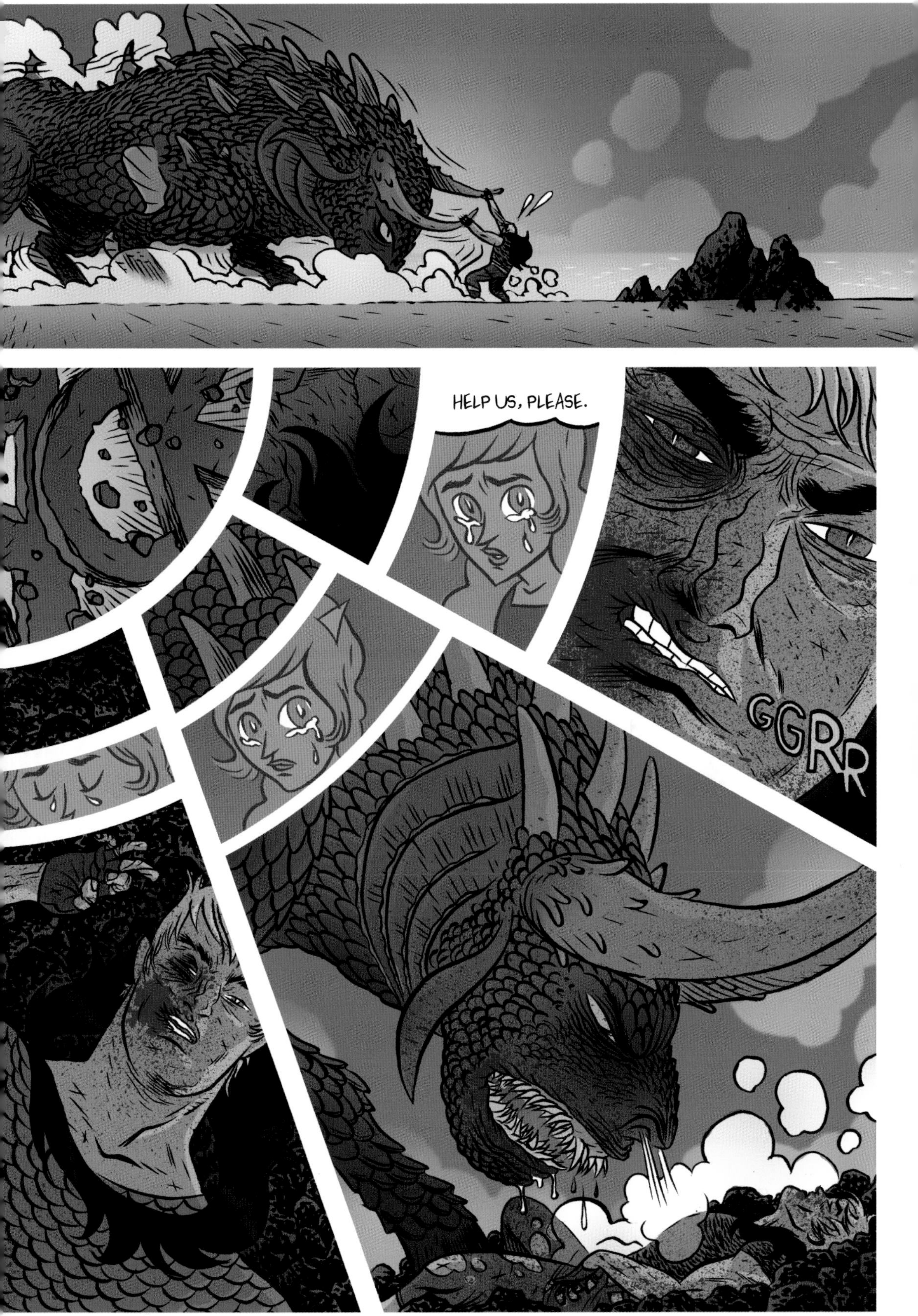
HELP US, PLEASE.
GGRRR

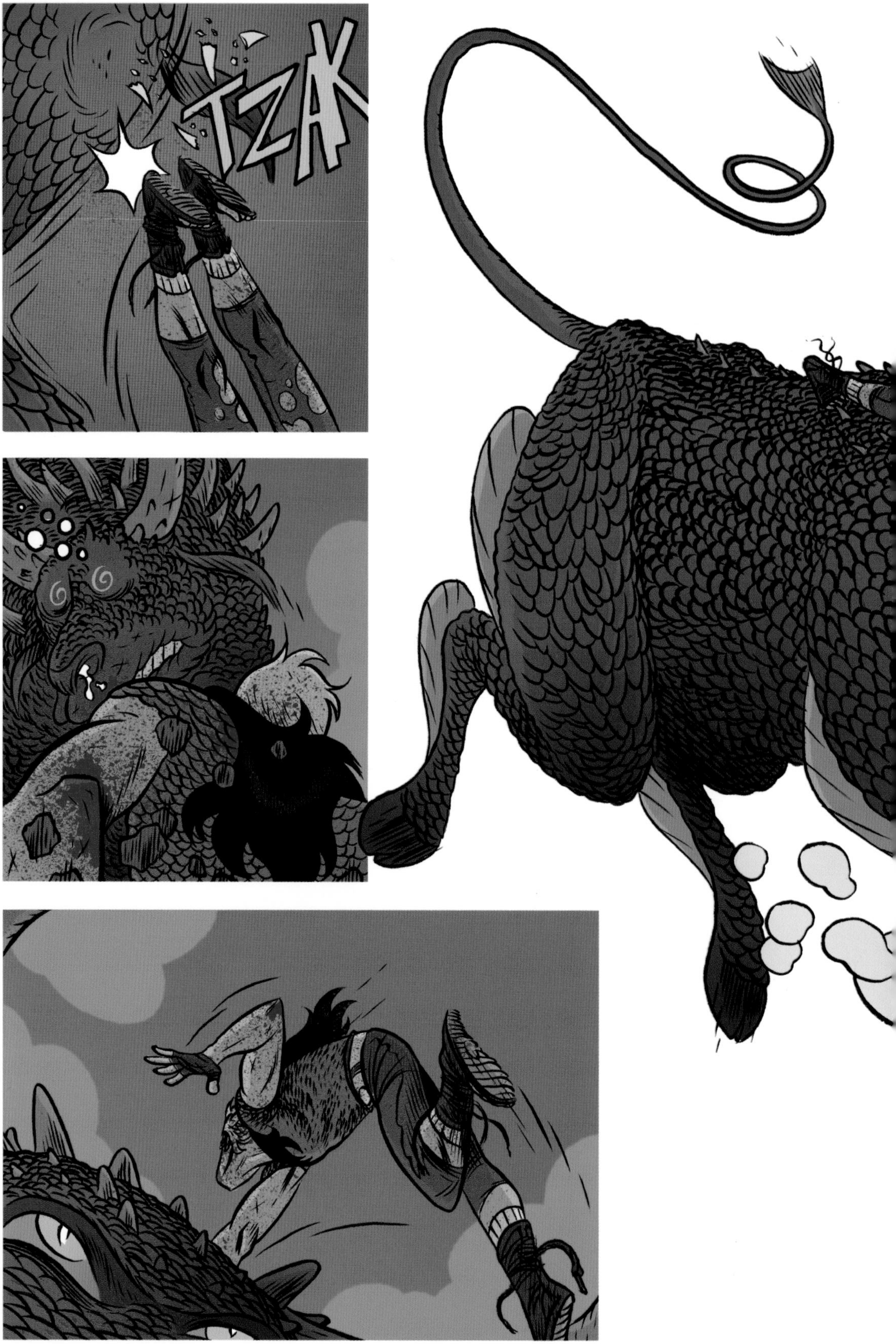
TZAK

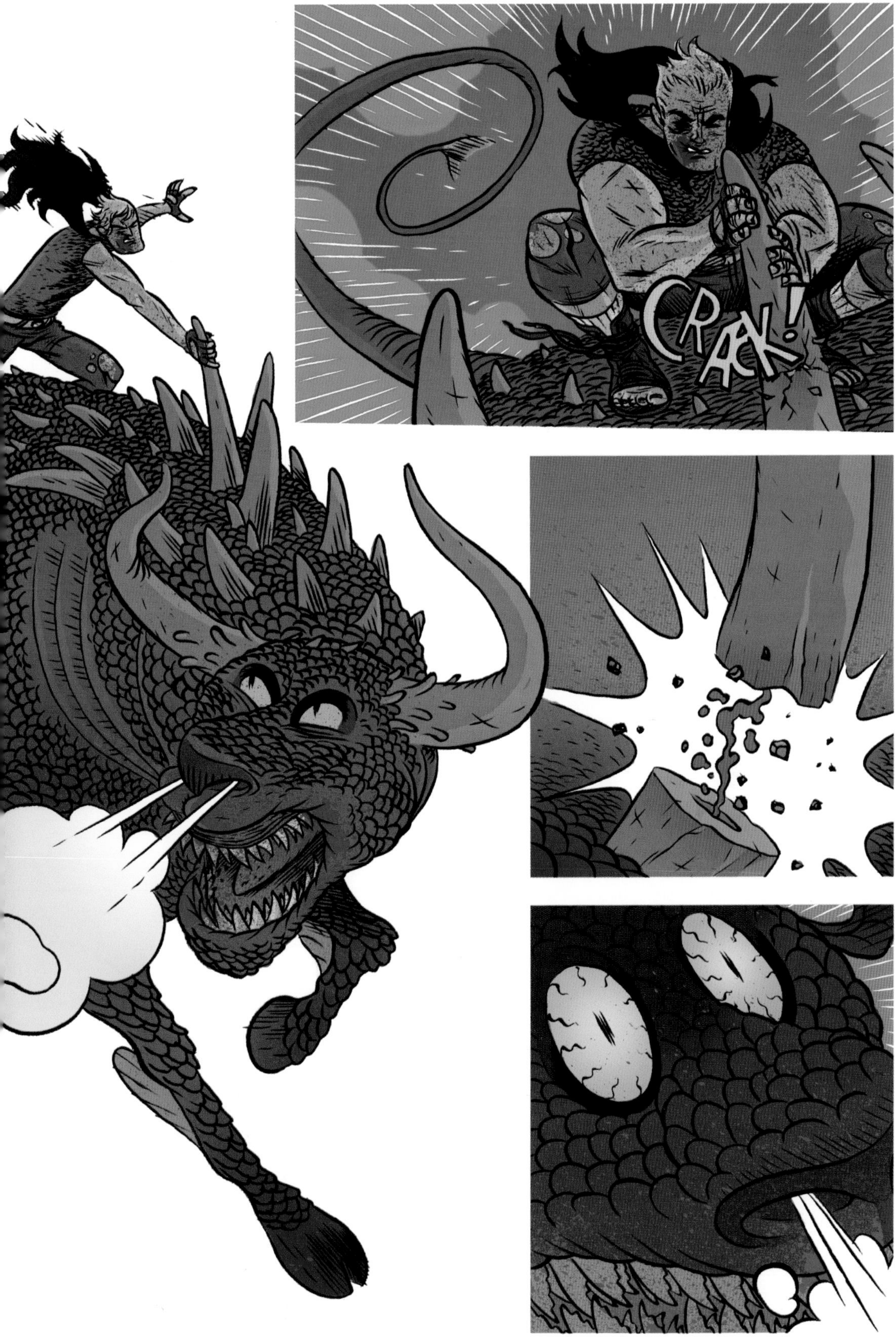
CRACK!

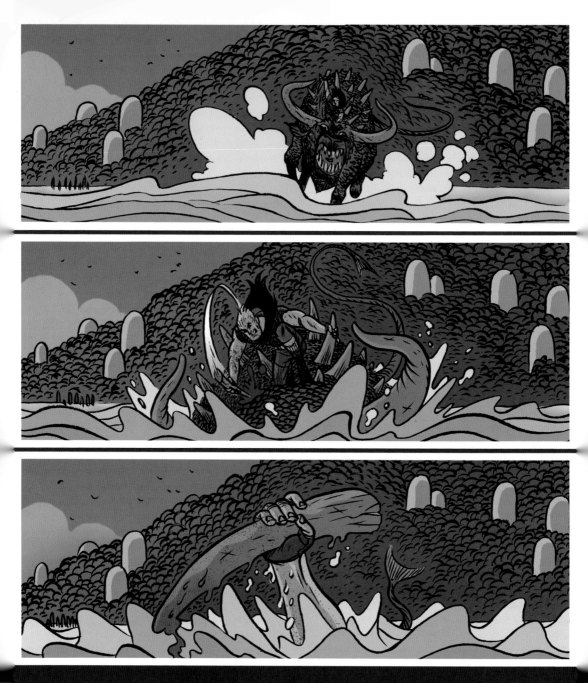

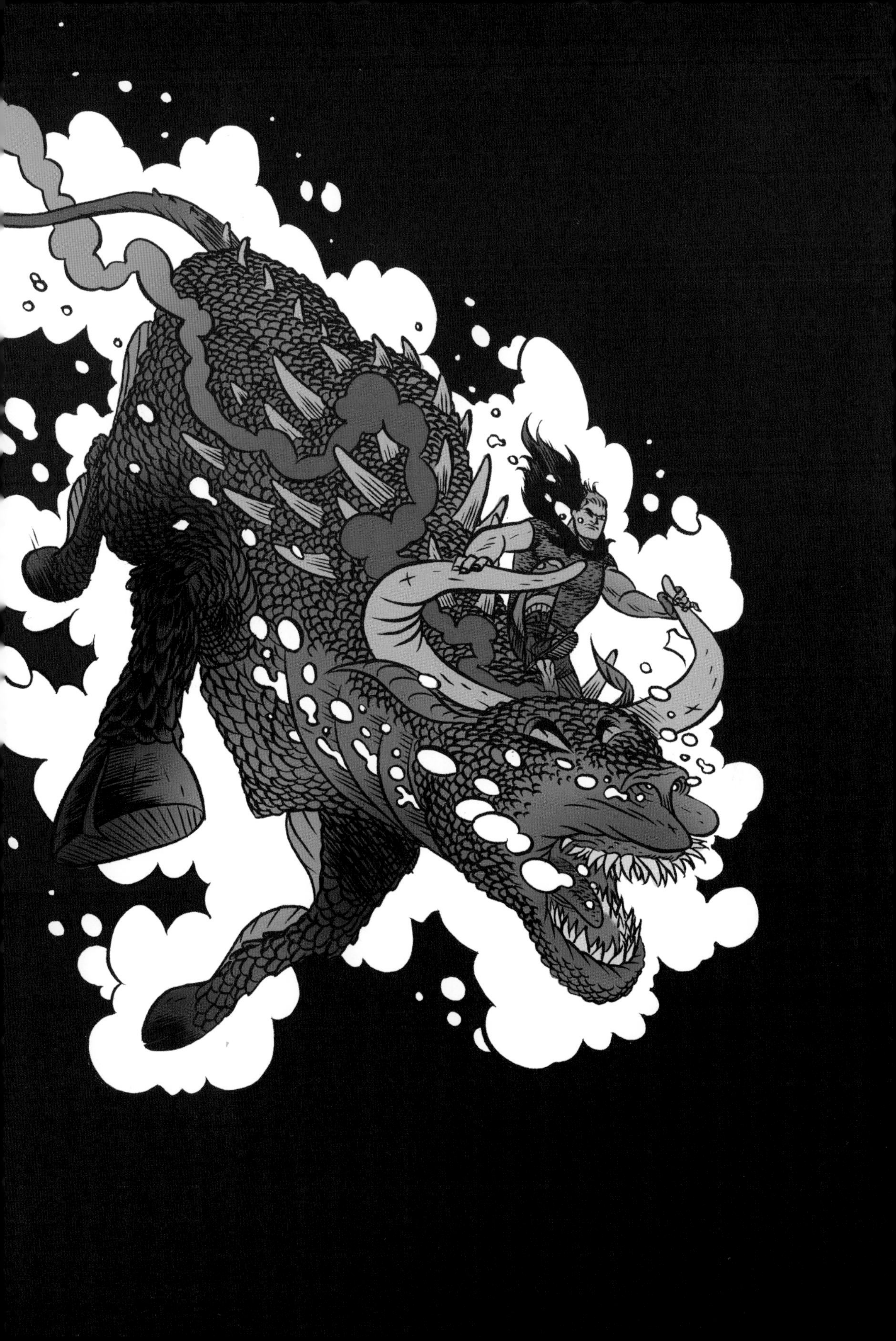

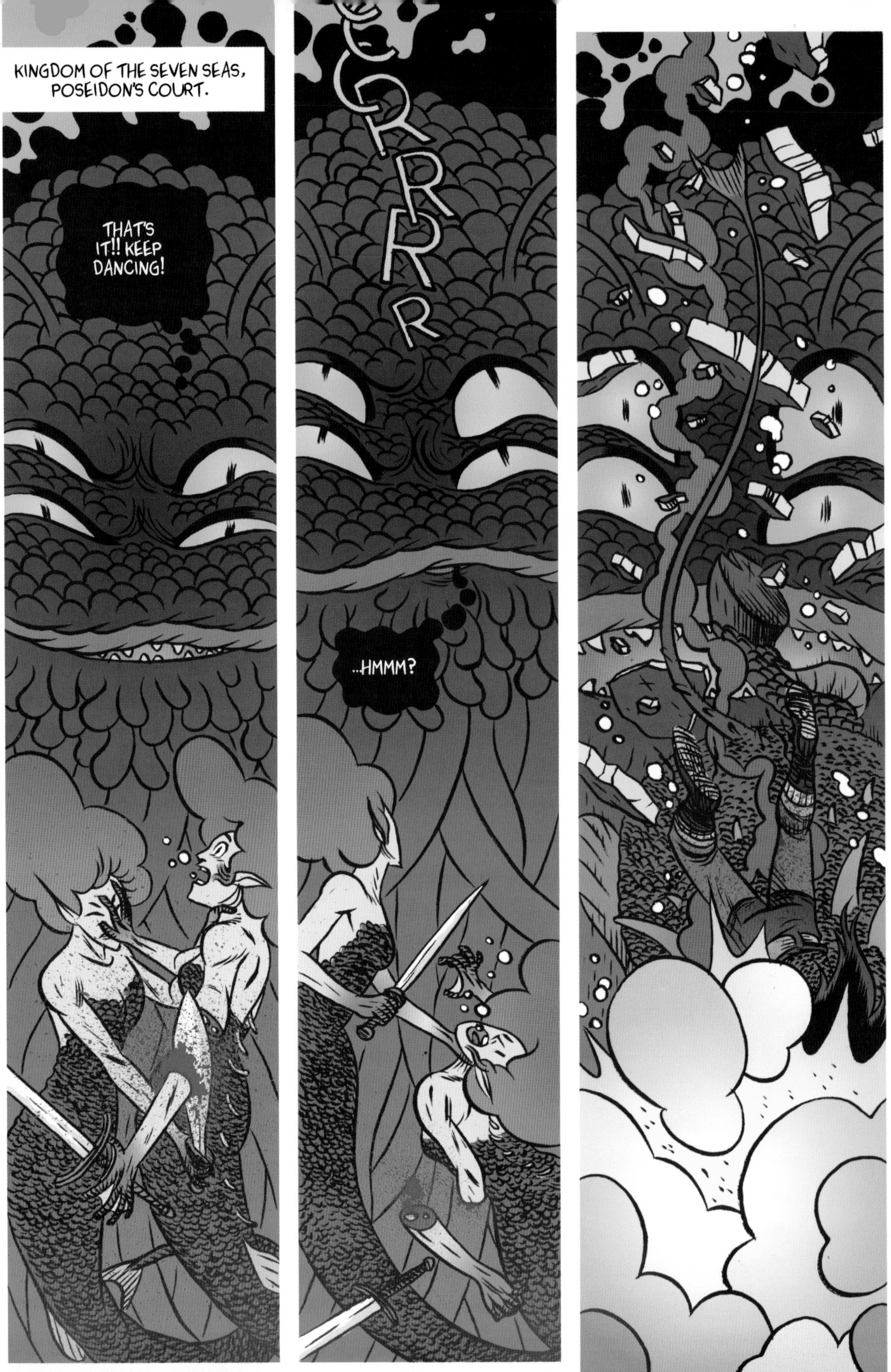
KINGDOM OF THE SEVEN SEAS, POSEIDON'S COURT.
THAT'S IT!! KEEP DANCING!
CRRRR
...HMMM?

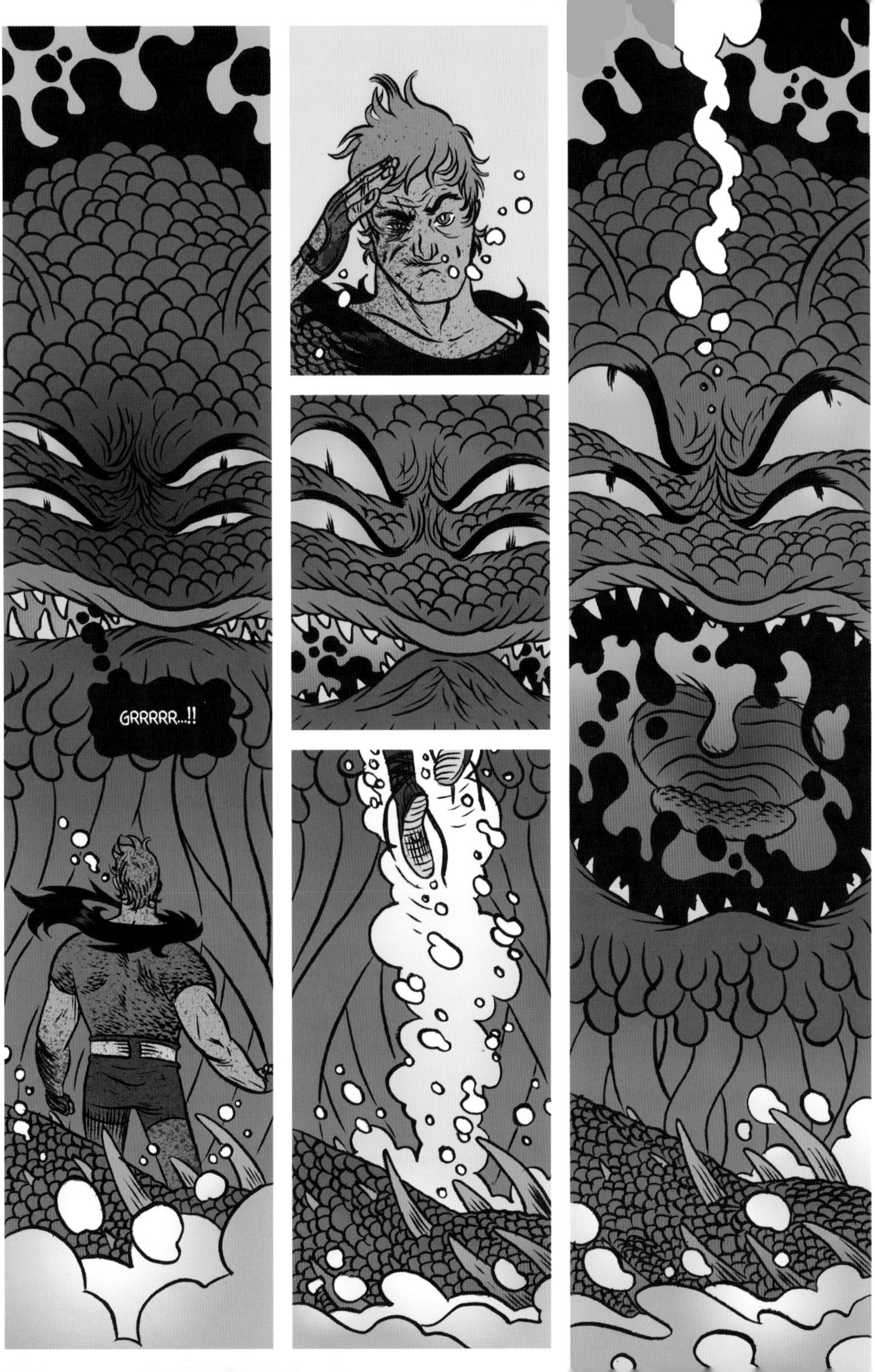
GRRRRR...!!

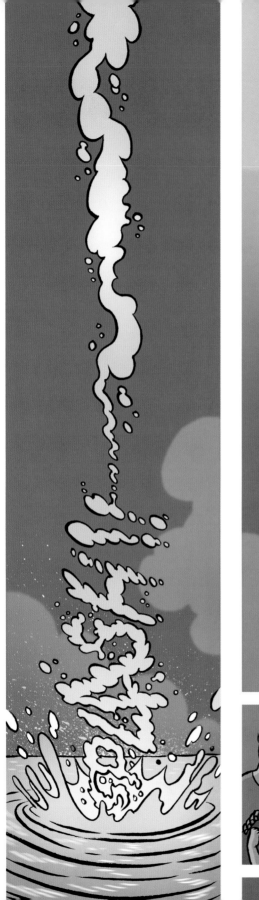

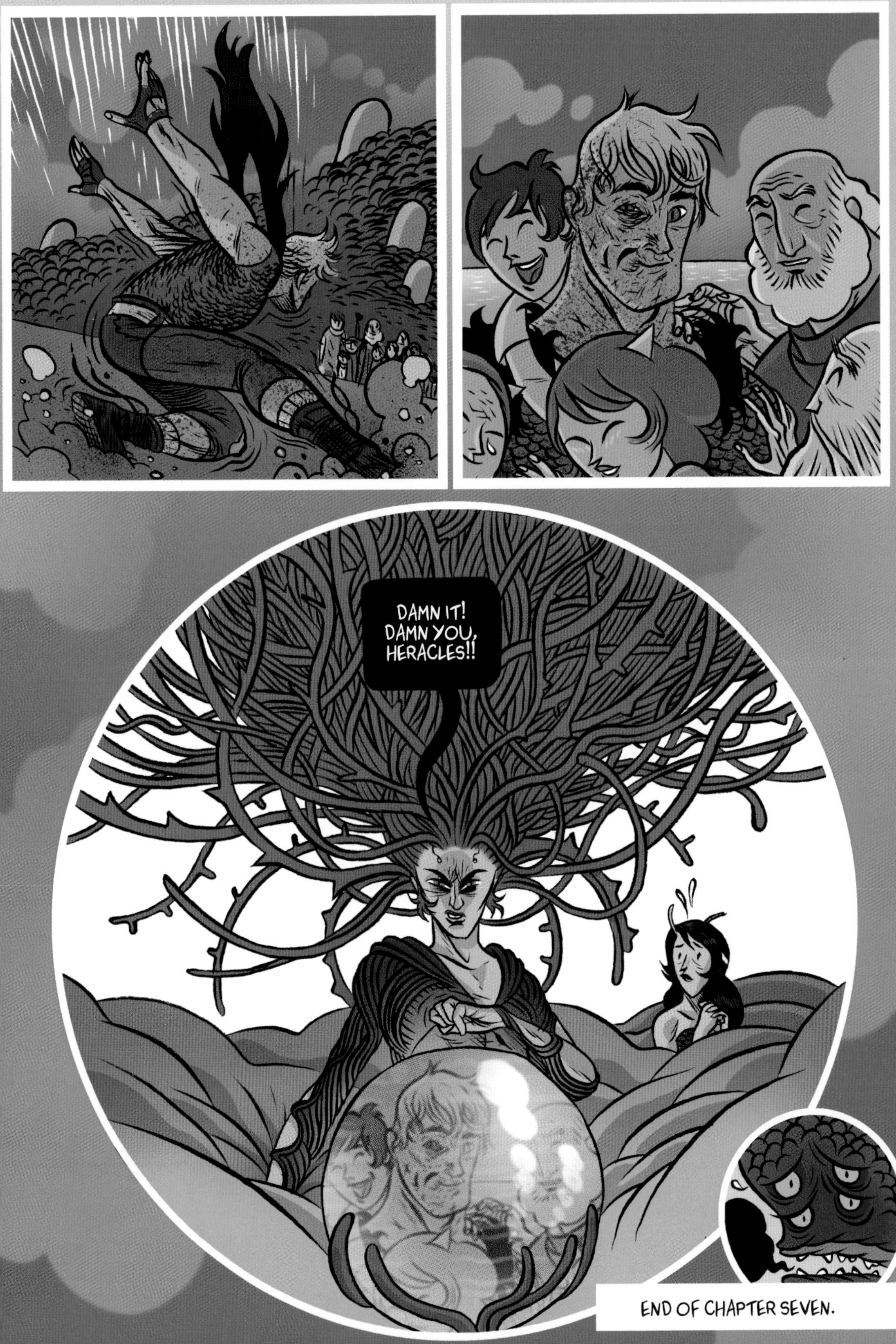
DAMN IT!
DAMN YOU,
HERACLES!!
END OF CHAPTER SEVEN.

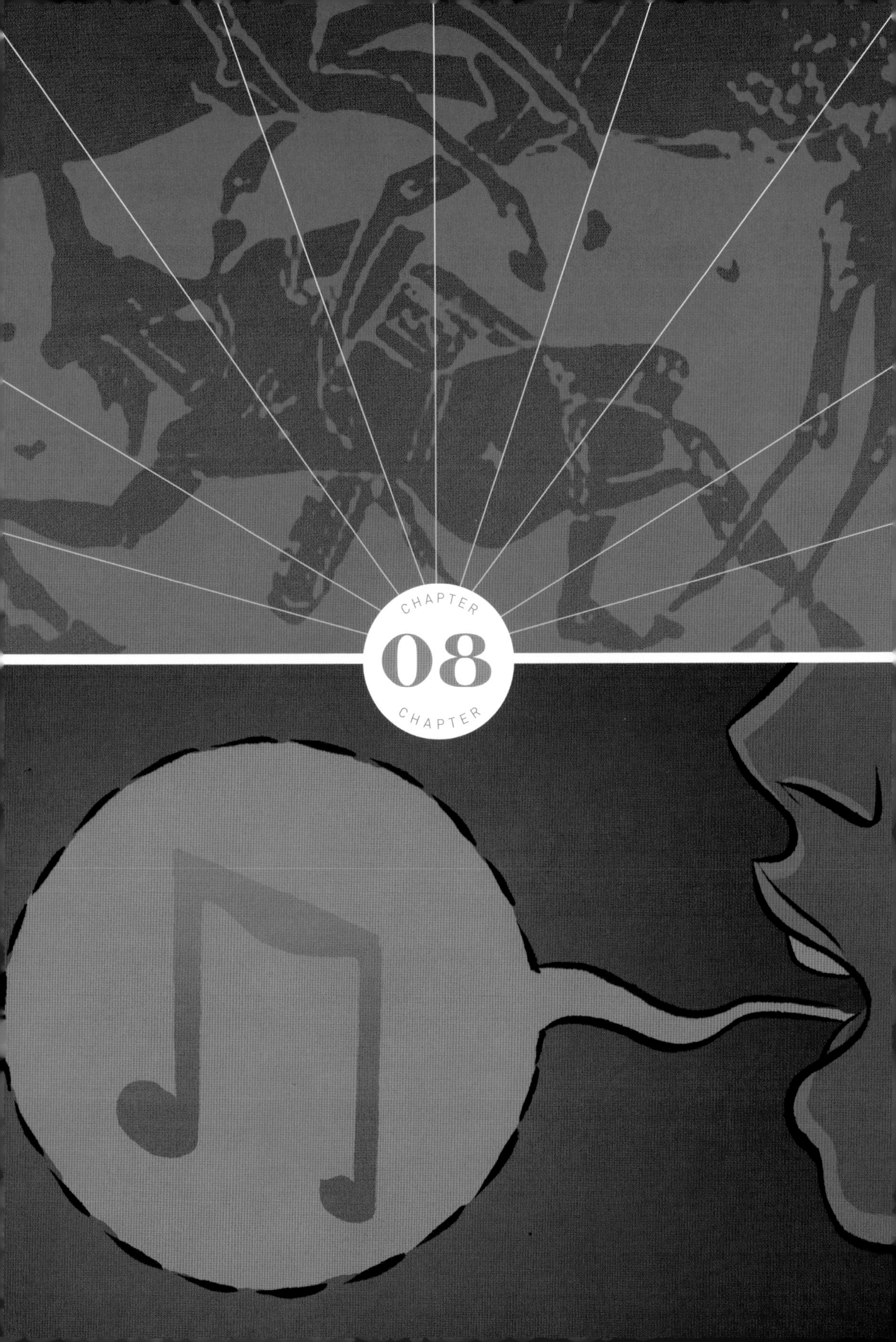
CHAPTER
08
CHAPTER

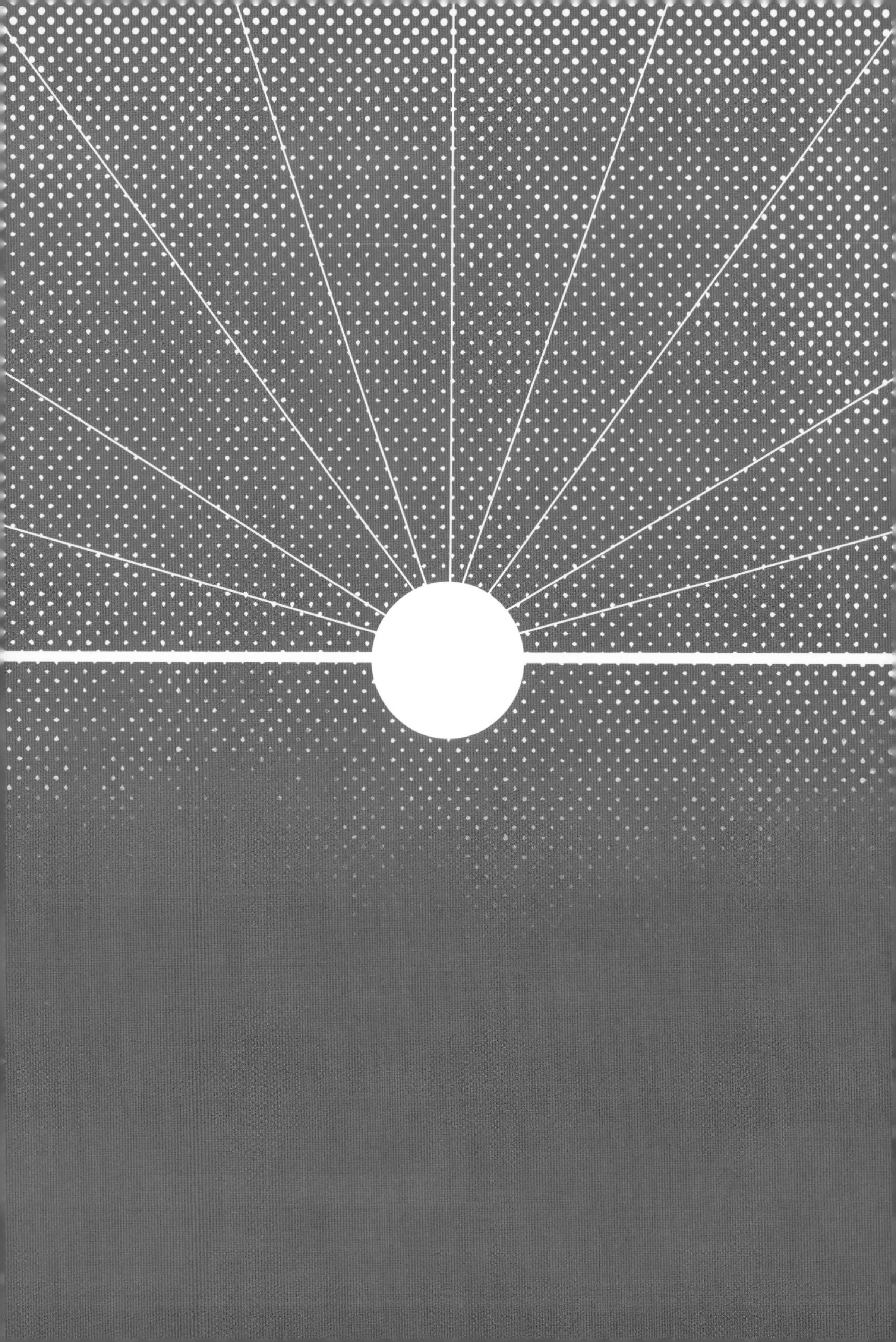

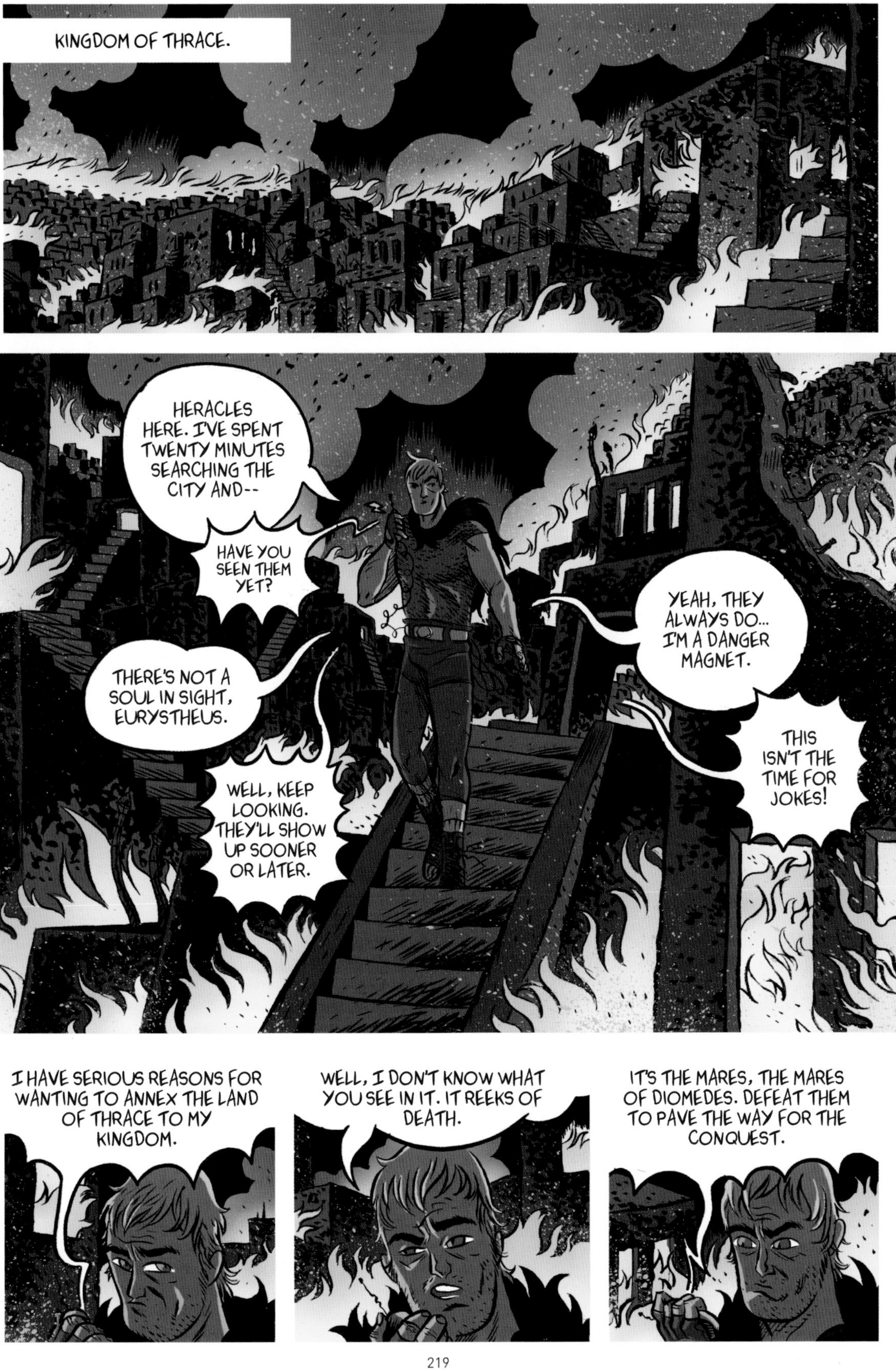
KINGDOM OF THRACE.
HERACLES HERE. I'VE SPENT TWENTY MINUTES SEARCHING THE CITY AND--
HAVE YOU SEEN THEM YET?
THERE'S NOT A SOUL IN SIGHT, EURYSTHEUS.
WELL, KEEP LOOKING. THEY'LL SHOW UP SOONER OR LATER.
YEAH, THEY ALWAYS DO... I'M A DANGER MAGNET.
THIS ISN'T THE TIME FOR JOKES!
I HAVE SERIOUS REASONS FOR WANTING TO ANNEX THE LAND OF THRACE TO MY KINGDOM.
WELL, I DON'T KNOW WHAT YOU SEE IN IT. IT REEKS OF DEATH.
IT'S THE MARES, THE MARES OF DIOMEDES. DEFEAT THEM TO PAVE THE WAY FOR THE CONQUEST.

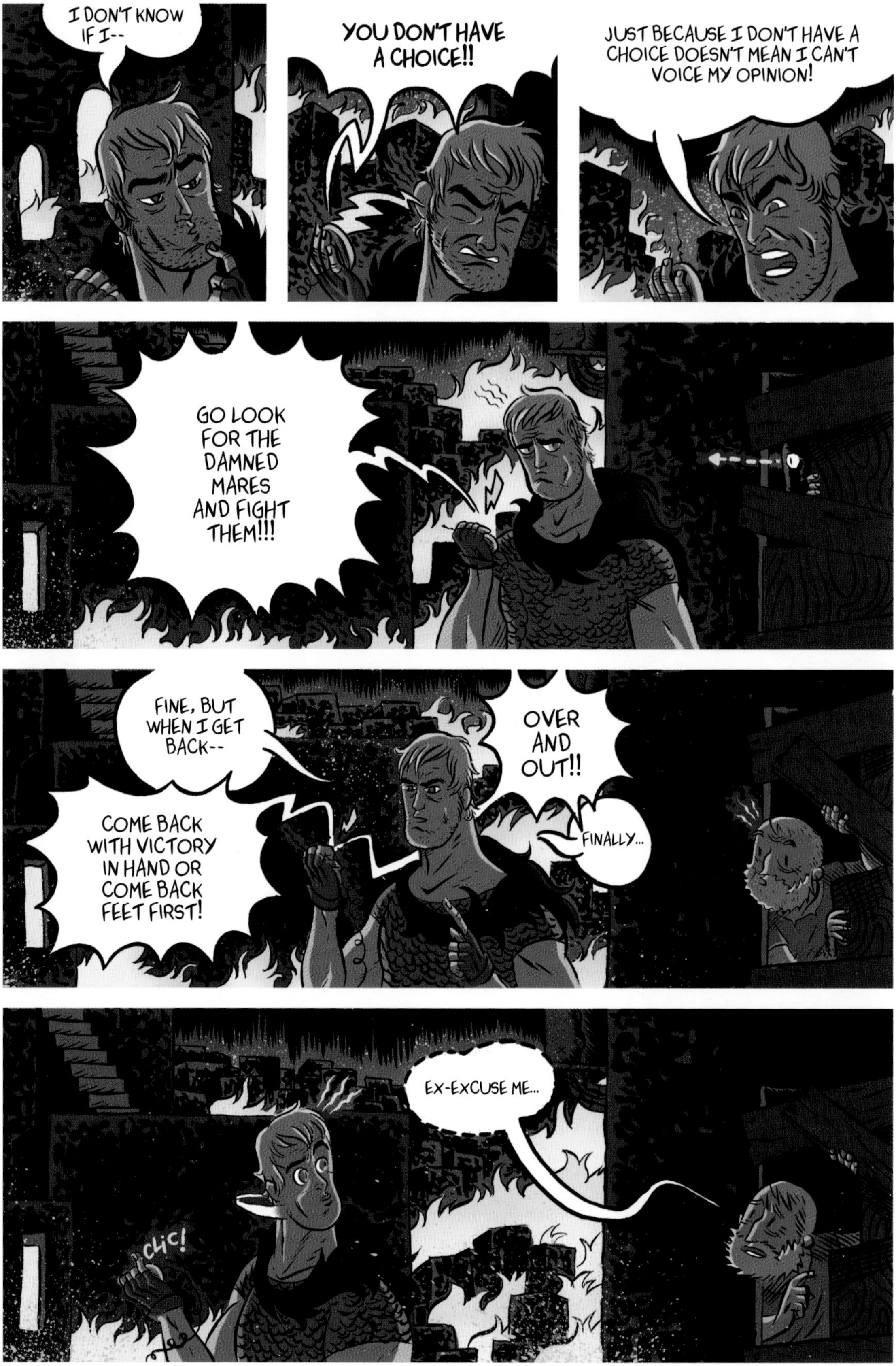

I DON'T KNOW IF I--
YOU DON'T HAVE A CHOICE!!
JUST BECAUSE I DON'T HAVE A CHOICE DOESN'T MEAN I CAN'T VOICE MY OPINION!
GO LOOK FOR THE DAMNED MARES AND FIGHT THEM!!!
FINE, BUT WHEN I GET BACK--
OVER AND OUT!!
COME BACK WITH VICTORY IN HAND OR COME BACK FEET FIRST!
FINALLY...
EX-EXCUSE ME...
CLIC!

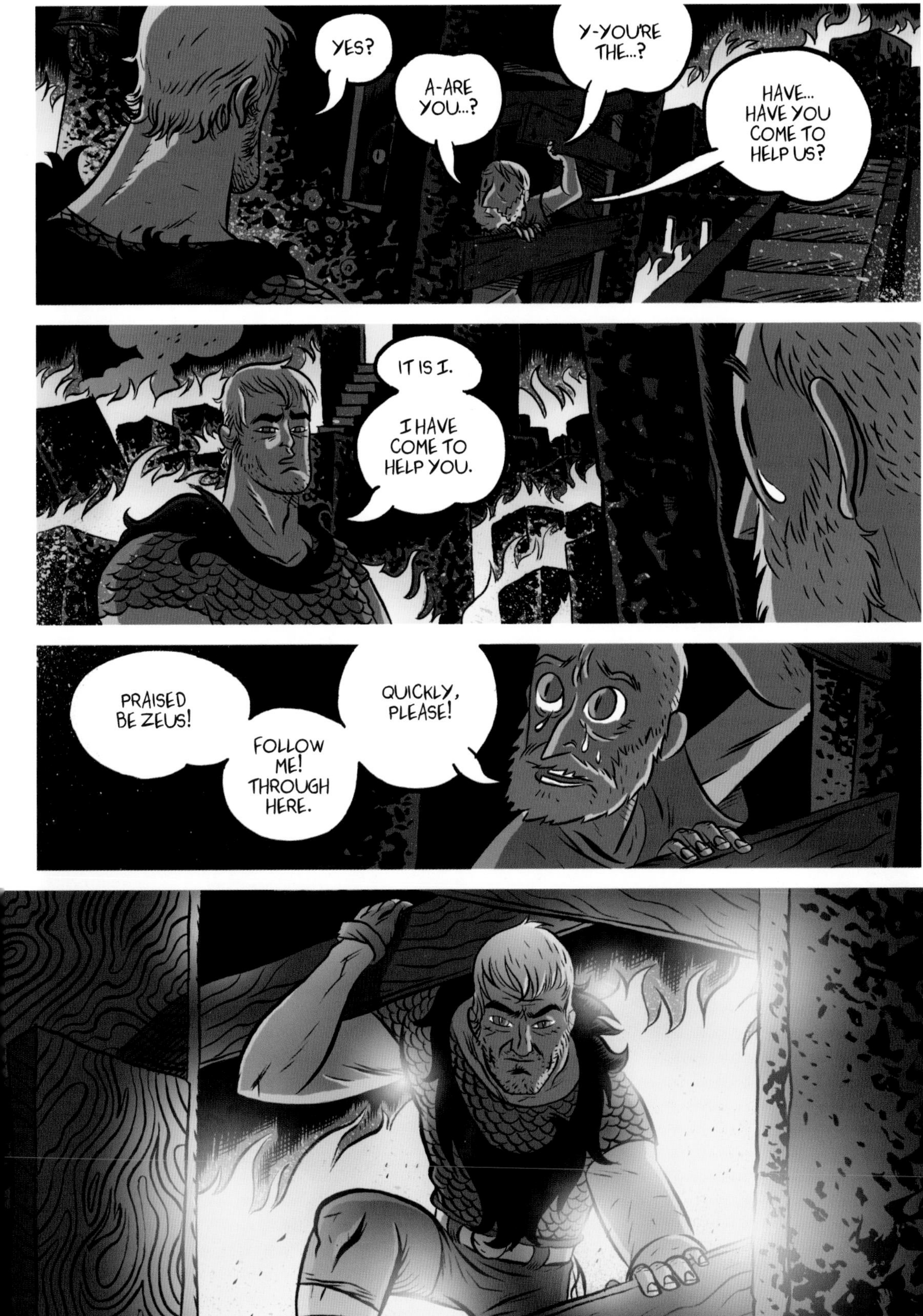
YES?
A-ARE YOU...?
Y-YOU'RE THE...?
HAVE... HAVE YOU COME TO HELP US?
IT IS I.
I HAVE COME TO HELP YOU.
PRAISED BE ZEUS!
FOLLOW ME! THROUGH HERE.
QUICKLY, PLEASE!

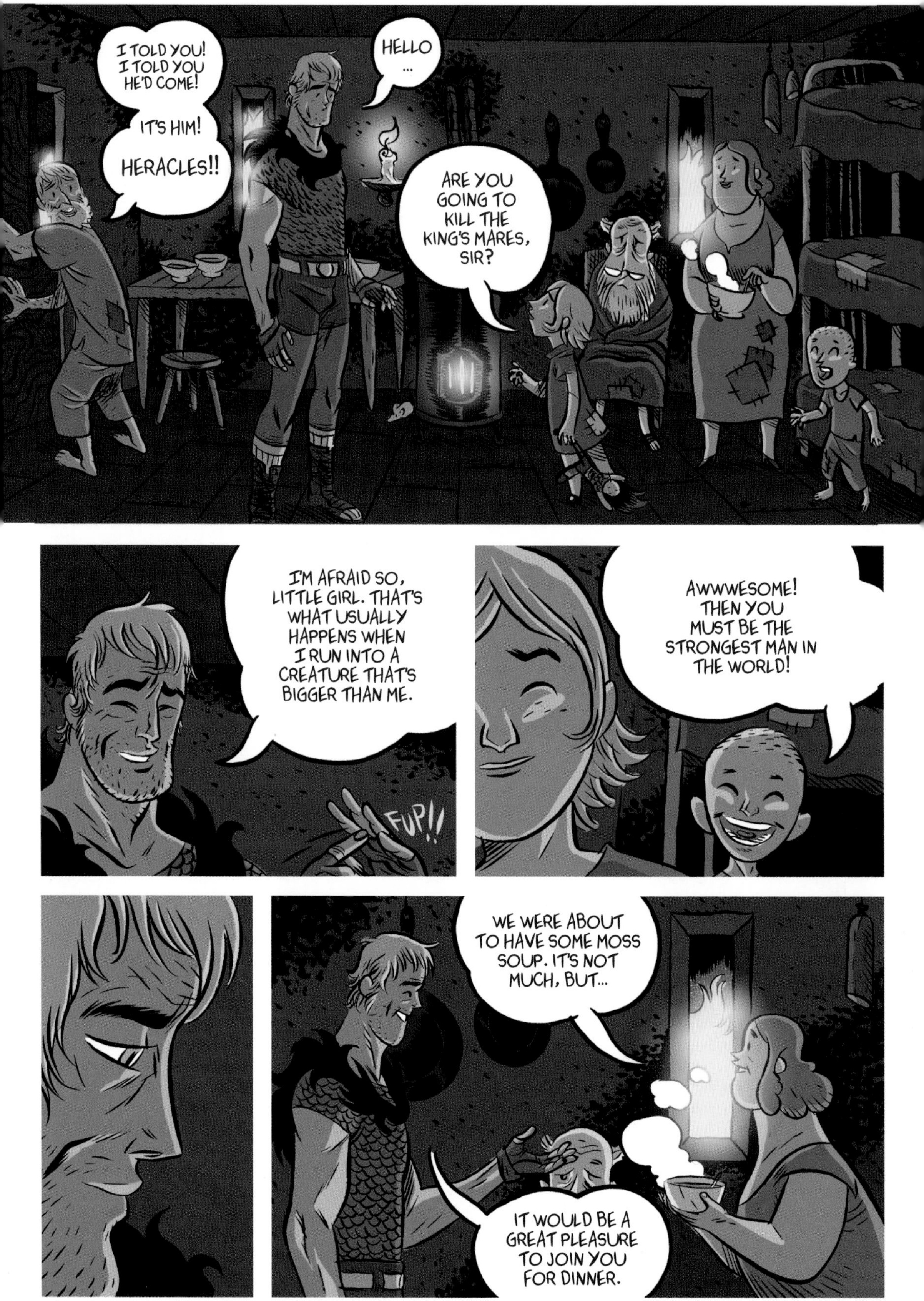
I TOLD YOU! I TOLD YOU HE'D COME!
IT'S HIM!
HERACLES!!
HELLO ...
ARE YOU GOING TO KILL THE KING'S MARES, SIR?
I'M AFRAID SO, LITTLE GIRL. THAT'S WHAT USUALLY HAPPENS WHEN I RUN INTO A CREATURE THAT'S BIGGER THAN ME.
FUP!!
AWWWESOME! THEN YOU MUST BE THE STRONGEST MAN IN THE WORLD!
WE WERE ABOUT TO HAVE SOME MOSS SOUP. IT'S NOT MUCH, BUT...
IT WOULD BE A GREAT PLEASURE TO JOIN YOU FOR DINNER.

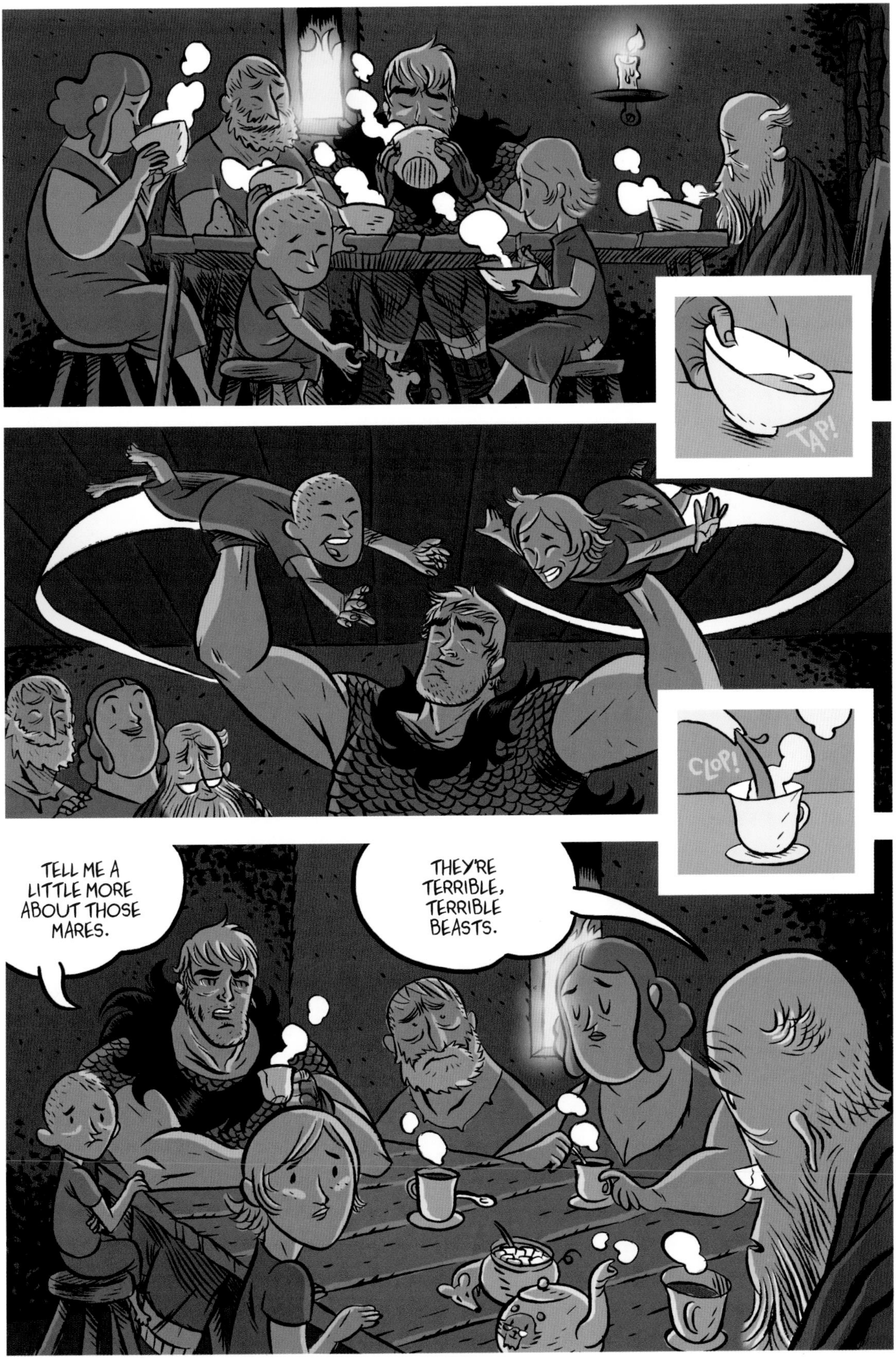
TAP!
CLOP!
TELL ME A LITTLE MORE ABOUT THOSE MARES.
THEY'RE TERRIBLE, TERRIBLE BEASTS.

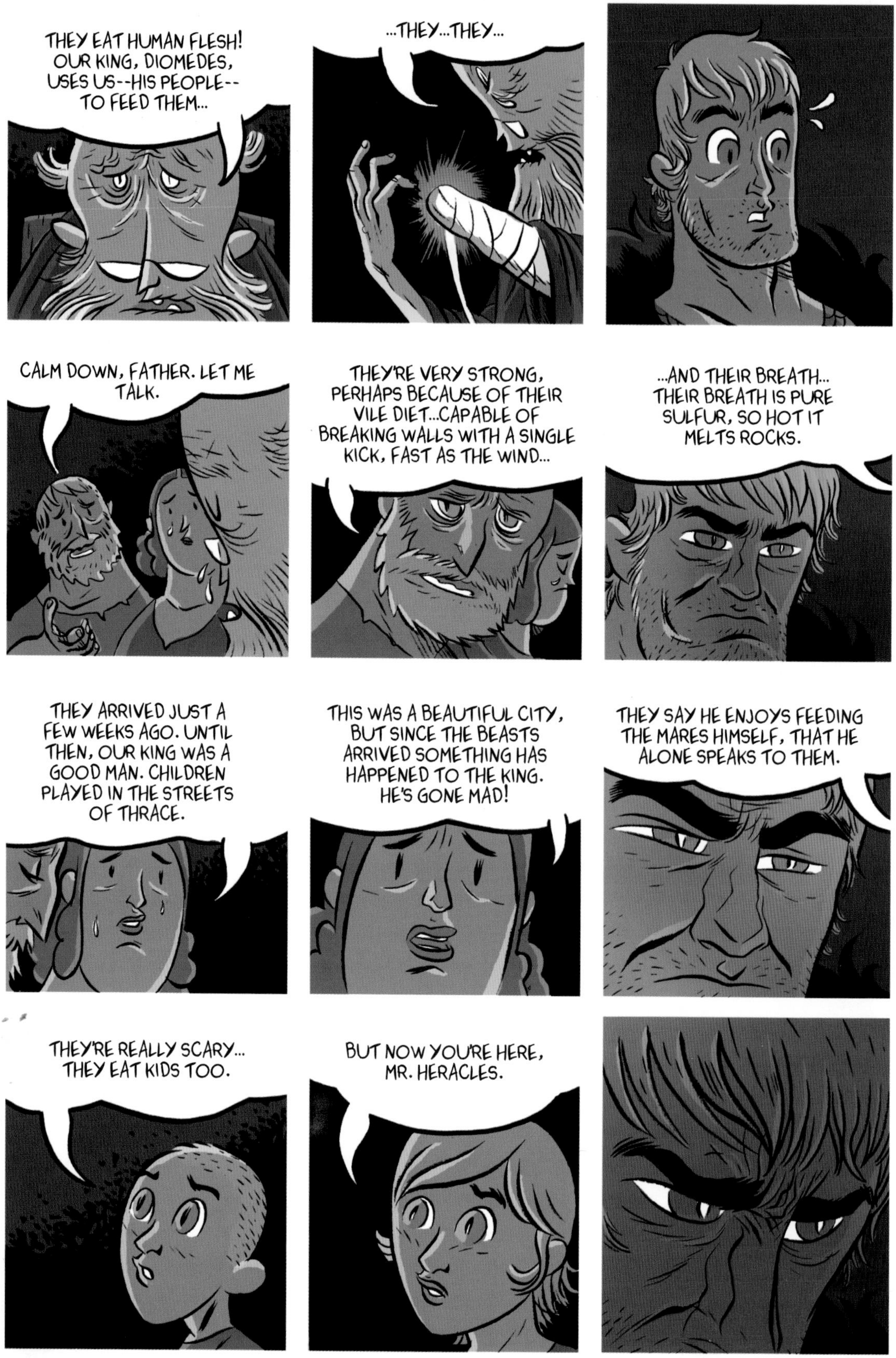
THEY EAT HUMAN FLESH! OUR KING, DIOMEDES, USES US--HIS PEOPLE-- TO FEED THEM...
...THEY...THEY...
CALM DOWN, FATHER. LET ME TALK.
THEY'RE VERY STRONG, PERHAPS BECAUSE OF THEIR VILE DIET...CAPABLE OF BREAKING WALLS WITH A SINGLE KICK, FAST AS THE WIND...
...AND THEIR BREATH... THEIR BREATH IS PURE SULFUR, SO HOT IT MELTS ROCKS.
THEY ARRIVED JUST A FEW WEEKS AGO. UNTIL THEN, OUR KING WAS A GOOD MAN. CHILDREN PLAYED IN THE STREETS OF THRACE.
THIS WAS A BEAUTIFUL CITY, BUT SINCE THE BEASTS ARRIVED SOMETHING HAS HAPPENED TO THE KING. HE'S GONE MAD!
THEY SAY HE ENJOYS FEEDING THE MARES HIMSELF, THAT HE ALONE SPEAKS TO THEM.
THEY'RE REALLY SCARY... THEY EAT KIDS TOO.
BUT NOW YOU'RE HERE, MR. HERACLES.

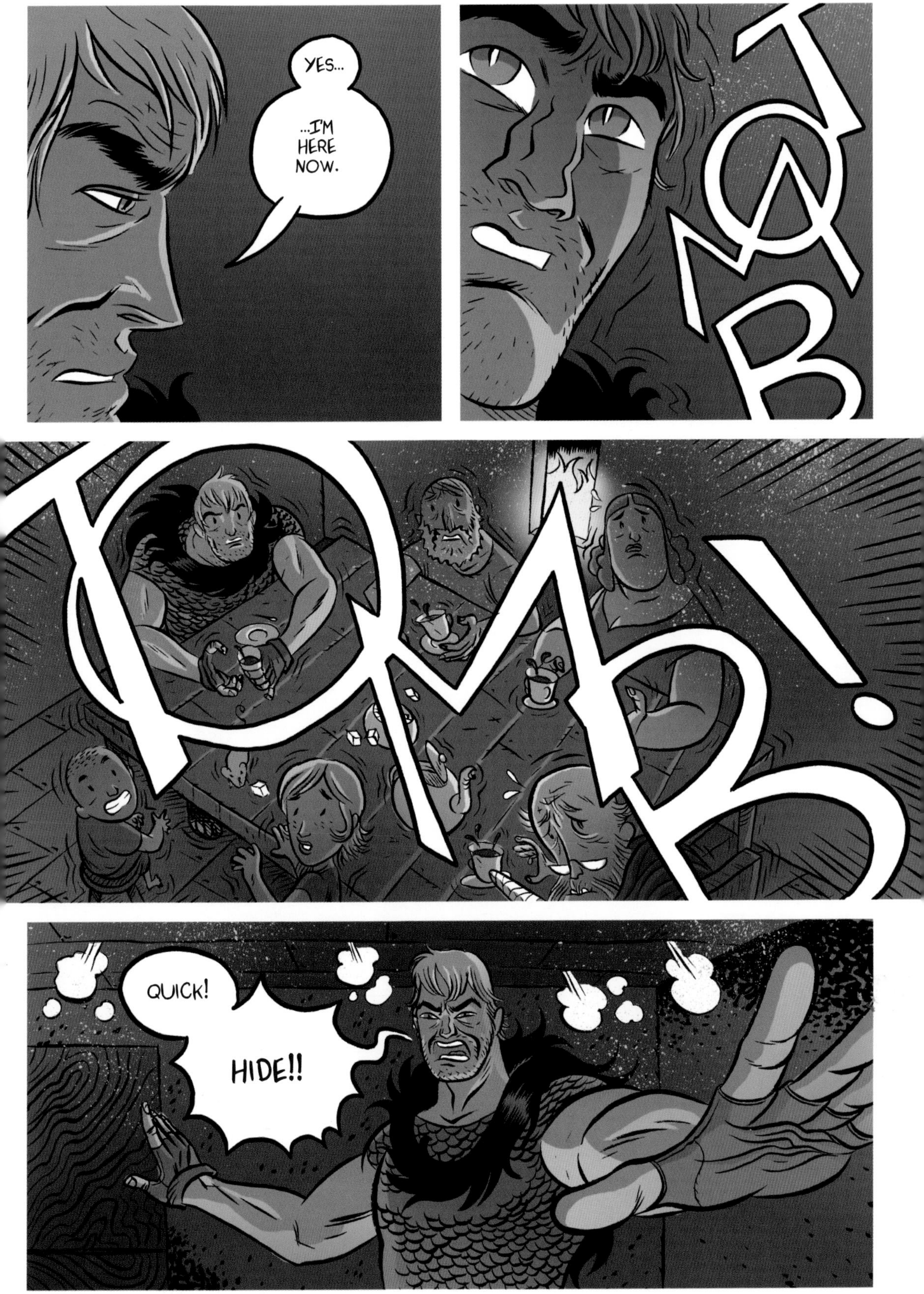
YES...
...I'M HERE NOW.
TOMB
TOMB!
QUICK!
HIDE!!

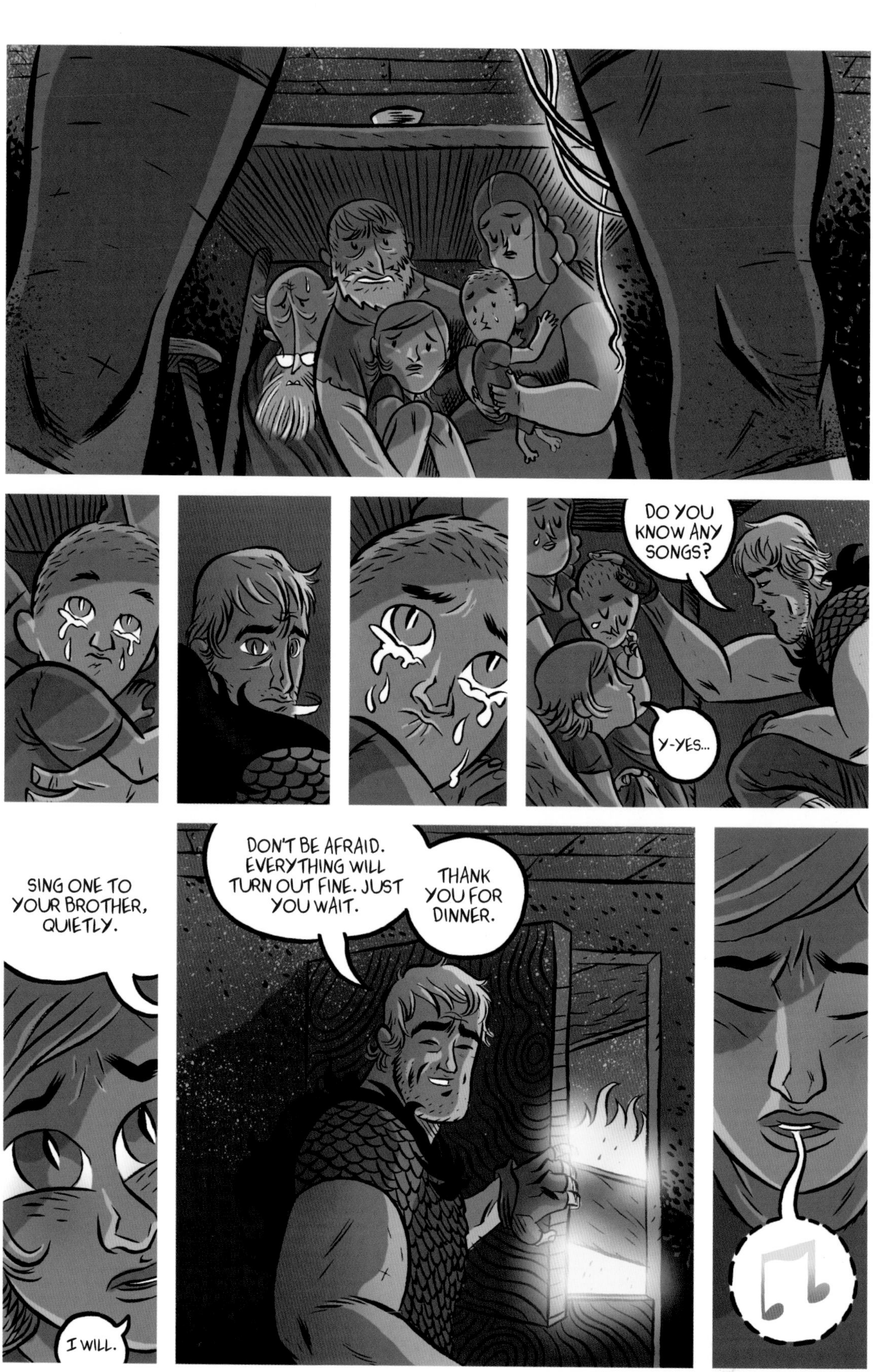
DO YOU KNOW ANY SONGS?
Y-YES...
SING ONE TO YOUR BROTHER, QUIETLY.
I WILL.
DON'T BE AFRAID. EVERYTHING WILL TURN OUT FINE. JUST YOU WAIT.
THANK YOU FOR DINNER.

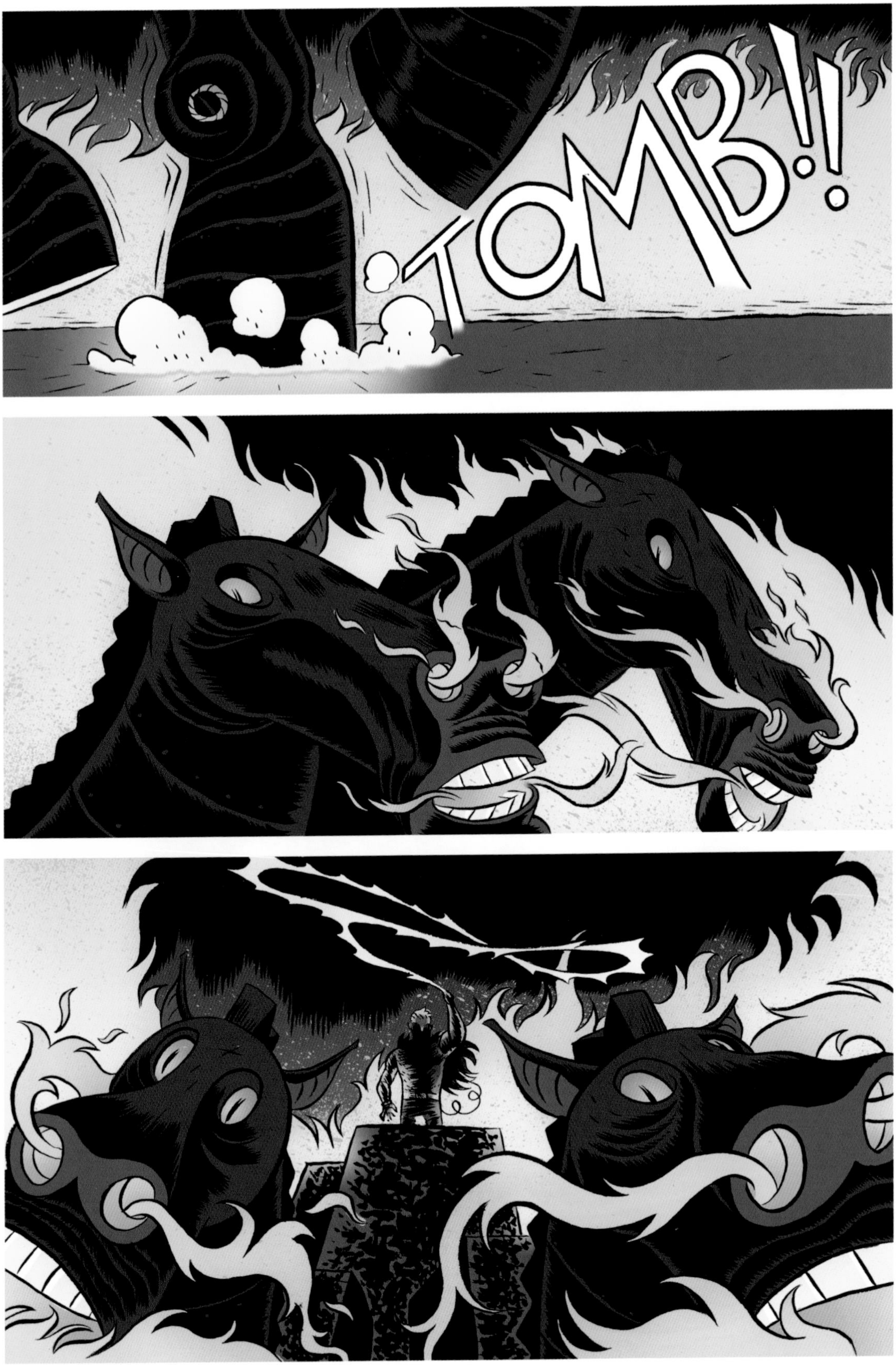
TOMB!!

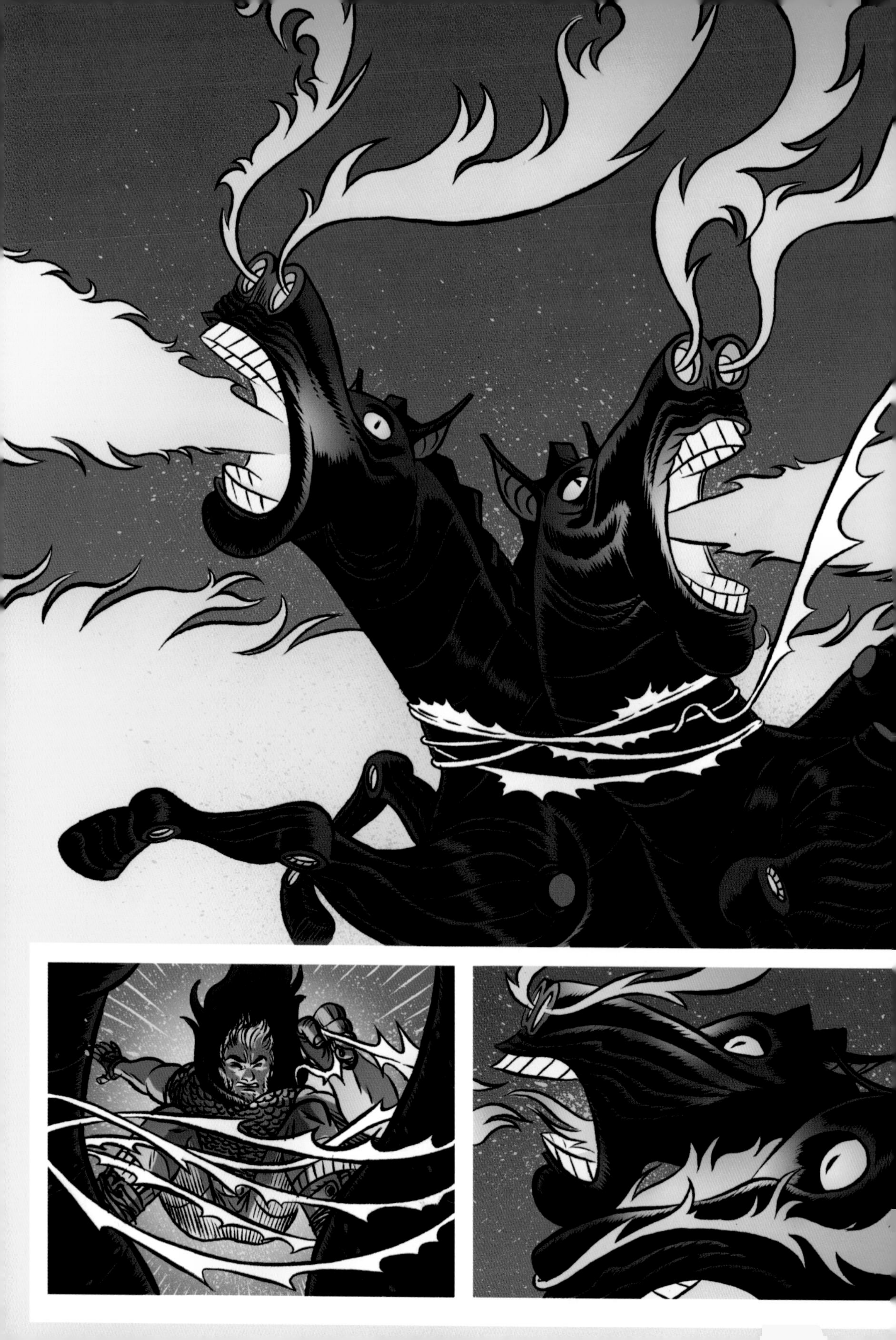

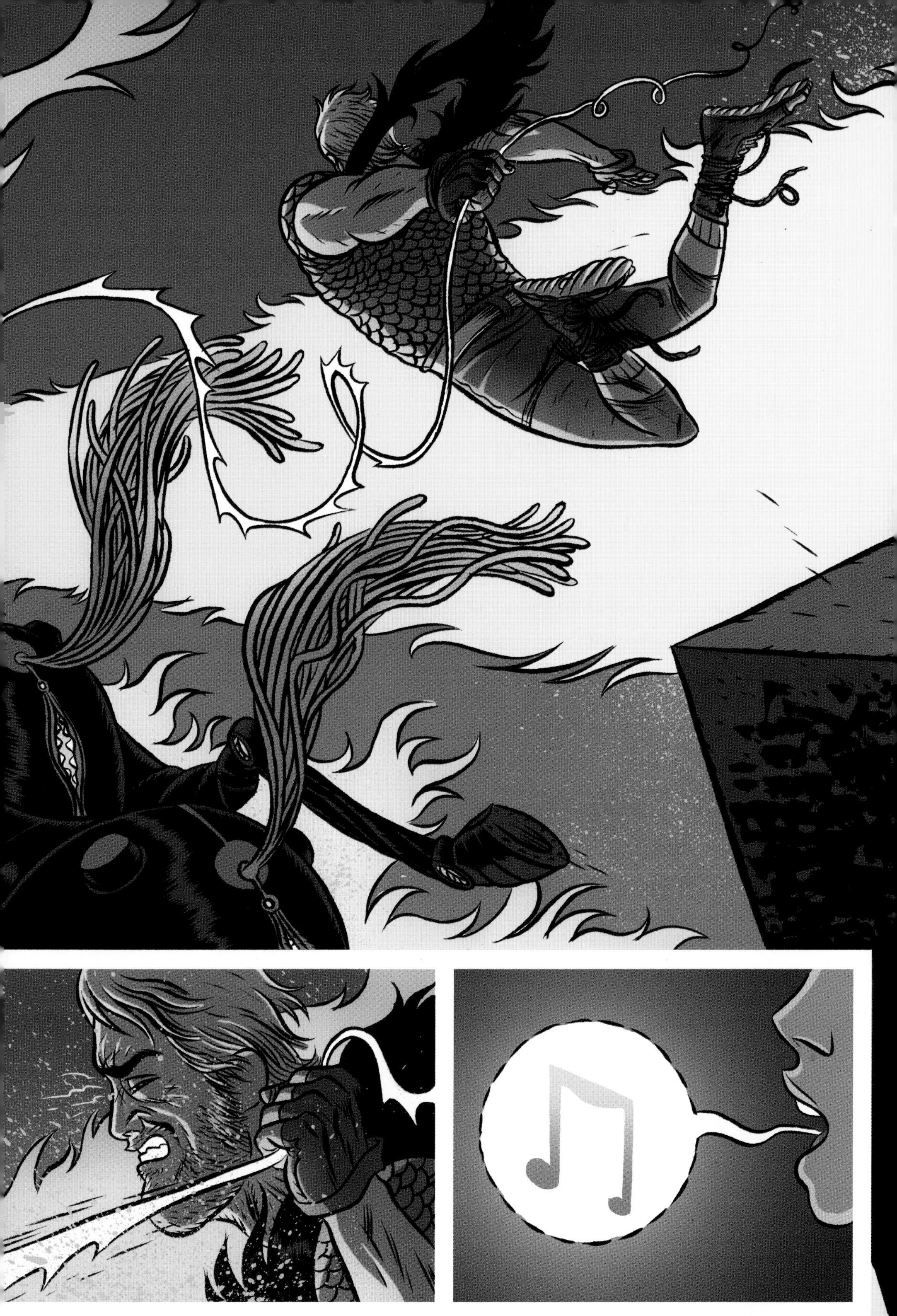

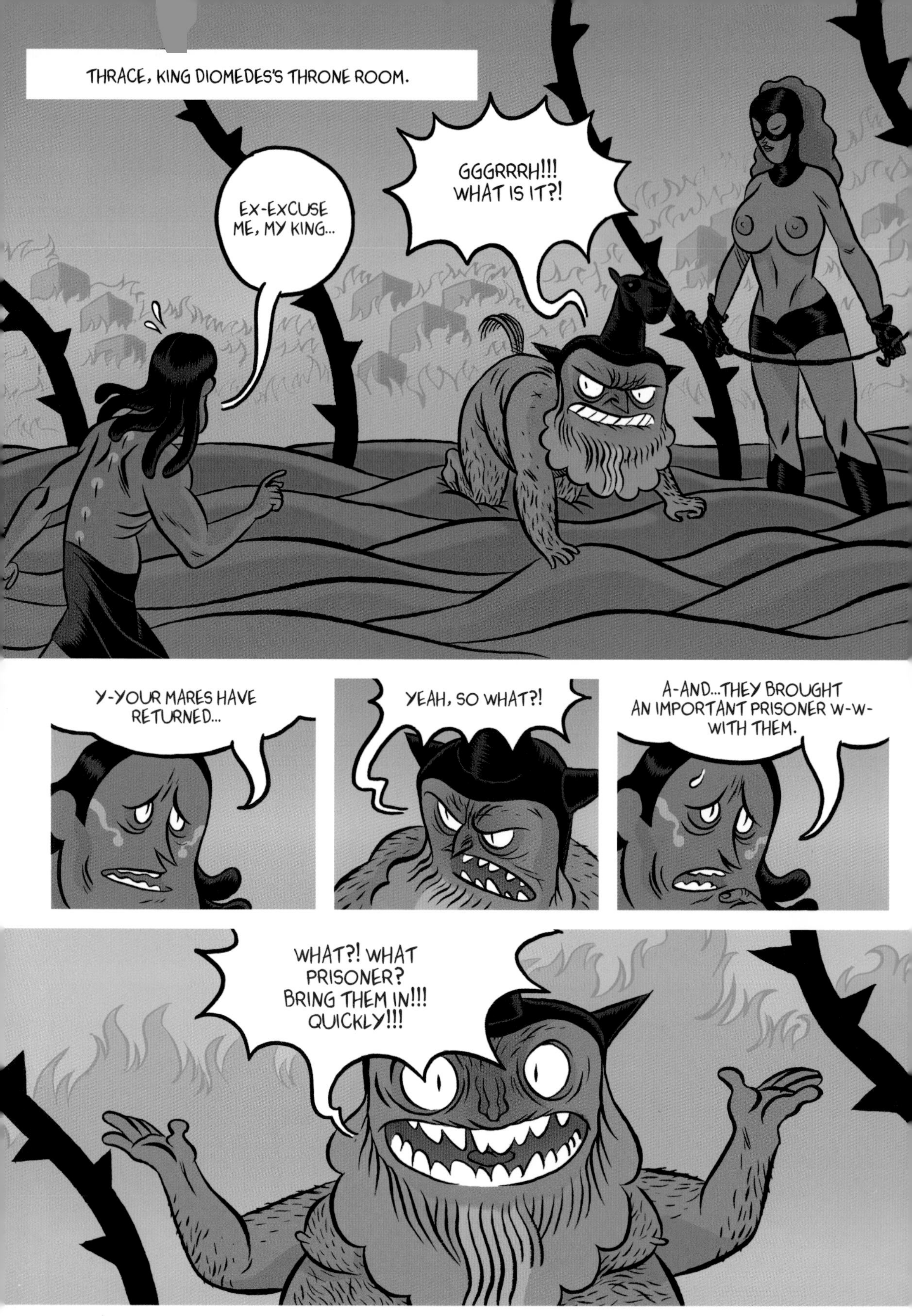
THRACE, KING DIOMEDES'S THRONE ROOM.
EX-EXCUSE ME, MY KING...
GGGRRRH!!! WHAT IS IT?!
Y-YOUR MARES HAVE RETURNED...
YEAH, SO WHAT?!
A-AND...THEY BROUGHT AN IMPORTANT PRISONER W-W-WITH THEM.
WHAT?! WHAT PRISONER? BRING THEM IN!!! QUICKLY!!!

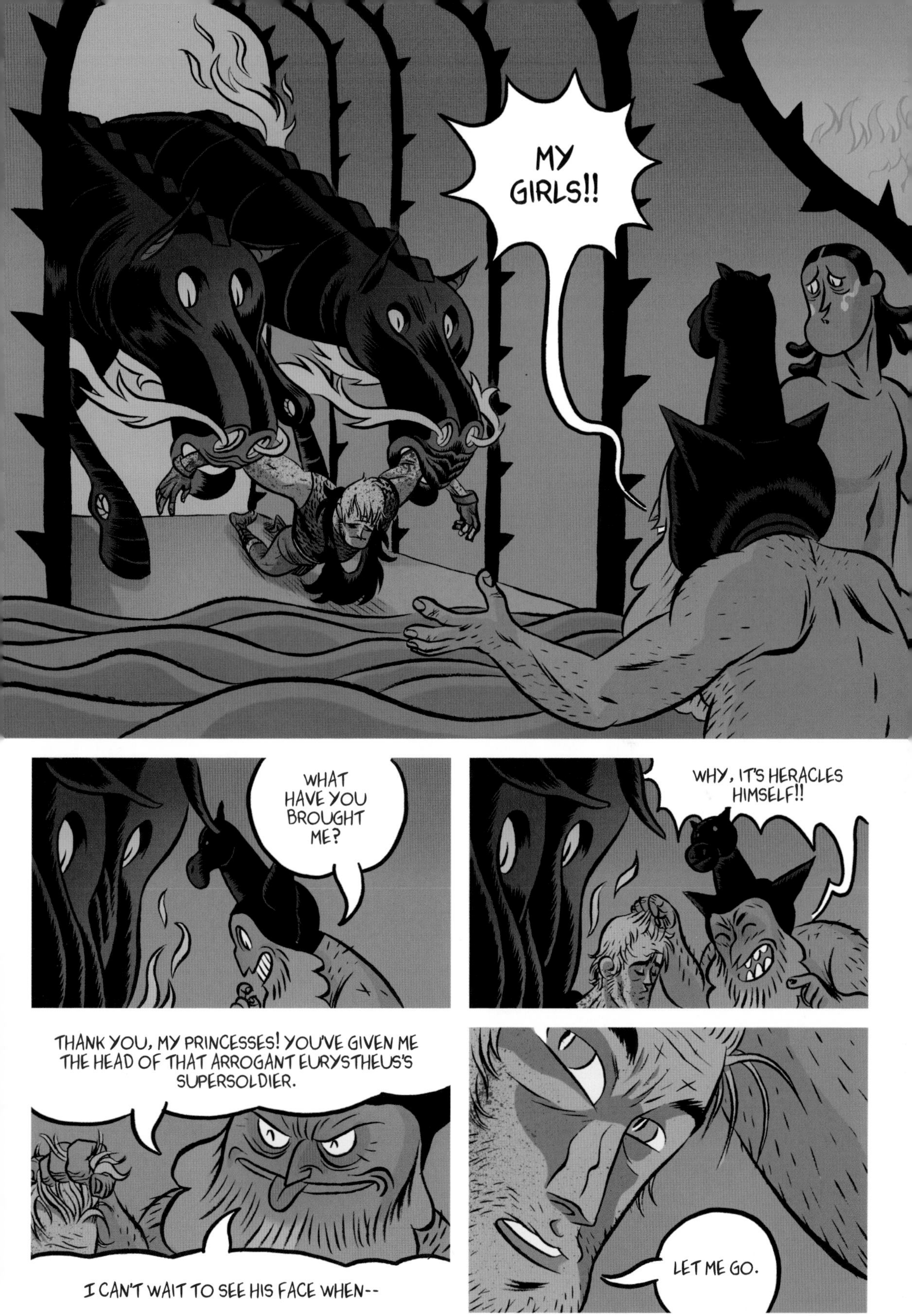
MY GIRLS!!
WHAT HAVE YOU BROUGHT ME?
WHY, IT'S HERACLES HIMSELF!!
THANK YOU, MY PRINCESSES! YOU'VE GIVEN ME THE HEAD OF THAT ARROGANT EURYSTHEUS'S SUPERSOLDIER.
I CAN'T WAIT TO SEE HIS FACE WHEN--
LET ME GO.

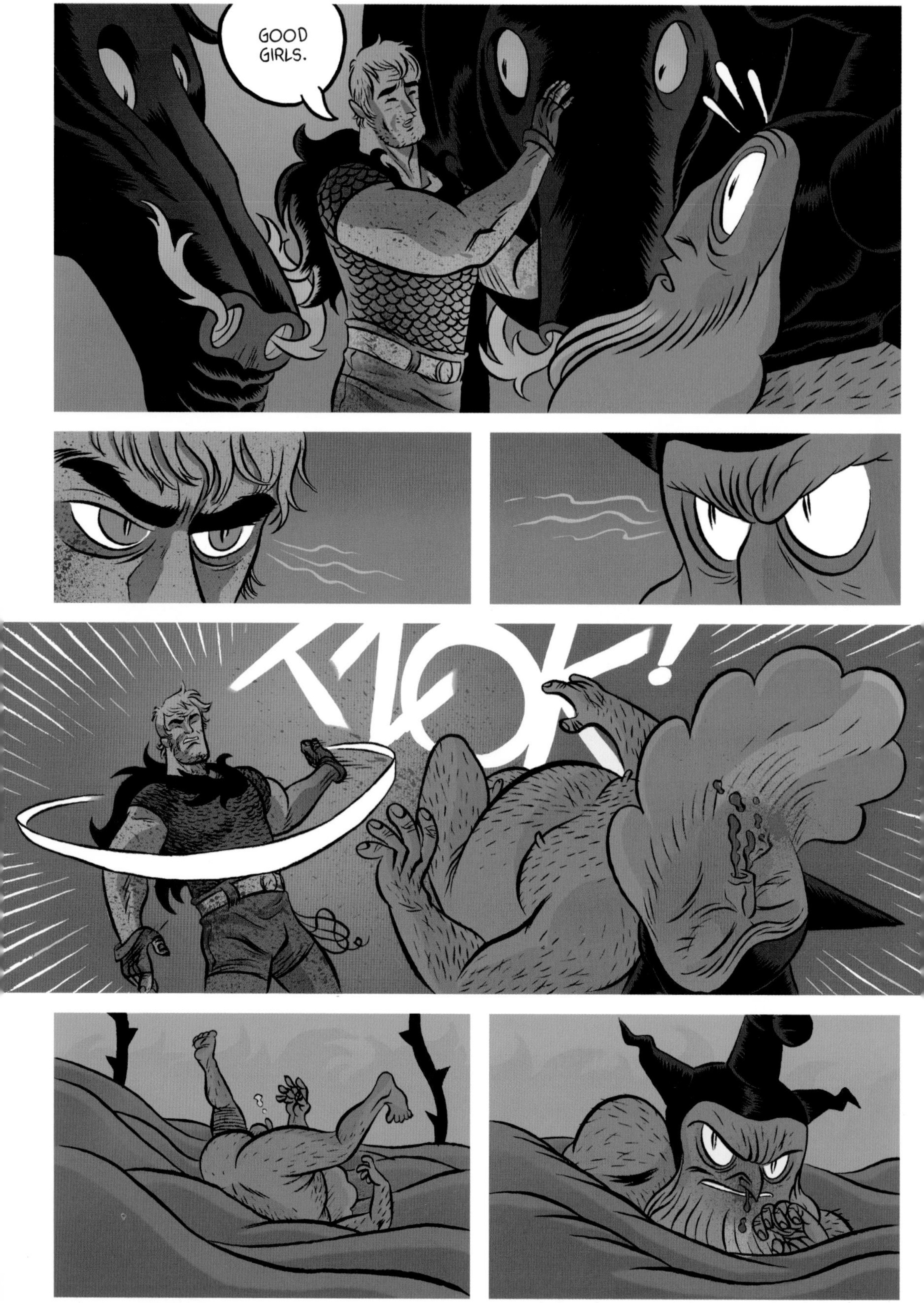
GOOD GIRLS.
KNOK!

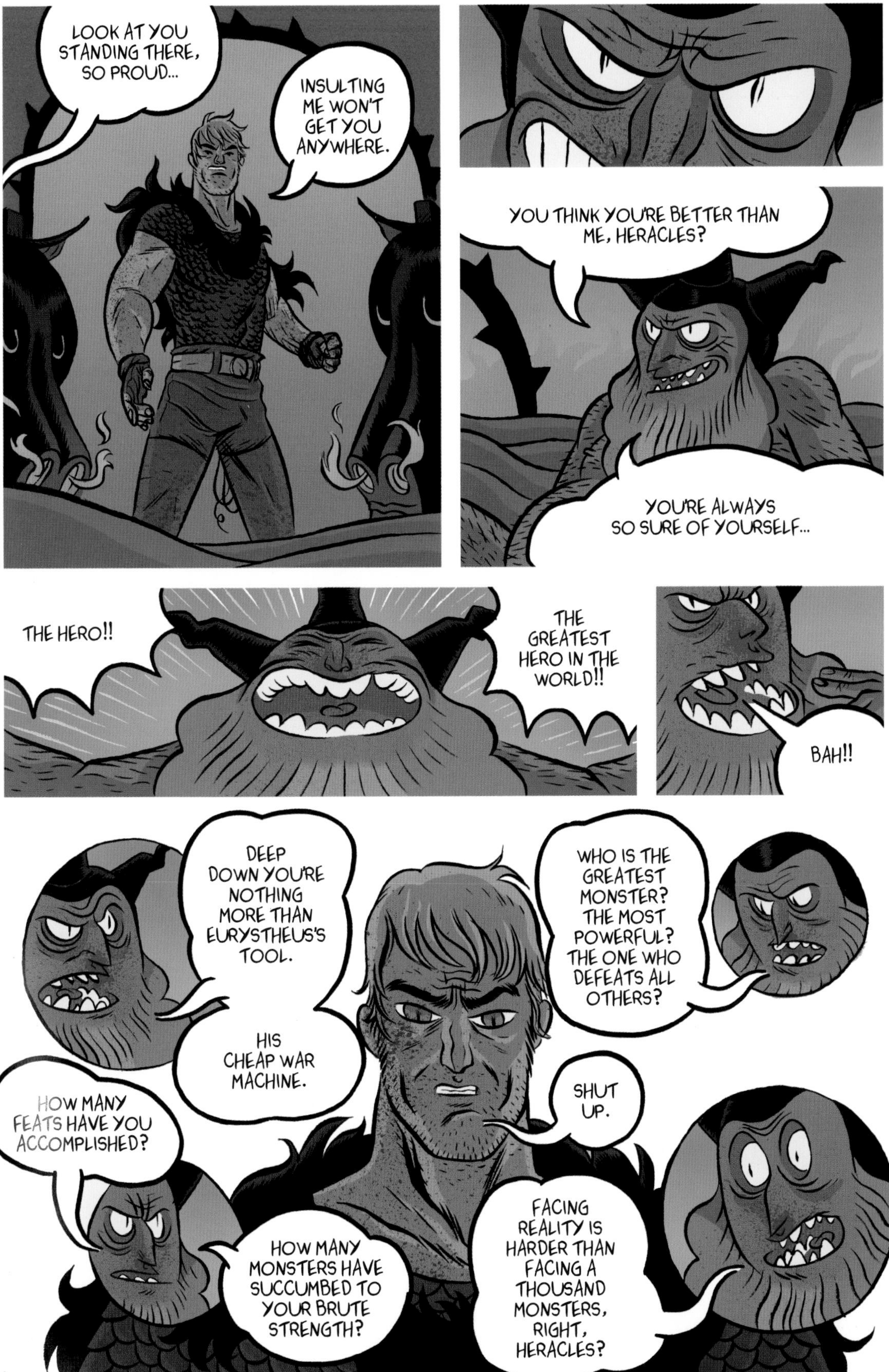
LOOK AT YOU STANDING THERE, SO PROUD...
INSULTING ME WON'T GET YOU ANYWHERE.
YOU THINK YOU'RE BETTER THAN ME, HERACLES?
YOU'RE ALWAYS SO SURE OF YOURSELF...
THE HERO!!
THE GREATEST HERO IN THE WORLD!!
BAH!!
DEEP DOWN YOU'RE NOTHING MORE THAN EURYSTHEUS'S TOOL.
HIS CHEAP WAR MACHINE.
WHO IS THE GREATEST MONSTER? THE MOST POWERFUL? THE ONE WHO DEFEATS ALL OTHERS?
HOW MANY FEATS HAVE YOU ACCOMPLISHED?
SHUT UP.
HOW MANY MONSTERS HAVE SUCCUMBED TO YOUR BRUTE STRENGTH?
FACING REALITY IS HARDER THAN FACING A THOUSAND MONSTERS, RIGHT, HERACLES?

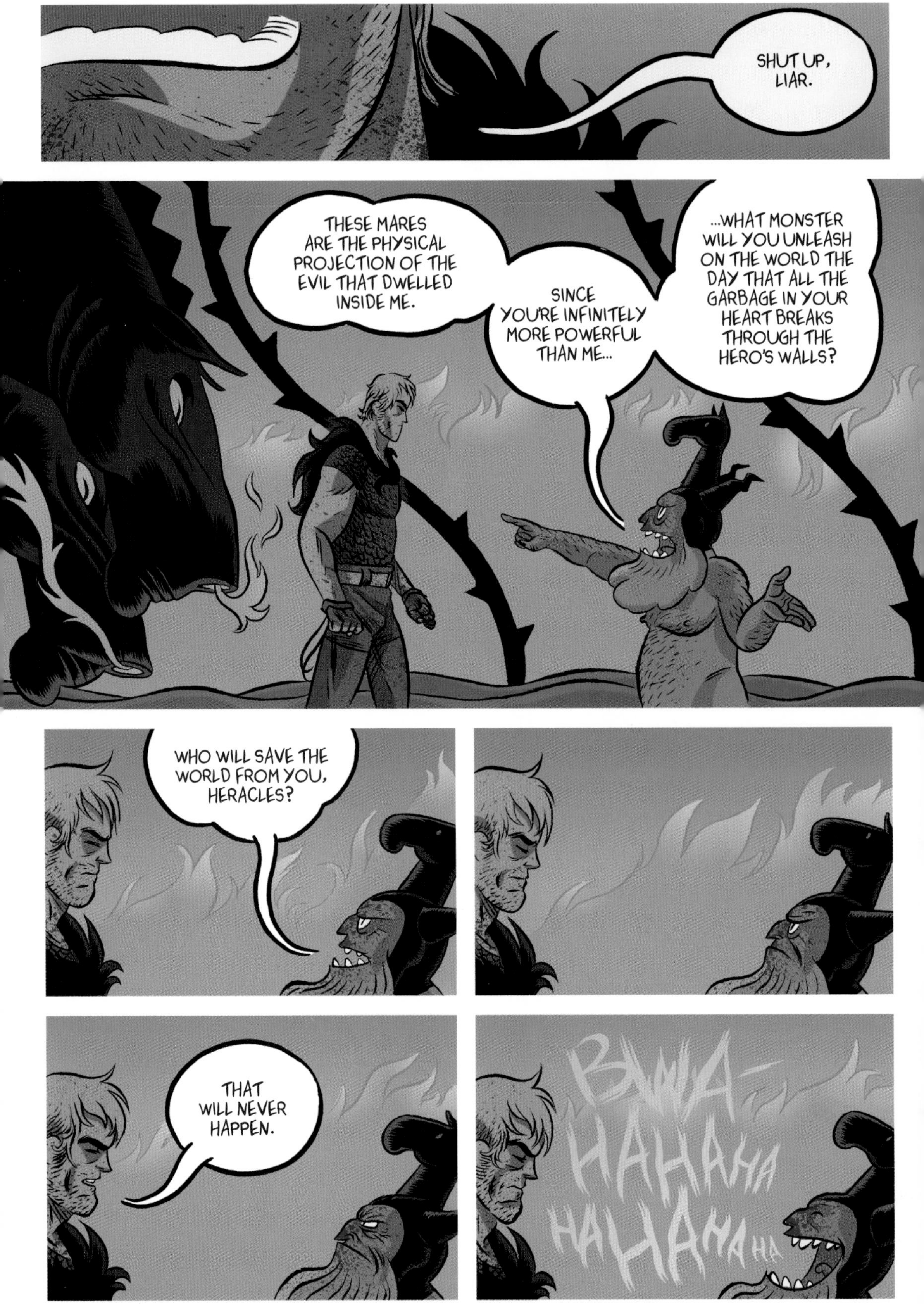
SHUT UP, LIAR.
THESE MARES ARE THE PHYSICAL PROJECTION OF THE EVIL THAT DWELLED INSIDE ME.
SINCE YOU'RE INFINITELY MORE POWERFUL THAN ME...
...WHAT MONSTER WILL YOU UNLEASH ON THE WORLD THE DAY THAT ALL THE GARBAGE IN YOUR HEART BREAKS THROUGH THE HERO'S WALLS?
WHO WILL SAVE THE WORLD FROM YOU, HERACLES?
THAT WILL NEVER HAPPEN.
BWA-HAHAHAHA HAHAHAHAHA

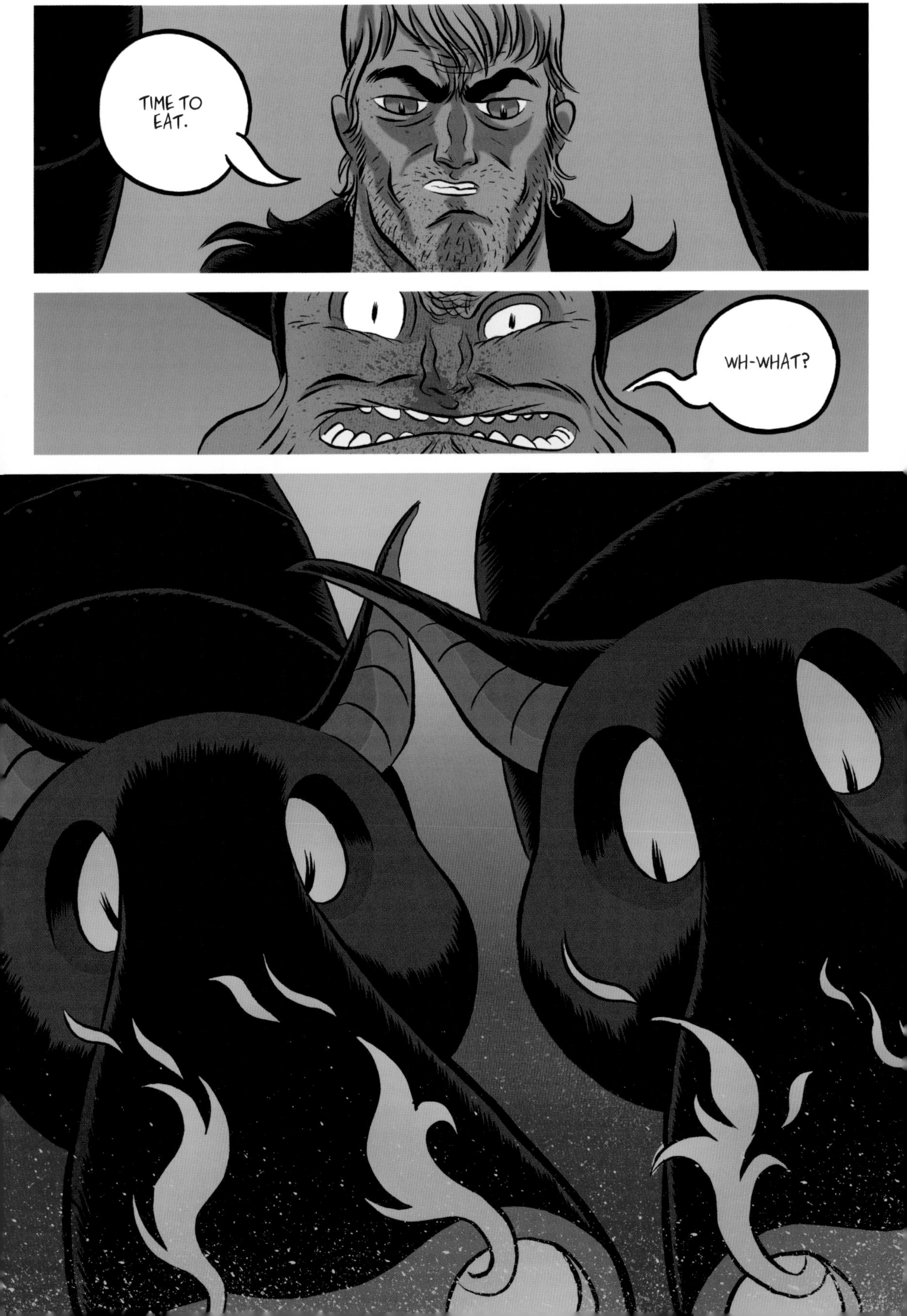
TIME TO EAT.
WH-WHAT?

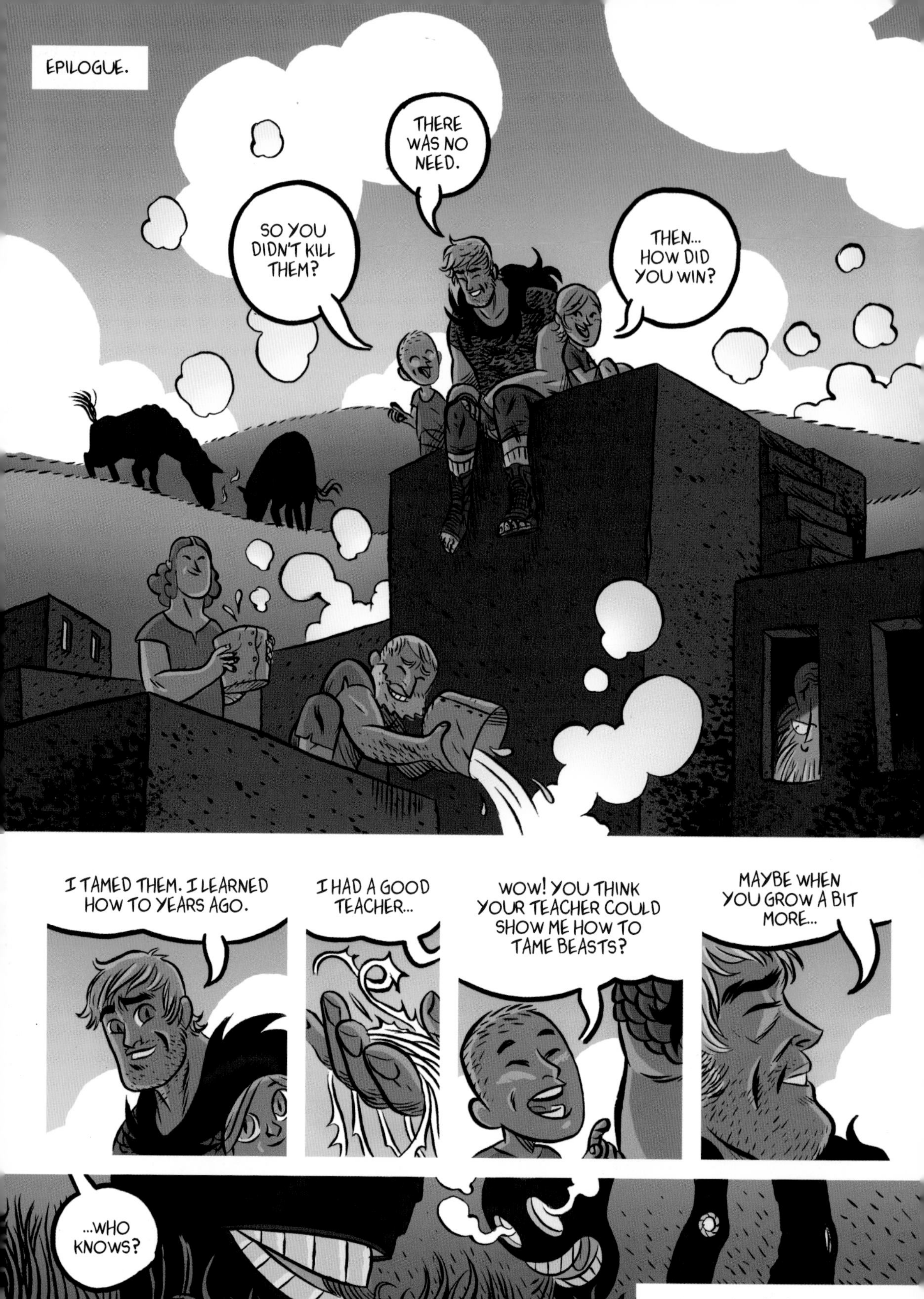
EPILOGUE.
SO YOU DIDN'T KILL THEM?
THERE WAS NO NEED.
THEN... HOW DID YOU WIN?
I TAMED THEM. I LEARNED HOW TO YEARS AGO.
I HAD A GOOD TEACHER...
WOW! YOU THINK YOUR TEACHER COULD SHOW ME HOW TO TAME BEASTS?
MAYBE WHEN YOU GROW A BIT MORE...
...WHO KNOWS?
END OF CHAPTER EIGHT.

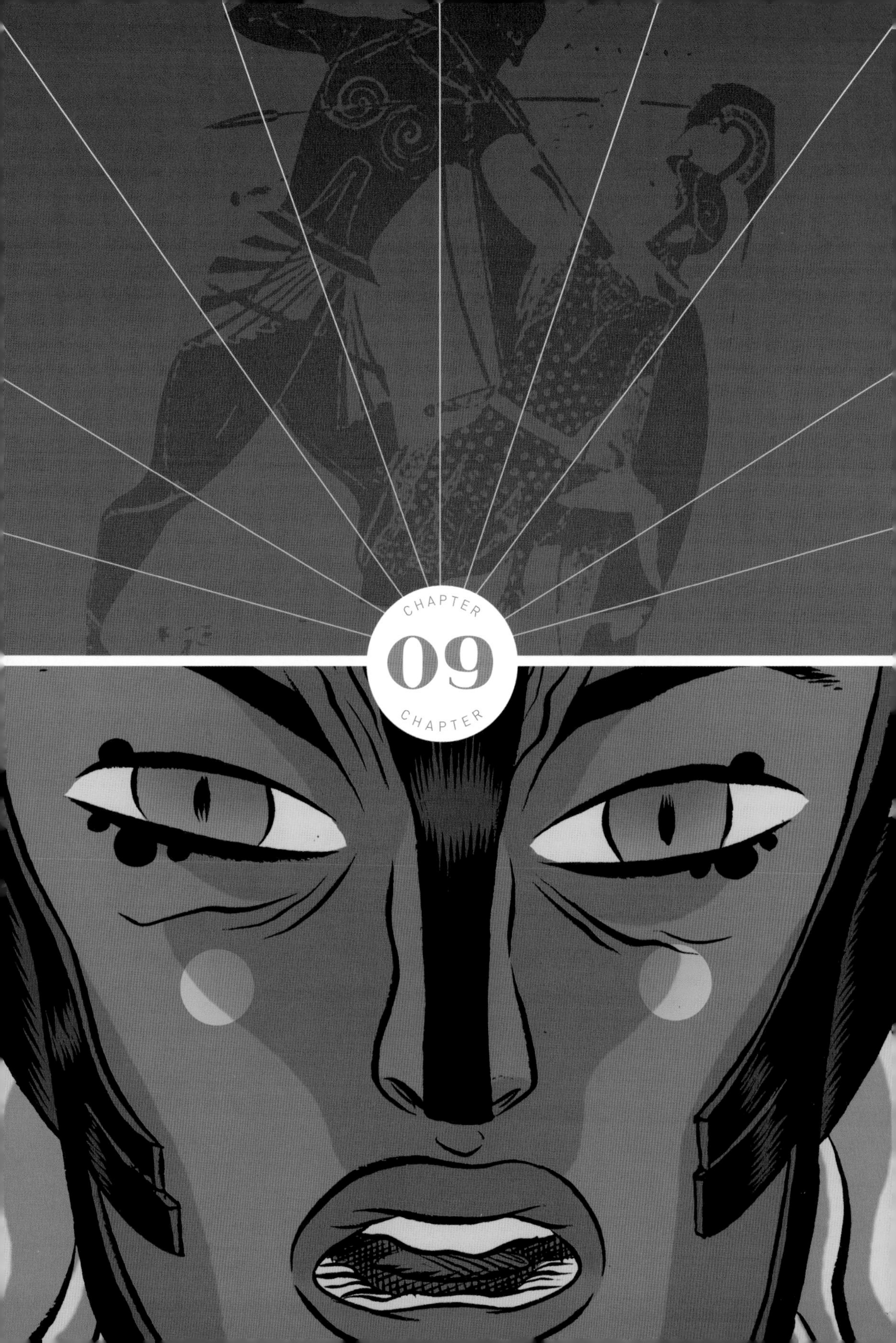
CHAPTER
09
CHAPTER

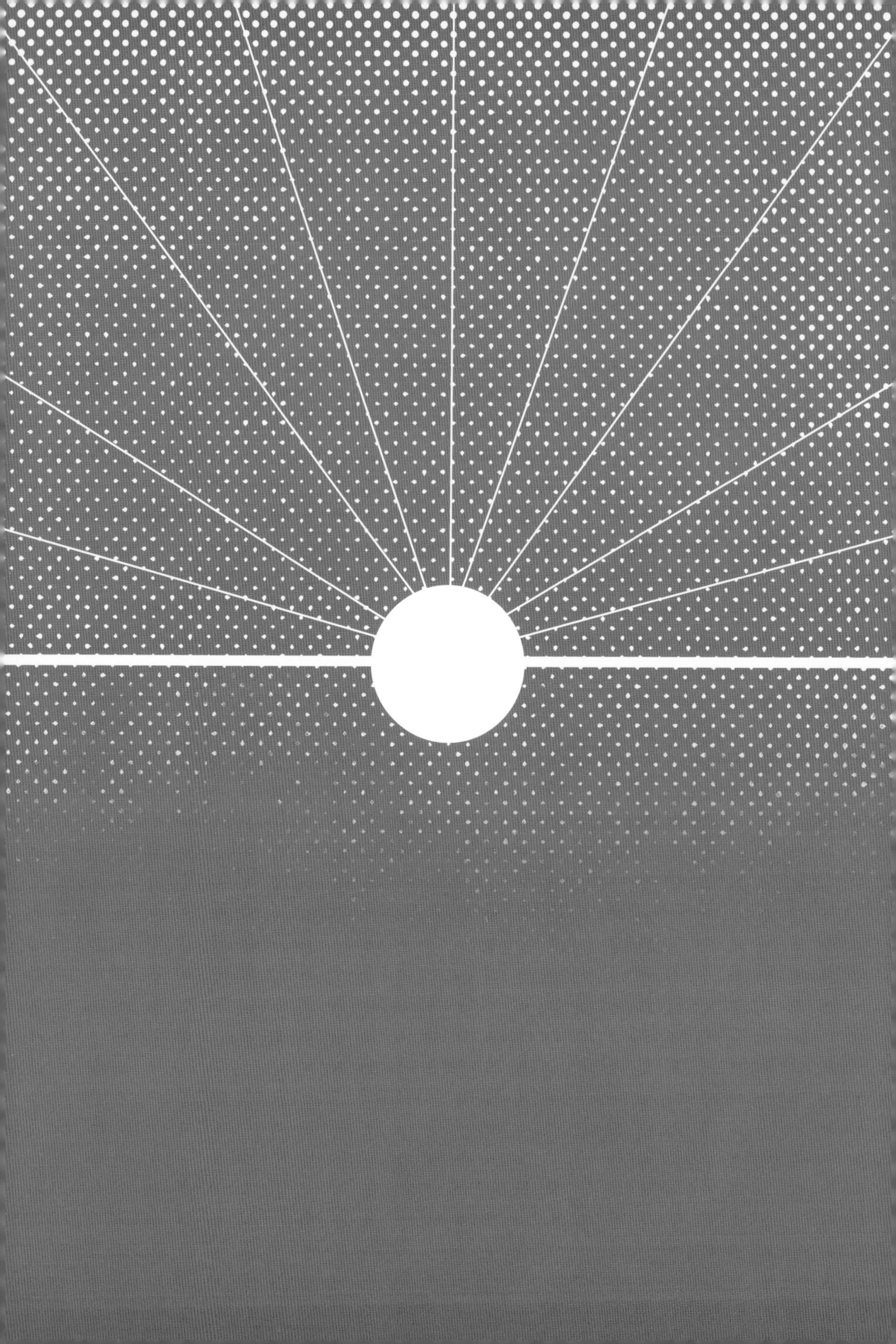

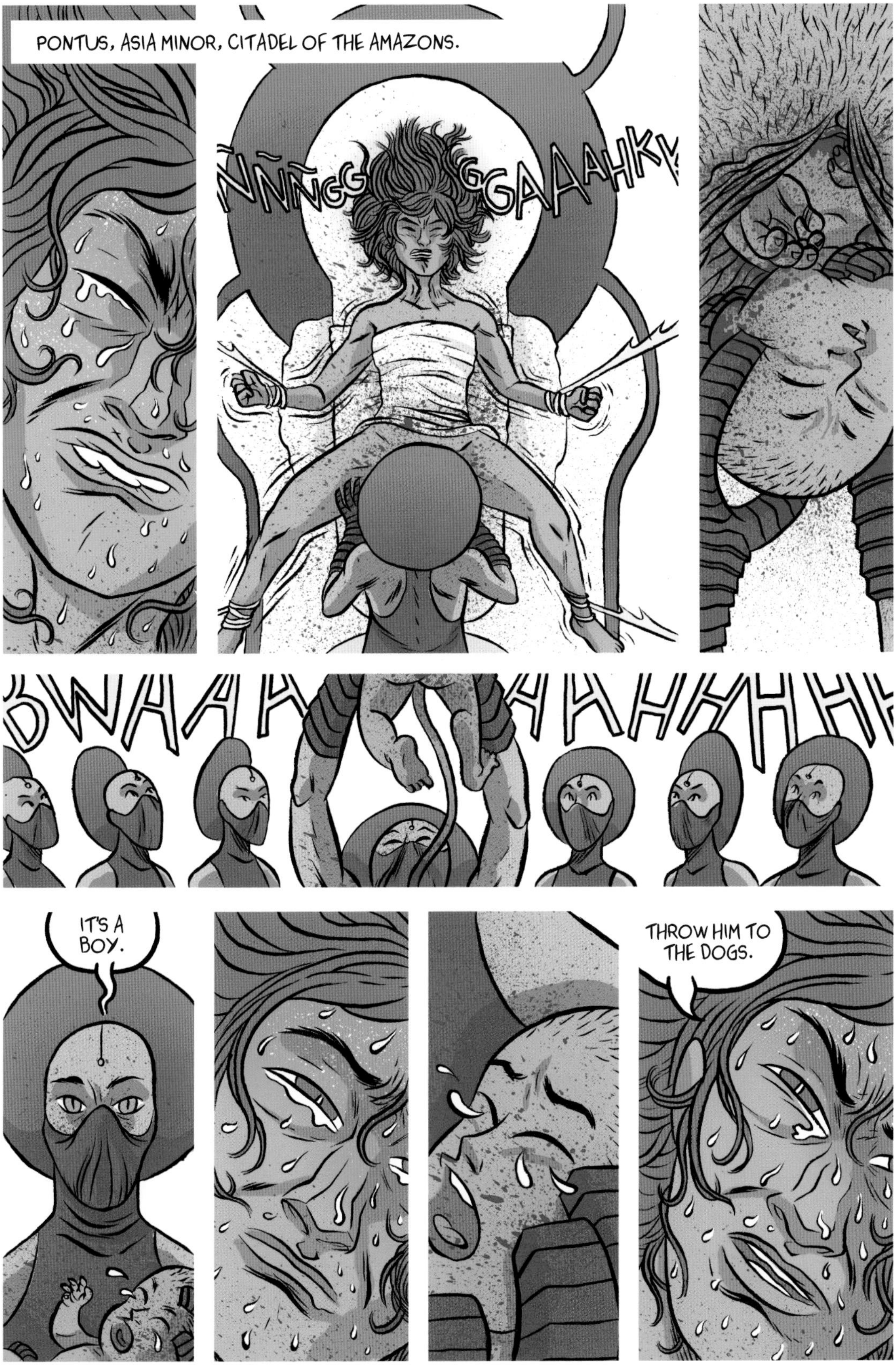

PONTUS, ASIA MINOR, CITADEL OF THE AMAZONS.
ÑÑÑGG GGAAAAHK!
BWAAAAAAAHHHHH
IT'S A BOY.
THROW HIM TO THE DOGS.

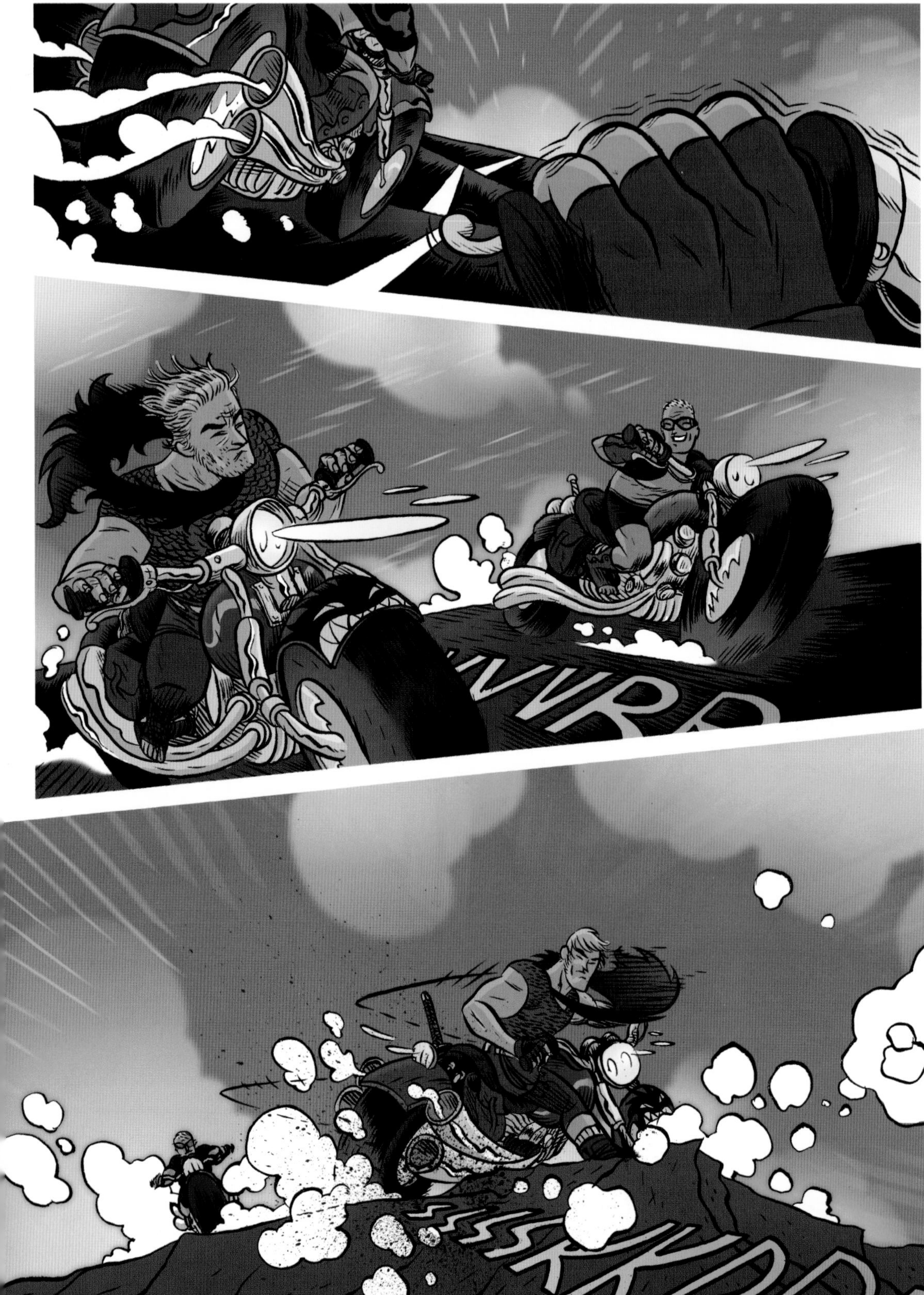

VVVRR
SSSKRRR

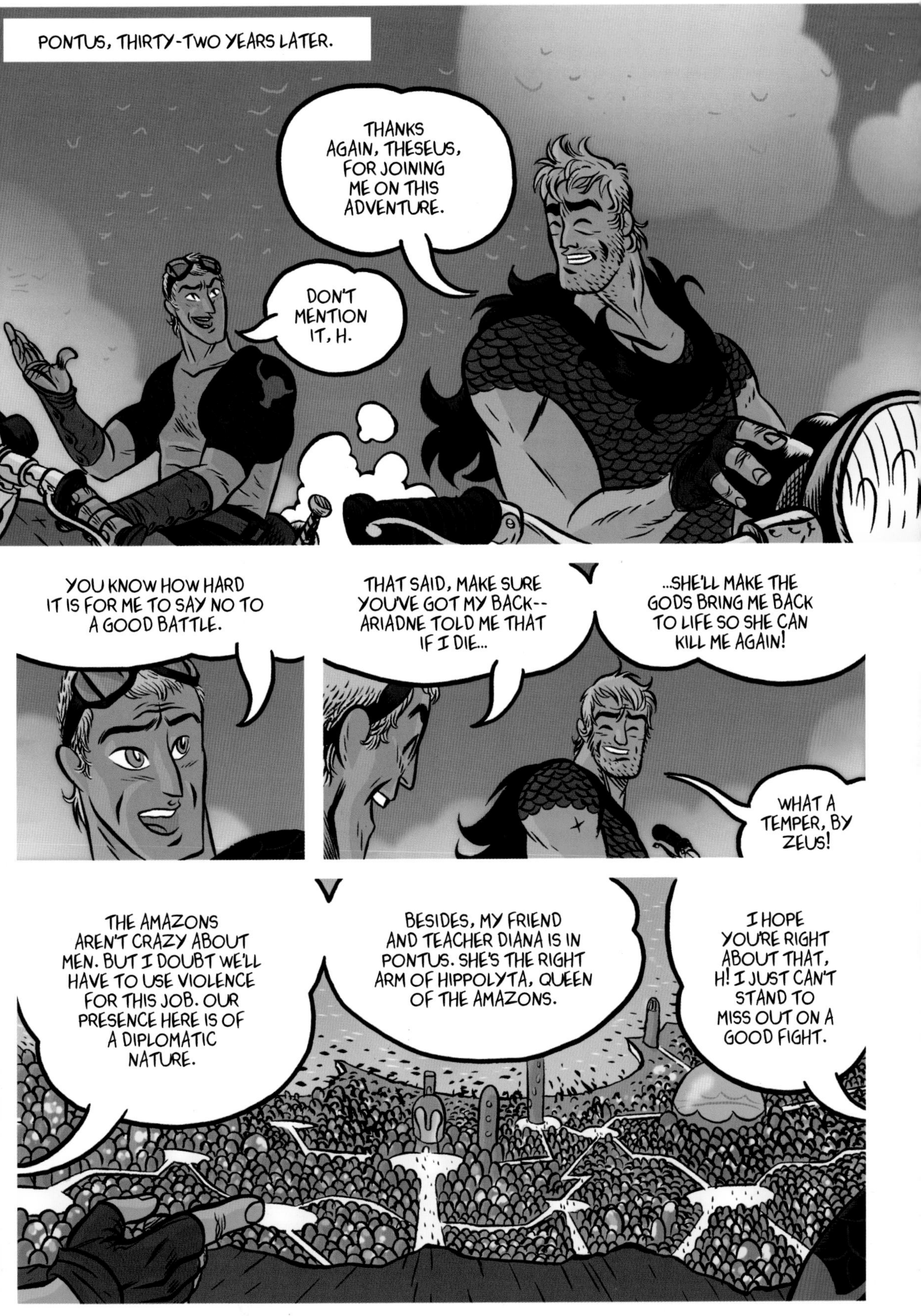
PONTUS, THIRTY-TWO YEARS LATER.
THANKS AGAIN, THESEUS, FOR JOINING ME ON THIS ADVENTURE.
DON'T MENTION IT, H.
YOU KNOW HOW HARD IT IS FOR ME TO SAY NO TO A GOOD BATTLE.
THAT SAID, MAKE SURE YOU'VE GOT MY BACK-- ARIADNE TOLD ME THAT IF I DIE...
...SHE'LL MAKE THE GODS BRING ME BACK TO LIFE SO SHE CAN KILL ME AGAIN!
WHAT A TEMPER, BY ZEUS!
THE AMAZONS AREN'T CRAZY ABOUT MEN. BUT I DOUBT WE'LL HAVE TO USE VIOLENCE FOR THIS JOB. OUR PRESENCE HERE IS OF A DIPLOMATIC NATURE.
BESIDES, MY FRIEND AND TEACHER DIANA IS IN PONTUS. SHE'S THE RIGHT ARM OF HIPPOLYTA, QUEEN OF THE AMAZONS.
I HOPE YOU'RE RIGHT ABOUT THAT, H! I JUST CAN'T STAND TO MISS OUT ON A GOOD FIGHT.

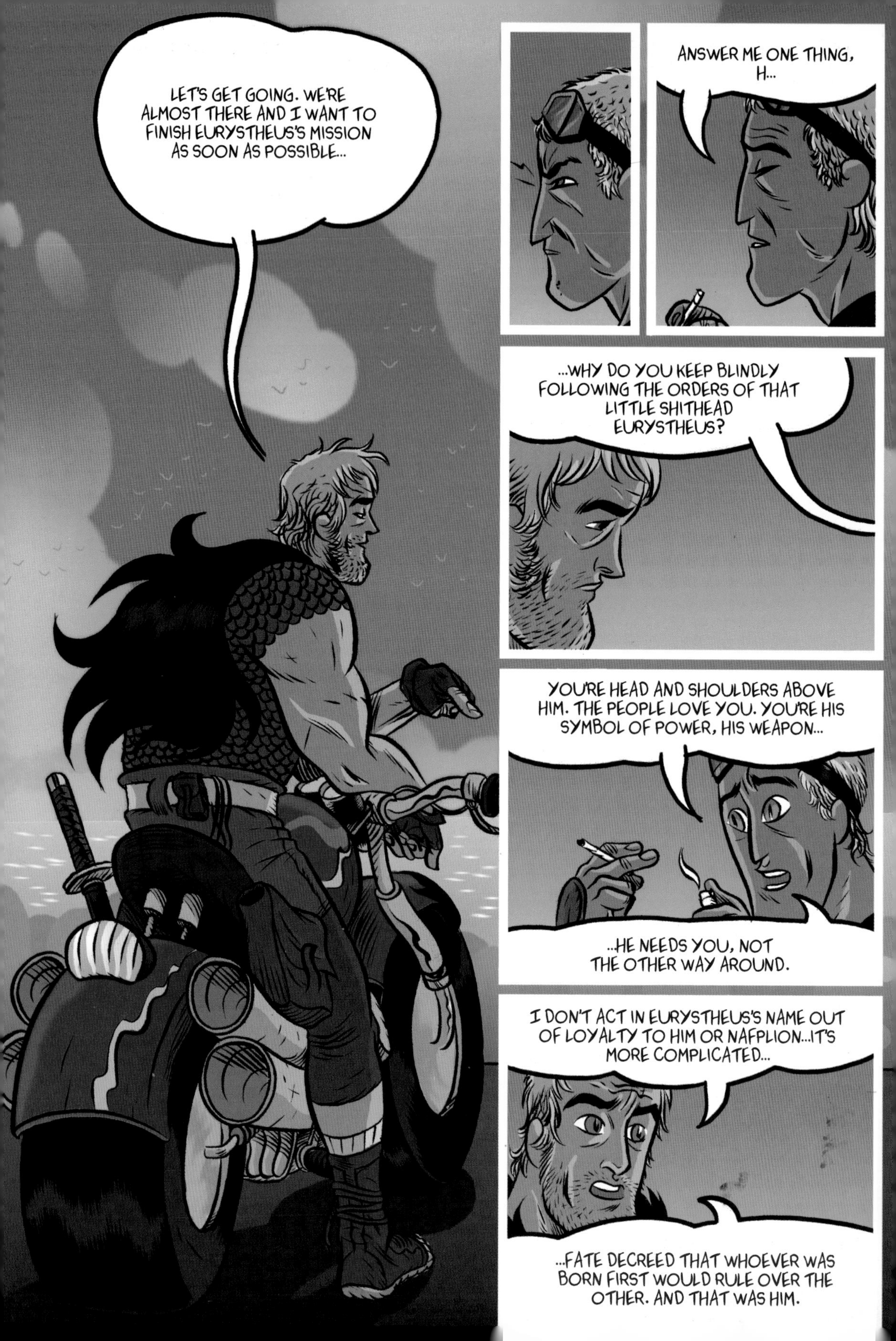
LET'S GET GOING. WE'RE ALMOST THERE AND I WANT TO FINISH EURYSTHEUS'S MISSION AS SOON AS POSSIBLE...
ANSWER ME ONE THING, H...
...WHY DO YOU KEEP BLINDLY FOLLOWING THE ORDERS OF THAT LITTLE SHITHEAD EURYSTHEUS?
YOU'RE HEAD AND SHOULDERS ABOVE HIM. THE PEOPLE LOVE YOU. YOU'RE HIS SYMBOL OF POWER, HIS WEAPON...
...HE NEEDS YOU, NOT THE OTHER WAY AROUND.
I DON'T ACT IN EURYSTHEUS'S NAME OUT OF LOYALTY TO HIM OR NAFPLION...IT'S MORE COMPLICATED...
...FATE DECREED THAT WHOEVER WAS BORN FIRST WOULD RULE OVER THE OTHER. AND THAT WAS HIM.

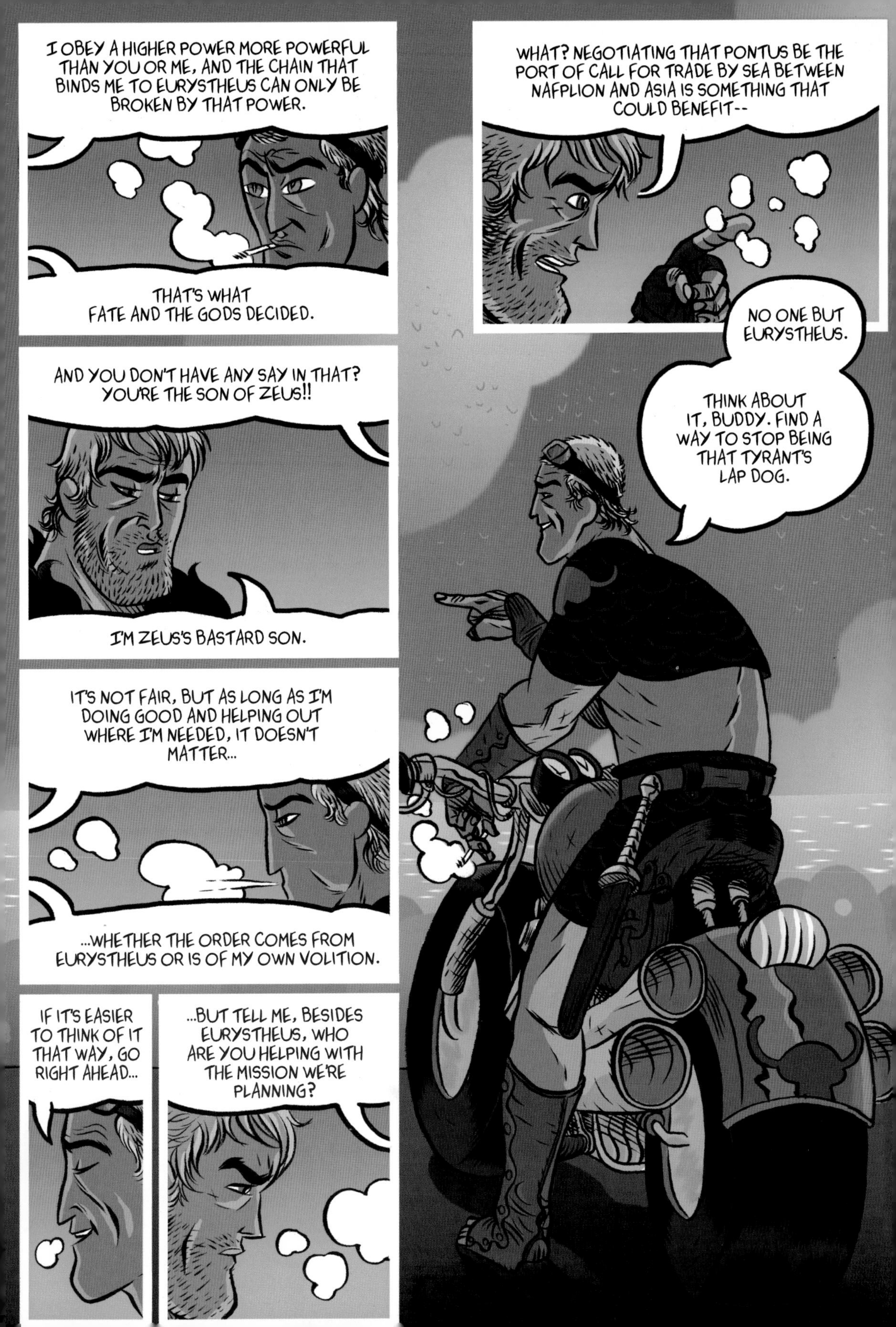

I OBEY A HIGHER POWER MORE POWERFUL THAN YOU OR ME, AND THE CHAIN THAT BINDS ME TO EURYSTHEUS CAN ONLY BE BROKEN BY THAT POWER.
THAT'S WHAT FATE AND THE GODS DECIDED.
AND YOU DON'T HAVE ANY SAY IN THAT? YOU'RE THE SON OF ZEUS!!
I'M ZEUS'S BASTARD SON.
IT'S NOT FAIR, BUT AS LONG AS I'M DOING GOOD AND HELPING OUT WHERE I'M NEEDED, IT DOESN'T MATTER...
...WHETHER THE ORDER COMES FROM EURYSTHEUS OR IS OF MY OWN VOLITION.
IF IT'S EASIER TO THINK OF IT THAT WAY, GO RIGHT AHEAD...
...BUT TELL ME, BESIDES EURYSTHEUS, WHO ARE YOU HELPING WITH THE MISSION WE'RE PLANNING?
WHAT? NEGOTIATING THAT PONTUS BE THE PORT OF CALL FOR TRADE BY SEA BETWEEN NAFPLION AND ASIA IS SOMETHING THAT COULD BENEFIT--
NO ONE BUT EURYSTHEUS.
THINK ABOUT IT, BUDDY. FIND A WAY TO STOP BEING THAT TYRANT'S LAP DOG.

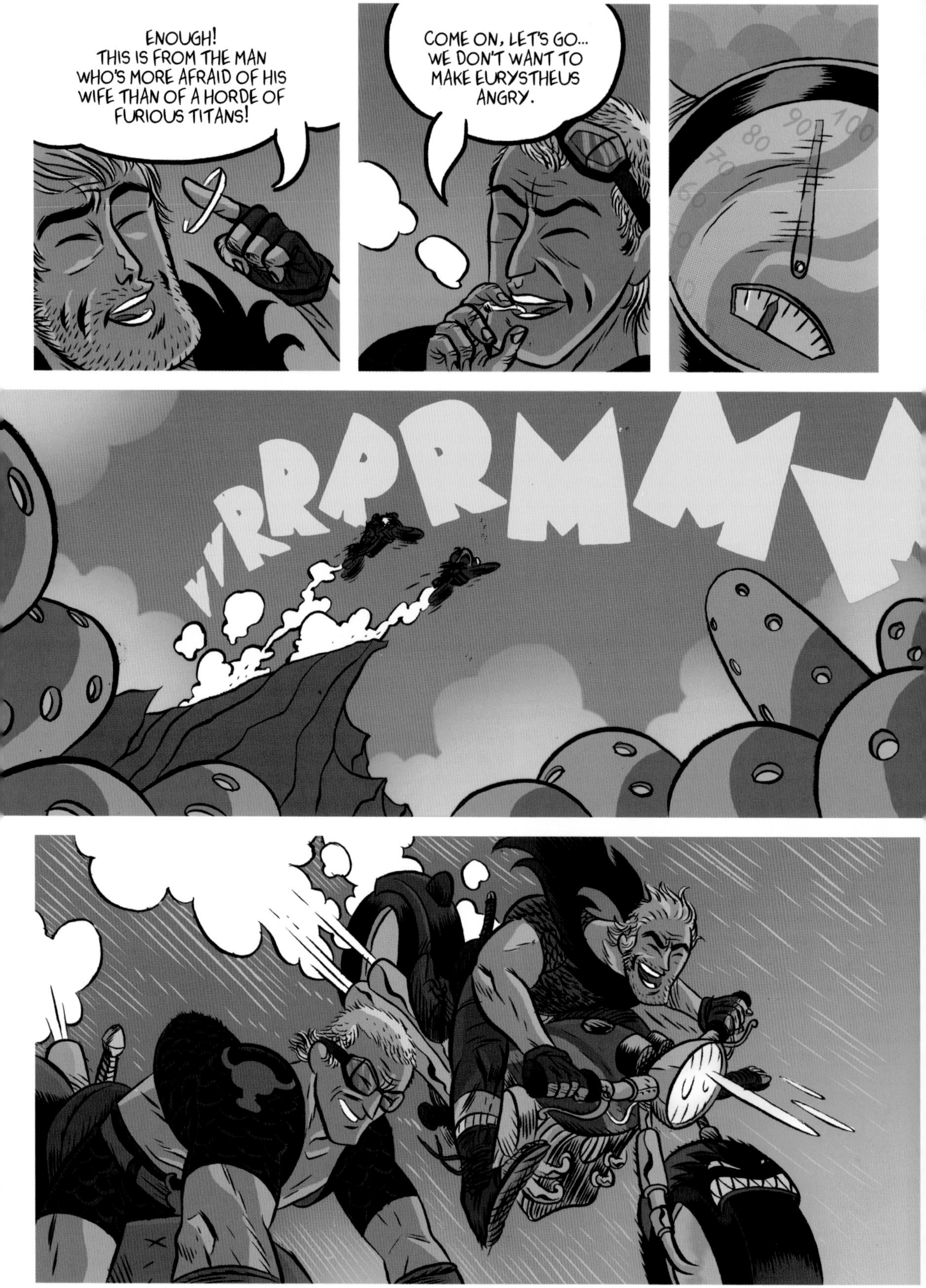
ENOUGH! THIS IS FROM THE MAN WHO'S MORE AFRAID OF HIS WIFE THAN OF A HORDE OF FURIOUS TITANS!
COME ON, LET'S GO... WE DON'T WANT TO MAKE EURYSTHEUS ANGRY.
VRRRPRMMM

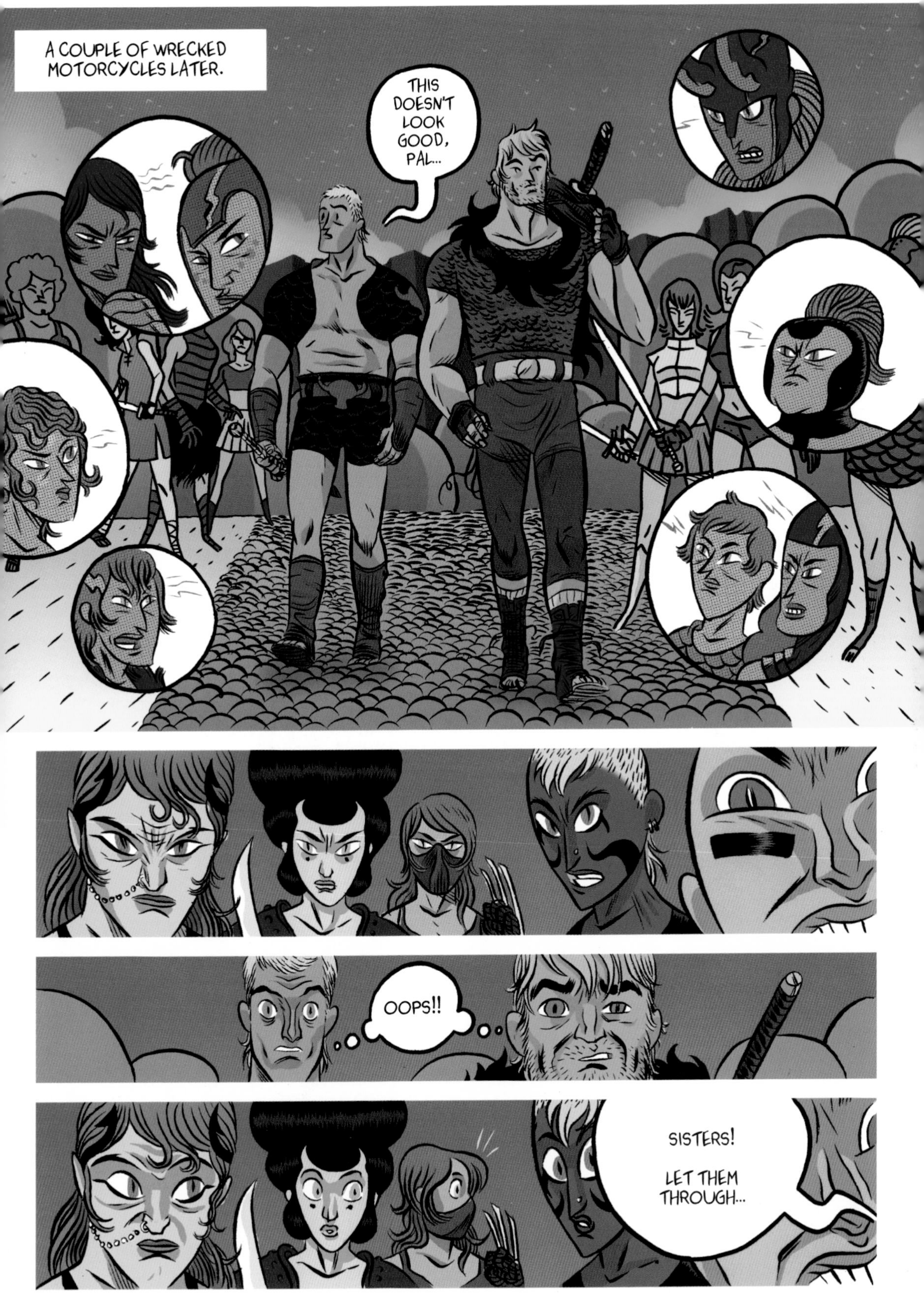
A COUPLE OF WRECKED MOTORCYCLES LATER.
THIS DOESN'T LOOK GOOD, PAL...
OOPS!!
SISTERS!
LET THEM THROUGH...

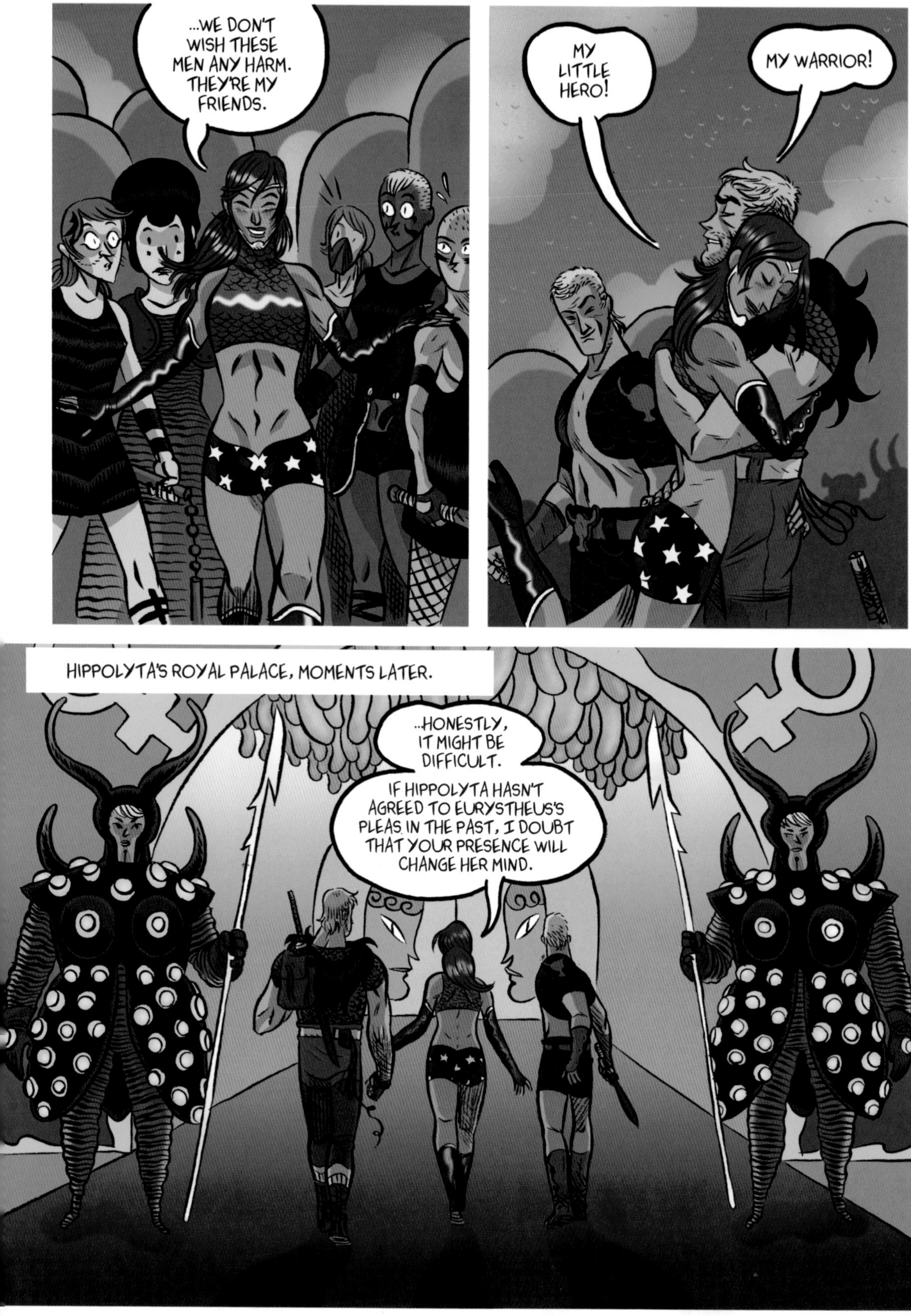
...WE DON'T WISH THESE MEN ANY HARM. THEY'RE MY FRIENDS.
MY LITTLE HERO!
MY WARRIOR!
HIPPOLYTA'S ROYAL PALACE, MOMENTS LATER.
...HONESTLY, IT MIGHT BE DIFFICULT.
IF HIPPOLYTA HASN'T AGREED TO EURYSTHEUS'S PLEAS IN THE PAST, I DOUBT THAT YOUR PRESENCE WILL CHANGE HER MIND.

AT ANY RATE, I'LL HELP YOU. I'LL INTERCEDE ON YOUR BEHALF BEFORE THE QUEEN. LET'S SEE WHAT WE CAN ACCOMPLISH.

THANK YOU, DIANA.

YOU CAN THANK ME LATER, KIDDO...

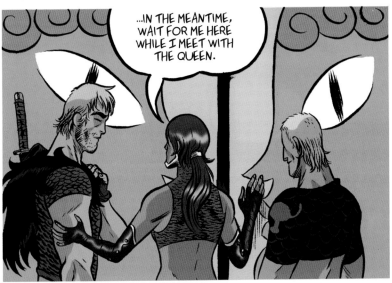

...IN THE MEANTIME, WAIT FOR ME HERE WHILE I MEET WITH THE QUEEN.

I WON'T BE LONG.

WHAT A WOMAN!

YEAH...

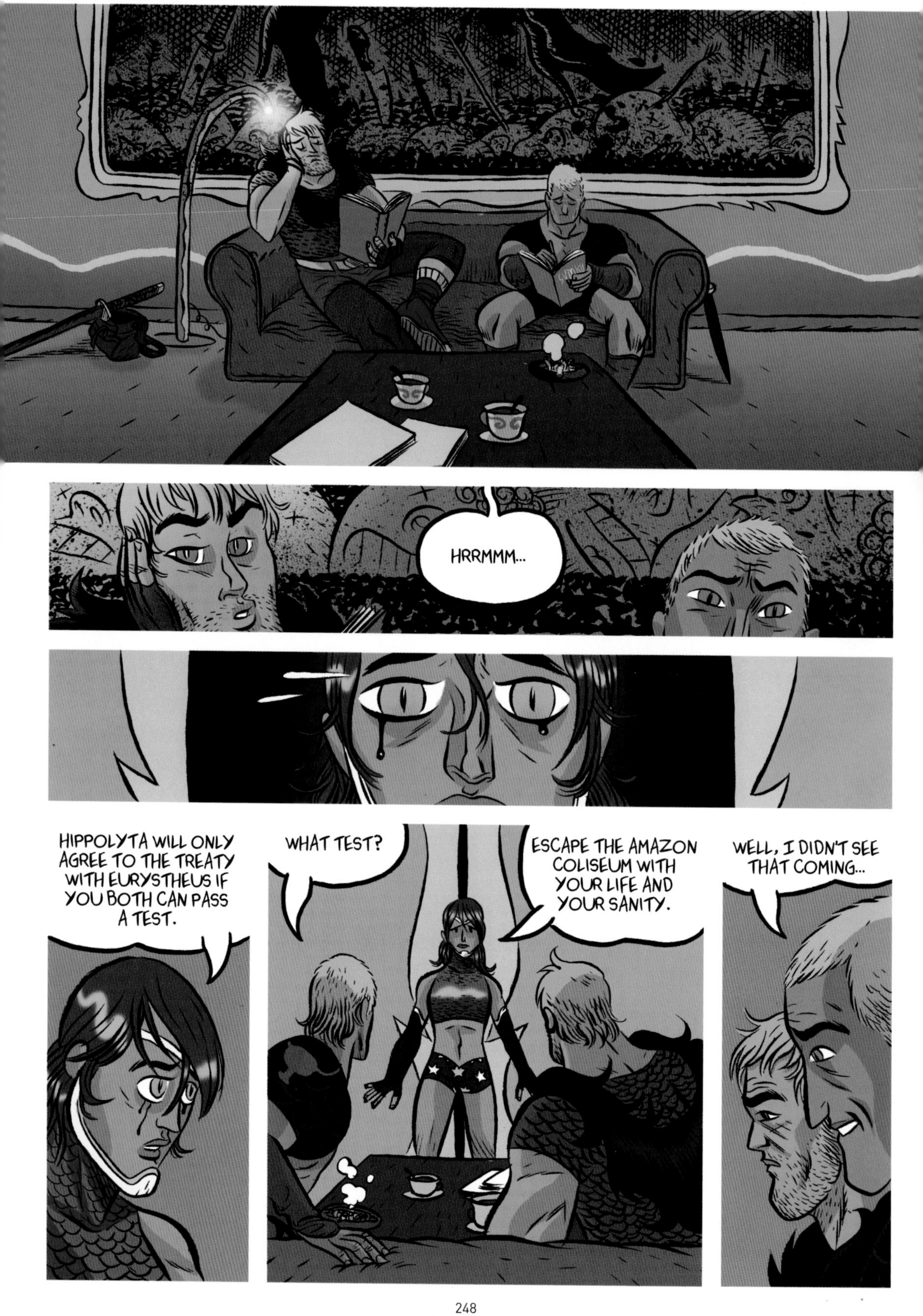
HRRMMM...
HIPPOLYTA WILL ONLY AGREE TO THE TREATY WITH EURYSTHEUS IF YOU BOTH CAN PASS A TEST.
WHAT TEST?
ESCAPE THE AMAZON COLISEUM WITH YOUR LIFE AND YOUR SANITY.
WELL, I DIDN'T SEE THAT COMING...

AMAZON COLISEUM.

SO THERE WON'T BE ANY BLOODSHED?

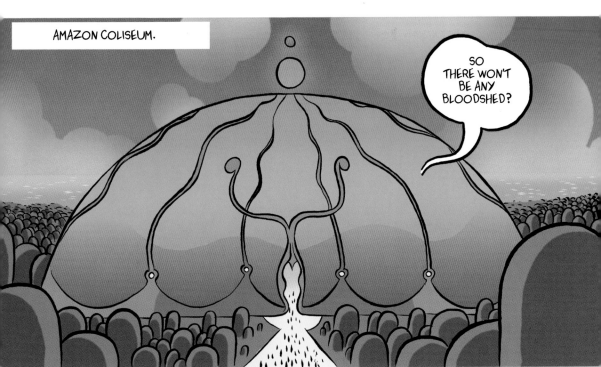

I DON'T WANT THERE TO BE.

RESPONSIBILITY! MATURITY!

TO THE ARENA!!

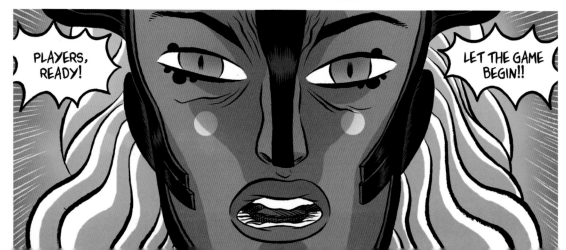

PLAYERS, READY!

LET THE GAME BEGIN!!

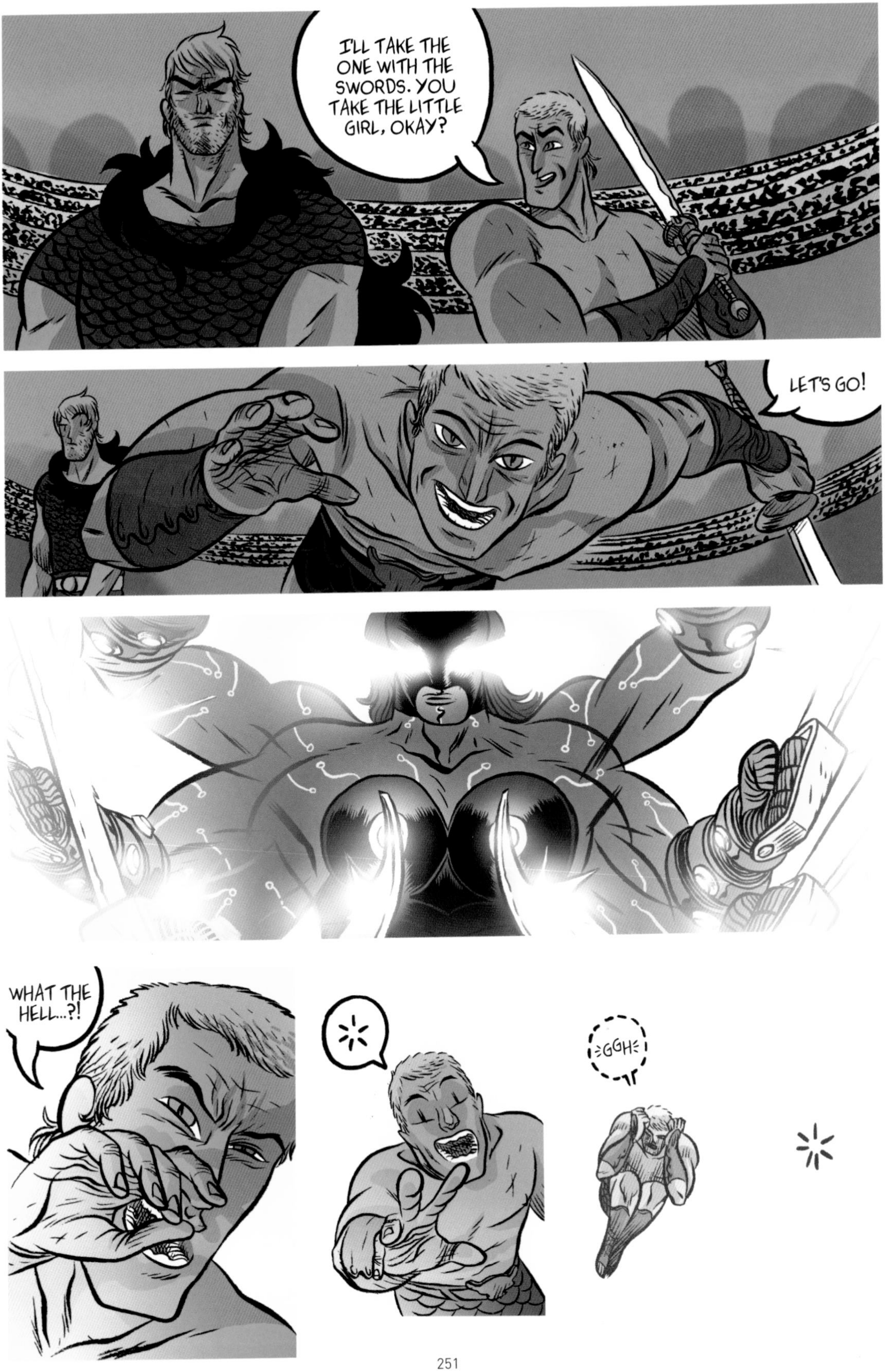
I'LL TAKE THE ONE WITH THE SWORDS. YOU TAKE THE LITTLE GIRL, OKAY?
LET'S GO!
WHAT THE HELL...?!
GGH

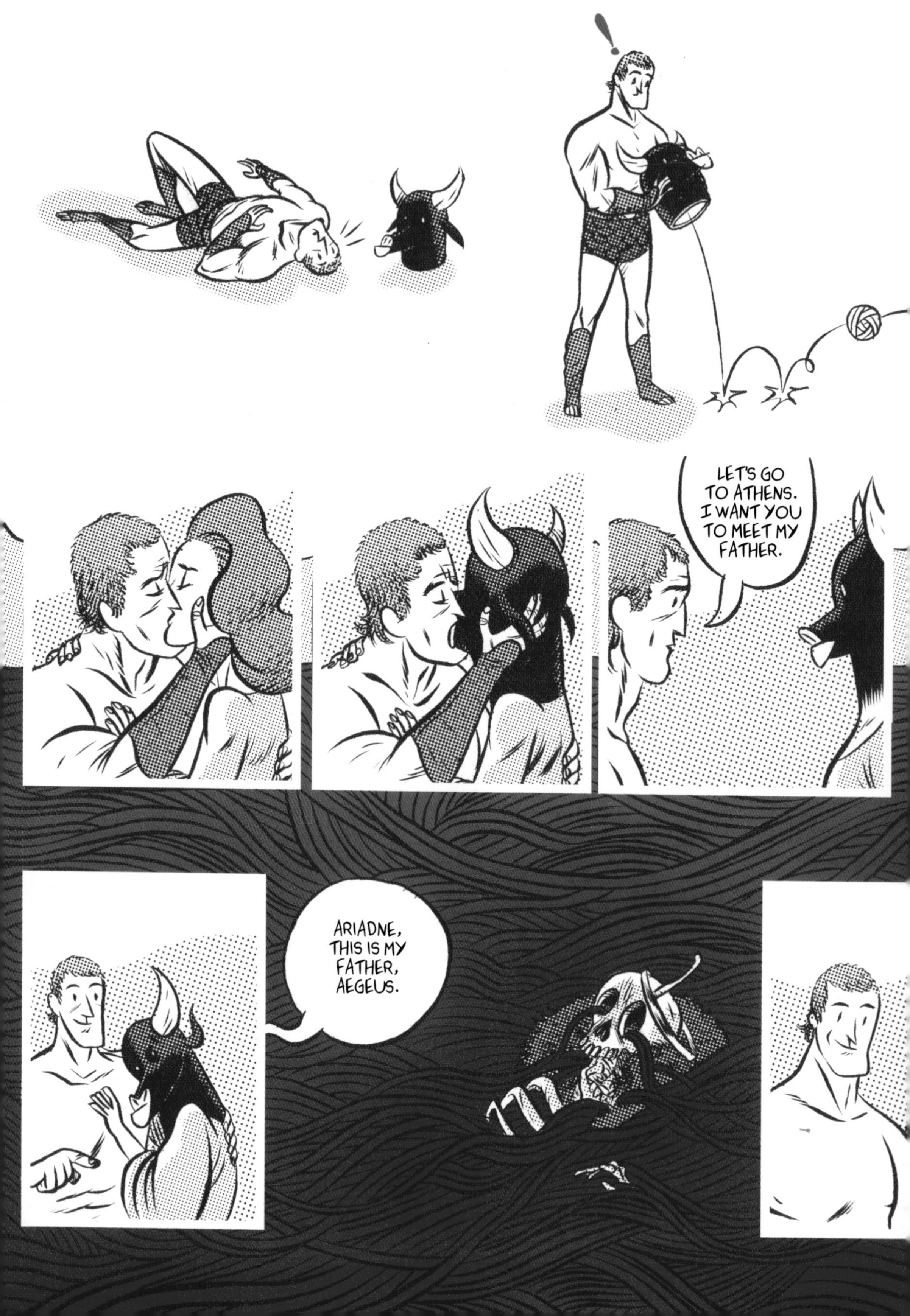
!
LET'S GO TO ATHENS. I WANT YOU TO MEET MY FATHER.
ARIADNE, THIS IS MY FATHER, AEGEUS.

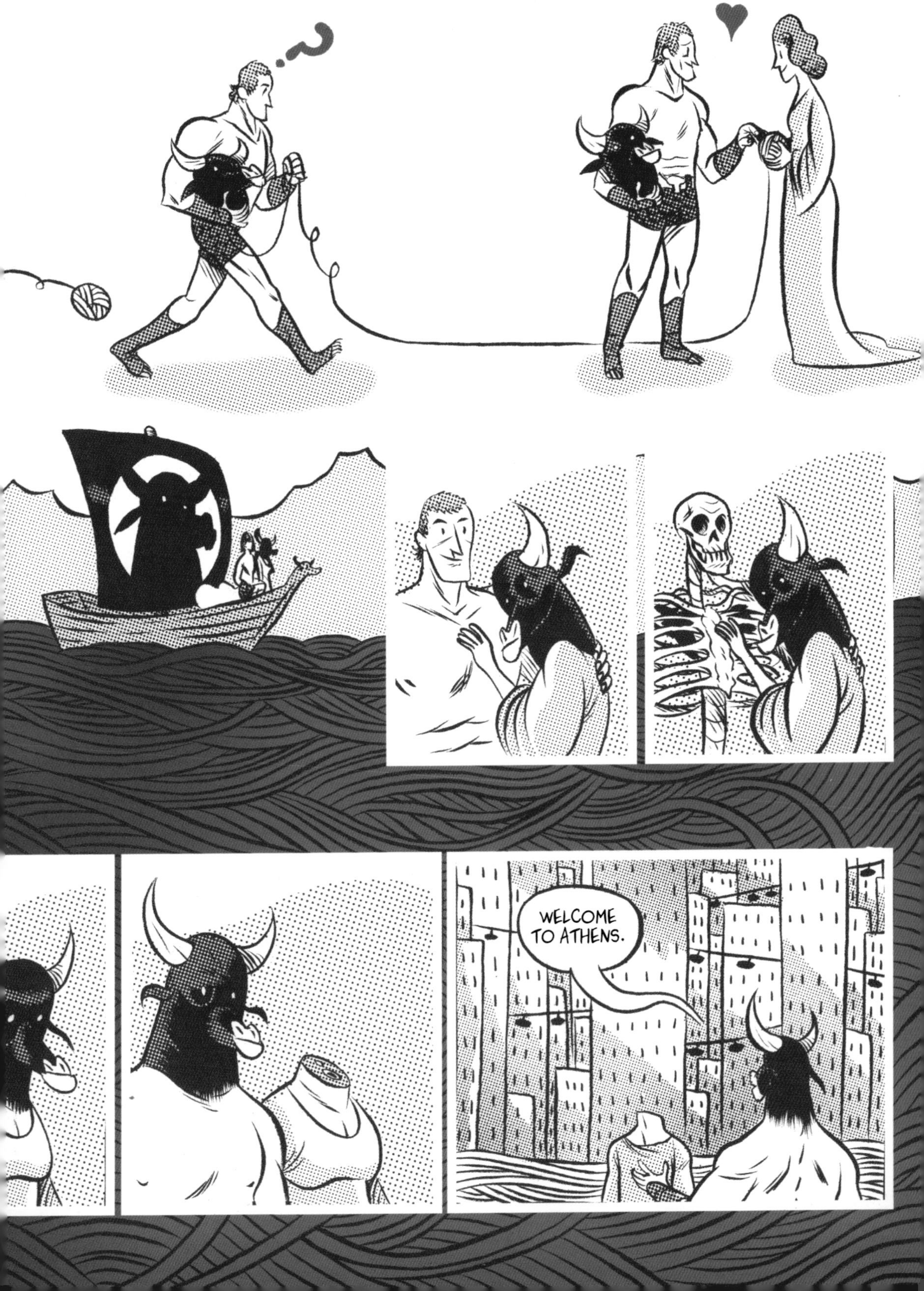
WELCOME TO ATHENS.

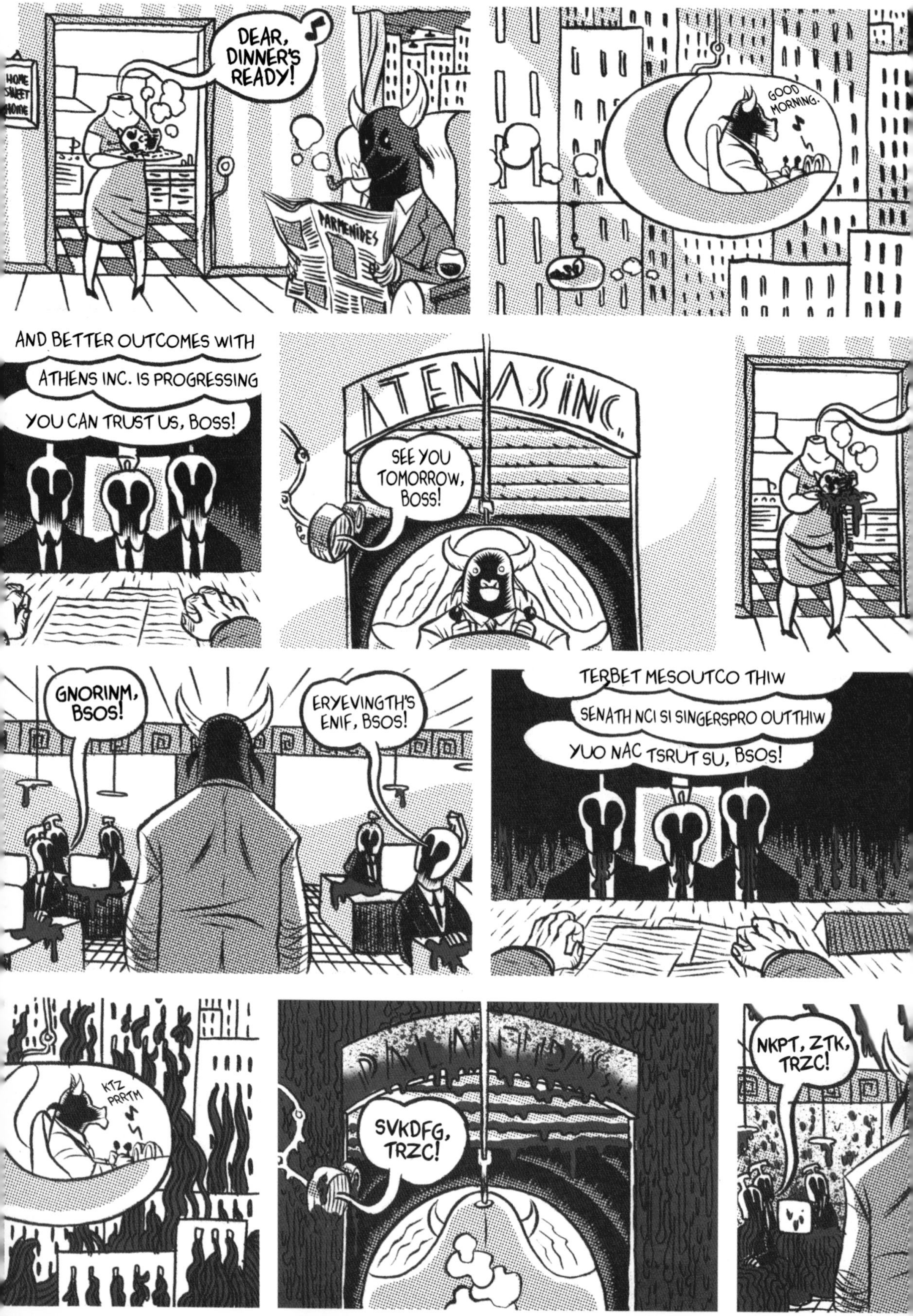
HOME SWEET HOME
DEAR, DINNER'S READY!
PARMENIDES
GOOD MORNING.
AND BETTER OUTCOMES WITH
ATHENS INC. IS PROGRESSING
YOU CAN TRUST US, BOSS!
ATENAS INC.
SEE YOU TOMORROW, BOSS!
GNORINM, BSOS!
ERYEVINGTH'S ENIF, BSOS!
TERBET MESOUTCO THIW
SENATH NCI SI SINGERSPRO OUTTHIW
YUO NAC TSRUT SU, BSOS!
KTZ PRRTM
SVKDFG, TRZC!
NKPT, ZTK, TRZC!

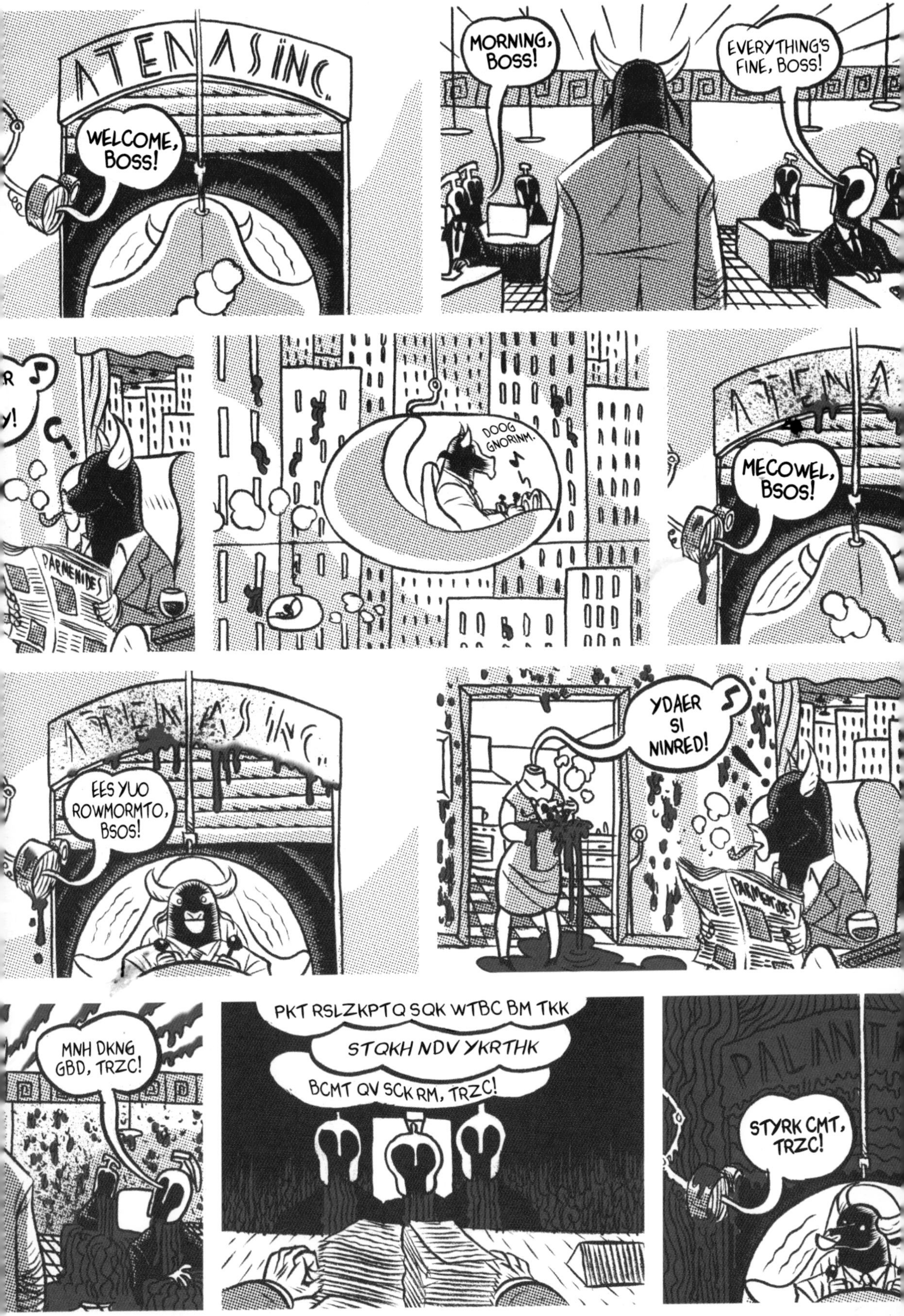
ATENAS INC.
WELCOME, BOSS!
MORNING, BOSS!
EVERYTHING'S FINE, BOSS!
PARMENIDES
DOOG GNORINM.
MECOWEL, BSOS!
ATENAS INC.
EES YUO ROWMORMTO, BSOS!
YDAER SI NINRED!
PARMENIDES
MNH DKNG GBD, TRZC!
PKT RSLZKPTQ SQK WTBC BM TKK
STQKH NDV YKRTHK
BCMT QV SCK RM, TRZC!
STYRK CMT, TRZC!

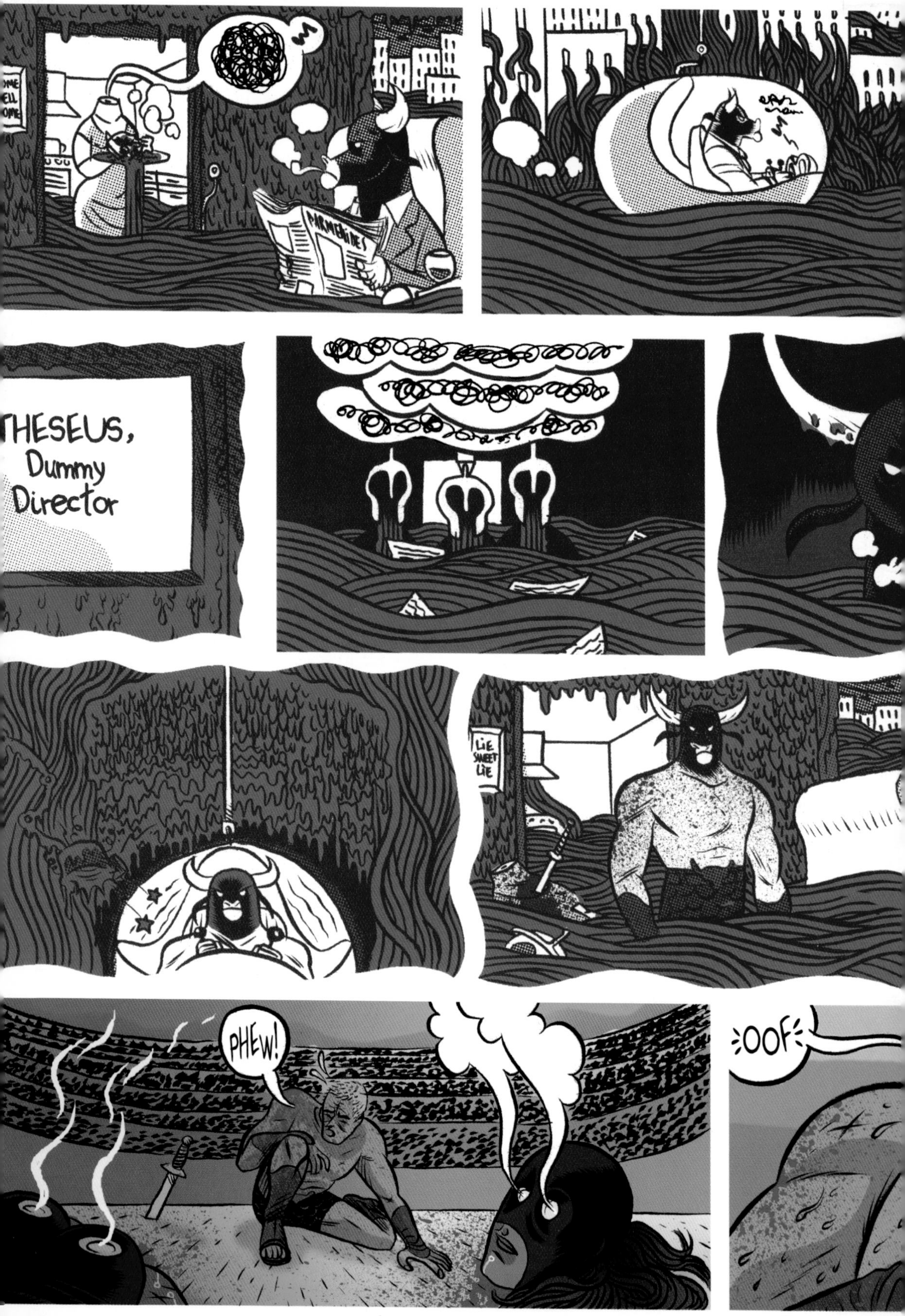
PARMENIDES
THESEUS,
Dummy
Director
LIE
SWEET
LIE
PHEW!
OOF

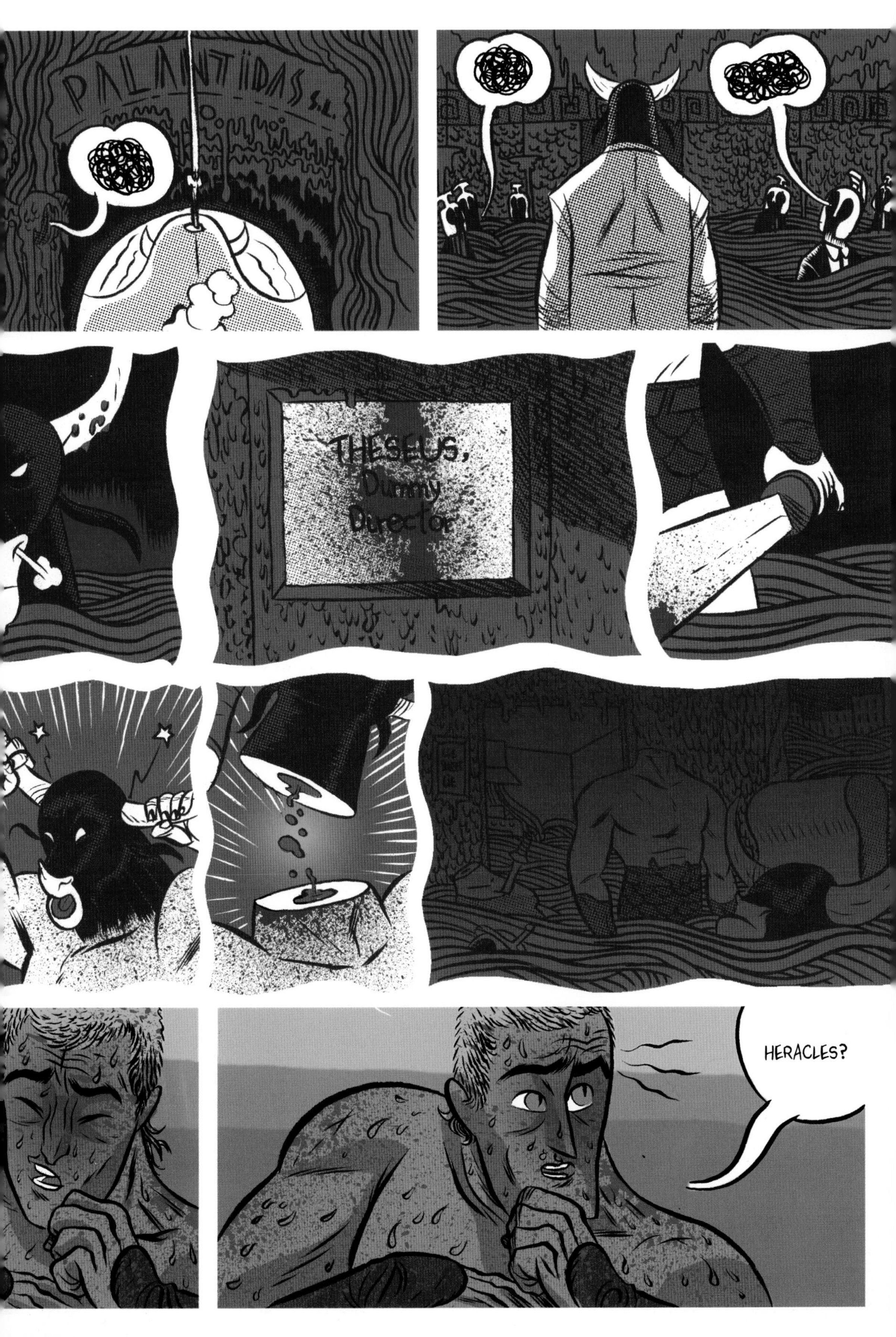
PALANTIDAS S.L.
THESEUS, Dummy Director
HERACLES?

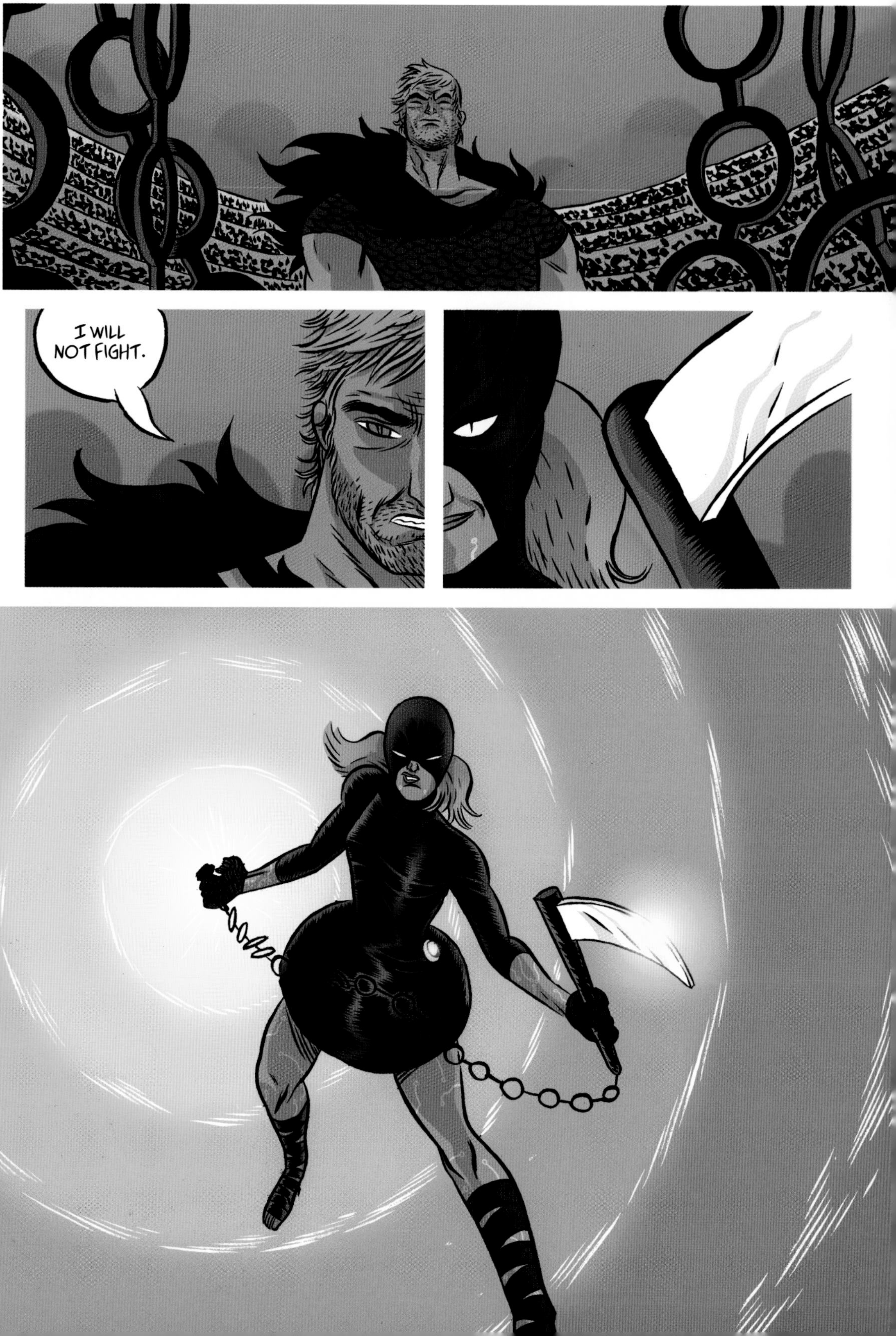
I WILL NOT FIGHT.

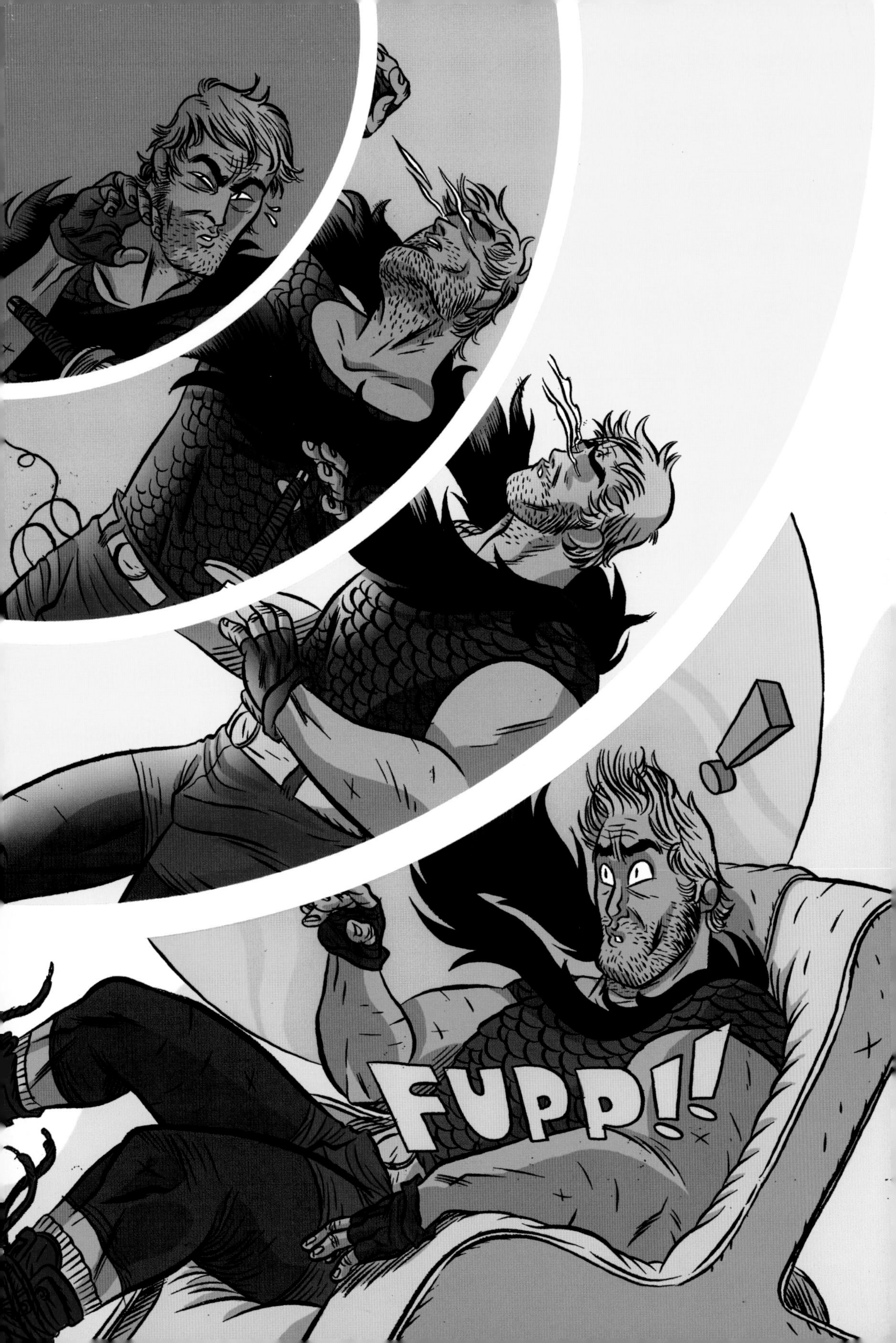
FUPP!!

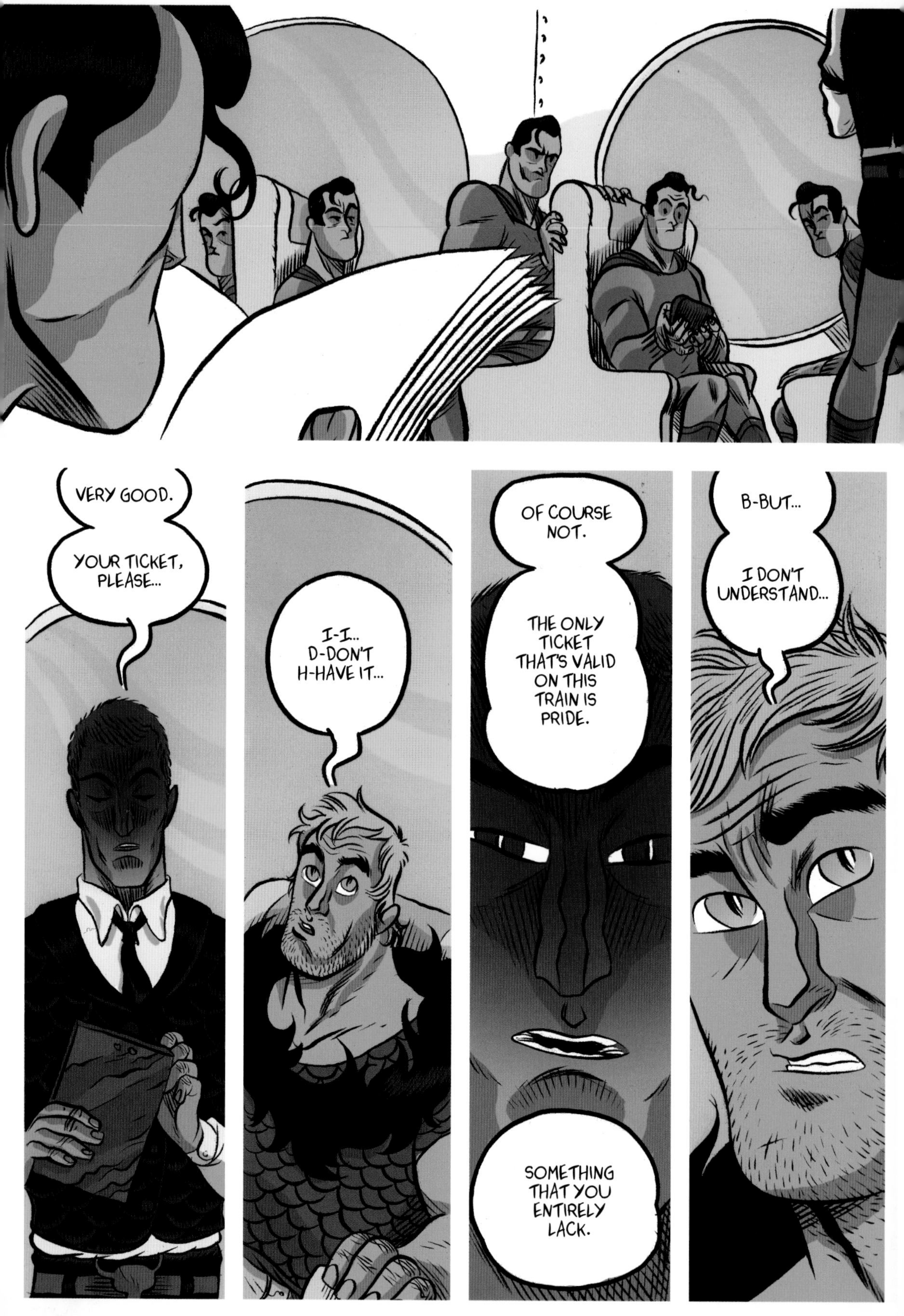
VERY GOOD.
YOUR TICKET, PLEASE...
I-I... D-DON'T H-HAVE IT...
OF COURSE NOT.
THE ONLY TICKET THAT'S VALID ON THIS TRAIN IS PRIDE.
SOMETHING THAT YOU ENTIRELY LACK.
B-BUT...
I DON'T UNDERSTAND...

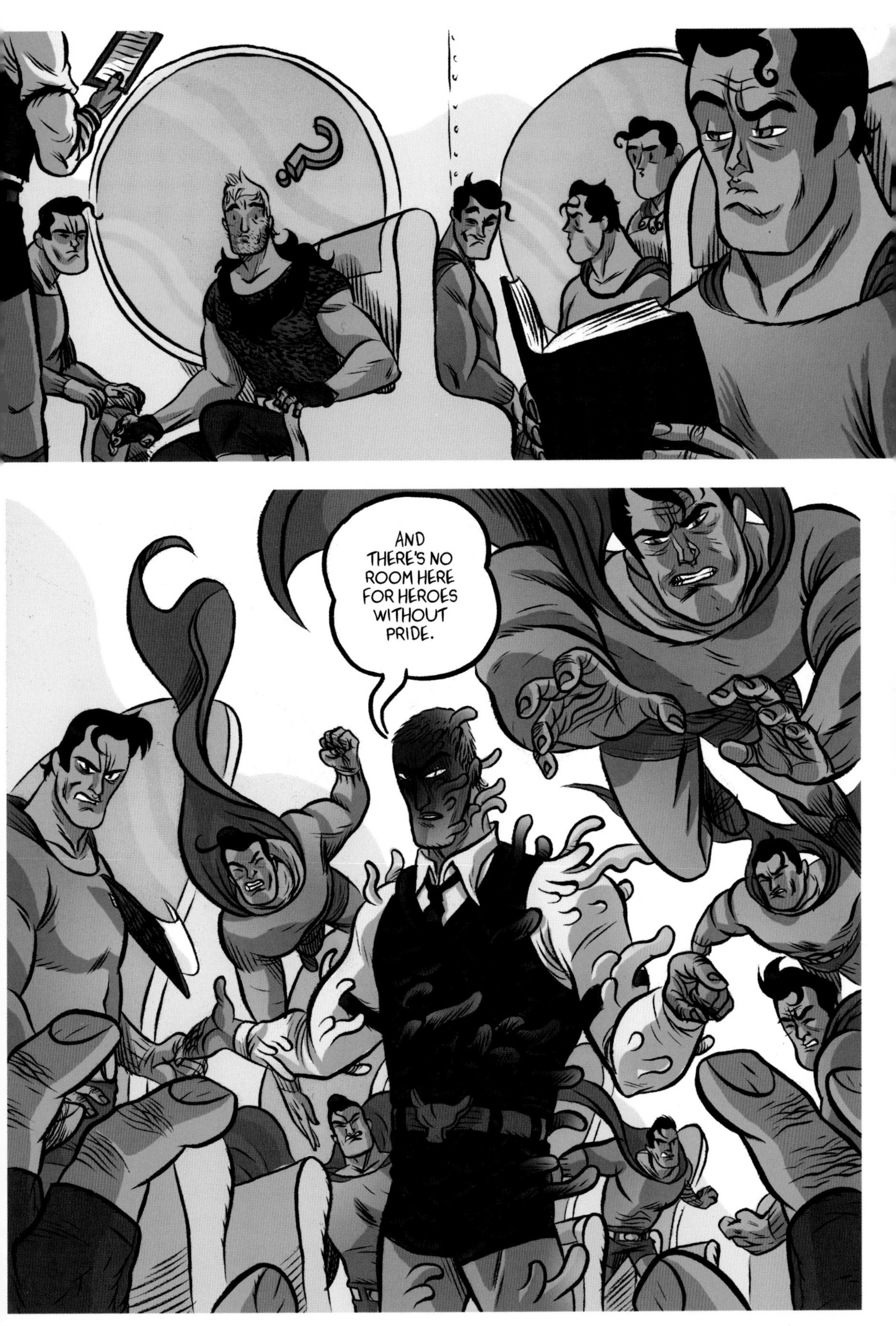
AND THERE'S NO ROOM HERE FOR HEROES WITHOUT PRIDE.

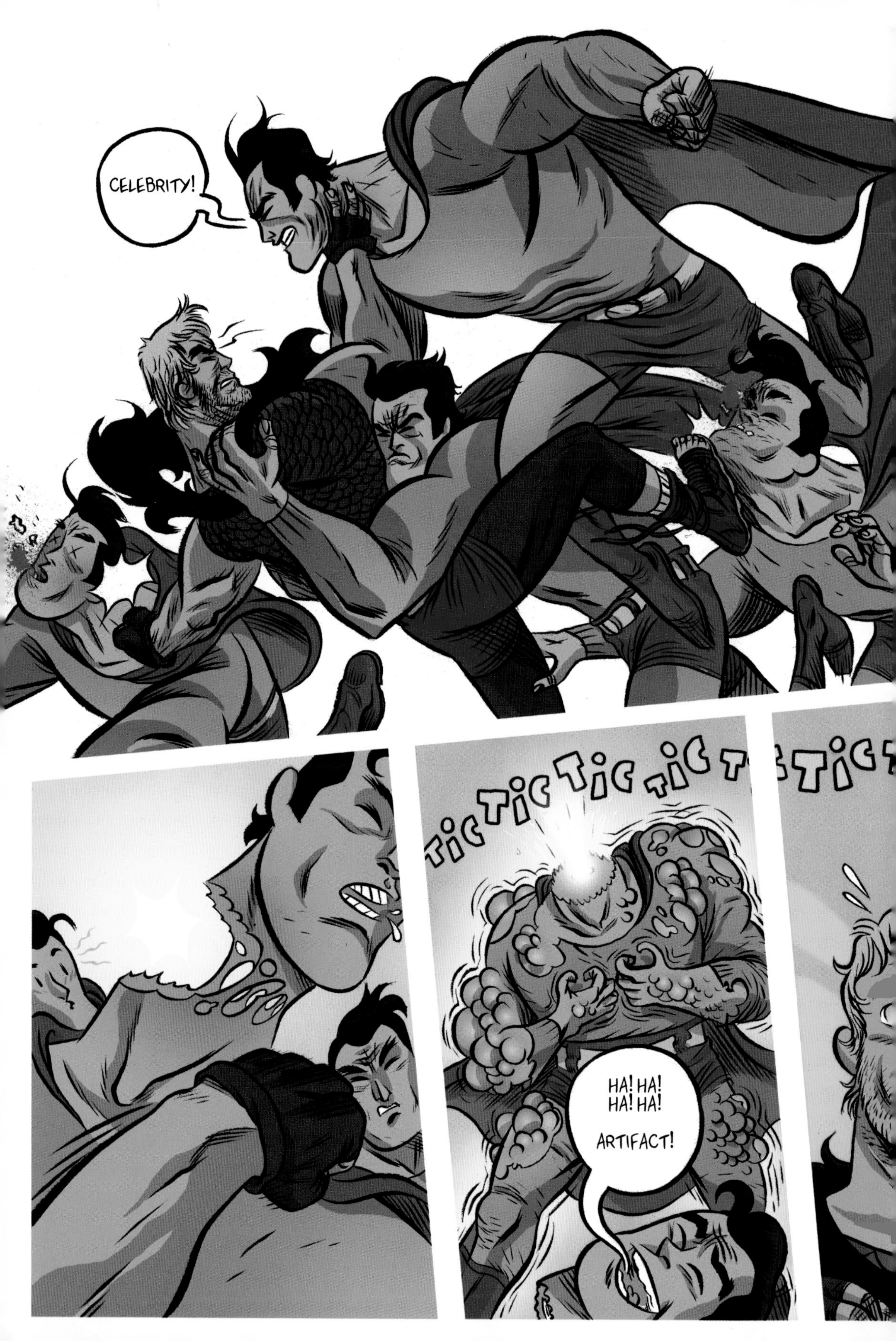
CELEBRITY!
TIC TIC TIC TIC
HA! HA!
HA! HA!
ARTIFACT!

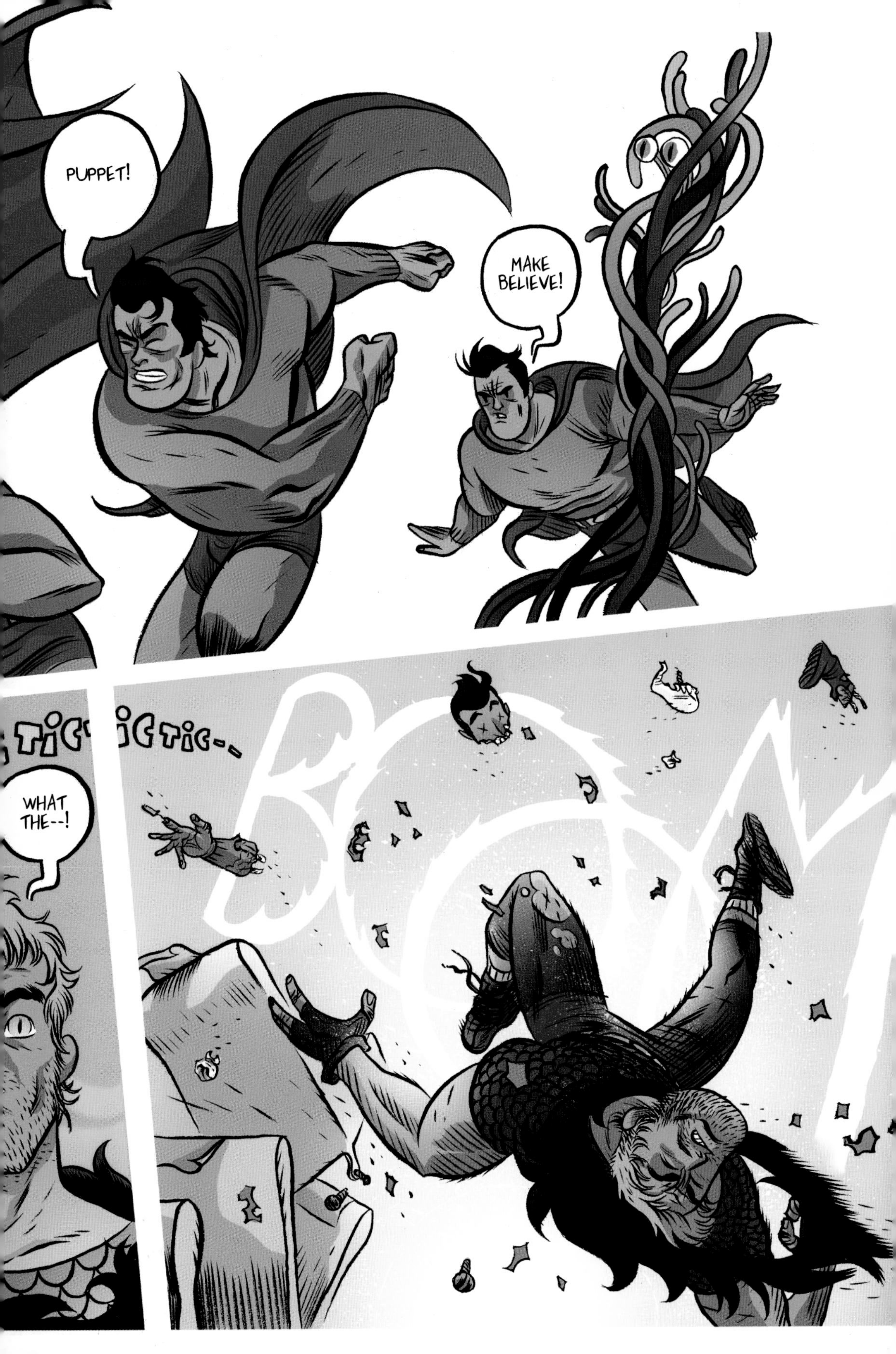
PUPPET!
MAKE BELIEVE!
TIC TIC TIC TIC--
WHAT THE--!

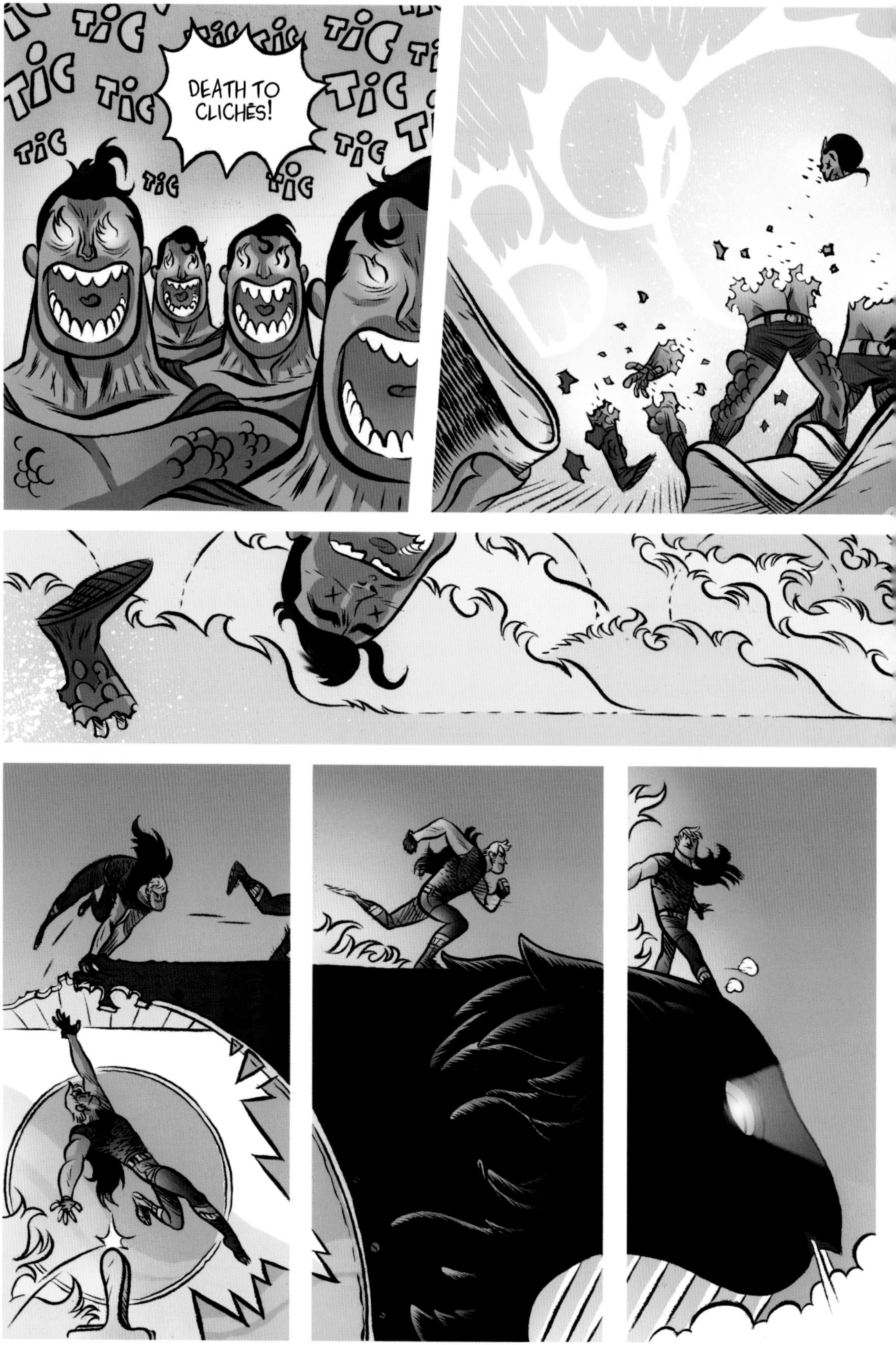
TIC TIC TIC TIC
DEATH TO CLICHES!
TIC TIC TIC TIC

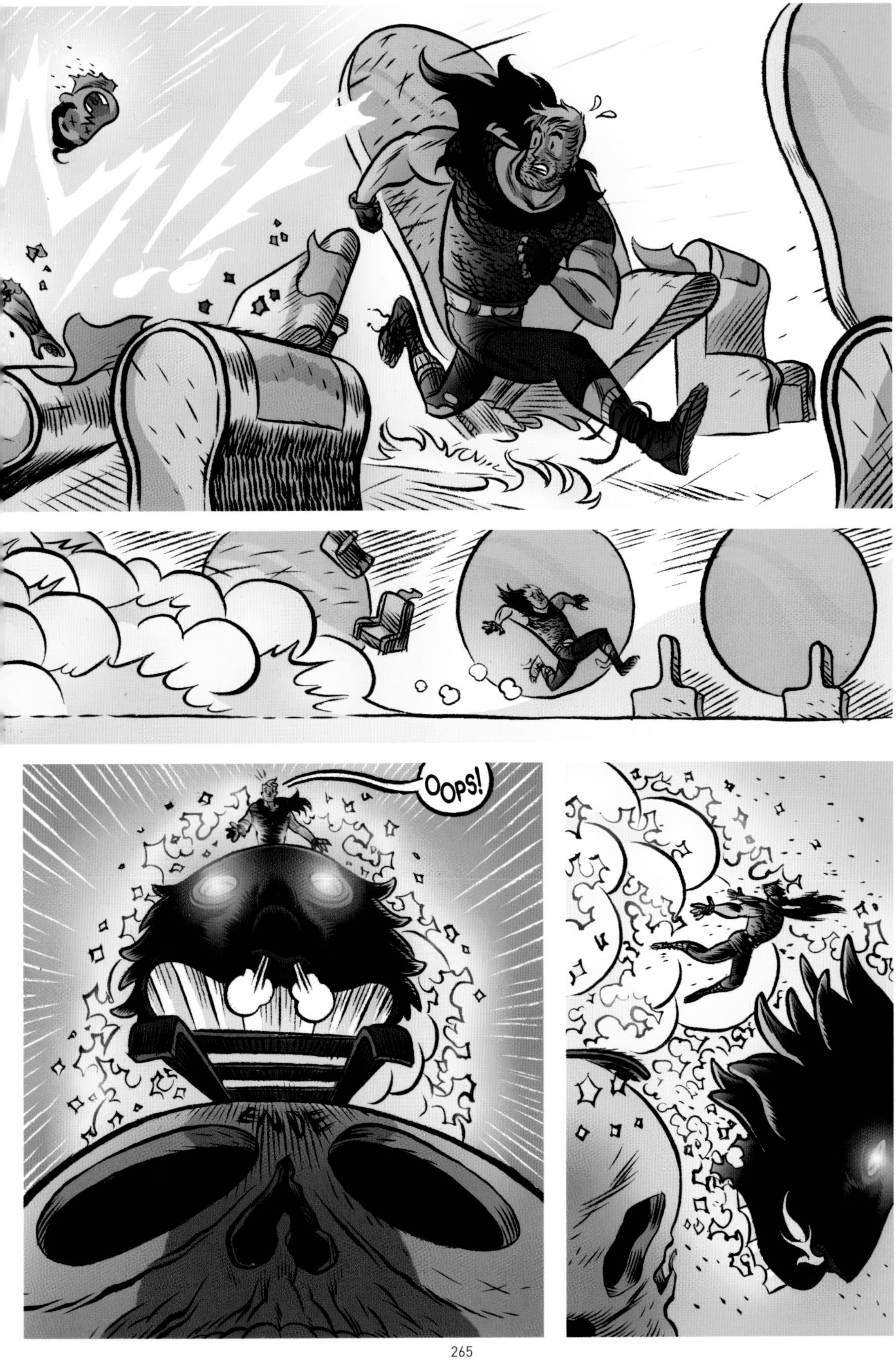
OOPS!

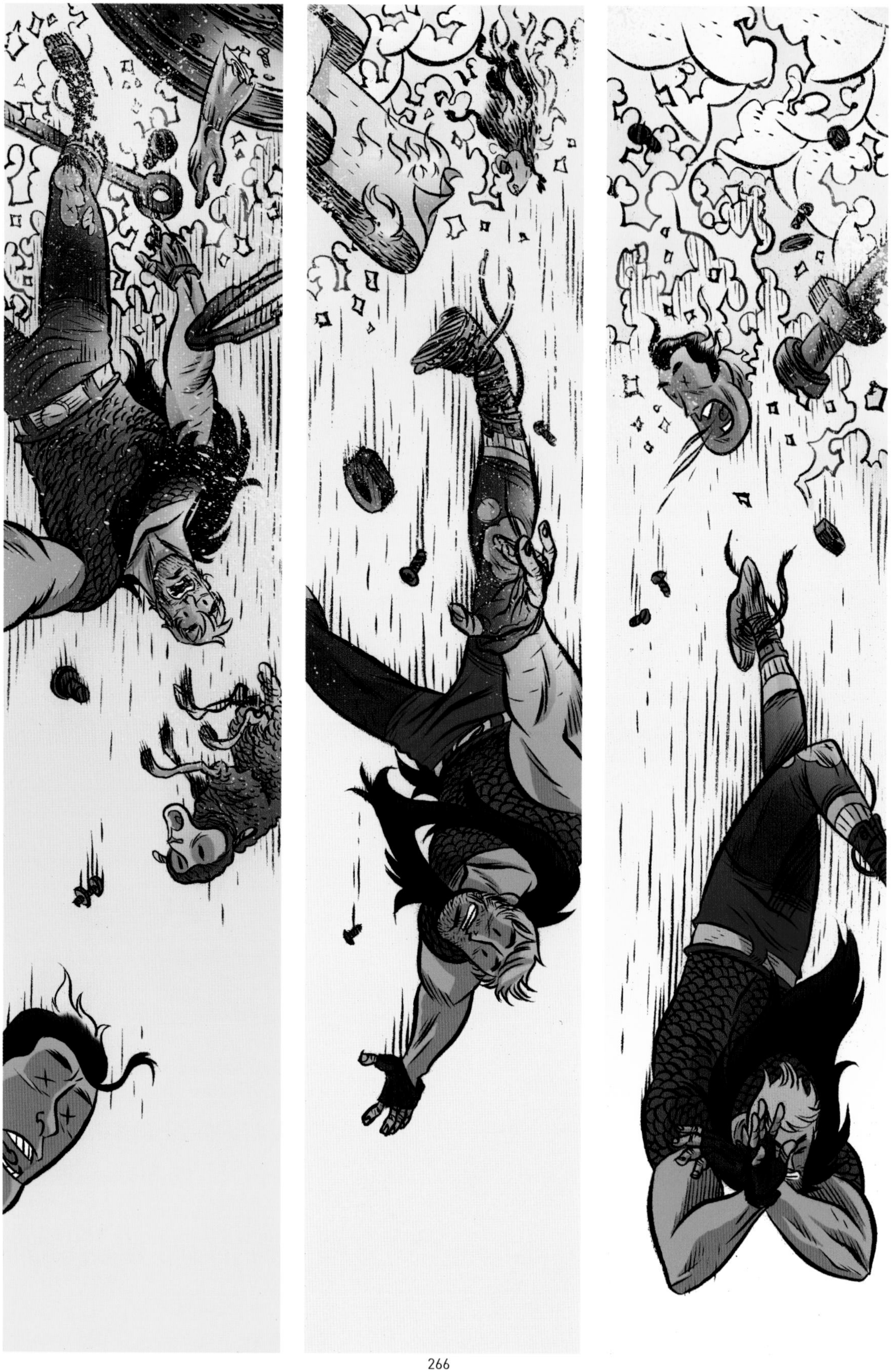

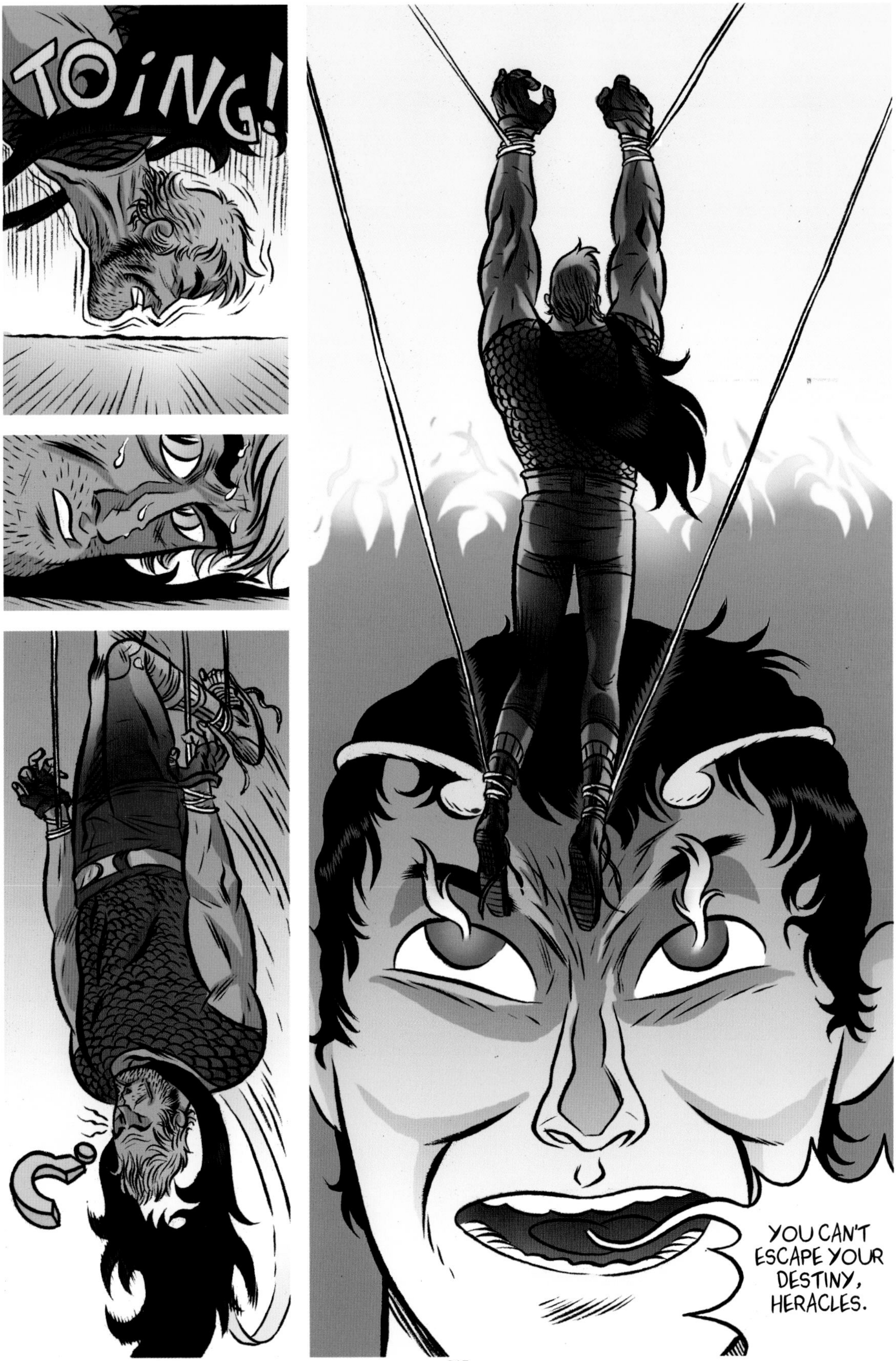
TOING!
?
YOU CAN'T ESCAPE YOUR DESTINY, HERACLES.

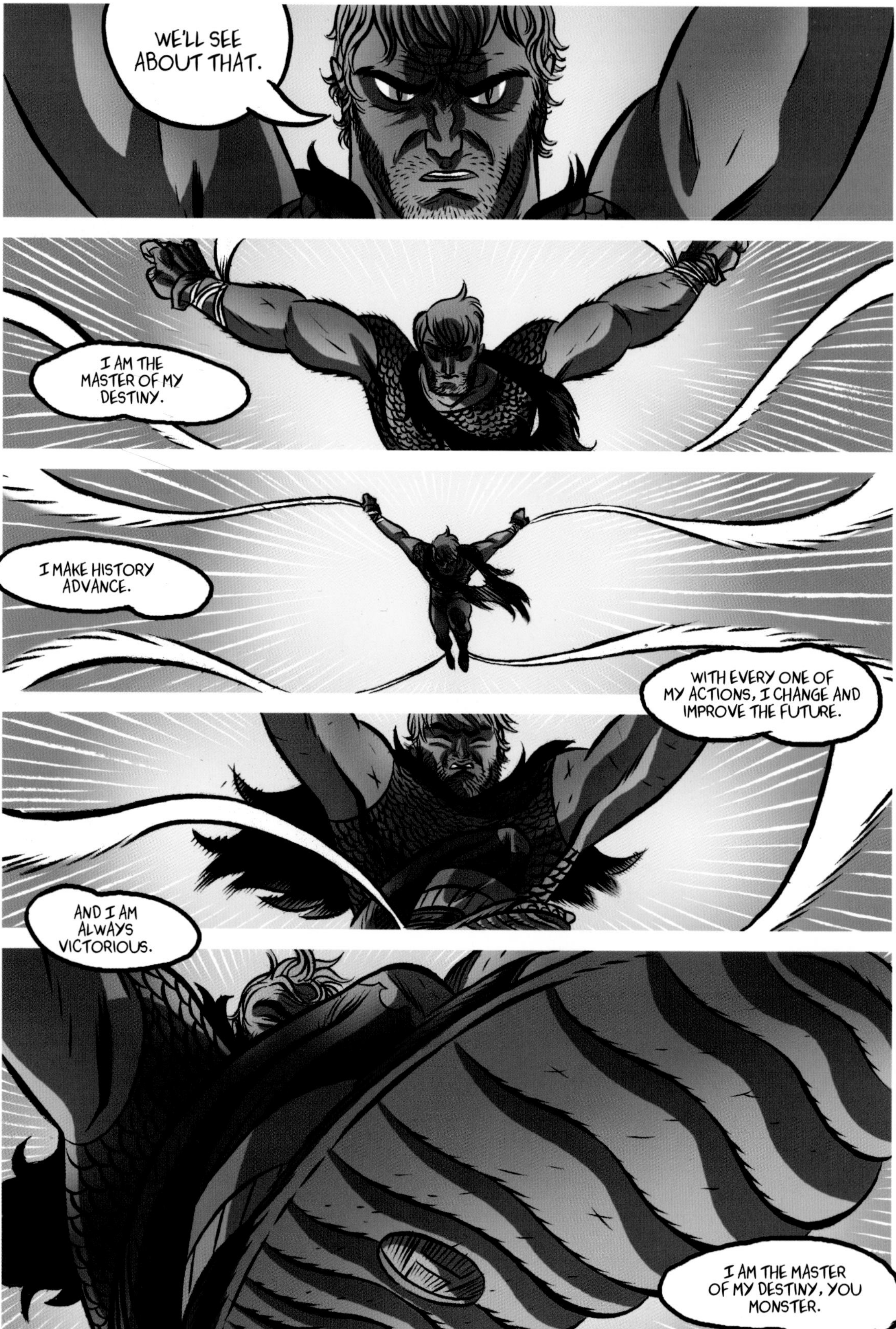
WE'LL SEE ABOUT THAT.
I AM THE MASTER OF MY DESTINY.
I MAKE HISTORY ADVANCE.
WITH EVERY ONE OF MY ACTIONS, I CHANGE AND IMPROVE THE FUTURE.
AND I AM ALWAYS VICTORIOUS.
I AM THE MASTER OF MY DESTINY, YOU MONSTER.

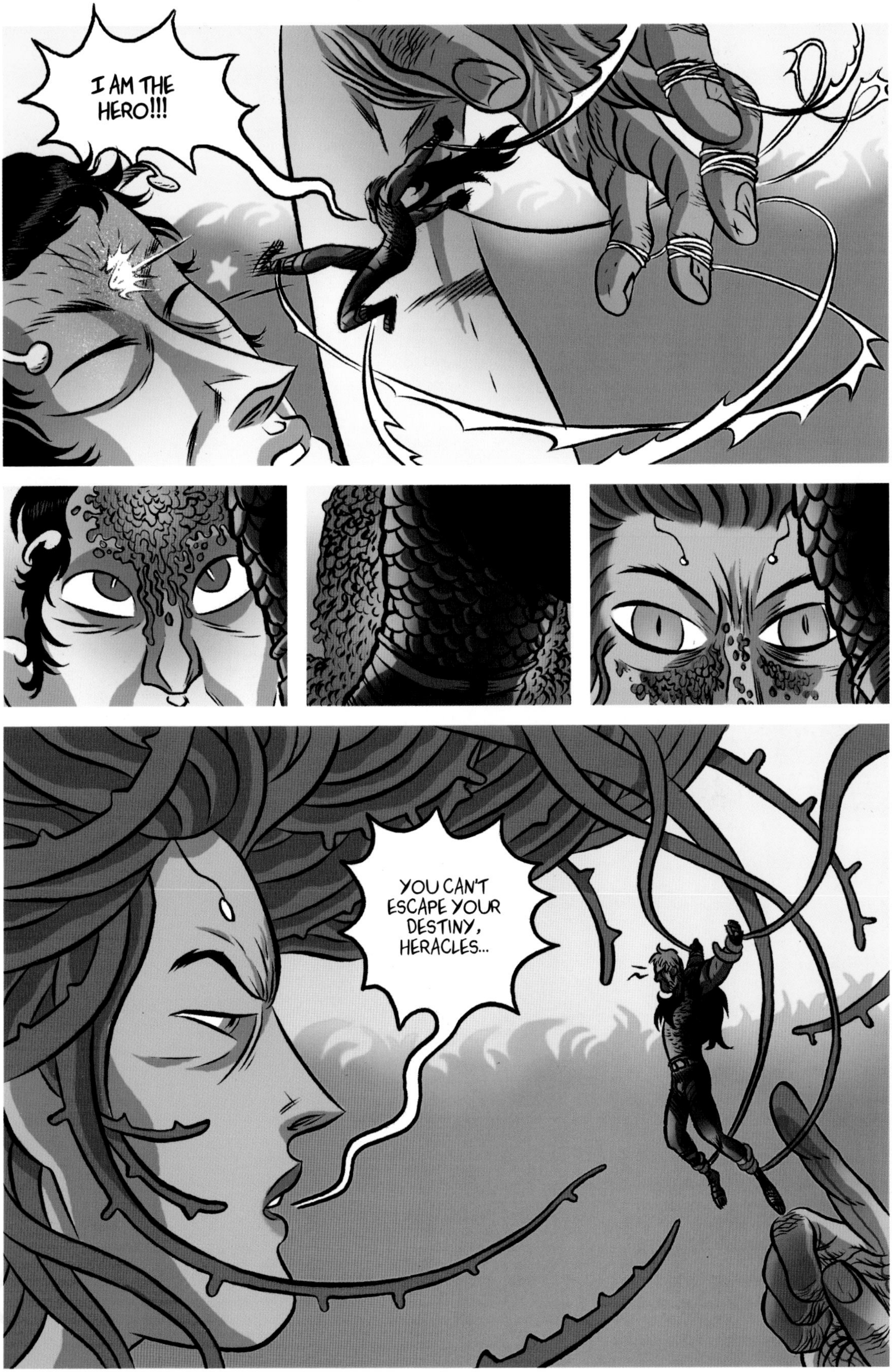
I AM THE HERO!!!
YOU CAN'T ESCAPE YOUR DESTINY, HERACLES...

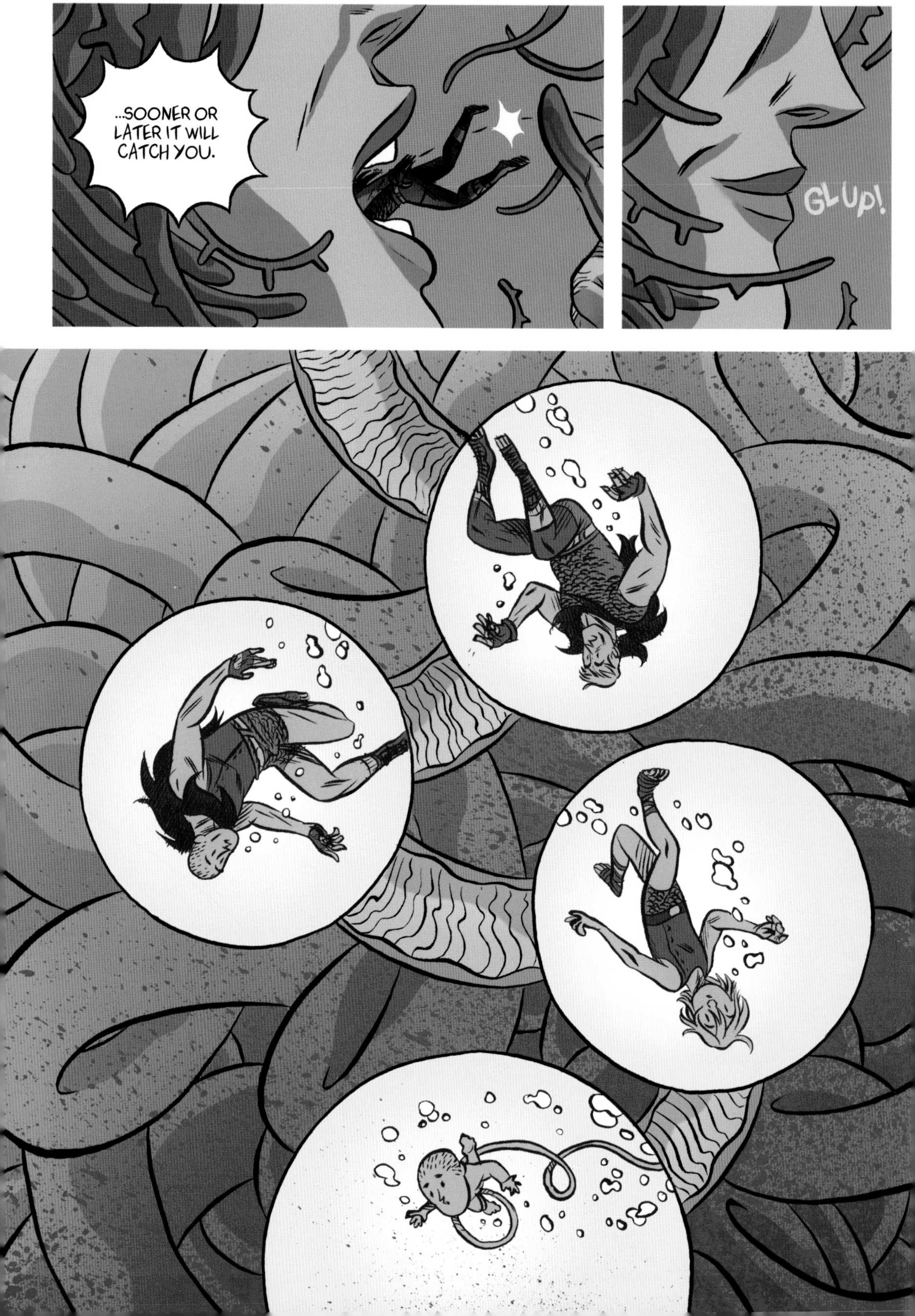
...SOONER OR LATER IT WILL CATCH YOU.
GLUP!

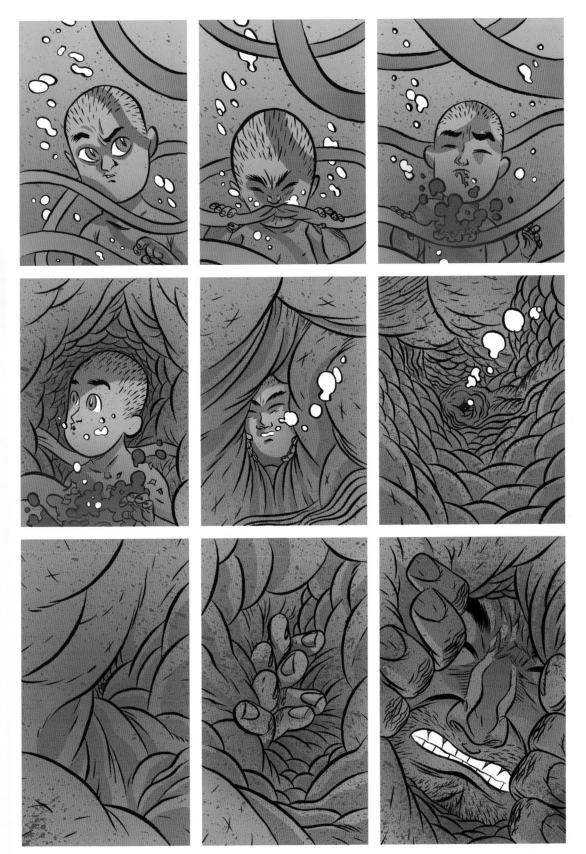

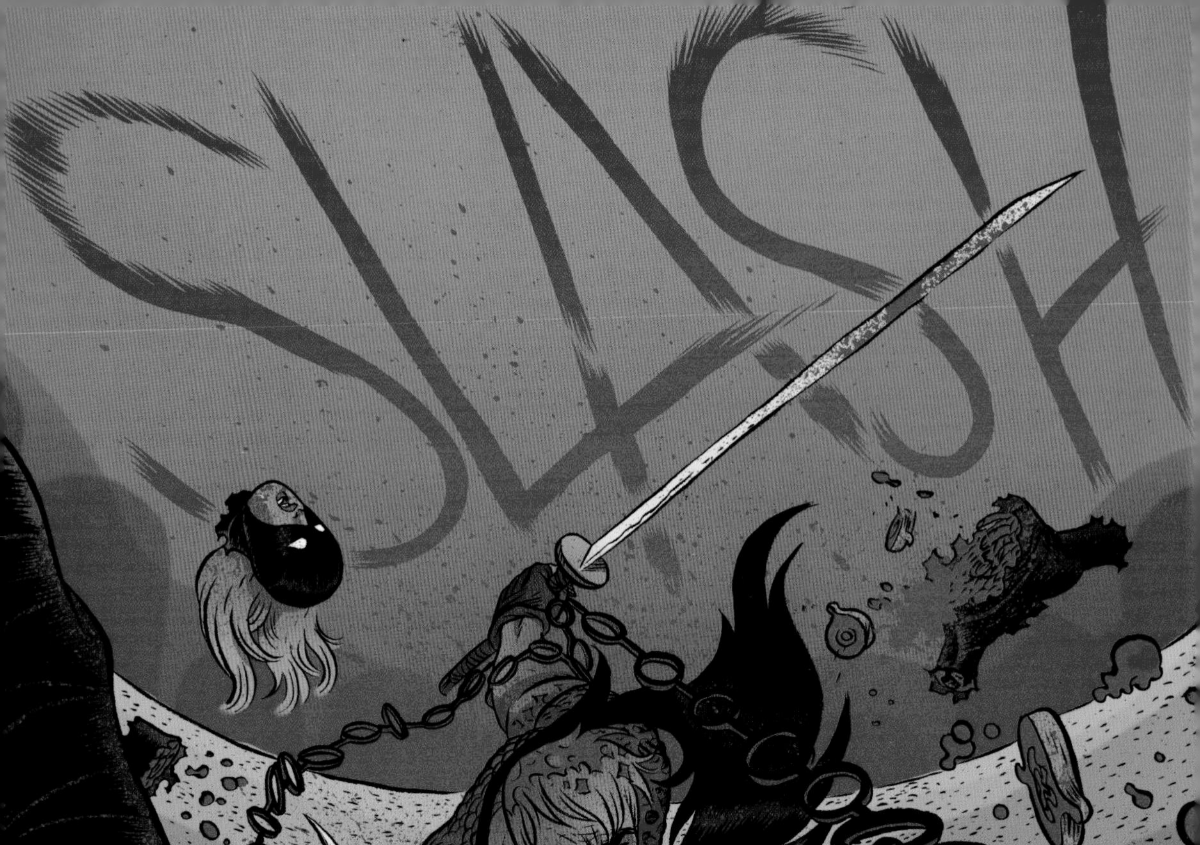
SLASH

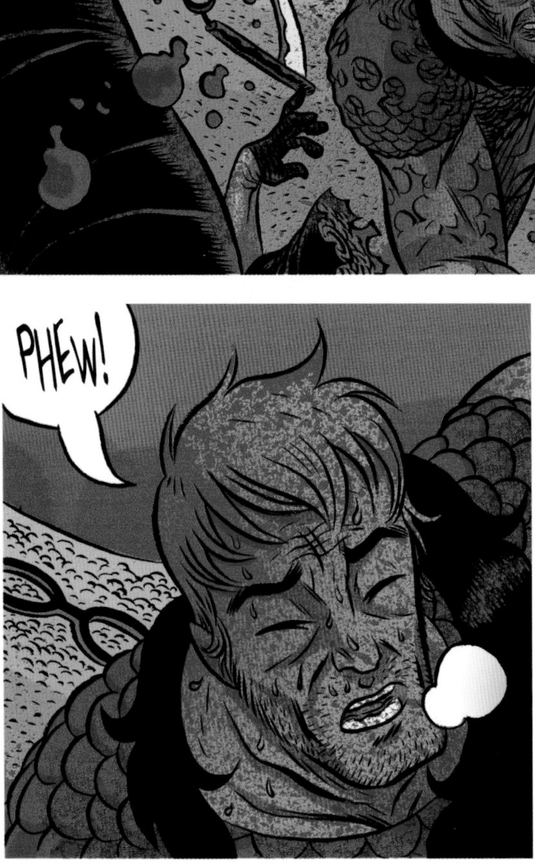
PHEW!

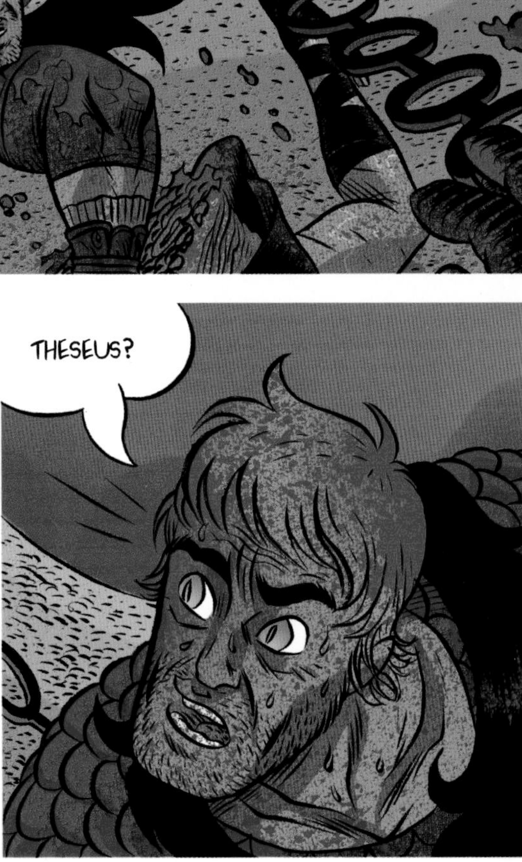
THESEUS?

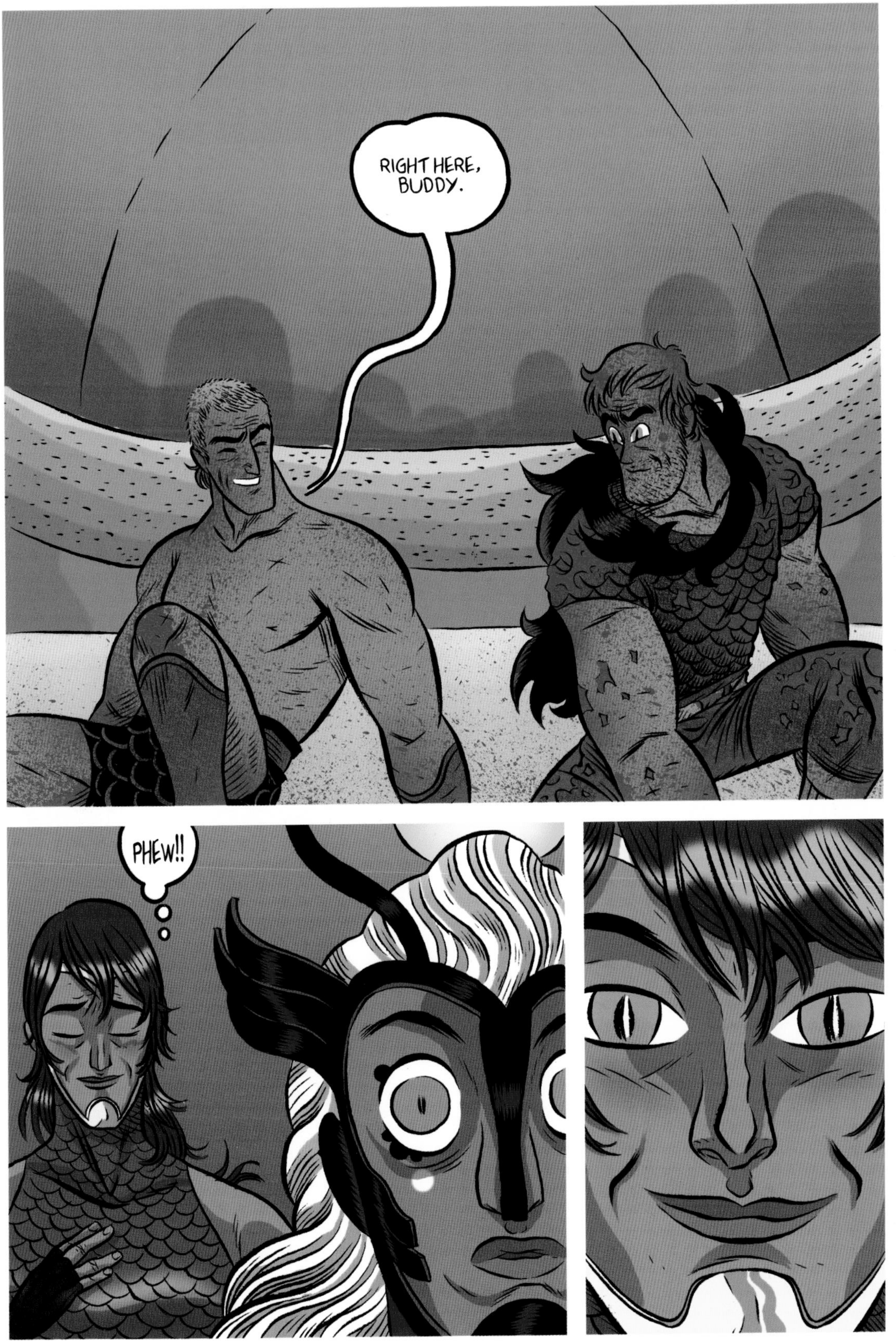
RIGHT HERE, BUDDY.
PHEW!!

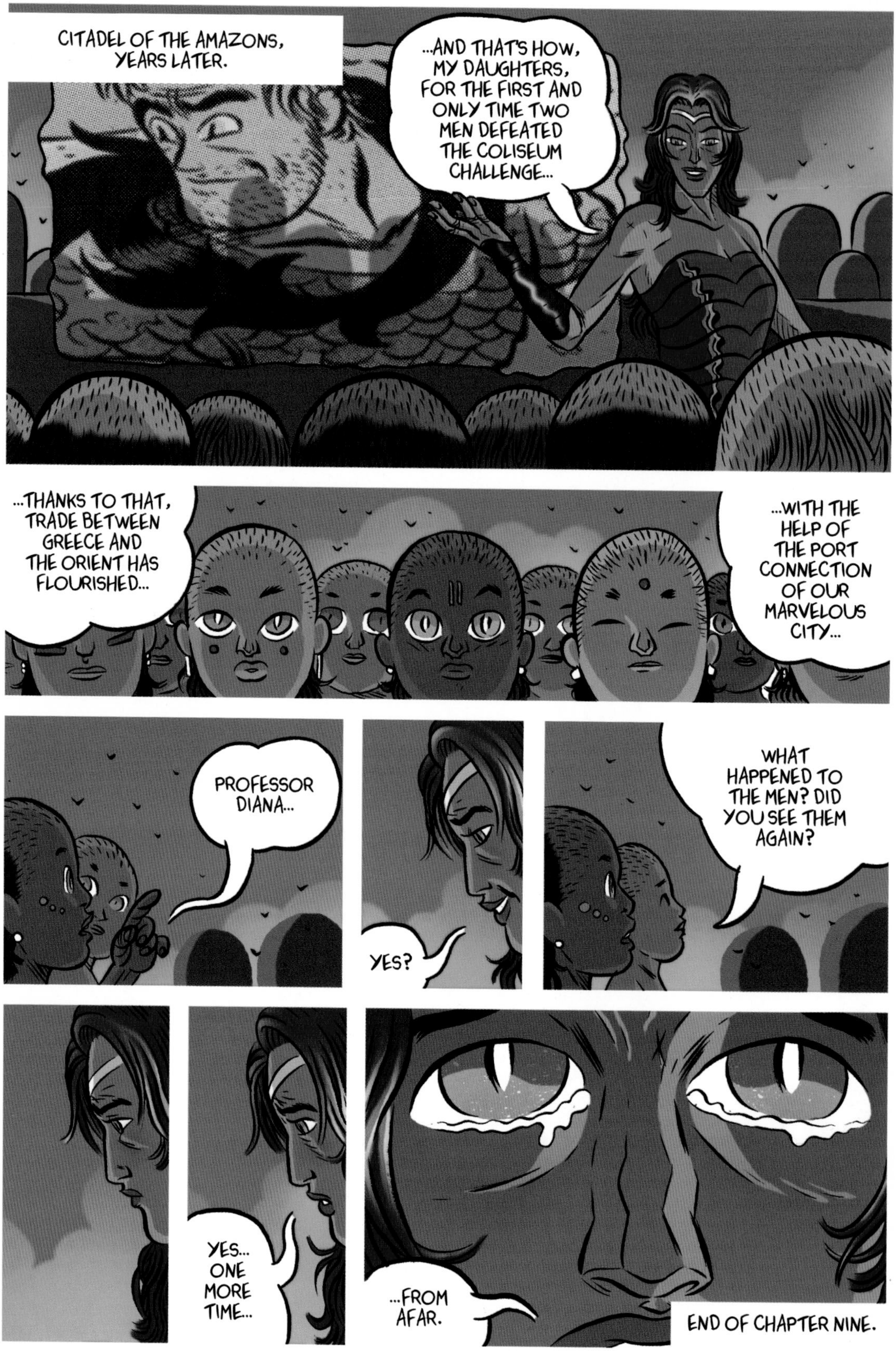
CITADEL OF THE AMAZONS, YEARS LATER.
...AND THAT'S HOW, MY DAUGHTERS, FOR THE FIRST AND ONLY TIME TWO MEN DEFEATED THE COLISEUM CHALLENGE...
...THANKS TO THAT, TRADE BETWEEN GREECE AND THE ORIENT HAS FLOURISHED...
...WITH THE HELP OF THE PORT CONNECTION OF OUR MARVELOUS CITY...
PROFESSOR DIANA...
YES?
WHAT HAPPENED TO THE MEN? DID YOU SEE THEM AGAIN?
YES... ONE MORE TIME...
...FROM AFAR.
END OF CHAPTER NINE.

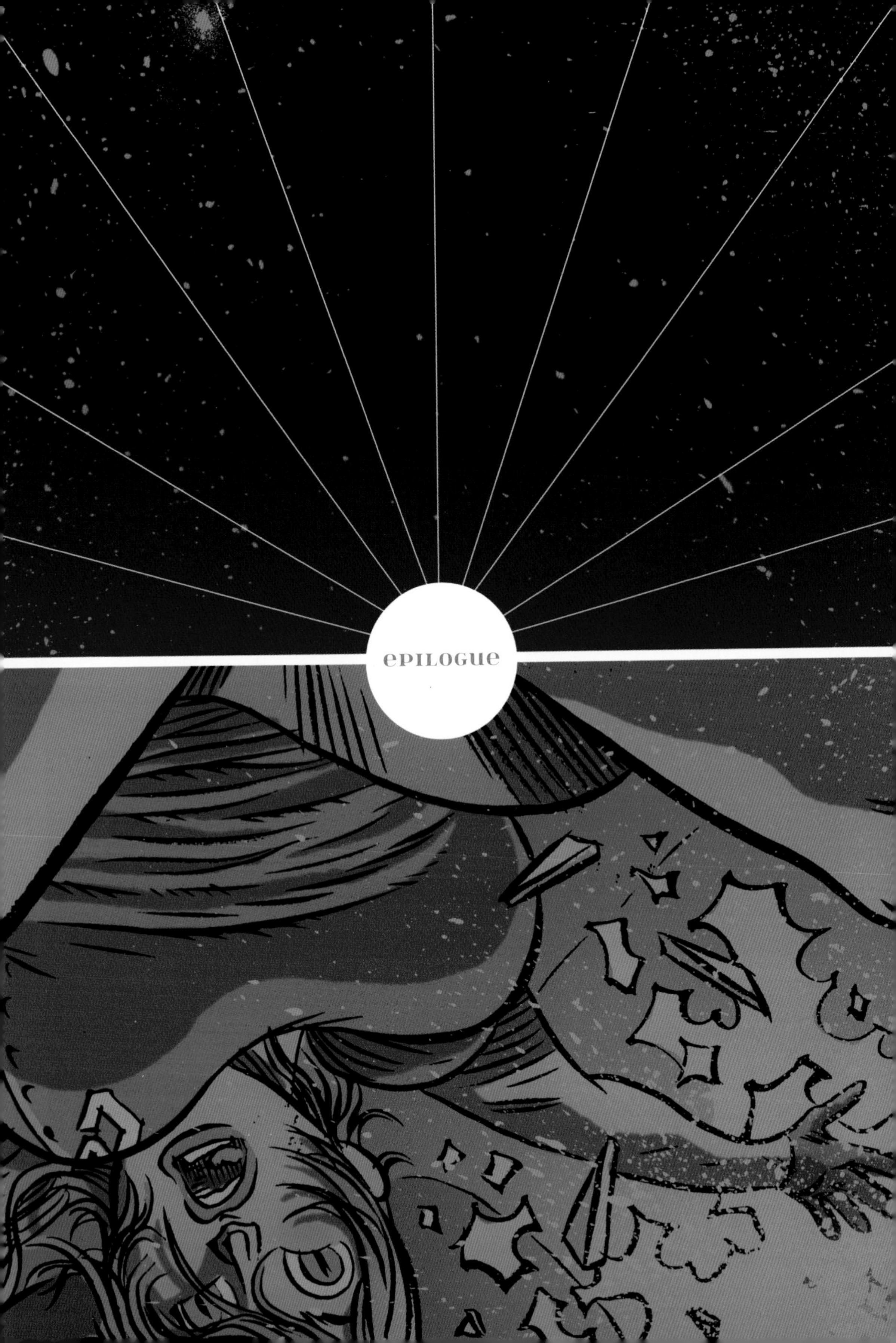
EPILOGUE

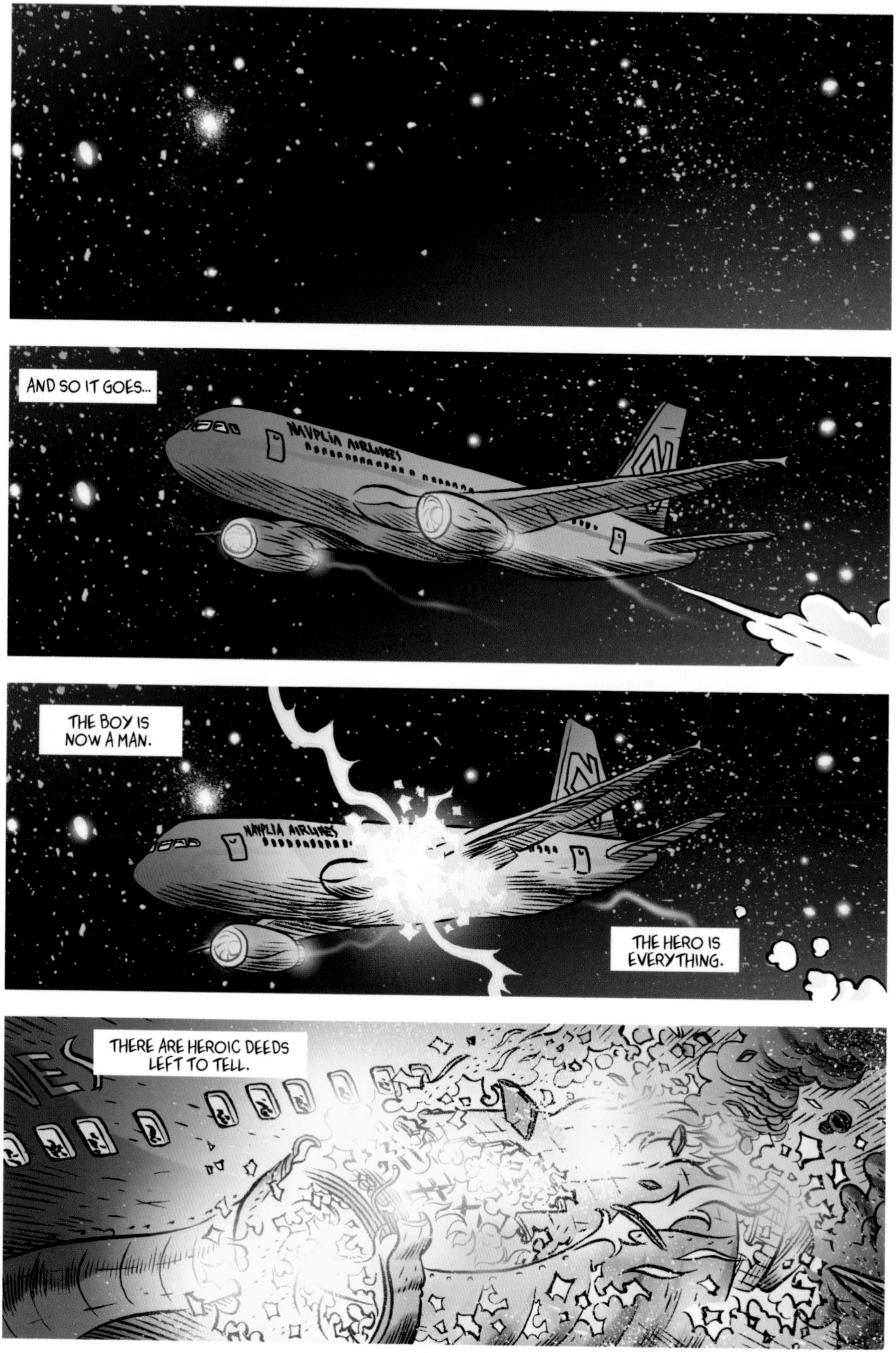
AND SO IT GOES...
NAUPLIA AIRLINES
THE BOY IS NOW A MAN.
NAUPLIA AIRLINES
THE HERO IS EVERYTHING.
THERE ARE HEROIC DEEDS LEFT TO TELL.

ROMANCE.

TRAGEDY.

DECEIT.

FICTION.

THE HOME STRETCH IS JUST AROUND THE CORNER.

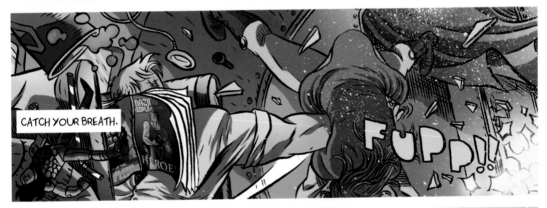

CATCH YOUR BREATH.

FUPP!!

THE ADVENTURE GOES ON.

STAY CALM. DON'T PANIC.

TO BE CONTINUED...

277

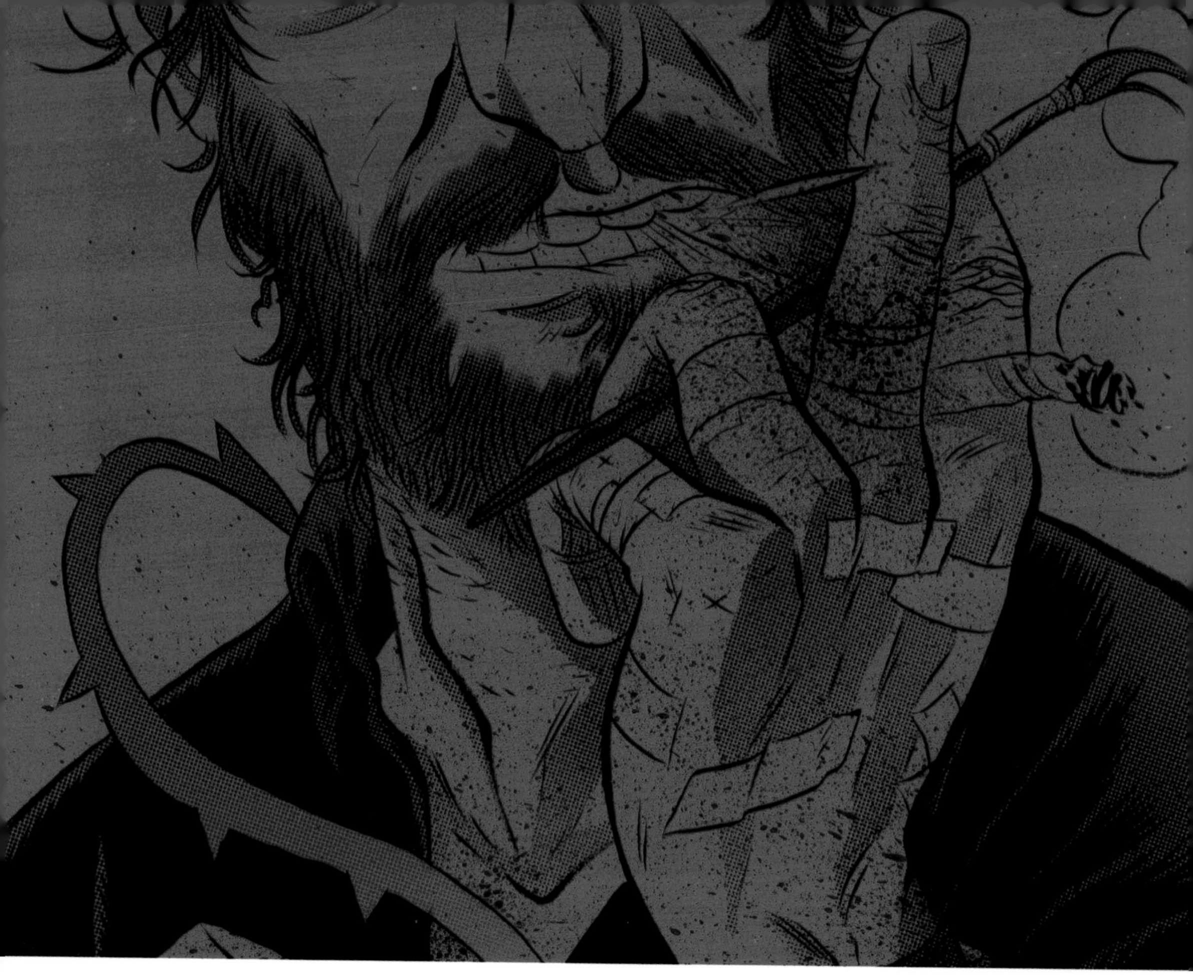

Acclaimed cartoonist David Rubín lives in Ourense, Spain, with his family. In 2011 he worked with writer Santiago García to adapt Beowulf, which will be available to English-language audiences in 2015 from Image Comics. He's currently working on the highly anticipated second chapter of Battling Boy: The Rise of Aurora West, written by Paul Pope and J. T. Petty, from First Second Books.

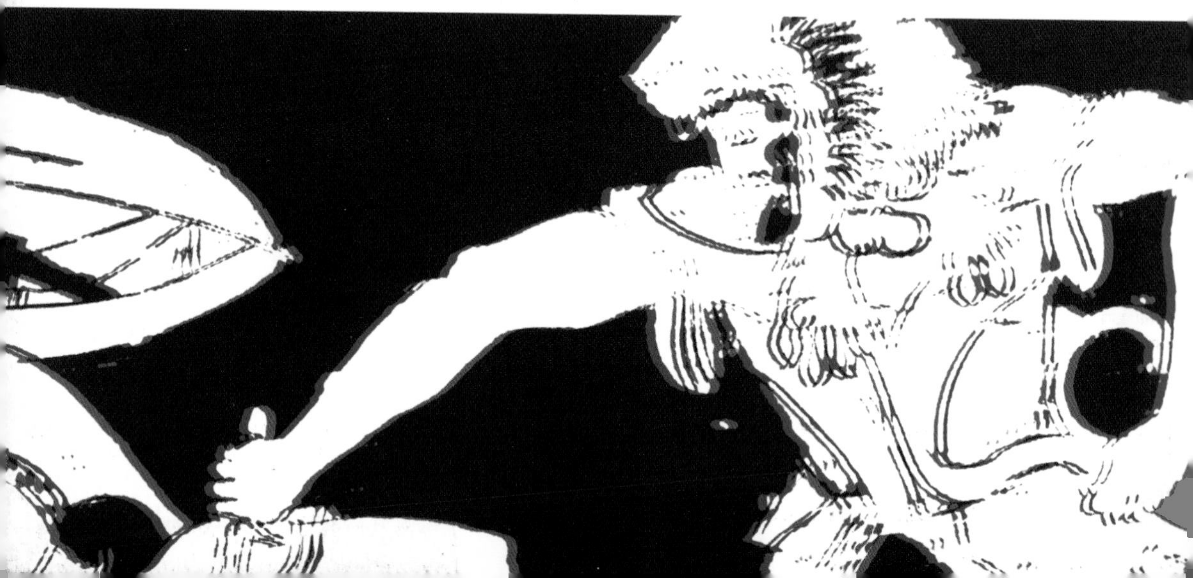

CREATIVE GIANTS!

GET YOUR FIX OF DARK HORSE BOOKS FROM THESE INSPIRED CREATORS!

MESMO DELIVERY SECOND EDITION - Rafael Grampá

Eisner Award–winning artist Rafael Grampá (*5*, *Hellblazer*) makes his full-length comics debut with the critically acclaimed graphic novel *Mesmo Delivery*—a kinetic, bloody romp starring Rufo, an ex-boxer; Sangrecco, an Elvis impersonator; and a ragtag crew of overly confident drunks who pick the wrong delivery men to mess with.

ISBN 978-1-61655-457-6 | $14.99

SIN TITULO - Cameron Stewart

Following the death of his grandfather, Alex Mackay discovers a mysterious photograph in the old man's belongings that sets him on an adventure like no other—where dreams and reality merge, family secrets are laid bare, and lives are irrevocably altered.

ISBN 978-1-61655-248-0 | $19.99

DE:TALES - Fábio Moon and Gabriel Bá

Brazilian twins Fábio Moon and Gabriel Bá's (*Daytripper*, *Pixu*) most personal work to date. Brimming with all the details of human life, their charming tales move from the urban reality of their home in São Paulo to the magical realism of their Latin American background.

ISBN 978-1-59582-557-5 | $19.99

THE TRUE LIVES OF THE FABULOUS KILLJOYS - Gerard Way, Shaun Simon, and Becky Cloonan

Years ago, the Killjoys fought against the tyrannical megacorporation Better Living Industries. Today, the followers of the original Killjoys languish in the desert and the fight for freedom fades. It's left to the Girl to take down BLI!

ISBN 978-1-59582-462-2 | $19.99

DEMO - Brian Wood and Becky Cloonan

It's hard enough being a teenager. Now try being a teenager with *powers*. A chronicle of the lives of young people on separate journeys to self-discovery in a world—just like our own—where being different is feared.

ISBN 978-1-61655-682-2 | $24.99

SABERTOOTH SWORDSMAN - Damon Gentry and Aaron Conley

When his village is enslaved and his wife kidnapped by the malevolent Mastodon Mathematician, a simple farmer must find his inner warrior—the Sabertooth Swordsman!

ISBN 978-1-61655-176-6 | $17.99

JAYBIRD - Jaakko and Lauri Ahonen

Disney meets Kafka in this beautiful, intense, original tale! A very small, very scared little bird lives an isolated life in a great big house with his infirm mother. He's never been outside the house, and he never will if his mother has anything to say about it.

ISBN 978-1-61655-469-9 | $19.99

MONSTERS! & OTHER STORIES - Gustavo Duarte

Newcomer Gustavo Duarte spins wordless tales inspired by Godzilla, King Kong, and Pixar, brimming with humor, charm, and delightfully twisted horror!

ISBN 978-1-61655-309-8 | $12.99

SACRIFICE - Sam Humphries and Dalton Rose

What happens when a troubled youth is plucked from modern society and thrust though time and space into the heart of the Aztec civilization—one of the most bloodthirsty times in human history?

ISBN 978-1-59582-985-6 | $19.99

EXPLORE THE MANY WORLDS OF THE EISNER AWARD—WINNING CREATORS OF *DAYTRIPPER*—

GABRIEL BÁ AND FÁBIO MOON!

"[De:Tales is] a perfect blend of fluid storytelling and contemporary style . . . A+." —Tom McLean, Variety

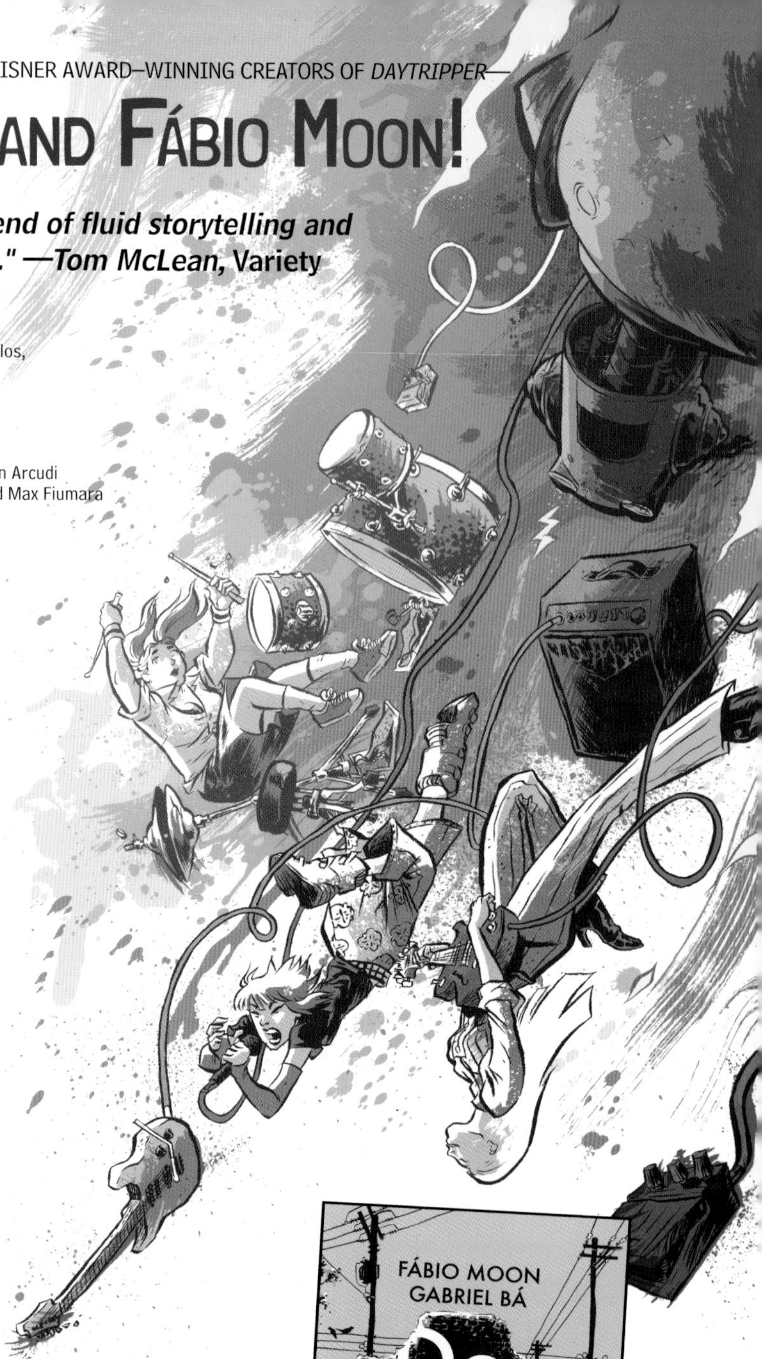

PIXU: THE MARK OF EVIL

Created by Gabriel Bá, Becky Cloonan, Vasilis Lolos, and Fábio Moon

ISBN 978-1-59582-340-3 | $17.99

B.P.R.D.: 1946–1948

Written by Mike Mignola,Joshua Dysart and John Arcudi
Art by Fábio Moon, Gabriel Bá, Paul Azaceta, and Max Fiumara

ISBN 978-1-61655-646-4 | $34.99

MYSPACE DARK HORSE PRESENTS

Volume 1

ISBN 978-1-59307-998-7 | $19.99

SUGARSHOCK

One-shot comic
Written by Joss Whedon
Art by Fábio Moon

$3.50

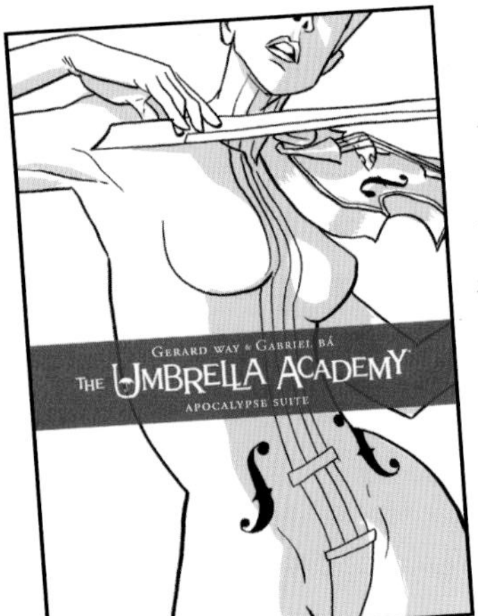

GERARD WAY & GABRIEL BÁ
THE UMBRELLA ACADEMY
APOCALYPSE SUITE

THE UMBRELLA ACADEMY: APOCALYPSE SUITE

Written by Gerard Way
Art by Gabriel Bá

TPB: 978-1-59307-978-9 | $17.99
Ltd. Ed. HC: 978-1-59582-163-8 | $79.95

THE UMBRELLA ACADEMY: DALLAS

Written by Gerard Way
Art by Gabriel Bá

TPB: 978-1-59582-345-8 | $17.99
Ltd. Ed. HC: 978-1-59582-344-1 | $79.95

DE:TALES

Story and art by
Gabriel Bá and Fábio Moon

ISBN 978-1-59582-557-5 | $19.99

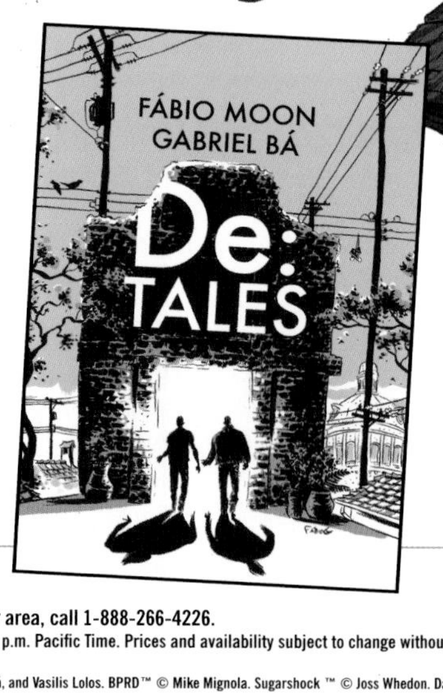

FÁBIO MOON
GABRIEL BÁ
De:
TALES

AVAILABLE AT YOUR LOCAL COMICS SHOP OR BOOKSTORE! • To find a comics shop in your area, call 1-888-266-4226.
For more information or to order direct visit DarkHorse.com or call 1-800-862-0052 Mon.–Fri. 9 a.m. to 5 p.m. Pacific Time. Prices and availability subject to change without notice.